FINTECH

ELGAR FINANCIAL LAW AND PRACTICE

Series Editor: Roger McCormick, *London School of Economics and Political Science, UK*

The Elgar Financial Law and Practice series is a library of works by leading practitioners and scholars covering discrete areas of law in the field of banking and finance. Titles in the series are both analytical and descriptive in approach, highlighting and unpicking the legal issues that are most critical and relevant to practice. Designed to be detailed, focused reference works, the books in this series offer an authoritative statement on the law and practice in key topics within the field, from Financial Collateral to Private Equity, from Secured Transactions to Financial Crime, and from Financial Derivatives and Hedge Funds to Bank Resolution and Bank Capital.

Titles in the series include:

The Law on Corporate Governance in Banks
Iris H-Y Chiu and Michael McKee

Yeowart and Parsons on the Law of Financial Collateral
Geoffrey Yeowart and Robin Parsons

The Governance of Credit Rating Agencies
Regulatory Regimes and Liability Issues
Andrea Miglionico

Mis-Selling Financial Services
Jonathan Kirk QC, Thomas Samuels and Lee Finch

FinTech
Law and Regulation
Edited by Jelena Madir

FINTECH

Law and Regulation

Edited by

JELENA MADIR

Chief Counsel, European Bank for Reconstruction and Development

ELGAR FINANCIAL LAW AND PRACTICE

Cheltenham, UK • Northampton, MA, USA

Published by
Edward Elgar Publishing Limited
The Lypiatts
15 Lansdown Road
Cheltenham
Glos GL50 2JA
UK

Edward Elgar Publishing, Inc.
William Pratt House
9 Dewey Court
Northampton
Massachusetts 01060
USA

A catalogue record for this book
is available from the British Library

This book is available electronically in the **Elgar**online
Law subject collection
DOI 10.4337/9781788979023

ISBN 978 1 78897 901 6 (cased)
ISBN 978 1 78897 902 3 (eBook)

Typeset by Columns Design XML Ltd, Reading

Printed and bound by CPI Group (UK) Ltd, Croydon, CR0 4YY

CONTENTS

PART IV   TECHNOLOGICAL INNOVATIONS IN LEGAL SERVICES

EXTENDED CONTENTS

FIGURES

TABLES

EDITOR AND CONTRIBUTORS

Sophia Adams-Bhatti is a public policy and regulation expert, having spent over 15 years in the regulatory and policy arena, working across a range of sectors, including legal services, financial services, economic regulation and healthcare. Sophia joined the Law Society of England and Wales in 2016 where, as a Director, she leads the Society's legal and regulatory policy team with oversight for policy development across the full breadth of the justice system, engaging with policy makers in government, and partner agencies. Specifically, Sophia leads the Law Society's programme of work on the impact of technology on the law and the justice system and practice of law. She is the creator and lead of the Law Society's ground-breaking Public Policy Commission on the use of Algorithms in the Justice System. In September 2019 Sophia joined forces with Wavelength Law leading on the intersection of public policy, legal innovation and technology.

Douglas Arner is the Kerry Holdings Professor in Law at the University of Hong Kong (HKU) and co-founder of HKU's Asian Institute of International Financial Law. He is a Senior Visiting Fellow of Melbourne Law School (University of Melbourne), an Executive Committee Member of the Asia Pacific Structured Finance Association, and an independent non-executive director of the Nasdaq-listed Aptorum Group. He led the development of the world's largest massive open online course (MOOC): Introduction to FinTech, launched on edX in May 2018, now with over 35,000 learners spanning every country in the world. Beyond academia, Douglas has served as a consultant for, among others, the World Bank, the Asian Development Bank and the European Bank for Reconstruction and Development in Europe, Asia Pacific and Africa.

Colleen Baker is an Assistant Professor of Legal Studies at the University of Oklahoma's Price College of Business and an Affiliate Faculty, College of Law. She is an expert in banking and financial institutions law and regulation, with extensive knowledge of the regulation of over-the-counter derivatives, clearing, the Dodd-Frank Act, bankruptcy, and dispute resolution (including being a mediator). She has taught courses at the University of Illinois Urbana-Champaign Business School, the University of Notre Dame Law School, Villanova University Law School, and the Wharton Business School. Colleen received a JD/MBA from the University of Virginia and a PhD from the Wharton School of the University of Pennsylvania.

Claude Brown is a senior member of Reed Smith's multijurisdictional FinTech Team and is head of the firm's EU FinTech practice. The team covers all aspects of FinTech, including fundraising, structuring, contracting, documentation, IP, regulation and enforcement. Claude's focus is on the design and structuring of cryptoassets, including a wide variety of token types, cryptocurrencies and ICOs in multi-jurisdictional offerings. His experience covers the use of cryptoassets in the financial, energy, commodities and media sectors, as well as providing advice to industry and trade associations on FinTech matters. He is a frequent speaker at conferences and seminars on cryptoassets, particularly on their treatment in cross-border insolvencies.

Ross Buckley is the KPMG Law – King & Wood Mallesons Professor of Disruptive Innovation, and a Scientia Professor, at the University of New South Wales in Sydney. His research focus is FinTech, RegTech, blockchain and digital finance. He chairs the Digital Finance Advisory Panel of the Australian Securities and Investments Commission, consults regularly to the Asian Development Bank, and has advised governments departments in ten other nations, including the U.S. He has twice been a Fulbright Scholar, at Yale and Duke universities.

Karen Butler is a senior associate in Reed Smith's Financial Regulation team. Karen advises UK and European clients on a broad range of UK and European financial services regulatory laws and regulations. She specialises in the payment services and e-money aspects of cryptoasset issuance and trading of them in the EU. She is an acknowledged authority on the collectivisation of investments and the impact of EU regulations on ICOs and securities tokens. Karen advises clients on how to structure, market and conduct their business in accordance with regulatory rules and requirements. Karen has written a number of papers on cryptoassets and their regulation and is a frequent contributor to FinTech publications.

Peter Chapman is a Partner at Clifford Chance in London. He advises financial institutions on a range of regulatory matters including new business development, mergers and acquisitions involving regulated businesses and regulatory change implementation. Peter has a specific focus on FinTech-related matters including in crowdfunding, cryptoassets as well as traditional and innovative payments platforms and businesses. Prior to joining Clifford Chance in 2007, Peter studied jurisprudence at St Edmund Hall, Oxford University.

Sofya Cherkasova is a graduate of Lomonosov Moscow State University. She currently works for a Russian law firm, ALRUD, in Moscow, and is completing a Master's of Technology Law. Sofya previously spent time with the International Bar Association's Legal Policy and Research Unit.

Tara Chittenden is a Technology and Learning Intelligence Officer in the Research Unit of the Law Society in London. Her PhD examined perceptual experiences of virtual reality technologies. Prior to her current employment, she worked at the British Museum. Her research interests include practices of interpretation, motion technologies, spatial narratives and technological interventions at museums and heritage sites. She publishes in all of these areas. Tara's research at the Law Society focuses on technology and process innovation, futures and horizon scanning, and she is the author of the Law Society's reports on the *Future of Legal Services* (2016) and *Capturing Technological Innovation in Legal Services* (2017), as well as numerous horizon scanning reports.

Daniel Cooper is a Partner in the Technology and Media group of Covington & Burling LLP in London. Daniel advises clients on information technology regulatory issues, particularly data protection, e-commerce and data security matters and is qualified to practice law in the United States, the United Kingdom and Ireland, and has been appointed to the advisory and expert boards of privacy NGOs and agencies, such as Privacy International and the European security agency, ENISA. He is a graduate of Princeton University (BA), Harvard Law School (JD), and Oxford (MSt).

Patricia L. de Miranda is a Senior Counsel at the World Bank in Washington, DC. Her current assignment in the World Bank's legal department institutional affairs practice group includes providing legal advice on information technology and data protection; cloud computing and related issues; non-licence issues of data processing; social media and other public statements; non-disclosure/confidentiality agreements; and access to information. Previously, Patricia provided legal advice on the World Bank's Access to Information Policy, on project finance in Brazil and East Asia and Pacific, and on corporate administrative matters. In Brazil, Patricia worked in litigation at Pinheiro Neto Advogados. Patricia received a Juris Doctor from Pontifícia Universidade Católica de São Paulo and completed her LLM in International Law at the American University in Washington, DC. She is admitted to practice in Brazil.

Hubert de Vauplane co-leads the Alternative Investment Management of Kramer Levin in Paris. Previously, he worked for various international banks including BNP Paribas, Oddo & Cie and Crédit Agricole, where he served as the Group General Counsel. Hubert is an expert on the French Financial Market Supervisory Authority, the European Commission and the European Central Bank. Hubert is also a member of various marketplace organisations, including the Financial Market Law Committee (London), Paris Europlace, P.R.I.M.E. (Panel of Recognized International Market Experts in Finance) and the French High Legal Committee for the Paris Finance Marketplace (Haut Comité Juridique de la Place Financière de Paris). He is a professor of international banking and financial law at the Paris Institute for Political Sciences (Sciences Po – IEP Paris).

Anton Didenko is a Research Fellow at the University of New South Wales in Sydney, specialising in banking and finance law, with the focus on FinTech and RegTech. He is a Russian qualified lawyer with ten years of experience as in-house counsel in major private commercial banks in Moscow and as a senior associate at a law firm in London. His experience covers advising on banking regulations and legislation applicable to financial intermediaries, as well as a wide range of financing transactions. Anton also specialises in the area of secured transactions law and transnational commercial law and is the editor of the *Cape Town Convention Journal*. Anton holds a law degree from the Russian Foreign Trade Academy, as well as Magister Juris and Doctor of Philosophy degrees from the University of Oxford.

Tim Dolan is the head of Reed Smith's Financial Regulation team. Tim has previously worked for several financial regulators and now advises UK and European firms on the application and interpretation of financial regulations relating to cryptoassets and tokenised interests. His focus is on ICOs and security tokens within the European regulatory environment. Tim assists clients to structure their tokens to fall within exemptions from the regulatory regime and, if exemptions are not available, to obtain authorisation from financial regulators. He has contributed to a number of publications on cryptoassets, blockchain and distributed ledger technology.

Mark Fenwick is Professor of International Business Law at the Faculty of Law, Kyushu University, Fukuoka, Japan. His primary research interests are in the fields of white-collar and corporate crime, and business regulation in a networked age. Recent publications include *New Technology, 'Big Data' and the Law* (2017) and *The Shifting Meaning of Legal Certainty in Comparative and Transnational Law* (2017). He has a master's degree and a Ph.D. from the Faculty of Law, University of Cambridge (Queens' College) and has been a visiting professor at Cambridge University, Chulalongkorn University, Duke University, the University of Hong Kong, Shanghai University of Finance & Economics, the National University of Singapore, Tilburg University and Vietnam National University.

Jane Finlayson-Brown is a Partner at Allen & Overy, and specialises in data protection, technology and outsourcing. She regularly advises companies and financial institutions on all aspects of data protection compliance, including data protection policies and procedures, the use of data in the provision of consumer and business products, Big Data issues, responding to data subject access requests, transfers of data in outsourcing projects and M&A transactions, cloud computing, data security breaches, cross border data transfers, transfers of data to overseas regulators, customer relationship management, employee monitoring and website compliance issues. Jane received her Bachelor of Arts degree from Oxford University.

John Ho Hee Jung is the Head of Legal, Financial Markets for Standard Chartered Bank (SCB), overseeing and providing legal advisory, transactional and documentation support for SCB's Financial Markets business globally, its branches and affiliates. John is the co-chair of the ISDA's South East Asia Legal and Regulatory Committee. He is an active participant in the industry's FinTech and blockchain events and has shared insights into the legal and regulatory framework relating to the development of FinTech. He is the chair of the FIA FinTech and Digital Assets Study Group. He is qualified as an advocate and solicitor in Singapore since 1995 and he received his law degree from the National University of Singapore.

Wulf A. Kaal is a Professor and Director of the Private Investment Fund Institute at the University of St. Thomas School of Law in Minneapolis. His research focuses on innovation, technology, emerging technology applications, smart contracts, initial coin offerings, hedge funds and dynamic regulatory methods. Before entering academia, he was associated with Cravath, Swain and Moore LLP, in New York, and Goldman Sachs in London. Wulf advises medium- to large-sized enterprises, crypto startups, venture capital funds, and international policy makers on emerging technology solutions. As an adviser and mentor, Wulf focuses on creating synergies for his clients and building successful new businesses.

Byungkwon Lim is a Partner at Debevoise and Plimpton, where he leads the firm's Derivatives, Blockchain and Hedge Fund Practice Groups. Byungkwon advises a wide range of clients, including banks, other dealers and end-users, on derivatives regulatory matters and transaction structuring. In the blockchain space, he advises technology companies and developers on regulatory matters, platform structuring and offering, and related documentation. Byungkwon received his LLB in 1981 from Seoul National University, an MPP from the John F. Kennedy School of Government at Harvard University in 1985, and a JD from Harvard Law School in 1988. He clerked at the Supreme Court of Korea from 1981 to 1983, and is admitted to the bars of the Republic of Korea and New York.

Charles Low is an Associate at Debevoise and Plimpton. His practice focuses on financing transactions, general corporate law, as well as blockchain technology and related regulatory matters (including regulatory sandboxes). Charles graduated from the University of Durham with an LLB in 2015 and completed the Legal Practice Course with distinction at BPP University in 2016. He is admitted as a solicitor of the Senior Courts of England and Wales.

Jelena Madir is a Chief Counsel at the European Bank for Reconstruction and Development (EBRD) in London. She heads the Financial Law Unit, which provides legal and regulatory advice to governments in the areas of access to finance, FinTech, corporate governance and insolvency. She also teaches FinTech: Law and Regulation at the University of London. Prior to joining EBRD, Jelena worked as a finance and capital markets lawyer at Cleary Gottlieb Steen & Hamilton LLP in Washington, DC; Shearman & Sterling LLP in Frankfurt, Germany; and Privredna Banka and DLA Piper LLP in Zagreb, Croatia. Jelena received her Juris Doctor from Columbia University School of Law and completed her undergraduate studies in Government and Asian Studies at Dartmouth College. She is admitted to practice law in Washington, DC and England and Wales; and to the Roll of Solicitors in the Republic of Ireland.

Gemma Nash is an Associate in the Technology and Media practice group of Covington & Burling LLP in London. Gemma advises emerging and leading companies on data protection issues, including cybersecurity, e-commerce and data security matters. Gemma also advises companies on how both existing and proposed legislation will impact on emerging technologies such as artificial intelligence and blockchain. She obtained her LLB degree from Cardiff University.

Kieran Pender is a legal adviser with the Legal Policy and Research Unit of the International Bar Association (IBA) in London. Kieran is project lead on the IBA's whistleblower protection work, including the *Whistleblower Protections: A Guide* (2018). He has spoken about whistleblower protection issues at the World Bank, European Parliament, Organisation for Economic Cooperation and Development, and University of Cambridge. Kieran is a graduate of the Australian National University, where he was awarded the university medal. He was formerly a research associate with Bradley Allen Love Lawyers in Canberra. Kieran is also a writer for *The Guardian* and *Monocle*.

Ben Regnard-Weinrabe is a Partner in the Financial Services Regulatory practice at Allen & Overy, with a particular focus on FinTech, payments, retail banking and consumer finance. Ben has extensive experience advising on EU and UK law and regulation, products, commercial contracts and transactions for the commercial and retail banking, e-money, payments, virtual currency and consumer finance industries. He also advises on non-sector specific legislation such as unfair terms, money laundering, e-commerce and data protection.

Lee Reiners is the Executive Director of the Global Financial Markets Center and a lecturing fellow at Duke University School of Law. At Duke Law, Lee teaches FinTech Law and Policy as well as seminars relating to financial policy and regulatory practice. He writes frequently on FinTech and other financial regulatory matters on the FinReg blog. Prior to joining Duke Law, Lee worked at the Federal Reserve Bank of New York (FRBNY), first as a supervisor of systemically important financial institutions and then as a senior associate within the executive office. In the latter capacity, he helped coordinate the FRBNY's engagement with international standard-setting bodies, such as the Bank for International Settlements and the Financial Stability Board.

Mirjana Stankovic is a Vice President for Emerging Technologies and Intellectual Property at Tambourine Innovation Ventures. Her work focuses on policy, legal, scientific and ethical aspects of intellectual property, technology transfer and emerging technologies. She consults for the World Bank, the United Nations Industrial Development Organization, the Inter-American Development Bank, the United States Agency for International Development, the African Development Bank, the Organisation for Economic Cooperation and Development, and other international organisations. The recent publications she co-authored include the World Bank's White Papers: *Exploring Legal, Ethical and Policy Implications of Artificial Intelligence* and *Patentability, Global Development and Ethical Considerations of Bioprinting*; the World Bank's publication *Ukraine: Intellectual Property and Technology Transfer Regulatory Review*; and the Inter-American Development Bank's Background Paper: *Social Services for Digital Citizens: Opportunities for Latin America and the Caribbean*.

Harriet Territt is a Partner at Jones Day, based in London. She works with clients on liability, risk and governance issues arising out of the cutting edge financial technology, including blockchain, artificial intelligence, alternative finance arrangements, and consumer-facing products. She is a founding member of Jones Day's blockchain initiative and the co-author of Jones Day's multi-jurisdictional blockchain overview.

Erik P.M. Vermeulen is a Professor of Business and Financial Law at Tilburg University and Tilburg Law and Economics Center in the Netherlands. He is also Senior Legal Counsel at Signify (a technology company, formerly known as Philips Lighting). He recently co-founded Governance Tomorrow, which helps develop strategies that enable governments, large corporations, start-ups and other organisations to make better choices in this new world. Erik regularly serves as an expert advisor to international organisations, such as the European Commission, the Organisation for Economic Co-operation and Development, the United Nations, the World Bank, and national and local governments around the world. He has a blog at medium.com/@erikpmvermeulen, where he shares insights and ideas about how the digital world is changing the way we live and work.

Kevin Werbach is a Professor of Legal Studies and Business Ethics at the Wharton School, University of Pennsylvania. A world-renowned expert on emerging technology, he examines business and policy implications of developments such as broadband, big data, gamification, and blockchain. Kevin served on the Obama Administration's Presidential Transition Team, founded the Supernova Group (a technology conference and consulting firm), helped develop the US approach to internet policy during the Clinton Administration, and created one of the most successful massive open online courses, with over 450,000 enrolments. His books include *For the Win: How Game Thinking Can Revolutionize Your Business* and *The Blockchain and the New Architecture of Trust.*

Anna Yamaoka-Enkerlin is a Competition, Innovation, and Information Law LL.M candidate at New York University, as well as a legal researcher at Urbanlogiq, a company that builds artificial intelligence analytics for governments. She was previously the editor-in-chief of the *Oxford University Undergraduate Law Journal* and president of Oxford Lawyers Without Borders. Anna is also the technology officer of the International Bar Association's North America Regional Forum.

Dirk Zetzsche is a Professor of Financial Law at the University of Luxembourg where he has helds the ADA Chair in Financial Law since March 2016. Dirk is also one of the Directors of the Center for Business and Corporate Law at Heinrich Heine University in Düsseldorf, Germany. He is the author of more than 200 publications and his current research focuses on FinTech/RegTech/CorpTech, corporate governance and alternative investment funds, as well as a number of finance topics. Dirk has advised, among others, the Financial Stability Board, the European Commission, the European Parliament, the European Securities and Markets Authority, the Hong Kong Monetary Authority, the German Secretary of Justice, the German Secretary of Finance, the Asian Development Bank, and the Alliance for Financial Inclusion on FinTech, RegTech, financial and banking law, shareholder rights, corporate governance, securities and investment law topics.

PREFACE

FinTech has become an inescapable buzzword in the last few years: the term is popularly used to describe internet- and smartphone-enabled financial innovations that have risen to prominence since the 2008 global financial crisis. Just as with other sectors, the tentacles of technology have coiled their way into the financial services industry. Agile disruptors in the form of innovative start-ups have been joined by large technology companies as they seek to take market share from incumbent financial services providers. In this context, there are new opportunities for innovation and growth, but also new challenges, particularly for regulators, who are often struggling to apply laws crafted decades ago and, in many cases, built on the assumptions now being challenged by technology.

This book falls into four parts. The first part explains what FinTech is, and examines legal and regulatory aspects of technology-enabled developments in the areas of banking, payments and fundraising – from open banking and alternative funding platforms, such as crowdfunding, to cryptoassets and initial coin offerings.

The second part focuses on blockchain, which is often held up as a signifier for innovation and is seen by many as the door to a distributed, decentralised internet. This part of the book examines potential blockchain applications in the financial services industry, with a particular focus on smart contracts. It also analyses legal and regulatory challenges to widespread adoption of blockchain – from data privacy and cybersecurity concerns to uncertainties about applicable law and allocation of liability in a decentralised ecosystem.

While some may argue that the promise of FinTech and blockchain is blindingly bright, regulators around the world are facing a heightened pressure to strike a sensible balance between, on the one hand, supportive space for innovation and, on the other hand, adequate consumer protection. In that context, the third part of the book examines the main regulatory and compliance issues surrounding FinTech developments – from the challenges of patenting FinTech inventions and regulating robo-advisors and e-commerce companies entering the financial services sector ('TechFins'), to the use of innovative solutions by both supervisory agencies and regulators to support innovation, including through regulatory sandboxes.

The fourth part examines the impact that the speed of technological change and the range of new entrants in the financial sector will have on the legal profession. The two chapters in this part suggest that, while lawyers should not feel threatened by these developments, it will not be possible for law firms to rise to the new challenges purely by looking within. Rather, lawyers will need to develop at least a basic understanding of technology, while law firms will have to move away from traditional decision-making structures and practices if they want to secure access and exposure to the technologies and skillsets required to operate successfully in the marketplace of the future.

As this area of law is not free of jargon, the book includes a glossary of terms, which I hope the readers will find helpful.

All websites cited in the volume were live as at 1 March 2019.

There is no doubt that the debate around the complex legal and regulatory issues surrounding FinTech has only just begun, but I believe that, equipped with the background that the chapters in this book offer, readers of this book will be able to follow this debate in the future, regardless of what policymakers ultimately decide.

Finally, I would like to acknowledge each and every author and co-author of this work for their contribution to a unique enterprise: the effort to analyse cutting-edge and often uncharted territory of FinTech laws and regulations. All of the 31 contributing authors, who come from four continents and ten countries, have worked towards a common project that I hope we will be able to develop over time as the technology-driven metamorphosis of the financial services sector continues to push boundaries of the traditional areas of law.

Jelena Madir

GLOSSARY OF KEY TERMS

algorithm	Software which uses a set of rules to create an automated process whereby outcomes are generated with little or no human intervention.
AML	Anti-money laundering.
application programming interface (API)	The underlying computer code behind applications which allow communication between software programmes or operating systems (for example, to allow information on a website to be displayed on both mobile devices and desktop browsers).
artificial intelligence (AI)	An area of computer science that emphasises the creation of intelligent machines that work and react like humans.
asymmetric encryption	Also known as public key cryptography, is a form of encryption where keys come in pairs. What one key encrypts, only the other can decrypt. Users typically create a matching key pair, and make one public while keeping the other secret (see private key and public key definitions below).
big data	A data set which derives value due to being very large in size, allowing it to be analysed in order to discover trends that would not be apparent with a smaller data set.
Bitcoin	Either a cryptocurrency or reference to the technology – a distributed network that maintains a ledger of balances of Bitcoin (the cryptocurrency).
blockchain	A type of distributed ledger taking the form of an electronic database that is replicated on numerous nodes spread across an organisation, a country, multiple countries, or the entire world. Records in a blockchain are stored sequentially in time in the form of blocks. Each block typically contains a cryptographic hash of the previous block, a timestamp and transaction data, which makes it inherently resistant to modification of the data.
business-to-business (B2B)	Refers to transactions between two businesses, rather than to transactions between a business and an individual consumer.
CFT	Countering the financing of terrorism.

chatbot	A computer program designed to stimulate conversation with human users, especially over the internet. It is often used for basic customer service and marketing systems, as well as in operating systems as intelligent virtual assistants, such as Siri and Alexa.
cloud computing	A model for storing data which allows access through the internet through using web-based tools, rather than requiring a direct connection to a particular server.
consensus	Refers to the act of more than 50 per cent of nodes concluding that a proposed block message is authenticated and verified, so that the block can be added to the distributed ledger.
consensus protocol	A computer protocol in the form of an algorithm constituting a set of rules for how each participant in a distributed ledger should process messages and how those participants should accept the processing done by other participants. The purpose of a consensus protocol is to achieve consensus between participants as to what a distributed ledger should contain at a given time.
crowdfunding	A method of collecting many small contributions, by means of an online funding platform, to finance or capitalise a popular enterprise, irrespective of whether that funding leads to a loan agreement, an equity stake or another transferable security-based stake.
cryptoassets	Digital assets recorded on a distributed ledger.
cryptocurrency (often used interchangeably with virtual currency)	A type of cryptoasset, which is a digital representation of value that is neither issued by a central bank or a public authority nor necessarily attached to a fiat currency, but is used by natural or legal persons as a means of exchange and can be transferred, stored or traded electronically (European Banking Authority). There are different types of cryptocurrencies. Bitcoin and Ethereum are among the best known.
cryptography	The science of taking information and transforming it in a manner in which it can be deciphered only by the intended recipient. It is used primarily to protect sensitive information.
cyber-attack	An attack, via cyberspace, targeting an organisation's use of cyberspace to disrupt, disable, destroy, or maliciously control a computing environment/infrastructure, destroy the integrity of the data or steal controlled information. It includes malware, phishing and spear phishing attacks, social engineering attack, denial-of-service and distributed denial-of-service, and advanced persistent threat.

cyber risk	The risk of financial loss, operational disruption, or damage, from the failure of the digital technologies employed for informational and/or operational functions introduced to a manufacturing system via electronic means from the unauthorised access, use, disclosure, disruption, modification or destruction of the manufacturing system.
cyber risk management	An ongoing process aimed at mitigating the impact of cyber-attacks by identifying the risks and adopting proper (a) pre-emptive measures to protect the IT infrastructure essential for conducting business with minimal or no interruption, and (b) remedies and response in case of a cyber-attack.
cyber threat	Refers to the threat of cyber-attack.
cyber threat actors	The actors responsible for cyber threats, including internal and external actors, varying from accidental or malicious insiders, hackers, hacktivists, petty criminals to organised crime, to nation states.
cyberwarfare	Refers to the most aggressive form of cyber-attack, usually carried out by a nation state, aimed at damaging another nation's computers or information networks, disrupting communities or countries and/or destroying critical infrastructure or industrial facilities in a manner that affects the national security of a state.
deep learning	A subset of machine learning that is concerned with emulating the learning approach that human beings use to gain certain types of knowledge. While traditional machine learning algorithms are linear, deep learning algorithms are stacked in a hierarchy of increasing complexity and abstraction.
denial-of-service attack	A cyber-attack in which the perpetrator seeks to make a machine or network resource unavailable to its intended users by temporarily or indefinitely disrupting services of a host connected to the internet.
digital currency	A type of currency available only in digital form, which can be fiat currency or cryptocurrency.
digital token	A digital representation of an asset. It typically does not have intrinsic value, but is linked to an underlying asset, which could be anything of value.
digital wallet	Software that allows users to make electronic payments, purchases and store their cryptocurrencies online.
distributed denial-of-service attack	A type of denial-of-service cyber-attack in which multiple compromised computer systems attack a target, such as a server, website or other network resource, and cause a denial of service for users of the targeted resource.

distributed ledger	A collection of records (making up a database), where identical copies of each record are held on numerous computers across an organisation, a country, multiple countries, or the entire world, either jointly or partitioned by the parties to which each record relates. A blockchain is a type of distributed ledger, but not all distributed ledgers are blockchains.
distributed ledger technology (DLT)	Software that creates a distributed ledger.
encryption	The method by which data is converted from a readable form to an encoded version that can only be decoded if a party has access to a decryption key.
Ether	A cryptocurrency whose blockchain is generated by the Ethereum platform.
Ethereum	An open software platform based on blockchain technology that enables developers to build and deploy decentralised applications.
EU	European Union.
FCA	UK Financial Conduct Authority.
FinTech	Refers to the use of technology in providing financial services that could result in new business models, applications, processes or products with an associated material effect on financial markets and institutions and the provision of financial services.
firmware	A software program or set of instructions programmed on a hardware device.
fork/forking	Occurs when participants in a blockchain system cannot immediately choose between two (or more) blocks upon which to continue the chain of blocks, so that two (or more) separate blocks are built on at the same time, creating a 'fork' in the chain.
GDPR	General Data Protection Regulation (EU) 2016/679.
hash/hashing	The process by which a grouping of digital data is converted into a single number, called a hash. The number is unique (effectively a "digital fingerprint" of the source data) and the source data cannot be reverse-engineered and recovered from it.
information technology (IT)	The study or use of systems (especially computers and telecommunications) for storing, retrieving, and sending information.
initial coin offering (ICO) (also referred to as a 'token sale')	The method of raising capital by an entity, whereby participants provide funds (in fiat and/or cryptocurrency) to the entity, in exchange for the issue, or right to future issue, of cryptoassets.

innovation hub	An institutional arrangement where regulated or unregulated entities engage with the competent authority to discuss FinTech-related issues (share information, views, etc.) and seek clarification on the conformity of business models with the regulatory framework or on regulatory/licensing requirements (i.e., individual guidance to a firm on the interpretation of applicable rules).
InsurTech	Refers to the use of technology innovations in the insurance industry.
Internet of Things (IoT)	A system of interrelated computing devices, mechanical and digital machines, objects, animals or people that are provided with unique identifiers and the ability to transfer data over a network without requiring human-to-human or human-to-computer interaction.
interoperability	The ability of databases, devices, or systems to talk with each other, exchanging information or queries. In some cases, interoperable databases or systems may be directly connected, allowing for the real-time exchange or updating of information; in others, databases or systems may be interoperable via a trusted third-party exchange layer that facilitates communication across disparate systems.
IP address	Unique address that identifies a device on the internet or a local network.
know your customer (KYC)	The process of a business verifying the identity of its clients and assessing potential risks of illegal intentions for the business relationship.
legacy system	Refers to computer systems, software, programming language, application programs or any other technology that is either out of date, obsolete or might be still in use because its application programs cannot be upgraded.
LegalTech	Refers to the use of technology and software to provide legal service.
machine learning	A variant of AI which involves creating a program to mimic learning, by which the programme adapts its approach based on past experience without the need for further programming to incorporate this.
malicious software (malware)	A simple, opportunistic and very common way to exploit vulnerabilities and flaws in a programme code. Malwares can affect a computer by being downloaded through accessing a malicious webpage or application, downloading a file from an email or even from a USB memory stick. It includes viruses, worms, Trojan horses, spyware, and ransomware.

man-in-the-middle cyber-attack	A cyber-attack where the attacker secretly relays and possibly alters the communication between two parties who believe they are directly communicating with each other.
Merkle tree	A data structure used for efficiently summarising and verifying the integrity of large sets of data. The root of a Merkle tree is a single hash representing all transactions. If a single detail in any of the transactions changes, so does the Merkle root.
metadata	A set of data that describes and gives information about other data. For example, information about the title, subject, author and size of the data file of a document constitutes metadata about that document.
MiFID 2	Markets in Financial Instruments Directive 2004/39/EC.
miners	Individuals or entities that run a special software to solve complex algorithms to validate cryptocurrency transactions. They get rewarded with the cryptocurrency created in the process.
mining	A process by which transactions are verified and added to the distributed ledger, and also the means by which new cryptocurrencies are released.
mining pools	A group of miners who combine their computational resources over a network.
native	Refers to assets, instruments or rights which exist only on the distributed ledger (i.e., in digital form). Cryptocurrencies are an example of a native asset.
natural language processing (NLP)	A field of artificial intelligence that enables computers to analyse and understand human language.
near-field communication	A set of communication protocols that enables two electronic devices, one of which is usually a portable device such as a smartphone, to establish communication by bringing them within 4 cm (1.6 in) of each other, and is used in contactless payment systems.
node	A single computer involved in processing a message in order to reach consensus. Nodes are connected to each other via the internet.
open banking	Refers to: (i) the use of open APIs that enable third-party developers to build applications and services around the financial institution, (ii) greater financial transparency options for account holders ranging from open data to private data, and (iii) the use of open source technology to achieve (i) and (ii).
open source software	Software with source code that is freely available for anyone to view, use and edit. Open source software may often be developed in collaborative, public manner.

oracle

An interface connecting a distributed ledger to a trusted data source or other input. In the context of blockchain, an oracle is a third-party information source that has the sole function of supplying data to blockchain, which allows for the creation of smart contracts. For example: Anna and Bob agree to bet on what the temperature will be on a Sunday. Anna bets that the temperature will be 20°C or above, while Bob bets that the temperature will be 19°C or below. They design a smart contract (to which they will both send funds), which will automatically pay out to the winner depending on what the temperature is. In order for the smart contract to determine the temperature, and thus, pay out to the winner, it must receive input from a trusted source – i.e., an oracle, and use the result to execute the smart contract. After receiving input from a local news website for the weather, the weather on Sunday is 24°C. The smart contract then executes on its conditions and sends all the funds to Anna.

permissioned/private distributed ledger

A distributed ledger is permissioned where its participants are pre-selected or subject to gated entry on satisfaction of certain requirements or on approval by an administrator of the ledger or some other mechanism. A permissioned ledger may use a consensus protocol for determining what the current state of facts should be, or it may use an administrator or sub-group of participants to do so.

permissionless/public distributed ledger

A distributed ledger is permissionless when anyone is free to submit messages for the purpose of, for example, processing and/or being involved in the process of reaching consensus. While a permissionless ledger will typically use a consensus protocol to determine what the current state of the chain should be, it could equally use some other process (such as using an administrator or subgroup of participants) to do so.

phishing and spear-phishing attacks

Digital scams that start by gaining a victim's trust; phishing targets numerous people, while spear-phishing is personalised by targeting specific people with specific information.

pilot

An approach to test a new proposition, often in the form of a minimum viable product, with a controlled subset of live customers to gain insight and feedback on functionality and satisfaction.

private key

An instance of data, privately held, and paired with a public key, used to initiate algorithms for text encryption and signing. A private key is created as part of a public key cryptography algorithm, and generates both the private and public key as a pair.

proof of concept   A realisation of a certain method or idea in order to demonstrate its feasibility, or a demonstration in principle with the aim of verifying that some concept or theory has practical potential.

proof of stake   A type of consensus protocol where, instead of mining, users can validate and make changes to the blockchain on the basis of their existing share ("stake") in the currency. This approach reduces the complexity of the decentralised verification process and can thus deliver large savings on energy and operating costs.

proof of work   A type of consensus protocol where each block is verified through a process called "mining" before information is stored. The data contained in each block is verified using algorithms that attach a unique hash to each block based on the information stored in it. Users continuously verify the hashes of transactions through the mining process in order to update the current status of the blockchain assets. Doing so requires an enormous number of random guesses, making it a costly and energy-intensive process – one that also faces speed constraints as the network grows.

PSD2   Payment Services Directive 2 Directive (EU) 2015/2366.

public key   An instance of data, available to anyone, paired with a private key to decrypt or verify text as part of public key cryptography.

public key infrastructure (PKI)   A set of roles, policies, and procedures needed to create, manage, distribute, use, store, and revoke digital certificates and manage public key encryption.

ransomware   A type of malware designed to block access to a computer system until a sum of money is paid.

RegTech (also known as regulatory technology)   A commonly recognised term for technologies that can be used by market participants to follow regulatory and compliance requirements more effectively and efficiently.

regulatory sandbox   Refers to a testing ground for innovative products, services and business models that can be tested without immediately being subject to all of the regulatory requirements. Sandboxes allow companies to test innovative products with temporary regulatory authorisation and under the regulator's supervision.

robo-advisor   A digital platform that provides automated, algorithm-driven financial advice with little or no human supervision. This usually involves clients answering a series of questions and providing an outcome based on their responses.

robotic process automation   Refers to software that can be easily programmed to do basic tasks across applications just as human workers do.

scale engagement   Moving a solution from a test or pilot state into a fully productionised and supported solution.

screen-scraping	Refers to a process of extracting and evaluating data from one application and translating it so that another application can display it.
smart contract[1]	Automatable and enforceable agreement: automatable by computer, although some parts may require human input and control; and enforceable either by legal enforcement of rights and obligations or via tamper-proof execution of computer code.
SMEs	Small- and medium-sized enterprises.
social engineering attacks	Explore human weaknesses to gain access to computer systems and networks by impersonating a friendly co-worker in need of help accessing a website.
start-up	Entrepreneurial venture often applying newly emerging technologies or business models to deliver an innovative new proposition or service with the intention of disrupting or materially enhancing established solutions.
SupTech (also known as supervisory technology)	The use of innovative technology by supervisory agencies to support supervision.
Sybil attack	A security threat on an online system where one person tries to take over the network by creating multiple accounts, nodes or computers.
tamper-proof technology	Typically refers to distributed networks of computers that are unstoppable and in a technological sense cannot fail regardless of malicious acts, power cuts, network disruption, natural disasters or any other conceivable event.
TechFin	A technology company offering financial services.
transmission control protocol/internet protocol (TCP/IP protocol)	A suite of communication protocols used to interconnect network devices on the internet.
UK	United Kingdom.
US	United States of America.

---

1 As described in Chapter 7, some define smart contract as a computer code that can automatically monitor, execute and enforce a legal agreement.

TABLE OF CASES

AUSTRALIA

EUROPEAN UNION

FRANCE

UNITED KINGDOM

UNITED STATES OF AMERICA

TABLE OF LEGISLATION

1

INTRODUCTION – WHAT IS FINTECH?

Jelena Madir

A. INTRODUCTION

Largely shrouded in hype and obscured by hyperbole, the word 'FinTech' is **1.01** simply a combination of the words 'financial' and 'technology'. It describes the use of technology to deliver financial services and products to consumers. This could be in the areas of banking, insurance, investing – anything that relates to finance. Increasingly, FinTech is coming to represent technologies that are disrupting traditional financial services, including mobile payments, money transfers, loans, fundraising and asset management. Yoshi Kawai, General Secretary of the International Association of Insurance Supervisors, a member organisation of the Financial Stability Board, offered a working definition of 'FinTech' as follows: it is a 'technologically enabled financial innovation. It is giving rise to new business models, applications, processes and products. These could have a material effect on financial markets and institutions and the provision of financial services'.[1]

This chapter proceeds as follows: Part B describes the development of **1.02** FinTech and its key features, Part C describes key players, products and

---

1 International Association of Insurance Supervisors Newsletter (June 2016), at 2.

trends, Part D analyses regulatory responses to FinTech and the impact FinTech will have on the legal practice. Part E concludes.

B. WHAT IS (AND ISN'T) NEW ABOUT FINTECH?

1.03 While some financial industry observers argue that FinTech has been around for decades and forms the lifeblood of all financial institutions (think ATMs), others posit that *this time is different* and that FinTech represents a phenomenon distinct from earlier eras of innovation. Both camps agree that it is the rapid evolution of FinTech over the past decades that has been transformational for the financial sector. A number of factors have conflated to turn FinTech into the poster child that continues to grab the headlines. First, following the 2008 global financial crisis, the brand image of banks was severely shaken. Such scandals as the LIBOR-fixing and foreign exchange price manipulation did not do banks any favours in terms of restoring public trust in the banking industry. For example, a 2015 survey reported that Americans trusted technology firms far more than banks to handle their money.[2] In addition, the global financial crisis damaged bank profitability and competitiveness, and the ensuing regulation drove compliance costs to record highs while simultaneously restricting credits. Requirements regarding ring-fencing, the preparation of recovery and resolution plans, and the performance of stress testing only contributed to rising bank costs. The crisis further led to large-scale redundancies, leaving many professionals seeking to apply their skills to new outlets.[3]

1.04 This, in turn, coincided with the rapid rate of technology development, high level of smartphone penetration and genuine sophistication regarding APIs. In today's digital age, people are seeking easy access, convenience, efficiency and speed. They want to conduct transactions via mobile technology platforms and applications, and such activities include managing their financial lives – from tracking their overall spending to applying for a loan and optimising their investment strategies. Given the level of service expectations from customers, there is no excuse for businesses not to embrace the latest technologies – and those who refuse will certainly be losing business. Moreover, the widespread adoption of mobile and internet technology is being driven by a change in

---

2   Banktech, Survey Shows Americans Trust Technology Firms More Than Banks and Retailers (25 June 2015), available at: https://gomedici.com/survey-shows-americans-trust-technology-firms-more-than-banks-and-retailers/.

3   Douglas W. Arner, Janos Barberis and Ross P. Buckley, FinTech and RegTech in a Nutshell, and the Future in a Sandbox, CFA Institute Research Foundation (2017), at 6.

demographics in emerging markets with a more technology savvy and connected generation of middle income investors. Investors between the ages of 18 and 34 are more likely to be internet and smartphone users and to participate in social media networks, compared to those aged 35 and older. As the income of this younger generation increases over time, it is expected that it will further drive the market size for FinTech.[4]

Importantly, not only is more information stored online, but the pace of **1.05** data-creation and its rapid availability to those seeking it has accelerated exponentially. For example, unlike in earlier decades, where information on underlying loans or mortgage-backed securities was sourced through central nodes of information, like credit rating agencies or conventional news organisations, the production of digital data is often decentralised, and emerges from a variety of websites, social media outlets and various types of news sources and databases.[5] Collectively, these developments are enabling the production of not only more data than in the past, but also *new* kinds of meta and secondary data not previously accessible. FinTech firms can scour the internet, including social media and mobile phone records for insight into customers. The cloud can help create secondary data based on the analysis and mining of original data.[6]

Closely related to the above is growing disintermediation driven by tech- **1.06** nology and the internet. For example, Tripadvisor combined with online travel agencies is disintermediating physical travel agencies, Amazon is disintermediating bookstores, iTunes is disintermediating CDs, Airbnb is disintermediating hotels, and Uber is disintermediating holders of official taxi operating licences. Similarly, innovative FinTech business models are disintermediating certain regulated activities. For instance, online equity crowdfunding platforms are disintermediating stock exchanges and underwriters and banks, peer-to-peer lending platforms are disintermediating banks and other lenders, and robo-advisers are disintermediating traditional financial advisers.[7] Advances in big data and machine learning have made it easier than ever for firms to cull information from traditional as well as alternative data sources, and develop new infrastructures designed to render irrelevant or bypass certain services of intermediaries like banks or securities

---

4   See Pew Global Research, Smartphone Ownership and Internet Usage Continues to Climb in Emerging Economies (2016).
5   Chris Brummer and Yesha Yadav, FinTech and the Innovation Trilemma (Spring 2018), available at: https://papers.ssrn.com/sol3/papers.cfm?abstract_id=3054770, at 28.
6   Ibid., at 29.
7   OICU-IOSCO, IOSCO Research Report on Financial Technologies (FinTech) (February 2017), at 7.

underwriters. By harnessing big data, algorithms and AI, firms are increasingly linking services and products directly with consumers, whether they are investors, entrepreneurs needing capital or borrowers.[8]

1.07 FinTech firms have attracted substantial investment in recent years, while public interest has grown significantly. Most firms have remained small – reflecting their knowledge-based business model, but investment in them has risen substantially. By June 2018, total global investment in FinTech companies reportedly hit USD 57.9 billion.[9] Venture capital investment has also risen steadily, from USD 0.8 billion in 2010 to nearly 20 billion by June 2018.[10]

C. KEY PLAYERS, PRODUCTS AND TRENDS

1.08 When people think of FinTech, they often focus on start-ups that are breaking into areas that banks and other legacy financial institutions have dominated. However, as illustrated in the Figure 1.1, the ecosystem of FinTech companies is considerably broader and covers:

- incumbent, well-established financial institutions such as HSBC, Barclays, Bank of America and Allstate, which are acquiring or working with FinTech start-ups and building their own innovative solutions;
- big technology companies that are active in the financial services space but not exclusively so, such as Apple, Google, Facebook, and Twitter;
- companies that provide infrastructure or technology that facilitates financial services transactions, such as MasterCard, Fiserv, First Data, various financial market utilities, and exchanges such as NASDAQ; and
- disruptors – the fast-moving companies, often start-ups, focused on a particular innovative technology or process, such as Stripe (mobile payments), Betterment (automated investing), Prosper (peer-to-peer lending), Moven (retail banking), and Lemonade (insurance).[11]

1.09 As an umbrella term, FinTech covers many technological disruptions related to finance. They can be classified in several categories: payments, insurance, investment advice, securities clearance and settlement, and alternative funding

---

8   Brummer and Yadav, *supra* note 5, at 37.
9   KPMG, The Pulse of FinTech 2018, available at: https://assets.kpmg/content/dam/kpmg/xx/pdf/2018/07/h1-2018-pulse-of-fintech.pdf, at 4.
10 Ibid., at 9.
11 PWC, What is FinTech? (2016), available at: https://www.pwc.com/us/en/financial-services/publications/viewpoints/assets/pwc-fsi-what-is-fintech.pdf, at 2.

Figure 1.1   FinTech players

platforms, all of which are enabled by cross-cutting technologies such as data analytics, distributed ledger technology/blockchain and cybersecurity. Table 1.1 lists key technologies and real-life examples associated with each of these categories.

Table 1.1   Real-life examples and technology disruptions related to finance

Category	Key technologies	Real-life examples
	FINTECH USE CASES	
Payments	Mobile payments, smartphone wallets, digital wallets, acceptance devices, Central Bank issued digital currencies	*Apple Pay, Android Pay, PayPal Mobile Express Checkout, Venmo, Square, TransferWise*
Insurance	Online insurance platforms, online brokers, peer-to-peer insurance	*Insureon, Knip, Oscar, Slice, Cuvva*
Investment advice	Robo-advisory, digital wealth management, digital investment tools, tailored financial messaging	*Motif, Wealthfront, Nutmeg, Juntos*
Securities clearing and settlement	Digital assets, DLT-based solutions	*Australian Stock Exchange (ASX) DLT settlement system, Hong Kong Exchange and Clearing Limited (HKEX)*
Alternative funding platforms	Equity-based crowdfunding and P2P lending platforms	*GoFundMe, Kickstarter, Lending Club, Funderbeam, Zelle, Crowdcube, Kabbage, Funding Circle*

Table 1.1 (continued)

Category	Key technologies	Real-life examples
CROSS-CUTTING ENABLING TECHNOLOGIES		
Data analytics	Big data, artificial intelligence, machine learning	*Equifax NeuroDecision credit scoring, Credit Benchmark, Bloomberg Social Sentiment Analytics, Solovis, Kreditech*
Distributed ledger technology/blockchain	Private key encryption, proof-of-work, proof-of-stake (and other protocols), cryptocurrencies, smart contracts	*Bitcoin, Ethereum, Ripple Payment Network, Coinbase*
Cybersecurity	Encryption, authentication, biometrics	*Diebold iris-scanning ATM, Mastercard Biometric Card, TeleSign, Experian CreditLock*

1.10 Let us look more closely at some of these:

1. Mobile payments and e-wallets

1.11 Mobile payments and e-wallets have made a huge impact on how people transact. Most mobile payment systems are based on a prepaid balance that is transferred by SMS, near-field communication, or using codes, but post-paid or real-time payments are also possible. As distinct from some other forms of electronic banking, the transferred money is available immediately and, depending on the system, a bank may not need to be directly involved.

1.12 A natural extension of mobile payments, mobile wallets let users store money and credit cards on their mobile devices and transact through their phones without ever opening their actual wallet. Google's Android pay and Apple's Apple Pay are two of the most well-known mobile wallets. Paypal has been considered as one of the pioneers of the digital payments industry. After its acquisition by eBay, Paypal payments rapidly gained popularity and became the choice of payment method for the majority of eBay users. This led to a chain effect, giving rise to a whole new segment concerned with digital payments – payment gateways, security companies and fraud detection software, to name a few.

2. Open banking/APIs

Open APIs are perceived by a number of institutions (particularly in the **1.13** European Union in view of the PSD2) as an opportunity to bring more tailored products to customers and offer new propositions. Through open APIs, institutions aim to ease the design and launch of new products to customers, taking advantage of the existing relationship of trust they may have built with customers, although it is yet unknown whether customers will consent to share their personal financial data with third-party providers.[12]

Recognising a number of potential risks that open APIs pose to consumers, **1.14** the European Banking Authority has developed regulatory technical standards, specifying the requirements for strong customer authentication, the requirements with which security measures have to comply to protect the confidentiality and the integrity of payment service users' personalised security credentials, and the requirements for common and secure open standards of communication.[13]

Mobile access and the internet have been transformational, allowing the gains **1.15** from technological progress to be shared directly with billions of individual consumers whose mobile devices are now portals for accessing a full range of financial services, and can be extended by third parties via APIs. This massive decentralisation is opening the door to crowdfunding platforms that disintermediate banks and directly connect those looking for financing with potential investors. Crowdfunding now means that one can raise money quickly and cheaply from people all over the world that one has never met. It has democratised the process of finding start-up capital and shortened the timeline from perhaps months of meetings to as little as a few weeks.

In addition, it is now also easier than ever for small businesses to accept **1.16** payments. Even farm stands in remote locations can accept credit and debit cards with tools like Square. Additionally, companies like TransferWise are providing ways to transfer money internationally, disrupting that sector by offering a 90 per cent discount on traditional bank transfer fees.

Another consequence of digitisation is that vast amounts of data now exist in **1.17** forms that can be readily aggregated and analysed with computing power.

---

12 Ibid., at 78.
13 European Banking Authority, Final Report, Draft Regulatory Technical Standards on Strong Customer Authentication and common and secure communication under Article 98 of Directive 2015/2366 (PSD2) (23 February 2017), available at: https://www.eba.europa.eu/documents/10180/1761863/Final+draft+RTS+on+SCA+and+CSC+under+PSD2+%28EBA-RTS-2017-02%29.pdf.

Online and mobile applications that draw on these data make it possible for consumers to view banking and other financial account information, often held at different financial institutions, on a single platform, monitor the performance of their investments in real-time, compare financial and investment products, and even make payments or execute transactions. Applications can also assist with automatic savings, budget advice, credit decisions, and fraud and identity theft detection in real-time.[14]

1.18 In short, digitised record-keeping and its applications have exponentially improved a consumer's ability to make financial decisions. They have given rise to a new sector of non-bank financial institutions focused on products and services utilising data aggregation, based on data obtained with the consumer's consent. The rise of such financial institutions presents questions regarding the way in which they operate and are currently regulated.

3. Artificial intelligence (AI) and big data

1.19 Artificial intelligence (AI) and big data can parse vast databases through advanced algorithms to derive patterns used to predict behaviour and prices, and in the end mimic human judgement in automated decisions. Related applications can automate credit approvals or advice, facilitate regulatory compliance and fraud detection, and automate the trading of financial assets.

1.20 Recent work from the Joint Committee of the European Supervisory Authorities has found that big data brings many benefits for the financial industry and consumers, such as more tailored products and services, improved fraud analytics or enhanced efficiency of internal organisational procedures. On the other hand, consumers should be made particularly aware of some of the risks posed by big data. The risks identified include the potential for errors in big data tools, which may lead to incorrect decisions being taken by financial service providers. In addition, the increasing level of segmentation of customers, enabled by big data, may potentially influence the access to and availability of certain financial services or products.[15]

---

14 See Letter from the Center for Financial Services Innovation to the Bureau of Consumer Financial Protection, CFPB-2016-0048 Request for Information Regarding Consumer Access to Financial Records (21 February, 2017), available at: https://www.regulations.gov/document?D=CFPB-2016-0048-0047.

15 Joint Committee of the European Supervisory Authorities: Joint Committee Final Report on Big Data (15 March 2018), at 14.

4. Machine learning

A sub-category of AI, machine learning is a method of teaching computers to **1.21** parse data, learn from it, and then make a determination or prediction regarding new data. Rather than hand-coding a specific set of instructions to accomplish a particular task, the machine is 'trained' using large amounts of data and algorithms to learn how to perform the task. Machine learning provides the financial sector with new methods of performing statistical analysis and performing tasks. Institutions and relevant service providers have already started using machine learning for a variety of purposes, such as credit scoring, for which it could improve services and pricing customisation, given its ability to process significantly larger amounts of data input than classic statistics analysis. For example, a number of new entrant FinTech firms are capitalising on this opportunity by leveraging on large amounts of data to produce challenger credit scoring models that assess creditworthiness faster and supposedly more accurately, and possibly also in cases where conventional data is not available.[16]

5. Biometrics

Biometrics identifies individuals through unique physical characteristics, such **1.22** as facial recognition, fingerprint and iris verification, as well as behavioural patterns, such as voice identification. Biometric authentication gives financial institutions independence from passwords, PINs, and tokens, which are susceptible to attack, and can offer significant opportunities, ranging from security to mobile payment solutions.[17] Notably, however, biometrics is not fool-proof and ramifications of any security breach involving biometric information is likely to be much more serious than a security breach involving a password or a PIN.

6. Robo-advice

Robo-advice is an online service that uses algorithms to automatically **1.23** perform many investment tasks done by a human financial adviser. Initially offered by start-ups, robo-advice is now part of the suite of services offered by major financial institutions such as Vanguard, Schwab and Fidelity.[18] Since they are less expensive than a human adviser, they democratise access

---

16 European Banking Authority, Report on the Impact of FinTech on Incumbent Credit Institutions' Business Models (3 July 2018), ¶ 83.
17 Ibid., ¶77.
18 The Rise of the Robo-advisor: How Fintech Is Disrupting Retirement, Knowledge@Wharton (14 June 2018).

to financial advice – they can take on customers with few savings since adding one more person will not cost much more. While an automated advice model could help mitigate some of the risks associated with human advisers and managing a large salesforce, ultimately the design of the robo-advice model is crucial and a poorly designed model could lead to systemic mis-selling. Managing risks is ultimately the responsibility of the individual firm and its senior management.[19]

7. Blockchain

1.24 Blockchain is a unique type of computerised ledger, which relies on cryptographic techniques and new methods for consensus to capture and secure the data. It is designed to be read by a computer, rather than by the human eye. The following traits characterise blockchain:

- the ledger is shared among and worked on by multiple participants, none of which has a single point of control over it;
- an ever-growing chain of ledger entries ('blocks') links the entire history in such a way as to prevent tampering with or rewriting past records;
- digitally signed transactions or instructions indicate intent to record or modify data, or to transfer digital assets.[20]

1.25 Blockchain technology offers a commonly agreed record of truth to multiple, mutually distrusting participants in an economic system. It uses a decentralised, peer-to-peer network comprised of many users, which maintains a ledger of transactions and relies upon multiple users to confirm the veracity and authenticity of such transactions using cryptography. Blockchain essentially provides a 'record book' of each component of a transaction and this record book is maintained and instantaneously authenticated on a network that is shared between a theoretically infinite number of computers. When all the members of the network approve a transaction, that transaction is added to the record book and such a transaction cannot be tampered with or altered.

1.26 A research report from Goldman Sachs offers a concise summary, explaining the core concept of how the consensus mechanism functions in a blockchain:

---

19 See *Robo Advice: an FCA Perspective*, a speech by Bob Ferguson, Head of Department, Strategy & Competition Division, Financial Conduct Authority (11 October 2017), available at: https://www.fca.org.uk/news/speeches/robo-advice-fca-perspective.

20 Michael Casey et al., *The Impact of Blockchain Technology on Finance: A Catalyst for Change*, Geneva Reports on the World Economy (2018), at 1, available at: http://www.sipotra.it/wp-content/uploads/2018/07/The-Impact-of-Blockchain-Technology-on-Finance-A-Catalyst-for-Change.pdf.

(1) It is a database containing transactions between two or more parties, where the copies of this database are replicated across multiple locations and computers being the nodes.

(2) This database is made of 'a chain of blocks', with each block containing data such as details of the transaction – the seller, the buyer, the price, the contract terms and other relevant details.

(3) The transaction information contained in each block is validated by all nodes in the network via an algorithm called 'hashing'. The transaction is valid if the result of hashing is confirmed by all nodes.[21]

For most financial data, however, the world still relies on central inter- **1.27** mediaries such as banks, accounting firms and governmental entities to create and maintain centralised, private databases, which keep track of such data and the transactions they comprise. In many cases, these databases are powered by obsolete, legacy computer systems that are inefficient, slow, costly and incompatible with other legacy systems. For most financial institutions, improving the customer experience has been their number one priority. Unfortunately, while the vast majority of banks and credit unions aim to compete and win new business by offering a personalised digital consumer experience that removes friction, existing bank infrastructure built on legacy systems may make this difficult.

A centralised database managed by one entity is susceptible to cyberattack and **1.28** error, and in some parts of the world, is affected by political and state manipulation. Effectively, the central intermediaries, through their own private databases, determine: (i) the status of each transaction; (ii) the ownership of certain goods; and (iii) the speed at which a transaction is completed. By contrast, the possibility of recording data and transferring value without the mediation of trusted third parties means that the speed of such matters can be increased, while the costs are reduced by not just avoiding transaction fees, but also, for instance, the costs of security, supervision and enforcement.

As described in more detail in Chapter 6, most of the blockchain platforms **1.29** being developed for use in financial services are 'permissioned', both in terms of who can access the network and who can update it. This means that access to the network is restricted to a list of known and approved parties, for example, banks who already trade with each other. The use of permissioned platforms might be preferable in some cases because financial institutions handle sensitive data and need to know who they are dealing with on the platform. There are also practical benefits to permissioned networks: if only

---

21 Goldman Sachs, Blockchain – Putting Theory in Practice (2016), at 8.

known and trusted users are admitted to the network, the consensus mechanism used can be significantly faster and more energy- and cost-efficient than in permissionless systems. Nevertheless, permissioned systems do not achieve the full potential of decentralisation that can be achieved through permissionless systems.

1.30 Many have recognised potentials of blockchain to, among other things, improve transparency and reduce transaction costs by better managing data and streamlining processes, improve supply chains, enable the tracking and management of intellectual property, improve reliability and traceability of records, reduce speed and cost of settlement, facilitate copyright and patent protection, and improve efficiency using automated reporting and smart contracts.

1.31 Yet, there are still significant challenges to broad application of blockchain:

(1) First, performance (particularly transaction capacity and scalability) of blockchain is still an issue – no blockchain has yet been able to process billions of transactions in a second in a way that the current banking payment systems can.[22]

(2) Second, there are concerns about privacy and security, with some stakeholders, particularly in the law enforcement and regulatory sectors being concerned that the pseudonymous nature of blockchain-based records obscures the identity of actors. Moreover, the fact that data once stored on the ledger cannot be erased may be at odds with the 'right to be forgotten' granted in some jurisdictions.

As illustrated in Figure 1.2, design choices made by blockchain developers, particularly with respect to the degree of data distribution and decentralisation of control, often lead to inevitable trade-offs that must be made between performance, privacy and resilience (i.e., the degree of decentralisation). Hopefully, future technical advancements will alter these trade-offs.

(3) Third, there are challenges relating to the interoperability: (i) between different blockchains, (ii) between applications built on the same blockchains, and (iii) between blockchain and legacy systems.[23] For example, in the potential area of application for post-trading settlement, it will be important to ensure interoperability among the systems of all current

---

22 House of Commons Treasury Committee, Crypto-assets, Twenty-Second Report of Session 2017–19 (September 2018), para 22.

23 See, e.g., European Parliament, Distributed Ledger Technologies and Blockchain: Building Trust with Disintermediation, P8_TA-PROV(2018)0373, para 40.

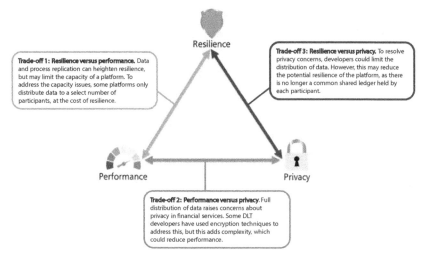

Source: HM Treasury, Financial Conduct Authority and Bank of England: Cryptoassets Taskforce: final report (October 2018), at 26.

Figure 1.2   Trade-offs in blockchain design

market participants (brokers, issuers, investors, trading venues and financial market infrastructure operators).

(4)   Fourth, there are concerns about the theft or loss of private keys, which allow the owners to control their digital assets and, if lost, the owners will lose such control. Private keys have been stolen in various high profile incidents. For example, hackers managed to steal nearly USD 500 million worth of Bitcoin from Mt. Gox in 2014 without breaching the Bitcoin blockchain protocol, which eventually led to the collapse of this Bitcoin exchange.[24]

(5)   Fifth, there are trade-offs relating to the governance of blockchains, particularly with regard to software updates: while in a centralised environment, some trusted authority controls much of the governance of a system and is responsible for software updates, in the blockchain universe, for certain software updates, there must be a consensus among a distributed network, for which there is no controlling entity.

(6)   Sixth, for blockchain technologies to reach their potential, they must be fully brought within public policy and legal frameworks. Only with clear rules will there be broad adoption of blockchain technologies.[25]

(7)   Seventh, as with the application of other new technologies, firms' use of blockchain may also raise a number of competition questions. For example, if a permissioned blockchain network developed to become

---

24   OICU-IOSCO, *supra* note 7, at 61.
25   Casey et al., *supra* note 20 at 10–13.

essential infrastructure (for example, in clearing and settlement), there could be competition concerns around access.[26]

1.32 While it is still early days, several authorities have issued views on blockchain. For example:

- In 2016, the French Parliament voted a law (Law n°2016-1691 (art 120)), which authorised the French government to determine, by an ordinance, the rules that could allow for the holding and transfer of non-listed securities via a blockchain system.
- In 2016, Japan enacted amendments to the Payment Services Act, which came into force on April 1, 2017 and introduced the registration requirement for operators of 'virtual currency exchange businesses' (defined as businesses involving the exchange of virtual currency to legal currency or another virtual currency). In order to prevent money laundering and the financing of terrorism, a registered operator of a virtual currency exchange business is required to implement certain identity verification procedures, among other steps.
- In 2018, 26 EU Member States and Norway agreed to sign a Declaration creating the European Blockchain Partnership and cooperate in the establishment of a European Blockchain Services Infrastructure that will support the delivery of cross-border digital public services, with the highest standards of security and privacy.[27]

1.33 In addition, international organisations such as the International Organization of Securities Commissions, the Financial Stability Board, the Bank of International Settlements, the World Bank Group and the International Monetary Fund (IMF) are observing the developments of FinTech under their respective objectives. For example, in October 2018, the World Bank and the IMF launched the Bali FinTech Agenda, which offers a framework for the consideration of high-level issues by individual member countries, including in their own domestic policy discussions.[28] After all, the rapid growth of FinTech products is an international phenomenon and is becoming an important component of the global financial system. As a result, regulators and standard-setting bodies are increasingly focusing their efforts on building a regulatory framework to support these new products, services and processes.

---

26 HM Treasury, Financial Conduct Authority and Bank of England, Cryptoassets Taskforce: Final Report (October 2018), ¶ 3.12.

27 See Digibyte, European Countries Join Blockchain Partnership (April 2018), available at: https://ec. europa.eu/digital-single-market/en/news/european-countries-join-blockchain-partnership.

28 The Bali FinTech Agenda, available at: https://www.imf.org/en/Publications/Policy-Papers/Issues/2018/10/ 11/pp101118-bali-fintech-agenda.

D. HOW SHOULD REGULATORS RESPOND AND WHY SHOULD LAWYERS CARE ABOUT FINTECH?

Evidently, FinTech offers wide-ranging opportunities, which national author- **1.34** ities are keen to foster. It holds the promise to reduce costs and frictions, increase efficiency and competition, narrow information asymmetry and broaden access to financial services – especially in low-income countries and for underserved populations – although the benefits of technological change may take time to fully materialise.

At the same time, however, national authorities are rightly concerned about **1.35** potential risks posed to the financial system and to its customers in terms of consumer protection, the clarity and consistency of regulatory and legal frameworks, the adequacy of existing financial safety nets, and potential threats to financial integrity. As technology alters financial service attributes and market structure, financial regulation must adapt to remain effective. In turn, regulation could also have an important influence on the development of technology. The following are some of the key issues that emerge:

1. Distributed ledgers and data privacy

Spreading data over multiple nodes may facilitate access to private data, which **1.36** in turn could violate data protection laws. The current regulatory landscape, following the recent implementation of the GDPR, raises data protection and customer consent as key requirements to be respected by all institutions.

2. Rules governing ownership and contractual rights and obligations

Digital transformation of the economy and financial services requires wide- **1.37** ranging changes to the regulatory system. For example, there is a need to modernise regulations for digitally communicating with consumers. Other regulations that should be implemented are discussed throughout this book and include: updating regulations to better facilitate secure access to digitised data; authentication of digital identity; and support for core financial service activities such as lending, payments, and investment advice.

Moreover, DLT records the transfer of ownership of 'digital tokens', which **1.38** are essentially units on a ledger. They can either have intrinsic value them-selves (e.g., a 'native asset' like Bitcoin), or be digital representations of a physical or digital asset that exists outside the ledger. The legal status of a digital token and the legal effect of its transfer are not clear. For example, would the transfer of an asset-backed token (e.g., representing a security) on a ledger transfer legal ownership of the security, or would registration outside the ledger (e.g., in a corporate share registry) still be required? Jurisdictions are trying to develop answers to these questions but country practice varies, and will therefore require thought from policymakers.[29]

3. Regulatory sandboxes

1.39 Regulatory sandboxes are testing grounds for innovative products, services and business models that can be tested without immediately being subject to all of the regulatory requirements. A regulatory sandbox provides valuable insights to policymakers in understanding new technologies and their applications, but is not a substitute for effective, permanent regulatory frameworks that will eventually need to be put in place.[30] For example, the UK Financial Conduct Authority (FCA), which was one of the first regulators in the world to introduce a FinTech sandbox, requires prospective participants to demonstrate that the product: offers genuine innovation – either ground-breaking or significantly different offering in the marketplace; creates a measurable benefit to consumers – either direct or indirect; is intended for the UK financial services market; needs to be tested in the sandbox alongside the FCA; and is ready to test (e.g., testing plans are well developed with clear objectives, parameters and success criteria; some preliminary testing has been concluded to date; the company has the tools and resources required to enable testing in the sandbox; and the company has sufficient safeguards in place to protect consumers).[31]

1.40 Arguably, the greatest tangible benefits to sandbox firms are contacts with the regulator and the credibility that the participation in the regulator's sandbox gives them vis-à-vis customers and financiers. On the flipside, one might argue that regulatory sandboxes create a 'two-tier' system of start-ups, where those that are selected in the sandbox are given a (possibly unfair) advantage. Moreover, one could also question if regulators have the requisite skillset to determine whether a business concept is innovative. Rather than emulating the model of corporate innovation accelerators, regulators may instead want to engage in a more open dialogue with all (or at least a less exclusive group) of innovative start-ups that need assistance navigating the maze of regulatory

---

29   International Monetary Fund Staff Discussion Note, Fintech and Financial Services: Initial Considerations, SDN/17/05 (June 2017), at 17.

30   Ibid.

31   See FCA, Applying to the Regulatory Sandbox, available at: https://www.fca.org.uk/firms/regulatory-sandbox/prepare-application; see also FCA, Regulatory Sandbox Lessons Learned Report (October 2017), available at: https://www.fca.org.uk/publication/research-and-data/regulatory-sandbox-lessons-learned-report.pdf.

requirements. This is partly achieved through *'innovation hubs'*. These are essentially schemes set up by competent authorities to enable firms to engage with the authorities on FinTech-related issues and seek clarification on licensing and regulatory requirements.

In China, which has quite a permissive regulatory framework and therefore, **1.41** arguably, does not need a regulatory sandbox approach, authorities have introduced a range of *regulatory pilot projects* tied to liberalising the country's financial markets and improving financial access. For example, the China Insurance Regulatory Commission (CIRC), the country's insurance regulator, has introduced a two-year pilot project designed to give insurance companies the regulatory room to offer services and products across city and state lines. Starting from February 2017, the CIRC lets insurance companies based in any of Beijing, Tijanjin or Hebei to conduct business across these regions. The objective of the pilot is to encourage insurance companies to set up shop in Tianjin or Hebei, where costs are lower than in Beijing, and to sell their services into Beijing and elsewhere within the permitted zone. The pilot illustrates the regulator's attempt to test-run regulatory innovations within a controlled setting.[32]

4. RegTech

RegTech is generally defined as the adoption of new technologies to facilitate **1.42** more efficient and effective delivery of regulatory requirements. Over the past ten years, financial institutions have faced an ever-increasing regulatory burden. The cost of compliance has skyrocketed for many financial institutions, particularly global institutions needing to comply with regulatory requirements across jurisdictions. The growing cost of compliance (particularly since the introduction of such financial regulations as GDPR, PSD2, the Markets in Financial Instruments Directive II/Markets in Financial Instruments Regulation).[33]

Most existing RegTech solutions operate along one or both of these dimen- **1.43** sions: reducing the cost of compliance via automation, or leveraging technology to increase the effectiveness of compliance (e.g., by accessing broader data sets or employing better data analytics). According to the Institute of International Finance, this wave of RegTech innovation 'stands out from

---

32 See, e.g., China: Pilot programme for insurance company and agency cross-regional business, available at: https://www.lloyds.com/market-resources/market-communications/regulatory-communications/regulatory-communications/regulatory-news-articles/2017/03/china-pilot-programme-for-insurance-company-and-agency-crossregional-business, and Brummer and Yadav, *supra* note 5, at 46–7.

33 KPMG, The Pulse of FinTech 2018, Biannual global analysis of investment in fintech (July 2018), at 6.

other software solutions by linking advanced models and algorithms, machine learning and advanced analytics, and real-time capabilities'.[34] Moreover, unlike FinTech's inherently financial focus, RegTech's applications span many regulatory contexts, including monitoring companies' compliance with environmental regulations and real-time tracking of the location of airlines, to name but two simple examples of how technology could be used to improve not only regulation but also the regulated industry itself.[35]

1.44 In addition to helping companies with their compliance processes, RegTech solutions can also help regulators explore leveraging new compliance software and surveillance tools to evaluate compliance with regulatory requirements. Increasingly, regulators are also starting to embrace the notion that blockchain has wider applications than cryptocurrencies, including the potential to provide greater transparency, innovative ways to solve problems and increased access for citizens. Particular areas of regulatory focus include developing new ways to manage and track physical and digital assets, record internal transactions and verify identities.

1.45 Excessive or indiscriminate reliance on RegTech solutions may, however, create new problems and could potentially cause system wide disruptions. For example, if multiple financial institutions rely on a single firm providing such solutions or on a single regulator to aggregate the data, this entity could be subject to a cyberattack or a malfunctioning of the underlying technology.[36]

1.46 In sum, the pace of technological development and its applications to financial services have increased dramatically. It is critical that financial regulators stay abreast of developments and establish mechanisms for adopting appropriate regulation and guidance accordingly without stifling innovations that require time to mature. Regulators must be more agile than in the past in order to successfully uphold their missions without creating unnecessary barriers to innovation. This requires principles- and performance-based regulation that enables the private sector to adopt innovative, technology-based compliance solutions. In addition, regulators need to understand technology on the same

---

34 Institute of International Finance, *RegTech: Exploring Solutions to Regulatory Challenges*, 29 October 2015, available at: https://www.iif.com/topics/regtech/regtech-exploring-solutions-regulatory-challenges.

35 Douglas W. Arner et al., *supra* note 3, at 10.

36 International Monetary Fund Staff Discussion Note, Fintech and Financial Services: Initial Considerations, SDN/17/05 (June 2017), at 18.

timeline as business. To do this, financial regulators need to engage with the private sector to test and understand new technologies and innovations as they arise.[37]

As FinTech continues to blossom, its impact will arguably creep into various **1.47** legal disciplines, just as the internet became an integral part of the modern-day law practice. As is happening now, more and more clients will demand sophisticated legal advice related to their complex use of FinTech products to evolve their businesses.[38] Moreover, it is quite probable that the software and database tools that lawyers use in their practices will incorporate blockchain technology, so the way that legal services are provided will inevitably change. For example, drafting of contracts with a simple 'if this, then that' logic may be somewhat displaced by blockchain-based smart contracts. In addition, lawyers may soon be confronted with more clients with issues arising from the use of blockchain. The creation of courts such as the Intellectual Property Enterprise Court and the Technology and Construction Court, both in the UK, demonstrates the need for lawyers with specialist knowledge to respond to the growing number of technology-related disputes.[39]

Finally, lawyers will likely be required to work more closely with technologists **1.48** and/or have some basic understanding of programming skills in order to be able to verify that contractual terms expressed in a computer code accurately reflect the natural language contract. This trend is already evident with law firms around the globe developing innovation labs and in-house technology for the legal sector in order to boost their competitive advantage against other firms.[40]

E. CONCLUSION

There is a lot of excitement when it comes to FinTech. After all, it erodes **1.49** intermediation and financial supply chains, introduces a cast of new characters and leaves familiar financial functions to be performed by sophisticated algorithms. Proponents believe that FinTech will fundamentally change and

---

37 US Department of the Treasury, A Financial System That Creates Economic Opportunities: Nonbank Financial, Fintech, and Innovation (July 2018), at 170–71.

38 International Bar Associate Legal Policy & Research Unit Legal Paper, Rule of Law Versus Rule of Code: A Blockchain-Driven Legal World (November 2017), at 42.

39 Ibid., at 38.

40 See, e.g., Allen & Overy, Second Group of Tech Companies Confirmed to Join Fuse in May (April 2018), available at: http://www.allenovery.com/news/en-gb/Pages/Second-group-of-tech-companies-confirmed-to-join-Fuse-in-May.aspx.

improve finance. One very obvious improvement, that every industry disrupted by technology has seen, is the lowering of costs and improvement of services. The other improvement that we are likely to see is better, data-driven decision making. Technology companies are able to identify better loan prospects based on algorithms driven by millions of data points. This is effectively able to overcome human bias and prejudice.

1.50 FinTech is still in its nascent stages, however. The disruptions caused by FinTech in the banking and finance sector pose a substantial risk to incumbent banking and finance service providers, but where there is risk there are also opportunities. The way regulators respond will have a heavy bearing on the shape of FinTech in the years ahead. In-house legal departments will need to cast a gimlet eye on the intricate requirements and jurisprudential uncertainty that attend this infant dynamic. The industry is changing rapidly, and shrewd businesses and lawyers alike will want to stay informed in order to stay at the forefront of their markets. Those that do not will lose out on opportunities, customers and market share.

Part I

PAYMENTS, ALTERNATIVE FINANCING AND CRYPTOASSETS

2

ADAPTING TO A CHANGING PAYMENTS LANDSCAPE

Ben Regnard-Weinrabe and Jane Finlayson-Brown[1]

A. INTRODUCTION

2.01 Technology is perhaps the primary force behind the changing payments landscape we see today. The digital revolution has made it easier for new entrants to access the market and scale up their businesses, by enabling them to rapidly develop and deliver attractively priced and presented payments products. This has helped to bring greater speed, transparency and convenience to many aspects of our lives, whether it be shopping, sending money to family and friends, managing our personal finances or paying suppliers, among other things.

2.02 This chapter examines trends, regulatory developments and policy initiatives which have informed and supported the growing popularity of digital payment

---

1 Written in collaboration with Kalila Bolton, Martin Dowdall, Rose Hall, Nikki Johnstone, Heather Luckhurst and Heenal Vasu.

methods across the world. Whilst the chapter mainly discusses the payments landscape from a European perspective, many of the themes and issues identified are also highly relevant in other countries and regions. The chapter is structured as follows: Sections B and C set the stage by describing trends in the online and mobile banking market, as well as contactless payments. Section D examines the second EU Payment Services Directive (PSD2), as an example of a broad-reaching piece of legislation that aims to bring about increased competition and greater transparency and security across the European payments landscape. Section E discusses the UK's Open Banking project, as one of the first examples of a regulatory initiative to develop consensus on the use of open APIs in the banking/payments sector. Whilst PSD2 and Open Banking are about creating access to personal data, the EU General Data Protection Regulation (GDPR) is about protecting it. Given that new payment services will require access to significant amounts of personal data, they will need to comply with GDPR; in that context, Section F examines the interplay between PSD2 and GDPR. Section G concludes.

B. ONLINE AND MOBILE BANKING

With mobile phones now practically ubiquitous, it is perhaps unsurprising that **2.03** mobile payments have been a particularly innovative sector of the payments market. Mobile phones have often been the delivery channel for the provision of payments and banking services to customers whom traditional banks have not reached. Perhaps the best known example of this is the M-Pesa product operated by Safaricom, which allows users to send, receive and store money as well as make payments via their mobile phones.[2]

Where innovation leads, regulation often follows and we have seen new **2.04** legislation introduced or proposed around the world in order to respond to, and foster, the increasing digitalisation of payment services. Some examples of recent regulatory developments include:

- PSD2,[3] whose implementation allows both traditional financial institutions and their FinTech rivals to provide payment services, increasing competition and – hopefully – efficiency, and which is described more fully at Section D below;

---

2 Vodafone: M-Pesa, available at: https://www.vodafone.com/content/index/what/m-pesa.html#.
3 Directive (EU) 2015/2366.

- Singapore's Payment Services Act which, amongst other things, seeks to update the existing regulatory framework to reflect technological developments and new types of products such as digital payment tokens;[4]
- a proposal by the US Federal Reserve for a service to facilitate real-time interbank settlement of faster payments which will be available 24 hours a day, seven days a week, 365 days a year;[5] and
- a proposal to overhaul South Africa's payment processing legislation to ensure it is fit for purpose following the emergence of new payments technologies.[6]

2.05 This trend towards fostering the digitalisation of payments is best reflected in today's online and mobile banking market. Online or internet banking typically refers to banking services accessible through a financial institution's website, while mobile banking refers to banking services accessible via a smartphone or other internet-connected device, usually by means of a specifically designed app. The driver for ongoing adoption of both mobile and online banking is convenience: consumers migrate to solutions which make their lives easier and take the friction out of everyday tasks, for example, by virtualising their plastic cards and helping them to track their spending.

2.06 The October 2018 quarterly consumer trends research from Fiserv, Inc. (conducted online by the Harris Poll) is one of several recent surveys which describes adoption of online banking as 'mature,' also claiming that the vast majority of consumers have accessed online banking with mobile banking trailing only slightly behind.[7] Whilst balance checking is reportedly the most common activity, Fiserv also reports that 44 per cent of online users and 36 per cent of mobile users pay bills online – showing growing levels of trust in mobile and online banking beyond simply viewing it as a source of information.

---

4   Payment Services Act 2019 (No. 2 of 2019).
5   Lael Brainard speech, Supporting Fast Payments for All (3 October 2018), available at: https://www.federalreserve.gov/newsevents/speech/brainard20181003a.htm.
6   Ashlin Perumall, South Africa starts review of payment processing legislation (14 January 2019), available at: https://www.scl.org/news/10396-south-africa-starts-review-of-payment-processing-legislation.
7   Fiserv, Fiserv research shows digital habits driving banking shifts (16 October 2018), available at: https://newsroom.fiserv.com/news-releases/news-release-details/fiserv-research-shows-digital-habits-driving-banking-shifts.

Traditional banking providers still appear to come out on top in terms of **2.07** consumer trust and adoption relative to new (often 'digital only') entrants.[8] There is nonetheless growing adoption of services offered by challenger banks and non-bank providers (including FinTech companies), which are often based on new business and pricing models, and often provide a distinctive user experience, typically appealing to particular demographics or aimed at meeting specific needs.

With the growth of smartphones, technology companies have launched a **2.08** variety of mobile payment products. For example, Facebook launched peer-to-peer payments through its Messenger service in the US in 2015 and in the UK in 2017, with continuing roll out globally. Facebook has also launched its own e-commerce platform, Facebook Marketplace, which allows users in certain countries to buy and sell goods via the site.[9] Google recently incorporated a peer-to-peer service – Google Pay Send – as part of its Google Pay app. Meanwhile, in China, payment by mobile phone has been completely normalised by the widespread adoption of Alipay and WeChat.

Among the challenger banks, the UK's Starling Bank grew from 43,000 **2.09** personal current accounts in November 2017 to 210,000 accounts in August 2018, with 60 per cent of customers using their account every month – demonstrating good ongoing engagement beyond initial customer acquisition, and that the bank's service had been accepted as more than a niche offering.[10] A striking example of a successful non-bank providing banking style services, is Revolut, again a UK company, which launched in 2015 and has enjoyed rapid growth, reaching two million users in 2018. It has already diversified into cryptocurrency exchange services and also has plans to offer share trading services which would bring it into direct competition with the likes of Robinhood, a US FinTech company.[11]

Further developments may come from cryptocurrencies and blockchain. As **2.10** described in Chapter 6, distributed ledger technology (DLT) holds out the promise of a rapid and low cost, low friction exchange of value between parties

---

8   *The Telegraph*, Future of Fintech. Consumer Survey 2017 presented by *The Telegraph* – 'What consumers really think', available at: https://www.telegraph.co.uk/content/dam/business/spark/Fintech/Telegraph_Fintech_Report%202017.pdf.

9   Mary Ku, Introducing marketplace: buy and sell with your local Community (3 October 2018), available at: https://newsroom.fb.com/news/2016/10/introducing-marketplace-buy-and-sell-with-your-local-community/.

10 Starling Bank, Letter from the CEO, No. 1, August 2018 (August 2018), available at: https://www.starlingbank.com/investors/2018/letter-from-ceo/.

11 Ryan Browne, Fintech start-up Revolut grabs 2 million users and plans to launch commission-free trading service, CNBC (7 June 2018), available at: https://www.cnbc.com/2018/06/07/revolut-has-2-million-users-to-launch-commission-free-trading-service.html.

without the need for clearing and/or settlement through traditional payment systems – or, potentially, traditional payment systems may be upgraded based on DLT. Many financial institutions are investing in the sector whether by way of bespoke projects or consortia for performance of inter-bank transfers. Ripple is one of the more high-profile players, with 100 banks globally signed up to its enterprise blockchain network, RippleNet.[12] Ant Financial has also partnered with Standard Chartered Bank to launch a blockchain cross-border remittance service.[13] Commentators also expect blockchain technology and DLTs to disintermediate various other key banking services which form part of a USD 134T industry.[14]

C. GROWTH IN CONTACTLESS PAYMENTS

2.11 As we look for greater convenience and lower costs of transacting, the growing popularity of contactless technologies to make payments has become a significant factor in the decline of cash.

2.12 Contactless payments are typically card, mobile, smartwatch or other device payments made on the basis of near field communication (NFC) technologies, with the device needing to be held in close proximity to a reader in order to make a low-value transaction without the need for authentication at the point of sale – for example, by personal identification number (PIN) or signature (albeit the device itself, such as a mobile phone, may already have required an authentication step before a contactless payment can be initiated).

2.13 Contactless payments are convenient for both customers and retailers: they are much quicker than conventional cash or card purchases and more secure since they use encrypted data which reduces the likelihood of card information being intercepted by fraudsters.

2.14 Global adoption is varied – but some markets, such as Australia and the UK, have seen contactless payments soar over the last ten years, with one report

---

12 Kelly Johnson, RippleNet Grows to More Than 100 Financial Institutions, *Ripple Insights* (10 October 2017), available at: https://ripple.com/insights/ripplenet-grows-to-over-100-financial-institutions/.

13 Standard Chartered, We have been appointed by Ant Financial as core partner bank for its new blockchain cross-border remittance service (25 June 2018), available at: https://www.sc.com/en/media/press-release/we-have-been-appointed-by-ant-financial-as-core-partner-bank-for-its-new-blockchain-cross-border-remittance-service/.

14 CBInsights, How blockchain could disrupt banking (12 December 2018), available at: https://www.cb insights.com/research/blockchain-disrupting-banking/.

stating that almost two-thirds of Britons were using contactless payments – with the number of payments made doubling over just one year.[15] Uptake of contactless payments in Asia has been remarkable and this success is also translating internationally. Ant Financial's Alipay business has reached 900 million users worldwide.[16] South Korean company, Samsung, has also achieved impressive global coverage with its Samsung Pay service now available in 24 countries across six continents,[17] with the mobile contactless payment service competing across the world with similar services rolled out by Google and Apple.

The rise of wearable tech is also accelerating contactless payment adoption. **2.15** Fully integrated solutions like the AppleWatch, Wear OS by Google, Samsung's Gear smartwatches and Jawbone's fitness tracking wristband all incorporate payment solutions, whilst a range of stickers and fobs can be added to physical products to enable contactless payments. Another example is Barclays bank teaming up with a number of watch brands such as Timex and Guess to put its payment chip into their products. Festivals, cruise ships and theme parks are popular use cases for wearable payment devices. For example, Disney World's 'Magic Band' enables visitors to pay for rides and food, and even enter their hotel rooms. A complex ecosystem however, means that we may still be some way off mass adoption of payments using wearables.[18]

The stakeholders in the contactless payments sector include banks, payment **2.16** systems, mobile operators, equipment manufacturers and technology providers. Apple Pay, for example, involves storage of cards provided by third-party banks or other issuers, with the card details being tokenised by the card schemes (such as Visa) for storage on an app stored on an iPhone enabled with contactless functionality. The device communicates with card acceptance terminals built by hardware providers to also incorporate contactless functionality in line with technical standards set by third-party bodies (likely with input from card schemes).

---

15 Visa, global payments technology: The rise of contactless payments around the globe (18 December 2017), available at: https://vision.visaeurope.com/blogs/the-rise-of-contactless-payments-around-the-globe.

16 Xinhua, China's Alipay now has over 900m users worldwide (30 November 2018), available at: http://www.chinadaily.com.cn/a/201811/30/WS5c00a1d3a310eff30328c073.html.

17 Samsung, Samsung Pay now available in six continents, accelerating global expansion (21 August 2018), available at: https://news.samsung.com/global/samsung-pay-now-available-in-six-continents-accelerating-global-expansion.

18 Smart Payment Association, Wearable tech: a growing payment opportunity (July 2017), available at: https://www.smartpaymentassociation.com/index.php/liste-documents/public-resources/position-papers/612-wearable-tech-growing-payment-opportunity-spa-july-17/file , at 6.

2.17 There are some concerns about contactless payments. One, at a public policy level, is that by taking too much of the friction out of payments, society might be encouraging consumers to spend too freely. Another is that without additional security, there is the risk of substantial payment fraud if devices are lost or stolen; in many countries, the payment card industry sets contactless 'floor limits' – for example, in the UK, this limit is GBP 30.[19] However, many retailers will allow higher value purchases by, for example, smartphone contactless payment services which provide for additional biometric authentication (e.g., fingerprint or facial recognition for payments via ApplePay).

2.18 With the payments landscape having changed so profoundly in the past decade, many countries are reviewing their regulatory framework to ensure that it serves the changing needs of customers and providers. Regulators are tasked with balancing the need to preserve consumer protection and enhance cybersecurity alongside responding to technological developments, improving competition and encouraging innovation. By way of example, recent (and ongoing) reforms to the European payments regulatory framework have brought about a series of changes designed to bring about technological, contractual and regulatory convergence to mobile payments.

D. PSD2 AND REGULATORY TECHNICAL STANDARDS ON STRONG CUSTOMER AUTHENTICATION AND SECURE COMMUNICATION

1. Second EU Payment Services Directive (PSD2)

2.19 PSD2 came into force on 12 January 2016 and EU Member States were required to transpose its provisions into national law by 13 January 2018.[20] PSD2 – which is supplemented by various delegated acts, technical standards and guidelines – repealed and replaced the first EU Payment Services Directive[21] (PSD1), which had been in force since 25 December 2007.

2.20 The European Commission considered PSD2 to be necessary to address what it considered to be gaps in the regulatory regime for payment services and to update the legal framework to address technological innovations (particularly

---

19   The UK Cards Association, News Release, £2.5bn spent using contactless cards in first half of 2015 as limit rises (September 1 2015), available at: http://www.theukcardsassociation.org.uk/wm_documents/010915%20 contactless%20payments.pdf.
20   At the time of writing, PSD2 has still not been fully implemented in all EU jurisdictions.
21   Directive 2007/64/EC.

internet and mobile payments) that had proliferated since the introduction of PSD1, some of which hitherto fell outside the existing regulatory perimeter.

The key objectives of PSD2, as articulated by the European Commission[22] **2.21**
were to:

- contribute to a more integrated and efficient European payments market;
- improve the level playing field for payment service providers (including new players);
- make payments safer and more secure; and
- protect consumers.

Changes under PSD2

In order to meet these policy objectives, PSD2 introduced numerous changes **2.22** to the existing EU payment services regime, some of which are described below. The changes were intended to create a more harmonised regulatory regime across the EU (and indeed the broader European Economic Area) with more consistent interpretation of the regulatory perimeter.

Scope of PSD2

Under PSD1, the transparency and conduct of business requirements applic- **2.23** able to payment service providers (PSPs) were triggered only in respect of payment services that took place entirely within the EU (i.e., where both the payer's and payee's PSPs were located in the EU) and were undertaken in relation to payment transactions denominated in euro or the currency of an EU Member State. PSD2 has extended the scope of these obligations so that in many respects they now also apply to:

(i)   'one leg out' transactions (i.e., transactions where only one of the payer's or payee's PSPs is located in the EU); and
(ii) transactions denominated in non-EU currencies.

Exclusions

The European Commission indicated that, in its opinion, certain exclusions **2.24** from regulation under PSD1 had been inconsistently applied and, in some cases, had been applied more broadly than had been intended.[23] Accordingly,

---

22   See response to question 3 in the European Commission's FAQ on the Payment Services Directive published 12 January 2018, available at: http://europa.eu/rapid/press-release_MEMO-15-5793_en.htm.
23   An example is the commercial agent exclusion. In its Proposal for a Directive of the European Parliament and of the Council on payment services in the internal market and amending Directives 2002/65/EC, 2013/36/EU and 2009/110/EC and repealing Directive 2007/64/EC, the European Commission stated that:

PSD2 brought about several significant changes to these exclusions, including the following:

(i) The 'limited network' exclusion (LNE) was narrowed to cover only services based on specific instruments which fall within one of three categories: (A) payment instruments which are only accepted within the issuer's premises (or a limited network of service providers); (B) instruments which can only be used to acquire a 'very limited range' of goods or services; or (C) instruments valid only in a single EU Member State issued for specific social or tax purposes.

(ii) Firms wishing to rely on the LNE are now required to notify the relevant competent authorities where transaction volumes shall exceed EUR 1 million over a 12-month period. PSD1's 'digital download' exclusion was replaced with an exclusion for transactions by electronic communication networks or services (which are provided in addition to electronic communications services) for subscribers for the purchase of 'digital content and voice-based services' or 'charitable activity or ... the purchase of tickets' via an electronic device.[24]

This exclusion does however have certain transaction limits; it is not available for (i) single transactions above EUR 50; or (ii) in the case of subscriptions, transactions above EUR 300 per month.

Changed and additional payment services

2.25 PSD1 regulated the 'acquiring of payment instruments,' but did not define the nature of the activity, which is likely to have led to some differences in interpretation. PSD2 relabelled the activity as the 'acquiring of payment transactions,' and defined it as 'a payment service provided by a payment service provider contracting with a payee to accept and process payment transactions, which results in a transfer of funds to the payee'.[25] The new definition, in combination with an emphasis on a narrower construction of the 'commercial agent' exclusion[26] under PSD2, has potentially brought a range of previously unregulated acquiring services within the scope of PSD2 (e.g., many online marketplaces have now obtained payments licenses in Europe or have instead partnered with an online payment provider, such as PayPal.)

'The "commercial agent" exemption ... has increasingly been used with regard to payment transactions handled by e-commerce platforms on behalf of both the seller (payee) and the buyer (payer). This use goes beyond the purpose of the exemption and should thus be further circumscribed.'

24 PSD2, art 3(l).
25 Ibid., art 4(44).
26 Ibid., art 3(b).

PSD2 introduced two new regulated payment services. Their introduction was **2.26** considered necessary to fill what had become something of a legal vacuum, whereby certain online service providers (such as account aggregators) fell outside the regulatory perimeter whilst still having (or wishing to have) access to either customer payment flow or account transaction data. Since these providers were not regulated, they were not subject to the same consumer protection or conduct of business requirements as apply to regulated PSPs. Post PSD2, these providers benefit from rights of access to the payments market by becoming regulated, as discussed below.

The two new services, referred to collectively as third party payment services **2.27** (TPPS), are:

(i)   Account information service (AIS), defined as:

'an online service to provide consolidated information on one or more payment accounts held by the payment service user with either another payment service provider or with more than one payment service provider',[27]

and covers a range of online account aggregation tools. Examples include such FinTech companies as Cleo, Money Dashboard and Plum.

(ii)   Payment initiation service (PIS), defined as:

'a service to initiate a payment order at the request of the payment service user with respect to a payment account held at another payment service provider',[28]

and facilitates payments direct from a customer's bank account (rather than via debit/credit cards). Examples include such FinTech companies as Sofort and Trustly.

The introduction of these TPPS extends the regulatory regime to cover new **2.28** technologies, encourage competition and innovation in the payments market, which – in principle – may lead to reduced prices for customers.

Access to payment accounts

Providers of TPPS appropriately licensed under PSD2 are, on behalf of their **2.29** customers, allowed to access third party accounts (and account information) without the need for bilateral agreements with the account provider (e.g., the customer's bank); in PSD2, this provider is referred to as the account servicing

---

27   Ibid., art 4(16).
28   Ibid., art 4(15).

payment service provider (ASPSP). ASPSPs are obliged to enable such access on a non-discriminatory and secure basis – for example, via a dedicated API.[29]

Access to bank accounts

2.30 PSD2 also seeks to address the challenge of bank 'de-risking,' which has meant that FinTech companies licensed under PSD2 have sometimes struggled to obtain access to banking services as necessary to deliver their regulated payment services. Banks are now required to provide certain FinTech companies with payment accounts at the bank 'on an objective, non-discriminatory and proportionate basis.' That access must be 'sufficiently extensive as to allow [the FinTech companies] to provide payment services in an unhindered and efficient manner'.[30] If a bank declines to grant such access, it must provide its competent authority with 'duly motivated reasons for any rejection'.

Access to payment systems

2.31 PSD2 introduces access requirements for certain PSPs seeking to use payment systems.[31] Rules of access must be: 'objective, non-discriminatory and proportionate and that they do not inhibit access more than is necessary to safeguard against specific risks such as settlement risk, operational risk and business risk and to protect the financial and operational stability of the payment system'.[32] This is a direct access requirement, which does not however apply to payment systems which are designated under the Settlement Finality Directive (SFD).[33] Indirect access to payment systems designated under the SFD must nonetheless be granted on 'an objective, non-discriminatory and proportionate basis'.[34]

Security

2.32 PSD2 introduces increased security requirements including around the secure storage and processing of customer and payment transaction data. One such measure is the introduction of strong (two-factor) customer authentication (SCA) for online payments, which is discussed in the following section.

---

29 Ibid., art 98(1)(d).
30 Ibid., art 36.
31 Ibid., art 4(7).
32 Ibid., art 35(1).
33 Directive (98/26/EC).
34 PSD2, art 35(2).

2. Strong customer authentication

As noted above, one of the main aims of PSD2 was to make payments safer **2.33** and more secure, most notably through the introduction of a requirement for SCA, and building on quasi-regulatory guidelines published by the European Banking Authority (EBA) in December 2014 on the security of internet payments (the EBA Guidelines).[35]

Accordingly, the EBA was mandated under PSD2 to draft Regulatory **2.34** Technical Standards on SCA (the RTS) to supplement PSD2.[36] The RTS were adopted by the European Commission and came into force on 14 March 2018 and apply from 14 September 2019.[37] As they take the form of a delegated regulation, they will be directly applicable and do not require implementing legislation in each EU Member State.

Scope

The scope of the RTS is broader than the previous EBA Guidelines, which **2.35** applied only to 'payment services offered through the internet' and excluded 'mobile payments other than browser-based payments'.[38] PSD2 is more neutral in scope, with article 97 stating that SCA must be applied where:

'... the payer:

(a)   accesses its payment account online;
(b)   initiates an electronic payment transaction;
(c)   carries out any action through a remote channel which may imply a risk of payment fraud or other abuses'.[39]

In particular, under limb (b) of this definition, the scope of SCA extends to **2.36** broader types of electronic payment transaction, including internet, mobile, in-app, and other electronic payments initiated by the payer (defined as the person 'who holds a payment account and allows a payment order from that payment account, or, where there is no payment account, a ... person who gives a payment order').[40] Per limb (a), SCA also applies to the simple act of a payer accessing its payment account online.

---

35   Final Guidelines on the Security of Internet Payments, EBA/GL/2014/12_Rev1, (19 December 2014).
36   PSD2, art 98.
37   Commission Delegated Regulation (EU) 2018/389 (27 November 2017).
38   EBA Guidelines, ¶¶ 2 and 11.
39   PSD2, art 97.
40   Ibid., art 4(8).

2.37 The scope of what triggers SCA on the basis that it constitutes an 'action through a remote channel which may imply a risk of payment fraud or other abuses' (as in limb (c)) is less clear. Various guidance suggests that this is aimed at the establishment by the payer of certain electronic mandates for *payee* initiated transactions (such as direct debits).[41] For example, the EBA states that 'if the payer's consent for a direct debit transaction is given in the form of an electronic mandate, it qualifies as falling under the category of "any action through a remote channel which may imply a risk of payment fraud or other abuses"'.[42] However, there is also guidance to suggest that SCA may only be triggered here if the payer's PSP is also involved in the establishment of the electronic mandate (and indeed such involvement would, presumably, generally be necessary as a practical matter since – for example – the PSP's platform would typically be used to input and transmit the details of a direct debit instruction). We understand that the exact scope of the SCA requirements in these and similar circumstances is subject to further clarification discussions among relevant authorities.

2.38 Geographically speaking, SCA is not expressly limited in scope. However, the EBA has in particular recognised that where card payment transactions are initiated through a payee (e.g., merchant) outside the EEA, SCA only applies on a 'best efforts' basis.[43]

What is SCA?

2.39 SCA is defined under PSD2 as:

> an authentication based on the use of two or more elements categorised as knowledge (something only the user knows), possession (something only the user possesses) and inherence (something the user is) that are independent, in that breach of one does not compromise the reliability of the others, and is designed in such a way as to protect the confidentiality of the authentication data.[44]

2.40 'Authentication' is defined as 'a procedure which allows the [PSP] to verify the identity of a payment service user or the validity of the use of a specific

---

41 See the FCA, Payment Services and Electronic Money – Our Approach, The FCA's role under the Payment Services Regulations 2017 and the Electronic Money Regulations 2011 (December 2018) (hereinafter: FCA Approach Paper), ¶20.55; EBA Final Report, Draft Regulatory Technical Standards EBA/RTS/2017/02 (23 February 2017) (hereinafter: EBA Final Report), ¶13; and EBA, Consultation Paper on the draft Regulatory Technical Standards specifying the requirements on strong customer authentication and common and secure communication under PSD2, EBA-CP-2016-11 (12 August 2016) (hereinafter: EBA CP).

42 EBA CP (12 August 2016), ¶18.

43 Opinion of the European Banking Authority on the implementation of the RTS on SCA and CSC, EBA-OP-2018-04 (13 June 2018), ¶32.

44 PSD2, art 4(1).

payment instrument, including the use of the user's personalised security credentials'.[45]

SCA is based on three elements: knowledge, possession and inherence. Table **2.41** 2.1 provides some examples to illustrate what these elements are likely to constitute in practice.

Table 2.1 Elements of strong customer authentication

Element	Description	Example
Knowledge	Something only the user knows	Static password, personal identification number, code
Possession	Something only the user possesses	Token, smart card, mobile phone
Inherence	Something the user is	Biometric characteristic, such as fingerprints

PSPs must ensure that the elements are mutually independent so that – if **2.42** there were a breach of one of the elements – the others would remain uncompromised. The question arises, therefore, as to how these elements could remain independent where one item may satisfy more than one element. For example, it is possible to see that at least two of the SCA elements could be met by use of a smartphone; the RTS suggest this is permissible provided there are separate execution environments installed on the smartphone.[46] By contrast, the EBA and the FCA make clear that whilst the customer verification number or expiry date of a debit card could be used to show possession, such information displayed on the debit card could not also be used to constitute a knowledge element.[47]

Dynamic linking

PSD2 requires that, for all remote electronic payment transactions initiated by **2.43** a payer, PSPs 'apply [SCA] that includes elements which dynamically link the transaction to a specific amount and a specific payee'.[48] This means that, as remote payments may be at a higher risk of fraud, extra processes should be in place to protect the customer, by linking the payee and payment amount to a specific transaction being authenticated[49] – for example, involving generation of an additional one-time password.

---

45   PSD2, art 4(29).
46   RTS, art 9.
47   FCA Approach Paper, ¶ 20.18.
48   PSD2, art 97.
49   Ibid., Recital 95.

Exemptions

2.44 A policy objective under PSD2 appears to be that SCA would ideally apply to all payment transactions where practicable and proportionate to do so, with the EBA stating that 'in a post-PSD2 world where SCA is the principle for all transactions, the balance has changed and any exemption in the RTS would need to be defined narrowly'.[50]

2.45 There are therefore only limited exemptions, which are set out in articles 10–18 of the RTS, from when SCA would otherwise be triggered under article 97 of PSD2. Exemptions apply to, for example:

(i)   accessing payment account information,[51] except where the user is accessing their account information online for the first time, or where the user has not accessed their account for more than 90 days;

(ii)   recurring transactions,[52] i.e., where the payee and amount are the same (but SCA is required when the payer sets up, amends or initiates the payments for the first time); or

(iii)   low-value transactions,[53] where: (A) the amount does not exceed EUR 30; and (B) since SCA was last applied, the cumulative amount of previous such transactions does not exceed EUR 100 or the number of previous such transactions does not exceed five transactions.

It should be noted that other requirements set out in the RTS apply to PSPs applying SCA or relying on exemptions from SCA.

2.46 It is still difficult to predict the precise commercial impact of SCA (both on PSPs and consumer behaviour). One key impact will be the prohibition on 'screen-scraping' by third parties of bank account data, which will force FinTech companies to access account information (including transaction data) via open-source technology.

2.47 Ever since PSD2 introduced the obligation on ASPSPs to enable access to payment accounts (see para 2.29 above), 'Open Banking' initiatives – the development of financial technology including the use of open APIs that enable third-party developers to build applications and services around the financial institution – have proliferated across Europe. The UK's Open

---

50   EBA Final Report, Section 4.3.1.
51   RTS, art 10.
52   Ibid, art 14.
53   Ibid, art 16.

Banking project was one of the first examples of a regulatory initiative to develop consensus on the use of open APIs in the banking/payments sector.

E. OPEN BANKING

1. Overview

Open Banking is a UK initiative likely to bring about a fundamental change in **2.48** retail banking, by improving competition and innovation in the payments industry.

Open Banking is 'a secure way for customers to take control of their financial **2.49** data and share it with organisations other than their banks without the need to share their credentials [username and password(s)] with third parties'.[54] Launched in January 2018, it is one of a series of regulatory remedies mandated by the UK Competition and Markets Authority, requiring a group of nine UK retail banks[55] to implement a common standard API in order to allow third parties to access customer bank accounts (with customers' explicit consent).

Commentators often discuss Open Banking in tandem with PSD2 which, as **2.50** noted above, introduced its own regime to encourage sharing of payment account data by banks and other PSPs. Both Open Banking and PSD2 aim to drive innovation in banking and payment services, by making it easier for banks and other PSPs to securely share data with each other and create a user experience which better suits customer needs.

Whilst PSD2 covers access to customer payment account information in **2.51** respect of any payment account accessible online, the initial roll-out of Open Banking was limited to online personal/business/current accounts. However, in the 2017 Budget, HM Treasury announced that Open Banking Standards would be created for all payment account types covered by PSD2, thereby allowing customers using credit cards, e-money accounts and prepaid cards the option to use Open Banking services.

---

54 Open Banking – About Us, available at: https://www.openbanking.org.uk/about-us/.
55 According to the Retail Banking Market Investigation Order 2017 (CMA Order), the following are the group of nine mandated institutions: Barclays plc, Lloyds Banking Group plc, Santander, Danske, HSBC, RBS, Bank of Ireland, Nationwide and AIBG.

2.52 The Open Banking ecosystem is also governed by GDPR, which provides an important framework under which customers' banking data can be accessed and shared (discussed further in Section F below).

2. What is the aim of Open Banking?

2.53 By requiring large banking incumbents to share data – via an Open API – on tariffs, bank services and customers' transaction data,[56] third party providers (TPPs) are able to provide specific comparisons tailored to the customers' individual profiles. Other types of innovative Open Banking services may include:

(i) allowing banking customers to register with a service provider that aggregates all of their accounts across multiple banks, thereby providing customers with a clearer and more comprehensive overview of their finances;

(ii) allowing customers to connect their bank account to an app that would analyse spending habits and recommend a new product, for example, a credit card or savings account to manage their finances more effectively; and

(iii) using a small business's transaction history to allow a potential lender (other than their bank) to accurately and reliably assess the business's creditworthiness and offer improved lending deals.

3. What sparked this initiative?

2.54 During the past decade, the UK banking industry was in the spotlight as the subject of various regulatory reviews and investigations. Some of the reviews highlighted the need to more closely scrutinise the retail banking industry, resulting in the retail banking market investigation report by the Competition and Markets Authority.[57] The report concluded that certain banks were not sufficiently competitive in endeavours to gain and retain customers. The report also noted that beyond the regulatory changes brought about post-2008, digitisation and technological developments necessitated a deeper reconsideration of the financial industry, its structure and the way it serves its customers. For example, since 2007, internet banking has 'doubled ... with over half of customers banking online and around a third of customers using mobile banking applications'.[58]

---

56 Such as balance information, transaction history and payment information.

57 Competition and Markets Authority, Retail banking market investigation, Final Report (9 August 2016), available at: https://assets.publishing.service.gov.uk/media/57ac9667e5274a0f6c00007a/retail-banking-market-investigation-full-final-report.pdf.

58 Ibid., at ¶ 12.

The perceived insufficient competition in the retail banking market, coupled **2.55** with the possibilities that emerge from technological advancements, lie at the heart of the current Open Banking initiative. Given the proliferation of the mobile phone and its app-dominated interface, there has been an unprecedented increase in the speed at which large amounts of information can be accessed. If harnessed efficiently and effectively, data can easily be made available in a clear, concise and customised way. Technology companies have paved the way, with '22.9m internet banking apps ... downloaded, an increase of 56 per cent in 2015, and Britons ... [logged] onto internet banking 9.6m times a day in 2015'.[59] The prevailing view has been that the information which banks and other financial institutions can make available to the public through the Open Banking initiative ought to lead to: (i) increased transparency of data; and (ii) the innovation of services that are tailored to customers' specific needs, thereby ultimately facilitating competition in the market.

4. Implementation of Open Banking

The Open Banking initiative is implemented through the development of an **2.56** open API standard for banking, which facilitates a data-sharing environment between banks and other providers by enabling their systems to interact directly with each other.

The Open Banking Implementation Entity (OBIE) is responsible for deliver- **2.57** ing the open API and data standards and security architectures. The Standards are intended to enable developers to 'harness technology which allows individuals and businesses to share their financial data held by their banks with third parties in a secure and standardised way'.[60] The OBIE is also responsible for integrating voluntary providers who wish to join the ecosystem and conform to the Standards.

From a customer perspective, individuals or businesses can grant authorised **2.58** providers access to their account data via Open Banking. The providers need to be appropriately authorised by the FCA or another EU regulator and will appear on the Open Banking Directory maintained by OBIE and/or the

---

59   The Open Banking Standard: Unlocking the potential of Open Banking to improve competition, efficiency and stimulate innovation, available at: https://www.paymentsforum.uk/sites/default/files/documents/Background%20Document%20No.%202%20-%20The%20Open%20Banking%20Standard%20-%20Full%20Report.pdf, at 15.
60   Open Banking: Open Banking ends managed roll out (17 April 2018), available at: https://www.open banking.org.uk/about-us/news/open-banking-ends-managed-roll-out/.

FCA's Register. In order to enhance security and maintain consumer confidence, the customer is able to choose when their data is accessible and at which point such access should terminate.

2.59 There are a number of authorised providers such as Yolt, a budgeting app, and Truelayer Limited. Additionally, some large banks have launched Open Banking services. For instance, in September 2018, Barclays launched a new Open Banking app feature in its mobile app which enables a customer to view current accounts from up to seven other banks together on one screen. HSBC also announced the new aggregation app 'Connected Money' in May 2018, and other challenger banks such as Starling Bank have partnered with Truelayer to offer similar aggregation services.

5. What are the potential advantages and disadvantages of Open Banking?

2.60 Whilst Open Banking is a UK-based initiative, the potential benefits for the banking industry and customers of Open Banking are far-reaching. With increased transparency and access to their personal banking data, customers will be in a position to make more informed decisions regarding their financial activities and their financial providers. Customer choice and individual control of data are both central tenets of Open Banking.

2.61 Access to banking data by newcomers including start-ups should create a more open and dynamically competitive banking industry. This may lead incumbent financial institutions to re-evaluate their pricing, products and services to ensure a competitive advantage. Additionally, with this open approach to data, banks could share fraud-detection operations with third-party detectors, offering individuals and businesses specialised fraud monitoring and notification services.[61]

2.62 On the other hand, transfer of banking data to third-party developers could raise concerns regarding data use, especially if this data is monetised through onward sale. In addition, Open Banking 'will allow financial data to be merged and analysed with other datasets'.[62] By way of example, a provider with access to customers' financial data might attempt to conceivably sell more products

---

61 Open Data Institute, Introducing the Open Banking Standard (2016), available at: https://www.payments forum.uk/sites/default/files/documents/Background%20Document%20No.%201%20-%20Introducing%20 the%20Open%20Banking%20Standard%202016.pdf, at 6.
62 Faith Reynolds, A Consumer Perspective (January 2017), available at: https://www.openbanking.org.uk/wp-content/uploads/Open-Banking-A-Consumer-Perspective.pdf, at 18.

and services than a customer would actually benefit from, on the basis that the provider would be privy to information regarding what the customer could afford.

The role of traditional banks may evolve, for example to be seen as trusted **2.63** guardians overseeing Open Banking. According to a report released by Ipsos MORI, 56 per cent of people would contact their bank first if they were to lose any money as a result of the fault of a third-party provider, and 39 per cent would expect the bank to compensate.[63] Another report by Accenture showed that 70 per cent of people would trust a bank more than a third party with their data.[64] In view of the reputational risks, and to preserve the banking-customer relationship, banks may therefore take on a greater protective role in the era of Open Banking.

6. The global perspective

While the UK has been diligently fostering and advancing Open Banking **2.64** initiatives, Open Banking is proving to be a global phenomenon. Other markets in the EU and beyond have begun to implement aspects of an Open Banking standard, according to a recent report by Capgemini and BNP Paribas.[65]

By way of example, the Hong Kong Monetary Authority recently unveiled a **2.65** regulatory framework to encourage Open Banking. Additionally, in Australia, four major banks were mandated to introduce Open Banking by July 2019.

The US has also been listed as a top ten pioneer of Open Banking according to **2.66** the Capgemini Report. Uniquely, in the US, the impetus to adopt Open Banking standards has been driven by banks looking to increase their competitive advantage and provide a higher quality of services and products to customers. Wells Fargo's announcement of a data exchange agreement in 2017 is a key example of this. In this context, Brett Pitts, the Head of Digital for Wells Fargo Virtual Channels noted that: 'This agreement creates a much

---

63 IPSOS, Open API Exploring the views of consumers and small businesses, available at: https://www.ipsos.com/sites/default/files/publication/1970-01/marketing-open-api-barclays-2015.pdf, at 7–8.

64 Accenture Payments, Consumers' initial reactions to the new services enabled by PSD2 (2016), available at: https://www.accenture.com/t00010101T000000Z__w__/gb-en/_acnmedia/PDF-29/Accenture-UK-Banking-PSD2-Consumer-Reactions.pdf, at 4.

65 World Payments Report, World Payments Report 2018, available at: https://worldpaymentsreport.com/.

better experience for our shared customers, gives them greater control over their financial data, and enhances the efficiency of the data-sharing process.'[66]

2.67 It seems then that across the world the trend towards Open Banking regulation is rapidly gaining traction and momentum, as countries recognise the economic importance of fostering market competition and consumer empowerment.

2.68 As consumers are able to interface and transact with a greater number of PSPs, data that records their personal details, financial health and spending history is now held in a far more fragmented manner. The responsibility of protecting this data thus now rests with a far larger number of actors. In the next section, we consider the challenges PSPs face in addressing the overlapping requirements of payments and data regulation.

F. PAYMENTS AND DATA PROTECTION

1. Overview

2.69 Both Open Banking and PSD2 aim to drive innovation in banking and payment services by making it easier to share data.[67] Provision of payment services entails processing of personal data and PSPs are obliged under PSD2 to give access to their customers' payment account data to certain TPPs to provide their services (both AIS and PIS).[68] Both PSD2 and GDPR impose obligations in relation to data processing to safeguard customer data, with serious enforcement implications for failing to do so. PSPs will want to adopt an integrated approach to simultaneous compliance with GDPR and PSD2. However, given the differing approaches in the regulatory frameworks, is this possible?

2. Consent, transparency and the legal basis for processing data

Legal basis for data processing – consent under PSD2 vs. GDPR

2.70 Whilst the individual's 'explicit consent' is required for data to be processed under PSD2, 'explicit consent' is not defined in PSD2 and there is no

---

66 Wells Fargo, News Release, Intuit Signs New Data-Exchange Agreement With Wells Fargo, available at: https://newsroom.wf.com/press-release/community-banking-and-small-business/intuit-signs-new-data-exchange-agreement-wells.

67 See Sections D and E above for further detail.

68 PSD2, arts 66(1), 66(4)(b) and 67(1); cf. above Section D for further details on the PSD2 requirements and Section E for further details on how Open Banking and the APIs assist account providers in meeting their PSD2 requirements and facilitate sharing data.

indication that it should be interpreted in the same way as 'consent' or 'explicit consent' under GDPR. It is a common misconception that personal data can only be processed under GDPR with the individual's consent. Consent is just one potential legal basis for processing and – given that the data subject can withdraw its consent at any time without reason and the extremely high requirements for valid GDPR consent – it is not the most practical one (depending on the circumstances, other more suitable legal bases include where processing is necessary for the performance of a contract, or necessary for the purposes of pursuing a legitimate interest). The difference in approach raises the question of whether PSD2 limits the alternative legal bases available under GDPR to 'consent' or 'explicit consent' under GDPR.

The European Data Protection Board (EDPB) provided helpful guidance by **2.71** taking the view that 'explicit consent' under PSD2 should be seen as contractual and not data protection consent. The consent requirement under PSD2 is therefore not a requirement to obtain a level of consent that meets the strict requirements under GDPR or to obtain GDPR consent at all. Rather, GDPR provides for alternative grounds to legitimise the use of data which are more likely to apply in relation to payment services than consent, such as for the purpose of fulfilling a contract, or for the purpose of a legitimate interest which is not overridden by the interests, rights and freedoms of a data subject. The EDPB contemplates in relation to payment services both of these bases as possibilities in addition to consent.[69]

'Silent party data'

Whilst PSD2 only requires explicit consent from the payment service user, the **2.72** questions of which GDPR legal basis applies and whether GDPR consent is required also arise in relation to processing personal data relating to the recipient of a payment, so-called 'silent party' personal data. This may result from a payment service user transferring money to a payee without there being a contractual, or any relationship between the payee and the PSPs, thereby becoming a 'silent party' in the transaction.

Such processing may be justified on the basis of the PSP's legitimate interest **2.73** in fulfilling a contract with the payment service user. The EDPB has endorsed this justification for silent party data in the context of PSD2.

---

69 Letter from EDPB to Sophie in 't Veld (5 July 2018), available at: https://edpb.europa.eu/sites/edpb/files/files/news/psd2_letter_en.pdf, at 3–4.

2.74 A further potential lawful ground for the processing of silent party data is the performance of a contract to which the data subject is a party, although this is not specifically addressed by the EDPB.

Practical measures

2.75 Both PSD2 and GDPR require transparency with the payment service user as to how and why their data are used and shared. PSPs should take this into account when framing PSD2 consent and privacy statements.

'Sensitive payment data'

2.76 Further restrictions apply under PSD2 in relation to 'sensitive payment data', including limitations on requesting or storing sensitive payment data (i.e., 'data, including personalized security credentials which can be used to carry out fraud'). This is not to be confused with 'special category data' under GDPR, which is described as particularly sensitive (e.g., health data), but does not include payment data.

2.77 PSPs need to be aware of these areas of specific compliance actions and ensure their procedures are sufficiently granular to ensure compliance with both regimes.

General principles

2.78 In any event, numerous safeguards, including processing which meets the reasonable expectations of the data subject (payer or payee), and wider data protection principles such as purpose limitation (see below for more detail), data minimisation ('only use the data necessary') and transparency (privacy statements) have to be complied with. PSPs should also ensure they implement privacy by design and default: integrating data protection in all aspects of the business and technology from the outset.

3. Purpose limitation: regulating the use of data

2.79 A potential future profit stream lies in the further use of payment data to improve products and services. Analysing what, where and when a product is bought can provide valuable insight into consumer behaviour, and crucially, how to influence purchasing habits. Whilst analysis of payment data brings great opportunity, it should not be used without careful consideration of the underlying data protection obligations, particularly the principle of purpose limitation.

Under GDPR, personal data can only be collected for 'specified, explicit and **2.80** legitimate purposes and not further processed in a manner that is incompatible with those purposes'.[70] In practice this means that parties should be transparent as to why they collect personal data and what they intend to do with it, e.g., by naming all relevant purposes in the privacy statement.[71] If personal data is to be used for a different purpose than originally specified (e.g., for marketing purposes or to merge financial data and analyse it with other datasets), the new use must be fair, lawful and transparent and not incompatible with the original. It may be necessary to obtain GDPR consent when using data for further purposes.[72]

PSD2 takes an even stricter approach, stating that TPPs shall not use, access **2.81** or store any data for any purpose other than the service explicitly requested by the payment service user.[73]

Privacy statements and PSD2 consents should therefore be carefully con- **2.82** structed to ensure they provide for new uses of data, where permissible under PSD2. An updated privacy statement cannot necessarily be relied upon to justify previous additional use of data. Regulators are likely to look at the privacy statement at the time of any data breach so it is imperative that these are up to date and provide sufficient detail.

4. Security and accountability

Whilst the potential benefits of new innovative payment services and initia- **2.83** tives such as Open Banking are far-reaching, security of payment services is fundamental for protecting the users' privacy and the development of a sound environment for e-commerce.[74] But keeping data secure is particularly challenging where Open Banking and PSD2 aim to make sharing data easier[75] and more players and technologies are involved.

Overlap in the regulatory regimes

Both GDPR and PSD2 require strong security measures. GDPR requires a **2.84** range of safeguards, including as an overarching principle that personal data must be processed in a manner which ensures appropriate security through

---

70 GDPR, art 5(1)(b).
71 GDPR, arts 13(1)(c) and 14(1)(c).
72 See ICO website: https://ico.org.uk/for-organisations/guide-to-the-general-data-protection-regulation-gdpr/principles/purpose-limitation/.
73 PSD2, arts 66(3)(g) and 67(2)(f).
74 Ibid., Recital 95.
75 See Sections D and E above for further information on PSD2 and Open Banking, respectively.

suitable technical and organisational measures[76] and more specific security measures under article 32 of GDPR, such as encryption and regular testing of security procedures. PSD2 also requires a robust security infrastructure adequate to the risk,[77] such as secure communication channels and secure customer authentication.[78]

2.85 From a liability perspective, security is of paramount importance to PSPs given the reputational risk of a data breach, but also the large potential fines. Under GDPR, fines for a breach of any of the security requirements in article 32 can reach EUR 10 million (or equivalent in GBP) or up to 2 per cent of the total annual worldwide turnover in the preceding financial year, whichever is higher.[79] If the breach is so extensive that the organisation is found to be non-compliant with the overarching principle of processing data in a manner ensuring appropriate security,[80] the fine may be up to EUR 20 million (or equivalent in GBP) or up to 4 per cent of the total annual worldwide turnover in the preceding financial year, whichever is higher.[81]

2.86 Another consequence of security breaches is reporting obligations: whilst both GDPR and PSD2 may require alerting the authorities, the two regimes provide for differences in the process, of which PSPs should be aware.

Incident reporting

2.87 Under GDPR, all incidents of a personal data breach[82] must be fully documented[83] and reported to the data protection authority 'without undue delay', and in any case, within 72 hours after becoming aware of the breach, unless it is unlikely that there will be a risk to the rights and freedoms of the data subject.[84] It may also be necessary to notify data subjects (e.g., payment service users or payees) 'without undue delay' where the breach poses a 'high risk' to them.[85]

---

76 GDPR, art 5(1)(f).
77 PSD2, Recital 96.
78 See, e.g., PSD2, arts 65, 66, 67 and 97 and Recitals 68, 91, 95, 96; for further information on security measures under PSD2 see Section D above.
79 GDPR, art 83(4).
80 Ibid., art 5(1)(f).
81 Ibid., art 83(5).
82 As defined in GDPR, art 4(12).
83 Ibid., art 33(5).
84 Ibid., art 33(1).
85 Ibid., art 34.

Separately, and in addition to the obligations under GDPR,[86] PSD2 requires **2.88** PSPs to notify the competent financial services regulator 'without undue delay' of any major operational or security incident.[87] The initial report should be provided within the much shorter time period of four hours from when the incident is first detected.[88]

In the event of a security breach (impacting customer data) PSPs therefore **2.89** have to satisfy two sets of reporting obligations and potentially notify two different authorities on different timescales. Practically speaking, the two responses should be aligned and made simultaneously to ensure that PSPs control communication to its regulators carefully.

Accountability

Whilst TPPs are likely to act as independent controllers under GDPR[89] (that **2.90** is, TPPs themselves control why and how customer data is processed and are therefore responsible for compliance with GDPR when providing their payment services), PSPs may still be held responsible for activities of the TTPs – either as so-called joint controllers[90] or by indirectly contributing to the TTPs' non-compliance. In October 2018, Facebook was issued the maximum fine[91] for failing to implement appropriate security measures preventing the misuse of data by a third party and was held to be ultimately responsible for the actions of another controller, a third-party app sharing information of Facebook users and their friends with companies who likely used the data for political campaigning. Whilst using the data for political campaigns may very well have hardened the authority's views in this case, it illustrates that PSPs should ensure that customer data is protected, even in seemingly clear controller-to-controller relationships with TPPs.

PSPs should consider apportioning responsibility for misuse of data relative to **2.91** their TPPs. This is made particularly challenging by articles 66(5) and 67(4) of PSD2, which prohibits PSPs from requiring TPPs to enter into a contractual agreement as a condition. The inability to impose a mandatory contractual

---

86 PSD2, Recital 92.

87 Ibid., art 96(1).

88 EBA: Guidelines on Incident Reporting Under PSD2 (27 July 2017), available at: (https://www.eba.europa. eu/documents/10180/1914076/Guidelines+on+incident+reporting+under+PSD2+%28EBA-GL-2017-10%29. pdf), at 10.

89 See Chapter 11 for a general introduction into the terms 'controller' and 'processor' under GDPR.

90 GDPR, art 26; joint controllers process personal data together and are therefore jointly liable and responsible.

91 The notice can be found here: https://ico.org.uk/action-weve-taken/enforcement/facebook-ireland-ltd/; the case is under appeal and was subject to the UK Data Protection Act 1998, but the relevant principles have not changed under GDPR.

relationship may hamper PSPs in imposing responsibility on TPPs for compliance with data protection obligations and security measures. PSPs should consider means of encouraging TPPs to enter into contracts addressing these issues. As a possible risk mitigant, strict controls should be placed on internal access to customer data. Employees working in the payment service industry should be trained on their data protection and security obligations.

G. CONCLUSION

2.92 New online and mobile payments technologies and innovative products will in many ways facilitate growth and data sharing in the payments industry. As FinTech products gain in popularity amongst consumers, PSPs must manage an increasingly complex set of regulatory requirements as well as preserving the security of customer funds and data.

2.93 Further technological change and greater regulatory alignment (particularly between payments and data laws) will hopefully deliver more compelling services that offer the best possible user experience and value for consumers. The FinTech revolution is only just beginning.

3

CROWDFUNDING

Peter Chapman

A. INTRODUCTION

Since the 2008 global financial crisis, alternative forms of finance have **3.01** proliferated. In a world where banks are required to hold more capital, investment funds have filled some of the credit gap, particularly for project financing. But in many markets, both developed and emerging, banks have especially chosen to reduce lending in the SME sector. Consequently, alternatives to bank lending have appeared. Crowdfunding platforms are taking off, encouraged in many jurisdictions by (relatively) lower regulatory hurdles. Crowdfunding is being talked up as part of the FinTech 'revolution' – the disintermediation of finance by ever-greater use of technology, and as a credible way for SMEs and early-stage businesses in the economy to raise capital. In fact, in its Crowdfunding Report, the European Commission has recognised crowdfunding as 'one of many technological innovations that have the potential to transform the financial system'.[1]

---

1   European Commission Staff Working Document, Crowdfunding in the EU Capital Markets Union, SWD (2016) 154 final, available at: https://ec.europa.eu/info/system/files/crowdfunding-report-03052016_en.pdf, at 31.

3.02 There are many benefits of crowdfunding. In addition to bringing together those with capital with those seeking finance, crowdfunding platforms also provide a means by which an investee business (an 'investee') may advertise its product to a broad audience of potential investors. There are also a range of potential wider societal benefits such as, for example, engaging individuals in investing capital and facilitating access to finance for minorities and women.[2] As the FCA notes, retail investors may also find it rewarding to be involved in a business or project as it develops, or to support a local initiative or other individuals.[3]

3.03 However, as with all investments, crowdfunding also entails a number of risks (such as that the investee fails, lack of liquidity and that the platform ceases to function) and concerns (for instance, investors' inexperience, minority shareholder protection and the potential for conflicts of interest). But, with appropriate safeguards, crowdfunding can be an important source of non-bank financing in support of entrepreneurship and economic growth.

3.04 This chapter is structured as follows: Section B examines the four principal types of crowdfunding; Section C considers the rationale for the regulation of crowdfunding; Section D analyses the regulatory approach to crowdfunding platforms focussing principally on the UK framework (with some international comparisons). Whilst there are many aspects of regulation, the section focuses on the key ones: authorisation requirements for crowdfunding platforms, investor protection, market integrity and market liquidity. Section E concludes.

B. FORMS OF CROWDFUNDING

3.05 There are four principal forms of crowdfunding: donation, reward, investment and debt. Each of these follows the same basic model of a large number (the crowd) providing small amounts of capital (the funding) to a borrower, a cause or a business, with a platform intermediating this transfer of capital – in other words, the platform is a marketplace bringing together those with capital to deploy and those seeking investment. The four principal types of crowdfunding are variations on this theme with their differences attributable to the purpose and form of fundraising.

---

2 Jason Greenberg and Ethan R. Mollick, Activist Choice Homophily and the Crowdfunding of Female Founders (2016), available at: https://papers.ssrn.com/sol3/papers.cfm?abstract_id=2462254.
3 FCA, Crowdfunding (18 April 2014), available at: https://www.fca.org.uk/consumers/crowdfunding.

1. Donation-based crowdfunding

Donation-based crowdfunding is very often charitable in nature, although not **3.06** necessarily – sometimes funding is sought for a particular project within a community, for example. Usually an appeal is made in relation to the project, cause or campaign and funding is provided by donors. Importantly, the donor does not receive any right to anything of value in return for the money provided to the cause or campaign; the donor may receive information on the success of the cause or campaign but does not have any entitlement to a product or service, a return of the capital or any income.

Perhaps one of the most famous historic examples of donation-based crowd- **3.07** funding was a campaign in the 1880s by the *New York World*'s Joseph Pulitzer, which raised over USD 100,000 from over 100,000 ordinary Americans to complete the Statue of Liberty's pedestal after the funds for the project ran dry. In the 16 March 1885 edition of the *New York World*, Joseph Pulitzer made the following appeal:

> We must raise the money! The World is the people's paper, and now it appeals to the people to come forward and raise the money. The $250,000 that the making of the Statue cost was paid in by the masses of the French people – by the working men, the tradesmen, the shop girls, the artisans – by all, irrespective of class or condition. Let us respond in like manner. Let us not wait for the millionaires to give us this money. It is not a gift from the millionaires of France to the millionaires of America, but a gift of the whole people of France to the whole people of America.[4]

2. Reward-based crowdfunding

Reward-based crowdfunding has its origins in *praenumeration*, a method of **3.08** raising funds which came to the fore in baroque Germany – a vibrant period for literature and the arts. Realising that they could finance the upfront costs of a print run or multi-volume works, book and manuscript publishers sought subscriptions prior to going to press – subscriptions would be offered at a discount to entice avid readers to part with their money. This arrangement, however, meant that the publisher had the certainty of its costs being covered and the subscribers would receive, in consideration for parting with their subscription funds up front, the printed work at a discount.

Unlike donation-based crowdfunding, those contributing funds in a reward- **3.09** based crowdfunding arrangement would expect to receive some form of

---

4   Joesph Pulitzer writing in the *New York World* (16 March 1885).

valuable return and, often, rewards are linked to the level of funding provided. Such returns, however, would not be financial in nature, but would rather be something tangible such as the product which was developed using the funds, although possibly even something less tangible such as the rights to name a character in a book. In this way, reward-based crowdfunding can be a valuable means of fundraising for businesses developing retail-focussed goods which has an obvious crowd from whom to raise funds but might be less useful for an industrial widget producing company whose product may not have mass appeal.

3.10 As a matter of English law, reward-based crowdfunding may be treated as a form of prepaid sale of goods or services, although there is no guarantee that the investor will actually receive the product or service, particularly where the funds extended are to be used to develop the relevant product, in which case, the characterisation may be that what the 'investor' purchases is the potential or the opportunity to receive the goods and services.

3. Investment-based crowdfunding

3.11 Investment-based crowdfunding is a more modern creature, originating in the US in the last decade and spreading to the UK and beyond. In more recent years, the growth of investment-based crowdfunding has been supported by specific regulation in a number of jurisdictions including the US[5] and the UK.[6]

3.12 Investment-based crowdfunding usually offers the investor some form of ownership by issuing shares in the investee. The rationale is that if the business does well, the investor will receive a share in the profit of that company by way of a dividend and/or a capital gain in the value of his or her share in the company. Typically, companies raising funding in this way will be unlisted SMEs, for which this type of fundraising can be attractive as, in return for this equity, there is typically no set repayment or interest period in relation to the funds invested.

3.13 Depending on the arrangements of the platform and/or the preference of the investee, however, investment-based crowdfunding can alternatively involve a business seeking capital by issuing financial instruments in the form of debt securities such as bonds with a set repayment period and coupons. This should

---

5   Jumpstart Our Business Startups (JOBS) Act (3 January 2012), Title III, available at: https://www. govinfo.gov/content/pkg/BILLS-112hr3606enr/pdf/BILLS-112hr3606enr.pdf.
6   Financial Services and Markets Act 2000 (Regulated Activities) Order 2001, Art 36H.

be contrasted with lending-based crowdfunding which is based on loans being entered into, rather than debt instruments being issued by the investee.

4. Lending-based crowdfunding

In lending-based crowdfunding, an investee will raise finance by way of a loan **3.14** from multiple lenders. In return, the investee agrees to pay back the capital plus interest in instalments set over a specified period. Unlike issuing shares in the context of investment-based crowdfunding, the investee does not surrender ownership and may be attractive in this regard for an investee. For the investor, the certainty of a capital and interest repayment schedule (as opposed to the possibility of a dividend and/or capital gain) may be attractive.

5. Initial coin offerings and securities token offerings

Whilst this is discussed in more detail in Chapter 4, it is worth noting that the **3.15** age of blockchain has given rise to new forms of crowdfunding in the so-called securities token offerings and initial coin offerings. These constructs can be thought of, in many ways, as effectively a new form of tokenised crowdfunding – an investee raising funds (in the form of tokens or coins) from multiple investors or backers with a view to those funds then being used to develop software or other products or services which, if the token or coin is a 'utility' token or coin, may be accessed or used by expending that token or coin.

The tokenisation aspect of securities token offerings and initial coin offerings **3.16** is important as one of the challenges faced by crowdfunding platforms and investors is liquidity. Usually, investments on traditional crowdfunding platforms are in private companies which are unlisted and often represent a minority stake. Therefore, there is not a ready marketplace for buyers and sellers to come together. Some platforms have sought to address this through a form of secondary market or buy-back facility, but the tokenisation and 'listing' the issued tokens or coins on a crypto-exchange accessible globally can be a powerful tool to increase liquidity for otherwise illiquid instruments.

C. RATIONALE FOR CROWDFUNDING REGULATION

1. Should crowdfunding be regulated at all?

Irrespective of whether a specific crowdfunding regulatory framework is **3.17** developed, the activities of crowdfunding platforms often involve the provision of services which would require the platform to obtain authorisation under an existing regulatory system and, consequently, it is appropriate that crowdfunding platforms maintain certain prudential, organisational and conduct standards.

3.18 For example, lending-based crowdfunding platforms may administer and enforce loans on behalf of investors. It is important that such loans are appropriately recorded and effectively administered by the platform. There is the same need for appropriate recording and administration in the context of investments arranged or made by the platform on behalf of investors in the case of equity-based crowdfunding. Furthermore, those investments need to be protected for investors in the event of the insolvency of the platform, something which regulation can provide for.

3.19 Notably, the failure to legislate or introduce regulation (at all, sufficiently and/or appropriately) may have a number of consequences – at best, it may give rise to barriers to entry, meaning that platform operators have insufficient clarity and certainty of the legal and regulatory framework that they consider conducting the business to be too high risk. In turn, this may shut off a potentially helpful source of finance for SMEs and a potentially attractive outlet for capital deployment by investors and lenders.

3.20 However, non-existent, insufficient and/or inappropriate regulation may also lead to gaps which may be exploited and a lack of suitable protections for investors and investees; for example, if there are no minimum standards to be adhered to by platforms, unscrupulous operators may establish platforms which are ill-managed and which do not protect the interests of investors or investees.

2. Is there a need for specific crowdfunding regulation?

3.21 Whether or not crowdfunding (and which types of crowdfunding) should be specifically regulated will depend on the type of activities that the crowdfunding platform is likely to carry out and the extent to which these activities are already regulated in the relevant jurisdiction. However, the application of existing generally applicable rules may not serve the specifics of crowdfunding. This may hamper the facilitation of platforms' activities, where the standards set by existing rules may be unsuited to crowdfunding platforms. For example, in the UK, lending to corporates is unregulated. Therefore, regulating the intermediation of such loans via a platform would increase regulatory hurdles.

By contrast, in respect of investment-based crowdfunding, most jurisdictions **3.22** already have an existing investment services regime which would be applicable to crowdfunding platforms as well. For example, in the EU, the activities of dealing in investments, receiving and transmitting orders and/or providing safeguarding and administration services are regulated under MiFID 2.[7]

3. The case for differing approaches to the different forms of crowdfunding

A distinction may be, and often is, drawn between, on the one hand, **3.23** crowdfunding platforms which facilitate investments in securities or lending, and, on the other hand, reward-based and donation-based crowdfunding platforms. There is a trend towards accepting that the latter do not give rise to financial services and, therefore, do not require specific financial services regulations or the need for operators to be licensed.

That said, even reward- and donation-based crowdfunding can, depending on **3.24** their specific activities, give rise to the provision of financial services if, for example, the platform is involved in making payments between parties using the platform.

4. Regulation to achieve more efficient capital markets

Whilst a number of EU Member States have introduced specific regulatory **3.25** frameworks for crowdfunding, there is no pan-European harmonised regime (except to the extent that the activities of platforms fall within the scope of existing EU financial services regulatory frameworks such as MiFID 2).

With this in mind, in March 2018, the EU Commission issued a FinTech **3.26** Action Plan and a draft Regulation on Crowdfunding. The aim of the new Regulation is to allow platforms to offer services not only in their home jurisdictions but across the EU and thereby harmonise the rules applicable to crowdfunding and improve the functioning of the EU capital markets.[8]

This proposed Regulation will also be accompanied by a Directive to amend **3.27** the existing investment services framework under MiFID 2. Interestingly, some of the early draft revisions proposed by the European Parliament have

---

7   Directive 2014/65/EU of the European Parliament and of the Council on markets in financial instruments (15 May 2014), available at: https://eur-lex.europa.eu/legal-content/EN/TXT/?uri=celex%3A32014L0065.
8   EU Commission proposal for a Regulation on European Crowdfunding Service Providers (ECSP) for Business (8 March 2018), available at: https://ec.europa.eu/info/law/better-regulation/initiative/1166/publication/181605/attachment/090166e5b9160b13_en.

also suggested including initial coin offerings and securities token offerings in its scope.[9] Whether this will come to pass will be seen in the future.

D. REGULATORY FRAMEWORK

1. Platform requirements

3.28 When considering the requirements for the operation of crowdfunding platforms, it is necessary to consider the authorisation and licensing requirements, the safeguards against platform failure and the platform governance standards. Each of these is examined in turn.

Authorisation/licensing

3.29 Some jurisdictions have introduced bespoke authorisation requirements for crowdfunding platforms. The Dubai International Finance Centre (the DIFC)[10] and France,[11] for example, have introduced such requirements for both investment- and lending-based crowdfunding, the UK has done so only for lending-based crowdfunding,[12] and the US has introduced a regime for investment-based crowdfunding.[13]

3.30 Where, however, crowdfunding activities sit within an existing licensing and regulatory framework, jurisdictions often introduce some crowdfunding-specific adaptations (although not specifically relating to authorisation). For instance, the UK's investment-based regime is regulated as part of the broader investment services framework, but the FCA has introduced restrictions on direct financial promotions to retail investors. Other countries such as Germany and Austria, have introduced exemptions or special rules which have allowed or encouraged platforms to operate within their existing regimes. For instance, the German crowdfunding exemption includes a higher threshold for certain types of loans brokered by platforms, below which a prospectus would not be not required. Across all regimes, the authorisations required will depend on the activities of the platform.

---

9 EU Parliament Draft Report on EU Commission's proposed Crowdfunding Regulation (10 August 2018), available at: http://www.europarl.europa.eu/sides/getDoc.do?type=COMPARL&reference=PE-626.662& format=PDF&language=EN&secondRef=02.

10 DFSA Rulebook, GEN 2 and COB 3 and 11, available at: http://dfsa.complinet.com/en/display/display. html?rbid=1547&record_id=1840.

11 Ordonnance n° 2014-559 *relative au financement participative* (30 May 2014), available at: http://www.legi france.gouv.fr/affichTexte.do?cidTexte=JORFTEXT000029008408&categorieLien=id.

12 Financial Services and Markets Act 2000 (Regulated Activities) Order 2001, Article 36H.

13 Jumpstart Our Business Startups (JOBS) Act (3 January 2012), available at: https://www.govinfo.gov/ content/pkg/BILLS-112hr3606enr/pdf/BILLS-112hr3606enr.pdf.

Whilst the type of authorisation or licensing will depend heavily on the **3.31** existing legal and regulatory regimes in place, a bespoke regime would allow for a framework to be developed in a way which is entirely tailored to crowdfunding business rather than retrofitting an existing authorisation framework (as well as the threshold and ongoing requirements that come with that existing authorisation framework).

Another benefit of a bespoke regime is that it can ensure that investors are not **3.32** misled as to the type of institution and products (and consequently the protections they may be afforded) with which they are engaging. For example, deposits held with a bank are in many jurisdictions protected to some extent by deposit insurance or governmental guarantees, whereas loans made through a platform would not typically benefit from such protections.

It is, however, quite possible to tailor existing regimes for lending and **3.33** investment services for crowdfunding. For example, where the provision of credit or loans requires a banking licence, a restricted authorisation could be developed for crowdfunding platforms permitting limited intermediation activities. More onerous authorisation threshold requirements best suited to large credit institutions providing a range of services could be waived, bearing in mind that lending-based platforms are not, for instance, engaged in maturity transformation, and may not necessarily act as principal to loans but rather as a marketplace. Notwithstanding this, a bespoke regime is likely to be clearer and more appropriate where platforms' activities fall outside the scope of existing regulated activities.

Platform continuity

There are many risks which can give rise to a crowdfunding platform failing. **3.34** For example, this could be due to financial distress of the platform, fraud, cyber-attack or IT system failure. Platform failure can result in disruption for investors. Without adequate regulation to identify and manage risks, investors' interests may not be adequately protected, and, in the event of platform failure, investors may not, for example, have access to their investments or be able to receive loan repayments.

From a prudential perspective, the UK utilises two commonly used tools to **3.35** ensure that a crowdfunding platform either remains a going concern or, if this is not possible, that there is an orderly process for winding down the business which protects investors in the event of a platform failure: (i) prudential standards and (ii) mandatory administration arrangements in the case of platform failure.[14]

Prudential standards

3.36 Minimum prudential standards can help minimise the risk of harm to investors by aiming to ensure that platforms have sufficient prudential resources to cover operational and compliance failures and/or pay redress to clients.

3.37 According to the FCA, prudential standards also serve a wider purpose:

> by ensuring that firms behave prudently in monitoring and managing business and financial risks. Experience suggests that if a firm is in financial difficulty or it fails, it can cause harm and disruption for consumers. A firm under financial/prudential strain is more vulnerable to behaving in a way that increases the probability of consumers suffering loss.[15]

3.38 For UK investment-based platforms, a capital requirement of between EUR 50,000 and EUR 730,000 will apply depending on the precise activities of the platform. For UK lending-based platforms, the capital requirement will be the higher of GBP 50,000 or a percentage of loaned funds.[16]

3.39 In other jurisdiction, platforms may be subject to a less intensive capital regime: for example, *conseils en investissement participatifs* (CIPs) in France and funding portals in the US, are not required to hold a minimum amount of capital. Typically, however, the amount of capital is likely to correlate to the level of the risk posed by the platform. Both the CIPs and funding portals are barred from holding client funds and may only offer securities for limited amounts, for example.[17] Similarly, in Germany, lending-based platforms broker credit agreements between credit institutions and investees, with the credit institution going on to lend to the investee and the platform having no further substantive role.[18] Given this limited function of facilitation, it is

---

14 FCA Handbook, IPRU-INV 12.2 and SYSC 4.1.8AR.

15 FCA: Consultation Paper 13/13, *The FCA's regulatory approach to crowdfunding (and similar activities)* (October 2013), available at: https://www.fca.org.uk/publication/consultation/cp13-13.pdf, ¶ 3.16.

16 0.2% per cent of the first GBP 50 million of the total value of loaned funds + 0.15 per cent of the next GBP 200 million of the total value of loaned funds + 0.1 per cent of the next GBP 250 million of the total value of loaned funds + 0.05 per cent of any remaining balance of total value of loaned funds outstanding above GBP 500 million. See FCA Handbook, IPRU-INV 12.2.

17 Art L. 548-2. III, Ordonnance n° 2014-559 *relative au financement participative* (30 May 2014), available at: http://www.legifrance.gouv.fr/affichTexte.do?cidTexte=JORFTEXT000029008408&categorieLien=id.

18 For further details on potential loan-lending-based crowdfunding structures in Germany, see: https://www.bafin.de/EN/Aufsicht/FinTech/Crowdfunding/Crowdlending/crowdlending_node_en.html;jsessionid=DCEB9B9B062ABA44B0D26514379C0243.1_cid372.

unsurprising then to note that strict platform continuity requirements are not imposed on these types of German lending-based platforms either.

Administration arrangements

The UK has imposed a new specific rule for lending-based platforms which **3.40** requires platforms to 'take reasonable steps to ensure that arrangements are in place to ensure that [loan agreements] facilitated by it will continue to be managed and administrated, in accordance with the contract terms' in the event of platform failure.[19]

Such arrangements could include entering into an agreement with a back-up **3.41** service provider or a guarantor, holding sufficient collateral in a segregated account to cover the cost of winding down the loan book and managing the loan book in such a way as to ensure that income is sufficient to cover the costs of a wind-down.[20]

UK investment-based platforms are subject to the existing FCA business **3.42** continuity rules which apply to investment firms generally;[21] there are no such rules applicable to crowdfunding investment-based platforms specifically.

Looking forward, the FCA has indicated that it intends to require lending- **3.43** based platforms to produce and keep up-to-date a manual containing information about their operations that would assist in resolving the platform in the event of its insolvency.[22] This 'resolution manual' would need to include a written explanation of how the platform administers loan agreements that it has facilitated, what the day-to-day operations of that business entails, and what resources would be needed to continue the platform's business if it ceased to carry it on.[23]

In the DIFC, lending-based platforms are also required to have a business **3.44** cessation plan in place.[24] The same rule applies to investment-based platforms

---

19   Ibid., SYSC 4.1.8AR.
20   Ibid., SYSC 4.1.8CG.
21   Ibid., SYSC 4.1.6R *et seq.*
22   FCA: Consultation Paper 18/20, Loan-based ('peer-to-peer') and investment-based crowdfunding platforms: Feedback on our post-implementation review and proposed changes to the regulatory framework (July 2018), available at: https://www.fca.org.uk/publication/consultation/cp18-20.pdf, ¶ 5.61.
23   Ibid., ¶ 5.62.
24   DFSA Rulebook, COB 11.1.20.

which are required to ensure 'the orderly administration of existing investments plus current and recently closed pitches, including holding and controlling client-assets (if applicable)'.[25]

Governance and risk management

3.45 Regulated crowdfunding platforms in the UK must also meet a range of minimum professional and organisational standards. For example, platforms are required to conduct business with due skill, care and diligence and take reasonable care to organise and control their affairs responsibly and effectively, with adequate risk management systems.[26]

3.46 Furthermore, platforms must have robust governance arrangements.[27] This includes having effective processes to identify, manage, monitor and report on the risks the platform is or might be exposed to. Other minimum standards for employees or officers, rules on system resilience and other administrative requirements such as record-keeping and outsourcing also apply.

3.47 These governance standards help mitigate the risk that conduct by the platform or its employees/officers might lead to customer detriment. In addition, the FCA is considering introducing more extensive risk management for lending-based platforms. In particular, it may require lending-based platforms to:

- have an independent risk management function;[28]
- maintain a permanent, effective and independent compliance function;[29] and
- establish and maintain an independent internal audit function.[30]

3.48 One key area of focus for regulators in the context of governance and risk management is conflicts of interest. In the UK, platforms must take all appropriate steps to identify and to prevent or manage conflicts of interest, between clients raising money and clients investing money, and between their interests and their clients' interests.[31]

---

25 DFSA: Consultation Paper 111, Crowdfunding: SME Financing Through Investing (13 February 2017), at 32.
26 FCA Handbook, PRIN 2.1.1R.
27 Ibid., SYSC 4.1.1R.
28 FCA, Consultation Paper 18/20, *supra* note 22, ¶ 5.27.
29 Ibid., ¶ 5.28.
30 Ibid., ¶ 5.31.
31 FCA Handbook, SYSC 10.1.3R.

The FCA has indicated that the steps that a lending-based crowdfunding **3.49** platform must take should account for the fact that the platform usually does much more than simply facilitate loans and therefore, platforms should not engage in practices that create a financial incentive for them to facilitate loans in a way that favours the platform or a certain cohort of investors/investees and is not transparent to all investors.

Such incentives may include, by way of example, opaque fee arrangements **3.50** between borrowers and the platform and group structures that generate additional and invisible layers of earnings for the platform itself. For example, this would occur if a company within the same group as a platform pre-funded loans and sold them to the platform via novation, but the group company retained a stake in each loan and the price of the loan was set at a higher rate of interest than that received by retail investors.

Another important governance-related issue is whether platforms should be **3.51** permitted to make investments in the businesses seeking capital. On the one hand, if a platform has 'skin in the game', it will be incentivised to ensure that the investee succeeds but, as the FCA notes, 'even though this can lead to a better standard of due diligence, it can also lead to conflicts of interest if [platforms] are able to use the secondary market to sell out early (possibly based on greater access to information), rather than holding to maturity'.[32] Ultimately, this is something that platforms will need to be mindful of and manage conflicts accordingly if they wish to invest.

2. Investor protection and business conduct

Investor protection is a significant element of crowdfunding regulation. The **3.52** consequence of democratising investment/lending is that more consumers are likely to become investors – indeed crowdfunding is typically marketed towards retail investors as a means of generating potentially higher returns, as compared with traditional savings account products, for example.

An important aspect of any financial services regulatory framework is to ensure **3.53** that retail investors are adequately protected and, as a result, a number of regulatory tools are deployed in the context of crowdfunding to limit the likelihood of unsustainable losses being incurred by retail investors. In the UK, the FCA provides an overarching framework for investor protection, but several additional specific consumer protection-focussed requirements also apply relating to, amongst other things, financial promotion restrictions,

---

32   FCA: Consultation Paper 18/20, *supra* note 22, ¶5.40.

disclosure and information, as well as investor appropriateness requirements.[33] Other jurisdictions have employed other tools such as investor caps, as well as substantial requirements on platforms to conduct due diligence on the investee.[34]

3.54 The sections that follow analyse key areas of investor protection: restrictions on the promotion of crowdfunding investments; disclosure and risk warnings to investors; assessment of the suitability and appropriateness of an investment for an investor; caps on the amounts that each investor may invest; due diligence that the platform should undertake on the underlying investment; protections of investors' assets and money; investors' right to withdraw from the commitment to invest; investors' rights as shareholders; lenders' rights in the event of the investee's default; contingency funds to cover losses that investors may suffer; and differentiation between retail and institutional investors.

Financial promotion restrictions

3.55 Investment-based platforms in the UK are required to classify retail investors to determine whether direct-offer financial promotions (i.e., financial promotions which include the means by which the recipient may go about making the relevant investment (such as a subscription form or link to an investment page)) for unlisted securities can be communicated to them. Only retail investors who are certified, or self-certify, as sophisticated investors, who are certified as high-net worth investors, who confirm they will receive regulated advice or who certify that they will not invest more than 10 per cent of their net investible portfolio in unlisted securities, may be sent direct offer financial promotions relating to securities.[35]

3.56 According to the FCA, 'this should ensure that clients are assessed as having the knowledge or experience to understand the risks involved before they can invest'.[36]

Disclosures, risk warnings and information

3.57 In the UK, clients of both lending- and investment-based crowdfunding platforms must receive information about the platform including contact

---

33 See FCA: *Principles of good regulation* (21 April 2016), available at: www.fca.org.uk/about/principles-good-regulation.
34 See, e.g., 17 CFR Part 227, Rule 301 in relation to US funding portals and DFSA Rulebook, COB 11.3.5 and COB 11.3.6 in relation to DIFC crowdfunding operators.
35 FCA Handbook, COBS 4.7.
36 FCA: Consultation Paper 13/13, *supra* note 15, ¶¶ 4.16 and 4.17.

details, a statement that the firm is authorised, details of what performance reports the client can expect, the platform's conflicts of interest policy, information on costs and charges and details of the firm's client money safeguards. Furthermore, UK crowdfunding platforms must have a written basic agreement setting out the essential rights and obligations of the platform and the client (although for lending-based platforms, this applies to retail clients only).[37]

Whilst the FCA does not mandate the exact content of investor disclosures, it **3.58** does require platforms to provide appropriate information to investors on the nature and risks of an investment.[38] Information disseminated to platform clients must give a fair and prominent indication of relevant risks when referencing potential benefits of an investment. The platform must provide clients with guidance on and warning of the risks associated with investments in financial instruments.[39]

The DIFC sets out a detailed list of information that must be displayed **3.59** prominently on the platform's website, including the main risks to lenders or investors of using a crowdfunding platform,[40] information about default or failure rates,[41] as well as information on the crowdfunding service, such as how the platform functions, how it deals with investee default, how it safeguards its clients' assets and how the platform is remunerated, including the fees and charges it imposes.[42]

Suitability/appropriateness assessments

There is a risk that a crowdfunding platform allows retail investors with little **3.60** experience or knowledge of investing easier access to potentially risky investments. Moreover, there is also a concern that these investors could put significant amounts of their investible assets into an investment without properly understanding the risks and lose all or much of their investment.

A tool commonly used to address this risk is the introduction of requirements **3.61** on platforms to have processes by which an assessment of whether an investment is suitable or appropriate is made by reference to a particular investor. These are more commonly used for investments in securities, perhaps reflecting the potentially more diverse and riskier nature of securities such as

---

37 FCA Handbook, COBS 8A and COBS 8 respectively.
38 Ibid., COBS 2.2 and COBS 2.2A.
39 Ibid., COBS 4.5 and COBS 4.5A.
40 DFSA Rulebook, COB 11.3.1.
41 Ibid., COB 11.3.2.
42 Ibid., COB 11.3.3.

shares (as compared with e.g., a loan). For example, in the EU jurisdictions, suitability and appropriateness rules would, subject to certain exceptions, apply.[43]

3.62 Investment-based platforms (but not lending-based platforms) in the UK must check that a client has sufficient knowledge and experience to understand the risks of the investment. In making this assessment, platforms may take account of:

- the types of service, transaction and investments the client is familiar with;
- the nature, volume and frequency of the client's investments and the period over which they have been carried out;
- the client's level of education, profession or former profession (if that profession is relevant to their understanding of the risks – for instance, if the client was previously a financial services professional).[44]

Investor caps

3.63 Caps on the amount an individual investor can lend, either per-project or over the course of a year, are a widely used investor protection tool. These caps aim to address the concern that investors, particularly inexperienced retail investors, could invest a significant proportion of their investible assets in a risky, illiquid investment without fully understanding the risks. However, the contrary argument is that investor caps can be blunt tools which can stifle market efficiency.

3.64 Whilst there is no general investor cap in the UK, the rules on direct financial promotions permit platforms to communicate direct financial promotions to a retail investor in reliance on that investor certifying that they will not invest more than 10 per cent of their net investible portfolio in unlisted shares/debt securities. This can therefore give rise to a *de facto* investor cap if this is the safe harbour that the platform is reliant on.

3.65 By contrast, in France, a EUR 2,000 per-project, per-investor cap for lending-based platforms applies.[45] The US,[46] Austria[47] and the DIFC[48] also all impose annual investment caps on investors.

---

43   MiFID2, Art 25, available at: https://eur-lex.europa.eu/legal-content/EN/TXT/?uri=celex%3A32014L0065.
44   FCA Handbook, COBS 10.2.2.
45   *Code monétaire et financier,* as amended by Décret n° 2016-1453 *relatif aux titres et aux prêts proposés dans le cadre du financement participative,* Article D. 548-1 (28 October 2016), available at: https://www.legifrance.gouv.fr/affichTexte.do?cidTexte=JORFTEXT000033317337&categorieLien=id.
46   17 CFR Part 227, Rule 100(a), available at: https://www.law.cornell.edu/cfr/text/17/part-227.

The reality is, however, that investor caps can be difficult to police in **3.66** practice.[49] For example, the Dubai Financial Services Authority (the DFSA) recognised that 'a Retail Client's risk exposure could be increased if they chose to invest through multiple other platforms'.[50] Whilst the DIFC regime imposes an obligation on platforms to have systems and controls in place to ensure that these investor limits are adhered to, in the US platforms are entitled to rely on investors' representations regarding compliance with caps. In Austria, it is an administrative offence to violate the investment caps of the Alternative Financing Act (under which most Austrian platforms operate) and both the platform and the investor may be subject to a fine of up to EUR 30,000 for breach.[51]

Investee due diligence

Another investor protection tool used in some jurisdictions is to require the **3.67** crowdfunding platform to carry out a certain level of due diligence on potential investments or on the investee that goes beyond AML/CFT checks. This might include, for example, requiring the platform to examine the soundness of an investment or financial strength of the issuer.

A range of approaches is taken to this. On the less interventionist end, the US **3.68** crowdfunding regime does not require specific due diligence checks to be performed (although platforms must deny access to issuers they believe pose a fraud risk).[52] In the UK, whilst the focus to date has been on ensuring that investors understand the amount of due diligence that has been undertaken by the platform, rather than imposing any requirement to conduct due diligence (beyond KYC identity checks), the FCA has more recently indicated that it would consider it unlikely that a platform could argue that it has met its obligations under Principle 2 (exercising skill, care and diligence) and Principle 6 (acting in the customers' best interests), if it has not undertaken enough due diligence to satisfy itself on the essential information on which any communication or promotion is based.[53] The FCA has also indicated that it is

---

47 *Alternativfinanzierungsgesetz*, art 3a (1 September 2015), available at: https://www.fma.gv.at/download.php ?d=3733.

48 DFSA Rulebook, COB 11.4.2, available at: http://dfsa.complinet.com/net_file_store/new_rulebooks/d/f/ DFSA1547_12383_VER310.pdf.

49 Nevertheless, the DFSA commented that it felt that other regulatory protections provided a suitable balance of protection for retail clients. See DFSA: Consultation Paper 109, *Crowdfunding: SME Financing through Lending* (31 January 2017), at 24; and DFSA: Consultation Paper 111, *supra* note 25, at 29.

50 DFSA, Consultation Paper 111, *supra* note 25, at 24.

51 *Alternativfinanzierungsgesetz*, Article 6 (1 September 2015), available at: https://www.fma.gv.at/download. php?d=3733.

52 17 CFR Part 227, Rule 301(c)(2), available at: https://www.law.cornell.edu/cfr/text/17/part-227.

53 FCA, Consultation Paper 18/20, *supra* note 22, ¶ 4.21.

incumbent on lending-based crowdfunding platforms to test statements made by investees regarding future commercial success.[54]

3.69 Similarly, the DIFC has stringent rules. The DIFC due diligence require-ments include, for example, verifying that the investee is compliant with applicable laws. The platform must also check the investee's fitness and propriety, financial strength and history, business valuation and business proposal. According to the DFSA, 'these checks are very important because [investees] are unable to carry out individual checks on [investees]'.[55]

3.70 The best practice probably entails a 'middle of the road' approach, which protects investors, but does not place an undue burden on platforms. Whilst mandating due diligence checks (that go beyond AML/CFT checks) on investees is a positive step towards investor protection, imposing minimum standards for such due diligence may not be appropriate for the platforms that act merely as facilitative entities. By contrast, where the platform provides a financial service itself (perhaps with the extended authorisations which accom-pany these activities), it may be appropriate to impose more extensive due diligence requirements on such a platform.

Client asset and client money protections

3.71 One of the most important investor protections (and indeed investee protec-tions) is ensuring that any client assets (including client money and securities in the investment context) received by the platform are appropriately pro-tected. The primary concern here is insolvency of the crowdfunding platform itself whilst in possession of such assets. Money or securities which are handled by platforms but not beneficially owned by platforms should not form part of the platform's estate in the event of failure.

3.72 Different jurisdictions take different approaches. In the UK, for example, lending-based crowdfunding platforms are subject to existing client-money rules, including the requirement to open segregated client bank accounts. The FCA has also prohibited lending-based platforms from taking on full owner-ship of lender monies under title transfer. In other words, this should mean that funds not yet invested by a lender on a crowdfunding platform should be protected from platform insolvency.

---

54 Ibid.
55 DFSA, Consultation Paper 111, *supra* note 25, at 25; and DFSA, Consultation Paper 109, *supra* note 49, at 22.

In the US, the more heavily regulated investment-based platforms, broker-dealers, can hold client money under existing rules,[56] whereas funding portals, crowdfunding-specific entities which are more lightly regulated than broker-dealers, are barred from holding client funds (and usually engage a third-party broker-dealer to deal in client payments on their behalf).[57] **3.73**

France similarly effectively prohibits its crowdfunding platforms from receiving funds from investors, unless they are specifically authorised to provide payment services (e.g., as a payment institution, electronic money institution, credit institution, etc.) or mandated as an agent of a payment services provider, in which case they may receive funds from investors subject to additional requirements – for example, opening a dedicated bank account for payment and subjecting these funds to segregation.[58] **3.74**

Cooling-off and cancellation rights

There is a risk that investors may change their mind about engaging in crowdfunding and, therefore, in some cases, it may be appropriate to allow for a period of time for investors (or perhaps retail investors, at least) to change their minds. However, this right to cancel needs to be balanced against the detriment which may be caused to the investee, where an investor has committed to funding a loan or make an equity investment. **3.75**

In the US, investors have unconditional rights to cancel until 48 hours before the deadline identified in the issuer's offering materials.[59] Similarly, the DIFC provides for mandatory cancellation rights for investors who have made an investment via an investment-based platform. The DFSA rules require a 'cooling-off' period of 48 hours during which an investor can withdraw its commitment without penalty and without giving a reason.[60] The DFSA decided not to extend this rule to investments made via lending-based platforms, but 'rather leave it up to the platforms to decide whether or not they will provide cancellation rights. If it is offered, then the operator is required to reflect that as part of its disclosure requirements'.[61] This difference in approach probably arises from the perceived higher risk nature of equity investments. **3.76**

---

56 Exchange Act, Rule 15c2–4, available at: https://www.law.cornell.edu/cfr/text/17/240.15c2-4.
57 17 CFR Part 227, Rule 402(a), available at: https://www.law.cornell.edu/cfr/text/17/part-227.
58 *Code monétaire et financier*, Art L522-17, available at: https://www.legifrance.gouv.fr/affichCodeArticle.do?cidTexte=LEGITEXT000006072026&idArticle=LEGIARTI000020862334&dateTexte=&categorieLien=cid.
59 17 CFR Part 227, Rule 201(j)(1), available at: https://www.law.cornell.edu/cfr/text/17/part-227.
60 DFSA Rulebook, COB 11.5.2, available at: http://dfsa.complinet.com/net_file_store/new_rulebooks/d/f/DFSA1547_12383_VER310.pdf.
61 DFSA, Consultation Paper 111, *supra* note 25, at 29.

3.77 In Europe, the Distance Marketing Directive provides consumers with a 14-day cancellation right in respect of financial services contracts made at a distance (i.e., on the internet).[62] However, the right of withdrawal does not apply to financial services whose price depends on fluctuations in the financial market outside the supplier's control, which may occur during the withdrawal period (such as services related to foreign exchange, money market instruments, transferable securities, units in collective investment undertakings, etc.).[63] In the UK, the FCA has previously stated that the most practical approach to cancellation rights in the context of lending-based crowdfunding is for the 'right to cancel to attach to the initial agreement with the platform, rather than to each loan contract'.[64]

Shareholder rights

3.78 One area in which there are relatively few regulatory requirements is the area of post-investment protection for shareholders in the context of investment-based crowdfunding. Investors purchasing shares via investment-based platforms can face particular risks as investments are highly illiquid, investments tend to be minority stakes in unlisted companies subject to significantly less stringent financial reporting and audit standards than publicly-listed firms. Moreover, the rights attaching to shares may not provide for voting rights or any protection against dilution.

3.79 It is also important to consider things from an issuer perspective. Issuers may be SMEs with little knowledge of corporate law or shareholder rights and those using crowdfunding platforms will usually raise relatively small amounts of capital from a large number of investors. This could impose significant administrative burdens on issuers – for example, communicating with investors and dealing with documentation relating to potentially hundreds of shareholders. Investees issuing shares should be aware that, where shares contain voting rights, they may need to seek approval from a large number of shareholders for certain corporate actions.

3.80 Most jurisdictions require at least some level of risk disclosure to be provided.[65] In the UK, the risk disclosure requirements are derived from Article 24 of MiFID 2.[66]

---

62   Directive 2002/65/EC, Art 6(1).
63   Ibid., Art 6(2)(a).
64   FCA, Policy Statement 14/4, The FCA's regulatory approach to crowdfunding over the internet, and the promotion of non-readily realisable securities by other media, Feedback to CP13/13 and final rules (March 2014), available at: https://www.fca.org.uk/publication/policy/ps14-04.pdf, at 29.
65   DFSA Rulebook, COB 11.3.
66   FCA Handbook, COBS 2.2A.

Loan enforcement

It is important that lending-based platforms which intermediate between **3.81** investee and investors take an active role to ensure that loans made through the platform are collected and, if necessary, enforced. The principal options available are for: (i) enforcement to be left to individual investors; (ii) the platform to take steps to enforce on behalf of investors; or (iii) a professional third-party enforcement provider to be appointed.

The first option is likely to be cumbersome, duplicative and inefficient (and **3.82** the likely small amount of investment means individual investors may not have the incentive to pursue defaulting borrowers). The DFSA commented, for example, that leaving it to individual lenders to obtain repayments on loans 'could be difficult, especially for individual retail lenders'.[67] This leaves a risk that, if a borrower defaults, no one is responsible or able to pursue the borrower for payment. By contrast, the second and third options provide for a coordinated, more efficient methodology.

Contingency funds

One approach taken by some lending-based platforms to mitigate the risk of **3.83** loss is the operation of a 'contingency fund', which is intended to cover losses that cannot be recovered from investees. These can operate by diverting a proportion of a customer's fee to a separately held fund which pays out upon the default of an investee.

There is a risk, of course, that such tools might give investors a false sense of **3.84** security and the FCA has stated that it is 'concerned that [default funds] can obscure the underlying risk to investors ... they can lead investors to believe that platforms provide a guaranteed rate of return on the loans they facilitate'.[68]

Measures to address different treatment of retail and institutional investors

Where both institutional and retail investors invest via crowdfunding plat- **3.85** forms, there is a risk that institutional investors could either gain preferential access to investments or obtain greater access through the platform to information about investments. This may be, for example, because of the platform's policies of providing broader/more detailed information, possibly in machine-readable formats, to institutional investors. This could disadvantage

---

67 DFSA, Consultation Paper 109, *supra* note 49, at 26.
68 FCA, Consultation Paper 18/20, *supra* note 22, ¶¶ 4.66 and 4.67.

retail investors who may be left with a lower quality choice of investments, or be less well, or later, informed.

3.86 The FCA has highlighted this as a potential concern as part of its post-implementation review of lending-based rules, noting examples where institutional lenders gained exclusive or early access to loans, greater access to information about the loans or the option to opt out from lending to segments of the market.[69]

3.87 In considering this issue, the FCA has noted that this indicates that firms may not be managing conflicts of interest adequately and, in practice, platforms cannot maintain structures that would result in higher-quality investment opportunities being made available to one class of clients, e.g. institutional investors. In particular, the FCA takes the view that 'it is unlikely to be possible to employ such arrangements and treat customers fairly'.[70]

3.88 Similarly, the DIFC has imposed specific rules which require the fair treatment of lenders through symmetrical information requirements. These rules require that all lenders have access to the same information or, where the platform uses systems which allow lenders to lend money ahead of other lenders, that platform discloses prominently that some lenders have preferential access to better proposals.[71] The DFSA comments that it 'appreciate[s] that not all lenders will in fact access this information, but regardless, they must have equal access to all information'.[72]

3. Market integrity and financial crime

3.89 There is a risk that platforms could be used by bad actors to launder money or to facilitate the use of money for the funding of criminal (including terrorist) activities. A report from the European Commission from June 2017 identified the vulnerability of crowdfunding to money-laundering and terrorist financing as 'significant'.[73] Crowdfunding platforms, however, are subject to the ambit of existing laws and rules on AML/CFT. In particular, platforms must take reasonable care to establish and maintain effective systems and controls for

---

69 FCA, Feedback Statement 16/13, Interim feedback to the Call for Input to the post-implementation review of the FCA's crowdfunding rules (December 2016), at 12.

70 Ibid.

71 DFSA, Consultation Paper 109, *supra* note 49, at 25.

72 Ibid.

73 European Commission: Supranational risk assessment report from the Commission to the European Parliament and the Council on the assessment of the risks of money laundering and terrorist financing affecting the internal market and relating to cross-border activities (26 June 2017), at 4.

compliance with applicable requirements and standards under the regulatory system and for countering the risk that the platform might be used to further financial crime.[74]

The FCA has provided further guidance stating that: **3.90**

> harm can arise if platforms do not take reasonable steps to counter the risk of the platform being used to further financial crime. Platforms' due diligence on fundraisers should assess whether they are legitimate. For example, obvious checks such as ensuring the company exists and that the founders are who they say they are should be carried out by all platforms as a minimum.[75]

The FCA's Financial Crime Guide provides extensive practical guidance on **3.91** how all regulated firms, including crowdfunding platforms, may counter financial crime.[76]

Overall, the level of the AML/CFT checks that crowdfunding platforms **3.92** should be required to undertake could be tailored to a risk-assessment performed by the platform (e.g., enhanced checks for higher-risk clients or activities) and should involve some ongoing monitoring of customers and transactions.[77]

4. Market liquidity

A key risk for investors is the mispricing of credit or an investment. This could **3.93** result because investments are priced by the platform or because the market on any platform is skewed. As with any market, accurate pricing of credit or investment risk requires a robust market of buyers and sellers to settle on prices that accurately reflect the underlying risk involved. For example, in the context of loans, too few investors or investees could lead to interest rates shifting too far towards being priced according to market demand and failing to accurately reflect the credit risk taken on by the investor.

Of course, achieving a balance of investors and investees is of paramount **3.94** commercial importance for any platform. The FCA addressed this issue in its 2013 Consultation Paper and commented that 'the platform provider needs to

---

74 FCA Handbook, SYSC 3.2.6.
75 FCA, Consultation Paper 18/20, *supra* note 22, ¶ 4.20.
76 FCA Handbook, FCG 1.1.
77 Clifford Chance and European Bank for Reconstruction and Development, Regulating Investment- and Lending-Based Crowdfunding: Best Practices (October 2018), available at: https://www.ebrd.com/documents/pdf-report-on-best-practices-for-regulating-investmentbased-and-lendingbased-crowdfunding.pdf, at 46.

acquire a sufficiently large number of investors and investees, which it can only do by building reputation'.[78] So, for now, there is no specific regulation addressing this risk.

3.95 Another risk is the inability of investors to sell investments they have made. Participants in investment-based crowdfunding platforms generally purchase shares in unlisted SMEs that are often in the early stages of growth. Indeed, as outlined above, investment-based crowdfunding markets are often designed specifically to provide funding for start-up businesses. As recognised by the DFSA, 'in the absence of a secondary market for trading in the securities, investors face the risk of not being able to sell their securities or having to sell them at a significant discount'.[79] An investor in unlisted securities could potentially have its investment locked up in shares for an indefinite period of time.

3.96 The FCA has also commented on this as follows: 'Consumers investing in such equity need to understand that they will probably have to wait until an event occurs, such as the sale of the company, a management buy-out or a flotation, before getting a return.'[80] The rules on direct offer financial promotions also serve as a brake on retail investors investing in illiquid securities.[81]

3.97 There has also been an emergence of secondary markets being offered by platforms. For example, a UK investment-based platform, Seedrs, introduced a secondary market in 2017 and subsequently widened access to allow any investor to purchase shares that were initially offered on the platform (previously, shareholders could only sell to other existing shareholders in the same company).[82]

E. CONCLUSION

3.98 The emergence of FinTech has driven the proliferation of new business models, such as crowdfunding platforms, which can provide access to finance where other traditional lenders and financiers may not have been prepared to

---

78 FCA, Consultation Paper 18/20, *supra* note 22, at 43.
79 DFSA, Consultation Paper 111, *supra* note 25, at 6.
80 FCA, Consultation Paper 18/20, *supra* note 22, at 15.
81 FCA Handbook, COBS 4.7.
82 Crowdfund Insider, *Seedrs Secondary Market is Now Open to All Investors* (5 February 2018), available at: https://www.crowdfundinsider.com/2018/02/127980-seedrs-secondary-market-now-open-investors/.

engage (or at least not at a commercially viable price). However, crowdfunding and the democratisation of finance come with risks and concerns, such as ensuring that investors are provided with adequate disclosures and risk warnings, and that crowdfunding platforms are adequately capitalised and properly governed. Regulation is therefore an important safety measure, and the regulatory framework for crowdfunding continues to mature.

This chapter has described the key issues that regulators have been grappling **3.99** with worldwide in trying to strike a sensible balance between creating a supportive space for innovation and growth of crowdfunding, on the one hand, and ensuring appropriate investor protection, on the other hand. Naturally, regulation will need to evolve, as crowdfunding itself develops. New rules will be needed to address the new risks presented by technological developments and new forms of crowdfunding such as initial coin offerings and securities token offerings.

4

CRYPTOASSETS AND INITIAL COIN OFFERINGS

Claude Brown, Tim Dolan and Karen Butler

A. INTRODUCTION

4.01 Distinct regulatory frameworks for cryptoassets are taking shape in key markets. Given that many of the non-crypto analogues to cryptoassets are subject to financial regulation, it is unsurprising that several jurisdictions have considered them in the context of financial instruments. That said, some have taken a different route and constructed a discrete legal regime for cryptoassets.

4.02 Motivations for this approach vary: some have found that the financial regulatory regime falls short of addressing these products. Others have sought to present a brand new regime to reflect the novelty of cryptoassets and thus associate their regulatory framework with the new technology and promote their jurisdiction as a contemporary and welcoming environment for new technologies and their proponents.

In contrast, some jurisdictions have set their face against cryptoassets by **4.03** seeking to ban activities relating to them. This approach reveals a longstanding regulatory dilemma: what should the regulator regulate (or ban)? In essence, there are three choices: (i) the product (although with a dematerialised, decentralised cryptoasset, the banning of the product is challenging); (ii) activities in or related to it (such as trading, marketing, broking); or (iii) categories of participants (for example, retail, market makers, exchanges or advisers).

The approaches taken in those countries which have taken the route of **4.04** prohibition show a variety of targets within these categories and are illustrative of the mosaic of approaches taken by those with a more liberal tendency. However, potentially incompatible regulatory and legal approaches to cryptoassets across key markets may have enormous implications for the development of the cryptoasset market in the longer term.

This chapter provides a high-level overview of the nature and use of crypto- **4.05** assets and initial coin offerings (ICOs) by analysing their regulatory treatment in several key markets. The chapter is structured as follows: Part B sets the scene by defining different types of cryptoassets and ICOs. Parts C–E analyse key legal and regulatory developments in relation to cryptoassets in each of the EU, the US and Asia. Part F concludes.

B. WHAT ARE CRYPTOASSETS AND INITIAL COIN OFFERINGS?

Broadly speaking, cryptoassets are digital assets recorded on a distributed **4.06** ledger. They are a secure digital representation of value or contractual rights that uses some type of distributed ledger technology (DLT) and can be transferred, stored or traded electronically.[1]

The cryptoasset market has also led to the development of 'tokenisation,' **4.07** which is a process whereby rights to an asset are recorded as digital tokens.

Most countries and regulatory authorities treat cryptoassets as assets or **4.08** commodities, rather than a traditional currency. Generally, the precise categorisation of a cryptoasset ultimately depends on whether it is backed by an underlying asset, whether it operates as a means of payment and the rights and entitlements that attach to its ownership.

---

1   HM Treasury, FCA and Bank of England Cryptoassets Taskforce, *Final Report* (October 2018), available at: https://www.gov.uk/government/publications/cryptoassets-taskforce, at 11.

4.09 Whilst the taxonomy of cryptoassets is still coalescing, and the terminology is subject to evolution and some strongly held and vociferously expressed views, broadly speaking, regulatory authorities have grouped cryptoassets into the following three core categories:

(1) *Cryptocurrencies* are generally those cryptoassets which are designed or intended to perform the roles of currency, principally to act as a medium of exchange, a store of value and a unit of account. Bitcoin is probably the most widely known example of cryptocurrency. Critics of the use of the term 'cryptocurrencies' challenge the ability of these cryptoassets to achieve these roles and their designation as 'currency' or even quasi-currency, pointing to their limited acceptance as a medium of exchange, volatility and near non-existent accounting role.[2] Whilst the use of the term cryptocurrencies is quite widespread, some (including certain regulators) use the term *'virtual currencies'*. An alternative term for crypto-currencies that is also sometimes used is *'exchange tokens'*, but this term is not without its issues. Tokens are typically representative of an entitlement to some asset or right. In the main, cryptocurrencies are not emblematic; they function as a medium of exchange, allowing their holder to use them by transfer to acquire goods and services, but they do not usually carry with them intrinsic rights and entitlements. Unlike security or utility token holders, exchange token holders do not have any rights or access to goods or services. Rather, these tokens are typically used as a way to reward market makers who create liquidity on a cryptocurrency exchange.

(2) *Utility tokens* confer on their holders the right or ability to access a product, asset or service. This is usually an item or service that exists outside the ecosystem in which the utility token operates. An example might be a utility token that entitles its holder to exchange it for a number of playing hours of a music streaming service. Some examples of utility tokens include Golem, Sonm, Siacom, OmiseGo and Augur.

Confusingly, some tokenised cryptoassets allow the holder to use them to acquire capacity within the token's own ecosystem, for example processing capacity. For example, Ether is marketed, sold, and serves as 'fuel' for the Ethereum blockchain. Ether is needed to pay for trans-actions and computational processes, and is also provided to miners as a reward for securing and validating transactions. In addition, like Bitcoin,

---

2   See, e.g., House of Commons Treasury Committee, Crypto-assets, Twenty-Second Report of Session 2017–19 (12 September 2018), at 4.

Ether can also be used as a payment instrument, and thus, arguably has a dual purpose – in that it operates both as a cryptocurrency and a utility token.

(3) *Security tokens* are generally issued by entities for purposes of: (i) capital raising (e.g., through an ICO), (ii) the tokenisation of ownership rights; or (iii) profit sharing. Once issued, this form of tokens can be traded on a secondary market, which can be either an organised platform or a more informal market. It is also the case that cryptocurrencies and utility tokens can be traded, based on their value, but this is more of a consequence of their characteristics, rather than their primary purpose as is the case with security tokens. Given that security tokens are a form of capital raising, there is a risk that these tokens will fall within the scope of the existing financial services regulatory perimeter as 'transferable securities' – for example, shares, contracts for differences or units in a fund, depending on how they are structured.

4.10 An ICO refers to 'a process in which companies, entrepreneurs, developers or other promoters raise capital for their projects in exchange for digital tokens that may represent payment for a good or service, or a security, commodity or derivative thereof, depending on the nature of the ICO's structure and the participants' activities'.[3] An ICO is a very light-touch form of an initial public offering (IPO), the difference being that, in an ICO, investors are offered the opportunity to purchase tokens. However, like the more traditional IPOs, ICOs may be deemed securities offerings if they meet certain regulatory criteria.

4.11 To launch an ICO, an issuer will typically produce a 'white paper', which describes the project itself, the DLT underlying the system, protocols and rules in general. The issuer will then typically announce the project to the public through social media, ICO aggregator websites and the project website itself, without the need for intermediaries. The issued tokens can be traded on particular exchange platforms (similarly to the securities offered in IPOs). Transactions in the tokens can be traced on websites such as Kraken, Poloniex or Livecoin. Given the dematerialised, digital nature of the tokens, investors who want to buy them need a 'digital wallet' into which the tokens that they subscribe for can be credited.

4.12 The earlier ICOs were used primarily to launch new cryptocurrencies. However, more recently, they have been used by start-ups to fund their projects and

---

3 Financial Stability Board, Crypto-asset markets, Potential channels for future financial stability implications (10 October 2018), at 3.

the services that they propose to offer. Currently, there are few regulatory burdens in launching an ICO, which has been seen by many as one of the key attractions of this type of fundraising.

4.13 Some ICOs have been highly successful, with USD 7 billion being raised via ICOs between January and June 2018.[4] That said, a large percentage of ICOs fail. For example, an estimated 55 per cent of ICOs failed to complete their fundraising targets in the second quarter of 2018[5]), and their popularity has somewhat declined since the 2017 'crypto bubble.'

4.14 ICOs have also begun to garner attention from regulatory authorities in the US, the EU and Asia, with some countries denouncing ICOs as a form of illegal fundraising (e.g., South Korea and China), whilst others have focussed on the potential risk of losses for investors, the heightened risk of financial crime, money laundering and market manipulation.

4.15 It is possible that future tailored regulation of this sector would be to its benefit by allowing it to have the stamp of legitimacy, and making it a viable and solid alternative to traditional securities. This has to be weighed against the increased burden of conducting an ICO which is subject to regulation and the loss of simplicity which attracts interest from those disposed to this form of fundraising.

4.16 At a national level, the differing philosophies of regulation, societal and economic drivers, the political climate and the sophistication of the financial markets have produced a patchwork of regulatory regimes. The sections that follow provide an overview of the rules and regulations applicable to crypto-assets in the UK (including the EU), the US and Asia, and describe the legal landscape impacting the issuance of, and dealings in, cryptoassets in these jurisdictions.[6]

---

4   Trustnodes, ICOs Have Raised $7 Billion This Year, $2 Billion Just in May, 3 June 2018, available at: https://www.trustnodes.com/2018/06/03/icos-raised-7-billion-year-2-billion-just-may.
5   ICORating, ICO Market Research Q2 2018, available at: https://icorating.com/report/ico-market-research-q2-2018/, at 7.
6   The referenced laws and regulations are as of February 2019.

C. UK AND EUROPE

1. Overview

It is important to note that there is currently no EU-wide regime for the **4.17**
regulation of cryptoassets, which means that each EU member state is
generally free to establish its own authorisation and regulatory requirements
for activities related to cryptoassets. Therefore, the analysis of whether the
activities related to cryptoassets need to be regulated and, if so, how, it differs
between EU member states. This country-by-country approach is challenging
for the growth of cryptoassets which, by their nature, are international in their
appeal, and cross-border in their application and infrastructure. It also presents a risk of regulatory arbitrage, with creators and promoters of cryptoassets
being drawn to those jurisdictions with the more benign regimes, which may
also provide the least amount of scrutiny and oversight.

It should also be noted that regulatory attitudes are not necessarily consistent **4.18**
within the same regulatory community. For example, central bankers, concerned with the supervision of their respective currencies and systemic risks,
have a different attitude to cryptoassets than their regulatory counterparts who
are charged with consumer protection or discouraging criminal endeavours.

The existing financial services regulatory framework in the EU was not **4.19**
designed with the use of cryptoassets in mind. Whilst certain activities relating
to derivatives of cryptoassets are currently regulated in the UK under the
Financial Services and Markets Act (FSMA), activities relating to cryptoassets
themselves are not currently subject to regulation or oversight by the UK's
Financial Conduct Authority (FCA) or the Prudential Regulation Authority
(PRA), unless the feature or functionality of the cryptoasset or the manner in
which it is structured or arranged results in it being categorised as a 'financial
instrument' (e.g., a security, a unit in a collective investment scheme, a warrant
or an alternative investment fund) or as a 'payment instrument' (e.g.,
e-money).

This means that, under the existing UK regulatory framework, subtle differ- **4.20**
ences in the legal structure and commercial function of a cryptoasset can have
significant regulatory consequences.

Due to the growing popularity of exchange tokens and the recent volatility in **4.21**
the price of some cryptocurrencies (notably Bitcoin), the FCA has issued
warnings to the market regarding the risks associated with investing in such

products,[7] whilst the PRA has issued a letter to top executives of banks, insurance companies and designated investment firms, warning them that cryptoassets raise concerns related to misconduct and market integrity, and stipulating a set of risk strategies and risk management systems that the PRA considers most appropriate to cryptoassets.[8]

2. Categorisation of cryptoassets

4.22 At present, cryptoassets may fall into one of the following categories:

(a) commodities or other forms of physical property, which means that they are largely unregulated from an EU financial services law perspective (save to the extent that any resulting contracts are classed as 'derivatives'). These would include cryptoassets such as Bitcoin and Ethereum, which utilise blockchain and can be used as a means of exchange but do not embody the types of rights or access provided by a security token or a utility token;

(b) financial instruments (e.g., a security, a collective investment scheme, or a unit in a fund (including a collective investment scheme, or an alternative investment fund, as described in more detail in Sections 5 and 6 below). This could be the case with security tokens; and

(c) e-money or the provision of a payment service, as described in Sections 3 and 4 below, depending on whether the relevant cryptoasset is seen as a medium of exchange or as having more narrow functions (e.g., such as solely enabling the payment for services provided within the particular cryptoasset's closed ecosystem). These would likely include certain types of utility tokens.

4.23 The reason that the regulatory categorisation of a cryptoasset is important is that it will determine the extent to which (if at all) any authorisation, prospectus, marketing restrictions, procedural, conduct of business or AML/CTF requirements apply.

---

7 See FCA, Consumer warning about the risks of investing in cryptocurrency CFDs (14 November 2017), available at: https://www.fca.org.uk/news/news-stories/consumer-warning-about-risks-investing-crypto currency-cfds and FCA: Cryptocurency investment scams (27 June 2018), available at: https://www.fca. org.uk/scamsmart/cryptocurrency-investment-scams.

8 Letter from Sam Woods, Existing or planned exposure to crypto-assets (28 June 2018), available at: https://www.bankofengland.co.uk/prudential-regulation/letter/2018/existing-or-planned-exposure-to-crypto-assets.

3. E-money and cryptoassets

It is possible that certain cryptoassets could be categorised as a form of **4.24**
e-money for UK regulatory purposes.

E-money is defined under the UK Electronic Money Regulations 2011 **4.25**
(which transpose in part the EU Directive 2009/110/EC) as electronically,
including magnetically, stored monetary value represented by a claim on the
electronic money issuer which: (i) is issued on receipt of funds for the purposes
of making payment transactions; (ii) is accepted by a person other than
the electronic money issuer; and (iii) is not otherwise excluded by the
Regulations.[9]

There is an explicit exclusion for monetary value stored in instruments that can **4.26**
be used to acquire goods or services only: (i) in or on the electronic money
issuer's premises; or (ii) under a commercial agreement with the electronic
money issuer, either within a limited network of service providers or for a
limited range of goods and services[10] (the so-called 'limited network exclusion'), which could be relevant for arrangements involving cryptoassets. The
UK Payment Services Regulations 2017 (PSR) introduced a notification
obligation on companies relying on this exclusion where the total value of the
payment transactions executed by the company under the limited network
exclusion exceeds EUR 1 million over a 12-month period.[11]

In many instances, the cryptoasset will not be treated as e-money because: **4.27**

(a) there is no claim against the issuer of the cryptoasset for the value of the
     cryptoasset acquired; in fact, in many instances, there will not even be an
     issuer;
(b) it does not have 'monetary value' (as it is not a traditional currency and
     therefore is not universally accepted as a means of payment); and
(c) the cryptoasset is not issued on receipt of funds (assuming the term
     'funds' refers to fiat currency).

However, there is a risk that the success of the cryptoasset over time could **4.28**
alter how it is categorised from a regulatory perspective. Cryptoassets such as
utility tokens that are centrally issued and widely accepted as a medium of
exchange by third parties may be viewed as e-money.

---

9   UK Electronic Money Regulations 2011, Part 1, s 2; see also Directive 2009/110/EC, art 2(2).
10 UK Electronic Money Regulations 2011, Part 1, s 3.
11 UK Payment Services Regulations 2017, Part 5, s 38.

4.29 If a cryptoasset is deemed to be e-money, this may require the issuer of the cryptoasset to be registered with the FCA, although there is a lighter touch regime for small e-money institutions.[12] E-money issuers are subject to certain capital requirements, systems and controls, reporting and operational requirements.

4. Payment services and cryptoassets

4.30 Consideration should also be given to whether certain activities related to cryptoassets could be classified as payment services for UK regulatory purposes.

4.31 The PSR, which transposes in part PSD2, regulates a broad range of services including those that enable: (i) cash to be placed on a payment account; (ii) cash withdrawals to be made from a payment account; (iii) the transfer of e-money; (iv) the execution of payment transactions where the funds are covered by a line of credit (e.g., direct debits, credit transfers); (v) customers to purchase goods and services through their online banking facilities or by e-money; and (vi) money remittance that does not involve the creation of payment accounts.

4.32 When a cryptoasset is used to facilitate a regulated payment service, the business carrying out this service may fall within the remit of the PSR, unless an exclusion applies.

4.33 In many cases, the issuance, as well as the purchase and sale, of the cryptoasset will not amount to the provision of a payment service under the PSR, on the basis that the arrangements do not:

(a) enable cash to be placed on a payment account or cash withdrawals to be made;

(b) enable direct debits or credit transfers (e.g., standing orders) to be made;

(c) facilitate payment transactions where the funds are covered by a credit line, since the cryptoasset holders have to pay for the cryptoasset upfront; and

(d) there is no money remittance service, as funds are not received from a payer for the sole purpose of transferring a corresponding amount to a

---

12 See FCA, Small electronic money institution (small EMI), available at: https://www.fca.org.uk/small-electronic-money-institution-small-emi.

payee or to another payment service provider acting on behalf of the payee, nor are the funds received on behalf of, and made available to, the payee.[13]

There is an exclusion for services based on specific payment instruments that can be used only in a limited way, which may be relevant in the context of cryptoassets, provided that they meet one of the following conditions: **4.34**

(a) they allow the holder to acquire goods or services only in the issuer's premises;
(b) they are issued by a professional issuer and allow the holder to acquire goods or services only within a limited network of service providers which have direct commercial agreements with the issuer;
(c) they may be used only to acquire a very limited range of goods or services; or
(d) they are valid only in a single European Economic Area country, are provided at the request of an undertaking or a public sector entity, and are regulated by a national or regional public authority for specific social or tax purposes to acquire specific goods or services from suppliers which have a commercial agreement with the issuer.[14]

Those who provide payment services in the UK may be required to be authorised by the FCA and must comply with certain systems, controls and conduct requirements. **4.35**

5. Collective investment schemes and cryptoassets

The UK's regime for collective investment schemes (CIS) is established principally under the FSMA. Arrangements will be considered a CIS if they fall within the basic definition of section 235 of the FSMA and are not excluded by the FSMA (Collective Investment Schemes) Order 2001, as amended (the CIS Order). **4.36**

Although the definition of a CIS is primarily intended to catch mutual investment funds, the definition is broad, technically complex and open to a number of differing interpretations. Unhelpfully, there is very little guidance on this topic. This therefore gives the courts latitude to interpret section 235 of the FSMA flexibly and purposively, and the affected parties may not even realise that the arrangement falls within the CIS definition. **4.37**

---

13 See Payment Services Regulations 2017, Part 1, s 1.
14 Ibid., Sch 2, para (k).

4.38 The definition of a CIS is deliberately broad and quite vague, and consequently capable of capturing a wide range of arrangements even if the parties to the arrangements do not intend to create or establish a fund or a collective investment.

4.39 Specifically, a CIS is defined as:

> any arrangements with respect to property of any description … the purposes or effect of which is to enable persons taking part in the arrangements … to participate in or receive profits or income arising from the acquisition, holding, management or disposal of the property or sums paid out of such profits or income.[15]

4.40 The arrangements must be such that the participants do not have day-to-day control over the management of the property, whether or not they have the right to be consulted or give direction.[16] Whilst this appears to assume that someone must have control over the 'management' of the property, management is not necessarily required for an arrangement to be classified as a CIS. There is no definition or guidance in the FSMA or given by the FCA on the meaning of 'management.'

4.41 Different types of management can arise depending on the nature of the property. In practice, two main types can be distinguished:

    (a)   management involving discretion (for instance, having the function of monitoring the property and deciding when to buy and sell); and

    (b)   management of a more administrative nature, not involving the exercise of discretion (for instance, ensuring that there is insurance of the property, security, cleaning, storage, etc.).

Whilst it is clear that 'management' at its most explicit means management involving the exercise of discretion, management of a more administrative nature may be sufficient, if it is more than the mere passive holding of property.

4.42 In addition, in order to be classified as a CIS, the arrangement must have either of the following characteristics:

    (a)   pooling of contributions and profits or income of the participants in the scheme (which would include cryptoassets); or

---

15   FSMA, s 235(1).
16   Ibid., s 235(2).

(b)   the property is managed as a whole on behalf of the operator of the scheme.[17]

Typically, a CIS takes in money from investors and invests it in some other **4.43** type of property. It is that other property, plus any uninvested contributions and undisbursed profits and income, which would normally be regarded as the underlying property of the CIS.

In the context of cryptoassets, arrangements are capable of being treated as a **4.44** CIS in circumstances where participants pay cash to an issuer of tokens in exchange for a token which gives the participants/investors an entitlement to certain underlying property (e.g., gold coins, silver, wine, art, etc.), if the underlying property is managed as a whole by a third party (including the issuer). In this context, the term 'managed' could entail administrative functions such as arranging for the property to be stored and/or insured. This means that arrangements relating to cryptoassets need to be carefully scrutinised to determine whether they fall under the UK CIS regime, even if the intention of the issuer is not to create a fund or a collective investment.

Even if the arrangements fall within the basic definition of a CIS, they could **4.45** possibly be exempt under the CIS Order, and these exemptions would have to be applied to each arrangement on a case-by-case basis.

The regulatory consequences of an arrangement relating to a cryptoasset being **4.46** categorised as a CIS are twofold:

(1)   it may trigger the requirement by certain parties to be authorised by a regulatory body (e.g., the FCA), which in turn will trigger the requirement to comply with certain rules; and regulations (e.g., the rules in the FCA Handbook, which are applicable to regulated financial services firms); and
(2)   it may restrict the ability to market the cryptoasset to certain professional investors, high net worth individuals or certified sophisticated investors.[18]

---

17   Ibid., s 235(3).
18   Ibid., s 238(1).

6. Alternative investment funds and cryptoassets

4.47 In the UK, there is a quite separate regime for alternative investment funds (AIF). Whilst there is some overlap in the definition of an AIF and a CIS, from a regulatory perspective, they fall under different rules and regulations.

4.48 An AIF is defined in the Alternative Investment Fund Managers Directive (AIFMD) as any 'collective undertaking including investment compartments thereof, which raises capital from a number of investors with a view to investing it in accordance with a defined investment policy and which is not required to be authorised under Article 5 of Directive 2009/65/EU'.[19] All elements of the AIF definition must be present in order for the cryptoasset to be treated as an AIF.

4.49 An AIF is a particular type of fund/collective investment vehicle, which overlaps in certain respects with the definition of a CIS, but the two are not exactly the same. For example, an arrangement structured as a close-ended body corporate is capable of being categorised as an AIF, whereas such an entity would not be categorised as a CIS.

4.50 A cryptoasset arrangement which meets the basic definition of an AIF under the AIFMD will not, however, constitute an AIF if it falls within an exemption under Article 2 of the AIFMD. These exemptions apply to holding companies, certain joint ventures and securitisation special purpose vehicles, and would have to be assessed on a case-by-case basis.

4.51 Arrangements which relate to body corporates, partnerships, unincorporated associations and funds set up as trusts, which pool together capital raised from participants/investors for the purposes of investment (e.g., the pooled capital is used to purchase gold, silver or art) with a view to generating a pooled return for those investors from investments[20] (e.g., the arrangements are capable of generating a return for the participants) may amount to an AIF.

4.52 As is the case with CISs, the regulatory consequences of an arrangement relating to a cryptoasset being categorised as an AIF may trigger a requirement for the manager to be authorised, the appointment of a depositary, as well as compliance with various procedures, controls, capital and conduct require-ments. There are also restrictions in relation to the marketing of AIFs,

---

19 AIFMD (which transposes in part Directive 2011/61/EU), art 4(1)(a).
20 FCA Perimeter Guidance (PERG) Ch 16.2, Question 2.3.

including the type of investors who can be marketed to, prior notifications to EU regulators and reliance on private placement rules.

7. Carrying on of a regulated activity

Arrangements relating to cryptoassets may entail the carrying on of a regulated activity for UK regulatory purposes. **4.53**

Section 19 of the FSMA states that a person may not carry on a regulated activity in the UK, or purport to do so, unless he is an authorised person or exempt person or an exclusion applies. This is referred to as the 'general prohibition,' and carrying on a regulated activity in breach of the general prohibition is a criminal offence and may result in certain agreements being unenforceable. **4.54**

A regulated activity is described in the FSMA as a specified activity that relates to a specified investment or property of any kind and is carried on by way of business.[21] Specified activities, in turn, include dealing as principal or agent in a specified investment,[22] making arrangements 'with a view' to persons buying and selling certain specified investments,[23] as well as safeguarding and administering assets.[24] **4.55**

Further, specified investments include shares, debt instruments, CISs, e-money and derivatives, as defined in the FSMA (Regulated Activities) Order 2001 (the RAO). Whilst cryptoassets are not specifically identified as a specified investment, the characteristics of cryptoassets would have to be assessed against the criteria of each specified investment to determine whether it is within scope. **4.56**

In addition, any platform on which the cryptoassets are traded or exchanged may be considered to be a regulated market, a multilateral trading facility or an organised trading facility if the cryptoasset is categorised as a specified investment. **4.57**

Even if a regulated activity is being performed, authorisation under the FSMA may not be required if an exclusion is available. There are various exclusions in the RAO that may be relevant in the context of cryptoassets, including in **4.58**

---

21 FSMA, Part 2.
22 FSMA (Regulated Activities) Order 2001, arts 14 and 22.
23 Ibid., s 25(2).
24 Ibid., s 40.

relation to activities carried out by an 'overseas person,' or in connection with the sale of goods or the supply of services, or there is the 'absence of holding out.'

4.59 Cryptoassets such as security tokens are capable of being treated as specified investments for the purposes of the RAO where they have the characteristics of securities such as shares, bonds or units in CIS.

4.60 If the issuer of a cryptoasset is deemed to perform a regulated activity and there is no available exclusion, there are three consequences of the cryptoasset being categorised as a specified investment under the FSMA and the RAO:

(i) the marketing of the cryptoasset may be restricted under the FSMA[25] or subject to compliance with certain conduct rules;

(ii) accessing the platform or exchange and its use by participants may be restricted; and

(iii) the operator of the platform, the custodian of the cryptoassets, the issuer of the cryptoasset and those who make arrangements for others to acquire the cryptoassets may have to be authorised. This in turn would trigger the requirement to comply with certain capital, systems, controls and conduct requirements.

4.61 Even if the cryptoasset is not categorised as a specified investment under the FSMA and the RAO, the platform or exchange on which the cryptoasset is bought or sold may be considered a commodity trading platform. Notably, there is no EU-wide regime for commodity trading platforms and so the analysis of whether a commodity trading platform needs to be regulated in a particular EU member state will have to be considered on a country-by-country basis. A pure commodity platform would not currently be required to be regulated in the UK under the FSMA.

8. Registry, settlement and clearing

4.62 Many cryptoasset systems will use DLT to register the transfer of cryptoassets between parties. The use of DLT itself does not mean that a cryptoasset will be subject to UK regulation. However, systems which involve the transfer of digital assets against value are being reviewed by a number of regulators, including in the UK, because of their resemblance to payment systems.

---

25   See FSMA, ss 21 and 238.

Cryptoasset arrangements may also require a settlement system in order to **4.63** transfer the cryptoasset from one account or e-wallet to another and record the transaction pursuant to which the cryptoasset is transferred, as well as the transfer of the corresponding 'consideration'. Indeed, if over time the cryptoasset becomes accepted as a medium of exchange for goods and services, it may be necessary either to expand its registry system into a payment system or a settlement system, or to develop interoperability between the cryptoasset settlement system and other cryptocurrency and/or fiat currency payment systems, which may result in it developing into a clearing system.

An entity which interposes itself between 'counterparties' to certain types of **4.64** contracts, thereby becoming the buyer to every seller and the seller to every buyer, may be required to be authorised or registered as a central clearing party (CCP). In the UK, CCPs are supervised by the Bank of England and are subject to various capital, systems and controls, margin and procedural requirements.

9. Future UK regulatory developments

As noted above, the volatility in the price of certain cryptoassets such as **4.65** Bitcoin has led to both the FCA and the PRA issuing warnings to the market regarding the risks associated with investing in such products and reminding investors that the purchase and sale of cryptoassets are not subject to safe-guards and protections, as they are unregulated in the UK.

The UK government, as well as the governments of other EU member states, **4.66** will extend certain AML and CFT requirements to cryptocurrency exchange platforms and certain custodial e-wallet providers through the implementation of the Fifth Anti-Money Laundering Directive[26] in 2019 (5MLD).

This will require cryptocurrency exchange platforms and custodial e-wallet **4.67** providers to conduct know your customer (KYC) due diligence checks on traders and users to determine their source of wealth and the source of their income. Additional checks will be required if the trader or user is located in a 'high risk' jurisdiction. In essence, this will require cryptoasset traders/users of exchange platforms to disclose their identities and exchange platforms and e-wallet providers will be required to report any suspicious activity to the national crime agency.

---

26   Directive 2018/843/EU of the European Parliament and the Council.

4.68 In March 2018, Her Majesty's Treasury (HMT), the FCA and the Bank of England established a taskforce (the Taskforce) to assess the current regulation of cryptoassets in the UK and to determine whether all cryptoassets should be subject to specific regulatory oversight. In October 2018, the Taskforce issued a report which indicated that cryptoassets would be subject to greater regulatory oversight and supervision in the coming years (the Report).[27]

4.69 The Report reflects on the use of blockchain and identified a number of potential barriers to its wider adoption, whilst also highlighting the UK regulators' support for innovation using blockchain and welcoming the opportunity to develop experience with blockchain applications and to explore how it can be used in a number of new areas, including real time settlement service, regulatory reporting, as well as in the public sector (e.g., with the GovTech Catalyst Fund[28]).

4.70 The Report notes that utility tokens are, in general, not regulated; exchange tokens may already be subject to regulation, whilst security tokens are already regulated.[29] The Report further observes that the regulatory perimeter depends not only on the characteristics of the token (e.g., whether it is an exchange, utility or security token), but also on the use to which the token is put (e.g., whether it is a means of exchange, a capital raising instrument or an investment). The FCA has provided further guidance on the regulatory treatment of cryptoassets in its January 2019 consultation paper.[30]

4.71 The Report also states that:

(a) the HMT will significantly extend the scope of 5MLD when it transposes it into UK law, following feedback to its proposed consultation paper;

(b) the FCA will consult on proposed guidance to clarify if and how certain cryptoassets fall within the current regulatory perimeter;

(c) the HMT will consult on whether the existing regulatory perimeter needs to be extended to capture other types of cryptoassets with comparable features to other financial instruments (such as shares or units in collective investment schemes);

---

27 HMT, FCA and Bank of England, *supra* note 1.

28 See the GovTech Catalyst challenge process, available at: https://www.gov.uk/guidance/the-govtech-catalyst-challenge-process.

29 HMT, FCA and Bank of England, *supra* note 1, at 40–43.

30 FCA, FCA consults on cryptoassets guidance (23 January 2019), available at: https://www.fca.org.uk/news/press-releases/fca-consults-cryptoassets-guidance.

(d)   the FCA will also consult on a proposed prohibition of the sale to retail clients of all derivatives referencing exchange tokens (such as Bitcoin) including contracts for differences, futures, options and transferable securities; and

(e)   the UK will engage with international governmental and non-governmental organisations to promote the harmonisation of laws relating to the supervision of cryptoassets.[31]

Whether this will ultimately lead to cryptoassets being subject to bespoke **4.72** general regulatory rules which introduce authorisation requirements, prospectus-like disclosures and marketing restrictions for ICOs, systems, controls, procedural, and conduct of business requirements remains to be seen.

D. UNITED STATES

1. Overview

In the US, market participants have to grapple with a patchwork of federal and **4.73** state regulators when operating in the cryptoassets space. This section provides a high-level overview of the federal regulation of cryptoassets in the US.

2. New York: the BitLicense regime

The state of New York has been at the forefront of cryptoasset regulation in **4.74** the US since 2014. On 3 June 2015, New York became the first state to implement a comprehensive cryptocurrency regulatory regime, popularly known as 'BitLicense'.[32]

Under the BitLicense regime, companies engaged in cryptocurrency business **4.75** activities are required to undergo a thorough application process, obtain a license, abide by numerous compliance requirements similar to banks and other financial institutions, and be subject to examinations by the New York Department of Financial Services.

The application of the BitLicense regulations has been controversial, and **4.76** some have criticised the burdens that they place on cryptocurrency-related businesses. Companies are faced with a stark choice: either apply for a license

---

31   HMT, FCA and Bank of England, *supra* note 1, at 42–5.
32   23 N.Y.C.R.R. Part 200 (Virtual Currencies), available at: http://www.dfs.ny.gov/legal/regulations/adoptions/dfsp200t.pdf (hereinafter: BitLicense).

that has only been granted to a select few companies and imposes burdensome compliance obligations on the licensee, or avoid doing business in the state of New York altogether. As a result, some cryptoasset companies have attempted to block users in New York from using their technology in an attempt to avoid bringing the business under the BitLicense regulations.[33]

4.77 Under the BitLicense, a 'virtual currency' is defined as a digital unit that is a digital medium of exchange or form of stored value (with specific exceptions for prepaid cards, customer rewards programs, in-game currency and reward points).[34] Companies that conduct 'virtual currency business activities,' as defined in the BitLicense regulations, and that operate in New York, or engage in business with New York-based customers, are subject to the BitLicense regime.[35]

4.78 Under the BitLicense, the following five activities constitute 'virtual currency business activities':

(i)   receiving virtual currency for transmission, or transmitting virtual currency through a third party;

(ii) maintaining custody of virtual currency or holding virtual currency on behalf of others;

(iii) buying or selling virtual currency as a customer business;

(iv) performing virtual currency exchange or conversion services (whether converting virtual currency to fiat currency or vice versa; or converting one type of virtual currency for another type of virtual currency); and

(iv) controlling, administering, or issuing virtual currency.[36]

4.79 The BitLicense exempts several activities from the licensing regime. For example, cryptocurrency mining on its own would not subject a party to the BitLicense regime.[37] Similarly, consumers or merchants only using cryptocurrency to buy or sell goods or services would not be required to obtain a license.[38] And finally, parties who engage purely in software development and dissemination do not fall under BitLicense.[39]

---

33   See, e.g., Daniel Roberts, Bitcoin company ditches New York, blaming new regulations, *Fortune* (11 June 2015), available at: http://fortune.com/2015/06/11/bitcoin-shapeshift-newyork-bitlicense/.

34   BitLicense, § 200.2(p).

35   Ibid., § 200.3(a).

36   Ibid., § 200.2(q).

37   Nermin Hajdarbegovic, Lawsky: Bitcoin Developers and Miners Exempt from BitLicense, *CoinDesk* (15 October 2014), available at: https://www.coindesk.com/lawsky-bitcoin-developers-miners-exempt-bitlicense.

38   Ibid.

39   BitLicense § 200.2(q).

There are many unanswered questions as to the particular circumstances in **4.80** which various exceptions would apply. For example, the BitLicense exempts from its licensing obligations the transmission of 'nominal amounts' of virtual currency for 'non-financial purposes'.[40] Whilst neither 'nominal' nor 'non-financial' have been defined, some have surmised that this is seemingly aimed at exempting blockchain companies that want to use cryptocurrency ledgers to record non-financial metadata (i.e., a document notary service or an identity validation tool).[41]

However, whether this exception would apply to the use of a nominal amount **4.81** of cryptocurrency to create a 'digital contract' is less clear. Likewise, there are several grey areas as to whether certain businesses are engaged in one of the five 'virtual currency business activities,' or in mere software development.

3.   Other state cryptocurrency statutes

Whilst several other federal states have enacted statutes governing crypto- **4.82** currencies, these statutes do not create a comprehensive cryptocurrency regulatory regime in the style of the New York's BitLicense, these statutes do add clarity to the treatment of virtual currency businesses under states' money transmission laws.

4.   Commodity Futures and Trading Commission

Whilst cryptoassets are not treated as 'currencies' under the US rules, **4.83** the Commodity Futures and Trading Commission (CFTC) treats cryptocurrencies (such as Bitcoin) as 'commodities' for the purposes of the Commodity Exchange Act (CEA).[42] The CFTC has interpreted the term 'virtual currency' broadly, to encompass any digital representation of value that functions as a medium of exchange, and any other digital unit of account used as a form of currency.[43] In addition, futures, options, swaps and other derivative contracts that make reference to the price of Bitcoin or another virtual currency that is considered a commodity, are subject to regulation by the CFTC under the CEA. Further, the CFTC also has jurisdiction over

---

40   Ibid. § 200.2(q)(1).
41   See, e.g., Peter Van Valkenburgh, BitLicense: It's not just for New Yorkers, *Coincenter* (13 July 2015), available at: https://coincenter.org/entry/bitlicense-it-s-not-just-for-new-yorkers.
42   See *In re Coinflip, Inc.*, CFTC No. 15-29, 2015 WL 5535736 (Sept. 17, 2015); see also *CFTC v. McDonnell*, No. 18-CV-361, 2018 WL 1175156, at *1 (E.D.N.Y. Mar. 6, 2018): 'A "commodity" encompasses virtual currency both in economic function and in the language of the statute.'
43   See Retail Commodity Transactions Involving Virtual Currency, 82 Fed. Reg. 60335 (Dec. 20, 2017), available at: http://www.cftc.gov/idc/groups/public/@lrfederalregister/documents/file/2017-27421a.pdf.

attempts to engage in market manipulation with respect to those virtual currencies that are considered commodities.

4.84 In 2017, the CFTC granted the cryptocurrency trading platform, LedgerX, registration as both a derivatives clearing organisation and a swap execution facility under the CEA. LedgerX is the first federally regulated cryptocurrency options exchange and clearing house in the US. The Chicago Mercantile Exchange and the CBOE Futures Exchange self-certified its futures contracts on Bitcoin with the CFTC and launched them in December 2017.[44]

4.85 Much like the FCA, the CFTC has also launched an innovation hub, LabCFTC, to foster responsible innovation in the FinTech space and to assist FinTech companies in understanding how the US commodities laws and regulations may affect their business.[45]

5. Financial Crimes Enforcement Network

4.86 In 2011, the Financial Crimes Enforcement Network (FinCEN) opened the door to the regulation of cryptocurrency businesses as money transmitters[46] when it revised the definition of money transmission business to include 'the acceptance of currency, funds or other value that substitutes for currency to another location or person by any means'.[47]

4.87 This means that persons engaged in the business of the transmitting of cryptocurrencies may be required to register with the FinCEN and comply with its rules on AML and regulatory reporting.

6. Securities and Exchange Commission

4.88 The US Securities and Exchange Commission (SEC) considers that certain cryptoassets issued in an ICO may be treated as securities for the purposes of the Securities and Exchange Act of 1934, if they meet the test set forth in *SEC v. Howey*. In order to qualify as an investment contract, the tokens must satisfy each of the three prongs of the test: (1) there is an investment of money; (2) the investment is in a common enterprise; and (3) the buyer of the token expects profits from the efforts of others. If a cryptoasset fails one prong of the

---

44   See CFTC press release, CFTC Statement on Self-Certification of Bitcoin Products by CME, CFE and Cantor Exchange (1 December 2017), available at: http://www.cftc.gov/PressRoom/PressReleases/pr7654-17.

45   See CFTC: LabCFTC, available at: http://www.cftc.gov/LabCFTC/index.htm.

46   31 C.F.R. § 1010.100(ff).

47   31 C.F.R. § 1010.100(ff)(5)(i)(A).

test, it will not be considered an investment contract from a federal securities law standpoint.[48]

If a cryptoasset passes the *Howey* test, the SEC may require certain partici- **4.89**
pants to be registered with the SEC and comply with its regulations, including mandatory requirements to conduct the trading of such cryptoassets through a registered broker-dealer.

The SEC has established a Cyber Unit and retail strategy task force to enable **4.90**
its Division of Enforcement to address cyber-based threats and protect retail investors. One area of the unit's declared focus will be potential violations involving blockchain and ICOs.[49]

7. Other federal agencies

Numerous other federal agencies have also issued guidance or consumer **4.91**
advisories on cryptoassets, including the Consumer Financial Protection Bureau (CFPB), the Board of Directors of the Federal Reserve System, and the Federal Deposit Insurance Corporation.

Notably however, whilst the CFPB has issued a consumer advisory regarding **4.92**
cryptocurrencies,[50] the agency explicitly declined to include regulation of cyptocurrencies as part of its recent Prepaid Rule.[51]

In conclusion, the explosion of cryptoassets over the past several years has not **4.93**
escaped the attention of regulators in the US. For at least the last several years, regulatory agencies have applied the already existing laws and regulations by adapting them to the cryptoasset landscape, notably the FinCEN, the CFTC and the SEC. In addition, New York's BitLicense regime became the first comprehensive regulatory regime aimed squarely at regulating crypto-currencies. The sustained growth and prevalence of cryptoassets will undoubt-edly continue to solicit attention from regulators, and additional regulations and enforcement actions at both the federal and state level.

---

48 *Securities and Exchange Commission v. W. J. Howey Co.*, 328 U.S. 293 (1946).
49 SEC Press Release, SEC announces enforcement initiatives to combat cyber-based threats and protect retail investors (25 September 2017), available at: https://www.sec.gov/news/press-release/2017-176.
50 Consumer Financial Protection Bureau, Consumer Advisory, Risks to consumers posed by virtual currency (August 2014), available at: http://files.consumerfinance.gov/f/201408_cfpb_consumer-advisory_virtual-currencies.pdf.
51 Bureau of Consumer Financial Protection, Final Rule: Prepaid Accounts Under the Electronic Fund Transfer Act (Regulation E) and the Truth in Lending Act (Regulation Z), 81 Fed. Reg. 83934, 83978 (22 November 2016).

E. ASIA

1. Overview

4.94 Generally speaking, Asian countries have more stringent regulations governing cryptoassets, relative to the rest of the world. For example, the use of Bitcoin and other cryptocurrencies is completely banned in Bangladesh, and the Bangladesh Central Bank has stated that anyone caught using cryptocurrencies may be sentenced to up to 12 years in jail under the country's strict AML laws.[52]

2. China

4.95 In China, although the use of Bitcoin and cryptocurrencies by individuals has not yet been declared as punishable, the introduction of a number of regulations has made it increasingly difficult, if not impossible, to conduct many activities involving cryptoassets. The growth of ICOs in China led the authorities to publish a notice in September 2017 (the Notice), prohibiting the raising of finance by offering tokens.[53] The Notice states that ICOs are a form of illegal public fundraising and also risk breaking Chinese laws on securities offerings. Further, the Notice reiterates the position under an earlier notice, issued in 2013, that tokens offered through ICOs will not be recognised as legal tender in China. Finally, the Notice also shut down cryptoasset trading platforms and websites and apps that facilitated the exchange of fiat currency into cryptocurrencies.[54]

4.96 Following the issuance of the Notice, ICOs and ICO platforms (such as ICOAGE, ICO365 and ICOINFO), as well as cryptocurrency trading platforms in China, have been shut down. On 24 August 2018, the China Banking Regulatory Commission, the Ministry of Public Security and other central government agencies jointly issued another notice warning against the risk of illegal fundraising under the guise of cryptocurrencies and blockchain,

---

52 *The Telegraph*, Why Bangladesh will jail Bitcoin traders (15 September 2014), available at: http://www. telegraph.co.uk/finance/currency/11097208/Why-Bangladesh-will-jail-Bitcoin-traders.html.

53 People's Bank of China, Cyberspace Administration of China, Ministry of Industry and Information Technology, State Administration for Industry and Commerce, China Banking Regulatory Commission, China Securities Regulatory Commission and China Insurance Regulatory Commission, Announcement on Preventing Financial Risks from Initial Coin Offerings (4 September 2017).

54 People's Bank of China, Ministry of Industry and Information Technology, China Banking Regulatory Commission, China Securities Regulatory Commission, and China Insurance Regulatory Commission, Notice on Precautions Against the Risks of Bitcoins (3 December 2013).

which represents the latest effort of the Chinese government to crack down on domestic cryptocurrency activity.[55]

3. Thailand

The regulatory status of cryptoassets in Thailand is far from clear. In 2013, **4.97** the Bank of Thailand informed a cryptocurrency-based business (Bitcoin Co. Ltd.) that its cryptocurrency activities were illegal in Thailand.[56] However, one year later, the Bank of Thailand concluded that Thai law did not have the means to regulate cryptocurrencies themselves, but that cryptoasset exchanges would not be allowed to operate unless they could prevent cryptoassets being exchanged for fiat currencies (except Thai Baht), presumably on the basis that cryptoassets could be used to facilitate foreign exchange speculation.[57]

In July 2018, the Thai Securities and Exchange Commission (TSEC) intro- **4.98** duced a set of ICO regulations. Under these regulations, companies registered in Thailand which issue tokens must be approved by the TSEC and have a minimum registered capital of five million Thai Baht (equivalent to approximately USD 150,000). Applications are made through an online portal which is operated under TSEC-supervision. Whilst there are no restrictions on the number of tokens that can be issued, the TSEC has placed an investment limit of 300,000 Thai Baht (approximately USD 9,050) per person per round of offering. The regulations also only allow seven approved cryptocurrencies to be used as consideration for the exchange of digital tokens issued through an ICO or to be traded as trading pairs.

4. Japan

Whilst several countries in Asia have taken a strict approach towards crypto- **4.99** assets and banned them or activities related to them, Japan has taken a markedly different approach. Initially, Japan's position was that, despite the fall of Japanese-based Bitcoin exchange Mt. Gox in 2014, it would not move to regulate cryptocurrencies in the immediate future.[58]

---

55   See, e.g., Evelyn Cheng, China clamps down on cryptocurrency speculation, but not blockchain development, CNBC (3 September 2018), available at: https://www.cnbc.com/2018/09/03/china-clamps-down-on-cryptocurrency-speculation.html.
56   See Kavitha A. Davidson, Bank of Thailand Bans Bitcoins, *The Huffington Post* (31 July 2013).
57   Pathom Sangwongwanich, Bitcoins back in the Thaimarketplace, *Bangkok Post* (20 February 2014), available at: http://www.bangkokpost.com/business/marketing/395952/bitcoinsback-in-the-thai-marketplace.
58   *Reuters*, Japan's ruling party says won't regulate Bitcoin for now (19 June 2014), http://www.reuters.com/article/2014/06/19/japan-bitcoin-idUSL4N0P01LS20140619.

4.100   However, in 2016, the Japanese lawmakers adopted amendments to the Payment Services Act (PSA) to define 'virtual currency' and to add regulations in respect of 'virtual currency exchange services providers'. The PSA defines 'virtual currency exchange services providers' as entities which: (i) buy or sell virtual currencies or exchange one virtual currency for another; (ii) act as an intermediary, agency, or as a delegated service provider for the purchase and sale or exchange of virtual currencies; or (iii) are involved in the management of a customers' money or their virtual currency in connection with any of the foregoing activities. The broad nature of this catches not only typical online cryptocurrency exchanges and platforms, but also those operating in the over-the-counter markets, such as brokers and participants with a physical presence in Japan, as well as ICO marketing and trading platforms.

4.101   Additionally, the Act on Prevention of Transfer of Criminal Proceeds was also amended to require virtual currency exchange service providers to implement KYC and other procedures.

4.102   In January 2018, however, Coincheck, Inc, one of the largest virtual currency exchanges in Japan, announced that it had lost approximately USD 530 million worth of virtual currencies through a hacking attack on its system.[59] Coincheck subsequently reopened its operations, after having been acquired by the Japanese internet broker Monex Group Inc, and having received a business improvement order from the Japanese Financial Services Agency (FSA), which demanded 'drastic' reforms to the exchange's management system, enhanced AML CFT measures, and revised assessment criteria for the risks for each crypto offering.[60]

4.103   In the aftermath of these developments, the FSA has taken a stringent approach towards the cryptocurrency industry. In deciding whether to grant licenses to prospective virtual currency exchanges, the FSA is said to be scrutinising business plans, anti-hacking measures and the effectiveness of

---

59   *Reuters*, The Coincheck cryptocurrency hack: everything you need to know (29 January 2018), available at: http://fortune.com/2018/01/29/coincheck-japan-nem-hack/.

60   See Marie Huillet, Japan: crypto exchange coincheck resumes NEM trading almost 10 months after major hack, *Cointelegraph* (13 November 2018), available at: https://cointelegraph.com/news/japan-crypto-exchange-coincheck-resumes-nem-trading-almost-10-months-after-major-hack; and Yuki Hagiwara and Yuji Nakamur, Japan expands cryptocurrency crackdown after coincheck hack, Bloomberg (8 March 2018), available at: https://www.bloomberg.com/news/articles/2018-03-08/japan-expands-cryptocurrency-crackdown-after-coincheck-hack.

shields put up against other misconduct, with applicants having to answer a 400-item questionnaire.[61]

5. Singapore

The Monetary Authority of Singapore (MAS), which operates both as the central bank and a unitary financial regulator in Singapore, has so far taken a 'technology-neutral' approach to regulating cryptoassets. The current Singaporean regulatory framework does not specifically regulate the trading of, the provision of advice on, or the intermediation of cryptoassets. Instead, the MAS has issued guidance clarifying that such activities may be regulated under its existing capital markets services regime (and, if applicable to a specific cryptoasset or activity, the financial advisory regime) if the relevant cryptoasset constitutes a capital markets product within the definitions of the MAS regulations (for instance, if a securities token or an exchange token were to fall within the definition of a 'security').[62]   **4.104**

The MAS has also issued several consumer alerts warning of fraudulent activities involving cryptoassets,[63] and has taken enforcement action against market participants (e.g., cryptoasset exchanges and ICO issuers) who conducted their activities in breach of the applicable MAS regulation.[64]   **4.105**

Depending on the characteristics of cryptoassets, they may also fall under other regulatory regimes administered by the MAS. For example, the issuance of utility tokens may fall under the framework governing stored value facilities, and providers of cryptoassets which facilitate the transfer of money to overseas recipients may be regulated as remittance businesses.   **4.106**

---

61 See Takero Minami and Keita Sekiguchi, Japan's Coincheck to gain license after $500m hack, *Nikkei Asian Review* (19 December 2018), available at: https://asia.nikkei.com/Spotlight/Bitcoin-evolution/Japan-s-Coincheck-to-gain-license-after-500m-hack.

62 MAS, Guide to digital token offerings (last updated 30 November 2018), available at: http://www.mas.gov.sg/News-and-Publications/Monographs-and-Information-Papers/2018/A-Guide-to-Digital-Token-Offerings.aspx.

63 See, e.g., MAS, Warning on fraudulent websites soliciting 'cryptocurrency' investments (29 January 2019), available at: http://www.mas.gov.sg/News-and-Publications/Media-Releases/2019/Warning-on-Fraudulent-Websites-Soliciting-Cryptocurrency-Investments.aspx.

64 See, e.g., MAS, MAS halts Securities Token Offering for regulatory breach (24 January 2019), available at: http://www.mas.gov.sg/News-and-Publications/Media-Releases/2019/MAS-halts-Securities-Token-Offering-for-regulatory-breach.aspx); and MAS, MAS warns digital token exchanges and ICO issuer (24 May 2018), available at: http://www.mas.gov.sg/News-and-Publications/Media-Releases/2018/MAS-warns-Digital-Token-Exchanges-and-ICO-Issuer.aspx.

4.107 On 14 January 2019, the Parliament of Singapore passed the Payment Services Act. The Act consolidates and replaces the Singaporean regulatory frameworks for payment services, and introduces a new licensing regime for specific types of payment services (including, among others, e-money issuance services and digital payment token services). This will result in certain providers and intermediaries of cryptoassets becoming subject to licensing and ongoing conduct requirements under the Act.

F. CONCLUSION

4.108 Whilst the global regulatory framework for cryptoassets continues to develop, its general contours can be seen developing in several jurisdictions. This chapter provides a high-level overview of the key legal and regulatory issues and the developments in the regulation of cryptoassets in the UK (including the EU), the US and Asia.

4.109 A particular challenge facing the regulatory community is that the regulators' attitudes may not necessarily be in synch with their confreres in the tax and revenue raising authorities or the views and aspirations of their political masters. In a global economy where growth is slow or slowing, any hot spot of commercial activity is likely to attract attention. For politicians, there is the opportunity to create an environment in which to stimulate economic growth and attract inward investment, with the added attraction of being at the forefront of the 'new economy'. For fiscal authorities in stagnant or stagnating economies, the prospect of taxable nascent but growing revenue streams is a welcoming proposition. The upshot can be a tension between the desire to protect investors and the financial markets, raising public finances and a political ambition to foster the 'new'.

4.110 To date, cryptoassets have not been of sufficient significance either to raise systemic concerns or to fall within the ambit of the global regulatory framework. Instead, their touch points with the existing financial regulatory regimes have been at a more localised, predominantly national level. At a global level, the international regulatory coordination is less pronounced and rendered harder to implement because of the differing national regulatory infrastructures.

4.111 However, as cryptoassets continue to attract growing attention from consumers, investors, banks, markets, governments and regulators globally, we can expect to see more interest in creating regulation that is less geographically fragmented and more internationally comprehensive and coordinated.

5

CRYPTOCURRENCIES AND CENTRAL BANKS

Hubert de Vauplane[*]

A. INTRODUCTION

5.01 Many central banks are considering issuing their own digital currencies (central bank digital currencies or CBDCs), and are currently analysing the economic and political implications and evaluating the corresponding regulatory reforms. There are, in addition, important legal issues to consider, including the possible need to adopt new legislation to address CBDCs.

5.02 One of the key legal questions associated with the issuance of CBDCs is whether CBDC should be subject to the regime applicable to existing currencies (including their status as legal tender); and if so, whether legislative measures may be needed to accomplish this, or alternatively, whether a new, stand-alone regime should be adopted for CBDCs.

---

[*] The author would like to thank his partner, Reid Feldman, for his contribution to this chapter, especially in relation to the US law developments.

This chapter is structured as follows: Section B describes the characteristics of **5.03** currency generally; Section C identifies some key legal issues presented by the issuance and use of currencies; Section D analyses the differences between traditional currencies and cryptocurrencies; Section E examines legal issues presented by the issuance and use of CBDCs; and Section F provides a brief conclusion.

B. CHARACTERISTICS OF CURRENCY

The notion of currency dates back to Aristotle, who defined its three **5.04** functions: (i) a unit of account, which allows the value of goods and services to be expressed in a common unit; (ii) a medium of exchange, which allows economic actors to engage in transactions without resorting to barter; and (iii) a store of value.[1] The idea that currency is essentially a substitute for, and an improvement of, barter is based on the economic interpretation of the role of currency, viewed through the prism of these three functions and in the context of exchanges through which it is possible to fulfil certain types of obligations.

However, in the wake of Karl Polanyi's work,[2] many scholars believe that the **5.05** role of currency should be viewed in relation to the concept of debt, rather than in relation to exchange. According to some of these scholars,[3] currency can be analysed as representing a set of debts and credits that arise through transfers of possession and/or ownership of real or symbolic property. Currency is therefore the vector for measuring and quantifying social relations, which take the form of reciprocal debts and claims among the members of society.

This may explain why many economists refer to the notion of trust in **5.06** describing the role of money. But what sort of trust is involved? There are arguably three types of trust:

(i)   Methodical, or daily trust, according to which 'one's word is one's bond'. This sort of trust makes it possible to create, exchange and satisfy debts and claims in the ordinary course of business.

---

1   Aristotle, *The Nicomachean Ethics*, Oxford University Press (2009), chapter V.
2   In his book *The Great Transformation* (1944), Polanyi criticises Adam Smith's paradigm of the 'bartering savage'.
3   See, e.g., Michel Aglietta et al., *La Monnaie souveraine*, Odile Jacob (1998).

(ii)   Hierarchical trust, which reflects the organisation of payment systems, clearing houses and settlement systems between private and central banks. In this context, the ultimate source of trust is the central bank, as the 'lender of last resort' in the event of a panic or financial crisis.

(iii) Ethical trust, which makes money a public good and not an arbitrary instrument in the hands of a few individuals or leaders. This ethical trust 'has the role of affirming that society depends on a monetary order'. It states that money is a common entity that allows us to live better and produce wealth, not an object to be appropriated.[4]

5.07 This concept of trust is a key element of cryptocurrencies. According to the classical approach to money as a medium of exchange, money is only recognised within a community because of the legitimacy that each person grants it. The sociological theory of money, introduced by Simmel, goes further and considers that trust in the ability to exchange money goes beyond interpersonal relationships. It requires what Simmel calls a 'supra-theoretical supplement of faith'.[5] 'Without confidence [in its legitimacy], the circulation of money would collapse', he argues.[6] It is therefore the social relationship maintained with money, more than its nature (coin, metal, silver, banknote or credit card), that is important. What matters is the intensity of the relationship of trust that surrounds the relationship with money. However, trust is not enough to explain why money is accepted by everyone when many of its modern forms can no longer claim any intrinsic value.

5.08 In fact, what leads to continued confidence in a currency is what the European Central Bank (ECB) refers to as its 'acceptability' as a medium of exchange and its attractiveness as a store of value.[7] As the International Monetary Fund (IMF) notes, a paper currency has no value 'other than that which a nation decides to assign to it'[8] – in other words, the belief in the currency's convertibility into something else. This belief is first and foremost the result of a legal phenomenon: it is because the law gives national currency the legal force to discharge obligations that one has confidence in its exchange value. If the statute that defines a currency as the national currency were removed from the law, few people would continue to use that currency. This is because,

---

4   Michel Aglietta, *La confiance dans la monnaie est l'alpha et l'oméga de la société* (2017), available at: http://equationdelaconfiance.fr/rencontre/michel-aglietta-cepii-la-confiance-dans-la-monnaie-est-lalpha-et-lomega-de-la-societe.

5   Georg Simmel, *The Philosophy of Money*, Taylor & Francis Ltd (2011), at 113.

6   Ibid., at 178.

7   European Central Bank, What is money? (24 November 2015), available at: https://www.ecb.europa.eu/explainers/tell-me-more/html/what_is_money.fr.html.

8   International Monetary Fund, What is money? (September 2012), available at: https://www.imf.org/external/pubs/ft/fandd/2012/09/basics.htm.

contrary to past practice, the quantity of money issued no longer has any relationship to reserves of gold or other precious metals.

C. LEGAL ASPECTS OF MONEY

Many of the legal questions related to cryptocurrencies involve practical issues **5.09** for both the holder and the recipient of cryptocurrencies. Specifically, the key legal question for the holder of cryptocurrencies is whether they can use cryptocurrencies to satisfy their payment obligations, while the key legal question for the recipient of cryptocurrencies is whether they will automatically acquire the cryptocurrencies' potential liabilities, defects of title, etc. In order to answer these questions, it is useful to examine the role of the State in regulating currencies, the meaning of legal tender in the context of currencies, convertibility and fungibility of currency, and the application of property rules to currencies, each of which is analysed in turn below.

1. The role of the State

There are several ways to define a 'legal currency' (i.e., currency that is **5.10** officially a legal instrument of payment in a country). In the European Union, in respect to the countries that use the Euro as the official currency, the currency is defined only by name.[9] There is no generic definition of the Euro. The Euro as a currency exists solely by the legislative declaration that designates the Euro as the legitimate currency.

Under US law, the term 'currency' is defined as: **5.11**

> the coin and paper money of the United States or of any other country that is designated as legal tender and that circulates and is customarily used and accepted as a medium of exchange in the country of issuance. Currency includes U.S. silver certificates, U.S. notes and Federal Reserve notes. Currency also includes official foreign bank notes that are customarily used and accepted as a medium of exchange in a foreign country.[10]

Similarly, the term 'money' is defined in the Uniform Commercial Code as: **5.12**

---

9 Article 106 of the Treaty on the European Union, which applies to the Euro area, states: 'The ECB alone is empowered to authorise the issue of bank notes in the Community. The ECB and the national central banks may issue such notes. Bank notes issued by the ECB and the national central banks are the only ones to be legal tender in the Community.' To clarify this notion, on March 22, 2010 the European Commission adopted a recommendation on the extent and effects of the legal tender of Euro banknotes and coins.
10 31 C.F.R. §1010.100 (m).

a medium of exchange currently authorised or adopted by a domestic or foreign government. The term includes a monetary unit of account established by an intergovernmental organization or by agreement between two or more countries.[11]

5.13 These definitions clearly establish that, at least within the US or the European Union, in order to be recognised as an instrument of legal exchange, a currency must be adopted or recognised as such by a governmental authority.

5.14 One legal feature of money today is that it is issued by a central bank. The concept of a central bank is relatively recent. While a number of central banks were created in the 17th century (the oldest is the Bank of Sweden, created in 1656, followed by the Bank of England, created in 1694), most of the central banks that currently exist were established after World War II.

5.15 The emergence of a new State on the international scene is typically accompanied by the creation of a central bank: a tool of sovereignty but above all of independence, giving the State its own currency, created by its own issuing institution, in charge of managing monetary reserves and monetary issuance.

5.16 Today, many consider that the regulation of the money supply:

> constitutes one of the modern extensions of the right to coin money, a sovereign right which is not limited to strict issuing power, but which extends more generally to the regulation of the entire national monetary system, which therefore includes the control of the volume of the money supply.[12]

5.17 From an economic point of view, monetary sovereignty is a set of prerogatives of an authority that gives itself the exclusive power to define the unit of account, the revenue it wishes to collect and the external marks of sovereignty. In that context, monetary sovereignty is first and foremost a question of exclusive prerogative:[13] the ability to issue money, to control the external value of money, and to control the scope of internal monetary practices and external flows. Internally, this sovereignty is exclusive and prohibits any person from modifying the monetary value or its use: monetary laws have mandatory application and it is not possible to deviate from them, in particular by monetary guarantee or indexation clauses (except as permitted by law).

---

11   Uniform Commercial Code, § 1 201(b)(24).
12   Geneviève Burdeau, *Internationalisation des monnaies et souveraineté des Etats*, in: Philippe Kahn: *Droit et monnaie. Etats et espace monétaire transnational*, Litec (1991) at 412.
13   Arthur Robert Burns, *Money and Monetary Policy in Early Times*, Routledge (1996) at 75–112.

2. Legal tender and the discharging power of money

A second characteristic of a legal currency is that it is a 'legal tender', i.e., it **5.18** must be accepted as payment for monetary obligations (subject to any applicable contractual provisions). Traditionally, the legal tender status of banknotes and coins has meant that they could not be refused as an acceptable means of settling a debt. Additionally, any such refusal may be punishable by a fine.

As noted by the IMF, the definition of legal tender varies from jurisdiction to **5.19** jurisdiction. In some countries:

> legal tender rules allow the debtor to make a valid 'tender' – that is, to take the necessary steps to complete a payment – but there is no obligation on the side of the creditor to accept the tender. A creditor, however, would be barred from recovering the debt in court, if he has refused to accept a valid tender. On the other hand, in other countries, it is unlawful to refuse legal tender in payment.[14]

In the UK, legal tender has a very narrow and technical meaning, which relates **5.20** to settling debts. It means that if you are indebted to someone, you cannot be sued for non-payment if you offer full payment of your debts using the legal tender. What qualifies as legal tender in the UK varies depending on the region. For instance, in England and Wales, legal tender consists of Royal Mint coins and Bank of England notes. In Scotland and Northern Ireland, only Royal Mint coins are considered legal tender. As indicated by the Bank of England:

> [s]even banks in Scotland and Northern Ireland are authorised to issue banknotes. These notes make up the majority of banknotes in Scotland and Northern Ireland and legislation is in place to ensure that note holders have a similar level of protection as they would for Bank of England notes. Despite this, Scottish and Northern Ireland banknotes are not classified as legal tender anywhere in the UK. Equally, Bank of England notes are not legal tender in Scotland and Northern Ireland.[15]

In the US, under the Coinage Act of 1965 the 'United States coins and **5.21** currency (including Federal reserve notes and circulating notes of Federal reserve banks and national banks) are legal tender for all debts, public charges, taxes, and dues'.[16] According to the US Treasury, 'there is, however, no federal

---

14 IMF Discussion Note, Virtual currencies and beyond: initial considerations (2016), SDN/16/03, available at: https://www.imf.org/external/pubs/ft/sdn/2016/sdn1603.pdf, at 16, footnote 12.
15 Bank of England, What is legal tender?, available at: https://www.bankofengland.co.uk/knowledgebank/what-is-legal-tender.
16 31 US Code 5013.

statute requiring a private business, a person or an organisation to accept currency or coins as for payment for goods and/or services. Private businesses may adopt their own policies on whether or not to accept cash as long this does not violate state law'.

5.22 In Europe, the legal tender status of Euro banknotes is governed by the Treaty on the Functioning of the European Union. Specifically, Council Regulation 974/98 on the introduction of the Euro sets forth the parameters on the legal tender of Euro banknotes and coins.[17] The same Regulation provides that the parties may deviate from this obligation by agreement. According to this recommendation, legal tender should be understood as the mandatory acceptance, at nominal value, allowing the debtor to be discharged. The text further clarifies each of these concepts: mandatory acceptance consists of the obligation for the beneficiary to accept Euro banknotes and coins, unless the parties have agreed on another method of payment; acceptance at nominal value means that the monetary value of Euro banknotes and coins is equal to the amount indicated on the banknotes and coins; as for the power of discharge, it consists in a debtor fulfilling a payment obligation by offering Euro banknotes and/or coins to its creditor.[18]

5.23 However, there are exceptions to the legal tender rule, so as to allow discharge of a debt by payment in another currency. For example, in the European Union, it is recognised that mortgage loans by consumers can be contracted in a currency that is not the legal currency of their place of residence, since the European Mortgage Directive introduces an exception to the concept of legal tender by allowing, under certain conditions, loans in foreign currency.[19]

3. Convertibility and fiat currency

5.24 A further characteristic of currency is 'convertibility', which is the potential to exchange the currency for something else, formerly metal (e.g. gold or silver)

---

17 Council Regulation (EC) No 974/98 of 3 May 1998 on the introduction of the Euro, available at: https://eur-lex.europa.eu/LexUriServ/LexUriServ.do?uri=CELEX:31998R0974:EN:HTML.

18 European Commission: Recommendation of 22 March 2010 on the scope and effects of legal tender for Euro banknotes and coins (2010/191/EU), available at: https://eur-lex.europa.eu/legal-content/EN/TXT/PDF/?uri=CELEX:32010H0191&from=EN; §1.

19 Directive 2014/17/EU of the European Parliament and of the Council of 4 February 2014 on credit agreements for consumers relating to residential immovable property, available at: https://eur-lex.europa.eu/legal-content/EN/TXT/PDF/?uri=CELEX:32014L0017&from=EN, Article 23. Notably, the currency used for payment of a debt (i.e., legal tender), may be different from the one used for calculation of obligations, which is the currency of account. Freedom to determine the currency of account may be restricted, e.g, as part of exchange control regulations, but it is a quite separate issue from the one involving currency payment.

or, today, foreign currencies.[20] However, a currency might function perfectly well in a given economy even if it is not convertible.

Finally, some currencies may have what is known as a fiat regime, which **5.25** requires the circulation of a currency at its nominal value, without any backing by a physical commodity. A fiat currency's value is therefore underpinned by the strength of the government that issues it, not its worth in gold or silver, and a fiat regime is based on a government's mandate that the paper currency it prints is legal tender for financial transactions.

4. Fungibility

Fungibility, or the mutual interchangeability of things, is an important **5.26** concept in relation to currencies. Things are fungible in three ways: by their nature because they are indistinguishable (as is the case with commodities such as wheat); as a result of the operation of a particular market or trade usage (as in the case of securities);[21] or as mandated by law, which is the case with a currency. The question of the fungibility of currency was not always settled law, and for different reasons with respect to coins and banknotes. For coins, it was often their poor quality and wear and tear over time that led to the refusal to consider two coins of the same face value as fungible. This is where legal solutions made it possible to achieve legal fungibility of coins. There are two types of laws that achieve this: the concept of legal tender and the so-called 'currency rule.'

The concept of legal tender requires debtors and creditors to accept all coins **5.27** considered legal tender by the authorities at their stipulated nominal value. Thus, even if two Louis or Shillings were not physically fungible – because one was cut and worn, and the other was new – holders of these Louis or Shillings were required to treat them as if they were perfectly interchangeable. But this concept also led to artificially granting the 'bad' coin (with less metal) the same purchasing power as the 'good' coin (the one with enough metal).[22]

The 'currency rule' is more relevant to banknotes.[23] Unlike coins, banknotes **5.28** have a unique identifier, a serial number. This specificity of banknotes makes

---

20 See, e.g., M.A. Heilperin, What is Monetary Convertibility?, 64(1) *Revue d'économie politique* (1954), at 14.
21 Geoffrey Fuller, *The Law and Practice of International Capital Markets*, 3rd edition (2012) LexisNexis, para 1.56.
22 The so-called 'Gresham Law' from Sir Thomas Gresham (1519–1579).
23 J.P. Koning, On currency (17 June 2017), available at: https://jpkoning.blogspot.com/2017/06/on-currency.html.

them identifiable, and even individualised, which is the opposite of fungibility. Moreover, in a case where several banks could issue banknotes, either in the same or separate territories, the question of the interchangeability of these banknotes quickly arose: to what extent were two banknotes of the same face value of the same currency issued by two different banks fungible?

5.29 It is on the basis of questions of property law (for example, the issue of stolen banknotes and the question of the *bona fide* holder (see paras 5.32–5.35 below)) that the issue of the total fungibility of banknotes has been recognised by the courts in both the UK and continental Europe. By allowing merchants to ignore the unique marks on each banknote, the court created fungibility by legal means. To this day, this 'currency rule' that was first established in Scottish courts in the 18th century[24] continues to apply to banknotes in most – if not all – legal systems.

5.30 For cryptocurrencies, the question is to what extent they are fungible. Cryptocurrencies are fungible assets and could be analogised to banknotes prior to the above-referenced 18th century court decisions that recognised the fungibility of banknotes notwithstanding the existence of different serial numbers. Cryptocurrencies are fungible in the sense that they all come from the same protocol with the same characteristics. It is only in the event of a fork of a cryptocurrency that the fungibility between the old and the new cryptocurrency disappears because the computer protocol has been modified. But in addition they are traceable: the entire history, from the day they were issued to the day they arrive in the last holder's account, is known to all.

5.31 The fact that these cryptocurrencies are traceable does not detract from their fungibility. However, due to their traceability, some traders refuse to receive cryptocurrencies, particularly if there is a risk that they have been used for illegal or prohibited purposes, such as the purchase of drugs or weapons. Again, this is a consequence of traceability and not of the very substance of the cryptocurrency, which is in itself fungible.

5. *Bona fide* holder

5.32 It is worth examining whether the paper currency issued by central banks benefits from any kind of legal qualification, in particular in the event of loss or theft, and therefore with respect to the protection of the third party *bona*

---

24   Reid Kenneth, Banknotes and their vindication in eighteenth-century Scotland, Edinburgh School of Law Research Paper No. 2013/19 (2013), at 11; and David Fox and Wolfgang Ernst (eds), *Money in the Western Legal Tradition*, Oxford University Press (2014), at 564–6.

fide acquirer.[25] For example, if a thief steals money from you, is it still yours? What if the thief gives it to a friend as a gift? Is the situation different if the thief spends the money in a store? The answer to these questions depends on the conditions under which transfers of ownership of scriptural money[26] are recognised. A person's title to a thing usually comes from the former owner, who is considered as not only a possessor, but also a legitimate owner. When the property is transferred to a third party, whether free of charge or not, the title that has vested in the transferor is simply transferred to the transferee, and the transferee cannot acquire a better title than that held by the transferor.

In common law as in civil law, there is a rule that protects the third party *bona* **5.33**
fide holder. Known in common law as *nemo dat quod non habet* ('no one can give what he does not have' and, conversely, a buyer cannot receive a better title to property than the seller), it has its civil law equivalent in the rule of *nemo plus iuris ad alium transferre potest transferre quam ipse habet* ('one cannot transfer more rights than one has').

Under English law, the title to banknotes passes by delivery and the *nemo dat* **5.34**
rule does not apply.[27] Coins and banknotes are also considered promissory notes for the purposes of the UK Bill of Exchange Act 1882 and, therefore, negotiable instruments. But in a study published in 2016 and subsequent papers, the Financial Market Law Committee (FMLC) explored these questions in depth, showing that to avoid the application of the *nemo dat* rule, legislation is probably necessary.[28]

In civil law, banknotes have gradually deviated from the legal qualification of **5.35**
commercial bills and promissory notes, in particular because banknotes no longer represent a claim against the issuing bank but have as their essential characteristic their status as legal tender, unlike commercial bills. In French law, as in most countries whose legal system is linked to the Napoleonic tradition, the question of proof of ownership resulting from the *nemo plus iuris* rule is resolved for movable assets according to the principle that possession creates valid title. This principle establishes a presumption of ownership for the benefit of the *bona fide* possessor. Thus, in the case of loss or theft, banknotes or metal coins are subject to the traditional rule that 'in matters of

---

25 David Fox, Bona Fide Purchase and the Currency of Money, 55(3) *The Cambridge Law Journal* (November 1996), 547–65.
26 Scriptural money is held by a bank in electronic or other non-cash forms.
27 Charles Proctor, *Mann on the Legal aspect of Money*, 7th edition, Oxford University Press (2012), at 43–5.
28 FMLC, Issues of legal uncertainty arising in the context of virtual currency (July 2016), at 12; and Joanna Perkins and Jennifer Enwezor, The legal aspect of virtual currencies, 10 *Journal of International Banking and Financial Law* (2016), at 569.

movables, possession is equivalent to title'. Even if currency is fungible, case law has recognised that it is possible to recover ownership of a fungible property, as long as the alleged owner of such property can prove that the property is indeed his. This has an interesting application for cryptocurrencies: since both Bitcoin and cryptocurrencies can be classified as moveable property, the civil law rules of possession should apply to them, and in particular the rule that 'in the case of movables, possession creates valid title', just like for paper money. Thus, in the event of theft or loss of Bitcoins or any other crypto-currencies, the aggrieved party should only be able to bring a successful claim under civil law if he can prove his title.

D. LEGAL DIFFERENCES BETWEEN LEGAL CURRENCIES AND CRYPTOCURRENCIES

5.36 There are several legal differences between cryptocurrencies and legal curren-cies. Cryptocurrencies are not issued by a central bank, they do not enjoy a legal tender status and therefore cannot be considered as a national currency or a currency at all. However, if they are not currencies in the legal sense, what are cryptocurrencies? They are monetary conventions between parties to a transaction. These conventions are not binding on third parties and the execution of these conventions depends entirely on the good faith of each party.

1. What cryptocurrencies are and are not

5.37 There are multiple definitions of cryptocurrencies. Most international and standard-setting organisations have provided their own definitions, and almost all of them overlap and lead to the definition of cryptocurrency as a digital representation of value that is not issued or guaranteed by a central bank or a public authority, that is not necessarily attached to a legally established currency and that does not possess a legal status of currency or money, but is accepted by natural or legal persons as a means of payment and which can be transferred, stored and traded electronically.[29]

5.38 The key characteristic that emerges from these definitions is the absence of the central bank as the issuer or the guarantor of these crypto assets. This is also

---

29 See, e.g., European Central Bank, *Virtual currency schemes: a further analysis* (February 2015), at 25; and Dong He et al., *Virtual currencies and beyond: initial considerations*, IMF, SDN 16/03 (January 2016), at 16–17.

why cryptocurrencies do not fulfil the three essential functions of a currency in the traditional sense, as described in 5.04 above. Specifically:

(i) Unit of account: the value of cryptocurrencies greatly fluctuates, which does not make it possible to make them units of account in a stable manner.

(ii) Medium of exchange: cryptocurrencies are less effective than the currency that is legal tender, to the extent that (a) the price volatility of cryptocurrencies makes it difficult to use them as a means of payment, (b) they lead to high transaction costs for simple retail operations and (c) they offer no guarantee of reimbursement in case of fraud.

(iii) Store of value: the lack of intrinsic value of cryptocurrencies also makes it impossible to make them stores of value. Cryptocurrencies are often issued based on a computing power, regardless of the needs of the economy and its trade, which does not make it possible to attach an intrinsic value to them.

Further, if we consider the legal criteria of currency, money, financial instru- **5.39** ments and payment services:

- cryptocurrencies are not a legal currency, as they are not legal tender in a sovereign geographical space;
- cryptocurrencies are also not electronic money within the meaning of the European law. Namely, the Electronic Money Institutions Directive defines 'electronic money' as 'electronically, including magnetically, stored monetary value as represented by a claim on the issuer which is issued on receipt of funds for the purpose of making payment transactions … and which is accepted by a natural or legal person other than the electronic money issuer'.[30] Decentralised and permissionless cryptocurrencies (e.g., Bitcoin) do not meet the legal conditions of electronic money within the meaning of the Directive because there is no issuer against which a claim can be made;
- cryptocurrencies are not financial instruments within the meaning of the European law in that they do not meet any of the financial instruments criteria under MiFID 2;[31]
- finally, while cryptocurrencies themselves do not constitute a payment service within the meaning of the European law, the exchange of

---

30 Directive 2009/110/EC of the European Parliament and of the Council of 16 September 2009 on the taking up, pursuit and prudential supervision of the business of electronic money institutions, Art 2.2.

31 Directive 2014/65/EU of the European Parliament and of the Council of 15 May 2014 on markets in financial instruments, Art 4.1(44).

currency against a cryptocurrency can be qualified as a payment service within the meaning of PSD2. This is the position of many regulators in Europe.[32]

5.40 Having established what cryptocurrencies are not, we must now consider what they are.

5.41 Pragmatically, cryptocurrencies can be considered as units of value, in the sense that they allow for the exchange of goods and services. They are not simply a unit of account, i.e., a monetary unit of measurement, but a unit of value, in the sense that they constitute in themselves a unit of exchange due to their own value.

5.42 However, like any other unit of value, cryptocurrencies are legally a convention between parties. In other words, it is only because the parties to a contract of sale or exchange (or any other contract) agree to be paid in cryptocurrency that these units of value fulfil a monetary function.

5.43 From the legal point of view, this could be analogised somewhat to contractual indexation clauses, which include a periodic adjustment to the prices paid for the goods or services based on the increase or decrease in the level of a nominated price index. The purpose of indexation is to take inflationary risk out of the contract. These clauses are often equated to foreign currency exchange clauses. The validity of these clauses depends on the specific legislation of each State, but it can be considered that the general tendency is to accept the validity of indexation clauses when the contract is of an international nature.

5.44 In the context of cryptocurrencies, since they cannot benefit from the status of a legal currency anywhere in the world, they are likely to be treated as mere commodities. Thus, a contract that provides for the debt to be paid in cryptocurrencies would be considered a contract in which the debtor's obligations are expressed not in legal tender, but in another form – which could be gold or another commodity, such as cryptocurrencies.

---

32 See Directive (EU) 2015/2366 of the European Parliament and of the Council of 25 November 2015 on payment services in the internal market; EBA: Report with advice for the European Commission on crypto-assets (9 January 2019); L'Autorité de contrôle prudentiel et de resolution: *Position de l'ACPR relative aux opérations sur Bitcoins en France* (20 January 2014); and Banque de France: *Les dangers liés au développement des monnaies virtuelles: l'exemple du bitcoin* (5 December 2013).

The practical question for a central bank is whether such indexation clauses **5.45** would be valid, and the answer depends either on national legislation and/or case law.

2. Personal right or intangible property?

Under both civil and common law, traditional legal classifications do not allow **5.46** cryptocurrencies to be included under an existing legal category of right or property.

More particularly, civil law distinguishes between movable and immovable **5.47** property, and between tangible and intangible property. Given the hybrid nature of cryptocurrencies, they tend to be considered as immaterial assets, a hybrid legal category whose emergence is relatively recent. Immaterial goods are services, skills, knowledge and training. These are goods of an economic nature. An intangible good is distinguished from a tangible good in that it has no material reality, and cannot be fully apprehended by hand or by eye.

Common law also distinguishes between tangible and intangible property. **5.48** Intangible property is traditionally divided into pure intangibles (such as debt, intellectual property rights and goodwill) and documentary intangibles, which obtain their character through the medium of a document (such as a bill of lading, promissory note or bill of exchange). In this respect, cryptocurrencies must be intangible property.

It is important to avoid making a frequent error that confuses the immaterial, **5.49** the virtual and the intangible. Virtual goods are goods that have no existence in the real world, goods devoid of any tangible reality. On the other hand, intangible goods are those that have no physical substance. The intangible should also not be confused with the immaterial. The intangible thing includes the monetary value recorded on the property (e.g., currency) or inherent in the property. Immaterial goods are characterised by their ability to be digitally recorded and stored on the internet without losing value or any of their components. They are composed of an intangible thing (information, knowledge, etc.) and a *corpus* (the recording medium). In this sense, crypto-currencies could fall within this definition of immaterial goods, both intangible and having a corpus: intangible for their monetary equivalent, and a *corpus* corresponding to the physical support of the private key.

Another important distinction is between choses in action and choses in **5.50** possession. A chose in possession is a tangible thing, capable of physical possession,[33] whereas a chose in action is essentially the right to sue. For example, a bank account is merely a chose in action, as there is no identified property available: only value.[34] As noted by the FMLC, were a virtual currency to be classed as a form of chose in action, the question would automatically arise as to the party against whom the action to enforce the rights of owner lies.[35] Further, the FMLC posits that if cryptocurrencies were choses in possession, and their value were realisable solely by virtue of their being exchanged for something else, then it would vital for a trustee in bankruptcy, liquidator or secured creditor to know by what means, if any, s/he is (they are) able to obtain possession of the coins or tokens.[36]

5.51 The FMLC concludes that:

> [o]n balance and considering the issues sketched very briefly above, it would seem that the legal uncertainty arising if [cryptocurrencies] are classified as choses in action is likely to be greater than if they are acknowledged to share the essential characteristics of choses in possession. Given that some virtual coins and tokens, at least, share certain characteristics of both intangible property and choses in possession, however, it may be convenient to understand them – where the currency is economically robust enough to be classed as 'property' – as a kind of hybrid: 'virtual choses in possession.' That is, intangible property with the essential characteristics of choses in possession.[37]

E. LEGAL ISSUES RELATED TO CRYPTOCURRENCIES

5.52 To what extent could a central bank issue cryptocurrencies that have the status of a legal tender? And are cryptocurrencies issued by a central bank intended to replace cash, or should this be seen as complementary to the use of paper money? CBDCs have recently become a focus of attention for many central banks. For instance, the Bank of International Settlement (BIS) encourages central banks to consider the possibility of issuing cryptocurrencies.[38]

---

33   Denis Keenan and Sarah Riches, *Business Law*, 11th edition, Pearson Longman (2013), at 610.
34   Alastair Hudson, *Equity and Trusts*, 8th edition, Routledge (2015), at 1294.
35   FMLC, *supra* note 28, at 7.
36   Ibid., at 8.
37   Ibid., at 6–15.
38   Morten Linnemann Bech and Rodney Garratt, Central Bank Cryptocurrencies, *BIS Quarterly Review* (September 2017), at 55.

1. Characteristics of Central Bank Digital Currency

While there is no single definition of a CBDC, and approaches to it vary by **5.53** institution, it can be viewed as a digital form of central bank money denominated in the official unit of account for general purpose users that can be exchanged, peer-to-peer, in a decentralised manner.[39] A CBDC could be a token representation of, or an addition to cash in physical form (banknotes and coins) and/or electronic deposits. It could be issued by the central bank directly to commercial banks and other payment service providers or to individuals, and would be exchanged at par with the central bank's other monetary liabilities.

CBDC, at the most basic level, is simply monetary value stored electronically **5.54** (digitally, or as an electronic token) that represents a liability of the central bank and can be used to make payment.[40] For the BIS:

> CBDC is potentially a new form of digital central bank money that can be distinguished from reserves or settlement balances held by commercial banks at central banks. There are various design options for a CBDC, including: access (widely vs restricted); degree of anonymity (ranging from complete to none); operational availability (ranging from current opening hours to 24 hours a day and seven days a week); and interest bearing characteristics (yes or no).[41]

Moreover, according to the BIS, two main CBDC variants can be issued: a wholesale and a general purpose one. The wholesale variant would limit access to a predefined group of users, while the general purpose one would be widely accessible.

Unlike currency exchanged by central bank accounts centrally, CBDCs would **5.55** be exchanged directly between the payer and the payee, without a bank intermediary and using DLT. The idea of central banks issuing cryptocurrencies is being studied by some central banks and universities, such as the FedCoin project.[42] More fundamentally, however, this phenomenon is in line with the idea of the disappearance of cash and bank notes. CBDCs would make it possible to maintain anonymity (to a certain extent) and thus facilitate the gradual abolition of physical monetary instruments while keeping the

---

39 BIS, Central Bank Digital Currency (March 2018), available at: https://www.bis.org/cpmi/publ/d174.pdf, at 6.
40 See Bank of Canada, Central Bank Digital Currency: Motivations and Implications, Staff Discussion Paper/Staff Analysis Paper 2017-16 (2017).
41 Ibid., at 1.
42 Sahil Gupta et al., FedCoin, a blockchain backed Central Bank cryptocurrency, Yale University (2017); available at: https://law.yale.edu/system/files/area/center/global/document/411_final_paper_-_fedcoin.pdf.

central bank's control over the circulation of the money supply and therefore the management of inflation, since central bank would be the only institution authorised to issue CBDCs. In fact, CBDCs would be nothing more than digitalised cash.

5.56 Central banks could create CBDCs for the general population. They could provide a digital means of payments, which would be claims against the central bank. The simplest solution would be to allow individuals and corporations (not only financial intermediaries) to directly hold accounts at the central bank, which might even be interest-bearing. Alternatively, central banks could resort to issuing their own cryptocurrencies, possibly using some decentralised and near anonymous technology to mimic and replace banknotes. A July 2018 study commissioned by the European Parliament Committee on Economic and Monetary Affairs found that CBDCs could be a 'remedy' for a lack of competition policy in the crypto sector.[43]

2. Specificities of CBDCs in comparison to paper money

5.57 A central bank's decision to issue CBDCs is primarily a political and economic one. However, some legal considerations must also be taken into account since, as the BIS notes, 'not all central banks have the authority to issue digital currencies and expand account access, and issuance may require legislative changes, which might not be feasible, at least in the short term'.

5.58 It is therefore the characteristics of each CBDC that will determine what legal framework will apply. However, CBDCs have specific features compared to traditional banknotes and coins.

3. Pseudonymity and traceability

5.59 Among the various cryptocurrencies that exist, some are pseudonymous and others are anonymous. For example, Bitcoin is pseudonymous because, although the IP address is not linked to a user, the user's identity may still be traced by other means. Specifically, transactions can be traced to a public key (an encrypted string) which, while not providing any material data about a user's identity, provides access to all transaction history and information for that Bitcoin holder. Thus, a participant on the blockchain – e.g., bank or merchant – who knows both the user's identity and his public key can cross-reference their own customer data with the transactional data from the

---

43 European Union Parliament, *Competition issues in the Area of Financial Technology* (FinTech), July 2018, at 66 and 73.

blockchain. As the use of blockchain becomes more commonplace, software tools for transaction analysis and identity knowledge will develop.

For CBDCs, the objective is to make it possible to trace their usage and even **5.60** identify their holders, either at any time or on request. Some central banks will prefer to stay as close as possible to paper money and use anonymous CBDCs; however, it is likely that most central banks will want to use the option of identifying CBDC users, either by pseudonym or by requiring CBDC users to reveal their identity when creating their accounts or using them, in order to facilitate the combatting of money laundering and terrorist financing. As noted by the BIS:

> CBDC might be an alternative to cash in some situations, a central bank introducing such a CBDC would have to ensure the fulfilment of anti-money laundering and counter terrorism financing (AML/CFT) requirements, as well as satisfy the public policy requirements of other supervisory and tax regimes.[44]

The implication of this profound change begs the question of whether and to **5.61** what extent the CBDC users will accept the lack of anonymity, and even identification during each transaction. The risk is that CBDCs will not be used and will be rejected by a significant part of the population. This is often a cultural issue, with some countries being more prepared than others for such a development.

4. Infringement and counterfeiting

Counterfeiting is a global scourge. It weakens confidence in the currency and **5.62** affects not only states but also citizens. Counterfeiting is generally defined as the circulation of an unauthorised currency sign, i.e., material representations of money, which refers to the fiduciary aspect of money. For this reason, counterfeit money only concerns paper money and not scriptural money. Indeed, only physical and material monetary signs, i.e., in practice, banknotes and coins, are covered by the legal and legislative provisions on counterfeiting. This is one of the reasons why cryptocurrencies do not generally fall within the scope of the provisions on counterfeiting.

As CBDCs are legal currencies, they will be protected in the same way as legal **5.63** currencies, but their introduction will most often require changes to the

---

44 BIS, *supra*, note 40, at 1.

regulatory framework to cover digital counterfeiting, even if today's technical solutions for protecting digital money offer solutions for central banks.[45]

5. Exchange control

5.64 Many countries have exchange control regulations aimed at preventing the flight of capital abroad under the control of a foreign exchange office. Exchange controls apply to all types of monetary representations: cash, scriptural money and electronic money. However, the emergence of cryptocurrencies has introduced new complications insofar as, given their characteristics, cryptocurrencies make it possible to circumvent national exchange control regulations. Indeed, as the IMF points out, cryptocurrencies can be used to carry out a cross-border transfer of paper money, while bypassing the traditional means of payment systems.[46] Specifically, 'as the applicability of national exchange control regimes to these systems is often unclear, the potential of cryptocurrencies to serve as an avenue for the evasion of capital controls is obvious'.[47] This was one of the main reasons why a number of countries, in view of the growing number of cryptocurrency transactions, have banned transactions with cryptocurrencies.

5.65 The practical question for many central banks is therefore whether the existing exchange control regulations allow cryptocurrencies to be included in these regulations in order to limit or even prohibit their purchase and holding. The answer will depend upon each country's regulatory regime. However, in the case of CBDCs, their use must also comply with national exchange control regulations, which will most often lead to the adaptation of the existing regulations in order to properly target this type of currency by the regulators. For CBDCs, exchange controls will likely be easier to design and implement than for coins and banknotes due to CBDCs' traceability.

F. CONCLUSION

5.66 This chapter has examined the characteristics of CBDCs and cryptocurrencies by reference to the features of legal currencies. The history of money suggests that, while the basic functions of money are constant, its form tends to evolve

---

45 Nicolas Christin et al., Monetary Forgery in the Digital Age: Will Physical-Digital Cash Be a Solution? 72 *A Journal of Law and Policy* (2012), at 172.
46 IMF, *supra* note 14, at 31.
47 Ibid.

in response to society's needs. Today's economy is being transformed by digitisation, prompting central banks to seriously consider the introduction of CBDCs.

There is currently no commonly agreed definition of CBDCs. Ultimately, this **5.67** definition will depend on the way in which central banks integrate future CBDCs into their existing legal systems, and whether CBDCs are simply a digitised representation of the fiat currency or a new form of currency, which exists alongside the legal currency. Depending on the approach taken by the relevant central bank, CBDCs may be subject to the same regime as the existing legal currencies or, alternatively, a new legal regime specific to CBDCs.

Ensuring acceptance of CBDCs among consumers by providing the same **5.68** standards of security as legal currencies – in particular in terms of traceability and protection against counterfeiting – will be critical to the success of CBDCs. Commercial banks and other financial institutions actively involved in the evolution of the monetary system should play an important role in the introduction of CBDCs to customers and in their day-to-day use.

Part II

BLOCKCHAIN AND DISTRIBUTED LEDGERS

6

BLOCKCHAIN IN FINANCIAL SERVICES

Colleen Baker and Kevin Werbach

A. INTRODUCTION

The financial services industry is among the areas predicted to benefit the **6.01** most from blockchain in the years to come. A key reason is that its 'core functions of verifying and transferring financial information and assets very closely align with blockchain's core transformative impact'[1] and it relies heavily 'on multiple ledgers to maintain transactional information and balances'.[2] Blockchain's promise for the industry lies in its potential to increase the efficiency of existing processes in the short term (dispensing with intermediaries and time-consuming administrative processes[3]), and to transform existing business models in the longer term. About 90 per cent of large North

---

1 Brant Carson et al., Blockchain Beyond the Hype: What Is the Strategic Business Value?, McKinsey & Company (June 2018), available at: https://www.mckinsey.com/business-functions/digital-mckinsey/our-insights/blockchain-beyond-the-hype-what-is-the-strategic-business-value. See also World Economic Forum, The Future of Financial Infrastructure: An Ambitious Look at How Blockchain Can Reshape Financial Services (August 2016), available at: http://www3.weforum.org/docs/WEF_The_future_of_financial_infrastructure.pdf.

2 Committee on Payments and Market Infrastructures, Distributed ledger technology in payment, clearing and settlement (February 2017).

3 McKinsey, *supra* note 1.

American, European and Australian banks are already investigating its potential.[4] Additionally, the financial services industry is home to about half of the 'identified blockchain uses cases' and '[f]inancial institutions are currently the biggest customers of blockchain technology providers'.[5]

6.02 However, the adoption of blockchain in financial services also presents significant challenges.[6] Financial services is a highly-regulated, global industry in which network effects are powerful. Many technology platforms in operation today are highly sophisticated and specialised. In interconnected global financial markets, changes in one area can produce unintended effects elsewhere. Legal uncertainty,[7] domestic and cross-border regulatory challenges and the need for coordinated action by industry participants on common standards (currently lacking) will make its widespread implementation a complex task. Hence, blockchain's adoption by the industry will likely be gradual and incremental in most cases.

6.03 This chapter is structured as follows: Section B briefly describes key aspects of blockchain-based systems; Section C analyses potential blockchain applications in the financial services industry; Section D discusses regulatory and compliance barriers to widespread adoption of blockchain; and Section E concludes.

B. TECHNOLOGY OVERVIEW

1. Definitions

6.04 The term 'blockchain' is often used in a generic sense, as in the title of this chapter, to describe a broad collection of systems.

---

4 Ibid.
5 Vedat Akgiray, Blockchain Technology and Corporate Governance, Technology, Markets, Regulation and Corporate Governance, Organisation for Economic Co-operation and Development (6 June 2018), available at: http://www.oecd.org/officialdocuments/publicdisplaydocumentpdf/?cote=DAF/CA/CG/RD(2018)1/REV1&docLanguage=En.
6 The Bank for International Settlements recently issued a highly critical report on the prospects for cryptocurrencies in financial services. See Bank of International Settlements, V. Cryptocurrencies: Looking Beyond the Hype (17 June 2018), available at: https://www.bis.org/publ/arpdf/ar2018e5.htm.
7 For example, the UK's Financial Conduct Authority (FCA) notes that courts would have to decide complex issues such as conflict of law questions that could surround cross-border contract execution using blockchain. See FCA, Discussion Paper on Distributed Ledger Technology, Discussion Paper DP17/3 (April 2017), available at: https://www.fca.org.uk/publication/discussion/dp17-03.pdf.

Distributed ledger technology (DLT) is the broadest category. As noted in the **6.05** Glossary, it involves a collection of records in which identical copies are held on numerous computers across an organisation, or multiple organisations. DLT systems are contrasted with centralised ledgers, such as traditional relational databases, in which one entity has ultimate control over the information recorded.

Distributed databases employing some of the techniques used in DLT have **6.06** been in use for decades.[8] However, earlier systems focused on fault tolerance within a centrally-controlled environment, such as a data centre in which one machine fails and the others must be shown to have an accurate copy of its records. DLT systems are designed to operate across organisational and other boundaries. They maintain consensus even though there is no controlling entity, and some nodes might actively attempt to cheat the network. The majority state of a DLT ledger is provably accurate and consistent up to a substantial number (usually between 33 and 50 per cent) of participants seeking to attack it.

Blockchain refers to a subset of DLT systems that organise transaction **6.07** histories as a linked series of time-stamped 'blocks'.[9] Each block is a collection of individual transactions, which are verified and added to the chain as a unit. The integrity of the chain is enforced through cryptography, specifically digital signatures to verify contributors and hash functions to verify stored information. Most of the prominent DLT solutions under development involve blockchains, although some solutions use similar mechanisms with slightly different information storage structures.[10] For the remainder of this chapter, we will follow the common practice of using the term 'blockchain' for both.[11]

---

8   See, e.g., Leslie Lamport, Paxos Made Simple (2001), available at: http://lamport.azurewebsites.net/pubs/paxos-simple.pdf.

9   Marco Iansiti and Karim R. Lakhani, The Truth about Blockchain, *Harvard Business Review* (2017): available at: https://hbr.org/2017/01/the-truth-about-blockchain, at 118–27.

10   The most prominent exceptions are the permissioned R3 Corda system for enterprise applications, and permissionless networks that employ a different information storage format. R3 is based on traditional relational database structures. See David E. Rutter, When is Blockchain not a Blockchain?, R3 Blog (24 February 2017), available at: https://www.r3.com/blog/when-is-blockchain-not-a-blockchain/. IOTA and Hedera Hashgraph are prominent examples of systems based on a directed acyclic graph (DAG) format rather than a chain of blocks. Jeff Kauflin, Hedera Hashgraph Thinks It Can One-Up Bitcoin and Ethereum With Faster Transactions, *Forbes* (13 March 2018), available at: https://www.forbes.com/sites/jeffkauflin/2018/03/13/hedera-hashgraph-thinks-it-can-one-up-bitcoin-and-ethereum-with-faster-transactions/.

11   Arvind Narayanan and Jeremy Clark, Bitcoin's Academic Pedigree, 15 ACM Queue 4 (29 August 2017), available at: https://queue.acm.org/detail.cfm?id=3136559.

6.08   As with other forms of DLT, many of the techniques used in blockchain systems were introduced in academic literature some time ago for decentralised digital time-stamping.[12] However, interest in blockchain increased dramatically after the 2008 release of the Bitcoin whitepaper by an anonymous author using the pseudonym Satoshi Nakamoto.[13] Bitcoin employed a blockchain to create a private, decentralised form of digital cash.

6.09   Unlike prior DLT solutions, Bitcoin is 'permissionless': anyone can participate in the network, with no verification of identities whatsoever. To ensure that hostile participants could not overwhelm the network by creating multiple virtual copies of themselves (known as a Sybil attack), Bitcoin employed a novel consensus algorithm called proof of work. In proof of work, verifiers of blocks known as miners are incentivised to waste significant amounts of computer processing power and electricity competing to earn a reward in the form of Bitcoin itself.[14] An attacker must compete against the aggregate computing power of the network, which is more expensive than the potential benefits.

2.   Key aspects of blockchain-based systems

6.10   All blockchain systems operate on the basis of decentralised consensus. There is no master party that maintains the canonical records or has the power to alter information recorded on the ledger. They are 'trust-minimised', in that confidence about the state of the ledger requires less trust in particular actors than traditional approaches.[15] For example, processing an international payment through the legacy SWIFT network requires trust in the monetary policy of the two central banks that issued the currencies, trust in the endpoint banks, trust in the intermediary correspondent banks, and trust in the operators of the SWIFT network. Sending the same payment across borders in Bitcoin does not involve any trusted issuer, intermediary, or operator.

6.11   There are three other major features of blockchain networks: access policies, immutability and transparency, each of which is described in continuation. In addition, blockchain networks can support sophisticated programmable functionality via smart contracts, which are described in Chapter 7. The particular

---

12   Ibid.

13   Satoshi Nakamoto, Bitcoin: A Peer-to-Peer Electronic Cash System (31 October 2008), available at: https://bitcoin.org/bitcoin.pdf.

14   Bitcoin with a capital 'B' is the network or protocol. The unit of currency is lowercase Bitcoin, similar to dollars or yuan.

15   Kevin Werbach, *The Blockchain and the New Architecture of Trust* (MIT Press 2018), at 28–31.

choices that systems make in their implementations affect their capabilities, appropriate uses, and legal/regulatory status.

(a) Access policies

Blockchain may be either permissioned or permissionless.[16] Permissionless **6.12** systems are more decentralised, in that not only is there no entity with control over the status of the ledger, there is none deciding who can participate in the first place. In a permissionless system, access simply requires a cryptographic public/private key pair, which anyone can generate.

Most financial services applications involving back-office functionality (such **6.13** as payments) or relationships among financial institutions (such as trade finance or loan syndication) are being implemented on permissioned networks. This is partly for performance reasons (particularly speed and scalability) and partly due to regulation, which often requires definite identification of the parties. Applications involving lending or trading of securities and other financial instruments are generally based on permissionless blockchains. Regulatory requirements for identification can be imposed on points outside the blockchain ledger itself, such as wallets, exchanges or token issuers.

(b) Immutability

Immutability means that once information is recorded on a blockchain, it **6.14** cannot easily be altered. At a technical level, all blockchains require immutable transactions. This is implicit in the fact there is no trusted party with the power to reverse a prior transaction. The strength of immutability in practice depends on the policies and practices of the key entities involved. For example, an issuer of tokens in an initial coin offering (ICO) may have the power to alter the rights associated with those tokens after the fact,[17] even freezing tokens in cases of hacking.[18] Or a majority of the miners in a proof of work network may agree to 'fork' the ledger to a new state, perhaps to reverse a fraudulent transaction.[19]

---

16   Tim Swanson, Consensus as a Service: A Brief Report on the Emergence of Permissioned, Distributed Ledger Systems (2015), available at: https://www.ofnumbers.com/wp-content/uploads/2015/04/Permissioned-distributed-ledgers.pdf.

17   Shaanan Cohney et al., Coin-Operated Capitalism, *Columbia Law Review* (forthcoming 2019), available at: https://papers.ssrn.com/sol3/papers.cfm?abstract_id=3215345.

18   Muyao Shen, $13.5 Million in Crypto Stolen from Token Platform Bancor, *Coindesk* (9 July 2018), available at: https://www.coindesk.com/token-platform-bancor-goes-offline-following-security-breach.

19   One of the most dramatic examples of a blockchain fork was in 2016, when the Ethereum network split in order to return funds stolen from a distributed crowdfunding application called The DAO, as described in more detail in Chapter 7. Joon Ian Wong and Ian Kar, Everything You Need to Know about the Ethereum 'Hard Fork', Quartz (18 July 2016), available at: https://qz.com/730004/everything-you-need-to-know-about-the-ethereum-hard-fork/.

(c) Transparency

6.15 On a permissionless blockchain network, all transactions are public, because they must be shared among all the network nodes as well as the verifiers in the proof of work process. The identities of those making the transactions, however, are represented by cryptographic keys rather than individual identities. Permissioned networks often have mechanisms that share transaction information only among the parties directly involved. As with the identity verification itself, this may be essential for operational business reasons (companies do not want to share their patterns with their competitors) or regulatory ones (certain transactions legally require confidentiality).

3. Potential benefits

6.16 We first identify the value propositions that this collection of technologies offers, and then address specific applications. The World Economic Forum lists six 'key value drivers' of this technology for the financial services industry: operational simplification; regulatory efficiency improvement; counterparty risk reduction; clearing and settlement time reduction; liquidity and capital improvement; and fraud minimisation.[20] We incorporate these into five more general potential advantages of blockchain solutions:

(a) Security

6.17 Blockchain has the potential to be significantly more secure than conventional financial systems. Because activities must be digitally signed and subject to a cryptographic consensus process, blockchain embeds information security deeply into the transactional process. And trusted intermediaries, which blockchain can eliminate, are single points of failure that can be significant security vulnerabilities. Blockchain systems do not eliminate security concerns entirely. Centralised entities may still be involved in storing and exchanging cryptocurrencies outside the blockchain itself, or the integrity of the blockchain may be vulnerable to hackers due to technical errors.

(b) Real-time gross settlement

6.18 In most financial transactions, each party keeps its own independent set of records. Settlement (the actual transfer of funds) is often a distinct process from trades or other transactions. One step transfers the legal rights among the parties; the other transfers the assets. This occurs either because the parties wish to verify the accuracy of the transfer and the availability of funds, or because it is more efficient to 'net' transactions between counterparties

---

20   World Economic Forum, *supra* note 1.

periodically as a batch than to keep track of them individually. When records do not agree, there must be a process of after-the-fact reconciliation to resolve the discrepancies.

With a blockchain, there is one distributed ledger that operates as the single **6.19** source of truth. Each transaction is simply a database entry. The costly and error-prone settlement process can be, at least in theory, eliminated.[21] Because there is no need for settlement, counterparty risk can be greatly reduced. Transactions that required pre-funding to ensure liquidity, thus tying up capital, may be executed directly in real time.

(c) Removal of intermediaries

Often, financial transactions require multiple hops, such as the international **6.20** payments process. Such transactions often go through intermediary correspondent banks in each country, which handle the currency conversion. This magnifies the duplication and inefficiency of settlement. Even a single intermediary that controls transactions, such as a stock exchange, may have incentives to extract unnecessary fees or even shape the market for its own proprietary advantage. Blockchain systems promise to reduce reliance on financial intermediaries in general, by giving all participants direct access to transaction ledgers and direct control over assets. At the same time, they can create new intermediaries such as cryptocurrency wallet providers and custody services for cryptographic keys.

(d) Automation

Because all transactions are on a common ledger, a blockchain creates a **6.21** software platform that can be the foundation for sophisticated smart contracts. Transactions can be automated, with the smart contracts immutably managing not only the trades but the associated execution. Because blockchain tokens are native digital assets, financial instruments can be combined in new ways and subject to complex software-defined rules that execute based on market developments.

(e) Auditability and compliance

Public blockchain ledgers are directly accessible to auditors and regulators. **6.22** This can remove the need to collect, process and reconcile data, which involves significant cost and possibilities for error, in the auditing process. Even for permissioned systems which keep transactions private to the parties involved,

---

21 In practice, there may be reasons to maintain some settlement delay. See Section C.2(b) below.

view-only access can sometimes be established and limited to authorised auditors and regulators.

C. BLOCKCHAIN APPLICATIONS IN FINANCIAL SERVICES

6.23 Blockchain's value proposition in specific areas of the financial services industry will ultimately rest upon a careful calculation of the benefits, costs, and risks of its use. Will the use of blockchain provide unique functionality or could improvements to existing technology enable such capabilities at lower cost and risk? The true impact of blockchain in the financial services industry will only become clear with time. Thus far, much attention has been focused on its potential in certain areas of the industry discussed in continuation: customer data and identity management, the trade life cycle, payments, financings, asset management, new currencies, cryptoassets, insurance, and corporate governance.

1. Customer data and identity management

6.24 The management of account customer data and identity information at financial institutions is a critical issue for the industry. As a heavily regulated industry, financial institutions are required by law and regulation to safeguard the privacy of much customer data.[22] These institutions are also legally required to know the background and identity of their customers, and to aid measures designed to prevent money laundering and terrorist financing. Such data is largely siloed as the importance of this task, especially potential liability considerations, often means firms conduct this due diligence on their own (though outsourcing does occur).[23] However, having data in discrete silos can make tracking criminal activity difficult.

6.25 Compliance with laws and regulations applicable in the customer data and identity management area is expensive. To cut costs, the idea of an industry utility for customer identity management has been considered in the past. The realisation of such a utility in practice, however, has been hampered by conflicting interests and by determining responsibility and accountability for

---

22 Lael Brainard, Cryptocurrencies, Digital Currencies, and Distributed Ledger Technologies: What Are We Learning?, Digital Currency Conference (15 May 2018), available at: https://www.federalreserve.gov/newsevents/speech/brainard20180515a.htm.

23 Bank of England, Cryptoassets Taskforce: Final Report (October 2018), available at: https://assets.publishing.service.gov.uk/government/uploads/system/uploads/attachment_data/file/752070/cryptoassets_taskforce_final_report_final_web.pdf.

any compliance-related issues.[24] These challenges would not be resolved merely by the use of blockchain technology.

The possibility of a government-run utility for such information has been **6.26** mentioned and might ultimately be the most viable common approach. But even with a government utility, there would likely be significant cross-border issues such as those experienced in the over-the-counter (OTC) derivative markets because of differing international regulations and political economy considerations. For example, international data privacy requirements are not uniform and might require that certain information about individuals remain in designated geographic areas.[25] National governments' regulation of OTC derivative markets and their differing regulations contribute to the fragmentation of what began as a global market. In theory, blockchain is a borderless technology. However, it is foreseeable that similar considerations could likewise fragment and localise its use. In the near term, blockchain might be most helpful in this area by enabling collaborative solutions for less sensitive, common industry data that might need to be included in a variety of transactions across the industry.

The reforms introduced in the aftermath of the 2008 global financial crisis **6.27** mandate centralised reporting of trade information in the OTC derivative markets. Industry utilities exist to store this information. For example, the Depository Trust and Clearing Corporation (DTCC)'s Trade Information Warehouse (TIW) 'provides lifecycle event processing services for approximately 98 per cent of all credit derivative transactions in the global market place',[26] a USD 8 trillion market.[27] DTCC, in cooperation with 15 global banks and MarkitSERV,[28] is in the process of 're-platforming' TIW, migrating its data to blockchain and cloud technologies.[29]

---

24 Martin Arnold, Five Ways Banks Are Using Blockchain, *Financial Times* (16 October 2017).
25 DTCC, Embracing Disruption: Tapping the Potential of Distributed Ledgers to Improve the Post-Trade Landscape (January 2016), available at: http://www.dtcc.com/blockchain-white-paper, at 9.
26 DTCC, *Trade Information Warehouse Learning Center*, available at: https://dtcclearning.com/products-and-services/trade-information-warehouse.html.
27 This is a notional amount. See Bank for International Settlements, Statistical release: OTC derivatives statistics at end June 2018 (31 October 2018), available at: https://www.bis.org/publ/otc_hy1810.pdf.
28 HIS Markit, MarkitSERV, available at: https://ihsmarkit.com/products/markitserv.html.
29 Kristi Morrow, DTCC Enters Test Phase on Distributed Ledger Project for Credit Derivatives with MarkitSERV and 15 Leading Global Banks (6 November 2018), available at: http://www.dtcc.com/news/2018/november/06/dtcc-enters-test-phase-on-distributed-ledger-project-for-credit-derivatives-with-markitserv.

2. The trade life cycle

6.28 Financial trades have a basic life cycle. In general, it begins when an order is placed, the trade is then executed, orders matched, the details confirmed, then cleared, and, finally, settled. Important differences do exist among the life cycles of different instruments. For example, securities settle within a short period of time (usually days), making the management of counterparty credit risk – the risk that one's counterparty will default on its obligations – minimal. In contrast, some OTC derivatives might last several years (credit default swaps contracts are frequently for a term of five years), making the management of counterparty credit risk a central function of the clearing process and, thereby, a more complex process to implement on a blockchain.

(a) Order flow and matching

6.29 Securities trade in both primary and secondary markets. Blockchain could be used to increase efficiencies and cut costs in both. An asset could be issued on, traded, and exist solely within a blockchain. For example, in August 2018, the World Bank issued a bond using blockchain for its entire life cycle[30] and Nasdaq has also used blockchain to issue and trade private securities.[31] Major oil companies, including BP and Shell, banks, and trading firms have launched a blockchain-based platform, Vakt, for energy commodity trading.[32] A blockchain-based trading platform, komgo SA, has also been launched to finance commodity trading.[33] Traded assets could also be issued using traditional approaches and then blockchain used to streamline their post-trade processing.

6.30 As part of the trade matching process, multiple information fields have to be matched and any trade exceptions (errors) handled. These are time-consuming, but necessary tasks. However, it is unclear whether using blockchain would be more efficient than the use of existing, centralised

---

30 The World Bank, World Bank Prices First Global Blockchain Bond, Raising A$110 Million (23 August 2018), available at: https://www.worldbank.org/en/news/press-release/2018/08/23/world-bank-prices-first-global-blockchain-bond-raising-a110-million.

31 Nasdaq, NASDAQ LINQ enables first-ever private securities issuance documented with Blockchain technology (30 December 2015), available at: http://ir.nasdaq.com/news-releases/news-release-details/nasdaq-linq-enables-first-ever-private-securities-issuance.

32 Ana Berman, Major Oil Firms, Banks Partner to Launch Blockchain Platform for Energy Commodity Trading (12 November 2018), available at: https://cointelegraph.com/news/major-oil-firms-banks-partner-to-launch-blockchain-platform-for-energy-commodity-trading.

33 Marie Huillet, Major Banks, Industry Players to Launch Blockchain-Based Commodities Platform (19 September 2018), available at: https://cointelegraph.com/news/major-banks-industry-players-to-launch-blockchain-based-commodities-platform.

approaches.[34] In entering trades, mistakes (known as 'fat fingers') also occur, which could require cancelation or reversal of transactions. Because of its immutability, blockchain could make correcting such common errors more difficult.

(b) Clearing and settlement

Clearing and settlement processes follow the completion of trade matching **6.31** and confirmation. These processes can take place bilaterally (between parties) or through centralised industry utilities. Post-financial crisis reforms have mandated use of such utilities for clearing standardised OTC derivatives.[35] Blockchain's potential to improve efficiencies and cut costs in these areas has received a significant amount of attention. It has been termed perhaps 'the most significant development in many years in payments, clearing, and settlement'.[36] This is largely due to its ability to instantaneously exchange assets and payments without a trusted intermediary.[37] Blockchain's potential to increase the resilience and reliability of such systems because information would be stored in multiple distributed ledgers rather than one central database also makes its use attractive. Some estimates suggest that big banks could see costs savings of around USD 10 billion annually with the use of blockchain in this area.[38] However, a blockchain based system could take longer to validate transaction settlement than a central entity.[39]

Clearing and settlement systems, along with payment systems, are often **6.32** referred to as the 'plumbing' of financial markets. Clearing refers to the process of calculating the obligations trade parties owe one another. For some instruments, such as over-the-counter derivatives, the clearing process could last many years. Settlement is the actual transfer and finalisation of this obligation exchange. On a daily basis, clearing and settlement systems process a tremendous number of transactions. For example, DTCC processes an average of 100 million trades a day.[40]

---

34 DTCC, *supra* note 25.
35 For an overview of OTC derivatives clearing, see Colleen Baker, Clearinghouses for Over-the-Counter Derivatives, Working paper, The Volcker Alliance, November 2016.
36 Lael Brainard, Distributed Ledger Technology: Implications for Payments, Clearing, and Settlement speech, Institute of International Finance Annual Meeting Panel on Blockchain (7 October 2016), available at: https://www.federalreserve.gov/newsevents/speech/brainard20161007a.htm.
37 DTCC, *supra* note 25, at 15.
38 Arnold, *supra* note 24.
39 Committee on Payments and Market Infrastructures, Distributed Ledger Technology in Payment, Clearing and Settlement (27 February 2017) available at: https://www.bis.org/cpmi/publ/d157.htm.
40 DTCC, *supra* note 25, at 15.

6.33 A time lag usually exists between the day a trade is made and the day its final settlement occurs. For example, in the US, the timetable for equity securities settlement is generally T+2 (trade date plus two days). Blockchain is often touted as offering the potential for real-time trade settlement. However, industry participants and policymakers note that current settlement delays are not necessarily due to the limitations of existing technology, which in some cases could perform real-time settlement. Rather, legal and regulatory considerations, market practices, and business processes are a stronger explanation for the time lag.[41] For example, faster clearing and settlement processes could impact credit and liquidity considerations in this area.[42] This is particularly true in the clearinghouse context. If clearing members have less time to meet margin calls, their liquidity risk will increase, and this could morph into a credit issue because an unmet margin call would trigger a default.[43]

6.34 Infrastructure systems, clearing and settlement processes must operate nearly flawlessly, even in crises; Federal Reserve policymakers note that '[s]afety and integrity in clearing and settlement is a critical, long-standing public policy objective of the Federal Reserve, and is critical for broader financial stability'.[44] The stability of global financial markets depends on the operational integrity of these systems. Otherwise, global markets risk coming to a standstill. For example, when the clearinghouse of the Hong Kong Futures Exchange collapsed in 1987, Hong Kong's capital markets shut down.[45] Hence, the stakes are high with any experimentation or changes in the area of clearing and settlement systems. However, incremental changes have begun. For example, the Australian Stock Exchange (ASX) is in the process of replacing its more than 25-year old system for post-trade processing of its cash equities market with a blockchain technology.[46]

6.35 Large-scale settlement systems must provide for what is known as settlement finality or legal certainty regarding when payment for a transaction or an asset transfer is final and irrevocable, that is, cannot be reversed because of a counterparty's insolvency. Principle 8 of the Principles for Financial Market

---

41   Ibid., at 3; see also FCA, *supra* note 7.

42   David Marshall and Robert Steigerwald, The Role of Time-Critical Liquidity in Financial Markets, 37(2) *Economics Perspectives* (2013), available at: https://www.chicagofed.org/publications/economic-perspectives/2013/2q-marshall-steigerwald.

43   Ibid.

44   Lael Brainard, The Use of Distributed Ledger Technologies in Payment, Clearing, and Settlement (14 April 2016), available at: https://www.federalreserve.gov/newsevents/speech/brainard20160414a.htm.

45   See Paul Tucker, Clearing Houses as System Risk Managers, Speech at the DTCC-CSFI Post Trade Fellowship Launch (1 June 2011) (explaining that when the Hong Kong Futures Exchange clearinghouse failed in 1987, it shut down Hong Kong's capital markets).

46   ASX, CHESS Replacement, available at: https://www.asx.com.au/services/chess-replacement.htm.

Infrastructures (FMI) states that '[a]n FMI's [financial market infrastructure's] rules and procedures should clearly define the point at which settlement is final'.[47] For financial markets to function, participants must have certainty from a legal perspective about the moment in which settlement finality has occurred. Hence, for a blockchain-based, large-scale settlement system to operate effectively, this issue, which is complicated by blockchain's use of probabilistic consensus processes for validation, must be clarified.[48] Also, any blockchain-based system would need to proactively address settlement risk between counterparties if the exchange of funds and assets does not occur simultaneously.[49]

With this difficulty in mind, several global banks are involved in the develop- **6.36** ment of 'utility settlement coins' to increase clearing and settlement efficiencies,[50] particularly in securities settlement, interbank payments, and international transactions, and to address settlement finality.[51] These coins would be used on blockchain platforms, and could be converted to multiple currencies in accounts at central banks. They would also enable dispensing with current time-consuming payment processes. Central banks themselves are exploring the use of such settlement assets.[52]

Blockchain could be used for asset custody and servicing (voting, dividend **6.37** distribution etc.). For example, banks such as Santander[53] and KAS Bank[54] have been testing the use of blockchain for shareholder voting.

---

47   Bank for International Settlements, Principles for Financial Market Infrastructures (April 2012), available at: https://www.bis.org/cpmi/publ/d101a.pdf.

48   For additional information on this issue, see Nancy Liao, On Settlement Finality and Distributed Ledger Technology, *Yale Journal of Regulation* (9 June 2017), available at: http://yalejreg.com/nc/on-settlement-finality-and-distributed-ledger-technology-by-nancy-liao/.

49   See Brainard, *supra* note 36. See also European Central Bank and Bank of Japan, Securities Settlement Systems: Delivery-Versus-Payment in a Distributed Ledger Environment (March 2018).

50   Adam Kissack, Utility Settlement Coin: A Pioneering Form of Digital Cash (5 September 2017), available at: https://www.clearmatics.com/utility-settlement-coin-pioneering-form-digital-cash/.

51   Brainard, *supra* note 22.

52   Ibid.

53   Sujha Sundararajan, Santander Conducts Proxy Voting Blockchain Pilot at AGM, *Coindesk* (18 May 2018), available at: https://www.coindesk.com/santander-conducts-proxy-voting-blockchain-pilot-at-agm.

54   Finextra, KAS Bank Moves Shareholder Voting to the Blockchain (23 April 2018), available at: https://www.finextra.com/newsarticle/31993/kas-bank-moves-shareholder-voting-to-the-blockchain.

3. Payments

6.38 Industry participants are highly interested in investing in blockchain-based solutions in the payments area.[55] Like clearing and settlement systems, systems for domestic and international payments, which can be consumer or commercial, are a critical part of the infrastructure of financial markets. Accordingly, similar considerations about the operational integrity of these systems are also relevant. Blockchain can also potentially increase efficiencies, speed, and cost savings in this area. International payments in particular involve significant friction due to currency conversions and intermediation. In theory, a cryptocurrency using a global shared ledger could eliminate the need for much of that infrastructure.

6.39 Indeed, blockchain is already being used for several applications. For example, Santander has teamed up with blockchain technology provider Ripple[56] to provide a mobile international payments application to its customers.[57] RippleNet is a permissioned, blockchain global payments network.[58] The Interbank Information Network (IIN),[59] a blockchain service launched by J.P. Morgan and including more than 75 banks, is being used to make faster, more efficient global payments: 'Using blockchain technology, IIN reduces the time correspondent banks currently spend responding to compliance and other data-related inquiries that delay payments.'[60] Japan, also using Ripple technology, recently launched the first domestic interbank payment system on blockchain: MoneyTap.[61] Ripple has begun signing up international money services businesses as customers for its xRapid offering, which uses the XRP cryptocurrency as a bridge to provide real-time liquidity for international payments.[62]

---

55 Herb Hozlov and James Wilkinson, Tech Control: How Fintech M&A is Shaping the Financial Future, Reed Smith (2018), available at: https://www.reedsmith.com/en/news/2018/11/tech-control-how-fintech-m-and-a-is-shaping-the-financial-future.

56 https://ripple.com/.

57 Team Ripple, Santander Launches First Mobile App for Global Payments Using Ripple's xCurrent, available at: https://ripple.com/insights/santander-launches-first-mobile-app-for-global-payments-using-ripples-xcurrent/.

58 https://ripple.com/ripplenet/.

59 J.P. Morgan, J.P. Morgan Interbank Information Network Expands to More Than 75 banks (25 September 2018), available at: https://www.jpmorgan.com/country/US/en/detail/1320570135560.

60 Ibid.

61 Samburaj Das, Ripple Blockchain Payments App 'MoneyTap' Goes Live in Japan, *Cryptocurrency News* (4 October 2018), available at: https://www.ccn.com/ripple-blockchain-payments-app-moneytap-goes-live-in-japan/.

62 Ryan Browne, Ripple's Cryptocurrency Product Goes Live for the First Time With Three Financial Firms, CNBC.com (1 October 2018), available at: https://www.cnbc.com/2018/10/01/ripple-xrp-cryptocurrency-product-xrapid-goes-live-for-first-time.html.

4. Financing

(a) Lending

The lending of money to corporations is a time-consuming, complex process **6.40** involving a number of parties who need to view much of the same data and transaction documentation.[63] Blockchain offers an efficient, cost-effective platform for such transactions and data sharing. The Spanish bank BBVA recently became the first global bank to issue a corporate loan (USD 75 million) from start to finish using blockchain technology. Using a permissioned blockchain, the bank both negotiated loan terms (traditionally, a lengthy process) and secured party signatures to the loan documentation. The loan agreement was then registered on Ethereum's public blockchain to ensure immutability.[64]

(b) Loan syndication and securitisation

In 2018, syndicated loans were a USD 4.6 trillion global market.[65] In a **6.41** syndicated loan, a lead or originating bank brings together a group of banks or financial institutions who commit to provide a certain amount of the total loan. Each institution then receives interest and principal payments proportional to its contribution commitment. Like corporate loans, syndications involve complex documentation that must be reviewed by multiple parties. Such transactions can take a while to settle.[66] To date, this area of the financial services industry also lacks significant standardisation. Because current processes are inefficient, paper-intensive, time-consuming, costly, and lack standardisation, blockchain's value proposition for this area is strong.[67] The Spanish bank BBVA, with MUFG (a Japanese bank) and BNP Paribas (a French bank), also first used blockchain to provide a syndicated loan (USD 150 million) to Red Electrica (a Spanish firm).[68] Using a permissioned blockchain, the parties were able to quickly negotiate, simultaneously access transaction data, instantaneously exchange information, and swiftly sign transaction documentation that was eventually registered on the Ethereum's public blockchain for transaction immutability.[69]

---

63 Laura Noonan, BBVA issues corporate loan using blockchain, *Financial Times* (25 April 2018).
64 Ibid.
65 *Dealogic, Global Landscape – Jumbo° deals on the rise*, https://www.dealogic.com/insight/loans-highlights-full-year-2018/.
66 Arnold, *supra* note 24.
67 See generally DTCC, *supra* note 25, at 17.
68 Laura Noonan, Banks Complete First Syndicated Loan on Blockchain, *Financial Times* (6 November 2018).
69 See generally ibid.

6.42 Blockchain could also facilitate loan securitisation. In a securitisation, a pool of loans is sold to a purchaser (generally a special purpose legal entity) who then uses these loan assets to collateralise securities that are sold to investors. The purchaser pays for the loans through the sale of securities. As borrowers make payments on their loans, these payments are collected and then used to make principal and interest payments to the investors. Here too blockchain could improve the efficiency of existing processes and offer cost savings. BBVA and the European Investment Bank Group recently completed a synthetic securitisation (EUR 1 billion) using blockchain.[70]

(c) Trade finance

6.43 Trade finance is an ancient industry that remains largely paper-based to this day. It too involves multiple documents (letters of credit, bills of lading, transportation receipts, etc.) and parties (banks, trading partners, shipping companies, customs officials, etc.) who need to share information. For example, an examination of the processes involved in a Danish shipping company shipping flowers from Mombasa (Kenya) to Rotterdam demonstrated that it 'generated dozens of documents and nearly 200 communications involving farmers, freight forwarders, land-based transporters, customs brokers, governments, ports and carriers'.[71]

6.44 Such extensive, international processes are vulnerable to errors, delay, and fraud. Blockchain platforms offer the possibility of increased efficiencies, security, and cost savings. For example, Voltron, which uses a blockchain platform, increases efficiency surrounding the use of letters of credit.[72] Tricon Energy (a Texas company) and Reliance Energy (an Indian company) used the system in a recent sale and purchase of polymers.[73] National authorities are also interested in the potential of blockchain to increase efficiencies in trade finance. For example, the Hong Kong Monetary Authority is collaborating with a group of banks in the creation of a trade finance platform.[74] It is also

---

70 BBVA, Investment Plan for Europe: BBVA and EIB Group sign the first synthetic securitization in blockchain of €1 billion (20 December 2018), available at: https://www.bbva.com/en/investment-plan-for-europe-bbva-and-eib-group-have-signed-the-first-synthetic-securitization-in-blockchain-of-e1-billion/.

71 Adam Green, Will Blockchain Accelerate Trade Flows?, *Financial Times* (9 November 2017).

72 R3, Trade Finance Solution Voltron Launches Open Platform on Corda Blockchain (22 October 2018), available at: https://www.r3.com/news/trade-finance-solution-voltron-launches-open-platform-on-corda-blockchain/.

73 Don Weinland, Banks Race to Make Money on Trade Finance Platforms, *Financial Times* (7 November 2018).

74 Wolfie Zhao, Hong Kong's Blockchain Trade Finance Platform to Go Live by September (16 July 2018), available at: https://www.coindesk.com/hong-kongs-blockchain-trade-finance-platform-to-go-live-by-september.

collaborating with the Monetary Authority of Singapore on a project aiming to use blockchain for a cross-border trade-finance infrastructure.[75]

However, commentators suggest that to effectively move trade finance to a **6.45** blockchain platform, the difficult task of migrating all of the steps involved in the entire trade finance process (from origination to completion, occurring anywhere in the world) to the use of this technology is also necessary because one critical, outstanding paper-based step could create a bottleneck in the whole process.[76]

5. Asset management

The potential impact of blockchain on the asset management industry has **6.46** received much attention because of its ability to improve cost efficiencies, particularly in the mutual fund trading life cycle. Additional potential applications include facilitating client onboarding and related regulatory compliance obligations, in addition to improving the management of third-party model portfolios.[77] Current processes are time-consuming and staff intensive. Estimates of potential industry cost savings from blockchain use are around USD 2.7 billion a year.[78]

Examples of developments in this area include: Calastone, a 'global funds **6.47** transaction network,' with more than 1,700 customers in 40 countries has announced plans to migrate its systems, which process more than nine million messages a month related to transactions totalling more than GBP 170 billion, to blockchain in May 2019;[79] and Melonport, an innovative technology company working to transform this space with a protocol designed for the management of cryptoassets.[80]

6. New currencies

Bitcoin was designed to operate as digital cash: a bearer instrument that is **6.48** widely accepted as a universal means of discharging financial obligations.[81] It, and other cryptocurrencies, can thus be employed as alternatives to traditional

---

75 Alice Woodhouse, Hong Kong and Singapore to Collaborate on Fintech, Blockchain, *Financial Times* (24 October 2017).

76 Arnold, *supra* note 24.

77 Ernst & Young LLP, Blockchain Innovation in Wealth and Asset Management (2017).

78 Attracta Mooney, Blockchain 'Could Save Asset Managers $2.7bn a Year', *Financial Times* (22 February 2018).

79 http://www.calastone.com/about-us/.

80 https://melonport.com/.

81 Nakamoto, *supra* note 13.

government-backed fiat currencies. These uses are distinguished from the payments applications where a cryptocurrency, such as XRP, serves purely a bridging function.

6.49 One scenario is that a cryptocurrency, most likely Bitcoin, could take the place of government-issued currencies as the base denomination for financial transactions within a country.[82] These scenarios usually focus on countries with unstable monetary policy and hyperinflation.[83] Alternately, a central bank could use blockchain technology to, in essence, tokenise and digitise its existing currency.[84] Such systems would be based on permissioned distributed ledger technology, with the government retaining control over which entities could participate or validate transactions. This would create a Central Bank Digital Currency (CBDC), still subject to traditional monetary policy.[85] The US Federal Reserve, the Bank of England, the People's Bank of China, and the Monetary Authority of Singapore have all expressed interest or engaged in technical trials of CBDCs.

6.50 Central bank implications of cryptocurrencies are described in greater detail in Chapter 5.

7. Cryptoassets

6.51 Cryptocurrencies can be traded like any other financial instrument. Using traditional trading infrastructure, both the CME Group and the Cboe Futures Exchange launched the trading of cash-settled Bitcoin futures contracts in

---

82 The extreme version of this scenario is called 'hyperbitcoinisation,' in which extreme inflation causes a rapid flight to Bitcoin globally. C. Edward Kelso, Hyperbitcoinization: $100Mil Per Coin By 2030 (7 July 2018), available at: https://news.bitcoin.com/hyperbitcoinization-bitcoin-100mil-per-coin-2030/.

83 Venezuela has established a cryptocurrency called the petro, backed by its oil reserves. Kirk Semple and Nathaniel Popper, Venezuela Launches Virtual Currency, Hoping to Resuscitate Economy, *The New York Times* (20 February 2018), available at: https://www.nytimes.com/2018/02/20/world/americas/venezuela-petro-currency.html. However, the petro is not widely accepted or used, and there is significant scepticism about the linkage between the digital currency and the physical oil reserves. Editorial Board: Venezuela's 'Crypto' Con, *Wall Street Journal* (22 February 2018), available at: https://www.wsj.com/articles/venezuelas-crypto-con-1519343990.

84 Aleksander Berentsen and Fabian Schar, The Case for Central Bank Electronic Money and the Non-case for Central Bank Cryptocurrencies, Federal Reserve Bank of St. Louis (28 February 2018), available at: https://research.stlouisfed.org/publications/review/2018/02/13/the-case-for-central-bank-electronic-money-and-the-non-case-for-central-bank-cryptocurrencies/.

85 International Monetary Fund, Casting Light on Central Bank Digital Currencies (12 November 2018), available at: https://www.imf.org/en/Publications/Staff-Discussion-Notes/Issues/2018/11/13/Casting-Light-on-Central-Bank-Digital-Currencies-46233, at 7–9.

2017.[86] Fidelity, which manages USD 7.2 trillion in client assets, has developed a platform for the trading and storage (custody) of cryptocurrencies.[87] Intercontinental Exchange, the parent company of the New York Stock Exchange, announced that it will begin trading physically-settled Bitcoin futures.[88] One major factor boosting cryptoasset trading is the rise of initial coin offerings (ICOs), in which projects pre-sell cryptocurrencies to the public to fund network development. It is estimated that over USD five billion was raised in ICOs in 2017, and over USD 16 billion in 2018.[89]

Speculative trading in cryptoassets and ICOs became widespread in 2017, as **6.52** prices spiked dramatically. Cryptocurrency prices dropped precipitously in 2018, with virtually all of them down 70–95 per cent from their all-time highs. There are also serious concerns about fraud, theft, and regulatory compliance to be addressed. Cryptoassets and ICOs are discussed in greater detail in Chapter 4.

8. Tokenisation

Blockchain could ultimately enable the 'tokenisation', or slicing up, of assets. **6.53** This would allow investors easier access to a far greater range of asset classes than just listed equities and bonds.[90] Cryptoassets can be associated with anything of value, physical or digital. Their smart contract code can directly embed the investor's rights and responsibilities. And because cryptoassets are native digital assets, they can eliminate friction traditionally involved with securitisation of assets such as real estate.[91] The potential here is not unlike that which gave rise to the innovative financial derivative markets in which the risks of various components of assets (credit, interest rate, foreign exchange risk, etc.) are bought and sold. A number of companies such as Templum and

---

86 Alexander Osipovich, First U.S. Bitcoin Futures to Start Trading Next Week, *Wall Street Journal* (4 December 2017), available at: https://www.wsj.com/articles/first-u-s-bitcoin-futures-to-start-trading-next-week-1512394201.

87 Nikhilesh De, Fidelity is Launching a Crypto Trading Platform, *Coindesk* (15 October 2018) available at: https://www.coindesk.com/fidelity-reveals-cryptocurrency-and-digital-asset-trading-platform.

88 Shawn Tully, The NYSE's Owner Wants to Bring Bitcoin to Your 401(k). Are Crypto Credit Cards Next?, *Fortune* (3 August 2018), available at: http://fortune.com/longform/nyse-owner-bitcoin-exchange-startup/.

89 Coindesk ICO Tracker, https://www.coindesk.com/ico-tracker. The precise numbers are in dispute, because there are no central registries or exchanges for ICOs.

90 Attracta Mooney, RBC GAM: blockchain will prevent us being Uberised, *Financial Times* (19 November 2017).

91 Jeff John Roberts, Real Estate on the Blockchain: $20 Million Sale 'Tokenizes' Student Residence, *Fortune* (27 November 2018), available at: http://fortune.com/2018/11/27/blockchain-harbor/.

T0 have received regulatory approval as alternative trading systems for 'security token' exchanges to support such activities.[92]

6.54 The bulk of the activity around tokenisation within financial services concentrates on either tokenising existing forms of securities, such as equity, or tokenising physical assets. Turning corporate stock into a tokenised crypto-asset offers several potential advantages. It would become a bearer instrument, eliminating potential discrepancies between brokerage records and central clearing houses. Companies could gain a real-time view of their shareholders, which would always be accurate. Investors would have access to greater liquidity. The state of Delaware has changed its corporate law to allow share issuance on a blockchain.[93] Going forward, tokens could be used in creative ways as 'programmable securities,' such as giving holders an automatic discount on a company's services along with their investment returns.

6.55 Tokenisation of physical assets promises even more significant opportunities. Investments in physical assets such as real estate or fine art are generally quite illiquid. Security tokens might make it possible to create dynamic investment markets in many assets where they do not exist today because tokenisation would essentially bundle all of a physical asset's property rights into a digital asset that could be easily and rapidly traded.

9. Insurance

6.56 Blockchain has the potential to increase efficiencies in the insurance industry and to transform business processes. Similar to other areas of the financial services industry, routine processes within the insurance industry such as underwriting and claims management are often paper-intensive, lack standardisation, require manual reconciliations, and involve multiple parties – sometimes in geographically remote locations – who need access to largely the same data and transaction documents. Blockchain could provide this distributed access more securely and at lower costs. For example, fragmented, sensitive, individual health history data could be centralised on a blockchain to improve patient diagnosis and care coordination, in addition to improving life insurance underwriting, including the application experience.[94] In August

---

92 Trevor M. Dodge, Implications for Launch to tZERO, First U.S. Registered ATS, *Nat'l L. Rev.* (14 January 2018), available at: https://www.natlawreview.com/article/implications-launch-tzero-first-us-registered-ats.

93 Jeff John Roberts, Companies Can Put Shareholders on a Blockchain Starting Today, *Fortune* (1 August 2017), available at: fortune.com/2017/08/01/blockchain-shareholders-law/.

94 See Deloitte, Blockchain in Insurance (2016), available at: https://www2.deloitte.com/content/dam/Deloitte/us/Documents/financial-services/us-fsi-blockchain-in-insurance-ebook.pdf.

2017, blockchain was used in the issuance of a USD 15 million catastrophe bond, Dom Re IC Limited 2017.[95]

The industry has established two consortia, RiskBlockAlliance[96] and B3i Participants.[97] Both are composed of brokers, underwriters, and reinsurers and aim to explore blockchain's possibilities in the insurance sector.[98] B3i estimates the industry could see a cost saving of 30 per cent from the use of blockchain.[99]   **6.57**

Ernst & Young suggest five areas of the industry as opportunity spaces for blockchain use: fraud detection and risk prevention, claims prevention and management, Internet of Things (IoT) and product development, new distribution and payment models, and reinsurance.[100] Blockchain could increase insurers' ability to authenticate customer identity, policies, and claims, in addition to helping identify duplicate claims across the industry. It is estimated that insurance fraud (non-health related) accounts for approximately USD 40 billion per year in costs.[101] Connections to the IOT could enable insurers to improve actuarial models, offer new programmes and products (e.g., healthy lifestyle choices could be collected and rewarded), and even provide notice of potential claims. Blockchain could centralise and share multiple data points both for claims prevention purposes and for more efficient processing of those created. The transparency of reinsurance contracts and related data could be increased by blockchain, enabling greater understanding of risk exposures within this area.   **6.58**

10. Corporate governance

Poor corporate governance is costly. It is also arguably 'the single most important cause of corporate scandals and financial crisis'.[102] However, the characteristic properties of blockchain – decentralisation, immutability, transparency and peer-to-peer communication – could enable tremendous   **6.59**

---

95   FitchRatings, Blockchain and Insurance – The Trust Machine (April 2018), available at: https://your.fitch.group/Blockchain-and-Insurance.html?utm_source=slipcase, at 6.
96   https://www.theinstitutes.org/guide/riskblock.
97   https://b3i.tech/home.html.
98   FitchRatings, *supra* note 95, at 6.
99   Ibid.
100   Ernst & Young LLP: Blockchain in Insurance: Applications and Pursuing a Path to Adoption (2017).
101   FitchRatings, *supra* note 95, at 5.
102   Vedat Akgiray, Blockchain Technology and Corporate Governance, Technology, Markets, Regulation and Corporate Governance, Organisation for Economic Co-operation and Development (6 June 2018), available at: http://www.oecd.org/officialdocuments/publicdisplaydocumentpdf/?cote=DAF/CA/CG/RD(2018)1/REV1&docLanguage=En.

improvements in corporate governance, whose core purposes include: transparency, accountability, responsibility, and fairness.[103]

6.60 For example, blockchain could increase the transparency of corporate asset ownership and trading. Maintaining accurate, timely ownership records of a corporation's stock has been a challenge in practice that could be ameliorated through blockchain use.[104] Heightened transparency could create profit winners and losers among various stakeholders such as managers, board members, activists, corporate raiders, and traders. And those benefiting from current opacity, such as corporate raiders and activists, could lose an important advantage. It could also decrease opportunities for corporate chicanery in areas such as financial statement reporting, earnings management, options backdating, and transactions involving insider conflicts of interest.[105]

D. REGULATORY AND COMPLIANCE CONSIDERATIONS

6.61 As part of participating in a highly-regulated industry, financial institutions have many regulatory reporting requirements that must be met timely and accurately. Indeed, the possibility of increased compliance and reporting efficiencies is among the greatest drivers of FinTech investment, including blockchain-related activity.[106] Smart contracts could increase the efficiency of compliance processes through automation. The transparency of blockchain ledgers could make it easier for auditors and regulators to track activity. The fact that all transactions among counterparties are recorded on a single shared ledger could eliminate the inefficiencies of assembling compliance data from multiple sources.

6.62 However, a potential barrier to widespread adoption of blockchain in the financial services industry is regulatory uncertainty. This is not unusual. In the past, new technologies have introduced regulatory uncertainty and, ultimately, required new regulatory paradigms as in the case of the dematerialisation of securities.[107] The UK's FCA has noted finding regulatory uncertainties in the custody and payments area.[108]

---

103   See ibid.
104   David Yermack, Corporate Governance and Blockchain, National Bureau of Economic Research, Working Paper Series No. 21802 (December 2015), available at: https://www.nber.org/papers/w21802.
105   Ibid.
106   Reed Smith, *supra* note 55, at 5.
107   Financial Conduct Authority, Discussion Paper on Distributed Ledger Technology, Discussion Paper DP17/3 (April 2017), available at: https://www.fca.org.uk/publication/discussion/dp17-03.pdf, at 23.
108   Ibid.

One of the most significant areas of concern is the difficulty of enforcing **6.63** AML, CFT and national currency controls on cryptocurrencies. While permissioned DLT systems require verification of participants' real-world identities, public blockchains do not. There is evidence that criminals take advantage of cryptocurrencies to engage in a significant level of money laundering.[109] This is one reason most banks still refuse to do business with cryptocurrency-related firms.

To address AML/CFT concerns, most large financial markets now require **6.64** cryptocurrency exchanges, especially those accepting fiat currencies, to engage in KYC processes and suspicious activity reporting analogous to regulated financial services firms. However, the requirements and coverage of these mandates are the subject of debate and global variation. The Financial Action Task Force (FATF), an intergovernmental body focused on these issues, outlined the AML/CFT risks of virtual currencies in 2014 and issued guidance the following year.[110] In 2018, it adopted new standards for cryptocurrency-related firms such as exchanges and wallet providers.[111]

A major area of regulatory uncertainty concerns the classification of crypto- **6.65** assets. Most ICOs in the 2017 boom disregarded the extensive requirements of securities regulation in all major jurisdictions. However, existing regulatory frameworks failed to specify the exact dividing lines between tokens properly classified as securities, currencies, commodities, consumptive assets, or other categories. Regulators in Switzerland issued a comprehensive framework on the legal treatment of cryptoassets in December 2018.[112] The Japanese Financial Services Agency published a study group report on virtual currency

---

109 Justin Scheck and Shane Shifflett, How Dirty Money Disappears into the Black Hole of Cryptocurrency, *Wall Street Journal* (28 September 2018), available at: https://www.wsj.com/articles/how-dirty-money-disappears-into-the-black-hole-of-cryptocurrency-1538149743.

110 Financial Action Task Force, Virtual Currencies Key Definitions and Potential AML/CFT Risks (June 2014), available at: https://www.fatf-gafi.org/media/fatf/documents/reports/Virtual-currency-key-definitions-and-potential-aml-cft-risks.pdf.

111 Samuel Rubenfeld, Financial Action Task Force Alters Rules to Cover Virtual Currency Firms, *Wall Street Journal* (19 October 2018), available at: https://blogs.wsj.com/riskandcompliance/2018/10/19/financial-action-task-force-alters-rules-to-cover-virtual-currency-firms/.

112 Swiss Federal Council, Legal Framework for Distributed Ledger Technology and Blockchain in Switzerland (December 2018), available at: https://cdn.crowdfundinsider.com/wp-content/uploads/2018/12/Legal-framework-for-distributed-ledger-technology-and-blockchain-in-Switzerland-Swiss-Federal-Council-December-2018.pdf.

exchange services the same month.[113] The SEC has promised further guidance on ICOs in 2019.[114]

6.66 The impact of new technology on risks in the industry is also initially uncertain, which is a cause of concern. New technologies such as blockchain can both decrease traditional risks and create new ones (for example, in the security area). Such considerations, in addition to the transparency and distribution of the new risks, are important to policymakers.[115] With new technologies, some problems may not be immediately obvious.

6.67 As described in more detail in Chapter 9, in implementing a distributed network such as blockchain in a highly-regulated industry like financial services, a fundamental question is who will ultimately be held responsible for regulatory and legal compliance. Such questions must also consider responsibilities of third-party providers. Relatedly, what should governance practices be in such a system?[116] In traditional systems, intermediaries and certain regulated entities are obligated to alter the content of ledgers to redress errors or fraud. Blockchain-based systems by design give no party the power to do so. Thus, for example, when Accenture designed an editable blockchain technology, its efforts were greeted with scorn.[117] In sum, '[o]ne of the core features of DLT is the ability to share information securely and efficiently. However, what may be arguably one of the technology's advantages may be the element which presents firms with the most regulatory and governance challenges.'[118]

E. CONCLUSION

6.68 Blockchain technology is likely to have a significant impact on financial services. It offers great potential benefits in a large number of industry sub-segments. Contrary to the visions of many early cryptocurrency advocates, however, it is quite unlikely to produce a radical disruption or decentralisation of financial institutions. Blockchain will be incorporated into the back-office

---

113 Financial Services Agency, Publication of the Report from the 'Study Group on the Virtual Currency Exchange Services' (28 December 2018), available at: https://www.fsa.go.jp/en/refer/councils/virtual-currency/20181228.html.

114 Nikhilesh De and Aaron Stanley, SEC Official Says 'Plain English' Guidance On ICOs Is Coming, *Coindesk* (5 November 2018), available at: https://www.coindesk.com/sec-official-says-plain-english-guidance-on-icos-is-coming.

115 Brainard, *supra* note 36.

116 Werbach, *supra* note 15, at chapter 7.

117 Martin Arnold, Accenture to Unveil Blockchain Editing Technique, *Financial Times* (19 September 2016).

118 FCA, *supra* note 7.

processes of financial services firms in order to increase efficiency, liquidity, transparency, and security. It will allow for the creation of new financial instruments and products, as well as the entry of new firms.

Alongside regulatory clarity, standards development will be a key topic in the **6.69** years ahead. If industry participants decide to implement blockchain solutions without common standards, they risk transitioning from 'multiple siloed databases' to 'multiple siloed blockchains'.[119] Such an approach could repeat costly historical patterns of individualistic responses to technological and market developments[120] that then require costly efforts for industry participants to reconcile. It would also risk failing to capture the potential value provided by blockchain: 'its network effects and interoperability'.[121] Some financial institutions are likely exploring multiple blockchain solutions in certain areas to hedge their bets until a clear winner emerges. However, as examples discussed above demonstrate, financial institutions are collaborating on blockchain solutions and in participating in multi-industry consortia such as R3 (developer of the Corda platform),[122] Enterprise Ethereum Alliance,[123] and Hyperledger.[124]

The boom and bust of cryptocurrencies in 2017–18 generated a great deal of **6.70** attention. Even at the peak, however, the total value of cryptocurrencies was small relative to traditional asset classes.[125] In the long run, blockchain's potential in financial services will depend on where it achieves its promised benefits for investors, regulated firms, service providers, and regulators.

---

119 McKinsey, *supra* note 1; see also Brainard, *supra* note 36.
120 See generally DTCC, *supra* note 25.
121 McKinsey, *supra* note 1.
122 https://www.r3.com/.
123 https://entethalliance.org/.
124 https://www.hyperledger.org/.
125 The Financial Stability Board concluded in 2018 that cryptocurrencies were too small and sparsely connected to the global financial system to represent a systemic threat to financial stability. Financial Stability Board: *Crypto-Asset Markets: Potential Channels for Future Financial Stability Implications* (10 October 2018), available at: http://www.fsb.org/wp-content/uploads/P101018.pdf.

7

SMART CONTRACTS

Jelena Madir

A. INTRODUCTION

7.01 The term 'smart contract' has entered the public consciousness following the rise to mainstream awareness of distributed ledger technology (DLT). The first thing many people think of when they hear the term 'smart contract' is a contract that is somehow transposed into computer code and runs without any human intervention. This misses the mark by a wide margin. Instead, smart contracts are better thought of as 'conditional transactions' because they refer to the logic written in code that has 'IF this, THEN that' conditions. For example, it can easily be programmed in a smart contract that 'IF on 1 October 2020, Bank A does not receive GBP 1,000 from Jack, transfer GBP 1,000 from Jack's account to Bank A's account.'

7.02 Smart contracts have the potential to increase commercial efficiency, lower transaction and legal costs, and increase transparency. They have a number of potential applications from the automatic payment of dividends, property transfers and automation of insurance claims to streamlining of clinical trials and more efficient data sharing. The US Chamber of Digital Commerce's report illustrates 12 possible use cases of smart contracts in different industries.[1] However, smart contracts also pose a number of challenges, starting from finding a suitable definition of a smart contract to the uncertainties around contract formation and allocation of liability in case of errors. This chapter will consider these challenges and whether they can be addressed within existing legal frameworks as follows: Sections B–D define and describe different types of smart contracts and automatability of contractual clauses; Sections E–L analyse legal issues related to smart contracts – from the existence of a valid and binding contract and capacity to enter into a contract to the allocation of liability and governing law and dispute resolution mechanisms; Section M concludes.

B. WHAT ARE SMART CONTRACTS?

Nick Szabo is widely credited for inventing the idea of a smart contract long before the emergence of DLT. In his article on smart contracts, he defines the term as 'a computerized transaction protocol that executes the terms of a contract'.[2] He gives an example of a drinks vending machine as something embodying these characteristics: if the correct coins are inserted into the slot, tip the bottle into the trough; if there are no bottles, return the coins. The transaction cannot be stopped in mid-flow. The money cannot be returned when the drink is supplied. The transaction's terms are in a sense embedded in the hardware and in the software that runs the machine.[3]   **7.03**

While smart contracts can exist entirely independently of DLT, with the advent of DLT, smart contracts can now be applied more efficiently between market participants around the world. Unlike the case of a vending machine, a smart contract can be effected without the physical presence of a person. Instead, parties can agree remotely on the computer code of the smart contract, programme it on the distributed ledger and then allow the ledger to execute automatically when the triggering event happens. This has the potential to reduce friction when transferring value between entities and opens the door to greater automation of transactions.   **7.04**

---

1 Chamber of Digital Commerce, Smart Contracts: 12 Use Cases for Business & Beyond: A Technology, Legal & Regulatory Introduction, available at: https://digitalchamber.org/wp-content/uploads/2018/02/Smart-Contracts-12-Use-Cases-for-Business-and-Beyond_Chamber-of-Digital-Commerce.pdf.

2 Nick Szabo, Smart Contracts (1994), available at: http://www.fon.hum.uva.nl/rob/Courses/InformationIn Speech/CDROM/Literature/LOTwinterschool2006/szabo.best.vwh.net/smart.contracts.html.

3 Nick Szabo, Smart Contracts: Building Blocks for Digital Markets (1996), available at: http://www. fon.hum.uva.nl/rob/Courses/InformationInSpeech/CDROM/Literature/LOTwinterschool2006/szabo.best. vwh.net/smart_contracts_2.html.

7.05   There is not yet a widely accepted legal definition of smart contract. For some, a 'smart contract' does not refer to a contract in a legal sense, but instead to a computer code that automates business processes without the need for recourse to the courts of law to resolve disputes – this is the so-called 'smart contract code'. For example, several states in the US have enacted legislation specific to smart contracts, which may not be so smart after all, given that it risks creating a patchwork system of inconsistent definitions, leading to further confusion. For example, in the State of Arizona, a smart contract is defined as: 'an event-driven program, with state, that runs on a distributed, decentralized, shared and replicated ledger and that can take custody over and instruct transfer of assets on that ledger'.[4]

7.06   The State of Tennessee modified and expanded on this definition, and defined smart contract as:

> an event-driven computer program, that executes on an electronic, distributed, decentralized, shared, and replicated ledger that is used to automate transactions, including, but not limited to, transactions that:
>
> (A) Take custody over and instruct transfer of assets on that ledger;
> (B) Create and distribute electronic assets;
> (C) Synchronize information; or
> (D) Manage identity and user access to software applications.[5]

7.07   Outside the US, in 2017, Belarus became the first country to legislate the smart contract, defining it in the Presidential Decree as: 'a programme code intended for functioning in the distributed ledger for purposes of automated performance and/or execution of transactions or performance of other legal actions'.[6]

7.08   Interestingly, the Decree establishes a rebuttable presumption that a person who entered into a transaction with the use of a smart contract is deemed to be fully familiar with the terms of the transaction, including those reflected in the smart contract.

7.09   Similarly, in February 2019, the Italian Parliament approved a decree aimed at simplifying and improving public administration and companies' operations (*Decreto Semplificazioni*). Among other things, the law recognises the full legal validity and enforceability of smart contracts in Italy, and defines them as: 'a

---

4   Ariz. Rev. Stat. Ann § 44-7061(E)(2) (2017).
5   State of Tennessee, Public Chapter No. 591, Senate Bill No. 1662, 47-10-201(2) (2018).
6   Decree of the President of the Republic of Belarus No. 8 (21 December 2017), unofficial translation.

computer programme that operates on DLT and whose execution automatically gives effect to the terms agreed between two or more parties'.[7]

Yet, for others, a 'smart contract' is a legal contract that is partly or wholly **7.10** represented and/or performed by software. In other words, the contractual obligations of a party to the contract are discharged through the automated performance of the software. In this chapter, references to 'smart contracts' are intended as references to smart legal contracts, rather than smart contract code.

These distinctions between smart contract code and smart legal contract can **7.11** cause confusion when smart contracts are discussed, and there is a risk that lawyers and computer scientists simply talk at cross purposes. However, rather than viewing smart legal contracts and smart contract code as two separate concepts, the reality is that there is a relationship between them: for a smart legal contract to be implemented, it will need to embed one or more pieces of code designed to execute certain tasks if predefined conditions are met – that is, pieces of smart contract code. Smart legal contracts, therefore, are functionally made up of pieces of smart contract code, but critically, under the umbrella of an overall relationship that creates legally enforceable rights. As a result, every smart legal contract can be said to contain one or more pieces of smart contract code, but not every piece of smart contract code comprises a smart legal contract.[8]

Taking into account both basic concepts and emphasising the aspects of **7.12** automation and enforceability, some authors have defined smart contracts as follows: 'A smart contract is an automatable and enforceable agreement. Automatable by computer, although some parts may require human input and control. Enforceable either by legal enforcement of rights and obligations or via tamper-proof execution of computer code.'[9]

Simply put: a smart contract is an agreement whose execution is automated. **7.13** This definition has the advantage that it is broad enough to cover both smart legal contracts and smart contract code. It captures what seems to be the fundamental essence of all conceptions of smart contracts: the automation and self-execution (and thereby enforcement) of a pre-set conditional action.

---

7   Camera dei Deputati N. 1550, Disegno di Legge Approvate dal Senato della Repubblica (29 January 2019), at 18–19.
8   ISDA and Linklaters, Whitepaper: Smart Contracts and Distributed Ledger – A Legal Perspective (2017), at 4–5.
9   Christopher D. Clack, Vikram A. Bakshi and Lee Braine, Smart Contract Templates: foundations, design landscape and research directions (2017), available at: https://arxiv.org/pdf/1608.00771.pdf, at 2.

7.14 It is important to note, however, that smart contracts are not artificially intelligent or capable of machine learning. They are designed to bring about a particular outcome every time a specific set of conditions is fulfilled. As such, they are suitable for binary 'if this, then that' conditions. Once a condition is met, the smart contract will take the next step necessary to execute the contract. For example, smart contracts would be ideal for parametric insurance, where payment is made upon the occurrence of a triggering event. In the event that your plane is delayed by a certain amount of time, or an earthquake reaches a particular magnitude, you will automatically receive payment instead of having to go through a lengthy claims process.

C. AUTOMATABILITY OF CONTRACTUAL CLAUSES

7.15 Not all of a smart contract needs to be expressed in code. In fact, as the technology stands, smart contracts are unlikely to be able to encode the subtlety and richness of contracts written in natural language which contain legal phrases whose meaning may not be settled at law. This is because computer code (like mathematics) is well adapted to represent terms which are expressions of logic, but not terms which are based on the exercise of discretion that is outside clearly defined parameters, such as, for example, 'material adverse change', 'best endeavours', 'reasonable endeavours', 'commercially reasonable manner', etc. These formulations involve judgment and are a question of degree. For instance, code could be used to represent the agreement that, if an event happened, the price will be adjusted by subtracting the product of x and y. However, it is unlikely that code can be used to represent that, if an event happened, the price is to be adjusted by the party *in a commercially reasonable manner.*

7.16 Smart contracts are therefore particularly effective for sectors that operate using highly standardised contractual terms without material deviation, and lend themselves well to agreements with clear conditions and repetitive transactions. For example, in the financial services sector, a loan agreement could be encoded so that the software automatically triggers a monthly loan repayment when the software receives an input confirming that it is the last day of the calendar month (i.e., without the need for human intervention or instruction) or so that the software automatically changes the monthly repayment amount where it receives an input confirming that there has been a reduction in the relevant reference interest rate (e.g., a central bank interest rate) – in each case the conditions can be objectively determined.

This is illustrated in Figure 7.1: Parties A and B enter into a smart loan **7.17** contract. The software is programmed to receive inputs from trusted data sources via an oracle and to automatically generate payment instructions based on those inputs, in accordance with the terms of the smart contract. When the smart contract receives an input that it is the last day of the month, it uses the interest rate input to calculate the correct monthly repayment amount under the smart loan contract. Then, the software automatically sends an electronic instruction to Party A's bank to transfer this amount from Party A's bank account to Party B's bank account. Party A's bank acts on the automatically generated instruction and transfers the payment to Party B's account.[10]

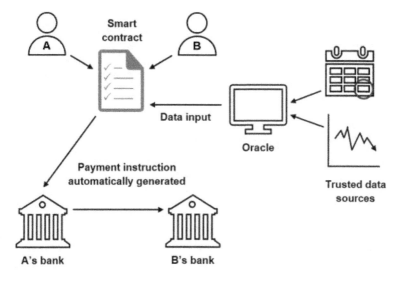

Source: Clifford Chance and European Bank for Reconstruction and Development, Smart Contracts – legal framework and proposed guidelines for lawmakers.

Figure 7.1 Smart loan contracts

Another example could entail the sale of a house on the blockchain: for **7.18** instance, after the buyer and the seller have executed the sale agreement, the buyer transfers the deposit amount to be held in escrow by the smart contract. In turn, and immediately prior to settlement, the lender can also send the loan amount to the smart contract escrow. After the total purchase price is sent to the smart contract escrow, the seller may finalise the transfer and trigger the smart contract to disburse the funds to its account and transfer the tokenised house to the buyer. The transfer is recorded on the blockchain and the state of

---

10 Clifford Chance and European Bank for Reconstruction and Development, Smart Contracts – Legal Framework and Proposed Guidelines for Lawmakers (September 2018), available at: www.ebrd.com/documents/pdf-smart-contracts-legal-framework-and-proposed-guidelines-for-lawmakers.pdf, at at 9–10.

title ownership is updated. There are a few key critical assumptions in this example: first, the house has been tokenised, which means that a blockchain token has been associated with the house. Despite media headlines about house sales on the blockchain,[11] there are a number of legal and technical challenges that need to be overcome for this to happen. Second, the transaction does not involve anything more than a simple transfer of property, free from encumbrances, between two parties. This is not often the case in practice.

7.19 Clearly, the potential applications for smart contracts are manifold. Although it remains to be seen which applications will take off in practice, the sheer potential increases the relevance of the question of how smart contracts are to be treated in legal practice and which problems may arise in this context.

D. DIFFERENT TYPES OF SMART CONTRACTS

7.20 It is a common misconception that there is only one type of smart contract. In fact, there is a spectrum of possibilities. As illustrated in Figure 7.2, the text of the contract may or may not be drafted in computer code. There can therefore be a contract which is (in whole or in part) written in a programming language, where the computer code forms an integral and binding part of the contract – i.e., some or all of the parties' rights and obligations are expressed in a programming language, rather than a natural language. For example, an agreement between Party A and Party B that Party A will transfer an asset to Party B at 10:00 am, might be agreed in computer code as follows:

If T = 10:00 CET, Execute Function: AssetTransfer X (Y to Z).
T = Time
X = Asset
Y = Party A
Z = Party B[12]

7.21 At the other end of the spectrum, a smart contract could be drafted entirely in natural language, but include an agreement between the parties to use specific software to perform and/or enforce (the whole or part of) the contract. For example, a company and an insurer may agree to use the insurer's automated

---

11 See, e.g., *The First House To Be Sold Entirely Through Blockchain* (October 2017), available at: https://www.leaprate.com/cryptocurrency/blockchain/first-house-sold-entirely-blockchain/, and *UK's First Blockchain Property Purchase Recorded in Manchester* (March 2018), available at: https://www.buy association.co.uk/2018/03/19/uks-first-blockchain-property-purchase-recorded-in-manchester/.
12 Clifford Chance and European Bank for Reconstruction and Development, *supra* note 10, at 12.

Smart Contracts Lie on a Spectrum			
Contract entirely in code	Contract in code with separate natural language version	'Split' natural language contract with encoded performance	Natural language contract with encoded payment mechanism

Encoding Natural Language   Automation

Source: Chamber of Digital Commerce, Smart contracts: 12 use cases for business and beyond: a technology, legal and regulatory introduction.

Figure 7.2   Smart contract models based on the level of integration of the computer code

claims-handling software. The software would review and determine claims made by the company and might even automatically instruct payments to be made in respect of determined claims.[13]

E. EXISTENCE OF A VALID AND BINDING CONTRACT

Smart contracts are essentially a slightly new form of an old phenomenon; **7.22** insofar as the 'new' features of smart contracts – e.g., their expression via computer code – fall within gaps in existing laws, it may be necessary to determine how to fill these gaps. As noted in Section B above, while certain jurisdictions have enacted legislation specific to smart contracts, there is no consistent set of laws for smart contracts. Perhaps none is needed if smart contracts are simply contracts being formed another way.

Under most common law jurisdictions, the following four elements need to be **7.23** present for a contract to exist in the legal sense: (i) offer and acceptance: (ii) consideration; (iii) intention to create legal relations; and (iv) certainty of terms. Civil law jurisdictions may prescribe other requirements. For example, under German law, parties need to have an intention to create a legally binding relationship (expressed through and offer and acceptance),[14] and 'essential terms' must be determined or sufficiently determinable.[15] For instance, in a car purchase, the 'essential terms' might be the identity of the

---

13   Ibid., at 13.
14   Bürgerlichen Gesetzbuch §145 *et seq.*
15   Ibid., §154(1).

seller and the purchaser, the obligation of the seller to transfer to the purchaser the ownership rights in a specific car (along with the car itself) and the obligations of the purchaser to pay a specific purchase price and to accept the transfer by the seller. Under Spanish law, there needs to be (i) consent through an offer and acceptance, (ii) object of the obligation, which must be determined or determinable (similar to the 'essential terms'), and (iii) cause of the obligation (similar to consideration).[16] French law has similar requirements.[17]

1. Offer and acceptance

7.24 Under both English and US law, smart contract code used on a distributed ledger would likely constitute an offer if other participants on the ledger are entitled to interact with and execute on the code. Under English law, e-mail messages are considered to be capable of constituting offers and acceptances.[18] Smart contracts are typically initiated by messages sent using PKI over the internet. It would be surprising if English courts were to draw conceptual distinctions between such messages and e-mail communications.[19] Under US law, '[a]n offer is an expression by one party of his assent to certain definite terms, provided that the other party involved in the bargaining transaction will likely express his assent to the identically same terms'.[20] Smart contract code used on a distributed ledger is therefore likely to constitute an offer if other participants on the ledger are entitled to interact with, and execute, the code.

7.25 Acceptance requires both an agreement by the counterparty to the substantive terms of the contract and an action by the counterparty to accept these terms within the time period and by the procedure required by the offer.[21] In the case of smart contracts, the offeree (or, in the case of a smart contract simply posted on a public ledger, any participant in the ledger) may indicate acceptance through signing the transaction with a private key. Signing the smart contract with a private key should constitute a valid offer and acceptance under US law.[22]

7.26 Some comparisons relating to how the courts have dealt with new technologies in the past may be of use. For example, smart contracts may evolve

---

16 Código Civil, § 1261.
17 Code Civil, § 1108.
18 See, e.g., *Golden Ocean Group Ltd v Salgaocar Mining Industries Pvt Ltd and Anr*, [2012] EWCA Civ 265.
19 R3 and Norton Rose White Paper: *Can Smart Contracts be Legally Binding Contracts?*, at 22.
20 Arthur L. Corbin et al., *Corbin on Contracts: 1*, Lexis Nexis (1993), § 11.
21 U.C.C. §2-206(1)(a)(1).
22 Miren B. Aparicio Bijuesca, The Legal Challenges Associated with Smart Contracts: Formation, Modification and Enforcement, in US Chamber of Commerce: *Smart Contracts: Is the Law Ready?* (September 2018), at 15.

like 'click-wrap' agreements.[23] These are contracts formed entirely over the internet. A party posts terms on its website, pursuant to which it offers to sell goods or services. To buy these goods, the purchaser is required to indicate its consent to be bound by the terms of the offer by his conduct – typically the act of clicking on a button stating 'I agree'. Generally, US courts have held click-wrap agreements to be enforceable, recognising that parties in a modern context do not need to consider and negotiate every term.[24] US courts are apprehensive of applying terms to a contract, however, if the consent was limited to other aspects of the contracting process. For example, US courts have found that clicking a 'Yes' button in connection with transmitting credit card data could not bind the purchaser to terms e-mailed to him after the enrolment process was completed.[25]

English courts have accepted that the parties are free to stipulate what acts will **7.27** constitute acceptance.[26] In the context of smart contracts, parties could therefore prescribe what particular message requirement will constitute acceptance of a previously messaged offer.

In Australia, the Electronic Transactions Act 1999 (the ETA) deals with the **7.28** formation of electronic contracts and provides some welcome clarity for the likely legal status of smart contracts under Australian law. For example, Section 15C of the ETA provides that a contract formed by the interaction of an automated message system and a natural person, or the interaction of automated message systems, is 'not invalid, void or unenforceable on the sole ground that no natural person reviewed or intervened in each of the individual actions carried out by the automated message systems or the resulting contract'. An 'automated message system' includes a computer program, without review or intervention by a natural person each time an action is initiated or a response generated by the system. This would mean that, even in cases where an agreement is reached through the interaction of two smart contracts, such an agreement will not be unenforceable purely because no natural persons were involved.[27]

---

23   R3 and Norton Rose White Paper, *supra* note 19, at 27.
24   See, e.g., *Hancock v American Telephone & Telegraph Co.*, 701 F.3d 1248, 1251 (10th Cir. 2012) and *Davis v HSBC Bank Nevada, N.A.*, 691 F.3d 1152, 1157 (9th Cir. 2012).
25   See, e.g., *Schnabel v Trilegiant Corp*, 697 F.3d 110, 121–22 (2d Cir. 2012).
26   See, e.g., *Holwell Securities Ltd v Hughes* [1974] 1 WLR 155.
27   R3 and Norton Rose White Paper, *supra* note 19, at 30.

7.29 Finally, under French law, in B2B contexts, there are no limitations on the use of electronic means to enter into a contract.[28]

2. Consideration

7.30 In assessing whether a smart contract is supported by consideration, an English court is likely to consider whether there has been an exchange of value, or mutual benefit and burden. English and Australian courts will not question whether 'adequate' value has been given. Similarly, under US law, consideration is generally anything of value, even if very slight, exchanged between the parties.[29]

3. Intention to create legal relations

7.31 Under English, US and Australian laws, the parties' intentions are assessed by reference to objective criteria: the status of their communication with each other is analysed by reference to what was communicated between the parties by words or conduct, and whether that leads objectively to a conclusion that they intended to create legal relations.[30] Therefore, if the other requirements for a legally binding contract are satisfied in the case of a smart contract, it may be difficult for a party to assert, as against the other party who acted in reliance on it, that there was no intention to create legal relations with respect to the smart contract.

7.32 One of the key characteristics of smart contracts, however, is that they can behave proactively: where parties have voluntarily entered into a smart contract (the primary contract), that contract itself can enter the parties into an additional contract (the secondary contract). For example, the bank and the borrower can agree on a framework agreement, whereby if the borrower's bank balance drops below a pre-agreed threshold, the software will automatically issue a loan request to the lender, and the loan request will be automatically accepted, provide that certain pre-programmed conditions are met. This involves the creation of new loan transactions from time to time (rather than a mere drawdown under the existing loan facility). Given that the parties made the initial decision to enter into the smart contract, one could argue that they indirectly agreed to be bound by the system in which it operates. One could also argue that if the parties intentionally coded a smart contract to make its

---

28 See, e.g., French Supreme Court: Cass. 1re civ., 1st July 2015, n° 14-19.781 and Paris Court of Appeals: CA Paris, 4 February 2016, n° 13-21057.

29 See, e.g., *Exch. Nat'l Bank of Chicago v Daniels*, 768 F.2d 140, at 143 (7th Cir. 1985).

30 See, e.g., *RTS Flexible Systems Ltd v Molkerei Alois Müller GmbH & Co KG* [2010] UKSC 14; *Empro Mfg. Co. v Ball-Co Mfg., Inc*, 870 F.2d 423, at 425 (7th Cir. 1989); and *Taylor v Johnson* (1983) 151 CLR 422.

own decisions, they must have intended to accept those decisions as their own. The borrower could therefore be characterised as making a conditional offer for a loan by coding the software to automatically request the loan when the relevant condition is met (i.e., when the borrower's balance reaches the relevant threshold). Similarly, the lender would make its conditional acceptance of the offer by coding the software to automatically accept any loan request that meets the pre-programmed conditions. The smart contract then automatically generates the loan request and acceptance communications when these conditions are fulfilled, thereby bringing about a new loan agreement.

This raises the question of whether the software itself might be seen as a party **7.33** to a smart contract and, if so, whether it would have the legal capacity to do so. One way to think about this question is by applying the law of agency – the software could be regarded as an agent for the party entering into the contract. There is no authority on this specific point, but the UK court considered a similar question in relation to a software programme in *Software Solutions Partners Ltd, R (on the application of) v HM Customs & Excise*, and found that an automated system could not be regarded as an agent, because only a person with a mind could be an agent in law. Therefore, it could be argued that the software is a mere messenger, which does not make its 'own' decisions, but executes human decisions within the limits of pre-set parameters. If the software is to be understood as a mere messenger, the parties' actions when programming the software could be characterised as the issue of a conditional offer and acceptance.

A similar concern arises under the German Civil Code, under which a **7.34** declaration of intent consists of an objective and a subjective element. The objective element requires that the behaviour of the declaring party implies a will to bring about legal consequences. The subjective element consists of: (1) the will to act; (2) the awareness to make a declaration; and (3) the will to engage in a transaction. The subjective element requires human behaviour and legal capacity, which are not present in smart contracts.[31] Under the existing legal framework, automated software may be able to qualify as a messenger of a declaration of intent issued by a contracting party, i.e., to submit or receive such declarations of a contracting party, given that under German law, being a messenger does not require a legal capacity to contract.[32]

---

31 R3 and Norton Rose White Paper, *supra* note 19, at 42.
32 *Münchener Kommentar zum Bürgerlichen Gesetzbuch*, 7th edn (2015), BGB §105, note 44.

4. Certainty of terms/essential terms

7.35 Smart contracts are (partly) written in a programming language and are often published on a distributed ledger in a 'compiled' form, which can be read only by computers.[33] This begs the question of whether a smart contract can provide determinable commitments. To avoid any difficulties around this, it is recommended that the commitments be described in a way that is understandable to all parties. A possible downside to agreements in natural language next to code is that there can be a discrepancy between the two. Nonetheless, one could argue that even natural language has many nuances and can be ambiguous. How one person interprets a clause might be different to another. Admittedly, well-drafted contracts should limit the degree to which such different interpretation might be possible, but the day-to-day business of the courts suggests that it is not always the case. Replacing parts of a contract with code may cause some translation issues, but natural language drafting itself is not free from the risk of incorrectly reflecting a contracting party's intention.[34] For example, German courts specifically recognised that a contract will be valid and binding even if one of the parties does not understand German well.[35]

7.36 However, even though the parties can agree to express specific terms of their agreement in computer code, it is important that this expression is admissible in any judicial and arbitration proceedings which arise out of that agreement. An inability to admit this record of the parties' agreement would impair its legal effectiveness, although courts may be willing to admit expert evidence as to the meaning of the code.

7.37 There is an additional concern that the terms agreed by the parties may be varied by law – for example, by implication, or if a court finds terms are void or have to be rectified because they do not reflect the true agreement between the parties. For instance, suppose that on the date of contract formation, the time a debtor needs to be in default for the creditor to repossess is 30 days and that after the contract is executed, the law changes, requiring that time period to be 90 days. The immutable nature of smart contracts would make it impossible to include such changes in the operation of the contract. A possible solution would be to leave certain terms of the contracts modifiable, while restricting others from modification. Thus, in the above example, the fact that payment is

---

33 Compiled form is a form converted from the programme written in a programming language, which is understandable to and written by humans, into a binary language form understood only by the computer.

34 See, e.g., ISDA and Linklaters, *Smart Contracts and Distributed Ledger – A Legal Perspective* (2017), at 17.

35 See Bundesarbeitsgericht, 5 AZR 252/12 (B) (19 March 2014).

necessary would be an immutable term, while the length of time a debtor has before (s)he is in default could be modifiable.[36] Another possible solution could be a system in which the relevant jurisdiction creates a publicly available database and API of relevant legal provisions. These would be provisions related to the terms of the contract. The smart contract would call these terms and would be able to update the relevant provisions in accordance with the jurisdiction's update of the database.[37]

In conclusion, it is reasonable to suppose that the usual rules relating to contract formation will probably apply to determine the legal status of a smart contract. Whether a particular smart contract amounts to a legally binding contract will likely depend on the type of smart contract at issue and the factual matrix within which it operates.[38] **7.38**

F. CAPACITY AND AUTHORITY

In the case of entering into a contract with a company, the counterparty will wish to determine whether the party signing on behalf of the company has the authority to enter into such a contract. Naturally, this is not unique to smart contracts; however, in the context of a smart contract, parties may want to verify such authority in an electronic or automated manner. This will be possible only if the relevant data sources (e.g., a company registry setting out the relevant information on the company and its authorised signatories, as well as other signature authorisation documents of the company) are accessible to the software, and if the software is sophisticated enough to parse the data contained in such documents to be able to establish whether a specific person is authorised to enter into a specific type of transaction on behalf of the company. **7.39**

If sufficiently intelligent, the software might be able to access and parse a board resolution or a list of directors itself. Otherwise, the software may simply seek an input confirming that the resolution was duly passed or that the person 'signing' the smart contract and purporting to have the authority to do so does in fact have such authority.[39] **7.40**

---

36   Max Raskin, The Law and Legality of Smart Contracts, 1 *Geo. L. Tech. Rev.* 305 (2017), at 327.
37   Ibid.
38   For further analysis of whether smart contracts have a legally binding effect in the US, the UK, Australia, Canada, Germany, France, China and South Africa, see R3 and Norton Rose White Paper, *supra* note 19, at 22–45.
39   Clifford Chance and European Bank for Reconstruction and Development, *supra* note 10, at 22.

G. FORM OF AGREEMENT

7.41 Sometimes the law requires that an agreement be concluded in writing. The law will typically also prescribe the conditions that must be met for an agreement that has been concluded electronically to be considered to be in writing. By way of example, under Dutch law, an agreement concluded electronically is deemed to be in writing if: (i) it can be consulted by parties; (ii) the authenticity of the agreement is safeguarded to a sufficient degree; (iii) the moment of the creation of the agreement can be determined with sufficient certainty; and (iv) the identity of the parties can be established with sufficient certainty.[40]

7.42 The first element is the most challenging one: if the agreement must be written in such a way that the parties are able to access and save its contents in order to be able to inform themselves later about the agreement, this can be difficult to achieve for a contract in compiled form, which is legible only to computers. It is highly doubtful whether even the most popular programming languages are widely enough understood to serve as a means of reducing the agreement to 'writing' in a way that ensures a meaningful 'meeting of the minds' between most contracting parties. The solution to this issue could be to ensure that a smart contract is accompanied by an attached 'natural language' written contract.[41] This should be incorporated as a design feature in the creation of any smart contracting system for a contract that is required to be 'in writing'.

7.43 The remaining three elements should be relatively straightforward: the obligation of authenticity is easily met as smart contracts cannot be changed unilaterally. Similarly, on the assumption that indisputable, automatic date/time stamps are used, the moment of an agreement's creation, or at least the smart contract portion of this, can be established with sufficient certainty.

7.44 Finally, with respect to the identity of the parties, the question remains as to whether, under the relevant laws, the cryptographic signature of a party qualifies as a proof of identity. In many jurisdictions electronic signatures are already considered as equivalent to handwritten signatures. The definition of 'electronic signature' is broadly similar across jurisdictions. For example, under the US Uniform Electronic Transactions Act (ETA), an 'electronic signature'

---

40   Article 6:227a of the Dutch Civil Code (English language translation available at: http://www.dutch civillaw.com/legislation/dcctitle6655.htm).

41   See Dutch Blockchain Coalition, Smart Contracts as a Specific Application of Blockchain Technology, available at: https://www.dutchdigitaldelta.nl/uploads/pdf/Smart-Contracts-ENG-report.pdf, at 23.

is defined as 'an electronic sound, symbol, or process attached to or logically associated with a record and executed or adopted by a person with the intent to sign the record'.[42] Under the EU Regulation No. 910/2014, 'electronic signature' is defined as 'data in electronic form which is attached to or logically associated with other data in electronic form and which is used by the signatory to sign',[43] and 'qualified electronic signature' (which is treated as equivalent to a handwritten signature) is defined as 'an advanced electronic signature that is created by a qualified electronic signature creation device, and which is based on a qualified certificate for electronic signatures'.[44]

A cryptographic key is likely to constitute a record of a 'process' (within the meaning of the ETA), which is logically associated with a record, or it may contain a symbol that constitutes a signature and is merely recorded on DLT. Whether or not it also meets the requirements of a 'qualified electronic signature' under the EU Regulation will depend on the characteristics of the DLT system in question and the way in which cryptographic keys are used under that system. **7.45**

Finally, as a matter of public policy, lawmakers will need to consider whether the role of such third parties as notaries should be retained or may be automated. This will, to a large extent, depend on the role that such third parties play in the transaction process, i.e., whether their role is limited to identifying parties or is broader and involves warning the parties about the implications of the contract they are entering into. Notably, real estate transactions may require agreements to be recorded by a notary and rights to be registered in the land registry, while lawmakers may be more confident in establishing a DLT-based land register (provided that the register satisfies the transparency and evidentiary functions adequately and is able to maintain public trust), they are less likely to be comfortable with removing the requirement for the notary recording to the extent this currently also serves to warn the contracting parties and to provide them with advice, rather than just verifying their identity.[45] **7.46**

---

42 Uniform Electronic Transactions Act, § 2(8).
43 EU Regulation No. 910/2014, Art 3(10).
44 Ibid., Art 3(12).
45 Clifford Chance and European Bank for Reconstruction and Development, *supra* note 10, at 28.

H. LIABILITY

7.47 What if there is a glitch somewhere in or between the programming language and the executable machine code and, consequently, the code does not do what it was intended to do when executed? Arguably, the risk of a glitch somewhere in the programming already exists in the use of any computer program. However, one of the main challenges concerning smart contract liability lies in the fact that there are many parties involved, but determining the relationship between them is far from easy. Namely, as described in more detail in Chapter 9, there are the core group that sets up the code design, the owners of additional servers running the distributed ledger code for validation purposes (such as Bitcoin or Ripple validation nodes), users of the distributed ledger (such as exchanges, lending institutions or owners of Bitcoin), and third parties affected by the system without directly relying on the technology (e.g., clients of brokers that hold cryptocurrency on behalf of clients). A number of issues and considerations arise from such complex relationships, which are examined in Chapter 9.

7.48 To prompt parties to at least consider the allocation of liability, smart contract templates should ideally contain a field indicating the contracting parties' choice of liability scheme in the event of a coding error. However, parties would still have the freedom to select no liability allocation mechanism. In such a case, there could be an automatic warning message asking the parties to confirm that they do not wish to specify what should happen in case the code deviates from the parties' expressed written wishes, and notifying them that failure to designate a liability mechanism could result in the allocation of losses wherever they fall.

7.49 Moreover, there are many potential non-contractual liabilities that may arise in relation to particular transactions effected through smart contracts, including, for example, claims for fraud, unfair trade practices, insider trading, market abuse, etc. There might be a possibility for insurance companies to fill in the liability space and insure liability risks in connection with smart contracts. Conditions under which such insurance applies will be far from easy to draft.

I. BURDEN OF PROOF

7.50 In many jurisdictions, applicable procedural rules will require each party to assert its own claims in court and to apply for its legal enforcement with a court. As a general rule, a claimant will often have to prove the facts on which it seeks to rely and will bear the risk that such facts cannot be proven. For example, if Party A fails to make a payment under a non-smart contract that obliges Party A to make the payment to Party B, Party B would have to assert and, generally, prove in court that it has a valid payment claim and that Party A has not paid. In addition, Party B would have to apply to the court for legal enforcement of a court judgment finding that Party B has a valid payment claim, if Party A still does not pay. Hence, Party B would bear the legal risk that it cannot prove its claim and the risk that Party A may enter into insolvency prior to legal enforcement of the judgment. While these general principles also apply to claims relating to smart contracts, the circumstances of the claim (and hence the burden of proof and associated risks) are likely to be reversed as a result of automation. If, in the above example, the payment were automated under a smart contract, Party B would automatically receive payment and so it would not have to assert its payment claim in court. Rather, Party A would now have to assert and, generally, prove in court its claim for repayment of the relevant amount if it considers that the payment should not have been made. As a result, Party A would bear the legal risk of having to prove its claim as well as the risk that Party B might enter into insolvency before the repayment is made. There may also be other legal consequences for Party B, such as an inability to exercise rights of retention or set-off either within or outside litigation.

The party benefitting from this procedural 'reversal' and shift in risk (Party B **7.51** in the above example) may therefore be more willing to enter into a contract with a pseudonymous third party. However, this procedural 'reversal' and shift in risk resulting from the automatic performance of a contract may not be desirable in certain cases. For example, certain types of parties (such as consumers) may be less able to assume such risk. Hence, legal systems may seek to prohibit any change to the usual burden of proof to the detriment of a consumer.[46]

J. GOVERNING LAW AND DISPUTE RESOLUTION MECHANISM

Because a smart contract automatically performs across distributed computing **7.52** systems, it may be difficult for a court to determine the place of that performance when attempting to decide what governing law ought to apply to the smart contracts. While this difficulty will not prevent courts from taking jurisdiction over smart contract disputes, it does prevent accurate prediction as

---

46 Clifford Chance and European Bank for Reconstruction and Development, *supra* note 10, at 43–44.

to which court will take jurisdiction and which governing law it will apply. Some comfort can be derived from the fact that courts are used to dealing with difficult jurisdictional issues in, for example, contracts formed over the internet (e.g., an online purchase of goods or services). Jurisdictional uncertainties in the case of smart contracts might be resolved (to some degree) by having a mandatory field in a smart contract for the parties to indicate which governing law applies. In many jurisdictions, courts will generally seek to uphold the parties' express choice of law to the extent possible. Notably, however, when selecting the governing law, parties should ensure that they choose the law that recognises contracts written in code, concluded electronically or with a pseudonymous counterparty as legally binding.

7.53 Still, there may be an issue concerning the location of the smart contract, which could be relevant for determining what professional regulatory or taxation regime applies, and these are not necessarily the areas where the parties' agreement is determinative. Instead, it can be a matter of objective determination based on the place of performance. Where the applicable conflicts of law rules provide that, in the absence of the parties' express choice of law, the applicable law is the law of the jurisdiction where an asset is located, an additional practical consideration arises in relation to native assets on permissionless blockchains. Namely, native assets on a public blockchain could be analogised to trade secrets or unregistered copyrights, which similarly have no central repository or registration authority. Participating in a permissioned blockchain with a centralised authority, or utilising a third-party intermediary (e.g., a known wallet provider) to hold blockchain-based assets, may give parties to smart contracts more reliability that these assets are held in the jurisdiction where the centralised authority or a third-party intermediary is located. Naturally, this will come at the expense of the decentralisation that many blockchain proponents desire.[47]

7.54 When it comes to dispute resolution mechanisms, recourse to the courts to enforce a smart contract can be cumbersome and ineffective. Instead, it has been suggested that a dispute resolution mechanism built into the smart contract itself could provide a solution. Such a mechanism would need to have the following characteristics:

- A provision in the code that causes delegation to an arbitrator, which would be triggered under the rules encoded in the smart contract: for

---

47   Jenny Cieplak: U.C.C. and State Law Issues in Smart Contracts, in The Legal Challenges Associated with Smart Contracts: Formation, Modification and Enforcement, in US Chamber of Commerce: *Smart Contracts: Is the Law Ready?* (September 2018), at 58.

example, by both parties asserting a defect and nominating the arbitrating entity. In fact, a number of organisations have already started developing arbitration clauses or 'libraries' that parties could include in their smart contracts.[48]

- A provision in the natural language version of the contract, agreeing to submit disputes to arbitration: this assumes that there is a natural language version of the contract and that it matches the delegation mechanism in the contract code.
- A forum for arbitration, which could be administered centrally, or via a relevant ledger, or by use of one of the many existing and experienced forums. The forum would identify these essential components: a body of rules for the arbitration, pool of possible arbitrators, and an administration capable of managing the cases as they are filed and decided.[49]

The arbitrator could also be (partially) automated and could, for example, have **7.55** control over funds deposited by parties to a smart loan contract, which it could automatically release where it resolves a dispute, deficiency or mistake by deciding that one party owes an amount to the other under the contract.

In due course and once we start seeing greater use of smart contracts in **7.56** practice, lawmakers may also wish to consider whether to establish courts that specialise in smart contract disputes, in the same way that, for example, specialist Intellectual Property Enterprise Court and the Technology and Construction Court have been established in the UK. Similarly, some continental European courts have established specialist chambers, for example, for construction, trade-related or medical disputes, which would be adjudicated by technical experts.

K. PRIVACY ISSUES

Privacy concerns the protection of personal information, which is data that can **7.57** be traced, directly or indirectly, to a living natural person. This covers such data as name, address and telephone numbers, but it may also apply to a set of other data that together have something to say about an identified or identifiable natural person such as, for instance, location data or video footage. If such information is included in a distributed ledger, it counts as personal

---

48 See, e.g., CodeLegit Conducts First Blockchain-based Smart Contract Arbitration Proceeding (July 2017), available at: https://datarella.com/codelegit-conducts-first-blockchain-based-smart-contract-arbitration-proceeding/, describing steps in the blockchain arbitration proceedings.
49 R3 and Norton Rose White Paper, *supra* note 19, at 19.

data. Within the European Union, on the basis of the GDPR, citizens have various rights with respect to their personal information. Among other things, this includes the right to correction of personal information, its deletion and the right to be forgotten. In the smart contracts context, data has been pseudonymised, and not anonymised, which means that it remains personal data for purposes of the GDPR.

7.58 As described in Chapter 11, the GDPR distinguishes between a data controller and a data processor. Identifying these persons and their roles can be challenging, particularly given the decentralised nature of permissionless DLT-based systems and the ability of network participants to enter into smart contracts directly with each other, share resources on a peer-to-peer basis and add information to the ledger, without requiring any authorisation from a central administrator. Arguably, any participant entering personal data in blocks of the ledger may be regarded as a controller of the data it has provided or to which it has access through the system, unless it is a mere technology service provider supporting the system, in which case it is likely to be characterised as a processor.

7.59 An option often used is not logging personal data directly in a blockchain, but instead inserting hyperlinks into a blockchain that can be linked to files containing personal data. Although this makes it easier to remove or amend personal data (see below), it does not detract from the fact that personal data is being processed. Whether or not the GDPR applies to a blockchain in which personal data is processed is therefore governed not by whether there are nodes situated within the EU, but whether processing is carried out in the context of the activities of an establishment of one of the controllers (or processors) in the EU. Recognising this challenge, the European Parliament has called on the European Commission and the European Data Protection Supervisor to provide further guidance on the compliance of blockchain-based applications with the GDPR.[50]

L. CONTRACTUAL AMENDMENTS

7.60 Although the immutability of smart contracts is seen by the proponents of DLT as a desirable feature, from a legal perspective, it can give rise to a number of issues. Natural language contracts often need to be amended to reflect changes to the underlying commercial arrangement, to correct errors, or

---

50 European Parliament, *Distributed Ledger Technologies and Blockchains: Building Trust with Disintermediation* (October 2018), ¶ 33.

to reflect changes in law. Any such desired changes will be impossible with respect to the encoded aspects of the smart contract on a distributed ledger. A possible solution to this issue may be to 'reverse' the transaction by a new transaction that exactly offsets an existing transaction, negating its effect. However, this solution is not ideal, because such reversal in performance could be void if it is entered into after one of the parties has become insolvent.

Indeed, the immutability of smart contracts deprives them of the flexibility of **7.61** traditional contractual relationships and prevents parties from being able to adjust their positions in response to changed circumstances. The problem these features can give rise to were revealed in June 2016, during the hack of the Decentralized Autonomous Organization (DAO) – a fundraising vehicle that raised USD 168 million when it was launched on Ethereum in 2016. When an attacker exploited a smart contract flaw to siphon off over USD 50 million from the DAO, the Ethereum community questioned the principle of maintaining the ledger's immutability. The Ethereum Foundation decided to intervene on the DAO investors' behalf – in effect, bailing them out – by rewriting Ethereum's core code to delegitimise the attackers' transactions and recover the funds. To do so, the Foundation, influenced by the platform's heavily invested founders, convinced most users to go along with its decision. In order to return the diverted funds, a fork was created, which changed the Ethereum protocol that restored the stolen tokens as if the hack had not happened. However, this breach of immutability was a controversial move, and one that prompted a split in the Ethereum community – a minority of the participants continued with the original, unamended code. As a result, Ethereum split into parallel crypto-universes, identical in most respects with one key difference: the forked Ethereum universe essentially treated the DAO's smart contracts as rescindable by all participants due to mutual mistake, and the non-forked Ethereum universe continued to treat the attack as a valid transaction within the terms of the DAO's smart contract.

Another problematic issue that arises as a consequence of the immutable **7.62** nature of smart contracts is the way in which a court's decision that a smart contract is void (i.e., never existed) would be effected. Clearly, 'reversing' the transaction by a new transaction that exactly offsets an existing transaction, negating its effect will not produce the same result as if the contract were treated as never having existed.

M. CONCLUSION

7.63 Given that smart contracts decrease transaction costs by cutting out inter-mediaries, they are likely to increase in relevance and scope. Admittedly, mainstream adoption is still a few years away, given that smart contracts need to be integrated with the industry's existing systems, which raises questions about the effort involved and the investment that will be required. However, just as companies are starting to identify the changes that will be required, including to IT systems, processes and change management policies, so too should regulators and lawyers capitalise on this momentum and focus on smart contracts as part of the broader FinTech innovation ambit.

7.64 Innovative technology does not necessarily require innovative jurisprudence and, in many instances, the existing legal systems will be perfectly sufficient to deal with the 'new' features of smart contracts – e.g., their expression via computer code. In other cases, the existing rules will need to be adapted to the new context of smart contracts (e.g., in relation to the signing via a crypto-graphic key and compliance with privacy regulations). Some of the solutions may even be provided by contracting parties through the design of their contracts (e.g., allocation of liability and specification of the governing law and dispute resolution mechanism). More broadly, smart contracts represent a unique opportunity for the legal profession to lead the development of a new, fast-evolving area.

8

GOVERNING THE BLOCKCHAIN: WHAT IS THE APPLICABLE LAW?

Harriet Territt[1]

A. INTRODUCTION

Both the functionality and the flexibility of distributed ledger technology **8.01** (DLT) systems can raise complex questions of applicable law for users. In particular, distance and national borders are largely irrelevant to the operation of distributed ledger technologies. The sheer variety and complexity of transactions conducted on DLT systems can also expose users and operators to multiple, national legal regimes, and therefore increase uncertainty for users.

This chapter will consider the challenge of establishing what laws or regu- **8.02** lations may be relevant to the operation and governance of DLT systems and transactions conducted on them. It will also consider practical solutions to this inherent uncertainty.

---

1 The summaries, views and conclusions in this chapter are the personal views of the author and do not necessarily reflect those of Jones Day.

B. ARE NATIONAL LAWS RELEVANT TO DLT SYSTEMS?

8.03 Early developers and proponents of blockchain-based systems often asserted that they could operate independently of national laws, regulations and court systems.[2] This was reflected in the development of permissionless, decentralised systems such as the Bitcoin network which enables peer-to-peer payments between global users without government or central bank oversight. Indeed, it is worth noting that the genesis block for the Bitcoin network contains the following message:

> *The Times 03 / Jan / 2009*
>
> *Chancellor on brink of second bailout for banks*

8.04 This message, included by Satoshi Nakamoto, reflected the launch of the Bitcoin network in the middle of a financial crisis, touted as a reaction to and potential solution for, the turmoil which was occurring within the traditional banking system.

8.05 The rationale behind this assertion (that laws and courts were irrelevant) varied – some developers believed that code-based systems could operate in such a way that disputes would either never arise, or could be resolved by self-governing dispute resolution systems, so that courts would become irrelevant.[3] Other parties focused on the lack of a central authority in control of permissionless systems and/or that a blockchain exists only because a copy of the relevant distributed ledger is stored on various computers linked to each other. In her 2015 paper 'Blockchain Technology and Decentralized Governance: Is the State Still Necessary',[4] Dr Marcella Atzori provides a more detailed analysis of these issues which she summarises as follows:

> Broadly speaking, the advocates of decentralization tend to have in common the same 'dissociative' attitude towards centralized institutions and the State in particular, 'failing to see its value adding contribution' … The dominant discourse mostly emerged through the media, and generally dominated by IT specialists and financial operators, sees governments 'as somewhat of an encumbrance – too slow, too corrupt, too lacking in innovation, and benefiting too few'.

---

2   See e.g., Mattheus Von Guttenberg, Crypto-Anarchists and Cryptoanarchists, *Bitcoin Magazine* (29 September 2014), available at: https://bitcoinmagazine.com/articles/crypto-anarchists-cryptoanarchists-2-1412033787/.

3   As discussed by Reggie O'Shields in Smart Contracts: Legal Agreements for the Blockchain, 21 *N.C. Banking Inst.* 177 (2017), available at: https://scholarship.law.unc.edu/ncbi/vol21/iss1/11.

4   Marcella Atzori, Blockchain Technology and Decentralized Governance: Is the State Still Necessary? (December 2015), available at: http://nzz-files-prod.s3-website-eu-west-1.amazonaws.com/files/9/3/1/blockchain+Is+the+State+Still+Necessary_1.18689931.pdf.

This approach is sometimes summarised as 'the code is the law' – meaning **8.06** that the programmed code in any DLT system sets out the only rules which any participant needs to take account of, and that no additional human intervention is required to operate the system or arbitrate any disputes. In practice, the last few years have shown that there is a multiplicity of national laws and regulations which can apply to DLT systems and which are, in some cases, expressly necessary for the smooth operation and execution of certain kinds of transactions. It is interesting to note that certain influential DLT developers have also moved away from the pure 'the code is the law' approach, to advocate specific decentralised solutions[5] to these problems.

However, regardless of the rationale, it is a fact that decentralisation of **8.07** information across a blockchain system also makes it difficult for any one country to assert sole jurisdiction over a DLT system with multiple, global users. In order for DLT systems to reach their full potential, it is important that participants have confidence that their transactions are legal, valid and binding, as well as clarity on how disputes will be resolved. The remainder of this chapter sets out the considerations which participants will need to take into account when considering blockchain structure and governance in this context.

C. WHY GOVERNING LAW AND JURISDICTION MATTER

1. Governing law

A contract, whether personal or commercial, written or oral, sets out the terms **8.08** on which the contracting parties agree to engage in a transaction. The interpretation and effect of those terms may vary significantly depending on which country's laws govern the contract. In the same way, the outcome of any dispute may be substantially affected by which courts can assert jurisdiction to determine any particular contractual dispute or non-contractual claim arising out of use of a distributed ledger (if, indeed, disputes are to be resolved by a court process). It is beyond the scope of this chapter to deal with applicable regulatory, administrative or criminal laws, but many of the same issues will

---

5   For example, in April 2016, one of the co-founders of Ethereum, Vitalik Buterin, proposed the creation of a decentralised dispute resolution system for DLT with similar features to traditional court systems:

> To achieve scalability, a multi-stage scheme where only a few randomly selected judges look at each question by default, and are incentivized by the threat of a larger 'supreme court' contradicting them, is probably optimal.

See Reddit at: https://www.reddit.com/r/ethereum/comments/4gigyd/decentralized_court/.

arise when considering whether such laws are applicable to business activities conducted on a distributed ledger.[6]

8.09 Generally, the governing law of the contract determines all questions in relation to its validity, interpretation, effect and discharge. It is common for parties to commercial contracts to include express governing law clauses in their agreements to provide certainty as to which law governs those issues and their respective rights and obligations. The inclusion of a governing law clause is not a 'silver bullet' which resolves all possible issues and outcomes but, in general, countries with developed legal systems will normally uphold the parties' choice of governing law in respect of contractual (and sometimes non-contractual) issues in commercial contracts, subject to certain exceptions.

8.10 Two common exceptions are for public policy or overriding mandatory provisions, as exemplified by the Rome I Regulation in the EU.[7] In practice, there is a significant overlap between the two areas, but the effect of the exceptions can be very different. Generally, a public policy exception will provide for an express choice of governing law to be entirely overridden where the effect is to permit the upholding of a contract which may harm society as a whole or otherwise offend public sensibilities.[8] An example would be a contract which generally offends society (e.g., for slavery or sexual exploitation) or where the performance of the contract in a particular country is prohibited (e.g., a contract involving Bitcoin which is to be carried out in Bolivia[9]).

8.11 In contrast, overriding mandatory provisions of the relevant country (separately from public policy issues) will not entirely overcome an express choice of governing law for a different country in a contract. In so far as any provisions of the chosen law would override local laws which are considered to be mandatory, the express governing law of the contract will not have full effect in respect of those provisions, but it will otherwise apply. A common example of an overriding mandatory provision would be national laws regulating the proper termination of employment. A contract with a governing law which provided for termination of employment on a shorter notice period than the statutory minimum in a country would be overridden in respect of that term to

---

6   It should be noted that the legal analysis and potential solutions for managing jurisdiction issues under regulations, criminal and administrative laws may, however, be very different from the analysis set out in this chapter.

7   Regulation (EC) 593/2008 on the Law Applicable to Contractual Obligations (otherwise known as Rome I or the Rome I Regulation).

8   Ibid., Art 21.

9   In May 2014, Bolivia's Central Bank issued a resolution which effectively banned the use of digital currencies within the country; see: https://www.bcb.gob.bo/?q=content/resolucion-de-directorio-n%C2%BA-0442014.

the extent it applied to employees located in that country. In a similar way, contracts providing that employees cannot use court processes to challenge termination, only private arbitration, will often be overridden in countries where it is not possible for employees to contract out of those legal challenge rights. Other areas where overriding mandatory provisions are common are agreements involving consumers or regulated activities and products. As a result, an express governing law clause in a consumer contract may be ineffective to the extent that the choice of law is inconsistent with mandatory local consumer laws.

In the absence of an express governing law clause, complex national and **8.12** supra-national rules apply to determine what the governing law of the contract should be. The approach taken by different national courts to determining the governing law varies and it is entirely possible that two different courts, looking at the same contract and factual background, could reach entirely different conclusions on the appropriate governing law (in the absence of an express governing law clause).

It is beyond the scope of this chapter to set out all possible approaches which **8.13** could apply to the determination of governing law for any contract in the absence of an express governing law clause. However, there are certain factors which are likely to have a substantial effect on the analysis. As a starting point, if the contract in question is entirely domestic, i.e., all the parties are domiciled in the same country and the contract involves supply of goods or services in that country, the governing law (in the absence of express choice) is very likely to be the law of that country. In a similar way, many jurisdictions will give particular weight to the law of the place in which the property which is the subject of the dispute is located (the *lex situs*) for tangible and/or immovable property. In contrast, Rome I[10] sets out specific rules depending on the type of contract, but if these rules are inapplicable or inconclusive, it provides that the governing law should be the law of the country where the characteristic performer of the contract is habitually resident,[11] although this rule can be disregarded if the contract is 'manifestly more closely connected' with the law of a different country.[12]

This brief summary highlights the potential difficulty and risks of an unfore- **8.14** seen outcome when establishing the correct governing law (in the absence of an express clause) for a cross-border contract involving tangible and/or

---

10   Which must be applied in all EU Member States (other than Denmark).
11   Rome I, Art 4(2).
12   Ibid., Art 4(3).

immovable property. That complexity is only heightened in the case of DLT systems, where the relevant contract is likely to relate to intangible property and/or digitised assets with the property or asset constituted or recorded in multiple copies of a ledger on a DLT system. The difficulties with applying traditional concepts of governing law to DLT systems are discussed in detail (in the context of English law and financial instruments) in the Financial Markets Law Committee's (FMLC) 2018 paper on Distributed Ledger Technology and Governing Law.[13] In particular, the FMLC Working Group noted the difficulties with applying the *lex situs* concept to DLT systems as follows:

> The *lex situs* does not, however, translate well when applied to a DLT system. The situs of an asset constituted on a DLT ledger—which by definition is distributed—is not immediately obvious. A network can span several jurisdictions and—in the case of a ledger which is fully decentralised—there is no central authority or validation point.[14]

8.15 At first sight, it may be easier to ascertain the governing law of a DLT system, based on the law of the country where the 'characteristic performer' of the contract is habitually resident, depending on the nature of the contract being performed. In the EU and elsewhere, there are long-established conventions as to what characteristic performance means in particular contexts. For example, the characteristic performance of a loan agreement is the act of lending, hence it is the lender's habitual residence which gives rise to the governing law. However, the particular technological features of DLT systems, particularly if contract terms are partly or fully automated via a smart contract, presents an additional challenge to identifying what the characteristic performance of any contract is and/or may introduce characteristic performance that is not, in fact, being carried out by any party to the transaction. At the least, it is a further operative fact which will need to be considered when identifying what the habitual residence is of the contracting party owing the obligation which is characteristic of the particular type of contract.

8.16 Similar issues may arise when considering the so-called 'escape clause' in Article 4(3) of Rome I that, where it is clear from all the circumstances of the case that the contract is 'manifestly more closely connected' with a different country, the law of that other country will govern the relevant contract. An important word in that statement is 'manifestly', implying a high standard of connection. In 2016, in the English case, *Molton Street Capital LLP v Shooters*

---

13   Financial Markets Law Committee: Distributed Ledger Technology and Governing Law 2018, available at: http://fmlc.org/report-finance-and-technology-27-march-2018/.
14   Ibid., para 4.6.

Hill Capital Partners LLP and another, the court described the necessary level of close connection as: 'the cumulative weight of the factors connecting the contract to another country must clearly and decisively outweigh the desideratum of certainty in applying the relevant test in Article 4.1 or 4.2'.[15]

As noted at 8.13 above, if an agreement is largely domestic, the governing law **8.17** doctrine of close connection remains entirely applicable in a DLT system. However, many likely successful applications of DLT systems are inherently cross-border. It is the challenges and delays to cross-border transactions and systems which DLT is best suited to solve, making it more likely that the doctrine of 'close connection' to any one particular country cannot be established (to the high standard required).

In short, there is a significant risk of multiple potential situses, inconsistent **8.18** approaches to governing law and/or to conflict of law issues when dealing with DLT systems, unless a clear choice of governing law has been made, as discussed at 8.43 below.

2. Jurisdiction

Where a dispute has an international element, questions of jurisdiction are **8.19** likely to arise – i.e. which country's court has jurisdictional competence to resolve any case. Differently from governing law issues, there may be more than one court which is able properly to hear the matter. This raises issues of whether there are any advantages or disadvantages for the parties of proceeding with the claim in a particular country (the so-called jurisdictional arbitrage). Where a case is heard can have a material impact on the process of the litigation, the cost to the parties and even to the outcome, both in terms of assessment of liability, availability of non-damage-based relief (such as specific performance) and to the calculation of damages.

In a similar way to the process for establishing governing law in the absence of **8.20** an express clause, courts must apply applicable national and supra-national rules in order to establish whether they have jurisdiction to hear a particular dispute. Generally, there are three broad concepts which are typically used to found jurisdiction – personal, territorial and subject matter:

- Personal jurisdiction is the authority of a court over a person – often, but not always, a national of that country, but always a person who has sufficient minimum contacts with the relevant forum to found personal

---

15 In *Molton Street Capital LLP v Shooters Hill Capital Partners LLP and another* [2015] EWHC 3419 (Comm).

jurisdiction. This includes where a party specifically submits to the jurisdiction of a particular court – for example, by agreeing to an express choice of jurisdiction clause and/or to accept service of court process within a particular jurisdiction.

- Territorial jurisdiction is the authority of a court over cases arising in the defined territory of that court – for example, the prosecution of a driving offence, even where the driver has no other connection to the relevant territory and was only passing through.

- Subject matter jurisdiction is the authority of a court to hear cases of a particular type or cases relating to a specific subject matter. For instance, specialist courts may have the exclusive authority to hear insolvency cases in a particular country.

8.21 Courts must also take account of particular laws, conventions or treaties which regulate jurisdiction within their territory. For example, the 'recast' Brussels Regulation[16] applies directly in all European Member States (including Denmark, which initially opted out of the legislative process) to civil and commercial proceedings instituted on or after 10 January 2015. The 'recast' Brussels Regulation, together with the Brussels Convention (which applies to certain dependent territories of EU Member States) and the 2007 Lugano Convention (which applies in Iceland, Norway and Switzerland) creates a single European-wide regime for establishing jurisdiction and priority as between the courts of those countries and territories. The regime principally provides that a defendant domiciled within the area of the regime should be sued in his country of domicile,[17] although there are exceptions and alternative grounds on which the court can take jurisdiction in relevant cases, including where an express choice of jurisdiction clause has been agreed. It is important to note that courts within the area of the European-wide regime will still apply the regime where there is an affected defendant, even if the claimant or other defendants are not domiciled within the area of the regime. Where the courts of more than one country within the European-wide regime could have jurisdiction, priority is generally given to the first court where proceedings were issued, subject to certain exceptions.

8.22 Other regimes include the Hague Convention on Choice of Court Agreements, which provides a more limited set of rules (to uphold express choices of jurisdiction in agreements) and applies to a more limited set of countries.[18]

---

16 Regulation (EU) 1215/2012 of the European Parliament and of the Council of 12 December 2012 on jurisdiction and the recognition and enforcement of judgments in civil and commercial matters.

17 Incorporated entities are entitled to be sued in the place of their statutory seat, central administration or principal place of business.

18 EU Member States and Mexico, Singapore and Montenegro, at the time of this writing.

In the same way that it is open to parties to a contract to agree which courts **8.23** should have jurisdiction over any matter, they can also generally opt for other forms of dispute resolution (typically arbitration or expert determination) so as to ensure the full and final resolution of any dispute. Arbitration awards are generally private, as opposed to court hearings which typically take place in public, and can normally be enforced under the New York Convention in a large number of countries. Arbitration may therefore be particularly suitable for cross-border matters with parties in countries where it is challenging to enforce a foreign court judgment.

D. DIFFERENT ASPECTS OF BLOCKCHAIN GOVERNANCE

Before considering what factors may be relevant to establishing the governing **8.24** law and/or jurisdiction in respect of any blockchain, it is first necessary to consider the different aspects of a blockchain which could be affected. Given the complexity and variation of the rules outlined above, it will be no surprise to learn that different aspects of DLT systems could well be subject to different governing laws and with different jurisdiction provisions depending on the situation.

1. Agreements concluded via DLT systems

The aspect of blockchain governance which fits most neatly into the above **8.25** summary of governing law and jurisdiction issues is where an agreement is concluded between two or more parties via the medium of a DLT system, possibly but not necessarily, utilising a smart contract. As noted in Chapter 7, it will be particularly important for parties to such agreements to ensure that the governing law will recognise agreements concluded by electronic means, for intangible/digital assets or written in code, and that the agreement meets the necessary formalities for contract formation in that jurisdiction, in order to give maximum assurance that the contract will be upheld.

2. Assets created or stored on DLT systems

The second aspect of blockchain governance where governing law or juris- **8.26** diction may be relevant is in respect of the creation or storage of digital assets or digital representations of assets on a DLT system. Whether the asset is a token, a unit of digital currency or a security, its applicable terms may have a distinct governing law or may give rise to jurisdiction issues, separately from any agreement to buy or sell that asset via a DLT system. An example would be a dematerialised debt security which exists only on a DLT system, where the terms and conditions attaching to any ownership of the security provide that the governing law will be English law and any disputes as to the interpretation of those terms would be dealt with in English courts.

3. Operation and management of DLT systems

8.27 Finally, the most complex aspect of blockchain governance relates to the governing laws or jurisdiction which may apply to the creation, operation and management of the blockchain itself. As a blockchain is not a legal entity, but rather a network of linked nodes, it can be difficult to ascertain, on a case-by-case basis, not only what the rules of operation are, but also who has the power to enforce or change those rules (if anyone). In the same way, it may not be obvious who could be legally responsible for any failure of the system.

8.28 There can also be fundamental differences in approach to governance between permissioned DLT systems and permissionless DLT systems. A permissioned DLT system restricts both access to, and ability to perform actions on, the relevant distributed ledger. As participant access is controlled, transactions are validated and processed by those who are already recognised by the ledger and a level of pre-existing trust is often assumed. The internal mechanics of a permissioned DLT system will vary (and may include an overall administrator type entity), but typically there will be a clear agreement on such issues as who is eligible to join the network, how permissions are managed between members, how the terms of the system can be changed, how transactions are validated, dispute resolution, software updates and regulatory reporting (if required). It is generally the case that this upfront agreement in a permissioned DLT system will include agreement on governing law and jurisdiction as part of the overarching governance agreement and/or require standard form contracts or incorporated terms for contracts between parties on that system, which include an express choice of governing law and choice of jurisdiction.

8.29 The approach may be quite different in a permissionless DLT system. Permissionless systems are open to any participant. They can also be based on open source software, meaning that the source code is made available by way of a license which permits any user the right to change and distribute the software to anyone else, for any purpose, providing it is on the same open source licence terms. Indeed, Bitcoin was first released as an open source project in January 2009.

8.30 Permissionless DLT systems have multiple groups of stakeholders, each of whom may have a different interest in the way that the ledger is governed. As described in Chapter 9, typical stakeholders include the day-to-day users of the ledger, any parties providing the computing power to run the ledger, application developers (to the extent that the blockchain allows third-party applications), and holders of any tokens or other digital assets which exist or can be transferred via the ledger. Each of these groups may have different interests and be differently affected by governance decisions. For example, a decision which increases the number of validators required to approve any particular transaction might increase security, but slow down transaction processing times.

Any governance structure of a permissionless DLT system needs to mediate **8.31** between these different groups of stakeholders, as well as wrestle with the practical issue that there may be no obvious primary entity or person to take the lead on governance issues and changes. Practically, the number of people who may be capable of properly assessing any proposed changes may be very limited, which raises the possibility that a small group of interested persons with technical knowledge are able to influence or control the governance of the ledger to their personal advantage.

There are two basic governance structures for permissionless DLT systems: **8.32** off-chain governance and on-chain governance. Off-chain governance requires users to manually update the software to incorporate any proposed governance rules, whereas systems with on-chain governance have governance rules coded into the ledger's protocol such that if the governance rules approve a change, it will automatically go into effect for everyone.

The largest and best-known permissionless DLT system (the Bitcoin block- **8.33** chain) uses off-chain governance based on allowing the persons supplying the computing capacity to run the ledger (i.e., miners) to decide whether to adopt a coding change. This raises the possibility that some miners will adopt the change and others will not, resulting in a blockchain being split, or 'forked', into two different blockchains operating under different rules. The ability to fork a ledger in the event of less than 100 per cent agreement on governance changes, gives users some protection in that they can choose the version of the ledger based on the code and governance process that they prefer. However, it also raises issues around scalability and security of the forked ledger as well as the potential for conflicts and disputes in respect of assets and transactions on the ledger.

In contrast, on-chain governance does not give rise to forks in the ledger (as **8.34** every user is forced to adopt the change) but it does require some kind of voting structure to be in place in order for code changes to be adopted, with the same risks of conflicting interests and overcontrol by a small group of interested persons as noted above.

8.35 In either case, it will be challenging to implement or even ascertain a single governing law for disputes which arise in respect of governance changes for a permissionless DLT system (although it is notable that claims were promptly filed in the US arising out of the hard fork of the Bitcoin blockchain alleging conspiracy by a 'tight knit network of individuals' to manipulate the market for Bitcoin Cash[19]).

E. FACTORS THAT MAY AFFECT THE APPLICABLE LAW

8.36 In a situation where a dispute arises on a DLT system and there is no clear governing law or choice of jurisdiction, the parties will need to assess the possible options. There are, at the time of this writing, no significant judicial precedents or other guidance which would assist in that analysis – even in jurisdictions which have promoted DLT by passing specific laws and regulations allowing its use.

8.37 However, it is possible to identify various factors which could be taken into account by any court or tribunal when determining governing law and jurisdiction. Some of these factors have already been identified and are obvious. Other factors are more technical in nature.

8.38 Two factors which fit within the traditional scope of assessment of governing law or jurisdiction (discussed at 8.13–8.18) are the place of business of the parties to the dispute and the place of performance of the agreement. For example, if the dispute relates to non-performance of an agreement concluded on a DLT system for the provision of goods by a German supplier, delivered in Germany, there will be clear arguments that (i) German law should be the governing law of that agreement (in the absence of an express clause); and (ii) German courts have jurisdiction over the dispute. However, those obvious factors could be much less relevant to a dispute involving several parties from different countries arising out of dematerialised assets created and stored on a DLT system.

8.39 There are then factors which are specific to DLT systems. In particular, the location of the various nodes which make up the blockchain is likely to be a

---

19 Ian Edwards, *American Firm Brings Lawsuit Against Bitcoin.com, Bitmain Over Hash War*, Bitsonline (7 December 2018), available at: https://bitsonline.com/lawsuit-hash-war/.

key factor in establishing jurisdiction, but also possibly the relevant governing law (in the absence of any express contractual clauses). At the most extreme end of the analysis, every transaction conducted on a DLT system could potentially be subject to the jurisdiction of the location of every node in the network. The practical implications and difficulties are obvious. While the location of the nodes may have some relation to the users in a permissioned DLT system, modern complex IT systems do not necessarily require key infrastructure to be located in the main place of business of any organisation. It is entirely possible that a user of a permissioned DLT system located in one country maintains its copy of the ledger on a node based in an entirely different country. The implications of multiple nodes in different countries are even greater in the context of permissionless systems where there is likely to be even less relationship between the locations of users and node providers. To the extent that any DLT system incorporates a concept of a 'lead node',[20] that may give rise to additional arguments that the law of the country of that node is particularly relevant to establishing jurisdiction and/or governing law. In a similar way, if a majority of nodes are located in one country, that may be an indication not only of the jurisdiction with the most connections to the blockchain, but also of what governing law should govern agreements concluded on that blockchain.

In a similar way to a lead node, if the DLT system has an administrator or **8.40** master key holder, that may also be an indication of a particular jurisdiction or governing law that should apply. This is, of course, a very fact-specific analysis, but the PROPA (Place of the Relevant Operating Authority/ Administrator) or PREMA (Place of the Encryption Master key-holder)[21] solutions may provide a simple and clear answer to governing law and jurisdiction issues for certain types of DLT systems.

Another factor to consider is whether a DLT system has a relevant DAO **8.41** which incorporates rules regarding governing law and/or jurisdiction. DAOs (distributed/decentralised autonomous organisations) are a comparatively new feature of certain programmable distributed ledgers such as Ethereum. DAOs are not easy to define, but in some ways can be thought of as investment vehicles or joint ventures, but where the partners do not necessarily know each other. A DAO is typically used by groups of persons jointly to invest in or promote a common economic goal, where the rules of the organisation are entirely defined by code. Participants become stakeholders in the DAO by

---

20   Typically, a node which is the most powerful on the ledger, or which may have particular rights or abilities to process transactions more quickly or with a different level of validation from other nodes on the ledger.
21   Financial Markets Law Committee, *supra* note 12, ¶6.15 *et seq.*

purchasing the DAO's digital tokens and in return the participant is entitled to a share in the profits of the DAO and/or an ability to become involved in the DAO's governance. The rules of the DAO are defined in the code and may include governing law or jurisdiction clauses. If the DAO is only one small part of the DLT system then those governing law or jurisdiction clauses will be largely irrelevant. However, on a specialised DLT system, where the DAO is the primary application, the rules of the DAO may well be imputed more widely to the entire blockchain.

8.42 Finally, some commentators have suggested that the most 'technically pure' solution to establishing applicable law in the context of DLT systems is to adopt the governing law of the code that was originally used to create the ledger (referred to as the *lex codicis*). This approach assumes that the original code has an express governing law or that it is possible easily to establish what the governing law is. One further suggestion is that the *lex codicis* should be the domicile of the original coder (but does not allow for teams of individual coders). In addition, it is unclear why the original coder should have any relevance to the ongoing management of a multi-party distributed ledger without some other ongoing involvement in the blockchain.

F. CONCLUSION

8.43 This chapter has highlighted the legal uncertainty and practical issues that can arise when establishing the governing law and appropriate jurisdiction for dispute resolution in respect of DLT systems. The use of multiple ledgers, the ability to run DLT systems seamlessly cross-border and the likelihood that the relevant contract will relate to intangible property and/or digitised assets all raise specific issues and, at best complicate and at worst make irrelevant, traditional methods of establishing the relevant law or jurisdiction.

8.44 As a result, the chapter concludes that the best way to manage issues of governing law and jurisdiction on any DLT system is to include comprehensive contractual clauses which cover all of the aspects of the blockchain that need governing, whether this is the blockchain itself or a contract concluded on a relevant blockchain system.

8.45 Where this is not possible, for example in a permissionless system, users should consider the risks identified in this chapter carefully and form their own view of the possible governing laws or courts which could have jurisdiction over any dispute as part of their risk assessment of the proposed transaction.

9

LIABILITIES ASSOCIATED WITH DISTRIBUTED LEDGERS: A COMPARATIVE ANALYSIS[1]

Dirk Zetzsche, Ross Buckley, Douglas Arner and Anton Didenko

A. INTRODUCTION

Over the past several years, interest in distributed ledger technology (DLT) **9.01** has exploded. Regulators, consultants, technology firms and academia are promoting DLT for financial services. The concept of distributed ledgers has moved beyond cryptocurrencies and is now being considered for all parts of the financial system and beyond. As described in Chapter 6, capital raising, trading, clearing and settlement, global payments, deposits and lending, property and casualty claims processing, digital identity management and authentication, and RegTech solutions (such as automated compliance and

---

[1] This chapter draws upon, and extends the comparative analysis in: D A Zetzsche, R P Buckley and D W Arner, The Distributed Liability of Distributed Ledgers: Legal Risks of Blockchain (2018) 4 *University of Illinois Law Review* 1361.

risk management, and AML and KYC checks) have all been identified as significant potential DLT use cases.

9.02 At the same time, legal concerns are emerging. The discussion so far has focused on investment fraud, the proper classification of cryptocurrencies, systemic risk regulation and central bank functions, as well as money laundering and taxation. This chapter seeks to add another, private law, dimension which has received little attention.

9.03 Even if distributed ledgers prove to be more secure or efficient than traditional centralised ledgers, recent events call for an analysis of who will bear the losses and responsibility for damages in connection with DLT platforms when things go wrong. Notable examples include the loss of 750,000 customer Bitcoins and 100,000 Bitcoins owned by the Japanese Mt. Gox Bitcoin exchange;[2] the hot wallet hack leading to the loss of 19,000 Bitcoins, by the world's second largest Bitcoin exchange, Bitstamp;[3] the misappropriation of USD 53 million held by the investor-directed, DLT-enabled Decentralized Autonomous Organization (DAO);[4] and the loss of 119,756 Bitcoins with a market value at the time of between USD 66–72 million by Hong Kong-based Bitfinex.[5]

9.04 As these examples show, risk does not simply vanish if financial services are provided via distributed ledgers, and it is essential to analyse how liability risk formerly concentrated in one ledger becomes distributed in distributed ledgers.

9.05 This chapter is structured as follows: Section B briefly explains the technology underlying distributed ledgers. Section C outlines the key risks associated with DLT. Sections D and E discuss the key parties involved in the DLT structure and legal consequences arising from the relationship between these parties. Section F provides a comparative analysis of potential liabilities arising under contract, tort, partnership and joint venture structures, specific legislation and breach of fiduciary duty. Section G concludes.

---

2 See The Troubling Holes in MtGox's Account of How It Lost $600 Million in Bitcoins, *MIT Technology Review*, 4 April 2014, available at: https://www.technologyreview.com/s/526161/the-troubling-holes-in-mtgoxs-account-of-how-it-lost-600-million-in-bitcoins/.

3 See Mariella Moon, Bitcoin Exchange Loses $5 Million in Security Breach, *Engadget*, 1 June 2015, available at: http://www.engadget.com/2015/01/06/bitstamp-bitcoin-exchange-hack/.

4 See Dino Mark et al., A Call for a Temporary Moratorium on The DAO, *Hacking Distributed* 27 May 2016, available at: http://hackingdistributed.com/2016/05/27/dao-call-for-moratorium/.

5 See Stan Higgins, The Bitfinex Bitcoin Hack: What We Know (And Don't Know), *Coindesk*, 3 August 2016, available at: http://www.coindesk.com/bitfinex-bitcoin-hack-know-dont-know/.

B. THE DISTRIBUTED LEDGER CONCEPT

How distributed ledgers work is best understood by looking at their counter- **9.06** part, the centralised ledger. Centralised ledgers are the most common data storage device in finance today. In a centralised ledger, data is stored on a single ledger, and the trusted administrator of the ledger maintains it and records transfers of assets. In this case, risks, just like the ledger itself, are centralised. The ledger could be destroyed, or hacked so that the original data are held for ransom or manipulated and replaced by new (inaccurate) data. The centralised ledger can implement robust cybersecurity measures, but with sufficient computing power, *any* server can be manipulated.

Distributed ledgers address this problem by raising the barriers for manipu- **9.07** lation of stored data. In distributed ledgers, many nodes are connected with each other and store all data simultaneously, together constituting the common ledger. DLT requires consensus of those nodes, rather than merely confirmation by one hierarchically structured storage device. The technical details of how to achieve consensus vary – technology allows for proof of work, proof of stake concepts and a range of others.

Perhaps the key benefit of DLT is its ability to replace multiple, competing **9.08** data sets with a single (distributed) one, thereby addressing the storage trust issue. DLT ensures the validity of data sets by spreading data over many nodes which have to agree, via the consensus mechanism, to confirm data validity. Instead of individually storing own data in isolated databases, all users of a DLT platform agree to treat the distributed database as authoritative. This agreement is the centerpiece of DLT functionality that makes it possible to build innovative applications on top of distributed databases, such as smart contracts, delivery versus payment (DVP) settlement systems[6] or electronic KYC platforms.

'Blockchain' is a term frequently associated with DLT which, nonetheless, has **9.09** a distinct meaning. It refers to how data are stored on the ledger. Rather than being stored individually, data are arranged in 'blocks'. The block serves as the container of multiple data points, and all blocks are stored in a specific order and linked together cryptographically (thus forming the 'chain'). In a Bitcoin blockchain, the link is generated by hashing the data in the preceding block, which means that the attacker needs to manipulate not only the block containing the desired data, but also every single block after it – while

---

6   Delivery versus payment (DVP) is a securities industry settlement procedure in which the buyer's payment for securities is due at the time of delivery.

outpacing the entire network of honest Bitcoin miners (due to the proof-of-work consensus algorithm). Blockchain's key benefit is in highlighting changes and evolution over time: in a hash-based blockchain database, any modification of data in any block will generate a different hash and any change will become evident from comparison with the hash recorded in the subsequent block. As a result, blockchain may be particularly useful in products and services that benefit from robust record-keeping.

9.10   At their core, distributed ledgers and blockchain are simply different ways of recording data – different database structures. These databases can be permissioned or permissionless. Permissioned systems are essentially private networks with a pre-defined governance structure where data authorisation depends upon the agreement of multiple pre-defined servers.

9.11   In contrast, permissionless platforms, such as Bitcoin, operate on public domain software and allow anyone who downloads and runs the software to participate. In some cases, even the code is further developed in the public domain. Participants in such distributed ledgers may not know who else is running another server functioning as a node at any given time. There is an additional security element from the unknown inherent in this structure: if the number of overall nodes is known, a cyber-attack may be planned with greater certainty.

9.12   These technical differences in how DLT systems are governed and operate impact not only the risks associated with such systems, but also, importantly, the liabilities which may arise from those risks. The next section explores these risks.

C. THE RISKS OF DISTRIBUTED LEDGERS

9.13   Despite its prospective advantages, DLT is not bulletproof, and implementation of distributed databases could result in undesirable data distribution, data loss or data manipulation. All of these lead to questions about responsibility and liability.

9.14   DLT commonly gives rise to at least three major sources of potential liability risk: ledger transparency risks, cyber risks and operational risks.

1. Ledger tansparency risks

DLT stores data by spreading them over multiple nodes. Every node operator **9.15** has access to the data. While data can be encrypted before being stored on a distributed ledger, making it readable only by those in possession of decryption tools, metadata is necessarily available to all node operators. This enhanced level of transparency may enable re-personalisation of data on the distributed ledger or enable node operators to make an informed guess as to identities of the parties entering into certain transactions.

For instance, Bitcoin reveals considerable information about users' profiles, **9.16** which means that anonymous data could potentially be linked to an individual, thus enabling the re-personalisation of pseudonymous data. Indeed, spreading data over multiple nodes may facilitate access to private data sets. In the context of Bitcoin, this largely means that, when it comes to criminal networks, its use is already limited, due to the potential for rapid identification of known identities.

Distribution of personal data over the ledger could be at odds with data **9.17** protection requirements. For example, and as described in more detail in Chapter 11, the right of a data subject to obtain erasure of one's own personal data (known as 'right to be forgotten' in the GDPR)[7] can be compromised if personal data are stored in DLT databases utilising blockchain, as such databases may have append-only design that does not permit the erasure of data.[8] In some jurisdictions, penalties for the violation of data protection rules are severe.[9]

Moreover, if DLT is used to store sensitive, valuable information, it may **9.18** facilitate a range of financial abuses including insider trading, tipping and market manipulation.[10] Responsible entities may face severe civil and criminal penalties,[11] and civil litigation in certain cases.

---

7   GDPR, Art 17.
8   Append-only design means that data can only be added to, but not removed from, the database. To eliminate a set of data that once entered an append-only database, one would have to create a new database without the undesirable data. On a blockchain, where any modification affects all subsequent blocks, a similar result is achievable through a chain split, i.e., creation of a new, accurate chain of blocks starting from the block immediately preceding the one which contains the undesirable data.
9   For instance, under GDPR, Art 83(5) regulators may impose penalties of up to 4 per cent of a firm's total worldwide annual turnover.
10 See European Securities and Markets Authority, Report – The Distributed Ledger Technology Applied to Securities Markets (7 February 2017), ¶38.
11 See 15 US Code § 78u-1 (civil penalties for insider trading), imposing penalties of up to three times the profit gained or loss avoided. In Europe, the penalties may be the higher of (i) 15 per cent of the entity's turnover and (ii) EUR 15 million. See Market Abuse Regulation (EU) No. 596/2014, Art 30(2).

2. Cyber risks

9.19 DLT does not solve the general issue that inaccurate data remains inaccurate however stored. For instance, if data from a financial transaction is stored on a distributed ledger, the data will often be generated by just two entities, e.g., transaction counterparties. If a so-called man-in-the-middle cyber-attack focuses on the transacting parties, rather than the storage device (DLT), users relying on the ledger may not realise the inaccuracies and rely upon it. While this is true of both centralised and distributed ledgers, for the latter the problem is more pronounced since it upsets the key perceived benefit of DLT – replacement of multiple data sets with a single authoritative database shared among, and trusted by, its end-users. Without trust in the contents of a distributed database, the latter is practically obsolete. Permissionless distributed ledgers are particularly exposed to cyber-attacks due to the absence of user/client enrolment/identity processes of the sort embedded into financial institutions' KYC/customer onboarding processes, which explains attacks on Bitcoin owners' wallets.

9.20 Cyber-resilience of distributed databases also has its limits. A brute force attack against a DLT platform becomes more difficult only if the security of nodes sufficient to achieve consensus surpasses the security of a centralised ledger. Yet, this scenario is unlikely to always be true.

9.21 First, transaction logic will lead to concentration among the nodes making some more important than others. For instance, in certain DLT platforms recording units of cryptocurrency, nodes are compensated per transaction they complete, thus providing incentives to compete for transactions. Some of the most active nodes will process a high proportion of transactions leading to a concentration of data generation in those nodes. For example, within the Bitcoin infrastructure, five mining pools together process about 85 per cent of all mining. If consensus building is capacity-oriented, as in some DLT platforms including Bitcoin, the attack must only result in control over more computing power than is retained by honest nodes, an instance referred to as a '51 per cent attack.' Thus, a cyber-attack that focuses on the handful or so of nodes in which most transaction validation is concentrated, is more likely to be successful. Alternatively, since brute force attacks require an enormous amount of computing power, an attacker may seek to 'convince' the necessary number of nodes to adopt a different version of the ledger software through which the desired change is implemented.

Second, some nodes will be safer than others, given that some owners will **9.22** invest more in cybersecurity. Attacking the nodes with weaker security may be more productive than a brute force attack on all nodes.

One perceived mechanism of self-defence of cryptocurrency DLT platforms **9.23** like Bitcoin lies in their self-perpetuating nature: it is expected that nefarious manipulation would lead to a general loss of trust, resulting in a plunge in the value of Bitcoin, thus harming the attackers who are presumably heavily invested in Bitcoin.[12] However, this disincentive is unlikely to stop attackers seeking to destroy the Bitcoin system as a form of terrorism, or to merely harm its users.

Another potential threat stems from distributed denial of service attacks **9.24** (DDOS). DDOS is more dangerous the more concentrated the ledger. For instance, in the Bitcoin ledger where a handful of miners control most computing power, DDOS has frequently brought mining to a halt.[13] The more widely used DLT becomes, the more likely are rogues or terrorists to turn to DDOS. Even if immediately detected due to intense monitoring, effects are potentially severe.[14]

Cybersecurity issues are described in Chapter 10.

3. Operational risks

While the standardisation and automatisation that form part of DLT mitigate **9.25** – in principle – operational risk, an error once implemented in the code may be shared across the whole database affecting a greater number of nodes than a concentrated ledger and at a faster rate.

In particular, poorly maintained, outdated or deficient code could open the **9.26** door for system hacks, such as those that occurred in the Mt. Gox and DAO cases. The governance deficiencies of permissionless ledgers may turn into real world issues in the context of poor coding.

---

12 One reason is that even control of the majority of hashing power does not allow a miner to spend someone else's Bitcoins. Nonetheless, it may allow double-spending of the malicious miner's own tokens.
13 See e.g., Julia McGovern, Official Statement on the Last Week's DDoS-attack against GHash.IO Mining Pool, CEX.IO (16 March 2015), available at: https://blog.cex.io/news/official-statement-on-the-last-weeks-ddos-attack-against-ghash-io-mining-pool-14156.
14 For details see Zetzsche et al., *supra* note 1.

9.27 Assuming that a distributed ledger ensures certain security and processing standards to market participants in an effort to enhance market share, the question of who is responsible will be asked if the ledger fails to meet these standards.

D. LEGAL CONSEQUENCES

9.28 All the DLT's limitations mentioned earlier translate into important legal questions. If a distributed database is broken or manipulated, who is liable for the resulting losses? If personal data stored on a distributed ledger cannot be deleted as directed by the data subject, who should bear the responsibility for breach of data privacy obligations? There are three important considerations to remember.

9.29 First, very few governments have as yet adopted a DLT or blockchain law.[15] That does not mean, however, that no law applies or that law's focus needs to shift from individuals to (web) communities. Rather, when facing innovation, the law will often provide an abundance of generally applicable principles, including the law of contracts, torts, property, data privacy, partnerships and companies, some of which are enshrined in legislation while others (in particular in common law jurisdictions) are in case law which applies in the absence of specific legislation.

9.30 Second, DLT – being a database structure – tells us nothing about the entities involved or their governance roles. For instance, multiple servers functioning as nodes can belong to one legal entity or financial group or multiple unrelated owners. In permissionless DLT platforms, node owners typically will not even know who operates the other nodes, while a permissioned ledger may have highly developed and legally sophisticated governance structures.

9.31 The second element – identity of entities involved in DLT operation – is critical for the functioning of any liability regime, at least for as long as individuals and their legally recognised forms of cooperation (and not computers) remain the subjects of liability. Broadly speaking, as illustrated in Figure 9.1, the following five groups intersect in the DLT hierarchy:

---

15 Arizona and California have each adopted a blockchain law. See An Act Amending Section 44-7003, Arizona Revised Statutes, Amending Title 44, Chapter 26, Arizona Revised Statutes, By Adding Article 5 Relating To Electronic Transactions, available at: https://legiscan.com/AZ/text/HB2417/2017; and California Assembly Bill No. 265 Chapter 875, an act to add and repeal Sections 11546.8 and 11546.9 of the Government Code, relating to blockchain technology, available at: https://legiscan.com/CA/text/AB2658/id/1821719. Others are considering implementation of the same approach.

(1) the *core group* that sets up the code design and (*de facto*) governs the distributed ledger, for instance by having the technical ability and opinion leadership to prompt a 'hard fork'[16] of the system (under certain conditions);

(2) the owners of *additional servers* running the distributed ledger code for *validation purposes* (such as Bitcoin nodes, Ripple validation nodes, etc.);

(3) *'qualified'* users of the distributed ledger (such as exchanges, lending institutions, miners, etc);

(4) *'simple'* users of the system (such as owners of Bitcoin,[17] Ether or investors in the DAO); and

(5) *third parties* affected by the system without directly relying on the technology (such as counterparties of, and banks lending to, 'simple users', clients of intermediaries that clear their financial assets via DLT and clients of brokers that hold cryptocurrency on behalf of clients).

Each of these parties plays a specific role in the ongoing operation of a DLT **9.32** system, which may result in legal liability if one of the risks detailed earlier comes to fruition.

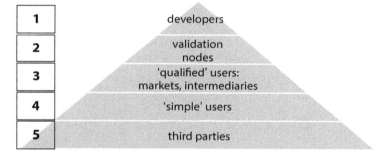

Figure 9.1   Ledger hierarchy

Third, DLT is a concept with multiple variations. Bitcoin, Ethereum and **9.33** Ripple[18] are all built using DLT so one is tempted to generalise, but up close they are very different. Each DLT application serves a certain defined use case ranging from currency and pegged services to automatic execution of functions (e.g., Bitcoin is intended to provide the functions of a currency, Ethereum is designed to provide a platform for the support of other applications, and Ripple is designed to facilitate cross-border payments). Moreover, they also

---

16 A hard fork results in a fundamental change in the nature of the system, with two networks resulting. It is a fork which results in a split in a system.

17 In the Bitcoin ledger, validation nodes (element 2) and owners (element 3) are identical.

18 Ripple is a real-time gross settlement system, currency exchange and remittance network created by Ripple Labs Inc., a US-based technology company.

have very different governance structures: Bitcoin and Ethereum both have distributed governance systems, while Ripple is a commercial entity; moreover, while Bitcoin has no legal structure, Ethereum has its foundation and Ripple a traditional corporate structure.

9.34 Depending on the DLT's design and use case, the number of users, the technical complexity and the delivery timeframe will vary – and so will the legal issues surrounding liability.

E. CONSEQUENCES OF JOINT CONTROL FOR LIABILITY

9.35 With regard to the question of the legal treatment of the cooperation underlying a distributed ledger, the type of cooperation created or evidenced by code is of legal relevance.

9.36 No legal system could afford to ignore DLT interactions, given the loopholes this would create. There is simply no good public policy reason to do so – in contrast to exceptions made for gambling and betting laws in some jurisdictions to prevent behaviour of questionable social merit. On the other hand, however, the perceived social and economic benefits of distributed ledgers are significant. It is both pragmatic and logical for the law to interfere and safeguard these benefits by allocating liability among various parties justly and efficiently. Where such allocation is not feasible, end-users are likely to remain disincentivised to use the technology altogether.

9.37 Further, individual transactions executed via a distributed ledger are likely to be contracts – with all related consequences, whether recorded only in code or in words. Each transaction is likely to give rise to liability in the event of failure.

9.38 The fact that law will apply is to be distinguished from the question of *which* law will apply. This will be determined by the application of conflicts of law rules by the courts with jurisdiction over the matter, including their treatment of the relevant choice of law provisions (if any), as described in more detail in Chapter 8.[19]

---

19 Dicey, Morris and Collins, *On the Conflict of Laws*, Sweet & Maxwell (5th ed. 2018); and Adrian Briggs, *Private International Law in English Courts*, Oxford University Press (2014).

1. System participants as related entities

From the outset, one is inclined to liken connections created by distributed **9.39**
ledgers to traditional 'business networks' (such as franchise systems, credit card
networks and supply chains involving multiple parties). However, networks
mimicking a distributed ledger differ from such traditional hybrid organisations[20] in one important respect. All members of the latter (e.g., franchisor
and franchisees) are linked together by a common business interest (for
instance, brand appeal), and traditional business networks follow a hub-and-
spokes model, where the spokes (e.g. the franchisees) are connected to other
spokes only indirectly through a contractual relationship to the 'hub' (for
instance, the franchisor).[21]

Yet, in a distributed ledger, all nodes (group 2 of the hierarchy in Figure 9.1) **9.40**
are linked together directly, in that they together communicate in the
consensus process and thereby determine the validity of data stored via the
'common ledger'. This connection removes the hierarchical relation of hubs
and spokes and justifies the term 'peer-to-peer networks'. In turn, the
difference between horizontal and vertical disappears – all links to other nodes
are by definition 'on the same level', pursuing a common objective.

From a legal perspective, the connection provides the (missing) link between **9.41**
the network partners. Where traditional business networks are mere virtual
networks, distributed ledgers are 'real' networks – with a real physical (tech)
link. While distributed ledgers vary in terms of software processes and thus
their legal consequences, we posit that such consequences follow from this
direct link among the nodes: it is the tipping point at which a loose assembly
of self-interested entities turns into a group of entities legally tied together.

2. Liabilities arising from 'shared control'

The very fact of data distribution among many ledgers which together perform **9.42**
a commercially relevant function renders legal consequence likely. At the same
time, joint performance assigns to all nodes together significant influence over
all users' positions in that they can together exclude any single user from
participation. For instance, if all but one user upload new software incompatible with the old, the value of the remaining user's position will suffer. In many
systems, agreement among a simple majority of nodes is determinative. The

---

20   Hugh Collins, Introduction to Networks as Connected Contracts, 11 *et seq.*, in Günther Teubner: *Networks as Connected Contracts*, Hart (2011).
21   For details, see Zetzsche et al., *supra* note 1.

operations of the information technologies interacting in a distributed ledger could be treated like those of the individuals controlling the servers and computers on which the software runs, or be treated like items a person is responsible for, similar to an animal or a car. In this case, the law would ask whether the person has engaged in negligent conduct, i.e., violated a standard of care when the item inflicted harm on someone.

9.43 Such quasi-organisational characteristics of the distributed ledger which go beyond mere economic interest imply that the whole ledger has a purpose or aim – the joint performance of the ledger service – from which obligations to cooperate, and of loyalty, as well as internal and external liability, could follow.

9.44 For instance, the distributed ledger could be deemed a platform establishing (or facilitating) a joint venture. The core group that sets up the system is a clear potential example, but this could extend further, for instance if nodes contribute and benefit to the same extent as the core group or even 'simple users' could be deemed joint venturers by third parties that rely on their service. One could also understand the joint performance to constitute a multi-party contract with the core group and all nodes functioning as contractors that commit to adhere to the processing rules and maintain a certain level of security. If the core group fails to deliver, or one or more of the nodes does not perform the necessary processes or does not maintain the minimum data security level, the fellow contractors could rely on contractual liability. In some jurisdictions we may also find sufficient ground to argue that the distributed ledger establishes or evidences an incorporated business organisation or partnership.

9.45 Once it is established that distributed ledgers create a sufficiently close organisational relation (regardless of how this is legally interpreted in any given jurisdiction), duties based on good faith, liability among users operating the nodes (internal network liability) and liability to third parties (external network liability) can be presumed to arise. In turn, one node operator could be deemed to owe to the other a duty of loyalty (for instance, not to turn off the computer to maintain the network's processing efficiency or regular software and hardware updates to maintain the ledger's performance) and to be directly liable for economic loss in case of its breach. Further, if a third party is damaged by inaccurate or insecure data storage, the third party could direct its claim based on tort law or special liability statutes to all node operators together.

9.46 From a legal perspective, some type of liability – joint, several or proportionate – could arise from this joint control towards third parties and among the node operators themselves. Which type of liability will arise will depend on the details of the DLT system, in particular the consensus mechanism, and on the rules of the applicable legal system. However, there are significant potential liability risks for entities involved in a distributed ledger, particularly those with design, control and/or maintenance roles.

F. COMPARATIVE ANALYSIS OF POTENTIAL LIABILITIES

Proponents of DLT often like to pretend that the technology is somehow **9.47** beyond the law, or at least, the law's reach. Yet, as noted in Section B, a distributed ledger is merely a different database structure. On its own, the concept of arranging data within a computer system is hardly contentious. This database can be used to record property rights, voting powers, access permissions, or entitlements to digital tokens, such as cryptocurrencies.

This section considers liability that may arise in one of five ways, by way of: **9.48** (i) contract; (ii) tort; (iii) partnership or joint venture; (iv) specific legislation; and (v) fiduciary liability. Of course, the specifics of each head of liability will be entirely jurisdiction specific, so our analysis is general.

1. Contractual liability

In contract law, each party is liable under the terms of the contract. The **9.49** parties to the contract are not the computer as a non-human electronic agent, but the person who exercises control (by virtue of ownership, management rights, or otherwise) of the non-human agent; the contractual acts – meeting of minds, breach of contract, performance – are attributed to this socio-technical ensemble.[22] In order to establish liability, a contract and a breach of the contract are required.

Most clearly, both contract and breach may be established in the relationship **9.50** between groups – group 4 of the distributed ledger hierarchy in Figure 9.1, on the one side, and group 5 on the other. For instance, if the Bitcoin broker breaches its promise to hold a certain amount of cryptocurrency on behalf of its client, the broker will be subject to a contractual claim by its client.[23]

---

22 Günther Teubner, Rights of Non-Humans? Electronic Agents and Animals as New Actors in Politics and Law (2006) 33:4 *Journal of Law and Society* 497.

23 Shaun Bayern, Dynamic Common Law and Technological Change: The Classification of Bitcoin (2014) 71 *Washington and Lee Review Online* 22, at 25–9.

9.51 Beyond this obvious case, contractual relations extend further into the direct relationships among groups 1–4 of our DLT hierarchy, given that both contract and breach can be established.

9.52 Broadly speaking, contractual agreement requires an offer and acceptance (to establish mutual assent), consideration (anything of value exchanged) and an intention to create legal relations. As to offer, acceptance and mutual assent, let us start with hierarchy groups 1 and 2 – the core group and validation nodes – as the parties to the 'distributed ledger contract', given that without them the system would not work. Even if some members of DLT hierarchy groups 1 and 2 do not wish to enter into legally binding relations, the fact they participate in the system knowing that third parties will rely upon it, may turn their participation in the distributed ledger into legally consequential conduct.[24] Even if one does not consider the validation nodes parties to the contract, their conduct may be significant if they are treated as agents of the 'core' group 1.

9.53 Consideration matters most in common law systems; however, not so much in civil law systems, particularly German civil law systems.[25] It may be less readily identifiable given the uncertain flows of assets in open source and permissionless systems, however, any type of consideration will suffice and courts will typically not question whether 'adequate' value has been given. Consideration can take the form of additional virtual assets (as in the case of Bitcoin miners), traffic (for advertisement purposes) or fee payments. The fact participants willingly enter into a distributed ledger, suggests they perceive value from doing so.

9.54 Whether there is a breach of contract depends on conduct in the context of the contract's terms. Warning language displayed prior to entering into the contract may constitute terms of the contract. Disclaimers and liability waivers may further limit obligations *if* they are upheld in court. For contractual liability, however, it makes no difference whether the damage resulted from an individual's misconduct or a machine's malfunction. The owner or node operator is liable for the machine's malfunction.[26]

---

24 In the UK or Australia, such conduct could give rise to remedies under statute: see *infra*. In the US, an implied contract is likely to exist; see *Baltimore & Ohio R Co v. United States*, 261 US 592, 597, 58 Ct.Cl. 709, 43 S.Ct. 425, 67 L.Ed. 816 (1923).

25 For instance, Section 311 of the Bürgerliches Gesetzbuch does not require consideration as a precondition for a *Schuldverhältnis* (best translated as 'obligation').

26 For French law, see Philippe Malaurie, Philippe Stoffel-Munck and Laurent Aynes, *Droit des Obligations* (2016), at 75.

Contractual liability is joint where the causes of actions are not distinct and **9.55** the defendants acted in furtherance of a common purpose.[27] Generally speaking, all multiple nodes functioning together to run the ledger (hierarchy group 2), and all core developers developing the code together (hierarchy group 1) would meet that test on their respective hierarchy levels. If nodes and developers cooperate, hierarchy groups 1 and 2 may find themselves tied together by joint liability vis-à-vis third parties.[28]

Some authors suggest that no contractual relationship exists in distributed **9.56** networks where the user is unknown and the userbase remains unstable, where the performance of the service depends on who is connected at what time, and none of the individual nodes is in itself essential (such as in permissionless distributed ledgers like Bitcoin).[29] Proponents of the idea that the DLT relationship does not give rise to legal rights refer implicitly to participants' lack of intent to grant contractual rights to co-users.[30] However, business entities are often unaware of all participants, and their roles, in complex business interactions. A distributed ledger can generate a complex network of users and contractual relationships that may change from time to time depending on who is participating in the ledger operation. While anonymity of the parties renders enforcement potentially difficult, it does not mean the actions of individuals who together 'operate' the distributed ledger are not legally relevant.

In a distributed ledger, IT-based messages and transactions may coincide, so **9.57** that any message a node sends is a declaration of intent and contribution to the transaction. It is inconsistent to deny legal relevance of cooperation where only reliance on others ensures access to one's own asset value and where this very cooperation by others is the precondition of contributing to the ledger in the first place. A simple example may demonstrate this point: assume miners on the Bitcoin platform find, for whatever reason, that no one will accept (today) the newly and properly generated Bitcoins, or (after 21 million Bitcoins are mined) the recycled split Bitcoins. The miner who invested significant processing power (energy) will either turn to the Bitcoin nodes that validate transactions (i.e., all who hold Bitcoins directly) for the fulfilment of the promise given to them that honestly mined coins would be added to the chain

---

27 For German law, see Section 421 of the Bürgerliches Gesetzbuch.

28 This does not mean that groups 1 and 2 are liable towards each other, nor that end-users necessarily have claims against the developers.

29 Aaron Wright and Primavera De Filippi, Decentralized Blockchain Technology and the Rise of Lex Cryptographia (unpublished manuscript, 12 March 2015), available at: https://ssrn.com/abstract=2580664; Bayern, *supra* note 22, at 31–3.

30 Bayern, ibid.

and thereby receive value, or to the core developers, for damages. In both cases the miner supposedly has standing to sue based on the promise received by all Bitcoin node operators together, regardless of the fact that the miner did not, at the time, know the nodes nor the developers. While enforcement may be difficult,[31] we should not confuse potential for legal liability with the challenge of enforcement.

2. Tortious liability

9.58 An entity operating in the distributed ledger may be liable in tort if its negligent act, omission or misstatement causes loss or damage, including loss due to a security breach or a coding error. A record on the system may be inaccurate causing losses to those relying on it.[32] An entity's liability in negligence will depend on whether it owes a duty of care and has breached that duty, whether the breach caused loss or damage, and whether it has effectively contractually excluded liability for this type of loss or damage.

9.59 The existence of a duty of care depends in part on the type of loss suffered and by whom it was suffered. In most potential distributed ledger actions, the relevant loss is likely to be 'pure economic loss' (that is, economic loss occurring in the absence of, or prior to, any damage to property or person). Courts in common law jurisdictions (and many civil law jurisdictions) have been reluctant to find that a duty of care exists in cases of pure economic loss for fear of 'imposing unreasonable burdens on the freedom of individuals to protect or pursue their own legitimate social and business interests'.[33] However, one may be liable in negligence for pure economic loss in certain situations, especially if the claimant was a member of a class exposed to foreseeable loss by the defendant's conduct whose members were ascertainable by the defendant and if imposing the duty does not unreasonably interfere with the defendant's commercial freedom.[34] Some common law jurisdictions also have statutory provisions that extend the duty of care to apply in cases of pure economic loss. For example, in New South Wales in Australia, the Civil Liability Act of 2002 includes 'economic loss' in the definition of 'harm' and a person may be negligent in failing to take precautions against a risk of harm if the risk was foreseeable and not insignificant, and a reasonable person in that person's position would have taken those precautions.[35]

---

31 The miner would turn to the nodes it could identify and ask them to pay damages.
32 See Vernon Valentine Palmer, A Comparative Law Sketch of Pure Economic Loss in Mauro Bussani and Anthony J Sebok, *Comparative Tort Law: Global Perspectives*, Edward Elgar (2015) 305–6.
33 *Perre v. Apand* (1999) 198 CLR 180, 218.
34 Ibid., at 204.
35 See, e.g., Section 5, 5B(1) of the Australian Civil Liability Act 2002 (NSW).

The relevant node operator might establish that no duty of care existed, **9.60** particularly if the claimant is a second- or third-line victim and not part of an ascertainable class. Liability for pure economic loss is therefore more likely in the case of smaller, permissioned blockchains where the class of claimants is readily ascertainable, although the claimant would still need to prove the defendant breached its duty of care (by, for instance, not meeting the standard of a reasonable node operator or software developer) and that this breach caused the claimant's loss.[36] Node operators may attempt to contractually exclude liability for negligence in these situations. However, such an exclusion clause may be void under consumer legislation or subject to narrow construction by the courts.

Over time, courts in jurisdictions that allow tort claims for pure economic loss **9.61** will shape the duties of care in the DLT context as distributed ledgers gain importance in business applications. This could result, for instance, in judicial pronouncements regarding the appropriate announcement time and method for code modifications, the required bit size and node computing power for the modification, and the necessary diligence prior to the new code's release. In a way, the strictest jurisdiction involved may determine the level of care for the whole ledger.

The important point here is, again, that groups 1–4 in our DLT hierarchy are **9.62** unlikely to enjoy the *laissez-faire* treatment, at least in the long run; as law develops, they may face the harsh reality that they need to keep in mind the reasonable expectations of all parties relying on the respective ledger, as well as the evolving case law in all jurisdictions where system users and beneficiaries can establish a court's jurisdiction in mind, and risk liability if they do not.

3. General partnership or joint venture

The criteria of when a group of joint actors will be a partnership differs from **9.63** jurisdiction to jurisdiction. While under the laws of some jurisdictions, the joint pursuit of a (joint) objective suffices to establish an unincorporated business,[37] the law of most common law jurisdictions requires the sharing of

---

36 See John C P Goldberg and Benjamin C Zipursky, Torts as Wrongs (2010) *Texas Law Review* 88.

37 For example, under German law, it has been held that certain developer associations in the open source domain qualify as unincorporated companies if, in addition to the joint purpose of further developing an open source software there is some, albeit purely factual, organisational structure. See Till Jaeger and Axel Metyger, *Open Source Software*, ¶193–200, Beck (4th ed. 2016).

profits. If a cooperation is deemed to be a partnership it will usually result in joint liability by its partners.[38]

9.64 For instance, while participation in a clearing and settlement distributed ledger system that relies on all nodes' mutual cooperation for identifying true transactions may be deemed a joint pursuit of a shared objective sufficient under some civil laws to establish a joint venture,[39] the fee and profit-sharing agreement will determine whether such cooperation is deemed a partnership under common law. As long as profit opportunities are held by a third-party distributed ledger sponsor/organiser and the nodes bear their own expenses and are rewarded on a predetermined basis as with Bitcoin, the risk that the system is a partnership at common law is very low indeed. However, if in a permissioned DLT system the network of validation nodes offers the services of the network to third-party users which pay 'the network' for these services, the system may be deemed to constitute a partnership, and in turn all validation node operators as partners may be liable vis-à-vis third parties.

9.65 The case of the DAO illustrates the potential magnitude of the risk. In the DAO, all investors jointly voted on investment proposals, all held jointly the assets acquired, no legal entity was positioned as a liability shield in between assets and investors, and all investors agreed that they were to share the profits generated by the assets. If the DAO's assets had generated losses rather than profits (for instance, people working in a factory held by the DAO were harmed in an accident), all investors could have been held to be partners and personally liable.

9.66 As a rule of thumb, the risk of liability associated with DLT participation based on partnership law is greater:

- the more a server owner benefits from participating in the ledger through profits (as long as there are others who benefit in the same way);
- the greater its influence on the server design, set-up or update, with 'creators' being more influential than 'simple users'; and

---

38 The extent of such joint liability may depend on specific circumstances. For example, under Russian law in a 'simple partnership' established for non-commercial purposes partners are jointly liable for contractual obligations pro rata to their contribution amount. Such limitation does not apply to non-contractual obligations or to any obligations of a 'simple partnership' established for commercial purposes. See Section 1047 of the Russian Civil Code.

39 An example could be provided by the Swiss giro network case Bundesgerichtsentscheid (BGE) 121 III 310, 314–15 where the Swiss Federal Court has taken the view that, for purposes of external liability, the network should not be regarded as a collection of bilateral contracts, but as a multilateral cooperative system similar to an unincorporated business organisation. On the common law perspective, see Dicey et al., *supra* note 19, at 64–71.

- the greater its influence on the decision to let others use or be excluded from using the distributed ledger. For example, the function of a validation node in a permissioned blockchain with a veto right against access or updates is more likely to lead to personal liability than the 'simple' mining function in Bitcoin.

4. Specific legislation

Regulators have suggested that DLT can pose a risk to fair competition and orderly markets.[40] For example, if DLT functions as a technological barrier that enables or facilitates monopolies, or if DLT participants refuse or impose stringent conditions on new members, additional liability may stem from competition/antitrust law.   **9.67**

This is of great importance since competition laws often impose antitrust liability on criteria that are different from contract or tort law. For instance, under European competition law, the definition of the responsible party may include the parent and subsidiary companies.[41]   **9.68**

While beyond the scope of this chapter, market participants involved in a distributed ledger system must keep this and other conduct-related legislation (such as data protection,[42] copyright laws, consumer protection laws, tax laws, AML/CFT, landlord-tenant laws[43]) in mind.   **9.69**

5. Fiduciary liability of core developers

Core developers of a DLT platform (group 1 in our hierarchy) play a critical role in the design and evolution of distributed networks. In permissioned   **9.70**

---

40   For example, Mary Starks, former Director of Competition at the FCA, highlights two competition-related issues in the context of DLT: access to permissioned platforms that form part of essential infrastructure (e.g., in clearing and settlement) and the dominance of early movers. See Mary Starks, Blockchain: Considering the Risks to Consumers and Competition, Speech at Authority for Consumers and Markets Conference Panel, Netherlands, available at: https://www.fca.org.uk/news/speeches/blockchain-considering-risks-consumers-and-competition.

41   See Arts 101, 102 and 106 of the Treaty on the Functioning of the European Union; see also W P Wils, The Undertaking as Subject of E.C. Competition Law and the Imputation of Infringements to Natural or Legal Persons (2000) 25 *Eur L Rev* at 99–116; and Pieter Van Cleynenbreugel, Single Entity Tests in US Antitrust and EU Competition Law (Working Paper, 21 June 2011), available at: https://ssrn.com/abstract=1889232.

42   See Matthias Berberich and Malgorzata Steiner, Blockchain Technology and the GDPR – How to Reconcile Privacy and Distributed Ledgers? (2016) 2 *European Data Protection Law Review* 422.

43   See Catherine Martin Christopher, *The Bridging Model: Exploring the Roles of Trust and Enforcement in Banking, Bitcoin, and the Blockchain* (2016) 17 *Nev L J* 139, 155, arguing access to an apartment governed by a blockchain may violate landlord-tenant laws if the blockchain inhibits the tenant's access following their default.

DLT systems with centralised governance, this fact does not raise serious implications – after all, liability channels in these cases are generally easier to establish. Yet, practice shows that the impact of a small group of 'masterminds' on the entire system may be pivotal even in permissionless databases.[44]

9.71 It has been suggested that this impact (as well as the overall structure of relationships between group 1 and the other groups in our hierarchy),[45] bears striking resemblance to the functionality of fiduciaries – service providers held to a higher standard of accountability to clients due to the clients' reliance on the service providers' skills and reputation.

9.72 There are many unknowns in the fiduciary equation in the context of permissionless distributed ledgers, such as the source of liability (contract, statute or case law), scope of fiduciary's duties, as well as entities entitled to fiduciary protections. Furthermore, there are possible negative implications stemming from characterising core developers as fiduciaries. For instance, developers may consider that they are not sufficiently compensated to be subject to fiduciary duties and the risk of additional liability and withdraw from further development of the platform.[46]

9.73 We acknowledge the underlying difficulties, but note the problem is not new, at least for the finance industry. In bond issues and other complex financial transactions, corporate trustees almost invariably seek to lower the scope of their duties and standards of liability, citing much the same reasons of insufficient compensation in comparison to the standard of performance requested from them. At some point, the law is bound to respond and clarify whether distributed ledgers do in fact give rise to fiduciary duties and liability. However, such response may take time and will have to be developed by each jurisdiction individually.

---

44 In 2013, the Bitcoin developers contacted miners to persuade them to switch to a certain version of the software following a hard fork resulting from the use of different versions of the Bitcoin protocol. This influence led to the creation of a single 'winning' ledger supported by the majority of miners. See Angela Walch, The Bitcoin Blockchain as Financial Market Infrastructure: A Consideration of Operational Risk (2015) 18 *NYU Journal of Legislation and Public Policy* 873. In 2016, following the DAO hack, Ethereum developers initiated a hard fork to reverse the theft, sacrificing the perceived 'immutability' of the entire distributed ledger – in doing so, they prepared explanatory notices and an advance poll among miners. Although the majority of miners migrated to the revised platform that created the hard fork, the dissenting operators retained the previous version of the software, thus splitting the Ethereum community. See Joon Ian Wong and Ian Kar, Everything you need to know about the Ethereum 'hard fork', *Quartz* (18 July 2016), available at: https://qz.com/730004/everything-you-need-to-know-about-the-ethereum-hard-fork/.

45 See Angela Walch, In Code(rs) We Trust: Software Developers as Fiduciaries in Public Blockchains (27 June 2018), available at: https://papers.ssrn.com/sol3/papers.cfm?abstract_id=3203198.

46 Ibid., at 18.

6. 'Liability cocoon' of software developers

End-users of DLT platforms developed by third parties may lack the pro- **9.74** gramming skills or resources necessary to verify the quality and design of computer code they use. In this case, it would seem logical to turn to the software developer with liability claims when programming defects or vulnerabilities expose customers to major losses. Nevertheless, customer-facing software agreements are routinely drafted with significant contractual limitations on liability of software developers (e.g., up to the amount of fees paid by the customer, regardless of the size of losses actually incurred by the latter). In other words, the current paradigm in software development can largely be defined in two words: *caveat emptor*. Surprisingly, the situation appears to be no different when the customer is a sophisticated commercial purchaser.[47] As a result, one generally observes in dismay a 'curious dearth of lawsuits by companies against security software ... vendors arising from a data security breach'.[48]

However entrenched current business and legal practices in software develop- **9.75** ment may seem, the situation may (have to) change in the context of the rollout of distributed ledgers on a commercial scale, at least in relation to certain public-facing platforms. We expect the wholesale liability waivers will be particularly difficult to retain in relation to DLT platforms developed by private parties for integration in major (sometimes nation-wide) infrastructure projects, such as DVP settlement platforms or central bank digital currencies. In many of these cases, the client of the software developer is a public entity, with enormous reputational risks (and the interests of the public at large) at stake in case the code does not function as expected. To offer the standard 'liability cocoon' to software developers of such DLT platforms would seem irresponsible.[49]

To demonstrate the deficiency of a wholesale *caveat emptor* approach in **9.76** software development, an analogy to the securities laws is illustrative. Non-sophisticated parties, such as individuals, are almost universally shielded from exposure to complex financial instruments, on the basis of a plausible excuse that only parties with sufficient resources and training can fully appreciate the underlying risks. In other words, not everyone is expected to be an expert in

---

47 See, e.g., Marian K. Reidy and Bartlomiej Hanus, It Is Just Unfair Using Trade Laws To Out Security Software Vulnerabilities (2017) 48 *Loyola University Chicago Law Journal* 1099, at 1111–14.
48 Ibid., at 1118–19.
49 Of course, establishing a higher liability standard in contract is not the solution. The responsible party must possess sufficient resources to compensate for the loss, or provide other satisfactory protections, such as insurance.

finance. But if this logic has any merit, and we certaintly believe it does, then it may be very difficult to accept that everyone is expected to be an expert in computer engineering. Yet, in contrast to the securities example, an outright prohibition for the masses to access distributed databases makes little sense, at least in the context of DLT forming the basis of key financial or other public infrastructure. Otherwise, what is the point in developing new infrastructure if it cannot be widely used? In any event, someone will have to accept responsibility – and we will be delighted to watch as this conundrum is resolved.

G. CONCLUSION

9.77 Risk does not vanish simply due to the use of a distributed ledger. Our analysis of the most important legal systems has revealed four general principles of liability:

9.78 First, the more the ledger is organised or based on a predetermined governance structure (most evident in permissioned ledgers), the greater the risk that participants, in particular those that are influential and 'control' the ledger, will be held liable for breach of contract or as partners of the 'ledger partnership'.

9.79 Second, cooperation in the context of sophisticated financial and business services requires organisation and, if the resource dealt with by the ledger is valuable, investors will demand control rights in return for their investment. Common sense and economic need will push for permissioned ledgers, so liability will be a major factor in designing DLT governance structures and arrangements. Large-scale economic use of the ledger will come with potential liability.

9.80 Third, permissionless ledgers are not the answer to the liability issue. Even in permissionless ledgers (for instance, Bitcoin), the liability risk is not zero, but rather highly case-specific. There is a strong differentiation of treatment of potential liabilties among countries and low levels of legal certainty, and thus higher legal costs and risk premiums, especially for transnational permissionless systems.

9.81 Fourth, some liability will arise from contract or liability statutes, some from special legislation, and some from tort or partnership law, but the net result of the joint/coordinated activity will most often be joint liability.

9.82 Firms will try to mitigate these risks with the choice of law and jurisdiction clauses, but this approach will be less effective with statutory, tortious and partnership liability, and with services offered to consumers (given the mandatory jurisdiction and applicable law typically associated with consumer transactions). Parties may choose the governing law to minimise liability, but liability risk may well harm, in particular, the development of cross-border ledger systems with many nodes.

Finally, liability will not be eliminated, but may instead be spread across the system, and financial intermediaries involved in a distributed ledger should arguably hold capital or acquire insurance for contingent liabilities stemming from DLT participation. Part of the thrill of blockchain to date has been its disregard of the law. With law in the picture, data are less attractively housed in distributed ledgers. Although this does not mean liability will exist in all cases, liability matters, and distributed ledgers may, in time, most often be legally structured (particularly in permissioned systems) as a joint venture where all servers are owned and operated – ironically – by one entity, or a small number of specified entities, rather than as a cooperation among multiple, and in some cases anonymous, entities. **9.83**

10

CYBERSECURITY AND BLOCKCHAIN

Patricia L. de Miranda

A. INTRODUCTION

10.01 As of December 2018, half the world's population uses the internet and 125 billion Internet of Things devices are expected by 2030.[1] Internet connectivity affects medical treatments, health care databases, power grids and other critical infrastructure and has been integrated into all aspects of private and public sectors for offering significant advantages: productivity, speed, cost-reduction and flexibility.[2] Such increased reliance on technology, communication, and interconnectivity has changed and expanded potential vulnerabilities and increased potential risk to operations. And to complicate matters further, online systems are inherently hard to secure.[3]

10.02 Despite the lack of standards, of the 30 reports issued by the World Economic Forum between January and October 2018, at least eight refer to some aspect

---

1 Infoblox, Assessing the DNS Cybersecurity Risk – 2018 Ponemon Report on DNS Cybersecurity and Protection, available at: https://info.infoblox.com/WW-PPC-FY19-2018-Ponemon-DNS-Risk-Cyber-Security-Report.html?ss=google&st=cyber%20threats&gclid=Cj0KCQiAxZPgBRCmARIsAOrTHSYYB XhRlr7Fg5tlYUOsIZGLe1HEEbS5l5GHstIIF2CD3207_6WLq9AaAuNTEALw_wcB.

2 I. Ghafir, J. Saleem, M. Hammoudehet al. J Supercomput (2018) 74: 4986, available at: https://doi.org/10.1007/s11227-018-2337-2 and *Global Cybersecurity Index & Cyberwellness Profiles*, 2015, available at: https://www.itu.int/pub/D-STR-SECU-2015.

3 Jonathan Bair, Steven M. Bellovin, Andrew Manley, Blake E. Reid and Adam Shostack, That Was Close! Reward Reporting of Cybersecurity 'Near Misses' (December 1, 2017). Forthcoming in *Colorado Technology Law Journal* 16.2; U of Colorado Law Legal Studies Research Paper No. 17-28, available at SSRN: https://ssrn.com/abstract=3081216 or http://dx.doi.org/10.2139/ssrn.3081216.

of digital technology.[4] Its annual Global Risks Report did not list cyber-attacks in 2016.[5] In 2018, cyber-attacks ranked third on the list of top ten risks for likelihood, behind extreme weather events and natural disasters, and sixth on the list of the top ten risks for impact.[6] In this context, as new technologies emerge, cybersecurity becomes increasingly important to keep data and information secure and businesses operating without disruption.

This chapter is structured as follows: Sections B–D explain what cybersecurity is, describe some of the most prominent cyber-attacks in the last few years and identify lessons learned from these cyber-attacks. Section E discusses whether and how blockchain could be used as a cybersecurity tool in the FinTech industry and beyond. Section F concludes. **10.03**

B. WHAT IS CYBERSECURITY?

Cybersecurity tends to defy precise definition and is easily confused with information security.[7] Agreeing on the terminology seems a work in progress naturally due to the constant advancement of technology and threats that inevitably accompany it. The National Institute of Standards and Technology (the NIST) offers a publicly available glossary comprising 6,753 terms on computer security.[8] The British Standards Institution also offers a publicly available glossary of cybersecurity terms and so does the European Union Agency for Network and Information Security, although much less comprehensively than the NIST.[9] **10.04**

---

4   See: https://www.weforum.org/reports/.

5   World Economic Forum, The Global Risks Report 2016 (14 January 2016), available at: https://www.weforum.org/reports/the-global-risks-report-2016.

6   Note that in 2017, cyber-attacks ranked sixth on the list of top ten risks in terms of likelihood, but did not appear at all on the list of the top 10 risks in terms of impact; see The Global Risks Report 2017, available at: https://www.weforum.org/reports/the-global-risks-report-2017.

7   Eric A. Fischer, Cybersecurity Issues and Challenges: In Brief (12 August 2016), available at: https://fas.org/sgp/crs/misc/R43831.pdf; and CISO Platform, Understanding Difference between Cyber Security & Information Security (22 July 2016), available at: http://www.cisoplatform.com/profiles/blogs/understanding-difference-between-cyber-security-information.

8   NIST: Computer Security Resource Center, Glossary, available at: https://csrc.nist.gov/Glossary. Nevertheless, in 2018, NIST was soliciting public comments to its Glossary, available at: https://csrc.nist.gov/publications/detail/nistir/7298/rev-3/draft.

9   British Standards Institution, Glossary of Cyber Security Terms, available at: https://www.bsigroup.com/en-GB/Cyber-Security/Cyber-security-for-SMEs/Glossary-of-cyber-security-terms/, and ENISA Overview of Cybersecurity and Related Terminology (September 2017), available at: https://www.enisa.europa.eu/publications/enisa-position-papers-and-opinions/enisa-overview-of-cybersecurity-and-related-terminology.

10.05 The core of cybersecurity seems to always involve safeguarding information and systems from harmful cyber threats.[10] There are plenty of definitions of 'cybersecurity', including:

(a) the ability to protect or defend the use of cyberspace from cyber-attacks;[11]

(b) protecting the confidentiality, integrity and availability of information systems (the so-called '*CIA triad*');[12]

(c) the practice of defending computers and servers, mobile devices, electronic systems, networks and data from malicious attacks. It is also known as information technology security or electronic information security. The term is broad-ranging and applies to everything from computer security to disaster recovery and end-user education;[13] and

(d) the practice of protecting systems, networks and programmes from digital attacks. These attacks are usually aimed at accessing, changing, or destroying sensitive information; extorting money from users; or interrupting normal business processes.[14]

C. CYBER-ATTACK CASE STUDIES

10.06 An online search for the biggest data breaches in history is overwhelming, including Facebook and Google, which are known to have the best cyber-security staff within their respective workforce.[15] By way of example:

(a) Marriott hotel: the personally identifiable information of 500 million people has been exposed since 2014, as publicly announced in November 2018.[16] Although publicised as a common data breach, the Marriott

---

10 McAfee, Cybersecurity in an Evolving Digital Landscape, available at: https://www.mcafee.com/enterprise/de-de/security-awareness/cybersecurity.html.

11 NIST, *supra* note 8.

12 Mike Gault, The CIA Secret to Cybersecurity That No One Seems to Get, *WIRED* (20 December 2015), available at: https://www.wired.com/2015/12/the-cia-secret-to-cybersecurity-that-no-one-seems-to-get/.

13 Kaspersky lab, *What is Cyber-Security*, available at: https://usa.kaspersky.com/resource-center/definitions/what-is-cyber-security.

14 CISCO, What is Cybersecurity?, available at: https://www.cisco.com/c/en/us/products/security/what-is-cybersecurity.html.

15 Mingis on Tech: Data breaches in a world of surveillance (12 October 2018), available at: https://www.youtube.com/watch?v=skGxxEAm3Vs.

16 Taylor Terlford and Craig Timberg, Marriott Discloses Massive Data Breach Affecting up to 500 Million Guests, *Washington Post* (30 November 2018), available at: https://www.washingtonpost.com/business/2018/11/30/marriott-discloses-massive-data-breach-impacting-million-guests/.

hack has been traced back to a Chinese intelligence-gathering effort combined with the 2014 hacks of the United States Office of Personnel Management and Anthem health insurance.[17]

(b)   Facebook: 50 million accounts were exposed in 2018.[18]

(c)   Google: more than 490,000 users' information was exposed in 2018.[19]

(d)   Equifax: data of 143 million people was exposed in 2017.[20]

(e)   Ashley Madison: 32 million users were affected in 2015.[21]

(f)   Sony Entertainment: confidential information including employees' salaries, addresses, and social security numbers was exposed in 2014.[22]

(g)   Yahoo: all of its three billion users were exposed in 2013 and 2014.[23]

Cyber-attacks disrupt business operations, cause legal and compliance prob- **10.07**
lems and costs to remediate the attack, and impact the organisation's reputation.[24] The ransomware attack against Bristol airport in September 2018
exemplifies business disruption as hackers took over control of display screens

---

17   David Sanger et al., Marriott Data Breach Is Traced to Chinese Hackers as U.S. Readies Crackdown on Beijing, *The New York Times* (11 December 2018), available at: https://www.nytimes.com/2018/12/11/us/politics/trump-china-trade.html; and Fareed Zakaria, On GPS: What's Behind the Marriott Hack?, CNN (15 December 2018), available at: https://www.cnn.com/videos/tv/2018/12/15/exp-gps-1216-sanger-on-marriott-hack.cnn.

18   Mike Isaac and Sheera Frenkel, Facebook Security Breach Exposes Accounts of 50 Million Users, *The New York Times* (28 September 2018), available at: https://www.nytimes.com/2018/09/28/technology/facebook-hack-data-breach.html; and Thomas Brewster, How Facebook Was Hacked and Why It's a Disaster for Internet Security, *Forbes* (29 September 2018), available at: https://www.forbes.com/sites/thomasbrewster/2018/09/29/how-facebook-was-hacked-and-why-its-a-disaster-for-internet-security/#458910392033.

19   Josh Constine, Google+ to Shut Down After Coverup of Data-exposing Bug (8 October 2018), available at: https://techcrunch.com/2018/10/08/google-plus-hack/; and Thomas Brewster, Google's Doors Hacked Wide Open By Own Employee, *Forbes* (3 September 2018), available at: https://www.forbes.com/sites/thomasbrewster/2018/09/03/googles-doors-hacked-wide-open-by-own-employee/#2bc5fbae3c7a.

20   Federal Trade Commission, The Equifax Data Breach, available at https://www.ftc.gov/equifax-data-breach.

21   Kim Zetter, Hackers Finally Post Stolen Ashley Madison Data, *WIRED* (18 August 2015), available at: https://www.wired.com/2015/08/happened-hackers-posted-stolen-ashley-madison-data/.

22   Aly Weisman, A Timeline of the Crazy Events in the Sony Hacking Scandal, *Business Insider* (9 December 2014), available at: https://www.businessinsider.com/sony-cyber-hack-timeline-2014-12; and Andrea Peterson, The Sony Pictures Hack, Explained, *The Washington Post* (18 December 2014), available at: https://www.washingtonpost.com/news/the-switch/wp/2014/12/18/the-sony-pictures-hack-explained/?noredirect=on&utm_term=.a49cab0ba4b3.

23   Nicole Perlroth, All 3 Billion Yahoo Accounts Were Affected by 2013 Attack, *The New York Times* (3 October 2017), available at: https://www.nytimes.com/2017/10/03/technology/yahoo-hack-3-billion-users.html.

24   The WannaCry case study in this chapter elaborates on the business disruption to hospitals.

around the airport making them unusable.[25] Airport staff had to resort to whiteboards and paper posters to constantly update flight information.[26]

10.08   Cyber-attacks can also have serious physical impact. For example, in 2008, a Turkish oil pipeline exploded without warning due to increased pressure.[27] Hackers gained access to the pipeline's control network by exploiting a vulnerability in the organisation's security camera software.[28] Damage to the pipeline caused thousands of barrels of oil to spill close to a water aquifer.[29] In 2010, the Stuxnet virus destroyed 1,000 centrifuges in an Iranian nuclear facility; it is reported that the US and Israel are responsible for the attack.[30]

10.09   Cyberwarfare is the most sophisticated type of cyber-attack, requires greater resources, and potentially has a much greater impact on the general public, the public and private sectors, and the environment than other types of cyber-attacks. The term refers to the most aggressive form of cyber-attack, usually carried out by a nation state, aimed at damaging another nation's computers or information networks, disrupting communities or countries and/or destroying critical infrastructure or industrial facilities, making it probably the greatest challenge to national security.[31] Its potential for collateral damage can affect any industry: the 2017 NotPetya attack illustrates the impact on the financial industry while the Maersk case illustrates the impact on the shipping industry with ripple effect to other industries.

---

25   Peter Newman, Airport Hack Shows a Need for Revamped Cybersecurity, *Business Insider* (18 September 2018), available at: https://www.businessinsider.com/bristol-airport-ransomware-attack-cybersecurity-2018-9.

26   Liviu Arsene, UK Airport Won't Negotiate With Ransomware Attackers; Falls Back to Whiteboards (17 September 2018), available at: https://securityboulevard.com/2018/09/uk-airport-wont-negotiate-with-ransomware-attackers-falls-back-to-whiteboards/; and Milena Dimitrova, Bristol Airport Hit by Ransomware, Officials Use Whiteboards to Announce Flights (17 September 2018), available at: https://securityboulevard.com/2018/09/bristol-airport-hit-by-ransomware-officials-use-whiteboards-to-announce-flights/.

27   Ariel Bogle, A Cyber Attack May Have Caused a Turkish Oil Pipeline to Catch Fire in 2008 (11 December 2014), available at: http://www.slate.com/blogs/future_tense/2014/12/11/bloomberg_reports_a_cyber_attack_may_have_made_a_turkish_oil_pipeline_catch.html; and Jordan Robertson and Michael Riley, Mysterious '08 Turkey Pipeline Blast Opened New Cyberwar, *Bloomberg* (10 December 2014), available at: https://www.bloomberg.com/news/articles/2014-12-10/mysterious-08-turkey-pipeline-blast-opened-new-cyberwar.

28   Ibid.

29   Ibid.

30   Nicole Perlroth and Quentin Hardy, Bank Hacking Was the Work of Iranians, Officials Say, *The New York Times* (8 January 2013), available at: https://www.nytimes.com/2013/01/09/technology/online-banking-attacks-were-work-of-iran-us-officials-say.html; and Kim Zetter, An Unprecedented Look at Stuxnet, the World's First Digital Weapon, *WIRED* (3 November 2014), available at: https://www.wired.com/2014/11/countdown-to-zero-day-stuxnet/.

31   Financial Times Lexicon, Definition of Cyberwarfare, available at: http://lexicon.ft.com/Term?term=cyberwarfare.

Nation states have emerged as the actors able to pull together the resources **10.10**
needed to break into sophisticated cybersecurity systems at least since 2007.[32]
This includes any country with capacity to carry out such cyber-attacks:
China,[33] France,[34] Israel,[35] Iran,[36] North Korea,[37] Russia,[38] the UK,[39] and the
US.[40]

1. The Ukraine cases: 2015 and 2017

(a) The 2015 power grid attack

On 23 December 2015, Ukraine experienced the first confirmed hack that **10.11**
shut down a power grid.[41] Hackers took control and shut down substations
and power distribution centres and disabled backup power supplies to two of
the three distribution centres, leaving more than 230,000 Ukrainians without
power.[42] The loss of power lasted up to six hours, but Ukraine's power control
centres were still not fully operating more than two months after the attack
and breakers were manually controlled.[43] The potential cyber threat to critical
infrastructure became indisputable.[44]

The attack was planned over many months by spear-phishing staff and system **10.12**
administrators working for companies distributing energy throughout
Ukraine.[45] Unsolicited emails were sent with a malicious Word document

---

32 Robert Windrem, Timeline: Ten Years of Russian Cyber Attacks on Other Nations, *NBC News* (18
    December 2016), available at: https://www.nbcnews.com/storyline/hacking-in-america/timeline-ten-years-
    russian-cyber-attacks-other-nations-n697111.
33 The Diplomat and Nicholas Lyall, China's Cyber Militias, *The Diplomat* (1 March 2018), available at:
    https://thediplomat.com/2018/03/chinas-cyber-militias/.
34 Pavel Polityuk and Alessandra Prentice, Ukrainian Banks, Electricity Firm Hit by Fresh Cyber Attack,
    Reuters (27 June 2017), available at: https://www.reuters.com/article/us-ukraine-cyber-attacks/ukrainian-
    banks-electricity-firm-hit-by-fresh-cyber-attack-idUSKBN19I1IJ.
35 Ibid.
36 Accenture, Cyber Threatscape Report 2018, Midyear Cybersecurity Risk Review (3 August 2018), available
    at: https://www.accenture.com/t20180803T064557Z__w__/us-en/_acnmedia/PDF-83/Accenture-Cyber-
    Threatscape-Report-2018.pdf.
37 David E. Sanger, David D. Kirkpatrick and Nicole Perlrot, The World Once Laughed at North Korean
    Cyberpower. No More, *The New York Times* (15 October 2017), available at: https://www.nytimes.com/
    2017/10/15/world/asia/north-korea-hacking-cyber-sony.html
38 Adrian Chen, The Agency, *The New York Times* (2 June 2015), available at: https://www.nytimes.com/2015/
    06/07/magazine/the-agency.html.
39 Polityuk and Prentice, *supra* note 34.
40 Ibid.
41 Kim Zetter, Inside the Cunning, Unprecedented Hack of Ukraine's Power Grid, *WIRED* (3 March 2016),
    available at: https://www.wired.com/2016/03/inside-cunning-unprecedented-hack-ukraines-power-grid/.
42 Ibid.
43 Ibid.
44 How Israel Rules the World of Cyber Security, *VICE on HBO* (14 March 2018), available at: https://
    www.youtube.com/watch?v=ca-C3voZwpM.
45 Zetter, *supra* note 41.

attached; once opened, the email asked the recipient to enable macros for the document which allowed hackers to access their systems by downloading a programme called BlackEnergy3.[46] This opened a backdoor to the hackers.

10.13   Hackers still had to access Ukraine's Supervisory Control and Data Acqui-sition network that controlled the power grid (the SCADA Network).[47] They studied the systems for months and, despite firewalls, successfully hijacked credentials to access the SCADA Network thanks to the lack of two-factor authentication, gaining access to systems that controlled the breakers.[48] Hackers wrote malicious firmware to replace the legitimate firmware at more than 12 substations, rendering them inoperable and unrecoverable.[49]

10.14   Hackers also accounted for contingencies and before the attack began, flooded customer call centres with fake calls to prevent customers from calling in to report the outage.[50] Lastly, the hackers used another malware called KillDisk to wipe and overwrite files from operator stations to render them inoperable by stopping infected computers from rebooting.[51]

(b)   The 2017 NotPetya attack

10.15   On 27 June 2017, cyber-attackers gained access to the source code of a widely used accountancy and bookkeeping package called M.E.Doc used by approxi-mately 80 per cent of all businesses in Ukraine at the time.[52] Around 90 per cent of Oschadbank's thousands of computers were locked in about 45 seconds, showing NotPetya's 'repairing disk' messages and ransom screens; a portion of one major Ukrainian transit hub was fully infected in 16 seconds.[53] Hospitals, six power companies, two airports, more than 22 Ukrainian banks,

---

46   Ibid. Exploiting the macros feature is an old-school method from the 1990s that attackers have recently revived in multiple attacks.

47   Ibid.

48   Ibid.

49   Ibid.

50   Ibid.

51   Ibid.

52   Mathew J. Schwartz, Ukraine Power Supplier Hit by WannaCry Lookalike, *Data Breach Today* (30 June 2017), available at: https://www.databreachtoday.com/ukraine-power-supplier-hit-by-wannacry-lookalike-a-10071. Four separate malware attacks targeting the country were identified, including NotPetya. See Mathew J. Schwartz, NotPetya Patient Zero: Ukrainian Accounting Software Vendor, *Bank Info Security* (4 July 2017), available at: https://www.bankinfosecurity.com/notpetya-patient-zero-ukrainian-accounting-software-vendor-a-10080

53   Andy Greenberg, The Untold Story of NotPetya, The Most Devastating Cyberattack in History, *WIRED* (22 August 2018), available at: https://www.wired.com/story/notpetya-cyberattack-ukraine-russia-code-crashed-the-world/.

ATMs and card payment systems, and practically every federal agency were all affected and inoperable.[54] It was a 'massive, coordinated cyber invasion'.[55]

NotPetya combines two hacker exploits: EternalBlue and Mimikatz. Eternal-   **10.16**
Blue is a software vulnerability in Microsoft's Windows operating system, specifically the Windows protocol M.E.Doc; it gives hackers free access to remotely run their own code on any unpatched machine.[56] This exploit was created by the US National Security Agency (the NSA), but was publicly leaked in April 2017 by a hacker group called 'Shadow Brokers'.[57] Microsoft announced patches[58] to fix EternalBlue on 12 March 2017, including to long-unsupported Windows XP and Windows Server 2003 operating systems, but many did not bother to patch their machines.[59]

Mimikatz was created as a proof of concept by a French security researcher in   **10.17**
2011 to exploit Windows users' passwords lingering on computers' memories then found by Mimikatz and used to access machines unlocked by those passwords.[60] Mimikatz allowed hackers to access passwords of computers that had been patched to fix EternalBlue's vulnerability and still spread NotPetya to patched computers.[61]

Reports show that Ukraine was not the only country affected by the attack.   **10.18**
The infected users were also in Germany, Poland, Serbia, Greece, Romania, Czech Republic and Russia.[62] Moreover, the attack also affected private sector industries such as Merck, TNT Express, and Saint-Gobain.[63] The collateral damage caused by NotPetya to the shipping industry is the subject of the next case study.

---

54   Ibid.

55   Ibid.

56   Ibid. See also Lily Hay Newman, The Leaked NSA Spy Tool That Hacked the World, *WIRED* (7 March 2018), available at: https://www.wired.com/story/eternalblue-leaked-nsa-spy-tool-hacked-world/; and A Hacker Explains Why the Internet Is Scarier Than You Think/Inc. (November 2018), available at: https://www.youtube.com/watch?v=lBSa5Acj7Q0.

57   Ibid., and Greenberg, *supra* note 53.

58   Patches are changes to the code of a software to update, fix security vulnerabilities and/or bugs, or improve the usability or performance of the software.

59   Microsoft, Customer Guidance for WannaCrypt Attacks (12 May 2017), available at: https://blogs.technet.microsoft.com/msrc/2017/05/12/customer-guidance-for-wannacrypt-attacks/

60   Greenberg, *supra* note 53.

61   Ibid.

62   Mathew J. Schwartz, Ukraine Power Supplier Hit by WannaCry Lookalike, *Data Breach Today* (30 June 2017), available at: https://www.databreachtoday.com/ukraine-power-supplier-hit-by-wannacry-lookalike-a-10071.

63   Greenberg, *supra* note 53. Merck had temporarily lost its ability to manufacture some medications and estimated the cost caused by NotPetya to be USD 870 million; TNT Express was crippled in the attack and required months to recover some data; it estimated the cost to have been USD 400 million, while French construction giant, Saint-Gobain, is estimated to have lost around the same amount. Ibid.

2. The Maersk case: June 2017

10.19 While Ukraine was frantically dealing with NotPetya, a finance executive for Maersk's Ukraine operation in Odessa asked IT administrators to install the accounting software M.E.Doc on one computer; unbeknownst to them, NotPetya entered and paralysed Maersk[64] in June 2017.[65] NotPetya infected Maersk's computer network and irreversibly encrypted the computers' master boot records, rendering the network useless.[66] Trucks could not get in or out of ports because gates operated by Maersk were inoperable; goods could not be shipped anywhere; trucks lined up along the roads causing major traffic backup at ports' gates; and the delivery of perishable goods and parts of supply chains were delayed.[67]

10.20 Maersk then established a recovery centre in the UK and outsourced its management to Deloitte. As it rebuilt its network from backups dating from between three and seven days before the attack, Maersk faced the challenge of overcoming NotPetya's simultaneous wipe of all its domain controllers. Out of pure luck, thanks to a blackout in Ghana that caused Maersk's computers in its local office to be offline during the NotPetya attack, Maersk was able to find one domain controller of its network that survived untouched by NotPetya. It took two weeks after the initial attack for Maersk to be able to reissue computers to its employees, and close to two months to fully rebuild Maersk's software setup.[68] Maersk did not have multifactor authentication, nor had it upgraded to Windows 10.[69] Maersk seemingly was still running Windows 2000 which was even no longer supported by Microsoft. The company estimated the cost of the cyber-attack to have been between USD 250 million and USD 300 million.[70]

---

64 Maersk is the world's largest container shipping company, operating in 130 countries, responsible for 76 ports worldwide, with nearly 800 seafaring vessels with container ships carrying millions of cargo worth millions of dollars, representing close to a fifth of the world's entire shipping capacity, and employing roughly 79,900 people. See Maersk: About Maersk, available at: https://www.maersk.com/about; see also Greenberg, *supra* note 53.

65 Greenberg, *supra* note 53.

66 Ibid.

67 Ibid.

68 *Ibid.* See also Catalin Cimpanu: Maersk Reinstalled 45,000 PCs and 4,000 Servers to Recover From NotPetya Attack, *Bleeping Computer* (25 January 2018), available at: https://www.bleepingcomputer.com/news/security/maersk-reinstalled-45-000-pcs-and-4-000-servers-to-recover-from-notpetya-attack/.

69 Greenberg, *supra* note 53.

70 Ibid.

3. WannaCry: May 2017

North Korea used EternalBlue to breed the WannaCry ransomware attacks in May 2017.[71] WannaCry affected more than 200,000 computers in more than 150 countries within 24 hours.[72] It impacted railways, banks and mobile phone operators in Russia; train stations in Germany; telecommunications companies in Spain; car manufacturers in France; universities in China; cinemas in South Korea; hospitals in Indonesia, Ireland and the UK; state police in India; FedEx in the US; and SMEs in Australia and New Zealand.[73] WannaCry highjacked the computers of the UK's National Health System (NHS) and demanded USD 300 worth of Bitcoin as ransom for every computer affected.[74] Health care is a popular target of ransomware for two reasons: one, it has an obviously urgent need to restore service and, therefore, is more likely to pay criminals to reinstate their systems, and, two, it tends to be very slow to address vulnerabilities.[75] For example, the NHS had to turn patients away, cancel non-urgent services and revert to backup procedures.[76] WannaCry's estimated cost is between USD 4 billion and USD 8 billion.[77]

10.21

WannaCry was accidentally stopped by a 22-year-old in the UK within 24 hours of its first attack. Wanting to help, he accidentally triggered a 'kill switch' that helped in stopping the WannaCry ransomware attack from spreading further.[78]

10.22

---

71 Newman, *supra* note 56 and Lily Hay Newman, The Ransomware Meltdown Experts Warned about is Here, *WIRED* (12 May 2017), available at: https://www.wired.com/2017/05/ransomware-meltdown-experts-warned/.

72 *BBC News*, Cyber-attack: Europol says it was Unprecedented in Scale (13 May 2017), available at: https://www.bbc.com/news/world-europe-39907965; and Elizabeth Dwoskin and Karla Adam, More Than 150 Countries Affected by Massive Cyberattack, Europol says, *The Washington Post* (14 May 2017), available at: https://www.washingtonpost.com/business/economy/more-than-150-countries-affected-by-massive-cyberattack-europol-says/2017/05/14/5091465e-3899-11e7-9e48-c4f199710b69_story.html?utm_term=.3d0296b70fce.

73 Dwoskin and Adam, ibid.

74 Newman, *supra* note 71.

75 Ibid.

76 Ibid.

77 Greenberg, *supra* note 53.

78 For a more detailed explanation of how the WannaCry attack was stopped, see, e.g., Thomas Tamblyn, This is how a 22-Year-Old Managed so Stop the WannaCry Ransomware from Spreading, *Huffington Post*, 15 May 2017, available at: https://www.huffingtonpost.co.uk/entry/this-is-how-a-22-year-old-managed-to-stop-the-wannacry-ransomware-from-spreading_uk_59197688e4b00f308cf66bf6; see also David Kennedy, *A Hacker Explains Why the Internet Is Scarier Than You Think/Inc.* (7 November 2018), available at: https://www.youtube.com/watch?v=lBSa5Acj7Q0.

D. LESSONS LEARNED

10.23 Human error and/or naiveté, as well as the lack of the two-factor authentication[79] were sufficient to expose critical infrastructure to cyber risk in the 2015 power grid attack in Ukraine. The lack of collaboration and reporting from those who first found EternalBlue contributed to the 2017 NotPetya and WannaCry attacks. The need for continuous and timely updates and patches is a common thread in all three of the cyber-attack case studies. And the importance to plan, prepare and have an incident response plan rises especially from the Maersk case. Arguably, all of them were preventable by adopting training and awareness, collaborating practices by exchanging information on cyber-attacks with other organisations or authorities when they occurred, and by timely updates to software and operational systems. They have been managed by adopting an incident response plan. Although there are many more lessons to learn, the sections that follow will briefly focus on the main ones identified in the three above-described cyber-attacks.

10.24 *The human factor.* Humans are highly vulnerable to social engineering, continue to be the largest attack surface[80] and the number one target for cyber-attacks by opening an email, a document, or simply by going to a website.[81] In 2018, 17 per cent of 2,216 data breaches in 65 countries were caused by human error.[82] In 2017, after sending 40 million simulated phishing emails to about 1,000 organisations, 91 per cent of the phishing emails were successful in tricking people into clicking on them and, thus, revealing how easy it is to breach an organisation's cybersecurity.[83] All it takes is for one person to enable a cyber-attack and cause the downfall of an entire company.[84] The best defence against a cyber-attack is investing in the human capacity to detect it before it happens.

10.25 Training and education are key.[85] The choice of a learning instrument (i.e., computer-based training and/or instructor-led training) is critical to the success of the learning process; each will have its own challenges to consider –

---

79 The two-factor authentication is the method to confirm a user's identity after successfully presenting two pieces of evidence to an authentication mechanism – e.g., a fingerprint and a password.

80 Attack surface of a software environment is the sum of the different points where an unauthorised user can try to enter data into or extract data from an environment.

81 Ghafir et al., *supra* note 3; and Kennedy, *supra* note 78.

82 Verizon, 2018 Data Breach Investigations Report, available at: https://enterprise.verizon.com/resources/reports/DBIR_2018_Report_execsummary.pdf, at 2 and 3.

83 Guest contributor, 91% of Cyber Attacks Start With A Phishing Email: Here's How To Protect Against Phishing, *Digital Guardian* (26 July 2017), available at: https://digitalguardian.com/blog/91-percent-cyber-attacks-start-phishing-email-heres-how-protect-against-phishing.

84 Kennedy, *supra* note 78.

85 Ibid.

for example, monitoring employee attendance or completion, employee retention of the information, and cost. Research found that after attending a business training session, employees, in general, tend to lose 50 per cent of the information within one hour, 70 per cent of the information is forgotten within 24 hours and 90 per cent within one week.[86] Certain companies specialise in offering such training to other companies, while some companies choose to run their own programmes.[87] Other organisations have customised training, such as IBM, which launched a 'training on wheels' programme in 2018 to run incident response drills with clients, provide on-demand cybersecurity support, and build cybersecurity awareness and skills with professionals, students and consumers.[88]

Every individual in an organisation must be aware of his/her duty to protect **10.26** corporate assets, data and information.[89] Top executives must be involved in cybersecurity to make budget decisions that impact the organisation's investment in cybersecurity.[90] A cybersecurity framework that incorporates and operationalises policies, procedures and standards must be developed and implemented by all employees, with consequences for non-compliance.[91]

Technical factors. The two-factor authentication should be used by all users **10.27** accessing any online account to bolster security and prevent account highjacking even if that does not stop breaches on the server side.[92] Such an authentication mechanism can limit the potential damage if credentials are lost or stolen.[93] The two-factor authentication will make it harder for a malicious actor, and also harder for a virus or malware to spread.

---

86 Ghafir et al., *supra* note 3; and Art Kohn, Brain Science: the Forgetting Curve – the Dirty Secret of Corporate Training, *Learning Solutions* (13 March 2014), available at: https://www.learningsolutionsmag.com/articles/1379/brain-science-the-forgetting-curvethe-dirty-secret-of-corporate-training.

87 *IBM News Room*, IBM Rolls Out Industry's First Cybersecurity Operations Center on Wheels, available at: https://newsroom.ibm.com/2018-10-15-IBM-Rolls-Out-Industrys-First-Cybersecurity-Operations-Center-on-Wheels. Some of the organisations offering cybersecurity training services include SANS Institute, Global Learning Systems scenario-based system, InfoSec Institute, AppSec Consulting, HITECH, NIST, NCSA (the National Cyber Security Alliance), FTC (the Federal Trade Commission), and SCIPP International.

88 Ibid.

89 Art Ehuan and Scott Harrison, Nation-State Cyber Threats: Corporations Must Be Proactive and Prepared, *ABF Journal*, November/December 2015, available at: http://www.abfjournal.com/%3Fpost_type%3D articles%26p%3D41656.

90 Orion Hindawi and Lou Modano, Bridging the Accountability Gap: Why We Need to Adopt a Culture of Responsibility (1 April 2016), available at: http://business.nasdaq.com/marketinsite/2016/Bridging-the-Accountability-Gap-Why-We-Need-to-Adopt-a-Culture-of-Responsibility.html.

91 Ehuan and Harrison, *supra* note 89.

92 Mingis on Tech, *supra* note 15.

93 Verizon, *supra* note 82.

10.28 Regular and timely updates and patches are not just good practice in keeping networks secure, but the lack of doing so causes a critical vulnerability that certainly opens organisations to a cyber-attack. The case studies in Section C above illustrate the damage caused by not timely updating and patching operating systems. In the case of EternalBlue, organisations were still being hit a year after WannaCry simply because they had not patched their systems.[94] Complacency, neglect, fear of updates and scheduling maintenance are other reasons why organisations may fail to regularly and timely update/ patch their systems.[95] Such situations can also result from third-party vendors outsourced to carry out technology responsibilities on behalf of an organisation; assessing third-party vendors' cybersecurity practices becomes a must to protect an organisation.[96]

10.29 *The need for collaboration.* NSA's secrecy of the EternalBlue vulnerability was highly criticised and exemplifies the consequences of lack of collaboration.[97] The Council on Foreign Relations has called for more international collaboration and exchange of information in cybersecurity to minimise politicisation and cyber risk.[98] The need for cooperation among nation states to mitigate cyber-threats on critical infrastructure, electronic espionage, bulk data interception, and offensive operations intended to project power by the application of force in and through cyberspace is even considered urgent.[99]

10. 30 *Cyber-risk management.* Maersk was lucky to have had a power outage in Ghana preserve one domain controller of its network free from NotPetya. But counting on luck is far from being close to any cybersecurity standard. Managing the inherent cyber risks in cyberspace is an on-going process to all organisations operating online. The never-ending technological advances make cyber threats evolve at a similarly rapid pace. Cyber-risk management is therefore crucial for the operation of any organisation; it aims at mitigating the impact of cyber-attacks by identifying the risks and adopting proper (i) pre-emptive measures to protect the IT infrastructure essential for conducting business with minimal or no interruption, and (ii) remedies and appropriate responses in case of a cyber-attack.

---

94 Newman, *supra* note 74.
95 Michael Trachtenberg: Why are we so bad at Cybersecurity? It's Mostly Neglect, *Forbes* (31 May 2018), available at: https://www.forbes.com/sites/forbestechcouncil/2018/05/31/why-are-we-so-bad-at-cyber security-its-mostly-neglect/#7bc3f51965af.
96 *Ibid.*
97 Newman, *supra* note 56.
98 Elena Chernenko, Increasing International Cooperation in Cybersecurity and Adapting Cyber Norms, *Council on Foreign Relations* (23 February 2018), available at: https://www.cfr.org/report/increasing-international-cooperation-cybersecurity-and-adapting-cyber-norms.
99 Ibid.

Cybersecurity requires planning, preparation and an incident response plan for **10.31** when a cyber-attack occurs. A robust incident response plan and process include prevention, planning, preparation, detection, analysis, containment, communication, eradication, recovery and post-event analysis. An organisation's capacity to detect and contain a cyber-attack can be the defining line of the organisation's survival and financial standing. Yahoo suffered a USD 350 million loss after the hack in 2014 in its merger with Verizon.[100]

The more organisations adapt to new technologies and approaches, the more **10.32** resilient their cybersecurity and cyber-risk management may be and, thus, the less the impact in case of cyber-attacks. Two well-known frameworks relied upon by organisations worldwide to develop their own cyber-risk management strategies are the ISO/IEC 27000 family[101] and NIST's cybersecurity framework.[102] These frameworks are voluntary road maps with best practices, common language, guidelines, principles, requirements and standards that can help organisations create and/or improve their own custom-made strategies to identify, assess, and manage cybersecurity.[103] NIST's cybersecurity framework, for example, is a risk-based approach to managing cybersecurity risk to critical infrastructure adaptable to any other industry based on three parts: (a) a framework core with five functions (i.e., identify, protect, detect, respond and recover); (b) four framework implementation tiers to characterize how organisations implement their cybersecurity practices (i.e., partial, risk informed, repeatable, to adaptive which includes the highest tier with adaptable cybersecurity practices to respond timely and effectively to evolving threats); and

---

100 Vindu Goel, Verizon will Pay $350 Million Less for Yahoo, *The New York Times* (21 February 2017), available at: https://www.nytimes.com/2017/02/21/technology/verizon-will-pay-350-million-less-for-yahoo.html.

101 ISO/IEC 27000 family – Information Security Management Systems, available at: https://www.iso.org/isoiec-27001-information-security.html.

102 NIST: Framework for Improving Critical Infrastructure Cybersecurity (16 April 2018), available at: https://www.nist.gov/cyberframework. Other frameworks exist, of course, but for purpose of this chapter, only the two most well-known are referred to. Other frameworks include:

    (a) CIS Top 20, available at: https://www.rapid7.com/solutions/compliance/critical-controls/;

    (b) NIST SP 800-53, available at: https://nvd.nist.gov/800-53;

    (c) The United States Federal Financial Institutions Examination Council, Cybersecurity Assessment Tool (specific to financial institutions), available at: https://www.ffiec.gov/cyberassessmenttool.htm;

    (d) Cloud Controls Matrix (CCM), available at: https://cloudsecurityalliance.org/working-groups/cloud-controls-matrix/#_overview;

    (e) NYDFS 23 NYCRR 500, available at: https://www.dfs.ny.gov/legal/regulations/adoptions/dfsrf500txt.pdf;

    (f) Security Standards Council, Payment Card Industry (PCI), available at: https://www.pci securitystandards.org/; and the United States Health Insurance Portability and Accountability Act of 1996 (HIPPA), HIPAA Security Rule, available at https://www.hhs.gov/hipaa/for-professionals/security/index.html.

103 NIST, *supra* note 1092.

(c) framework profiles to help businesses assess their cyber-risk management approach, as well as gaps and priorities, and what they want to achieve.[104]

10.33 Cybersecurity also requires a good governance structure with well-defined roles and authority for leadership in the organisation to assign the proper importance and priority, and to allocate sufficient resources – both budgetary and human – to cybersecurity. Leadership needs to foster a strong cyber-security culture that empowers every employee in an organisation to properly handle cyber-threats in a timely manner, in a way that the human error in cybersecurity can be highly mitigated. Such structure should also include a data governance structure, especially in light of the GDPR which has certainly raised privacy and data protection needs to a higher standard.

10.34 Finally, no organisation should overlook its physical security, including personnel and facilities. For example, the Stuxnet virus (mentioned in 10.08 above) illustrates how the breach of physical security can enable a cyber threat to enter.[105] The human factor is not limited to the cyberspace, however. As social engineering gains territory in cyber-attacks, physical security becomes just as important as any other security. However, both physical and cyber-security teams must communicate and coordinate efforts to avoid undermining cybersecurity efforts.

E. BLOCKCHAIN AS A CYBERSECURITY TOOL OR BLOCKCHAIN AS A RISK?

10.35 Despite numerous use cases for blockchain, it is somewhat surprising that one does not see many cybersecurity use cases. It is still unclear whether cyber-security can benefit from blockchain. Blockchain is subject to the same cybersecurity risks from human error, social engineering, unintended sharing of private keys, malware and other exploits.[106] Users are hard to control and can negatively contribute to the risk; blockchain does not address the security of users or the applications that connect to its network.[107] Authentication and authorisation controls, together with encryption, are needed in a blockchain

---

104 Ibid.
105 See Natgeotv, The Future of Cyberwarfare | Origins: The Journey of Humankind (6 April 2017), available at: https://www.youtube.com/watch?v=L78r7YD-kNw.
106 McAfee: Blockchain Threat Report, June 2018), available at: https://www.mcafee.com/enterprise/en-us/ assets/reports/rp-blockchain-security-risks.pdf.
107 Ibid.

even if its public/permissionless nature conflicts with such controls.[108] Identifying the risks by comparing what blockchain offers with the safeguards offered by the current and physical systems is one approach, e.g., monetary policies and cryptocurrencies, physical and digital archival practices.

On the other hand, however, blockchain may be able to contribute to **10.36** cybersecurity by monitoring and analysing network traffic against cyber-attacks to minimise breach detection gaps, i.e., the delay between when a breach occurs and when the organisation detects the breach, which can be before or after the breach has caused damage.[109] Detecting breaches in a timely manner allows more time to respond to a breach that has not yet caused damage.[110] If a breach can be quickly detected, it is possible to reduce or even prevent the impact of a cyber-attack from occurring. A permissioned 'blockchain-enabled federated cloud computing framework' could continuously monitor for deviations in behaviour on the network, but would need to reduce voting response time to reach consensus to an acceptable time frame to mitigate the risk of rendering the exercise useless.[111]

Another potential for blockchain as a cybersecurity tool is to leverage it as a **10.37** blockchain-based identity management system to enhance the security of online identification. It would also facilitate the detection of unauthorised access, detection of rogue devices, and improve tracking and reporting of unauthorised access or data modification.[112]

Some argue that blockchain may cause more problems than it proposes to **10.38** solve.[113] While blockchain offers potential to improve efficiency of keys and certificate distribution, its immutability requires negotiations with all nodes to reach consensus to resolve disputes and correct the ledger, potentially being too rigid in case a transaction needs to be reversed.[114]

Others argue that blockchain is impenetrable and can be used to protect data **10.39** from cyber-attacks, prevent fraud and data from being lost, stolen, or damaged

---

108 Deloitte, Blockchain and Cybersecurity, An Assessment of the Security of Blockchain Technology, available at: https://www2.deloitte.com/tr/en/pages/technology-media-and-telecommunications/articles/blockchain-and-cyber.html.

109 O.O. Malomo, D.B. Rawat and M. Garuba, J Supercomput (2018) 74: 5099. https://doi.org/10.1007/s11227-018-2385-7.

110 Ibid.

111 Ibid.

112 Jon Cawley, Using Blockchain to Enhance Health Care Security, *Sentara* (16 May 2018), available at: https://www.sentara.com/aboutus/news/news-articles/using-blockchain-to-enhance-health-care-security.aspx

113 Maria Korolov, Can Blockchain Fix Cybersecurity? *Sentara* (3 December 2018), available at: https://www.datacenterknowledge.com/security/can-blockchain-fix-cybersecurity.

114 Ibid.

thanks to blockchain's immutability. Arguably, blockchain can also improve cybersecurity across industries by better protecting networks from distributed denial-of-service attacks by decentralising the domain name system and protecting data from cyber-attacks thanks to blockchain's rigorous encryption and data distribution protocols on a network.[115] In that context, blockchain technology has been used to create a formally verifiable security system for Estonia.[116] The Estonian blockchain, called Keyless Signature Infrastructure (KSI), has securely stored Estonia's one million health records with asymmetric encryption and public keys maintained by a centralised certificate authority.[117]

10.40 Blockchain is also said to have an inherent connection to cybersecurity by being the culmination of decades of research and breakthroughs in cryptography and security.[118] Companies like Guardtime and REMME have tapped into blockchain to offer cybersecurity services.

10. 41 Guardtime's KSI is a blockchain platform designed with security, scale and performance built-in.[119] Its applications provide cybersecurity defence to Lockheed Martin[120] and include the world's first (a) blockchain platform for marine insurance launched in partnership with several organisations including Maersk and Microsoft Azure cloud platform,[121] and (b) blockchain-supported personal care record platform covering up to 30 million NHS patients in the UK.[122] Guardtime signed a global pledge to fight cyber-attacks, the Cybersecurity Tech Accord – a public commitment among more than 60 global companies to protect and empower the public online to improve the security, stability and resilience of cyberspace.[123]

---

115   Yuliia Horbenko, Using Blockchain Technology to Boost Cyber Security, *Steel Kiwi*, available at: https://steelkiwi.com/blog/using-blockchain-technology-to-boost-cybersecurity/.

116   Guardtime, KSI Technology Stack, available at: https://guardtime.com/technology.

117   Omri Barzilay, 3 Ways Blockchain Is Revolutionizing Cybersecurity, *Forbes* (21 August 2017), available at: https://www.forbes.com/sites/omribarzilay/2017/08/21/3-ways-blockchain-is-revolutionizing-cybersecurity/#244c171e2334.

118   Ibid.

119   Guardtime, https://guardtime.com/.

120   See Lancaster, Lockheed Martin Bets on Blockchain for Cybersecurity, CNet (2 May 2017), available at: https://www.cnet.com/news/lockheed-martin-bets-on-blockchain-for-cybersecurity/.

121   Martin Ruubel, World's First Blockchain Platform for Marine Insurance Now in Commercial Use, 24 May 2018, available at: https://guardtime.com/blog/world-s-first-blockchain-platform-for-marine-insurance-now-in-commercial-use.

122   Martin Ruubel, World's first blockchain-supported Personal Care Record Platform launched by Guardtime and partners to up to 30 million NHS patients in the UK, Guardtime (June 20, 2018), available at: https://guardtime.com/blog.

123   Meelis Vill, Guardtime Signs a Global Pledge to Fight Cyber Attacks, Guardtime (17 April 2018), available at: https://guardtime.com/blog/guardtime-signs-a-global-pledge-to-fight-cyber-attacks; and Tech Accord: https://cybertechaccord.org/.

REMME's blockchain leverages a distributed public key infrastructure to **10.42** authenticate users and devices without the need for a password.[124] Instead of a password, REMME gives each device a specific certificate managed on the blockchain.[125] The platform also uses the two-factor authentication mechanism to further enhance security for its users.[126]

To provide an effective, scalable and safe application, blockchain, as well as **10.43** any other technology, must be evaluated from the cybersecurity risk perspective. The CIA triad of confidentiality, integrity, and availability of computer data and systems is at the heart of cybersecurity. Blockchains must protect the CIA triad to offer a secure cyber environment. Some believe in blockchain's potential to do so because of blockchain's immutable nature that can serve to protect data from tampering.[127] This argument would respond favourably to keeping the integrity of data, but not necessarily securing the data's confidentiality and availability.

One way of protecting the confidentiality, integrity and availability of the CIA **10.44** triad on a blockchain is to use blockchain as the instruction of where the data is located, but not contain the data on the blockchain itself; in a way, blockchain would serve as library reference cards instead of providing direct access to the data.[128] This approach, however, may not be suitable for all blockchain applications, because it would certainly require an additional system to digitally store the information, instead of having it all on the blockchain, and decrease the transparency value of a blockchain.

As described in more detail in Chapter 6, the financial services industry may **10.45** consider blockchain as a way to develop and achieve more efficient alternatives to resource-intensive processes – for example, those that rely on intermediaries to establish trust and facilitate communication between multiple entities across borders.[129] Potential uses of blockchain in the financial services industry

---

124 REMME: https://remme.io/.
125 Ibid.
126 Ibid.
127 Rachel Wolfson, How A Leading Cyber Security Company Uses Blockchain Technology To Prevent Data Tampering, *Forbes* (3 July 2018), available at: https://www.forbes.com/sites/rachelwolfson/2018/07/03/how-a-leading-cyber-security-company-uses-blockchain-technology-to-prevent-data-tampering/#727c00174529.
128 Elizabeth M. Renieris, Global Policy Counsel, Evernym, Can Blockchain and Other Innovative Technologies Help Solve the Refugee Crisis?, at the Law, Justice and Development Week 2018 (6 November 2018), available at: http://pubdocs.worldbank.org/en/627571540505017333/LJD-Week-2018-FINAL-FOR-PRINT-WEB.pdf.
129 Erin English et al., Advancing Blockchain Cybersecurity: Technical and Policy Considerations for the Financial Services Industry, Microsoft (2018), available at: https://www.microsoft.com/en-us/cybersecurity/content-hub/advancing-blockchain-cybersecurity, at 6.

include enhancing trade finance, cross-border payments, compliance and audit functions including anti-money laundering and know-your customer, and the settlement and clearing of securities and derivatives transactions.[130]

10.46 Blockchain's resilience and potential to enhance cybersecurity, compared to other technologies and especially for the financial industry and its challenges, derive from the following:

(a) The distributed architecture of blockchain, which inherently avoids a single access point or a single point of failure. This has the potential to deter or minimise the effect of a cyber-attack, as the majority of the nodes would need to be compromised for the success of a cyber-attack.[131] On the other hand, such distributed architecture means that the different nodes participating in the blockchain may also have their own firewalls, which opens an external vulnerability to the blockchain. Moreover, it also raises challenges to manage different identities, participation rights and limitations, public/private key storage, and security configurations across multiple nodes.[132]

(b) Encryption: on 14 November 2018, while visiting Washington DC, Vitalik Buterin was asked about the main cybersecurity weaknesses in a blockchain. Vitalik noted that the use and management of private keys, no central authority to effectuate changes if things go wrong, is a risk, and the loss of a private key has severe consequences as private keys are not recoverable. Indeed, the majority of attacks related to blockchains have targeted cryptographic keys and key management services, not necessarily attacking the blockchain itself, which underscores the importance of key management to mitigate the risk of keys being stolen or otherwise compromised.[133] Accessing a blockchain account from multiple devices also raises the risk of losing control of private keys; developing secure key governance practices is crucial for lowering such risk.[134] Key management has also been flagged as one of the biggest risks to blockchain security.[135]

(c) The consensus mechanism of the peer-to-peer network aims at providing a continuous check on the integrity of transactions and of new blocks of data, and mitigates the possibility that a hacker or one or more compromised network participants can corrupt or manipulate the

---

130 Ibid.
131 Ibid., at 4 and 11.
132 Ibid., at 14.
133 Ibid., at 12.
134 Deloitte, *supra* note 108, at 6, and English et al., *supra* note 129, at 10.
135 English et al., *supra* note 129, at 10 and 12.

ledger.[136] Yet, in case of a Sybil cyber-attack, the attacker may be able to out-vote the honest nodes by creating enough fake identities and reaching the 51 per cent of the consensus mechanism necessary to control the transactions on a blockchain. In the proof of work consensus protocol, an attacker must compete against an aggregate of computing power of the network, which is more expensive than the potential benefits. One way to mitigate the risk of a Sybil attack may be by using a multi-tenant cloud-based directory and identity management service that certifies the identity of the persons permitted to access the blockchain since any cyber threat actor would be identified by the service and refused access.[137]

(d)   Transparency of blockchain is believed to offer another degree of cybersecurity protection, and makes it relatively easy to identify an attempt to corrupt the blockchain.[138] Other advantages of transparency in blockchains include: (i) the deployment of enhanced compliance processes, including real-time auditing or monitoring thanks to the sharing of identical records among various nodes, and (ii) quick identification of vulnerabilities and threats, provided good risk management and compliance controls are in place.[139] However, depending on the type of data to be added to the blockchain, data protection and privacy requirements apply – for example, the GDPR and/or health and drugs regulations, and transparency may cause non-compliance instead.

Vitalik also noted that blockchain needs better infrastructure to overcome the risk of single mistakes compromising the whole system, such as software coding errors. As described in Chapter 7, coding errors can cause problems, and because of the immutable nature of blockchains, it is difficult to change the code as a majority of the nodes would need to agree to any change in coding. It is therefore crucial for those writing the codes to ensure the published code is good from the outset. Secure coding procedures, the application of security by design principles,[140] a robust quality assurance programme, extensive security testing, the avoidance of rushed coding processes and production schedules, as well as greater clarity regarding the allocation of liability for coding errors, as described in Chapter 9, can help mitigate coding defects.[141]   **10.47**

---

136   Ibid., at 11.
137   Ibid., at 13 and 14.
138   Ibid., at 12.
139   Ibid.
140   'Security by design' means that the software has been designed from the foundation to be secure.
141   English et al., *supra* note 129, at 13.

10.48 Since no software code is 100 per cent free from defects, the need to update and patch software in a timely manner may apply in a similar fashion to blockchain. In the case of blockchain, due to its consensus mechanisms, most nodes need to agree to upload the patch. While blockchain's consensus mechanism is beneficial for the immutability and integrity of the record, it may be a hurdle when the blockchain's code needs a patch or when data needs to be recovered in case of fraud or malicious transactions added to a blockchain. If there is no consensus to adopt a patch, there will be a fork with part of the blockchain being patched and breaking up from the part that is not patched, as was the case after the hack of the Decentralised Autonomous Organisation, described in greater detail in Chapter 7. The problem is that records are still in both routes and the unpatched route will be vulnerable.

10.49 Other challenges to the blockchain's cybersecurity capacity include the quality of the data added to the blockchain and evolving cyber-attack technology. If the source of such data is compromised, the blockchain will be compromised too. With respect to evolving cyber-attack technology, new threats to cybersecurity in general may emerge with quantum computing.[142] Training and awareness remain crucial to mitigate risks, help anticipate and proactively protect against cyber-attacks, and to adapt and upgrade security protocols.

10.50 As described in Chapter 6, and in paragraph 10.45 above, in the financial services industry, permissioned blockchain has been used more than permissionless blockchain, and is expected to enhance the efficiency of trade finance, cross-border payments, asset management, customer data and identity management, and settlement and clearing of securities. Any technology applicable to banking and financial services must first and foremost comply with the applicable laws and regulations which can include specific control requirements including access controls, threat modeling, encryption, employee background checks, audit programmes and incident response plans.[143] Voluntarily adopting frameworks on cybersecurity and other matters such as NIST, the Payment Card Industry Data Security Standard for network-branded payment cards, Service Organization Control audit standards and how auditing can help with cybersecurity, help assess technologies against cybersecurity requirements that trump the adoption of any technology.[144] Since there is no

---

142   Ibid., at 14.
143   Ibid., at 17.
144   The Payment Card Industry (PCI) Data Security is a global forum founded by American Express, Discover Financial Services, JCB International, MasterCard, and Visa Inc., to develop, enhance, disseminate and assist with the understanding of security standards for payment account security aimed at merchants and other entities involved in payment card processing. See PCI, About Us, available at: https://www.pcisecuritystandards.org/about_us/. The PCI Data Security Standard consists of 12 requirements,

cybersecurity standard specifically applicable to blockchain solutions in the financial services, the industry is subject to general cybersecurity standards.

Additionally, to better assess how blockchain can contribute to the cyber- **10.51** security of the financial services industry, it is useful to consider what types of cyber-attacks are most common to such industry. Cyber-attacks against the financial services industry include the theft of keys or passwords, malware, web application attacks (when hackers infiltrate web applications, such as web browsers, with malicious codes to intercept data),[145] credential stuffing (i.e., when hackers automatically inject large numbers of breached username/password combinations into websites until they are potentially matched to an existing account to fraudulently gain access to user accounts),[146] distributed denial-of-service attack, man-in-the-middle cyber-attack and ransomware.[147] Even NotPetya affected the banking industry in Ukraine, as illustrated above. Knowing how to mitigate these cyber-attacks has become crucial for blockchain's potential.

Ultimately, blockchain's decentralised, immutable and transparent architec- **10.52** ture, coupled with its consensus mechanism, must be considered against the purpose for which blockchain may be adopted. Depending on what issue is to be addressed, a centralised system may respond to certain business needs better than a decentralised system (e.g., in law enforcement). On the other hand, a decentralised system may allow for a quick recovery, as illustrated by the DAO hack[148] when, within hours of the hack, the community connected to the DAO created a recovery plan and stopped the hack.[149]

Some propose the creation of third-party entities to serve as contractual **10.53** intermediaries between DAO-type communities and regulatory mechanisms

---

ranging from installing a firewall configuration to protect cardholder data, to maintaining a policy to address information security for all personnel. See PCI DSS Quick Reference Guide – Understanding the Payment Card Industry Data Security Standard version 3.2.1 (July 2018), available at: https://www.pci securitystandards.org/documents/PCI_DSS-QRG-v3_2_1.pdf?agreement=true&time=1546894768175, at 9.

The Service Organization Control provides resources to help organisations and businesses, including CPA firms, to assess risks, and assists CPAs as they provide advisory or assurance services on clients' risk programs. See AICPa, Cybersecurity Resource Center, available at: https://www.aicpa.org/interestareas/frc/assuranceadvisoryservices/cyber-security-resource-center.html.

145   Acunetix, What is a Web Application Attack and how to Defend Against it (2018), available at: https://www.acunetix.com/websitesecurity/web-application-attack/.
146   OWASP Foundation: Credential Stuffing, available at: https://www.owasp.org/index.php/Credential_stuffing.
147   English et al., *supra* note 129, at 9 and 10.
148   Deloitte, *supra* note 108, at 8.
149   United Nations Office of Project Services, *The Legal Aspects of Blockchain* (2018), Chapter 3 – Some general remarks about blockchain and the law, Jeroen Naves and Olivier Rikken, available at: https://www.blockchainpilots.nl/home-eng, at 27.

or third-party partners.[150] The decentralised nature of the blockchain also raises the issue of identifying the person behind the transactions. Some companies are in the business of trying to identify people on the blockchain, usually for purposes of crime prevention.[151] A system adaptable to change, rather than an immutable system, may be a better option in some situations, as privacy requirements may need to be prioritised. Every participant in a blockchain has access to information, which is a concern not only from the privacy standpoint, but also from the confidentiality of information perspective. For this reason, it would behove those who own or control the information to assess and decide whether a public/permissionless blockchain is suitable. If the information to be added to a blockchain application is confidential, using a blockchain-based application may not be advisable. If the information is public already, then no such concern applies, regardless of the technology.

F. CONCLUSION

10.54 As described in this chapter, given the scale of damages that cyber-attacks can cause, cybersecurity should be at the forefront of any business decision. Specifically, cybersecurity must trump any technology underlying a potential application to be deployed into production if such technology fails to provide sufficient basis to ensure the protection of the CIA triad or in any other way threatens the organisation's business operations, reputation and/or compliance with laws and regulations. The credibility and operability of any business depends on its capacity to protect the CIA triad of computer data and systems at the core of cybersecurity. Adopting any technology must be assessed against the latest developments in cybersecurity and accepting any residual risk must be carefully considered. The purpose and the data to be recorded in the blockchain are also important considerations in any decision on whether blockchain is the proper technology to satisfy a specific business need.

10.55 With increased sophistication of cyber-attacks, organisations will unlikely be able to protect their data by storing it on on-premises servers. Regardless of any technology underlying an application solution, one must consider which well-structured platforms are available to mitigate cyber risks. Such platforms should adhere to industry-leading standards, including from ISO and NIST,

---

150   Ibid., Chapter 5 – Implications of Blockchain / DLT on the UN System, Benedetta Audia, at 80.
151   Chainalysis, available at: https://www.chainalysis.com/, and J.P. Buntinx, Top 4 Companies Providing Bitcoin Blockchain Analysis Services (12 February 2017), available at: https://nulltx.com/top-4-companies-providing-bitcoin-blockchain-analysis-services/.

and have robust physical and cybersecurity controls. No such consideration, however, takes away the added need to carefully consider any technology, including blockchain, in deploying it as an application.

11

BLOCKCHAIN AND PRIVACY

Daniel Cooper and Gemma Nash

A. INTRODUCTION

11.01 It is becoming increasingly apparent that blockchain, as a technology, will transform a multitude of industries and reap vast rewards, and this is nowhere more apparent than in the financial service sector. Indeed, it is perhaps hardly surprising that one of the first reported deployments of blockchain – Bitcoin – challenged the traditional paradigm by which modern financial transactions are conducted. Blockchain, along with the rise of blockchain-enabled crypto-currencies, undoubtedly will continue to have broader implications for the financial services sector in relation to trading, clearing and settlement, as well as middle- and back-office business functions.[1]

11.02 That said, the implementation of blockchain in real-world scenarios has not been without its challenges, in part because conventional legal norms and doctrines often appear ill-suited to regulate it. This is hardly surprising, as lawmakers and courts traditionally struggle to keep pace with new technologies, and blockchain still remains novel enough today to escape heavy and targeted regulation under most legal frameworks. Whether blockchain merits

---

1 While the focus of this book is on FinTech, we note that blockchain technology is also set to revolutionise many other industries, e.g., its potential to increase efficiencies with regard to government operations, such as e-governance; see, EU Blockchain Observatory and Forum, Blockchain for Governance and Public Services (7 December 2018), available at: https://www.eublockchainforum.eu/sites/default/files/reports/eu_observatory_blockchain_in_government_services_v1_2018-12-07.pdf?width=1024&height=800&iframe=true.

more focused and extensive regulation is a question that inspires strong views either way. If that were to occur, as appears inevitable, then such regulation would need to achieve the right balance, avoiding stifling an innovative technology with obvious benefits, on the one hand, while deterring parties from using the technology to infringe other deeply held rights and values, on the other.

One topic that has attracted attention is the perceived conflict between **11.03** blockchain and legal rules designed to protect personal data, illustrated in data protection laws like the EU's General Data Protection Regulation (GDPR),[2] Canada's Personal Information Protection and Electronic Documents Act, South Korea's Personal Information Protection Act, Turkey's Law on the Protection of Personal Data and a host of regional and national data protection laws that have appeared in recent times. Simply put, blockchain technology has certain defining features that challenge some of the basic assumptions underpinning many of these laws. For instance, blockchains are essentially decentralised and collaborative endeavours; there typically is no single owner of a blockchain but multiple actors, none of whom arguably can 'control' the operation of the ledger. They are permanent and immutable, meaning that information, including any personal data, generally will not be deleted once stored on the blockchain. These characteristics distinguish blockchain from a standard ledger and have helped to give the technology its notoriety and utility. However, these same features operate in tension with concepts found in most data privacy legislation, which imposes responsibility and liability upon parties in a position to control the relevant data, and presumes that all data are capable of editing and correction. It remains an open question whether blockchain inherently conflicts with such laws.

At the time of writing,[3] the EU's institutions and the EU data privacy **11.04** regulators in particular have been devoting significant attention to understanding how blockchain and the GDPR can peacefully co-exist. This effort is instructive for other parts of the world, where the same concerns have arisen. In October 2018, the EU Blockchain Observatory and Forum, a European Parliament pilot project overseen by the EU Commission, published a report,

---

2 Regulation (EU) 2016/679 of the European Parliament and of the Council of 27 April 2016 on the protection of natural persons with regard to the processing of personal data and on the free movement of such data, and repealing Directive 95/46/EC, OJ L 119.

3 This chapter was written in January 2019, and reflects the law and guidance as of that date. Given the attention this topic is attracting from regulators, academics and policymakers, further guidance and possibly decisional case law can be expected to emerge in the coming months.

entitled 'Blockchain and the GDPR',[4] which discussed some possible GDPR compliance concerns associated with blockchain. Around the same time, the European Parliament called upon the EU Commission and the European Data Protection Supervisor to provide further guidance in this area.[5] Shortly thereafter, in November 2018, the widely respected French data protection authority, the *Commission nationale de l'informatique et des libertés* (the CNIL), released its own opinion paper,[6] proferring some suggestions aimed at mitigating conflicts between blockchain and the GDPR, although the authority tellingly left some important questions unanswered. It was the first serious effort by an EU regulator to explore the intersection of blockchain and EU data privacy laws, and clearly a sign of things to come.

11.05 Given the increasing attention from, and concerns raised by, those in the data privacy field with regards to blockchain, it seems appropriate to critically examine the technology through the lens of the EU GDPR, increasingly a benchmark for data protection frameworks around the world.[7] While we primarily consider here the legal issues associated with the EU's data privacy framework, many of the issues are highly relevant to other national and regional data protection laws, particularly those implementing privacy legislation influenced by the GDPR.[8]

11.06 This chapter is structured as follows – Section B gives a brief overview of EU data privacy law, to provide background and context. In Section C, we discuss

---

4   The EU Blockchain Observatory and Forum, Blockchain and the GDPR (16 October 2018), available at: https://www.eublockchainforum.eu/sites/default/files/reports/20181016_report_gdpr.pdf?width=1024& height=800&iframe=true.

5   European Parliament Resolution of 3 October 2018 on distributed ledger technologies and blockchains: building trust with disintermediation (2017/2772(RSP)), available at: http://www.europarl.europa.eu/sides/ getDoc.do?pubRef=-//EP//NONSGML+TA+P8-TA-2018-0373+0+DOC+PDF+V0//EN, at 33. The European Parliament reiterated this point in a report published in November 2018, see European Parliament Report on Blockchain: a forward-looking trade policy (2018/2085(INI)), available at: http:// www.europarl.europa.eu/sides/getDoc.do?pubRef=-//EP//NONSGML+REPORT+A8-2018-0407+0+DOC +PDF+V0//EN, at 14.

6   CNIL, Blockchain and the GDPR: Solutions for a responsible use of the blockchain in the context of personal data (6 November 2018), available at: https://www.cnil.fr/en/blockchain-and-gdpr-solutions-responsible-use-blockchain-context-personal-data.

7   While this chapter focuses on the tensions associated with the use of blockchain and emerging data privacy laws, some have noted the potential for blockchain to promote data privacy rights: for instance, blockchain potentially offers more transparency and accountability with regard to the processing of personal data, and could be used to give data subjects more control of their data. In addition, blockchain solutions could be used as a method of demonstrating compliance, such as recording consents. For further reading see Natalia D'Agostini, GDPR and Blockchain: What does this Mean for In-House Counsel? (2018) 11(45) *International In-House Counsel Journal*, 5563; Luis-Daniel Ibáñez et al., On Blockchains and the General Data Protection Regulation (2018), available at: https://eprints.soton.ac.uk/422879/, at 11.

8   For example, California's new Californian Consumer Privacy Act of 2018 and Brazil's General Data Privacy Law (*Lei Geral de Proteção de Dados Pessoais*).

aspects of blockchain that are attracting attention from a data protection point of view. This includes the extent to which personal data are stored on a blockchain (C.2); blockchain's immutable qualities and the difficulties this poses when complying with data subject rights and data minimisation rules (C.3); the decentralised nature of blockchain and what this means with respect to the roles, responsibilities, and liabilities of the critical actors operating in any given blockchain network (C.4); and other privacy challenges that block-chain technology poses (C.5). Section D concludes.

B. EU DATA PRIVACY LAW

1. The EU GDPR and its origins

Following a four-year period marked by heated debate, the EU institutions – **11.07** the EU Commission, Council and Parliament – reached agreement in December 2015 on the final text of the GDPR, which eventually made its way into the Official Journal of the EU on 27 April 2016. The GDPR did not enter into force immediately, as organisations were given roughly two years, or until 25 May 2018, to comply. The GDPR's passage into EU law was a watershed moment, as it represented the most significant and comprehensive overhaul of the EU's data protection rules since 1995, when the EU's Data Protection Directive[9] (the Directive) was passed, and sought to harmonise the EU's divergent Member State data privacy laws.

Many saw the GDPR as a harbinger of a new era of data protection law in the **11.08** EU, and still do. It is expected to give individuals greater control over the processing of their 'personal data', such as by bestowing additional data privacy rights. It is ambitiously intended to combat the emerging privacy threats associated with the internet, social networking, 'big data' initiatives, more sophisticated IT networks, online profiling capabilities and other tech-nological advances that were less well developed or simply absent when EU lawmakers debated the Directive. As the European Commission noted with remarkable understatement when publishing its proposal for the GDPR, '[r]apid technological developments have brought new challenges for the protection of personal data. The scale of data sharing and collecting has increased dramatically'.[10]

---

9   Directive 95/46/EC of the European Parliament and of the Council of 24 October 1995 on the protection of individuals with regard to the processing of personal data and on the free movement of such data, OJ L 281.
10   Proposal for a Regulation on the protection of individuals with regard to the processing of personal data and on the free movement of such data, COM (2012) 11 final, at 1.

11.09   During the GDPR's fraught four-year gestation, however, blockchain remained a relatively nascent technology, familiar to a technologically-savvy few and raising only vaguely understood privacy concerns. Not surprisingly, EU lawmakers paid little attention to blockchain as the GDPR text snaked its way through the EU institutions, attracting more and more proposed amendments from lawmakers. It is hardly a surprise therefore that the GDPR, when it was finally birthed by the EU in 2016, contained no specific provisions aimed at regulating blockchain, unlike, by contrast, provisions meant to manacle the more widely known proliferation of online behavioural advertising or harmful automated decision-making.

11.10   This is not to say that personal data were not robustly protected prior to the GDPR. The Directive, as well as various EU instruments, including the Charter of Fundamental Rights, established a firm bedrock of protections that the GDPR amplified and embellished.[11] Indeed, the GDPR wrought some substantive changes to the fabric of the law, including enhancing existing data subject rights and establishing new rights, as well as imposing additional compliance obligations upon organisations, such as new 'accountability' requirements, that did not previously exist. Perhaps garnering most media attention, the GDPR dramatically increased the potential sanctions arising from an infringement, up to an eye-watering 4 per cent of the relevant undertaking's last annual turnover. That said, some pundits have, quite accurately, described the GDPR as more of an evolution, and less of a revolution, of EU data protection law, by building on the firm foundations set by the Directive and EU instruments.

2.   Scope and core concepts

11.11   The GDPR left many of the foundational concepts and definitions that informed the Directive relatively untouched. For instance, the GDPR regulates the 'processing' of 'personal data', which is defined as 'any information relating to an identified or identifiable natural person ("data subject")', and an 'identifiable natural person is one who can be identified, directly or indirectly' by reference to an identifier, which includes a name or an online identifier.[12] Online identifiers may include device IDs and other unique IDs, such as an internet user's IP address or a device fingerprint.[13] The GDPR also spells out

---

11   Art 16(1) of the Treaty on the Functioning of the European Union and Art 8 of the EU Charter of Fundamental Rights.

12   GDPR, Art 4(1).

13   GDPR, Recital 30; see also UK Information Commissioner's Office, What is Personal Data?, available at: https://ico.org.uk/for-organisations/guide-to-data-protection/guide-to-the-general-data-protection-regulation-gdpr/what-is-personal-data/.

special, or sensitive, categories of personal data, which are afforded greater privacy and security protections. 'Special data' refers to data revealing an individual's racial or ethnic origin, political opinions, religious or philosophical beliefs, or trade union membership, and the processing of genetic data, biometric data for the purpose of uniquely identifying a natural person, data concerning health or data concerning a natural person's sex life or sexual orientation.[14] 'Processing' remains very broadly defined to include almost any use of personal data, such as collection, storage or even deletion.[15]

The GDPR defines particular legal actors with regard to the processing of personal data, the two primary roles being that of a 'controller' and that of a 'processor'. These roles dictate which of the GDPR's substantive obligations will apply to an organisation, with (not surprisingly) a more fulsome set of obligations applied to the former.[16] More specifically, a 'controller' is defined as a party that 'alone or jointly with others, determines the purposes and means of the processing of personal data'.[17] This would include, by way of example, a financial institution that processes customer details for purposes of providing financial services to the customer or that processes customer data ingested via a website that the institution makes available to customers for online banking purposes. There is even scope for 'joint controllers' under the GDPR, relevant in situations where two or more controllers 'jointly' control the purposes and means of the processing. **11.12**

A 'processor', by contrast, is a party that 'processes personal data on behalf of the controller', and effectively serves the aims set by the controller.[18] Processors lack a critical aspect of autonomy when processing data, and for this reason have lesser obligations under the GDPR. For instance, a third-party service provider engaged by a financial institution to store the institution's customer data on its computer servers, such as a cloud provider, would likely be deemed a processor given its lack of control over the purposes for which the data are processed. The service provider does not decide the purposes and means of processing, but merely stores the data for the data controller's own use.[19] To the extent the service provider can be said to decide the technical **11.13**

---

14   GDPR, Art 9(1).
15   GDPR, Art 4(2).
16   Both a data controller and a data processor can be a natural person, legal person, public authority, agency or another body; see GDPR, Art 4(7) and (8).
17   GDPR, Art 4(7).
18   GDPR, Art 4(8).
19   See recent guidance from the ICO, How do you Determine whether you are a Controller or Processor?, available at: https://ico.org.uk/for-organisations/guide-to-data-protection/guide-to-the-general-data-protection-regulation-gdpr/controllers-and-processors/how-do-you-determine-whether-you-are-a-controller-or-processor/.

means by which the data are stored, EU regulators have been clear that determining processing purposes has greater evidential weight when assessing a party's status. It is expected that the service provider will apply its own skill, judgment and expertise to the processing, and this contribution will not necessarily convert the provider into a controller in its own right. In this, the GDPR largely transposes concepts that already appeared in the Directive.

11.14 The GDPR, further mirroring the Directive, applies both to controllers and processors that are established in the EU and processing data there, as well as those controllers and processors outside the EU that process personal data 'in the context of the activities of' an EU establishment. Thus, the GDPR applies to organisations processing data outside the EU where there is a sufficient causal nexus to an EU establishment, such as a branch, affiliate, subsidiary or even permanently situated employees. However, the GDPR did bring about more substantial changes to the Directive's remaining applicable law doctrines. More specifically, the GDPR now applies to controllers and processors established outside the EU in cases where they: (i) offer goods or services to data subjects in the EU (the 'targeting' doctrine); or (ii) monitor the behaviour of data subjects as far as their behaviour takes place within the EU (the 'monitoring' doctrine). Consequently, many organisations established outside the EU, but doing business inside the EU, are now focused on EU data protection law like never before.

3. Key principles and rules

11.15 In addition to applicable law doctrines, the GDPR also brought about some important changes to the substantive rules of EU data protection law, notably with the obligations imposed upon controllers and, for the first time, processors. Supplementing these new obligations and requirements is a broader base of data subject rights, including novel rights intended to empower individuals and give them choices regarding their data. We summarise some of these key requirements below.

- *Principles of processing:* The GDPR requires controllers to process personal data lawfully, fairly and in a transparent manner (this includes augmented notice obligations), only for specified purposes, and to a minimum degree (also referred to as data minimisation). Personal data also must be accurate and kept up-to-date, stored only for as long as needed to fulfil identified processing purposes, and subjected to adequate security measures.[20] Processing data can only occur where there is an appropriate legal basis arising in the GDPR.

- *Data subject rights:* The GDPR codifies certain new data subject rights, such as the right to data portability,[21] the 'right to be forgotten',[22] and the right to restrict or suspend further processing of one's data, thereby empowering individuals to a higher degree, but stops short of bestowing rights of data ownership. Other data subject rights, such as rights of access, rectification, and objection are carried over, and strengthened in certain respects, from the Directive.

- *Accountability:* The GDPR gave birth to a new buzzword – 'accountability'. Controllers are now required to demonstrate their compliance with the GDPR's data processing principles.[23] Tangible examples of this concept include novel record-keeping requirements, privacy impact assessments and, in some cases, obligatory appointment of a data protection officer to monitor compliance.

- *Coordinated enforcement:* The GDPR introduces a 'one-stop-shop' mechanism for enforcement, albeit weaker than the mechanism originally proposed by the European Commission. In brief, each controller or processor is expected to deal with one 'lead' data protection authority, allocated based on the location of the controller or processor's 'main establishment', for pan-EU infringements of the GDPR.[24] And, as touted in the media and made known to many corporate boards of directors, the GDPR permits regulators to sanction infringing firms up to 4 per cent of an undertaking's total worldwide annual turnover, or up to EUR 20 million, whichever is higher.[25]

Due in large part to these more muscular rules and sanctions, the GDPR is **11.16** seen today as one of the most, if not the most, mature data privacy frameworks globally and its influence in other countries and regions is just beginning to be seen as new laws mirroring the GDPR are passed. The GDPR's persuasive appeal in other countries undoubtedly will continue to be seen in the years ahead, and its effects are even being seen in the US, historically less attuned to EU-style data privacy rights, where states such as California have passed significant new data privacy laws. Indeed, California's law shares many features found in the GDPR, including more robust data subject rights. The inevitable upshot of this is that the concerns that some have raised regarding

---

20 GDPR, Art 5(1).
21 GDPR, Art 20.
22 GDPR, Art 17.
23 GDPR, Art 5(2).
24 GDPR, Art 56.
25 GDPR, Art 83.

blockchain and the EU's GDPR in time will be repeated in other parts of the world, as the technology begins to take hold. This makes it highly relevant, both from an EU and broader global perspective, to examine some of the complex issues that blockchain has thrust up in the data privacy field.

C. DATA PRIVACY AND BLOCKCHAIN

1. Introduction

11.17 Today, organisations contemplating the use of blockchain have had to accept that, as with the use of many transformative technologies, there are associated risks. This is a by-product of blockchain's capacity to operate in a manner that challenges well-settled assumptions underlying some important regulatory frameworks, including data protection frameworks. This is somewhat ironic, given that many modern data privacy laws, like the GDPR, were implemented in part to address concerns associated with a variety of new technologies. In the case of the GDPR, the roughly 20-year interim period between passage of the Directive and enactment of the GDPR saw some of the most remarkable advances seen for ages, many of them privacy-confounding and posing risks to data protection. However, blockchain technology was simply not well-enough known at the time to play a significant factor in the policy deliberations that took place during the drafting of the GDPR. The result is that today, applying GDPR rules to real-world blockchain use cases is like trying to fit a round peg into a square hole.

11.18 Naturally, the extent to which the GDPR-related issues and concerns will materialise in any particular scenario will depend on the precise characteristics of the relevant blockchain, as no two blockchains are identical, and a bevy of other factors. Blockchain networks that involve the processing of more limited amounts of personal data – for example, a blockchain-based land registry – as opposed to blockchain networks that process very large amounts of sensitive personal data – for example, a blockchain-based patient health record repository – will give rise to varying degrees of risk under the GDPR (as well as regulatory scrutiny).

11.19 Put another way, a blockchain network's particular qualities and features will materially influence the extent to which the network can or needs to comply with the GDPR. The fact that blockchain can be either public or private helps to illustrate this basic point. Public blockchains are those that can be accessed by almost anyone armed with an internet-enabled computer, while private blockchains can only be viewed by designated parties that have been author-ised to use the blockchain. Public and private blockchains, by virtue of who can use them, give rise to much different GDPR challenges and risks.

2. Blockchain and personal data

It is axiomatic, but bears repeating, that the GDPR only applies where the processing of some personal data occurs. Accordingly, for a blockchain network to raise GDPR compliance issues, some personal data must be involved, either by virtue of being stored within the blockchain or by being associated with it somehow. For most blockchains, there often will be personal data that enables the participants on the network to be identified, i.e., through unique attributes, including their activities vis-à-vis the ledger, or personal data may actually be stored within the blockchain in some format, or both. **11.20**

To take the former scenario, involving identification of the network partici-pants, individuals who have access to a blockchain network are assigned a public and a private key. Every time an individual is linked to a particular transaction on the network, by interacting with the blockchain ledger, that individual's public key, which uniquely identifies that user, will be displayed. A user's public key will be considered personal data where it constitutes 'infor-mation relating to an identified or identifiable natural person'. While a user's public key does not itself directly disclose that particular user's identity, i.e., his/her name, the use of that key over time by the user may lead to his/her identification or allow other individuals to construct a profile of that user's behaviour in relation to ledger-related events. Moreover, as EU law has controversially developed to date, merely being able to 'single out' someone based on their online behaviour often suffices to qualify data as personal, even when their real names are never known.[26] This means that real-world attribution of blockchain interactions to a living individual, via their public key display, is not a necessary condition for determining whether the data in question is personal data. **11.21**

This expansive interpretation of the term 'personal data' is now well settled in EU law, and is reflected in case law of the European Court of Justice. For example, in *Patrick Breyer v Germany*,[27] the court determined that even dynamic IP addresses, associated with an internet user's computer, could **11.22**

---

26 Article 29 Working Party, Opinion 2/2010 on Online Behavioural Advertising (22 June 2010), available at: https://ec.europa.eu/justice/article-29/documentation/opinion-recommendation/files/2010/wp171_en.pdf, at 9.
27 Case C-582/14, *Patrick Breyer v Germany* (2016).

qualify as personal data on the basis that the addresses could relate to an identifiable user when combined with account data held by the user's internet service provider (ISP). It was not necessary that the party possessing the IP address could itself make the attribution, so long as another party – the ISP, for instance – could do so. As such, just because one party is not able to identify an individual with the information they possess, the fact that a second party has additional information that could identify that individual when used in combination with the original information may be enough to convert it into personal data for the first party. *Breyer*, and cases like it, have the potential for bringing many blockchain applications within the scope of the GDPR, simply on the grounds that blockchain participants are or may become identifiable through observable interactions with the blockchain.

11.23 A more concrete example may be helpful. An internet user, called Claire, buys products using a blockchain-enabled cryptocurrency. Every time Claire buys a product using the cryptocurrency, the transaction will be published on the blockchain network, which will associate Claire's public key with that transaction. A third party viewing transactions on the blockchain network will not at first be able to identify Claire as the natural, living person initiating the transaction. However, over time, as Claire continues to spend using her cryptocurrency, it is conceivable that the third party could begin to associate her transactions with other information available to that party or other parties, thereby facilitating the ultimate real-world identification of Claire. Quite naturally, the risks will be variable depending on a multitude of factors, including the purpose of the blockchain, the size of the blockchain community, the number of blockchain interactions, and so forth, such that quantifying this risk is impossible. However, the EU data privacy regulators have, if anything, demonstrated a willingness to treat data as personal, even in circumstances where the risks of identification are remote, if not speculative. And, applying the rationale of the *Breyer* court, if a party participating in the blockchain network, such as an administrator, has additional information that would associate Claire with her public key, the public key alone could amount to personal data, similar to the IP address in *Breyer*, for other members of the blockchain.

11.24 What about situations where personal data are actually embedded within a blockchain and become a constituent part of it? Most believe that this scenario presents a clearer case for the application of the GDPR. More obvious forms of personal data, such as an individual's name, stored in a blockchain network will amount to the processing of regulated personal data, and thereby trigger the application of the GDPR. For example, a blockchain network that is used to store medical records and that physically incorporates patient data on the blockchain network will, and undoubtedly should, bring the protections afforded by the GDPR to bear. It would be wrong to assume that where personal data stored on the blockchain are encrypted or encoded, the GDPR will not apply. The GDPR expressly applies to 'pseudonymised' data, and encryption techniques, while useful, are treated merely as a matter of data security, rather than a means of anonymising data. As such, neither encryption nor encoding would exclude the GDPR from applying. Others have proposed anonymising personal data retained on the blockchain, which, if possible, would take it outside the ambit of the GDPR. But, as we discuss in 11.32 below, there are significant challenges with this approach given how broadly 'personal data' is defined under the GDPR and how narrowly EU authorities regard what is truly anonymised data.

3. The immutable nature of blockchain

Another aspect of blockchain that worries privacy advocates is its unforgiv- **11.25** ingly immutable nature, which means that information contained within the blocks can persist indefinitely and can only be deleted or modified with extreme difficulty. Each 'block' is produced by generating a hash using information derived from a transaction, with links to the hash in the preceding block. As each block becomes affixed to the previous block *ad infinitum*, like a daisy chain, the ability to delete or amend a block in the chain becomes almost impossible because of the knock-on effect this would have on all other blocks. Blockchain adherents regard this as one of the virtues of the technology, by making it resistant to tampering and a more trustworthy system for recording information.

While this is one of the proclaimed advantages of blockchain, there are **11.26** concerns that, where the blocks do incorporate personal data, this characteristic may be incompatible with some key principles of the GDPR. There is angst that by freezing personal data in the blockchain and making it impervious to change, it becomes impossible to comply with core data retention and minimisation norms. The GDPR, like most privacy frameworks, requires that personal data only be retained for as long as is necessary to satisfy an identified processing aim or purpose. Or, as stated in the GDPR, personal data shall be 'limited to what is necessary in relation to the purposes for which they are processed' and only 'kept in a form which permits identification of data subjects for no longer than is necessary for the purposes for which the personal data are processed'.[28] Data privacy laws aim to ensure the eradication of personal data once they have served their purpose, and debates will arise as to

---

28 GDPR, Art 5(1)(c) and (e).

the purposes served by the personal data residing in a block. For instance, is the purpose served at the time the blockchain transaction that led to its generation is concluded or is there a purpose served in permanently recording even the earlier transactions on the blockchain? For some blockchains, there may be good arguments for storing the data for long periods of time, such as a blockchain reflecting shifting rights in property or some other asset. For other blockchains, the arguments are weaker. It could be questioned, and generally has been by the EU data privacy regulators, whether any technology that *inevitably* results in the indefinite retention of personal data can be compatible with these basic data retention principles.

11.27 Concerns have also been raised over blockchain immutability in another respect, namely with respect to compliance with data subject rights that allow individuals to correct, alter, amend or delete their personal data, as well as object to its further processing, in particular circumstances.[29] Although the GDPR qualifies each of these rights in important respects, it is possible to imagine a situation where a blockchain participant asserts a right that is fundamentally incompatible with how the blockchain actually operates. This further assumes that there is a clearly identified data controller (or controllers) in the blockchain positioned to respond to such a request. As we discuss below, the decentralised nature of a blockchain creates difficulties in this respect as well.

11.28 Focusing on the 'right to be forgotten', or data erasure, helps to illustrate the dilemma. Under the GDPR, data subjects have 'the right to obtain from the controller the erasure of personal data concerning him or her without undue delay' where certain conditions are met.[30] This includes, but is not limited to, situations where personal data are no longer necessary given the purposes for which the data were collected, where the legal basis for processing is based on consent and the data subject subsequently withdraws their consent and there is no other legal ground to justify the retention of the data, and where the personal data must be erased to comply with a legal obligation.[31] The right is not absolute, however, and there are circumstances in which erasure requests can be denied, for instance where the processing relates to freedom of expression, implicates public interests and or relates to an overriding legal obligation.[32]

---

29 The GDPR establishes many other data subject rights, such as rights of access and portability, which controllers in a blockchain network will also have to comply. However, the CNIL has recently opined that blockchain is not incompatible with all of these rights; see CNIL, *supra* note 6, at 8.
30 GDPR, Art 17(1).
31 Ibid.
32 GDPR, Art 17(3).

In a blockchain context, where a data subject asserts such a right, compliance **11.29** can be expected to pose a severe challenge. In fact, the CNIL has recently recognised this limitation of blockchain, observing that 'it is technically impossible to grant the request for erasure made by a data subject when data are registered on a blockchain'.[33] For example, a company uses blockchain technology as a method of recording and storing employee information relating to compensation, vacation time and sick leave. An employee of the company subsequently resigns, and several years later, requests that the company deletes their personal data. It will prove difficult, after a number of years, for the company to legitimately argue that it has a business need to store the data. Unless the company is under a legal obligation to retain this information, it is likely that the company will have to delete the employee's information under the GDPR. However, as it has been stored on a blockchain network, it will be extremely difficult for the company to go back and delete the relevant blocks in the chain that contain that employee's personal data. Or, returning to the scenario described above, an employee books a holiday and this is recorded incorrectly in the system, due to human error. The employee later wishes to rectify this information, fearing that it will lead to disciplinary sanctions. As the information is inaccurate, the employee is entitled to have this corrected applying his or her right of 'rectification'. However, again, this is very difficult for the company to do, given the information is captured in a blockchain.

While extremely difficult to delete or amend such data, it is not impossible. **11.30** Provided that a majority of the users on the blockchain network approve the alteration or deletion and have the requisite computing power to modify all the blocks, deletions or changes can be made.[34] With a public and permissionless blockchain, this inevitably will be far more difficult an undertaking, especially if the number of participants that are required to validate the change on the network is high. For private and permissioned blockchains, where the number of participants on the network can be expected to be lower, this is more viable, although whether this is desirable can be questioned. Normally, blockchain developers will establish a minimum number of participants who must validate transactions in order to ensure that unauthorised third parties cannot re-write the blocks. Allowing validators to go back and modify or delete blocks in the chain to any degree, including to honour data subject rights requests, inevitably weakens the reliability of the ledger, undermining

---

33   CNIL, *supra* note 6, at 8.
34   Michèle Finck: Blockchain and Data Protection in the EU, Max Planck Institute for Innovation and Competition Research Paper No. 18-01, at 4.

one of the most appealing features of blockchain as compared with traditional ledger systems.

11.31 All of this of course assumes that there is someone positioned and capable of responding to rights requests. As alluded to above, it can prove deeply difficult to identify which, if any, parties are data controllers in a given blockchain network, particularly a public blockchain, and this legal obligation, and others like it, may prove difficult to exercise in practice. In an ideal world, EU data protection authorities would be willing to waive compliance with these obligations, and the right to erasure more specifically, in this limited context.[35] But, given these rights are fundamental under EU law, and grounded in the EU Charter, this is unlikely and regulators have been disinclined historically to permit it. The CNIL, in its 2018 guidance paper discussed above, emphasise that controllers and processors should be questioning the appropriateness of using blockchain technology, given the 'difficulties for data controllers in terms of compliance with the obligations set out by the GDPR'.[36] This is arguably a naive view, which ignores the inevitable march of this technology, a modern version of King Canute trying to hold back the tide.

11.32 The immutable nature of blockchain is undoubtedly a thorny issue, as seen through a GDPR lens. One 'solution' that has been raised, which would help to avoid the application of the GDPR altogether, is to structure the blockchain such that personal data are never deposited within it. Certain blockchains would operate by keeping data off the 'blocks' and processing data in a parallel database separate from the blockchain network, with the blockchain network only referencing the database. This lends itself to additional complexities and challenges, and in many instances may be impractical. The separate database, meanwhile, would itself be subject to regulation under the GDPR, although it would at least avoid the immutability problem to the extent that the database is responsive to amendment and deletion requests, although strict protocols for responding to such requests would be required to avoid degrading the integrity of the blockchain. Relatedly, there is a near universal consensus that personal data should not be stored on a blockchain in a 'clear (i.e., unencrypted) way',[37] given the privacy risks this presents. Otherwise, the GDPR would require and regulators would certainly expect there to be safeguards in place, including encryption techniques, to limit or restrict access. The CNIL recommends using various types of cryptographic mechanisms to reduce the ability to identify personal data on the blockchain network.

---

35   Ibid., at 24.
36   CNIL, *supra* note 6, at 5.
37   The EU Blockchain Observatory and Forum, *supra* note 4, at 19.

However, these techniques will not amount to anonymisation, though they do lower the risks and are more aligned with GDPR doctrines.

Anonymisation solutions, for the time being, could be deemed aspirational **11.33** given the high standards set under EU law for anonymising data. The GDPR itself does not define the term 'anonymisation', but it is commonly understood to mean a technique used to *permanently* and *irretrievably* strip personal data of all identifiers, such that it is no longer possible to identify a natural person. While this sounds like a perfect solution in theory, anonymisation in practice is a tall order, as regulatory guidance papers make abundantly clear. The Article 29 Working Party[38] has expressed its views on the validity of various anonymisation techniques,[39] and warned that 'the creation of a truly anonymous dataset from a rich set of personal data … is not a simple proposition'[40] and that 'anonymisation practices and techniques exist with variable degrees of robustness'.[41] The EU Blockchain Observatory and Forum, in its report, noted that advanced cryptographic techniques are currently being developed in the blockchain context that could allow for even more 'robust data anonymisation approaches'.[42] However, according to EU regulators, these techniques need to take account of any existing risks of re-identification, and also may need to account for potential future threats that could lead to re-identification, even though these threats may be difficult to anticipate or foresee.[43] Notwithstanding the above, at least one academic has postulated that in time, either the EU courts or the European data protection authorities will declare certain cryptographic processes as being capable of anonymising data.[44] If or when they do, this will make blockchain a more attractive proposition from a privacy standpoint.

Inevitably, the extent to which any of these potential solutions are possible will **11.34** depend on the particular blockchain use case, and the features of the blockchain network itself. Private and permissioned blockchain networks may pose less of a privacy risk in this regard, and the use of encryption techniques alone may be enough to adequately balance the privacy risks against the efficiencies derived from using the technology. In a public and permissionless blockchain network, these concerns appear greater, given the greater number of participants and opportunity for unauthorised access and processing of the data. The

---

38   The predecessor to the European Data Protection Board prior to the GDPR.
39   Article 29 Working Party, Opinion 05/2014 on Anonymisation Techniques (10 April 2014).
40   Ibid., at 5.
41   Ibid., at 11.
42   The EU Blockchain Observatory and Forum, *supra* note 4, at 23.
43   ICO, Anonymisation: Managing Data Protection Risk Code of Practice (2012) at 21.
44   Finck, *supra* note 34, at 11.

EU Blockchain Observatory and Forum observes that personal data should be stored off-chain, but where this is not possible they recognise that storing the data in a private blockchain network is a better solution from a privacy perspective.[45] The nature of the personal data will also be relevant when assessing the risks associated with the technology. Regulators could expect organisations to conduct so-called 'privacy impact assessments', which the GDPR requires of controllers before engaging in any 'high risk' processing activity, especially those involving novel technologies, so that they are forced to consciously weigh up the benefits and privacy risks associated with the use of blockchain.[46]

4.   Decentralised networks and issues of responsibility

11.35   Blockchain is a decentralised peer-to-peer network, meaning that no one central organisation controls the network. In essence, all users of the network obtain a copy of the blockchain, and roles and responsibilities are allocated to different individuals, such as adding and validating transactions on the chain. This has been heralded as one of blockchain's most attractive features, as it removes the need for a meddlesome or unwanted intermediary, frequently leading to greater efficiency or cost savings. It challenges our thinking about how many traditional services should be supplied. With information comes power, and many–- including many privacy advocates – rightly fear that certain organisations, whether in the public or private sector, will amass and control large amounts of personal data to the detriment of the relevant individuals. Blockchain may do away with the need for centralised actors in situations where they are common today, as instead, data will be stored across decentralised blockchains, eliminating the need for this middleman.[47]

11.36   Unhelpfully, the GDPR, like most data privacy frameworks, was not drafted with decentralised processing scenarios in mind; in fact, quite the reverse is true. The GDPR's concept of controller, for instance, somewhat simplistically assumes there to be a single, or possibly joint, controllers of data, dictating processing purposes and 'controlling' the data, aided by data processors acting on the instructions of the controller. Fitting these pre-defined roles into a decentralised blockchain ecosystem is not easy, given that there are many different actors with varying roles and responsibilities within the network. As

---

45   The EU Blockchain Observatory and Forum, *supra* note 4, at 30.

46   Under the GDPR, where a type of processing, particularly one involving new technology, is likely to result in a high risk to the rights and freedoms of natural persons, a data controller must carry out a data protection impact assessment, see GDPR, Art 35.

47   R. Danes, Peer-to-peer Blockchain Could Disrupt or even Destroy the Cloud (20 August 2018), available at: https://siliconangle.com/2018/08/20/peer-peer-blockchain-disrupt-even-destroy-cloud-blockchainweek/.

one academic has noted, 'blockchains … and the GDPR are profoundly incompatible at a conceptual level as the data protection mechanism developed for centralized data silos cannot be easily reconciled with a decentralized method of data storage and protection'.[48] In effect, no one 'controls' the data, as *everyone* controls the data.

The fact that 'everyone' might control the data is a difficult concept for those who embrace modern data privacy laws to accept. The GDPR, for instance, presumes two clearly defined roles – the controller, who determines the purposes and means of processing, and a processor, who processes data on the instructions of a data controller. A bank will collect and store personal data about its customers, e.g., name, contact details and financial information, for the purposes of providing them banking and related services. The bank will be positioned as a controller due to its autonomy and ability to make independent decisions about the data. The bank may hire vendors to assist with the processing of its customers' data, such as a cloud storage provider or a marketing firm. These third-party providers are typically data processors, as they process the bank's customers' personal data on the bank's instructions, and it is the bank that determines the purposes and means of processing. The example above, which sits easily with the GDPR's controller/processor distinction, is as remarkable for its simplicity as it is for its failure to reflect modern-day realities of how data may actually be processed, particularly in a blockchain setting. **11.37**

With a blockchain network, there is often no one centralised agent that determines how data are collected and processed on the network. Depending on the particular blockchain, there are likely multiple actors that can use the network for their own purposes or to advance the purposes of others. Participants on a blockchain network, or nodes, will store local copies of information held on the blockchain. And different nodes will play different roles, such as 'participating nodes' that decide what information (or transactions) will be submitted to the blockchain for validation, and 'validating nodes' that validate transactions that are submitted to the blockchain network prior to their being uploaded to the chain. In addition, there will be the individual users of the blockchain networks, i.e., persons that use the network to achieve certain desired ends. In this complex environment of multiple actors serving different functions, the question of who is a controller, who is a processor and who might be 'nothing' in data protection terms is far from clear. And, even where their status might be clear, there may be challenges in discharging their respective GDPR obligations. **11.38**

---

48 Finck, *supra* note 34, at 1.

11.39 To illustrate the difficulties here, a simple example will suffice. Data controllers are required by the GDPR to subject their data processors to quite robust data processing contracts.[49] If participating nodes were deemed data controllers, for the sake of argument, and validating nodes were deemed data processors, the participating nodes then would be required to put in place contractual agreements with the validating nodes that comply with the particular prescribed rules set out in the GDPR. Yet, trying to put such contracts in place in the context of a large public and permissionless blockchain network, like Bitcoin, would be impossible as a practical matter. All of this of course assumes that the parties agree that participating nodes are controllers and validating nodes are processors, which is a contentious proposition in itself.[50]

11.40 The CNIL, for one, has considered the roles of the different actors in a blockchain network, and concludes that in many cases participating nodes are likely data controllers, as they 'define the purposes (objects pursued by the processing), and the means (data format, use of blockchain technology, etc.) of the processing'.[51] In addition, CNIL has opined that validating nodes (or 'miners', as the CNIL refers to them), could be considered data processors as they 'follow the data controllers' instructions when checking whether the transaction meets technical criteria'.[52] Whether other regulators will endorse the CNIL's views is yet to be seen. Ambitiously, the CNIL specifically refers to the need for participating nodes to establish contracts with the validating nodes, as well as suggesting that groups of participating nodes, who intend to use the blockchain technology for a common purpose, should designate a sole or primary controller beforehand. Or, they might even create a separate legal entity that they can designate as the sole data controller, to avoid all participants being considered joint controllers, which would require even more complicated contractual arrangements.[53]

11.41 Of course, this suggestion critically assumes that the relevant parties are in a position to conduct such a discussion, reach agreement and then act on what has been agreed. With a private and permissioned blockchain, the ability to put in place a centralised agent may be possible, but with a public and permissionless blockchain, where the ability to identify every participant on the network would be quite difficult, to say the least, this suggestion appears overly optimistic. In any event, the CNIL could be rightly criticised for

---

49   GDPR, Art 28(3).
50   See The EU Blockchain Observatory and Forum, *supra* note 4, at 17.
51   CNIL, *supra* note 6, at 1.
52   Ibid., at 3.
53   Ibid., at 2.

attempting to convert a decentralised arrangement into one that more neatly fits existing data protection doctrines by forcing its participants to appoint a single controller, overlooking the fact that the suggestion runs counter to one of the key features of blockchain technology.

5. Other privacy challenges with blockchain

A further problematic aspect of blockchains with any international dimension **11.42** is the issue of cross-border data transfers. It is common for data privacy frameworks, and the GDPR is no exception, to impose significant restrictions on the transmittal of personal data to other third countries, unless they have been designated as furnishing adequate protections for the data. In the EU, for instance, the European Commission may formally designate a country as 'adequate',[54] although only few countries to date have been awarded an adequacy determination. In the absence of such a decision, the transfer must be protected by means of appropriate data transfer mechanisms unless there is an applicable statutory derogation. This can require parties to use the European Commission's standard contractual clauses, or 'model clauses', implement internal 'binding corporate rules' (for intra-company transfers),[55] or seek the consent of the relevant individuals.[56]

Because many blockchain networks today operate across national borders, the **11.43** problem of international data transfers rears its ugly head. Where this is the case, appropriate safeguards are needed, and the deployment of these in a blockchain scenario is likely to be extremely difficult. For instance, it could require participants on the network to collectively enter into standard contractual clauses, which remains (in ordinary circumstances) one of the more popular compliance solutions. But, where the relevant parties are numerous and distributed across multiple jurisdictions, problems inevitably will arise. As with other GDPR rules, parties involved in private blockchain networks may find compliance easier because collaboration and agreement may be easier to achieve. For example, an international corporation that wishes to use an internal blockchain solution to process customer transactions may find it less challenging to ensure the participants agree to a set of common contract clauses because of its ability to manage the behaviour of the parties and administer the execution of the clauses. In a public blockchain, however, these compliance measures are considerably less viable to deploy. Entering into

---

54   GDPR, Art 45.
55   GDPR, Art 46.
56   GDPR, Art 49.

standard contractual clauses with every participant who accesses personal data originating from the EU is aspirational, to say the least.

11.44 Finally, there is the question of which party or parties involved in the blockchain should be liable for a breach of any applicable data protection rules. This question is a close cousin to the problem of allocating controller and processor status to blockchain participants. Where allocation of controller or processor status is unclear, so is the allocation of responsibility and, ultimately, liability. In practice, blockchain participants are less likely to comply with applicable data privacy rules, including the GDPR, where their legal status remains ambiguous. This ambiguity may feed into a belief that the risk of enforcement, whether through regulatory enforcement or through civil claims brought by individuals or their representatives, is low. Arguably, this remains a more pressing issue for a public blockchain where there are a number of participants located all over the world. Regulators could, of course, enforce the rules against those parties within their jurisdiction, even when the relevant breach was committed by a participant outside the jurisdiction. If all participating nodes are deemed joint data controllers, then in theory, they are all individually and severally liable for any breach of the GDPR. However tempting this doctrine may be to authorities, the obvious inequities in pursuing one innocent party having virtually no hope of recourse against another party may dissuade the authorities from enforcing the rules. But, without the threat of enforcement, the motivation to be compliant is likely to be low. Issues surrounding the allocation of liability on distributed ledgers are described in Chapter 9.

D. CONCLUSION

11.45 This chapter has identified some of the inherent challenges blockchain technology creates when it comes to ensuring compliance with the GDPR. Given that many jurisdictions are adopting privacy frameworks similar to the EU's, it is likely that these issues will be similarly felt across the world. The extent to which these challenges are easier or harder to overcome will depend on the particular use case, and features of the blockchain network. The debates on possible solutions to the challenges raised by blockchain are ongoing, and it is likely, and in fact necessary, that regulatory guidance at an EU level is needed to overcome some of the biggest unknowns: when is personal data considered erased from a blockchain network, and what roles do different participants on the blockchain network play (i.e., controller or processor)?

While solutions to these challenges are not yet obvious, it cannot be denied **11.46** that blockchain is likely to create incredible efficiencies and cost savings across various industries, and as such, regulation should not become an obstacle to this revolution. Conversely, the rise of new technologies, while beneficial, should not thwart the fundamental rights of individuals, and particularly individuals' rights to privacy. How data protection authorities are dealing with these tensions is ongoing. Notably, the UK Information Commissioner's Office (the ICO) recently held a public consultation on the adoption of a regulatory sandbox, similar to the UK Financial Conduct Authority's regulatory sandbox,[57] which would allow organisations to be supported by the ICO in developing innovative products and services with the use of personal data.[58] Blockchain was specifically identified in the ICO's calls for views as a developing technology that would benefit from inclusion in the regulatory sandbox.[59] Initiatives such as these, and clearer guidance from regulators, will be fundamental to blockchain's future development in Europe and more globally.

---

57 FCA, Regulatory Sandbox, available at: https://www.fca.org.uk/firms/regulatory-sandbox.
58 ICO, ICO Call for Views on Creating a Regulatory Sandbox (10 September 2018), available at: https://ico.org.uk/about-the-ico/ico-and-stakeholder-consultations/ico-call-for-views-on-creating-a-regulatory-sandbox/.
59 Ibid.

Part III

REGULATION AND COMPLIANCE

12

REGTECH AND SUPTECH: THE FUTURE OF COMPLIANCE

John Ho Hee Jung

A. INTRODUCTION

Regulatory Technology, also known as RegTech, has been described by the UK Financial Conduct Authority (the FCA) as a subset of FinTech that focuses on technology within the financial industry to facilitate the delivery of regulatory requirements more efficiently and effectively than existing capabilities.[1] RegTech can take the form of any tool, application or platform that makes regulatory compliance more efficient through automated processes and reduction in costs. However, unlike FinTech, RegTech offers financial firms the opportunity to rethink the way that regulation and finance work together. **12.01**

In the UK, the FCA emphasises the importance of using 'tools and systems' to identify, establish and monitor mandatory controls. In its 2018–19 Business **12.02**

---

1 FCA, Call for Input on Supporting the Development and Adoption of RegTech, Feedback Statement FS16/4 (July 2016), available at: https://www.fca.org.uk/publication/feedback/fs-16-04.pdf, at 3.

Plan, the FCA stated that RegTech would be crucial in enabling it to take forward work to deliver cost savings, both for firms submitting regulatory returns to the FCA and in the way in which the FCA uses the information.[2]

12.03 The term Supervisory Technology, also known as SupTech, was first coined by Mr Ravi Menon, Head of the Monetary Authority of Singapore (the MAS) in 2017,[3] who queried: 'Why should regulated entities have a monopoly over the use of technology? Regulators too can harness technology to enhance the efficiency and effectiveness of supervision and surveillance.'[4] In that context, SupTech has been described by the Bank for International Settlement (the BIS) as the use of innovative technology by supervisory agencies to support innovation.[5] It helps supervisory agencies to digitise reporting and regulatory processes, resulting in more efficient and proactive monitoring of risk and compliance at financial institutions.

12.04 SupTech enables regulators to conduct supervisory work and oversight more effectively and efficiently. It differs from RegTech in that the former supports financial supervision, while the later aims at improving risk management and compliance in financial institutions.[6]

12.05 This chapter is structured as follows: Section B describes the development of RegTech and its key features; Section C describes key players, drivers and applications in RegTech; Part D analyses the risks and challenges of adopting RegTech; Section E describes the potential benefits, challenges and growth of SupTech; Section F examines the future trends of both RegTech and SupTech; Section G discusses the future of compliance; and Section H concludes.

---

2   FCA, Business Plan 2018/19, available at: https://www.fca.org.uk/publication/business-plans/business-plan-2018-19.pdf, at 27.

3   Ravi Menon, Financial Regulation – the Forward Agenda (2017), available at: http://www.mas.gov.sg/News-and-Publications/Speeches-and-Monetary-Policy-Statements/Speeches/2017/Financial-Regulation.aspx.

4   Ibid.

5   Bank for International Settlements, Financial Stability Institute, Insights on Policy Implementation No. 9, (2018), available at: https://www.bis.org/fsi/publ/insights9.pdf, at 1.

6   Toronto Centre, SupTech: Leveraging Technology for Better Supervision (July 2018), available at: https://res.torontocentre.org/guidedocs/SupTech%20-%20Leveraging%20Technology%20for%20Better%20Supervision.pdf, at 2.

B. DEVELOPMENT OF REGTECH

The development of RegTech has been characterised by a series of stages.[7] **12.06**
The first stage, RegTech 1.0, occurred in the 1990s and 2000s and was led by
large financial institutions that integrated technology into their internal
processes to combat rising compliance costs and complexity, as epitomised in
the complexity of complying with Pillar 1 (regulatory capital) of the Basel II
Capital Accord.[8] Supervisors and financial institutions wishing to implement
Basel II needed to build considerable additional infrastructure, i.e., data and
reporting systems, and verification and validation capacity.[9] However, this
pre-2008 paradigm was largely driven by the financial industry in partnership
with regulators, and was focused on the digitisation of manual reporting and
compliance processes.

In the aftermath of the 2008 global financial crisis (GFC), financial insti- **12.07**
tutions faced the regulatory burden of having to comply with the much-
needed regulatory reforms. Many responded by increasing compliance staff,
but continued to use the same systems. This resulted in increased compliance
costs for these companies in an environment of enhanced regulatory scrutiny
and complexity in meeting regulatory obligations. The second stage, RegTech
2.0, was driven by the post-GFC regulatory requirements and the costs of
their implementation. At the same time, regulators have been trying to mirror
the increasingly digitised nature of the markets they monitor and to enhance
their capacity to analyse the rising volumes of data generated by the post-GFC
reporting obligations.

RegTech 2.0 heralds a new regulatory landscape in response to the GFC as a **12.08**
catalyst for greater use of technology by financial institutions and regulators to
enhance regulatory compliance and streamline its processes.[10] RegTech is
perceived as a solution to bring down the cost of compliance by leveraging
technology to meet heightened regulatory obligations more efficiently and
effectively.

---

7   See Douglas W. Arner et al., Fintech and RegTech in a Nutshell, and the Future in a Sandbox, CFA Institute
     Research Foundation (2017).
8   BIS, Part 2: The First Pillar – Minimum Capital Requirements, available at: https://www.bis.org/publ/
     bcbs128b.pdf.
9   IMF, Implementation of Basel II—Implications for the World Bank and the IMF (2005), available at:
     https://www.imf.org/external/np/pp/eng/2005/072205.htm, III(19).
10 Patrick Armstrong, Developments in RegTech and SupTech, ESMA RegTechs: Feedback from First
     Experiments (2018), available at: https://www.esma.europa.eu/sites/default/files/library/esma71-99-1070_
     speech_on_regtech.pdf, at 1.

12.09 According to the Institute of International Finance, this wave of RegTech innovation 'stands out from other software solutions by linking advanced models and algorithms, machine learning and advanced analytics, and real-time capabilities'.[11] Primary technological drivers are the widespread use of cloud computing, the increased acceptance of application programming interfaces (APIs) and advances in the fields of artificial intelligence and machine learning (AI/ML). RegTech has grown from a niche to one of the most promising and exciting areas in the financial and regulatory landscape. The range of services is broad and includes activities such as customer identification/verification and transaction monitoring in such areas as AML/CFT, anti-fraud surveillance, risk assessment and management, market conduct services, origination processes and regulatory requirement monitoring.

12.10 RegTech aims to shift the risk/cost curve by reducing costs of compliance through automation and/or leveraging technology to increase the effectiveness of compliance.[12] One report on RegTech firms estimates that 'governance, risk and compliance (GRC) costs account for 15 to 20 per cent of the total "run the bank" cost base of most major financial institutions. GRC demand drives roughly 40 per cent of costs for "change the bank" projects under way'.[13] Streamlining onerous processes by utilising RegTech allows organisations to maximise time spent on value added projects, rather than time-consuming manual processes.[14] Additionally, RegTech reduces exposure to the risk of human error, permitting organisations to automate compliance without relying on individuals.[15] RegTech not only promises to not only improve reporting and compliance, but also to achieve cost savings.

12.11 For regulated financial institutions, compliance with applicable laws and regulations is mandatory. The costs of non-compliance are punitive and can include fines, loss of business, loss of licences, sanctions, penalties and reputational damage. In 2018, the US Securities and Exchange Commission (the SEC) alone issued 821 enforcements, amounting to approximately USD

---

11 Institute of International Finance, Regtech: Exploring Solutions to Regulatory Challenges (October 2015), available at: https://www.iif.com/topics/regtech/regtech-exploring-solutions-regulatory-challenges.

12 Jonah M.A. Crane, RegTech: Bending the Risk/Cost Curve or Breaking It?, 20(4) *Thomson Reuters Fintech Law Report*, (July/August 2017), at 4.

13 Bain and Company, Banking Regtechs to the Rescue? (2016), available at: https://www.bain.com/contentassets/0952af5e941e4e0aaa84902e3fceae53/bain_brief_banking_regtechs_to_the_rescue.pdf, at 1.

14 Thomson Reuters, Regtech 2020 and Beyond – What Does the Future Hold?, available at: https://www.refinitiv.com/content/dam/gl/en/documents/reports/regtech-2020-and-beyond.pdf, at 3.

15 Ibid.

4 billion in fines.[16] In the same year, the FCA issued fines for compliance breaches totalling nearly GBP 60 million.[17]

Regulators seem optimistic about RegTech. For example, in the UK, RegTech **12.12** has for many years benefited from the FCA's RegTech sandbox which allows businesses to test products, services, business models and delivery mechanisms in the real market, with real consumers.[18] In the US, the Commodity Futures Trading Commission (the CFTC) launched the LabCFTC programme to promote RegTech innovations that can benefit the American public.[19] Regulatory bodies are also interested in RegTech's growth to better utilise their limited oversight and enforcement resources. In Singapore and Hong Kong, for instance, the regulators have opened their FinTech supervisory sandboxes for RegTech projects or ideas generated by financial institutions and RegTech firms.

RegTech firms have attracted substantial investment in recent years, while **12.13** interest from financial institutions and regulators has grown significantly.[20] The growth potential and market size of RegTech serves as a magnet for developers of cutting-edge technologies. According to KMPG's 2018 report, RegTech investment reached USD 1.37 billion in the first half of 2018, thereby already surpassing the 2017 annual totals.[21] RegTech developments are growing rapidly particularly in the areas of transaction monitoring, regulatory reporting, risk management and compliance. Bloomberg estimated that the global demand for regulatory, compliance and governance software is expected to reach USD 118.7 billion by 2020, which represents a great opportunity for RegTech firms.[22]

Another noteworthy study is Accenture's 2018 Compliance Risk Study,[23] **12.14** which surveyed executive-level compliance professionals from 150 financial

---

16 See SEC Press Release, SEC Enforcement Division Issues Report on FY 2018 Results, available at: https://www.sec.gov/news/press-release/2018-250.

17 See FCA, 2018 Fines, available at: https://www.fca.org.uk/news/news-stories/2018-fines.

18 See FCA, Working with us, available at: https://www.fca.org.uk/firms/regtech/working-with-us.

19 See CFTC: LabCFTC Overview, available at: https://www.cftc.gov/LabCFTC/Overview/index.htm.

20 KPMG, The Pulse of FinTech 2018, available at: https://assets.kpmg.com/content/dam/kpmg/xx/pdf/2018/07/h1-2018-pulse-of-fintech.pdf, at 4.

21 Ibid., at 3.

22 Marco Antonio Cavallo, How RegTech Closes the Gap Between Technology and Financial Services (April 2017), available at: https://www.bloomberg.com/professional/blog/regtech-closes-gap-technology-financial-services/.

23 Accenture, Overcoming Barriers in the Growing RegTech Space (March 2018), available at: https://financeandriskblog.accenture.com/regulatory-insights/reg-tech/overcoming-barriers-in-the-growing-regtech-space.

institutions across 13 countries, and showed the following key statistics for respondents related to technology:

- 57 per cent of compliance respondents rank compliance technology transformation as one of their top three strategic initiatives for 2019; and
- in the 12 months from the date of the survey, nearly half of compliance executives surveyed were planning to leverage innovative technology such as surveillance tools as part of their compliance operating model, and move towards adopting AI capabilities over the next three years.

12.15 In the future, RegTech will exhibit its greatest potential in the third stage of its development—RegTech 3.0—a move from 'know your customer' (KYC) to a 'know your data' (KYD) approach.[24] This is underpinned by an emerging trend of financial institutions leveraging advanced technology and data-centric solutions to comply with their compliance requirements and realise internal efficiencies. The shift from customer-centric to data-centric focus of the RegTech and SupTech segments encourages regulators and supervisory authorities to roll out data-centric agile regulations, paving the way for truly revamping financial regulation. In the long term, beyond regulatory compliance and cost efficiency, the key benefit of RegTech will be its ability to enable innovation while enhancing consumer confidence through better customer experience.[25] Financial institutions and regulators will need to work together to provide a roadmap for a sustainable and robust RegTech agenda that keeps pace with digital transformation, while maintaining the safety and soundness of financial markets.

C. KEY PLAYERS, DRIVERS AND APPLICATIONS IN REGTECH

1. Players and drivers

12.16 Many RegTech firms tend to be relatively young, having come into existence in the aftermath of the 2008 global financial crisis. As illustrated in Table 12.1,[26] the ecosystem of RegTech firms includes the following key players: RegTech companies; regulators; financial institutions and professional service providers, such as accounting, legal, compliance and tax experts and advisers.

---

24 KPMG, There's a Revolution Coming (2018), available at: https://home.kpmg/content/dam/kpmg/uk/pdf/2018/09/regtech-revolution-coming.pdf, at 18.

25 EY, Innovating with RegTech (2015), available at: https://www.ey.com/Publication/vwLUAssets/EY-Innovating-with-RegTech/$FILE/EY-Innovating-with-RegTech.pdf, at 9.

26 Ibid., at 5.

Table 12.1   Ecosystem of RegTech companies

Player	Current Focus	Anticipated Role
RegTech firms	Developing understanding of engagement between businesses and the regulator to align solutions with regulatory and risk management frameworks	• Developing solutions to meet business and regulator needs • Confirming that developed solutions are compatible with wider risk management frameworks and regulatory requirements
Financial institutions	Developing RegTech strategy and roadmap	• RegTech adopters • Internal development of RegTech solutions
Regulators	Encouraging dialogue and collecting market views	• Continuing to promote innovation around regulatory compliance • Adopting an increasingly proactive role in driving efficiency and collaboration across the different parts of the RegTech ecosystem • Assisting in the creation of common integrated standards and development of guidance on the rules of engagement • Progressing initiatives focussed on managing internal change resulting from RegTech, including horizon scanning from a global perspective
Professional service firms	Working across the ecosystem to understand requirements, needs and solutions	• Driving cohesion of regulatory standards, institution needs and vendor solutions • Using industry insights and network to connect providers and users • Supporting due diligence for new market entrants • Providing regulatory, systems and compliance transformation advisory support, including proactively managing risks associated with implementing new RegTech solutions

12.17 RegTech is well positioned to further enhance the interface between financial institutions and regulators, with the regulator playing a more prominent role.

For example, according to Nick Cook,[27] the FCA's Head of RegTech and Advanced Analytics, the FCA tries to play three key roles in developing the RegTech sector:

(a)   The first is as an engaged market participant, publishing calls for input and meeting with RegTech companies and accelerator programmes to work out the ways in which the technology can be used to meet the needs of regulated firms.

(b)   The second is as 'a convener of new solutions' through the hosting of regulatory sandboxes and TechSprints – two-day events that bring together participants from across and outside financial services to develop technology-based ideas or proof of concepts to address specific industry challenges.[28]

(c)   Finally, the FCA is also an ambassador of RegTech through experimentation, research and development of its own. The regulator is piloting a series of tests to develop 'machine executional reporting' – in layman's terms, writing law as code, and is also looking at how machine learning technology and natural language processing technology can be implemented in the regulatory process.

12.18   In Hong Kong, the Hong Kong Monetary Authority (the HKMA) is encouraging a closer interaction and dialogue between financial institutions and the regulator. As an illustration, the regulator has launched a series of RegTech projects, through its Banking Made Easy initiative and the Balanced and Responsive Supervision programme.[29] Specifically, Banking Made Easy focuses on minimising regulatory frictions in bank customers' digital experience, including remote onboarding, online finance and online wealth management.[30] The HKMA plans to open the FinTech Supervisory Sandbox to RegTech projects through its Banking Made Easy initiative, focusing on four areas: AML/CFT surveillance technologies, RegTech for prudential risk management and compliance, study of machine-readable regulations and the HKMA's exploration of SupTech.[31]

---

27   FCA, RegTech at the FCA (2018), available at: http://www.fsclub.co.uk/public-servfile.cfm?f=Nick %20Cook%20FCA%20Presentation.pdf.

28   See: https://www.fca.org.uk/firms/regtech/techsprints.

29   Artur Yuen, RegTech in the Smart Banking Era – a Supervisor's Perspective (2018), available at: https:// www.bis.org/review/r181012g.pdf.

30   See HKMA Press Release, A New Era of Smart Banking (September 2017), available at: https:// www.hkma.gov.hk/eng/key-information/press-releases/2017/20170929-3.shtml.

31   Ibid.

RegTech is developing in response to various demand and supply drivers.[32] **12.19**
Demand is linked to regulatory changes and the need for financial institutions
and regulators alike to process large amounts of data. Supply factors primarily
focus on advances in technology.

Demand for RegTech solutions is driven by an increase in the complexity and **12.20**
scale of financial regulation activity across the world, which has grown
significantly since the GFC. This is seen in the transformation of the
European regulatory landscape with the enactment of extensive legislation
such as Markets in Financial Instruments Directive II, European Market
Infrastructure Regulation, Market Abuse Directive II, Undertakings for
Collective Investments in Transferable Securities V and Payment Services
Directive II, which has resulted in significant reporting obligations. In
addition, compliance with stringent data privacy laws and regulations across
the globe such as the GDPR and the US Personal Data Protection and Breach
Accountability Act have all increased the demand for RegTech.

The second demand driver cited for the rise of RegTech adoption[33] is the **12.21**
sheer volume of transactions and data that many financial institutions need to
handle as the economy and business continue to grow. If we take the mobile
wallet market as an example, research predicts cumulative annual growth of
32 per cent in the global e-wallet transactions between 2017 and 2022.[34]
According to the HKMA, '[s]uch a scale of transactions means it would
simply be impracticable for some financial institutions and e-wallet operators
to effectively manage the associated risks using traditional or manual risk
management approaches'.[35]

The supply drivers underpinning the growth of RegTech are the combination **12.22**
of advancements in the development of AI/ML, enhancements in computing
power, wider availability of RegTech solutions, reduction in costs of computing power and storage.[36]

2. RegTech applications

Technology now plays an increasingly fundamental role in financial services **12.23**
and is also a catalyst for change and innovation.

---

32 Armstrong, *supra* note 10, at 3.
33 HKMA, Regtech in the Smart Banking Era – A Supervisor's Perspective (2018), available at: https://
    www.hkma.gov.hk/eng/key-information/speech-speakers/akhyuen/20180927-1.shtml.
34 Ibid.
35 Ibid.
36 Armstrong, *supra* note 10, at 3.

The FCA has identified three types of RegTech applications:[37]

(a)   those aimed at supporting regulatory compliance in firms;
(b)   those aimed at improving regulatory oversight and modernising regulators; and
(c)   those aimed at re-engineering or reforming regulatory systems.

Whilst there are numerous potential use cases and applications of RegTech, according to the Toronto Centre,[38] the following areas of RegTech (Table 12.2) have received significant attention:

Table 12.2   Areas of RegTech application

Area of RegTech   Use cases

	Area of RegTech	Use cases
1	Compliance	Enterprise-wide solutions for identifying and keeping track of changes in regulatory requirements, at local or global levels, and solutions for automated real-time monitoring of compliance levels and compliance risk, based on the analysis of operational and other data (e.g., employee monitoring, historical email analysis, human behaviour analysis, trade communication analysis).
2	Identity management and control	Solutions that digitise client or partner onboarding processes, digitise and share customer/partner information, gather and analyse customer and transaction data, and identify suspicious transactions based on automated triggers and constantly updated customer/partner profiles.
3	Risk management	Tools to improve the risk management process at financial institutions, by bringing efficiencies to the generation of risk data, risk data aggregation, internal risk reporting, automatically identifying and monitoring risks according to internal methodologies or regulatory definitions, and creating alerts and automated actions triggered when pre-determined risk levels are reached.
4	Regulatory reporting	Solutions that help automate and integrate regulatory reporting requirements to cut costs, and streamline and increase the accuracy and timeliness of reporting, including making real-time reporting possible.
5	Transaction monitoring	Solutions that offer real-time transaction monitoring and auditing, such as by using DLT, end-to-end integrity validation, anti-fraud and market abuse identification systems, back-office automation (post-transaction settlement, closing procedures), and risk alerts.

---

37   FCA, *supra* note 27, at 6.
38   Toronto Centre, FinTech, RegTech and SupTech: What They Mean for Financial Supervision (2017), available at: https://res.torontocentre.org/guidedocs/FinTech%20RegTech%20and%20SupTech%20-%20What%20They%20Mean%20for%20Financial%20Supervision.pdf, at 9–10.

| 6 | Trading in financial markets | Solutions that automate numerous procedures related to transacting in financial markets, such as calculating margins, choosing central counterparties and trading venues, assessing exposures, complying with good conduct-of-business principles, etc. |

These examples are certainly not exhaustive, as rapid developments in technology create new application segments for the adoption of RegTech.

Let us now examine the main RegTech technologies used in the financial **12.24** sector. Whilst the use of technology for compliance is not new, RegTech promises agility, speed, increased integration and analytics.[39] This is enabled by new or emerging technologies including AI/ML, robotic process automation (RPA), natural language processing (NLP), big data, cloud computing, API and DLT, including blockchain.

Specifically, AI/ML techniques can be used to find patterns in large amounts **12.25** of data from increasingly diverse and innovative sources. Big data is used broadly to describe the storage and analysis of large and/or complicated data sets using a variety of data elaboration techniques, which can discover trends that would not be apparent with a smaller data set. AI/ML tools are generally used in a big data environment, allowing the implementation of new data management platforms that can capture, store and analyse enormous volumes of structured and unstructured data. APIs refer to protocols and tools that allow different systems to interact with each other. Biometrics is the use of people's unique physical and behavioural characteristics to authenticate their identity. RPA refers to the application of computer technology in order to process relatively simple, repetitive tasks in a consistent and automated fashion. Cloud computing refers to the use of an online network of hosting processors to increase the scale and flexibility of computing capacity. NLP is an interdisciplinary field of computer science, AI and computation linguistics that focuses on programming computers and algorithms to parse, process and understand human language. All of this means that both financial institutions and regulators need to look at smart solutions for infrastructure, data and analytics.

Financial institutions have used AI/ML technologies in the following areas: **12.26** (i) customer-focused uses such as credit scoring, insurance and chatbots; (ii) operational uses, including capital optimisation, model risk management and market impact analysis; and (iii) trading and portfolio management in

---

39 BBVA Research, RegTech, the New Magic Word in FinTech (2016), available at: https://www.bbva research.com/wp-content/uploads/2016/03/Banking-Outlook-Q116_Cap6.pdf.

financial markets.[40] Moreover, financial institutions and insurance companies are also using AI in the automation of repetitive tasks, such as KYC and AML checks, claims processing, trade reconciliations and fraud identification.[41] Increased automation of compliance processes through RPA has allowed financial institutions to minimise the need to perform repetitive tasks, such as collecting data and analysing information across systems, thereby reducing errors and freeing up resources to focus on higher-value work.[42] For example, Commonwealth Bank of Australia and ING have collaborated with the FCA on the use of NLP to simplify processing of information and implementation under MiFID 2.[43]

D. RISKS AND CHALLENGES OF REGTECH ADOPTION

12.27 The advent of new technologies has been accompanied by the emergence of new and complex risks that need to be considered. Below are examples (which are by no means exhaustive) of a number of major barriers to achieving effective collaboration among financial institutions, RegTech firms and regulators.

1. Onerous procurement process

12.28 Financial institutions' procurement and approval processes are among the main barriers to RegTech adoption. The long sales, decision and onboarding cycle and approval processes, coupled with the typical need to get buy-in from legal, compliance, risk, finance and IT groups, which in some instances may take a year or longer to complete, constrain the mass adoption of solutions offered by RegTech firms.[44] Recent research from Burnmark shows that for nearly 50 per cent of financial institutions surveyed, procurement is a challenge

---

40 Patrick Armstrong, Developments in RegTech and SupTech, ESMA RegTechs: Feedback from First Experiments (2018), available at: https://www.esma.europa.eu/sites/default/files/library/esma71-99-1070_speech_on_regtech.pdf, at 3

41 Bloomberg Professional Services Blog, The Race to AI Utilization in Finance is a Marathon, Not a Sprint, (2017), available at: https://www.bloomberg.com/professional/blog/race-ai-utilization-finance-marathon-not-sprint.

42 FINRA, Technology Based Innovations for Regulatory Compliance ('RegTech') in the Securities Industry (2018), available at: http://www.finra.org/sites/default/files/2018_RegTech_Report.pdf, at 6.

43 See Finextra, CBA and ING Partner on RegTech Pilot (22 February 2018), available at: https://www.finextra.com/newsarticle/31721/cba-and-ing-partner-on-regtech-pilot?utm_medium=newsflash&utm_source=2018-2-22&member=82535.

44 DLA Piper, Digital Transformation in Financial Services (2018), available at: https://www.dlapiper.com/en/uk/insights/publications/2018/10/digital-transformation-in-financial-services/, at 18.

for the adoption of RegTech.[45] Most likely, this is because many firms are still approaching disruptive technologies from top-down by asking how such technologies can improve their bottom line. By contrast, a bottom-up approach that identifies problems and then looks for good solutions is more likely to align decision-makers across the organisation.[46] Moreover, the lack of necessary investment, as well as the lack of staff expertise and skills in delivering digital transformation, present a challenge for many financial institutions. This may explain why RegTech has been relatively slow to take off in some of them. In particular, the shortage of technology expertise appears to have led to a conservative approach to adopting technology.[47]

2. Preference for large and established providers

Many new RegTech firms face challenges in convincing financial institutions **12.29** to adopt their RegTech solutions in particular where they do not have a track record or sufficient financial resources to persist in the long term. Financial institutions typically ask for years of corporate history as part of their due diligence requirements, which can be a challenge for relatively young RegTech firms. Unlike start-ups, incumbent large and established technology firms have greater trust and credibility based on their track record, financial resources and experience as trusted partners.

3. Fragmented market

Many RegTech firms tend to offer specific or targeted solutions that are not **12.30** easily scalable and typically do not provide solutions across multiple jurisdictions. This creates a fragmented environment and financial institutions are hesitant to adopt RegTech solutions that are limited in scope and jurisdiction given the complexity of integrating them within their existing systems and processes. A possible solution is a RegTech model that offers flexible enterprise solutions that can be applied to a variety of tasks. For example, IBM RegTech offers a comprehensive solution portfolio that leverages deep expertise in risk and compliance with advanced AI and analytics technology. These solutions are transforming how firms manage their risk and compliance

---

45 LhoFT, A SWOT Analysis of the $100B Regtech Market (April 2018), available at: https://www.lhoft.com/en/insights/a-swot-analysis-of-the-100b-regtech-market.

46 Crane, *supra* note 12, at 8.

47 Jonathan Frieder, Overcoming Barriers in the Growing RegTech Space (2018), available at: https://financeandriskblog.accenture.com/regulatory-insights/reg-tech/overcoming-challenges-in-helping-regulatory-technology-grow, at 2.

function by enabling more informed decisions—from regulatory change management to specific compliance processes, such as AML, KYC, conduct surveillance and stress testing.[48]

4. Regulatory uncertainty

12.31 The constantly evolving regulatory landscape creates difficulties for financial institutions to choose the areas of compliance modernisation to invest in. Adoption and implementation of RegTech solutions have not always been consistent due to the evolving nature of compliance taxonomies and technical requirements. For example, the GDPR, which is designed to strengthen and unify data protection for every individual across the European Union, places certain transparency requirements on organisations that cannot be ignored especially in the context of AI and the use of algorithms to process or handle personal data. Transparency is a major obligation under the GDPR, which expands the notion that personal data must be lawfully and fairly processed.[49] Specifically, Article 22 of the GDPR states that '[t]he data subject shall have the right not to be subject to a decision based solely on automated processing, including profiling, which produces legal effects concerning him or her or similarly significantly affects him or her'. Consequently, data controllers need to clearly communicate with data subjects, such as by informing them of the specific purpose of the data processing and obtain relevant consent in accordance with the GDPR rules. This poses a problem for certain AIs that are considered 'black-boxes', which are opaque where the underlying algorithms are not disclosed to individual consumers. However, the GDPR highlights the right to an explanation of the decision reached,[50] which arguably entitles users to be given an explanation for an algorithm's output. The challenge with transparency for firms using AI is that very rarely do they want to share their all-important algorithm source codes that underpin their decisions.

---

48 IBM, IBM RegTech, available at: https://www.ibm.com/industries/banking-financial-markets/risk-compliance.

49 See Natasha Lomas, AI Spots Legal Problems with Tech T&Cs in GDPR Research Project (2018), available at: https://techcrunch.com/2018/07/04/european-ai-used-to-spot-legal-problems-in-tech-tcs/.

50 The debate centres on the single occurrence of the phrase 'right to explanation' in Recital 71 of the GDPR, available at: https://gdpr-info.eu/recitals/no-71/.

5. Concentration risk

Operational risk in the form of concentration risk may arise from a move to a greater use of data and risk management tools via third party service providers. More particularly, data provided by the Monetary Authority of Singapore[51] shows that: **12.32**

- in 2018, the top four cloud service providers in the world held a market share of 80 per cent;
- about 25 per cent of the core banking systems of global systemically important banks is now residing on the cloud; and
- a large supplier of cloud services could potentially become a single point of failure when many financial institutions rely on it.

Moreover, excessive or indiscriminate reliance on RegTech solutions may create new problems and could potentially cause system-wide disruptions.[52] Regulators have expressed concern about the operational risk of many institutions relying on RegTech firms for the provision of critical activities, and the need for adequate back-up recovery plans.[53] In addition, concentrations of outsourcing providers may lead to increased systemic risk, for example when technical problems or solvency issues lead to the disruption of services covered by RegTech firms.[54] Regulators and financial institutions will therefore need to devise and implement appropriate strategies to manage this operational risk. In this regard, regulators around the world have issued either regulations or guidance notes on the management of outsourcing risks pertaining to cloud services.[55] **12.33**

6. Data protection security and cyber threats

As regulators and financial institutions move towards digitalised infrastructures, new risks related to data protection, privacy and cyber threats will inevitably emerge due to increased interconnectivity. As many RegTech **12.34**

---

51 Ravi Menon, Financial Regulation – 20 Years after the Global Financial Crisis (June 2018), available at: http://www.mas.gov.sg/News-and-Publications/Speeches-and-Monetary-Policy-Statements/Speeches/2018/Financial-Regulation.aspx.

52 International Monetary Fund Staff Discussion Note, Fintech and Financial Services: Initial Considerations, SDN/17/05 (June 2017), at 18.

53 See Mark Wetjen, Cloud Computing: A Blueprint for Market Infrastructures (2017), available at: http://www.dtcc.com/news/2017/july/05/a-blueprint-for-market-infrastructures.

54 ESAS, Joint Committee Report on Risks and Vulnerabilities in the EU Financial System, available at: https://esas-joint-committee.europa.eu/Publications/Reports/Joint%20Committee%20Risk%20Report.pdf, at 14.

55 Menon, *supra* note 51.

solutions are based on cloud-based computing, regulators in such jurisdictions as the US, the UK, the EU, Hong Kong and Singapore have issued guidance on the use of cloud solutions and in certain instances treat cloud solutions as outsourcing to third parties. For example, the European Banking Authority has issued guidance on outsourcing to cloud service providers and the EU-wide supervisory expectations if institutions in the European Economic Area intend to adopt cloud computing, so as to allow them to leverage the benefits of using cloud services, while ensuring that any related risks are adequately identified and managed.[56]

12.35 There are specific concerns around cross-border data flows and determination of applicable law for borderless technologies such as DLT (as described in more detail in Chapter 8), as well as audit trails for the automated decision-making. Cyber resilience, security and data protection are therefore areas where further regulatory guidance will be needed. Broadly speaking, regulators expect financial institutions to take appropriate actions to promote effective management of cyber risk, with sufficiently robust systems and controls to minimise the potential impact on their businesses, reputation and the financial system.

12.36 Notwithstanding these barriers to the adoption of RegTech solutions, financial institutions, regulators and RegTech firms are increasingly collaborating to address some of these concerns and map out a path for closer innovation and technology engagement industry-wide.

E. BENEFITS, CHALLENGES AND GROWTH OF SUPTECH

12.37 SupTech is altering the way in which supervisory agencies supervise markets and has the potential to transform financial supervision.[57] It helps supervisory agencies to digitise reporting and regulatory processes, resulting in more efficient and proactive monitoring of risk and compliance in financial institutions.[58] According to the BIS, the experience of early users suggests that SupTech can enhance supervisory effectiveness, cut costs and increase capability.[59]

---

56 European Banking Authority: Recommendations on Outsourcing to Third Party Providers (2017), available at: https://eba.europa.eu/regulation-and-policy/internal-governance/recommendations-on-outsourcing-to-cloud-service-providers.
57 Armstrong, *supra* note 10, at 4.
58 Bank for International Settlements, *supra* note 5, at 3.
59 Ibid.

Whilst still in the early stages of development, generally SupTech applications **12.38** can be found in the areas of data collection and analysis.[60] Specifically, in data collection, SupTech applications can be found in reporting, data management and virtual assistance. In data analytics, SupTech applications cover market surveillance, misconduct analysis, micro prudential supervision and macro prudential supervision.[61] Figure 12.1 summarises the key areas identified by the BIS in which SupTech applications can be found.[62]

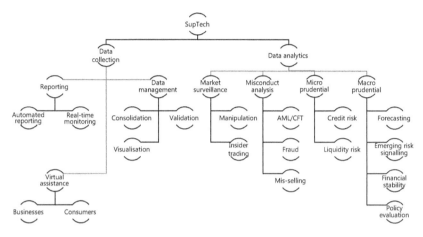

Figure 12.1   SupTech applications

SupTech solutions are increasingly being used to make supervision more **12.39** effective, improve surveillance and reduce compliance requirements imposed on financial institutions. For example, the European Central Bank and the US Federal Reserve are using NLP to help them identify financial stability risks.[63] The FCA has been using AI/ML to analyse big data sets with the aim of identifying suspicious trading behaviour.[64] The Monetary Authority of Singapore has been using NLP and ML to analyse suspicious transaction reports and find potential money laundering networks.[65] The Australian Securities and Investments Commission is using SupTech to analyse real time and historical trade data, create alerts and assess complex thematic risks.[66] The US Financial Industry Regulatory Authority has leveraged cloud computing and

---

60   Ibid.
61   Ibid., at 5.
62   Ibid., at 4.
63   Armstrong, *supra* note 5, at 4.
64   Ibid.
65   BIS, *supra* note 5, at 10.
66   Ibid., at 7.

ML in its surveillance space.[67] The Philippines' central bank, Bangko Sentral ng Pilipinas, has developed a prototype for an API-based data input approach to extract regulatory reports directly from banks.[68] Whilst DLT is still in a nascent stage, regulators such as the CFTC envision that rulebooks will be digitised, compliance increasingly automated or built into business operations through smart contracts, and regulatory reporting satisfied through real-time DLT networks.[69]

12.40   One of the main promises of SupTech is the potential to move away from templates and manual procedures to support data pull approaches,[70] data accessibility, reporting utilities,[71] making sense of unstructured data, data quality management, as well as regulatory submissions. Compared to the high false positive detection rate from traditional rule-based surveillance systems, through mathematical optimisation techniques, the ML-based surveillance systems have been able to reduce false positive rates.[72] SupTech solutions are automating and streamlining administrative and operational procedures, digitising data and working tools, and improving data analytics. The adoption of SupTech by supervisory agencies therefore promises to help streamline the digestion, analysis and reporting of financial trends on a global basis across multiple markets and supervisory agencies.

12.41   Despite these promises, there are also risks associated with the adoption of SupTech. While some of the risks are similar to the risks faced by financial institutions in the adoption of RegTech, there are also some specific risks related to technology and data used in SupTech. Some of these issues relate to

---

67   FINRA podcast, How the Cloud and Machine Learning Have Transformed FINRA Market Surveillance (2018), available at: http://www.finra.org/industry/podcasts/how-cloud-and-machine-learning-have-transformed-market-surveillance.

68   BIS, *supra* note 5, at 7.

69   Keynote address of Chairman J. Christopher Giancarlo at FinTech Week, Georgetown University Law School: Quantitative Regulation: Effective Market Regulation in a Digital Era (7 November 2018), available at: https://www.cftc.gov/PressRoom/SpeechesTestimony/opagiancarlo59.

70   The National Bank of Rwanda (BNR) is one of the first supervisory agencies to use a data pull approach:

This technology extracts data directly from the IT systems of supervised institutions. Data-pulling is done automatically every 24 hours or, in some cases, every 15 minutes. For other data, the frequency is monthly. Combined with data from BNR's internal systems, the SupTech application streamlines the reporting process and produces meaningful information for supervisors and policymakers.

BIS, *supra* note 5, at 6.

71   Reporting utilities refers to centralised structures that function not only as a common database of reported granular data, but also as a repository of the interpretation of reporting rules. See Toronto Centre, FinTech, RegTech and SupTech: What They Mean for Financial Supervision (2017), available at: https://res.toronto centre.org/guidedocs/FinTech%20RegTech%20and%20SupTech%20-%20What%20They%20Mean%20for %20Financial%20Supervision.pdf, at 12.

72   Financial Stability Board, Artificial Intelligence and Machine Learning in Financial Services – Market Developments and Financial Stability Implications (2017), available at: http://www.fsb.org/wp-content/uploads/P011117.pdf, at 24.

computational capacity constraints, increased operational risks, including cyber risk, data quality, finding the right talent, management support and buy-in from supervision units, and rigid rules in project management. The lack of transparency in some of the data analytics applications is also a critical issue.[73] In this regard, it is crucial for regulators, supervisory agencies and financial institutions to work together to manage these risks and promote effective management and mitigants of these risks.

F. FUTURE TRENDS IN REGTECH AND SUPTECH

Looking towards the future, the adoption of RegTech and SupTech by financial institutions, supervisory authorities and regulators is likely to increase. We can already see this in the Basel Committee's Principles for Effective Risk Data Aggregation and Risk Reporting, which require systemically important financial institutions to have a high degree of automation in risk data aggregation and reporting.[74]   **12.42**

Emerging trends that could shape the future of RegTech and SupTech are as follows: **12.43**

1. Quantitative regulation

The term 'quantitative regulation' was coined by the CFTC Chairman J. Christopher Giancarlo when he unveiled the CFTC's response to increasing centrality of data and the CFTC's role as a quantitative regulator.[75] Even though market regulation is increasingly powered by data automation and machine learning, Giancarlo explained that quantitative regulation means 'melding machines and humans, not separating them.' He explained:[76]   **12.44**

> In fact, the objective of quantitative regulation is to more firmly support the skilled teams that carry out the agency's ongoing activities in market surveillance, enforcement, regulatory compliance and rule examinations, market intelligence, policy development, and market reform. It means freeing agency staff from repetitive and low value tasks to focus on high value activities that require their expert judgment and

---

73   Financial Stability Institute: FSI Insights on policy implementation no 9 – Innovative technology in Financial Supervision (SupTech) – the Experience of Early Users (2018), available at: https://www.bis.org/fsi/publ/insights9.pdf, at 1.

74   See Basel Committee on Banking Supervision, Principles for Effective Risk Data Aggregation and Risk Reporting (January 2013), available at: https://www.bis.org/publ/bcbs239.pdf.

75   Financial Stability Institute, *supra* note 78, at 1.

76   Ibid.

domain knowledge. It means marshalling quality data that is efficiently and, perhaps, algorithmically analyzed upon which human judgement can be deployed, unfurled and expanded.

12.45 Whilst the term 'quantitative regulation' may be novel, the concept of such an agile supervisory and regulatory approach is not new and is receiving similar attention from the regulators in the UK, continental Europe, Hong Kong, Singapore, Australia and other jurisdictions. This is likely to translate to regulators applying regulatory data collection, automated analyses and data-driven policies to achieve better regulatory outcomes.

2. Machine-readable regulations

12.46 A number of regulators, including the CFTC, the UK Prudential Regulatory Authority, the MAS and the HKMA, are exploring the possibility of introducing machine readable regulation to cope with the growing sophistication of regulations and to process new or amended regulations in a timely manner.[77] This is useful when there are changes to the regulatory requirements, which require financial institutions to examine necessary changes to their compliance processes and reporting obligations.[78] In theory, one of the principal objectives of this initiative is to enable financial institutions to make use of technologies to automate their interpretations of regulatory requirements.[79] The potential outcome is that 'rule books are digitised, compliance is increasingly automated or built into business operations through smart contracts, and regulatory reporting is satisfied through real-time DLT network'.[80] To that end, the CFTC (through its LabCFTC) is looking to crowdsource such ideas via 'Request for Input' on innovation competitions.[81] In the UK, the FCA is taking a similar approach via hackathons and TechSprints, which provide an opportunity to collaborate across sectors to develop RegTech solutions. In November 2017, the FCA and the Bank of England held a two-week TechSprint to examine how technology can make the current system of regulatory reporting more accurate, efficient and consistent.[82]

---

77 Yuen, *supra* note 29.
78 Ibid.
79 Ibid.
80 Keynote address, *supra* note 69.
81 CFTC, TAC Panel III: RegTech & Robo-Rulebooks (2018), available at: https://www.cftc.gov/sites/default/files/2018-10/tac100518_LabCFTC.pdf, at 3.
82 FCA, Digital Regulatory Reporting (2018), available at: https://www.fca.org.uk/firms/our-work-programme/digital-regulatory-reporting.

3. Agile regulation

In harnessing the benefits of machine-readable regulations via technology, **12.47** regulators have the opportunity to provide for agile regulation.[83] Rather than relying on static rules and regulations, regulators may be able to measure data, real-world outcomes and success in satisfying regulatory objectives.[84] This enables regulators to be more proactive and nimble in order to make regulations easier to adopt and comply with. To illustrate, in October 2018, the FCA published the feedback statement of its call for input on how technology could achieve smarter regulatory reporting. The call for input outlined a 'proof of concept' developed at the FCA's November 2017 TechSprint, which makes it easier for firms to meet their regulatory reporting requirements and improve the quality of the data that they provide. The benefits of the digital regulatory reporting that the FCA identified are: (i) a reduced need for firms to interpret FCA's rules, making the information they send to FCA more accurate and consistent; (ii) increased efficiency, producing significant cost savings for industry, freeing up resource and capital to innovate, improve products and services and reducing barriers to new firms entering markets; (iii) changes to regulatory requirements being able to be implemented more quickly and cheaply; and (iv) higher quality data, allowing regulators to identify and monitor issues and risks more efficiently, diagnose harm and potentially intervene earlier.[85]

4. Regulatory sandboxes

If technology is to play its proper role in innovation, it needs the right **12.48** ecosystem to support it. Increasingly, regulators and financial institutions are working closely to test innovative products via regulatory sandboxes, innovation hubs, technology labs or similar initiatives to crowdfund new ideas and solutions. As described in more detail in Chapter 14, regulatory sandboxes allow FinTech start-ups to launch products on a limited scale to actual customers without incurring the large regulatory burdens and cost that they would otherwise face. This controlled environment makes it easier for innovators and start-ups to navigate the often cumbersome regulatory process. Additionally, successful testing and cooperation with the regulator of new products helps later efforts to raise capital for a larger scale launch of the product. This approach has gathered momentum globally since the FCA

---

83 Ibid.
84 Ibid.
85 FCA, Digital Regulatory Reporting – Feedback Statement on Call for Input (2018), available at: https://www.fca.org.uk/publication/feedback/fs18-02.pdf, ¶ 2.1.

launched its regulatory sandbox in May 2016 and regulators across the globe have followed suit with similar frameworks. There are now regulatory sandboxes in Abu Dhabi, Australia, Canada, Hong Kong, Lithuania, Singapore, Switzerland and Thailand, to mention only a few.

5. International cooperation

12.49 The Bali Fintech Agenda 2018, jointly issued by the International Monetary Fund and the World Bank, has as one of the key principles the encouragement of international cooperation and information-sharing across the global regulatory community to share knowledge, experience, and best practices to support effective regulatory frameworks.[86] As new technologies increasingly operate across borders, international cooperation is essential to ensure effective policy responses to foster opportunities and to limit risks that could arise from divergence in regulatory frameworks. Sharing experiences and best practices with the private sector and with the public at large would help catalyse discussion on the most effective regulatory response, considering country circumstances, and to build a global consensus. To this end, a number of countries and regulators have entered into cooperation agreements to exchange ideas and information and to align their positions to ensure effective policy responses.

12.50 Similarly, and as described in Chapter 14, in August 2018, the FCA, in collaboration with 11 financial regulators and related organisations announced the establishment of the Global Financial Innovation Network to act as a network of regulators to collaborate and share experience of innovation in respective markets, including emerging technologies and business models, provide a forum for joint policy work and discussions, and to provide firms with an environment in which to trial cross-border solutions.[87]

G. FUTURE OF COMPLIANCE

12.51 As the financial services industry becomes increasingly digitalised and data-driven, we can expect the regulatory structure to shift from a rule-based regulatory framework to a more data-driven and proactive approach to compliance and supervisory monitoring. This RegTech 3.0 approach will

---

86 The Bali FinTech Agenda (11 October 2018), available at: https://www.imf.org/en/Publications/Policy-Papers/Issues/2018/10/11/pp101118-bali-fintech-agenda.

87 Ibid.

involve a regulatory approach that is data-centric and will provide the regulatory framework for the digital age.

RegTech is bringing compliance processes in line with other parts of banking, such as middle office, trading and risk management, which are already digitalised. In response to these challenges, compliance functions have increasingly adopted RegTech solutions to automate activities, streamline processes and facilitate the delivery of regulatory compliance. However, the adoption of technology alone is not sufficient, as there is a corresponding need to upgrade compliance capabilities and transition to a dynamic regulatory compliance environment that combines machines and human input. In order to ensure that the RegTech solutions are successfully adopted, compliance staff will need to acquire knowledge of technology solutions that are pertinent to their practice areas. This includes both the general knowledge of the state of technology solutions in the practice area concerned, as well as training to use specific solutions effectively.
12.52

Technological advances such as AI/ML, big data analytics, RPA and DLT are forcing financial institutions and regulators alike to re-examine their compliance design, readiness, capability and skill set to cope with the adoption of new technologies. RegTech is serving as a catalyst for financial institutions to rethink how their compliance functions should be re-configured to ensure that their institutions have the right tools, systems and people with the relevant skills to address the regulatory challenges. In addition, it is important for compliance teams to partner with their innovation and technology teams to collaborate and adopt strategic application of the RegTech solutions. Engaging with industry associations will also benefit from understanding how other financial institutions are leveraging technology to solve specific compliance obligations.
12.53

As far as regulators are concerned, the Transatlantic Policy Working Group (TPWG), an organisation set up by Innovate Finance and its partners, which is dedicated to FinTech policy discussion between the US and the UK, has considered possible ways in which regulators may approach technology solutions for regulatory compliance in the future. The key conclusion of the TPWG Report can be summarised as three broad approaches that can be adopted singularly or collectively to help regulators encourage more digital reporting, competition and innovation:[88]
12.54

---

88 Transatlantic Policy Working Group Fintech, *The Future of RegTech for Regulators* (June 2017), available at: https://www.innovatefinance.com/wp-content/uploads/2017/06/tpwg-regtech-paper-digital.pdf, at 5.

- *Ecosystem support*: Governments should engage more with the financial industry via such bodies as the LabCFTC in the US and the FCA's regulatory sandbox in the UK in order to help identify new technology and market developments and encourage cross-border engagement among governments. This will allow regulators to work closely with technology innovators and understand any process and regulatory infrastructure adjustments that may be necessary to mainstream new, innovative products.
- *Digital financial infrastructure*: Implementing new technologies, such as real-time reporting, shared utilities and API architecture that can be easily accessed by all, can help facilitate innovation. APIs should also streamline the way that banks can develop and submit applications for new products, settle payments, clear securities and report their compliance with regulations.
- *Rule and process changes*: Implementing new rules and processes to encourage and allow innovative solutions to be tried out on regulatory compliance procedures would be beneficial for the regulator. This could include defining new regulation in a machine-readable format, for instance, so that the regulation can be applied automatically. Alternatively, a regulator's handbook could be adjusted to accommodate the application of new technologies, such as blockchain-compatible data protection or digital identification.

H. CONCLUSION

12.55 The importance of financial institutions, regulators and supervisory agencies being 'digital-ready' in the RegTech and SupTech ecosystem cannot be overstated. The business models and operations of financial institutions are changing rapidly in line with technology advances. Both RegTech and SupTech offer a significant opportunity for financial institutions, regulators and supervisory agencies to improve compliance, reduce costs and promote innovation. Increasingly, financial institutions have embraced RegTech and SupTech solutions to help them keep up with the pace of change. Getting a strong grip on the data and customers' profile by leveraging on technology would enable better provision of services and improved customer experience. There are, however, no all-encompassing technological solutions. Financial institutions must first identify gaps and understand their specific compliance needs before exploring possible solutions offered by RegTech and SupTech. New technological abilities bring with them new challenges and new risks, including operational risk. Nonetheless, provided they are implemented correctly and monitored effectively, RegTech and SupTech tools have the potential to improve a financial institutions' ability to meet regulatory demands in a cost-efficient manner.

Finally, the key to success for all parties, whether supervisory agencies, **12.56** regulators, financial institutions or RegTech providers, is collaboration. Cross-industry dialogue and discussions on innovative technologies, priority use cases and regulatory or policy clarification from regulators and supervisory agencies will help to shape the direction of the future regulatory and supervisory landscape. Such active collaboration can accelerate the use of emerging financial technologies, open clear channels of communication and achieve regulatory and supervisory consistency by setting standards to get everyone on the same framework. All parties will need to adopt a strategic long-term view and create a roadmap to foster an innovative ecosystem that can facilitate the delivery of optimal regulatory and supervisory outcomes.

13

THE RISE OF TECHFINS: REGULATORY CHALLENGES

Dirk Zetzsche, Ross Buckley and Douglas Arner

A. INTRODUCTION

13.01 This chapter focuses on the regulatory and legal challenges associated with the trend of non-financial businesses such as technology, e-commerce and telecommunications companies (tech companies) entering the financial services sector. China is at the forefront of this change, notably with Alibaba establishing the online financial conglomerate Ant Financial in 2014. Ant Financial was valued at USD 150 billion in April 2018.[1] The global tech

---

1 Alibaba's financial services (including payment services) operate from a separate finance holding company, Ant Financial, in which Alibaba is the controlling shareholder. Ant Financial offers short-term loan services to Chinese customers and runs Alipay, the largest payments network worldwide with 520 million customers (as of December 2018). Alipay also distributes loans from other companies to Alibaba.com users (see Alipay

company behemoths of Amazon,[2] Apple[3] and Google[4] are also replicating Alibaba's business model of entering and potentially disrupting the financial services sector. With established tech companies entering the finance services sector, the question is: how do tech companies fit within the framework of financial regulation?[5]

This chapter is structured as follows: Sections B and C describe the features **13.02** of, and opportunities offered by, TechFin and how they differ from those of FinTech. Section D analyses the challenges that the shift from financial intermediary (FinTech) to data intermediary (TechFin) raises for incumbent traditional financial services institutions, and regulators. Section E discusses possible regulatory responses aimed at balancing the competing interests of innovation, development, financial stability, financial inclusion and consumer protection. Section F concludes.

B. FINTECHS AND TECHFINS, DIGITISATION AND DATAFICATION

1. Features of FinTech and RegTech

FinTech's current expansion is principally driven by new market participants. **13.03** Prior to the 2008 global financial crisis (the GFC), FinTech was driven by incumbent financial institutions to support their operations, for example the introduction of internet banking. Since the GFC a 'new wave' of start-ups have been the major catalyst for FinTech's growth and development.[6] This FinTech start-up trend, combined with post-crisis regulatory reforms pushing

---

https://intl.alipay.com/); see also, Gabriel Wildau, Alibaba's finance arm bans high-interest consumer loans, *Financial Times* (24 November 2017), available at: https://www.ft.com/content/778d9338-d0d4-11e7-b781-794ce08b24dc.

2　See Alistair Barr, Amazon offering loans to its online sellers, *Reuters* (28 September 2012), available at: https://www.reuters.com/article/net-us-amazon-lending-idUSBRE88Q1CC20120927 and Maria Lamagna, Amazon's next customer: Americans who don't have a bank account, *MarketWatch* (27 April 2017), available at: https://www.marketwatch.com/story/amazons-next-customer-americans-who-dont-have-a-bank-account-2017-04-04.

3　See Apple's Apple Pay, available at: http://www.apple.com/apple-pay/.

4　See Google's Google Pay, available at: https://pay.google.com/about/. Google also offers 'Financial Services Solutions', which is a data storage and management service (Google Cloud Platform) for incumbent financial institutions; see Google, Financial services solutions, described at: https://cloud.google.com/solutions/financial-services/.

5　See, e.g., the recent inquiry into the regulation of the digital environment in Australia, Financial System Inquiry, Interim Report – Regulation in a digital environment, Commonwealth of Australia (2014–15), available at: http://fsi.gov.au/publications/interim-report/09-technology/regulation-digital-environment/.

6　Laurens Kolkman, Bank-less future: how FinTech Start-ups might take over the Financial System, 4 *TopQuants Newsletter* 1 (May 2016), at 9–10.

structural change, is compelling incumbent financial institutions to embrace technological innovation to remain competitive.[7]

2. Features of TechFin

13.04   The critical distinction between a technology company offering financial services (TechFin), a FinTech start-up and a traditional financial institution is simple: TechFins lever innate technology and data to seamlessly introduce financial services to supplement their value chain.[8] A TechFin utilises existing customer relationships in a non-financial services setting to collect large amounts of data which is monetised by offering, among other things, financial services. FinTechs, on the other hand, are typically start-ups that identify a 'pain point' in financial services,[9] something traditional financial institutions do poorly or not at all, which seek to sell a solution directly to customers or incumbents, and/or become an acquisition target.[10] FinTechs do not enter the financial services sector from the same starting point or position as a TechFin. Finally, traditional financial institutions, such as banks, historically focused on customer relationships. Banks have only recently begun considering supplementing customer risk analysis with more broadly derived data.

13.05   The provider with the most accurate, detailed and extensive customer information will be in the best position to analyse that information for the pricing of credit and insurance services through 'datafication' (that is, the process of analysing and using data).[11] In the past, this was a customer's bank.[12] Banks relied on detailed customer questionnaires to garner information on income and expenses. Objectives, experience and risk tolerance were collated over time from the bank's knowledge of the customer's financial history. The financial data advantage that banks once enjoyed is diminishing fast.

---

7   Nathaniel Popper, 'Fintech' start-up boom said to threaten bank jobs, *New York Times* (30 March 2016), available at: https://www.nytimes.com/2016/03/31/business/dealbook/fintech-start-up-boom-said-to-threaten-bank-jobs.html.

8   Ryan Shea, Fintech versus techfin: does technology offer real innovation or simply improve what is out there?, *Refinitiv* (26 July 2016), available at: https://www.refinitiv.com/perspectives/ai-digitization/fintech-versus-techfin-technology-offer-real-innovation-simply-improve/.

9   Matthew Smith, When technology trumps finance, *Finsia* (11 April 2017), available at: http://www.finsia.com/insights/news/news-article/2017/04/11/when-technology-trumps-finance.

10 See Imran Gulamhuseinwala, Thomas Bull and Steven Lewis, FinTech is gaining traction and young, high income users are the early adopters, *3 Journal of Financial Perspectives* 3 (2015).

11 Jens-Erik Mai, Big data privacy: the datafication of personal information, *32 The Information Society* 3 (2016), at 193.

12 See Banks in Insurance Report, Using customer data effectively (July 2000).

TechFins' data superiority is derived from information collected from several **13.06** sources, which when combined, provide a comprehensive personification of the customers' preferences and behaviours. This data can be derived from:

(A) software companies (e.g., Microsoft and Google) aggregating information about users' activities;

(B) hardware companies (e.g., Huawei, Tesla and Apple) and 'internet of things'[13] companies utilising sensors which continually monitor usage behaviour and location;

(C) social media services (e.g., Facebook[14] and Tencent) and search engines (for example, Google[15] and Baidu) providing insight into social preferences and activities;

(D) e-commerce companies (e.g., Amazon, Alibaba and major retail chains with large market shares, such as WalMart) providing insight into consumer demand and payment history;[16] and

(E) telecommunications services providers (e.g., Vodafone) providing data on mobile activities.[17]

The data provided by these five sources is typically expansive, covering a large **13.07** population of the reference market and is often deep in the number of data points for each customer.[18]

TechFins can relatively efficiently collect most financial information (compar- **13.08** able to information accumulated by a bank or asset manager) to supplement their detailed knowledge of a customer's choices and preferences.[19] This information is processed through algorithms that have established correlations between preferences and creditworthiness[20] to formulate a more nuanced assessment of creditworthiness (in contrast to traditional bank assessments).

---

13 See Sachin Modak, The 'Fin'-ternet of Things: how IoT affects financial services (3 August 2015), available at: http://www.fintech.finance/01-news/the-fin-ternet-of-things-how-iot-affects-financial-services/.

14 See Steve Lohr, The age of big data, *The New York Times* (11 February 2012), and Strategy& PwC, Benefiting from big data: A new approach for the telecom industry (2013), available at: https://www.strategyand.pwc.com/tlecommunications.

15 See Leonard Kile, Apple and Google yield control over consumer data, *CRM Magazine* (1 January 2016), available at: https://www.destinationcrm.com/Articles/ReadArticle.aspx?ArticleID=108307.

16 See Janos Barberis, From FinTech to TechFin: data is the new oil, *The Asian Banker* (16 May 2016), available at: http://www.theasianbanker.com/updates-and-articles/from-fintech-to-techfin:-data-is-the-new-oil.

17 Nick McKenzie and Richard Baker, Your mobile phone records and home address for sale, *Sydney Morning Herald* (16 November 2016), available at: http://www.smh.com.au/business/your-mobile-phone-records-and-home-address-for-sale-20161116-gsqkwe.html.

18 The founder of Alibaba, Jack Ma, has stated that Alibaba holds on average 20,000 to 25,000 data points on any customer. Statistics from Jack Woo in a presentation entitled 'China's Financial Innovation' on 15 October 2015.

19 See generally, Barberis, *supra* note 16.

20 Mikella Hurley and Julius Adebayo, Credit scoring in the era of big data, 18 *Yale J. L. & Tech.* 148 (2016).

Once a client relationship is established, TechFins can seamlessly lever existing levels of trust to expand service offerings.

13.09 To summarise, a FinTech is a 'financial' intermediary, while a TechFin is a 'data' intermediary. For TechFins, data accumulation and analytics are key: starting with self-developed algorithms that find and measure data correlations which later progress to machine learning and artificial intelligence.

3. TechFin stages

13.10 TechFins push into financial services typically in three stages:

(1) The 'data broker' stage is when the TechFin aggregates data from its customer-connected business model. For example, aggregate data is licensed to incumbent financial institutions or FinTechs, to carry out data analytics (for lending or investment decisions) or to test data sets which may eventually be offered for sale. Buyers are typically financial institutions which use the information to formulate customer correlations.

(2) The 'vertical integration' stage is when data sets are used to guide business decisions. For example, TechFins can use innate data to improve risk management, micro-loan approvals (such as Amazon Lending) or to optimise payments (such as Alipay[21]).

(3) The 'horizontal diversification' stage is when the TechFin becomes or establishes a financial institution. Some TechFins will start by offering financial services and competing with incumbents, while others will evolve into or establish a regulated financial institution.

13.11 When a tech company moves from the non-financial business model to stage one, or from stage one to stage two, the core issue from a regulator's perspective is: When does the technology company become a regulated financial institution? Some activities clearly attract regulation, such as when client funds are taken onto the tech company's balance sheet, when discretion over client money is exercised or when client assets are pooled. Formal banking and financial services characteristics may materialise late in the evolutionary process. Most TechFins reach the second stage before applying for a financial services license or authorisation. It is not unusual for TechFins to provide credit or sophisticated payment services to individuals or small- and medium-sized enterprises (SMEs) without a financial services license.[22]

---

21   See generally, Barberis, *supra* note 16.
22   See examples described in notes 2–4 above.

Financial regulation normally requires intermediaries to be licensed when **13.12** accessing client funds (either from a bank account or security deposit), soliciting clients and marketing or arranging financial services and products. In the TechFin world, clients often voluntarily contact the TechFin for services. Technically speaking, this may not constitute solicitation, marketing or arranging, and thus falls outside financial licensing requirements. This is because TechFins do not seek access to a client's assets but rather their data: from that all else follows. The critical distinction is that TechFins derive their influence from access to data, not access to money.

When TechFins have direct access to client funds, such as through Alipay's **13.13** money market funds,[23] they will (or at least should) be subject to mandatory regulation. Where the part of the business that must be licensed is quarantined in a subsidiary of the parent company, only a tiny fraction of the overall data set and algorithms will be regulated. Accordingly, regulators will only supervise a small part of the tech company conglomerate and a fraction of its overall risk.

Development from stage one to three can occur rapidly. For example Alipay **13.14** introduced Yu'e Bao and its associated mobile application 'Alipay Wallet' in June 2013.[24] Yu'e Bao is essentially an online money market fund, in which Alipay customers can invest surplus money from their Alipay accounts to earn interest at rates higher than those offered by traditional banks.[25] Yu'e Bao's advantages over traditional financial products include a minimum investment amount which enabled it to quickly become China's largest online money market fund[26] and the fourth largest worldwide.[27]

---

23 See generally, Tracey Xiang, Alipay's 10 years: from payment service to online finance pioneer, *Technode* (8 December 2014), available at: https://technode.com/2014/12/08/alipays-ten-years-from-payment-service-to-online-finance-pioneer/, and Alizila Staff, Alipay Yu'e Bao is largest money market fund in China (28 October 2013), available at: http://www.alizila.com/alipay-yue-bao-is-largest-money-market-fund-in-china/.

24 See Jon Russell, China's Alipay relaunches its e-payment app as Alipay Wallet with online-to-offline payments, *The Next Web* (18 January 2013), available at: https://thenextweb.com/asia/2013/01/18/alipay-wallet/#.tnw_439CO2Jv.

25 See Moran Zhang, Alibaba's online money market fund Yu'e Bao: 8 things you need to know, *International Business Times* (11 March 2014), available at: https://www.ibtimes.com/alibabas-online-money-market-fund-yue-bao-8-things-you-need-know-1560601.

26 Ibid.

27 Tjun Tang, Yue Zhang and David He, The rise of digital finance in China – new drivers, new game, new strategy, Boston Consulting Group (October 2014), at 4, available at: https://slidex.tips/download/the-rise-of-digital-fiance-in-china-new-drivers-new-game-new-strategy.

4. Over time the distinctions will disappear

13.15 As noted in 13.04 above, there are stark differences between traditional financial institutions, FinTech start-ups and TechFins. As the importance of data analytics increases, these differences will diminish. For example, large international banks could buy more aggregated data sets to factor into their business decisions. Some TechFins may ultimately apply for full banking and financial services licenses and become global financial conglomerates. E-commerce provides an apt analogy: ten years ago, buying products online constituted engaging in e-commerce. Today this is simply shopping. We are concerned with what happens in the meantime and how regulators will respond to these challenges.

C. NEW OPPORTUNITIES PROVIDED BY TECHFINS

1. Reducing transaction costs

13.16 Technology and the data underlying TechFins can reduce transaction costs. Traditional financial institutions have fixed transaction costs for each contract. If technology can automate procedures, transaction costs should reduce once the initial investment in software and server set-up (i.e., sunk costs) has been recuperated. Reducing transaction costs is not unique to TechFins: this is the rationale for most FinTech and information technology innovations such as distributed ledger technologies or even interbank electronic payment systems.[28]

2. Improved business decisions and risk management

13.17 TechFins' big data approach should improve business decisions. This is because TechFins' data sets are typically more comprehensive and therefore of higher quality than those of incumbent financial institutions. Traditional banks only practice the 'back-end' of transactions: the cash flow processed from bank accounts, accompanied by qualitative statements from the client on projected income and expenses. The 'front-end' of transactions is the client relationship: customer product preferences, which network participants contacted the client and for what reasons, which contracts were entered into or terminated, and which goods were returned and why. This information enables a TechFin to form a far more accurate representation, in close to real

---

28   Kim Kaivanto and Daniel Prince, Risks and transaction costs of distributed-ledger fintech: boundary effects and consequences (2017) at 2, available at: https://arxiv.org/pdf/1702.08478.pdf.

time, of the actual financial position of an individual or business when considering offering financial services.

TechFin data sets comprise a large cross-section of society and the economy. **13.18** This is because TechFins originate and leverage data derived from social media and e-commerce into financial services to an extent which is unattainable for traditional financial institutions. For example, correlations may indicate that the purchase of door stoppers to prevent doors from damaging walls correlates with conscientious homeowners who are slightly more creditworthy.[29] The challenge of the next decade is identifying which correlations are random and which function as appropriate bases for prudent business decisions.[30]

3. Financial inclusion

TechFins can also facilitate financial inclusion by replacing the need, common **13.19** in traditional banking, for interpersonal relationships.[31]

a. SMEs and consumer loans

In the past, relationship banking was characterised by a high level of personal **13.20** trust from long-standing business relationships.[32] From a big data perspective, the relationship banker (located at a branch) collected an enormous number of client data points based on multiple transactions and information collected from, for example, discussions, business lunches, referrals from other clients and so on. Relationship banking for small clients has been replaced by the 'rule of the quants' because costs have become too high. Traditional financial institutions are now focusing on relationship services for large clients, while SMEs and small clients are offered either standardised services or excluded altogether.

29　Example provided by Paul Schulte during the launch of his book *Next Revolution in Our Credit-Driven Economy: The Advent of Financial Technology* (Wiley & Sons, 2015), on 4 September 2015.

30　For example, Facebook has applied for a patent to use friend connection as a metric for creditworthiness: see Robinson Meyer, Could a bank deny your loan based on your Facebook friends?, *The Atlantic* (25 September 2015), available at: https://www.theatlantic.com/technology/archive/2015/09/facebooks-new-patent-and-digital-redlining/407287/, and Gil Press, Big data news roundup: correlation vs. causation, *Forbes* (19 April 2013), available at: https://www.forbes.com/sites/gilpress/2013/04/19/big-data-news-roundup-correlation-vs-causation/#68ca6bab5db4.

31　See Susan Wolfe, Banks seek balance of interpersonal relationships, online convenience, *Mintel* (20 May 2014), available at: http://www.mintel.com/blog/finance-market-news/banks-seek-balance-of-interpersonal-relationships-online-convenience.

32　Ross P. Buckley, The changing nature of banking and why it matters, in Ross Buckley, Emilios Avgouleas and Douglas Arner (eds) *Reconceptualising Global Finance and Its Regulation* (Cambridge University Press, 2016), at 9–27.

13.21   In contrast, withTechFins, the costs of an automated contract are basically the same regardless of volume after sunk costs have been recuperated. Once automated (and in the absence of costly regulation), the risks associated with a transaction will determine business strategies and decisions.

13.22   From a risk perspective, big data should drive strategic change. The general assumption in the past has been that lending to small businesses is high risk,[33] whether from a higher likelihood of failure[34] or a lack of professional management. By compiling more comprehensive data sets and extracting more accurate data analytics, TechFins are in a better position to assess risk and the customer's credit rating, and to 'personalise' the financial relationship through algorithms. Data-based finance could simultaneously be more attuned to customers' real risk profile (only if the data-based methodology is sound) and more inclusive by providing affordable 'personalised' financial services.

b.   Developing countries

13.23   Lower transaction costs and better access to risk-related data also explains the remarkable tech-based financial inclusion prompted by TechFins in developing countries, such as through M-Pesa and M-KESHO.[35] While the details are beyond the focus of this chapter,[36] we note that technology which is tried and proven in an environment of (more or less) weak public institutions should work in developed countries. Examples include the mobile phone-based M-Pesa services offered in societies where a large portion of the population cannot read and write.[37] Although service costs reflect a less competitive environment, TechFins can advance financial inclusion by enabling a far broader range of people to enjoy the benefits of digital financial services.

---

33   See, e.g., Bank for International Settlements, Basel III: international regulatory framework for banks, available at: http://www.bis.org/bcbs/basel3.htm.

34   See, e.g., Financial System Inquiry, Small- and medium-sized enterprises, Commonwealth of Australia (2014–15), available at: http://fsi.gov.au/publications/interim-report/03-funding/small-med-enterprises/.

35   See African Development Bank Group, Financial inclusion and integration through mobile payments and transfer (March 2012), available at: https://www.afdb.org/fileadmin/uploads/afdb/Documents/Project-and-Operations/Financial_Inclusion_and_Integration_through_Mobile_Payments_and_Transfers.pdf; and Financial Access Initiative, M-KESHO in Kenya: A new step for M-PESA and mobile banking (27 May 2010), available at: https://www.financialaccess.org/blog/2015/7/16/m-kesho-in-kenya-a-new-step-for-m-pesa-and-mobile-banking.

36   See Ross P. Buckley and Sarah Webster, FinTech in developing countries: charting new customer journeys, 44 *Journal of Financial Transformation* (2016), at 151–9, and Jonathan Greenacre, Ross P. Buckley and Louise Malady, The regulation of mobile money: a case study of Malawi, 14 *Global Studies Law Review* 3 (2015) at 435–97.

37   Janet Kamana, M-PESA: How Kenya took the lead in mobile money, Mobile Transaction (7 April 2014), available at: https://www.mobiletransaction.org/m-pesa-kenya-the-lead-in-mobile-money/.

D. FINANCIAL LAW AND REGULATION CHALLENGES

1. Systemic issues and false predictions

Data correlations can raise the risk of false predictions if not tested for **13.24** causation.[38] If the algorithm is wrong at a systematic level,[39] the data advantage of TechFins may be diminished by increasing risk, including systemic risk. When a TechFin reaches a certain size, businesses linked to the TechFin may be impaired by its insolvency. For example, if a TechFin website links customers to a licensed financial services provider, their prospects may be interrelated and adversely affected by the failing TechFin because the financial institution will have lost the portal through which it was interacting with its customers.

Regulators will seek to mitigate the systemic risk from TechFins licensed for **13.25** financial services. The systemic dimension of algorithms is covered by the risks of defective risk models and of model misuse.[40] Financial regulation requires a licensed entity to review its data and risk models regularly and justify assumptions unique to the firm vis-à-vis the regulator.[41] Furthermore, regula-tors require diversification to hedge against concentration risk of a business model focused on a narrow demographic. While the regulation of risk is not foolproof, some safeguards are necessary to strengthen financial stability during financial crises.

2. Protected factors

TechFins need to be regulated as licensed financial institutions to prevent **13.26** discriminatory practices. Within the financial services sector the law protects certain values by prohibiting discrimination based on certain factors, which we term 'protected factors'.[42] Yet, the effectiveness of protected factors may be undermined by data analytics. If for example data analytics produces a correlation between a certain race or gender generally having higher credit

---

38   Hector Zenil, Algorithmic data analytics, small data matters and correlation versus causation (26 July 2017), at 16–17, available at: https://arxiv.org/pdf/1309.1418.pdf.

39   Joshua A. Kroll et al., Accountable algorithms, 165 *U Pa. L. Rev.* 633 (2017), at 683.

40   Ignacio Crespo et al., *The Evolution of Model Risk Management*, McKinsey & Company (2017), available at: https://www.mckinsey.com/business-functions/risk/our-insights/the-evolution-of-model-risk-management.

41   For example, see the US Office of the Comptroller of the Currency, *Comptroller's Handbook: Bank Supervision Process* (June 2018), at 21 and 56. For Europe, see ESMA/EBA/EIOPA – Joint Committee of the European Supervisory Authorities: Joint Committee Discussion Paper on the use of Big Data by Financial Institutions, JC 2016 86 (2016), at 28–9.

42   The US federal law provides for two 'fair lending' statutes, the Equal Credit Opportunity Act (ECOA), 15 U.S.C. § 1691 (1974); and Fair Housing Act, 42 U.S.C. §§ 3601–3619 (1968).

scores, this outcome could be derived from preconceived bias. Algorithms are quite capable of wrongly discriminating against certain demographics.[43]

13.27 Data-led discrimination combined with automated decisions 'enhances the ability to conceal acts of intentional discrimination'.[44] The more often data analytics substitutes human judgement, the greater importance will be placed on shielding protected factors from abuse and enforcing anti-discrimination laws to prevent a new type of racial or other profiling engendering financial exclusion.[45]

13.28 Regulators have imposed safeguards to ensure that protected factors are maintained. For example, in some jurisdictions financial institutions must provide an affordable payments account while in others they are required to serve all members and segments of society. Most government efforts attach these duties to entities which satisfy the customary definition of a financial institution – TechFins will typically do this in the later stages of their development cycle. The future effects that algorithms and machine learning will have on protection factors is still unclear.

3. Real power, unreal responsibility

a. Denial of services

13.29 TechFins also have an impact at the individual level. For example, assume that the purchaser of a choker chain (which correlates to a higher risk premium) intends the purchase as a gift for another. Using the choker chain as a proxy results in the incorrect pricing of credit or insurance. Similarly, a housemaid who is responsible for purchasing items for a dog and likes to display pictures of herself walking the dog, may be penalised with a higher premium (assuming owning a dog correlates with higher risk), while the dog owner would not. Algorithms can of course be much more sophisticated.

13.30 Although these statistical outliers will be removed by data smoothing on a system-wide basis, the credit and insurance pricing for those individuals who are real outliers will be inaccurate. Despite this being a trivial example, it is

---

43 See, Sarah Ludwig, Credit scores in America perpetuate racial injustice. Here's how, *Guardian* (13 October 2015), available at: https://www.theguardian.com/commentisfree/2015/oct/13/your-credit-score-is-racist-heres-why. In the context of TechFin, Uber's algorithm has been qualified as discriminatory. See, Gillian B. White, Uber and Lyft are failing black riders, *The Atlantic* (31 October 2016), available at: https://www.theatlantic.com/business/archive/2016/10/uber-lyft-and-the-false-promise-of-fair-rides/506000/.

44 Solon Barocas and Andrew D. Selbst, Big data's disparate impact, 104 *Calif. L. Rev.* 671 (2016), at 677. See also, Kroll et al., *supra* note 39, at 680.

45 See Kroll et al., ibid., at 683.

easy to imagine more severe interference with human lives, perhaps resulting in the denial of credit or other financial services.

Non-users may also be subjected to financial and other forms of exclusion: for **13.31** example, opting to not share personal data may result in people becoming *de facto* second-class digital citizens. If big data applications are used for background checks, real front-end interactions could rectify this problem. When big data is used principally for front-end analytics in an unregulated environment, rectification will become impossible because the factors considered for calculating risk premiums may be discriminatory with no recourse for a remedy.

These problems could be mitigated if TechFins were licensed. The impact of **13.32** business decisions on clients is covered by a multitude of customer, client and investor protection laws. At a minimum, these require transparency and a contact point for recourse and customer complaints. For example, the US Office of the Comptroller runs the website (HelpWithMyBank.gov) to ensure that federal banks and credit associations treat customers fairly and comply with the applicable laws and regulations.[46] A regulator will also be available to intervene and protect the consumer and punish a non-compliant TechFin.[47] While these solutions are not perfect, financial regulation can provide some safeguards, particularly for vulnerable consumers.

b. Pay for display

Given that TechFins control the front-end customer relationship and the **13.33** marketing fee business model, their 'pay for display' schemes often dominate the 'selection of services or products for display' schemes based on quality or price. For example, paid announcements on Google's search engine hold the top positions in many countries. Linking a tech-based strategy with financial services creates serious concerns for consumer choice and market efficiency.

---

46 ESMA/EBA/EIOPA – Joint Committee of the European Supervisory Authorities, Joint Committee Discussion Paper on the use of Big Data by Financial Institutions, JC 2016 86 (2016), at 27–8.

47 For the OCC's consumer protection mandate, see OCC, Consumer Protection, available at: https://www.occ.gov/topics/consumer-protection/index-consumer-protection.html. Similarly, the mandate of European financial regulators has been widened to include consumer protection, prompting the European Banking Authority to issue a number of standards, see European Banking Authority, Consumer protection and financial innovation, available at: https://www.eba.europa.eu/regulation-and-policy/consumer-protection-and-financial-innovation.

13.34 Social media data could also be used to target less educated and financially inexperienced people for high-cost predatory loans and risky financial products.[48] Financial regulation is designed to mitigate such abuses. Fees received by investment firms must not impair compliance with the firm's duty to act honestly, fairly and professionally in accordance with the best interests of its clients.[49] As for predatory lending, financial law generally imposes fair lending policies and charges regulators with enforcing these duties.[50] While financial regulation is not perfect, it does attempt to counter misbehaviour. None of this currently occurs in the world of unlicensed tech companies.

4. Fiduciary status

13.35 The conceptual legal question of to whom TechFins owe duties matters. Financial law assigns to financial advisers, asset managers and fund managers the status of a fiduciary, which means all their business activities must be aligned with the interests of their clients.[51]

13.36 To the same extent that TechFins may tailor products to the customer's needs, data-driven micro-segmentation could unlock income-generating insights which draw on customer weaknesses. For example, TechFins can adjust prices upward for customers who are either insensitive (inelastic) to price movements or unwilling to switch products and providers. Exploitation of brand loyalty and other customer traits would violate financial law requirements to treat customers fairly, honestly and act in their best interests.[52] The fact that

---

48 For example, Facebook can use its data to allow advertisers to target people on the basis of sexual orientation or religion without their consent. See, Miguel Helft, Marketers can glean private data on Facebook, *The New York Times* (22 October 2010), available at: http://www.nytimes.com/2010/10/23/technology/23facebook. html.

49 When investment firms are not fulfilling their obligations in this context, see e.g., Art 24(9) Directive 2014/65/EU of the European Parliament and of the Council of 15 May 2014 on markets in financial instruments and amending Directive 2002/92/EC and Directive 2011/61/EU, OJ L 173/349 of 12.6.2014 ('MiFID 2').

50 In the US, bank credit must meet communities' needs, banks must have safe and sound lending practices, and ensure fair access and equal treatment of all customers, see OCC, Licensing Manual (September 2016), Appendix A: Directors' Duties and Responsibilities, Qualifications, and Other Issues, at 78, available at: https://www.occ.gov/publications/publications-by-type/licensing-manuals/charters.pdf.

51 For example, the Securities and Exchange Commission in the US issued guidance on 23 February 2017 for automated digital investment advisory programmes (robo-advisers) which are subject to substantive and fiduciary obligations pursuant to the Investment Advisors Act 15 U.S.C. § 80b-1 (1940). See also, Stephen Cohen, et al., SEC staff issues guidance update and investor bulletin on 'robo-advisers', *JDSupra* (15 March 2017), available at: http://www.jdsupra.com/legalnews/sec-staff-issues-guidance-update-and-31449/.

52 In the US a safe and sound manner, provide fair access to financial services, treat customers fairly and comply with applicable laws and regulations, see National Bank Act 12 U.S.C. §1(a). In Europe, financial institutions using big data have general consumer protection requirements based on negative obligations, see ESMA/EBA/EIOPA – Joint Committee of the European Supervisory Authorities, *supra* note 46, at 17–18.

financial law does not apply to TechFins may create undesirable opportunities to exploit customers.

5. Legal obligations

In the early stages of development, TechFins will often fall outside the ambit **13.37** of financial regulation. This may be because TechFins will be able to rely on legal exemptions when functioning as a conduit between clients and financial institutions, even in circumstances where the institution is dependent on the TechFin to provide client access and data.

TechFins are not subject to the 'solicitation', 'marketing' or 'arranging' rules **13.38** originally drafted for those controlling client access in the financial services sector. In this context, data delivery to financial institutions is a regulated activity only in some countries, and even in those countries, only under strictly defined conditions typically limited to credit rating agencies and market data providers.[53] The shortcomings of TechFin activity may not be addressed, which will leave clients and investors exposed to unregulated big data analytic risk.

Access to more comprehensive data may enable TechFins to provide the **13.39** financial intermediary function more efficiently than traditional financial institutions. TechFins currently operate for the most part in an unregulated environment. Until the third stage of the development cycle is reached and financial services licenses are required, TechFins will not be subject to client/customer/investor protection rules, market conduct obligations nor measures that ensure the functioning of financial markets and preventing the build up of systemic risk – these being the three pillars of modern financial regulation.[54]

6. Fair competition

From the perspective of licensed intermediaries, TechFins provide unbalanced **13.40** and arguably unfair competition. The fixed costs of an initial license and the

---

53 For example, credit rating agencies in the US, see generally, Dodd–Frank Wall Street Reform and Consumer Protection Act P.L. 111-203 (2010). For credit rating agencies in Europe, see Regulation (EC) No. 1060/2009 of the European Parliament and the Council of 16 September 2009 on credit rating agencies, OJ L 302/1. For data reporting services providers in Europe, see Title V, MiFID 2, governing 'approved publication arrangements' (APA), 'consolidated tape provider' (CTP) and an 'approved reporting mechanism' (ARM).

54 Dirk Zetzsche, Investment Law as Financial Law: From Fund Governance over Market Governance to Stakeholder Governance? in Hanne S. Birkmose, Mette Neville and Karsten Engsig Sørensen (eds): *The European Financial Market in Transition* (Kluwer Law International, 2012), at 339 and 343.

ongoing costs of supervision and reviews will result in licensed intermediaries bearing higher costs. In the long run, licensed intermediaries will be at a competitive disadvantage, given their higher cost base and limited flexibility to respond to challenges.

13.41 There are three ways for incumbents to respond:

(1) Lobby for the removal of some or all regulation for financial institutions. Yet, in the aftermath of the 2008 global financial crisis, de-regulation remains a very unlikely outcome, and deregulation will not, in any event, solve the underlying problem.

(2) Combine the strengths of traditional financial institutions and TechFins. Potential solutions include allowing traditional financial institutions to rely on TechFin data in addition to their own (insourcing rules) and allowing TechFins to acquire licensed financial service providers (under a merger model). In the absence of uniform regulatory requirements, TechFins are unlikely to forego their competitive advantage.

(3) Safeguard the areas in which TechFins undermine financial regulation with an appropriate regulatory response. This is discussed in the remainder of this chapter.

7. Differences from FinTech

13.42 In respect of client protection, the first and foremost asset of financial services providers is their clients' trust. Without trust, clients will not place their money with the provider.[55] Unlike FinTechs, TechFins start with the client relationship (and the trust engendered in this relationship) before adding the financial dimension. To build the financial dimension of the business model, the TechFin levers its control over client data by selecting clients for financial services on the basis of loyalty and comfort with data-driven contact.

13.43 Size creates systemic risk.[56] FinTechs are problem-driven businesses and though they aim to grow large, they tend to start small.[57] Although the relationship between FinTechs and traditional financial institutions, such as banks, creates a conduit for indirect regulation, this may not be sufficient to

---

55 Torben Hansen, Understanding trust in financial services: the influence of financial healthiness knowledge, and satisfaction, 15 *Journal of Service Research* 3 (2012).

56 Luc Laeven, Lev Ratnovski and Hui Tong, Bank size and systemic risk, IMF Staff Discussion Note (May 2014), available at: https://www.imf.org/external/pubs/ft/sdn/2014/sdn1404.pdf.

57 See generally, Daniel Drummer, et al., Fintech – Challenges and Opportunities, McKinsey & Company (May 2016), at 2, available at: https://www.mckinsey.de/files/160525_fintech_english.pdf.

address systemic risk.[58] A proposal to supervise and issue rules for large FinTech payment providers is equally pertinent to TechFins which are often behemoths outside the regulatory ambit of the financial services sector.[59] Due to their sheer size, TechFins are connected to many institutions from the moment they enter stage one. By the time they enter stage three, they often tend to control whole market segments.

In the financial services sector, trust and control over important market **13.44** participants being concentrated in a few behemoths has led to major financial crises. Some recent examples include accounting frauds in the early 2000s[60] and the infamous role of rating agencies[61] and systemically important financial institutions prior to the 2008 global financial crisis.[62] With more TechFins moving into the financial services sector, it will be essential to protect society from TechFin failures.

E. POLICY CONSIDERATIONS

In the present regulatory environment, TechFins often do not pay for their **13.45** systemic exposure or risk. TechFins do not endure inhibited market access nor do they pay regulatory fees and often avoid national taxes. The concern is: if the competition from unregulated entities destabilises regulated financial institutions, the rise of TechFins may well reduce client protection and promote systemic risk.

1. Costs of doing nothing

If the regulators do nothing, the 'uneven playing field' will persist. This will **13.46** result in licensed intermediaries losing business, the level of compliance being gradually undermined and the role of enforcement agencies weakened as their mandates narrow. Systemic risk will build-up unobserved, unmitigated and

---

58 See generally, Deloitte, The evolving Fintech regulatory environment (2017), at 2–3, available at: https://www2.deloitte.com/content/dam/Deloitte/us/Documents/regulatory/us-aers-the-evolving-fintech-regulatory-environment.pdf.

59 Ibid.

60 See, e.g., Sean Farrell, The world's biggest accounting scandals, *The Guardian* (21 July 2015), available at: https://www.theguardian.com/business/2015/jul/21/the-worlds-biggest-accounting-scandals-toshiba-enron-olympus.

61 See generally, Amanda J. Bahena, What role did credit rating agencies play in the credit crisis? (March 2010), available at: http://www.spaeth.ru/HS20152016/artikel_16.pdf.

62 For a discussion in the context of Australia, see Financial System Inquiry, Too-big-to-fail and moral hazard, Commonwealth of Australia (2014-15), available at: http://fsi.gov.au/publications/interim-report/05-stability/too-big-to-fail/.

uncontrolled. Looking to the long term, the next global financial crisis may well come from TechFins rather than regulated financial institutions.

13.47 There is evidence to support the systemic dimension of TechFins. For example, within ten months from launch, Yu'e Bao was the fourth largest money market fund in the world, leading to a hasty response from Chinese regulators.[63] We can also assume that the systemic importance of TechFins such as Amazon and Alibaba in SME niche markets, and M-Pesa for consumers in some underdeveloped African countries[64] is a precondition for the well-being of society and enterprises in those markets.

13.48 One counterargument is that the early stage TechFin conduit function is data delivery which is not an activity warranting regulation. Regulators have addressed data provisioning in highly concentrated markets by requiring financial institutions to diversify data sources. The difference for TechFins is that data delivery is a back-end function, while providing overlay services to financial institutions is a front-end function. TechFins' conduit function cannot be addressed by diversification since the financial institution cannot change being a service provider as readily: terminating cooperation with the TechFin would cost the financial institution the conduit or link to the TechFin's clients.

2. Costs of catch-all mandatory licensing

13.49 The cost of a catch-all mandatory licensing requirement for data analytics is likely to stifle innovation. TechFins have the ability to fill gaps in the provision of financial services, such as Ant Financial's targeting of 'Tier 2' cities and the provision of SME finance, an area in which the traditional Chinese financial services sector has performed poorly.[65] Regulators should assess the financial and social benefits before intervening prematurely.

---

63 Weihuan Zhou, Douglas Arner and Ross Buckley, Regulation of digital financial services in China: last mover advantage?, 8 *TCLR* 1 (2015), at 38.

64 See, e.g., Kiarie Njoroge, Report: This is what would happen to Kenya's economy if M-Pesa was to collapse, *Nairobi News* (30 November 2016), available at: http://nairobinews.nation.co.ke/news/treasury-report-reveals-fears-m-pesas-critical-role-economy/, and Frank Jacob, The role of M-Pesa in Kenya's economic and political development, in Mickie Mwanzia Koster, Michael Mwenda Kithinji and Jerono P. Rotich (eds) *Kenya After 50: Reconfiguring Education, Gender, and Policy* (Palgrave Macmillan, 2016), at 89–100.

65 See generally, Douglas W. Arner and Janos Barberis, FinTech in China: from the shadows in EY, Who will disrupt the disruptors? *The Journal of Financial Perspectives* (Winter 2015), at 83–6, available at: http://www.ey.com/Publication/vwLUAssets/ey-the-journal-of-financial-perspectives-fintech-winter-2015/$FILE/ey-the-journal-of-financial-perspectives-fintech-winter-2015.pdf.

3. Other regulatory options

a. *Widening existing definitions*

Rules from the era of analog technology could be widened, notably for existing **13.50** definitions such as solicitation, marketing and arranging. Regulators pursuing this approach will face protracted court cases and uncertainty likely lasting for years. A general widening of definitions may prove overly burdensome for innovative businesses and stifle innovation. For example, if rereading 'solicitation' and the other terms to include websites, the regulatory definition could extend to all website providers. Widening existing definitions requires carefully considering exemptions, otherwise enforcement will be unworkable. TechFins require an entirely new regulatory approach because the established reference mechanisms for 'carve outs' will not work (for example, assets on the balance sheets, under management and so on).

A variation of this approach can be found in delegation rules, which address **13.51** the core underlying problem: what is the legal nature of the relationship between the conduit TechFin and the financial intermediary? If there is a service agreement between the financial service provider and the TechFin, delegation rules could apply and therefore so would indirect supervision.

b. *Private law alternatives*

Another approach is to consider imposing joint liability for damages on the **13.52** back-end financial institution and the front-end TechFin. This is also unsuitable. Private law disregards the systemic risk dimension. Segments of society financial law seeks to protect are particularly vulnerable, but non-litigious: the poor rarely sue. In the absence of additional legislation, claimants face significant challenges in court, given the difficulties of gathering evidence and the costs of civil procedure.

4. Data

a. *Open data policy*

Proponents of open data might suggest that one way of dealing with TechFins **13.53** is to reduce the value of data by providing access to everyone. In this scenario all entities can build algorithms. This solves only one side of the problem: data access. Algorithms can be profoundly misleading. The creation of an open data world runs into legal barriers such as data protection issues and would take years to be fully operational (if it ever happens).

b. Independent data banks

13.54 Another market-based solution is the use of data banks. Data banks act as data repositories controlled by end users instead of FinTechs or TechFins. The user grants access rights to their data depending on the product or service. Providers adjust services based on the data and algorithm. This would also allow the customer to make comparisons between providers. A data bank model nonetheless suffers from initial data collection issues and the differentiation between data ownership and control. Another problem is that the market price for raw data creates little economic incentive for customers to support data sovereignty. The privatisation of data which underlies this model requires cross-border data access which, similar to the open data policy, will require years or decades of coordination to be operational.

5. Balanced risk analysis

13.55 A balanced risk analysis should follow the hierarchical evolution of any business from (A) too small to care, (B) too large to ignore and (C) too big to fail.[66] As TechFins often do not seek direct access to client funds, many established financial regulatory thresholds will not be triggered by entry to the financial services sector. Despite this, TechFins can be much more influential in the financial services sector. To set appropriate regulatory thresholds, new criteria needs to be developed. Criteria could encapsulate substantial data sets such as an overall number of data points or holding data on a large portion of a population in the reference market.

13.56 Systemic risk measures should apply when TechFins become a threat to financial stability. This will depend on the 'too big to fail' or 'too complex to fail' tests. If a TechFin provides an essential facility to a systemic bank (e.g., the TechFin is the systemic bank's main data analytics provider), the TechFin can be viewed as systemic financial infrastructure and be required to diversify its data delivery channels. If the TechFin is the main client channel for a systemic bank or for many banks which together are systemic, an analogy can be made with the TechFin and to the appointment of a new CEO operating under a new financial business model. To the same extent that the new CEO and other key staff would be subject to regulatory scrutiny, the TechFin would need to meet and maintain a 'fit and proper' requirement. This is where the systemic risk perspective necessitates the regulation of TechFins.

---

66 Douglas Arner et al., FinTech, RegTech and the reconceptualisation of financial regulation, 37 *Northwestern Journal of International Law and Business* 371 (2017), at 403–4 and 412 (fn 178).

6. Licensing requirement for data gathering and analytics

The need for regulation is supported by analysing the customer/client/investor **13.57** (collectively, '*individuals*') protection dimension: if TechFins affect individuals' lives, regulators should become involved. Once the TechFin's effect on individuals' lives passes a threshold, regulators should ensure client data is being appropriately collected and processed.

From the above discussion regulators may consider requiring licensing for data **13.58** gathering and analytics when used for financial services, either directly as a financial services provider, or indirectly as a conduit for data delivery or access to customers, subject to certain qualifications.

First, regulators can impose information rights linked to data gathering and **13.59** analytics, such as those in the GDPR. To support enforcement of such rights, the TechFin should be asked to declare its jurisdictional scope by reporting on: (1) data gathering; (2) the location of clients; and (3) data delivery to intermediaries. If a TechFin refuses to cooperate, regulators could seek enforcement by imposing a variant of geoblocking called 'datablocking' (meaning that no data from that jurisdiction can be used by the TechFin).

Exemptions are necessary to, among other things, promote market growth and **13.60** competition. In this context 'too small to care' businesses should be subject to a generous exemption threshold. For example, if a deep data analysis on a single person amounts to 25,000 data points,[67] a data business that processes the data of 400,000 people will manage 10 billion data points in the market. It can be presumed that the business does not pose any systemic risk. If a regulatory threshold for the data business is set at 10 billion data points (which is not significant for the market), to remain under this threshold the business could be given a choice of either deriving and analysing fewer client specific data points for more than 400,000 clients or over 25,000 data points on fewer than 400,000 clients.

Once the TechFin reaches a certain size including processing a certain volume **13.61** of data points which indicates it is reaching the 'too large to ignore' threshold, regulators should have access to the TechFin's data-based business models and algorithms to ensure sound methods and adherence to protected factors relevant to the reference market. Regulators could be empowered to require

---

67 Note that this figure is taken arbitrarily. The real number may be higher or lower, and the figures in our example should be adjusted accordingly.

data analytics to demonstrate process regularity, upholding protected factors and review algorithm specifications.

13.62 Once regulators reach the conclusion that the TechFin is of systemic importance, measures should be implemented to control and limit systemic risk. In the first instance, this would require diversifying data sources. In the second instance, regulators could consider (1) structural requirements for TechFins (quarantine provisions as to the regulated financial services elements of the entity with respect to the (a) information technology and capital; (b) minimum capital for maintenance and clean-up and (c) country-by-country segregation of activities), (2) empowering regulators to shut down the activity (while preserving customer data) or (3) appointing a commissioner to run the quarantined TechFin part of the business in the public interest.

F. CONCLUSION

13.63 TechFin may be the single most important development in financial services going forward, as digitisation enables datafication.[68]

13.64 TechFins are not simply a progression of FinTechs, but instead represent a new type of market participant. They originate in technology or e-commerce environments which are typically connected to a multitude of clients (both consumers and/or small businesses) and have access to very deep pools of data. TechFins can enter the world of finance by providing data, either raw or processed, to incumbent financial institutions and/or FinTech start-ups. Over time the likelihood is that many TechFins will start providing financial services directly to their customers.

13.65 Efficient financial services can be provided by TechFins to society. In particular TechFins can reduce transaction costs and improve decision-making by using a more comprehensive data set than that of established financial intermediaries. These two advantages can lead to an increased level of financial inclusion for SMEs, consumers and the underprivileged.

13.66 Established thresholds for the imposition of financial regulation such as the solicitation of customers, deposit-taking, pooling of assets, or discretion over

---

68 Ericsson, *The Impact of Datafication on Strategic Landscapes* (2014), at 4–5, available at: https://www.ericsson.com/res/docs/2014/the-impact-of-datafication-on-strategic-landscapes.pdf, and Viktor Mayer-Schönberger and Kenneth Cukier, *Big Data: A Revolution that will Transform How We Live, Work and Think* (John Murray, 2013).

client assets often fail to capture TechFins. Regulators are unable to enforce customer protection measures to monitor and mitigate systemic risk. Protection factors are often put at risk by TechFins.

If financial regulation matters in furthering market efficiency[69] and customer protection,[70] TechFins should be regulated when offering financial services. An imbalance of competition will arise if TechFins are not regulated in the 'too large to ignore' phase of their development cycle and will not bear the regulatory costs of licensed financial services providers.   **13.67**

In the world of TechFin most customers provide their data for free in exchange for a free service. Therefore the 'follow the money' traditional financial legal approach is likely to fail. The new regulatory approach should be 'follow the data', not as a mere policy choice but as a necessity. In a world where data is the new currency and where legislation regulates intermediaries managing financial assets (for example banks and asset managers), there is an urgent need to regulate data intermediaries in a similar way.   **13.68**

Regulators should consider defining financial data collecting and analytics as a regulated activity when the activity exceeds certain thresholds. A threshold set as a percentage (perhaps 1–5 per cent) of the overall population in the reference market could represent the threshold between 'too small to care' and 'too large to ignore'. Above this threshold TechFin regulation should focus on information collecting and ensuring regulatory access to data-based business models. This will ensure sound analytical methods and adherence to protected factors relevant to that reference market. If the risk analysis arising from the regulatory inquiry reveals systemic risk, systemic risk prevention measures should apply.   **13.69**

---

69   See Randall Dodd, The economic rationale for financial market regulation, Financial Policy Forum Derivatives Study Center (December 2002), available at: www.financialpolicy.org/fpfspr12.pdf.

70   For example in the Australian context, see Financial System Inquiry, Consumer protection framework in financial services, Commonwealth of Australia (2014–15), available at: http://fsi.gov.au/publications/interim-report/06-consumer-outcomes/consumer-protection-framework-in-financial-services/.

14

REGULATORY SANDBOXES

Byungkwon Lim and Charles Low

A. INTRODUCTION

14.01 The global financial industry has been experiencing rapid and broad changes fuelled by technological innovation, including the emergence of novel products, delivery mechanisms and business models (collectively, FinTech products). The ever-changing financial industry landscape has not always been a snug fit with legacy regulatory schemes. National regulators often struggle to enforce existing regulations or implement new ones in the evolving business environment in a timely and proper manner, leaving many FinTech companies and financial institutions uncertain about how they may implement innovative technologies in a regulation compliant manner.[1] Regulators around the world thus face a heightened pressure to tackle the regulatory challenges of today and tomorrow to ensure that their national regulatory regimes adequately manage

---

1 Hilary J. Allen, *A US Regulatory Sandbox?* (Draft, 8 February 2018), available at: http://dx.doi.org/10.2139/ssrn.3056993, at 11.

FinTech developments without stifling innovation and compromising on consumer protection, and, in some cases, to attract FinTech investment in competition with their foreign counterparts.[2] Enter the FinTech regulatory sandbox, a unique regulatory solution in the FinTech sphere being embraced by a growing number of national regulators to tackle these challenges.

This chapter is structured as follows: Sections B–D consider the general **14.02** characteristics, including certain benefits and shortcomings, of the regulatory sandbox model; Sections E and F examine the regulatory sandbox models adopted in two distinct legal systems (the UK and the US) as a focal point for a wider consideration of the various issues related to its implementation. Section G discusses the conception of a global regulatory sandbox model. Section H concludes.

On balance, our view is that the adoption and proper administration of **14.03** regulatory sandboxes will generate substantial social benefits, but national regulators must carefully consider the design of any proposed regulatory sandbox in light of their particular circumstances and, in designing and administering a regulatory sandbox, they must be guided by their mandates to protect consumers and the integrity of the financial system. In addition to the 'why?' of regulatory sandbox implementation, we will consider the equally crucial question of 'how' and 'when' regulatory sandboxes should be implemented and the nuances involved in identifying some key considerations to designing a regulatory sandbox that upholds the typical objectives of consumer protection and promoting innovation.

B. THE REGULATORY SANDBOX IN GENERAL

The regulatory sandbox is a regulatory framework under which FinTech **14.04** companies can test their products on real-world consumers in a controlled, demarcated, market space, while benefitting from certain temporary exemptions[3] from full compliance with the relevant regulatory regimes but under the supervision of a regulator. The regulatory sandbox thus facilitates a form of

---

2 Ibid., at 3.
3 Or, as in the case of some EU member states, the benefit of favourable exercises of 'supervisory powers or levers for proportionality' available to the regulators. See European Securities and Markets Authority et al., Report: FinTech: Regulatory sandboxes and innovation hubs, available at: https://eba.europa.eu/documents/10180/2545547/JC+2018+74+Joint+Report+on+Regulatory+Sandboxes+and +Innovation+Hubs.pdf, at 20.

'structured experimentalism'[4] akin to clinical trials in which FinTech companies can test their products on consenting participant consumers.[5]

14.05 A regulatory sandbox can be established to achieve numerous objectives, including the lowering of barriers to entry for new entrants into the financial services industry and consequently promoting competition and socially beneficial innovation. Whatever the objectives, a regulatory sandbox should not be adopted simply to lure FinTech investment with the promise of relaxed regulation at the expense of consumer protection or financial stability. Existing and proposed regulatory sandboxes have different designs and structures, but they generally share certain characteristics as described below.

1. Covered FinTech products and eligible participants

14.06 The testing scope of FinTech products within a regulatory sandbox will be limited according to the authority of the regulatory sandbox administrator. Some existing regulatory sandboxes are open to FinTech companies generally, while others are not. For example, the Hong Kong regulatory sandbox only admits authorised financial institutions, and the Thai regulatory sandbox only admits institutions regulated by the Bank of Thailand or the Thailand Securities and Exchange Commission. These restrictions may limit access to and, ultimately, the utility of the sandbox regime.[6]

2. Parameters

14.07 Regulatory sandbox parameters include the length of the testing period, and the number and type of participating consumers. For example, the length of testing may range, subject to permitted extensions, from six months (UK[7] and Brunei[8]) to 24 months (Abu Dhabi[9]). Some regulatory sandboxes are more

---

4   Dirk A. Zetsche, Ross P. Buckley, Janos N. Barberis and Douglas W. Arner, Regulating a revolution: from regulatory sandboxes to smart regulation, *Fordham Journal of Corporate & Financial Law*, Vol XXIII (2017), at 32.

5   The FCA has drawn parallels between the sandbox and clinical trials. See Financial Conduct Authority, Regulatory sandbox (November 2015), available at: https://www.fca.org.uk/publication/research/regulatory-sandbox.pdf, at 9.

6   Jason Corbett, Thailand Launches Regulatory Sandbox for FinTech Services, *Silk Legal* (19 June 2017), available at: https://www.vantageasia.com/thailand-launches-regulatory-sandbox-for-fintech-services/.

7   Financial Conduct Authority, Default standards for sandbox testing criteria, available at: https://www.fca.org.uk/publication/policy/default-standards-for-sandbox-testing-parameters.pdf.

8   Autoriti Monetari Brunei Darussalam, *Guidelines No. FTU/G-1/2017/1*, available at: https://www.ambd.gov.bn/SiteAssets/fintech-office/FTSG%20v1_final.pdf, at Appendix B.

9   Abu Dhabi Global Market, The Fintech Regulatory Laboratory – the Regime for FinTech Innovation (February 2018), available at: https://www.adgm.com/media/125942/adgm-fintech-reglab-brochure.pdf.

flexible when it comes to the duration of testing for any particular innovation.[10] However, there are obvious costs associated with indefinite or extensive regulatory sandbox testing, and the prospect of impending full regulatory compliance under the time-limited testing model may compel timely project development.[11]

In relation to the number and type of participating consumers, some regulators **14.08** adopt a risk- and proportionality-based approach. For example, the FCA requires not only that the type of customers being tested on is appropriate for the type of innovation and the intended market, but also that the risks these customers are exposed to are also appropriate: if wholesale clients are sophisticated enough to comprehend the risks, it may be sufficient for participants to simply disclose their 'limited authorisation' regulatory status. On the other hand, regulatory sandbox participants seeking to test on retail clients will likely be subject to greater regulatory requirements.[12] Other regulatory sandbox boundaries are more prescriptive. For example, the Australian Securities and Investments Commission (ASIC) imposed a 200 participant limit on retail clients, but did not impose such a limit for testing on non-retail clients.[13] Given the limited history of FinTech regulatory sandboxes, it is premature to identify a 'most successful' regulatory sandbox model.

3. Regulatory safe harbour

Whilst most regulatory sandboxes do not specify which regulatory require- **14.09** ments would be waived or relaxed, some regulators have strict expectations of compliance in particular areas. For instance, the Monetary Authority of Singapore (MAS) is flexible on requirements relating to, among others, licensing fees, participant's capital requirements, leadership composition and credit ratings. However, the MAS has expressed that it will not relax compliance standards in relation to the confidentiality of customer information, management fitness, the handling of customer money and assets by intermediaries, and AML/CFT measures.[14]

---

10   For example, Singapore and Hong Kong.
11   Allen, *supra* note 1, at 53.
12   Zetsche et al., *supra* note 4, at 74.
13   Australian Securities and Investments Commission, *Licensing Exemption for FinTech Testing*, available at: https://asic.gov.au/for-business/your-business/innovation-hub/licensing-and-regulation/licensing-exemption-for-fintech-testing/.
14   Monetary Authority of Singapore: *Fintech Regulatory Sandbox Guidelines* (November 2016), available at: http://www.mas.gov.sg/~/media/Smart%20Financial%20Centre/Sandbox/FinTech%20Regulatory%20Sandbox%20Guidelines%2019Feb2018.pdf, at Annex A.

14.10   The scope of relief will also depend on what measures a particular regulator has the power to waive or exempt. As described in 14.44 below, the US Consumer Financial Protection Bureau's (CFPB) Project Catalyst could have waived certain consumer product disclosure policies and permitted its staff to grant no-action letters on certain matters, but it could not have provided any waiver or no-action relief on any matter that fell under the exclusive jurisdiction of other agencies.[15]

4.   Post-sandbox engagement

14.11   Successful testing generally leads to the full or tailored registration or authorisation of the participant. Alternatively, a regulator may grant permanent waivers of certain regulatory requirements for FinTech firms successfully leaving a regulatory sandbox. In the long term, a regulator may even be compelled by its regulatory sandbox experience to initiate a change of the applicable rules.[16]

14.12   There may be concerns about participants being particularly vulnerable to market forces upon graduating from a regulatory sandbox.[17] However, there must be an end, for practical reasons, to any regulatory sandbox administrator's commitment towards any particular participant. Further, the benefits of being a participant, including having increased investor appeal and thus potentially benefitting from external financing and support, should have contributed to preparing the FinTech product for its exit from the regulatory sandbox.

14.13   This is not to say that the regulator-participant relationship must completely terminate upon exit. There may be benefits to be reaped by regulators from maintaining post-regulatory sandbox engagement with participants, even if they have successfully become fully authorised firms.[18] For example, monitoring a FinTech product beyond the regulatory sandbox would provide regulators with insight on the product's actual impact on the financial markets.[19] Similarly, how the innovations fare in practice could inform improvements to the regulatory sandbox programme itself. On the flipside,

---

15   For example, the US Securities Exchange Commission and the Commodity Futures Trading Commission. Similarly, the UK FCA will not be able to grant relief with respect to any national or EU law matter.

16   Rosael Ng, Jeffrey Lim, Tian Sion Yoong and Hannah Ng, Inside and outside Singapore's proposed Fintech Regulatory Sandbox: Balancing Supervision and Innovation, 10 *Journal of International Banking and Financial Law* 596(2016).

17   Allen, *supra* note 1, at 54.

18   Ibid., at 53.

19   Ibid.

repeated failures of projects post-testing could be indicative of a regulator's incompetence in identifying the 'correct' participants to admit. From the participant's perspective, failure to survive post-testing would be a strong indicator that the product was lacking in one critical aspect or another, including commercial viability or scalability.[20]

C. BENEFITS OF THE REGULATORY SANDBOX

1. Participant-regulator dialogue

A regulatory sandbox presents an opportunity for FinTech companies and **14.14** regulators to collaborate and exchange information relating to, amongst other things, the innovative product, developments in the product's industry generally, and the state of the regulatory landscape from the participant's perspective.[21] Direct access to such information places regulators in an informed position to chart the development of financial regulatory frameworks in a more sustainable way and possibly identify risks before they materialise, furthering the objective of consumer protection. FinTech companies will have a better sense of the regulator's priorities and thus greater certainty of the future regulatory landscape. This open dialogue and active engagement may help avoid 'reactionary' relationships between regulators and participants so as to minimise regulatory hurdles without compromising on consumer protection and market integrity.

2. Reduced time and cost of market penetration

FinTech companies, particularly start-ups, will benefit from savings from, **14.15** amongst other things, reduced expenditure on legal advice regarding the regulations applicable to their FinTech products.[22] As many FinTech products may fail to fit squarely within existing regulatory regimes or may span several, obtaining definitive legal advice could prove problematic. It would thus be more prudent to obtain guidance directly from the regulators where possible. In addition, there may be potential costs related to the risk of harm to consumers from innovative financial products, for which FinTech companies may have to compensate. Consultation with and supervision by a regulator during live testing will aid in the early identification and mitigation of these

---

20 For the avoidance of doubt, we are referring to products that have undergone a full regulatory sandbox programme.

21 Zetsche et al., *supra* note 4, at 101.

22 Allen, *supra* note 1, at 11.

risks and thereby minimise potential liabilities. This does not mean that admission to a regulatory sandbox spares FinTech companies from all legal advice expenditure whatsoever. As is noted in this chapter, in support of an application to a regulatory sandbox, regulators would expect applicants to indicate which regulations they are seeking dispensation of and show that some prior market testing had been engaged in, all of which would inevitably require some preliminary expenditure on legal advice.[23]

14.16 On a similar note, a FinTech company could prepare for an application for full or modified authorisation with the aid of the regulator whilst in the regulatory sandbox. The regulator, being more familiar with such FinTech company and its product, should be able to process the application more expeditiously.

14.17 Lastly, the opportunity to test products in the regulatory sandbox environment prior to a full-fledged launch in the market could help FinTech companies assess the commercial viability of their products, tweaking the product in response to market reactions and, in the case of failed projects, sparing valuable resources from being needlessly invested in unprofitable ventures by terminating them at an earlier stage of development.

3. Stronger appeal to stakeholders

14.18 Increased regulatory certainty would give potential investors of regulatory sandbox projects the confidence that they are investing in products that are regulation compliant and, assuming dialogue with the regulators is maintained post-testing, would not be blindsided by future changes to the regulatory landscape. For unauthorised firms,[24] the quicker route to authorisation offered by regulatory sandboxes may provide further comfort to investors. This particular feature of the regulatory sandbox model has been criticised as being a 'stamp of approval' that regulators are in no position to give.[25] Likewise, the FCA has stated in response that their regulatory sandbox programme is not meant to serve that purpose. So why do sandbox administrators not just provide guidance to participants in confidence? To do so would spawn issues relating to the sandbox administrator's exercise of its discretionary powers to

---

23 Amongst other things, the FCA eligibility criteria for the FCA Sandbox applicants positively views applicants with well-developed testing plans and clear objectives, parameters and success criteria.

24 Almost all entities offering financial services in the UK must be authorised by the FCA. See Financial Conduct Authority, Unauthorised Firms and Individuals, available at: https://www.fca.org.uk/consumers/unauthorised-firms-individuals.

25 Jemima Kelly, A 'fintech sandbox' might sound like a harmless idea. It's not, *Financial Times* (5 December 2018), available at: https://ftalphaville.ft.com/2018/12/05/1543986004000/A–fintech-sandbox–might-sound-like-a-harmless-idea–It-s-not/.

choose participants, as described in more detail in 14.26–14.28 below. If the sandbox involves the regulator giving bespoke regulatory advice and support to a select number of entities (which, at least in the case of the FCA, have gone through a relatively rigorous selection process), it is simply a matter of public accountability that the processes are kept transparent. Perhaps this criticism should be reversed, demanding even more transparency where possible, particularly in relation to how participants are selected. Perhaps another counter-enquiry could be: so what if it is 'exploited' as PR?[26] The fact that these firms are subjecting themselves to closer scrutiny as part of the process of developing their products prior to market launch is, quite objectively, a legitimate selling point to potential consumers and investors who might be concerned about risks associated with embracing new FinTech products.

It has also been suggested that regulatory sandbox participation sends a **14.19** negative signal – that a participant is not fully regulated and thus riskier to conduct business with.[27] The FCA regulatory sandbox (the 'FCA Sandbox'), at least, has shown strong evidence to the contrary[28] – at least 40 per cent of firms, which completed testing in the first cohort of the FCA Sandbox programme, received investment during or following their regulatory sandbox tests.[29] This is not to say the 'negative stamp' effect is only a theory. If a regulatory 'race-to-the-bottom' situation arises between national regulators, the 'winning' regulatory sandbox might very well have such a negative reputational mark.

4. Market signalling

The implementation of a regulatory sandbox signals to all stakeholders, **14.20** including FinTech companies and consumers, a regulator's desire to facilitate FinTech innovation.[30] Such regulators would be perceived as 'collaborators' rather than 'enforcers'.

---

26   Kelly, *supra* note 25.
27   Zetsche et al., *supra* note 4, at 79.
28   Deloitte and Innovate Finance, A Journey Through the FCA Regulatory Sandbox (2018), available at: https://www2.deloitte.com/content/dam/Deloitte/uk/Documents/financial-services/deloitte-uk-fca-regulatory-sandbox-project-innovate-finance-journey.pdf, at 7.
29   Financial Conduct Authority, Lessons Learned Report (October 2017), available at: https://www.fca.org.uk/publication/research-and-data/regulatory-sandbox-lessons-learned-report.pdf, at 6.
30   Zetsche et al., *supra* note 4, at 78.

D. SHORTCOMINGS OF REGULATORY SANDBOXES

1. Multi-tiered regimes

14.21 One of the main criticisms of the regulatory sandbox model, as levelled by the French Autorité des Marchés Financiers (AMF), is that it would create a split, and thus discriminatory, regulatory regime with three classes of participants: (a) established companies that wish to implement FinTech innovations but are subject to the full extent of applicable regulation; (b) participants, chosen by the regulator, which enjoy a lower level of regulatory compliance; and (c) newly established companies, not selected by the regulator, and therefore subject to the same rules as the companies in (a).[31]

14.22 Instead, the AMF opted to pass new regulations to address specific forms of new FinTech products and institutions. For example, to address the proliferation of blockchain technology in the financial services sphere, the AMF implemented a two-stage regulation aimed at creating a formal legal framework for the use of blockchain technology in the issuance and transfer of unlisted securities – the first phase being a governmental order, and the second involving an implementing decree.[32] This approach may provide regulatory consistency and certainty since it affects all relevant entities generally, but in light of the breakneck pace of technological development, there is a high risk that any new regulation would not be imposed fast enough to comprehensively manage the disruptive effects of such FinTech products, or would quickly become outdated.

14.23 If only start-ups or new companies are admitted into a regulatory sandbox, then labelling the regulatory sandbox as 'discriminatory' distracts from how it serves to level the playing field for FinTech start-ups seeking to enter a market dominated by large financial institutions. However, whilst only admitting start-ups rationalises the tier divide between (a) and (b) above, it leaves the divide between (b) and (c) unaddressed. Adverse consequences of the latter divide may be mitigated through a transparent and objective admission process, but the extent of such mitigation would depend on the ability of regulators to adequately understand the technology of the FinTech products

---

31 Michelle Abraham, Leading Role: How France is Tackling Crypto, *International Financial Law Review* (29 May 2018), available at: http://www.iflr.com/Article/3810438/Leading-role-how-France-is-tackling-crypto.html.

32 See Ordonnance no 2016-520 du 28 Avril 2016 relative aux bons de caisse; and Décret no 2016-1458 du 28 Octobre 2016 relatif aux titres et aux prêts proposés dans le cadre du financement participative, both published in the French official journal.

they are admitting, and make selections that best achieve their regulatory sandbox objectives.

In other markets that have shown a reluctance to embrace the regulatory **14.24** sandbox model, regulators already have an established practice of dispensing with the relevant regulations, including by way of no-action letters, restricted licencing and piloting.[33] This mitigates the uneven competition regulatory sandboxes create and is akin to a 'boundless sandpit' – careful dispensation focuses most of the regulator's resources on the initial phase of the imaginary regulatory sandbox, namely, participant filtering. There is no discrimination between participants and non-participants *per se* because anyone is a 'potential participant'. However, a regulator of a regime based centrally on enforcement, forbearance, or regulation dispensation will have to predict, perhaps unrealistically, the outcome of any one FinTech innovation from the outset. Further, this foregoes one of the key mutual benefits of regulatory sandboxes – the open and continuous cooperation with national regulators *whilst* the FinTech product is being tested.

There are also services provided through dedicated points of contact with **14.25** regulators to direct enquiries on FinTech-related regulatory advice without the product testing element.[34] For example, the FCA's Innovation Hub service may give 'an informal steer or potential regulatory implications at an early stage of developing an innovative product or business model'. However, access to the Innovation Hub is also limited by criteria that vaguely echo those of the FCA Sandbox (including genuine innovation, consumer benefit and background research)[35] – this is essentially a return to square one on the 'discrimination issue'. There is, however, a distinct difference from regulatory sandboxes – in this model, regulators advise but do not grant exemptions or regulatory dispensations. The degree of regulatory scrutiny is also different – regulators will not monitor the development of a FinTech product as closely in this model.[36] As described in 14.45 below, certain US federal agencies have adopted similar 'Innovation Hub'-style services, rather than regulatory sandboxes.

---

33 Zetsche et al., *supra* note 4, at 79.
34 European Securities and Markets Authority et al., *supra* note 3, at 7.
35 Financial Conduct Authority, Eligibility for Innovation Hub, available at: https://www.fca.org.uk/firms/project-innovate-innovation-hub/eligibility.
36 Ibid.

2. Pre-judging innovative value

14.26 Administering a regulatory sandbox, including the individual monitoring and engagement of each separate testing participant, can be a costly affair. The case-by-case approach means that the demands of administering the regulatory sandbox for each participant will vary. 'Demands' also encompasses the technological aptitude of the administering regulators. Given the wide range and complexity of technologies being developed in the FinTech sector, it is unlikely that regulatory sandbox administrators would have expertise on all products being tested. This means that additional resources will be necessary to hire experts to ensure that the appropriate expertise is available to the regulatory sandbox administrator throughout testing. The reality of resource scarcity imposes upon the regulator the duty to choose, amongst many candidates, a few lucky participants for the regulatory sandbox. Even the criteria of 'genuinely innovative' and 'identifiable consumer benefit'[37] do little to narrow down the disparity between the number of candidates and available spaces.

14.27 These criteria inadvertently force regulators to prematurely decide whether a new FinTech product is technologically innovative and meets a market need. Are the regulators even qualified to have such discretion?[38] Some may find it unsettling that a financial regulator, whose central mandate is to protect consumers, is, as regulatory sandbox administrator, effectively allowed to steer FinTech innovation. There is also a risk of a regulator setting off a self-perpetuating and misleading feedback loop in relation to their perception of the direction of FinTech innovation. The composition of participants in a regulatory sandbox programme may skew the regulator's understanding of 'innovation' and its trend, and consequently skew any regulation subsequently imposed in response to observations drawn from them. Some have suggested the adoption of a formal selection criterion anchored to the regulatory sandbox's other overarching regulatory goals (including financial stability and consumer protection in particular), as these would provide greater certainty to applicants and also provide the regulator with justifications for its selection of participants.[39] But, the prevention of *any* risk to consumers or financial stability is not an objective of a regulatory sandbox – it is an integral operating standard. Also, it is often difficult to predict *ex ante* the risks a FinTech product may entail.

---

37 Financial Conduct Authority, Applying to the Regulatory Sandbox, available at: https://www.fca.org.uk/firms/regulatory-sandbox/prepare-application.

38 Allen, *supra* note 1, at 41.

39 Ibid., at 42.

At this point in time, it is not clear if this is a real issue in practice. If it is, a **14.28** regulator could 'democratise' the selection process by launching public consultations prior to finalising applicant nominations or have the general public vote on projects. However, responses to public consultations might be disproportionately skewed towards favouring financial institutions that are threatened by FinTech innovations. Also, allowing the general public who might not have the technological expertise to vote on complex FinTech products simply defeats the purpose of seeking the public opinion for an informed choice. Perhaps the best a regulator could do for now is to simply keep its decision-making processes transparent to the public and maintain an openness to suggestions and criticisms from the industry and all other stakeholders.

3. Scalability

There are generally two scalability-related issues – one in relation to the **14.29** validity of testing within a limited perimeter, and the other in relation to the scalability of a regulatory sandbox itself. With regard to the former, what can appear to work on a small scale in a controlled environment may not necessarily work in a large-scale setting. FinTech products in particular rely on or are embodied within computer software programmes, and thus may encounter unanticipated issues when running in an uncontrolled live environment. Secondly, a FinTech project successfully tested in a regulatory sandbox may prove to be less beneficial or even harmful to consumers and the financial system at large once removed from the confines of the regulatory sandbox.[40] Lastly, this scalability concern may manifest itself when participants seek to implement their projects on a cross-border basis because different countries have different consumer protection and financial regulatory regimes and their financial markets are of varying maturities. In this regard, a global sandbox might provide a solution – the opportunity to test their innovations on a larger pool of consumers and across jurisdictions.

The second scalability issue relates to regulatory sandboxes themselves. For **14.30** example, the existing conception of the FCA Sandbox is hardly scalable. Out of 99 applicants for its fifth cohort, only 29 were admitted into the FCA Sandbox. As regulatory sandboxes become increasingly popular, the number and variety of applicants will increase, and so will the imperative for regulators

---

40 Zetsche et al., *supra* note 4, at 62. One example of the scalability problem is embodied by Bitcoin's limited block size which creates a transaction processing bottleneck – the transaction processing capacity maximum is estimated between 3.3 and 7 transactions per second. See Xuan Han et al., A User-Friendly Centrally Banked Cryptocurrency, in Joseph K. Liu and Pierangela Samarati, *Information Security Practice and Experience*, Springer (2017), at 26.

to accommodate more applicants to ensure that the benefits of the regulatory sandbox programme can be enjoyed by as many eligible interested parties as possible.[41]

14.31 The scarcity issue is thus inexorably linked to the selectivity issue – regulators cannot admit all innovations, or even all good innovations, into the regulatory sandbox, and are thus forced to pick and choose. For this reason, it has been argued that regulatory sandboxes need to be made 'smarter and equipped to self-monitor activity within them', but to what extent will such streamlining solutions begin to erode the 'case-by-case' attention that has become a key feature of the regulatory sandbox in the first place?[42] Until a solution for scalability is forthcoming, a short-term solution might be to prioritise the admission of smaller start-ups over established financial institutions in order to ensure that regulatory sandbox programmes admit those who need it most.[43] This is not to suggest that larger financial institutions should face a blanket exclusion from regulatory sandboxes. Rather, regulators could instead prefer the admission of start-ups and large institutions partnering with start-ups.[44]

4. Race to the bottom

14.32 A large extent of the social benefits of a sandbox programme stems from the potential for in-depth knowledge exchange between innovators and regulators. In this regard, the regulatory sandbox signal is less credible for regulators with little experience with FinTech products. If a regulator cannot attract participants to its regulatory sandbox with its reputation for high programme quality, its next most convenient competitive strategy might involve the lowering of the entry criteria, an expansion of the regulatory exemptions on offer, and/or lax supervision during the testing period. Regulators who compete this way would find themselves embroiled in a race-to-the bottom style competition which, in the longer run, is bound to lead to compromises on consumer protection and financial stability. This, in turn, would lead to the erosion of a regulator's credibility in the eyes of all stakeholders, including consumers.[45] Serious participants would seek to avoid being associated with such regulatory sandboxes that could inadvertently mark their products as risky or inadequately regulated.

---

41 Zetsche et al., *supra* note 4, at 46.
42 Ibid., at 85.
43 Allen, *supra* note 1, at 45.
44 For example, Tradle, an app and web-based service that creates personal or commercial identity and verifiable documents using DLT, partnered with Aviva to participate in the first cohort of the FCA Sandbox.
45 Kelly, *supra* note 25.

Joining the race to the bottom inflicts another handicap on regulatory sandbox **14.33** programmes – by adopting standards that deviate so far from those of reputable regulatory sandboxes, regulators could disqualify themselves from inclusion in cross-border regulatory sandbox collaborations as further discussed in 14.56 below. This is because, as with passporting regimes,[46] one basic requirement for such cooperation would likely be for a participant in one country to adopt regulations that are at least as stringent as those of other global regulatory sandbox members – a highest common denominator standard.

E. THE FCA SANDBOX

As noted, the FCA is a pioneer of the FinTech regulatory sandbox model. In **14.34** June 2016, the FCA Sandbox admitted its first cohort of participants with the aim of fostering innovation in financial products and services and promoting effective competition in the interests of consumers.[47] By May 2019, the FCA Sandbox had supported more than 100 firms in testing innovative new FinTech products including blockchain technology-based money transfer services, automated debt solution advisors, biometric digital ID verification, and flight delay insurance.[48]

Non-authorised participants in the FCA Sandbox would be granted a **14.35** restricted form of FCA authorisation specifically in relation to the product or activity that is being tested,[49] and all participants may benefit from a number of measures aimed at addressing concerns about being subject to enforcement action stemming from the activities tested, including individual guidance on

---

46   For example, under the EU Alternative Investment Fund Managers Directive (2011/61/EU) (AIFM Directive) an Alternative Investment Fund (AIFM) from one EU member state can market their fund in another EU member state but must apply the minimum AIFM Directive standards to AIFMs under the AIFMD regime.

47   Financial Conduct Authority, UK FinTech: Regulating for Innovation, available at: https://www.fca.org.uk/news/speeches/uk-fintech-regulating-innovation.

48   Financial Conduct Authority, Regulatory sandbox – cohort 5, available at: https://www.fca.org.uk/firms/regulatory-sandbox/cohort-5.

49   Financial Conduct Authority, Regulatory Sandbox, available at: https://www.fca.org.uk/firms/regulatory-sandbox. This contrasts with the ASIC's regulatory sandbox. Unlike the FCA's restricted authorisations (which still require sandbox firms to apply to the FCA for authorisation), ASIC's FinTech licensing exemption allows start-ups to avoid applying for any license for a 12-month period. So long as start-ups meet the eligibility criteria for the licensing exemption, there is no application process at all – all that is required is a notification to ASIC of the intention to rely on the exemption and the provision of certain information. But, the applicable exemptions are only available to firms advising on or dealing in certain specified products, such as listed stocks, government bonds, and certain general insurance products. See Australian Securities & Investments Commission, *Regulatory Guide 257: Testing FinTech Products and Services Without Holding an AFS or Credit Licence*, available at: http://download.asic.gov.au/media/ 4160999/rg257-published-24-february-2017.pdf.

the interpretation of the rules applicable to the activities being tested; 'No Enforcement Action' letters (NALs), stating that the FCA will not take enforcement action during the testing period where the FCA is reasonably satisfied that the activities being tested do not breach the conditions agreed with the FCA or their objectives;[50] and waivers of certain applicable FCA rules to participants who meet the statutory criteria.[51]

14.36 Each participant is assigned a case officer who will support the design and implementation of tests on the proposed project and provide guidance on how each project would fit within the regulatory framework.[52] Projects that entail the introduction of new technologies or the application of existing technologies in new ways will be subject to technology and cyber resilience reviews to minimise potential harm to consumers.[53]

14.37 A set of standard safeguards will be imposed on all FCA Sandbox tests, but the final suite of safeguards may include additional bespoke parameters to suit each individual project. For example, whilst the FCA requires all participants to establish an exit plan upon termination of testing for any reason,[54] firms proposing to test the use of digital currencies in money remittance have been required to guarantee a full refund of any amounts lost.[55]

14.38 Participants must apply for full FCA authorisation to launch their FinTech products outside the FCA Sandbox once testing is complete, and the FCA has observed that the majority of firms initially issued with restricted authorisation proceeded, post-testing, to secure full authorisation.[56] On the other hand, some firms that had completed testing in the FCA Sandbox sought confirmation from the FCA that their projects did not require full FCA authorisation or chose to revamp their business models to avoid falling under the FCA's regulatory purview.[57]

---

50 It should be noted that NALs only address FCA's enforcement actions and do not affect a regulatory sandbox participant's liability towards the consumers being tested on.

51 For instance, under s 138A(a) of the Financial Services and Markets Act 2000, a waiver may be granted where compliance by the person with the rules would be unduly burdensome or would not achieve the purpose for which the rules were made and such waiver would not adversely affect the advancement of any of the regulator's objectives.

52 Financial Conduct Authority, Lessons Learned Report, *supra* note 29, at 4.

53 Ibid., at 6.

54 Ibid.

55 Ibid., at 11.

56 Ibid., at 5.

57 Deloitte and Innovate Finance, *supra* note 28, at 6.

1. Admission into the FCA Sandbox

Firms are admitted to the FCA Sandbox on a cohort basis, with two **14.39** six-month test periods each year. There are a number of requirements firms must fulfil to apply for FCA Sandbox testing, including having a significant UK presence (e.g., a certain level of staff and a head office in the UK) and a contractual relationship with all relevant partners, if any. The success of an application generally depends on the demonstration of a need for regulatory sandbox testing. For example, applicants should show that the innovation does not easily fit the existing regulatory framework or it is prohibitively costly to bring the innovation to the UK market, as well as the promise of direct or indirect material benefits to the UK financial sector – participants will have to demonstrate that their projects embody 'genuine innovation', consumer risks have been identified, and they will promote effective competition.[58]

In an October 2017 report, the FCA identified a number of notable obstacles **14.40** that applicants may encounter.[59] First, smaller firms and start-ups might face difficulty in acquiring participant customers for regulatory sandbox testing relative to larger institutions with well-established customer bases. One solution is for smaller firms to enter into partnerships with larger institutions, such as banks – the smaller firms gain access to a larger pool of existing customers for testing, while their partners benefit from access to their innovations and technological expertise.[60] However, FinTech firms that do not provide financial services themselves, but instead create products and services for regulated financial services firms, must recognise the risk that they may become subject to regulatory scrutiny because of their relationship with a regulated financial institution.[61]

Another obstacle relates to meeting the conditions for FCA authorisation **14.41** itself. Some applicants found the FCA Sandbox authorisation process, and specifically navigating and interpreting the FCA handbook, fairly daunting. Applicants will still need to invest a significant amount of resources to ensure that they and their projects meet the eligibility criteria, particularly in relation to the authorisation requirements. Further, depending on the nature of the proposed product, heightened authorisation requirements may have to be met. For example, firms that proposed projects involving the underwriting of insurance products had to qualify for FCA authorisation as insurers. Likewise,

---

58 Financial Conduct Authority, Applying to the Regulatory Sandbox, *supra* note 37.
59 Financial Conduct Authority, Lessons Learned Report, *supra* note 29, at 57.
60 For example, in December 2016, HSBC Bank collaborated with FinTech start-up Pariti to test HSBC's SmartSave app in the FCA Sandbox.
61 Allen, *supra* note 1, at 10.

some firms seeking to operate multilateral trading facilities have struggled to meet the requirement to hold a sufficient level of initial capital reserves.[62]

14.42 Third, whilst most firms will need a UK bank account before they can participate in the FCA Sandbox, many banks refused to offer banking services to certain types of firms due to perceived greater money laundering and terrorist financing risks. This is the case particularly for firms seeking to leverage DLT or become payment institutions. Perhaps the increasing openness of the FCA to explore these technologies within the FCA Sandbox would encourage banks to open bank accounts for such applicants in the future.[63]

2. Reception of the FCA Sandbox

14.43 The FCA Sandbox has proven reasonably popular – for its first cohort, the FCA received 69 applications and accepted 24 for testing. In its fifth cohort in May 2019, increased interest was shown with 99 applicants and 29 admissions.[64] Participants in the earlier cohorts have expressed, unequivocally, that the regulatory sandbox has delivered real value to firms, with a number of participants expressing an intention to join the FCA Sandbox for future projects.[65]

F. REGULATORY SANDBOXES IN THE US

1. Federal-level experiment

14.44 In the US, a number of attempts have been made to implement a regulatory sandbox. In 2016, the CFPB initiated Project Catalyst, in which FinTech companies were encouraged to pitch for pilot programmes or novel disclosure trials to achieve enhanced consumer protection, but this project was not embraced by the FinTech industry for a number of reasons, including an inevitable collision on jurisdictional oversight with other regulatory agencies and an almost useless no-action letter scheme. From a policy perspective, the absence of a mandate to protect financial stability has left many to question

---

62 Financial Conduct Authority, Lessons Learned Report, *supra* note 29, at 18.

63 In the third FCA Sandbox cohort, only four participants tested products incorporating DLT. For its fourth cohort, the FCA admitted 12 applicants which sought to test products incorporating DLT. See Financial Conduct Authority, FCA Reveals the Fourth Round of Successful Firms in its Regulatory Sandbox, available at: https://www.fca.org.uk/news/press-releases/fca-reveals-fourth-round-successful-firms-its-regulatory-sandbox.

64 Ibid.

65 Deloitte and Innovate Finance, *supra* note 28, at 7. Etherisc applied to both the third and fourth cohort of the FCA Sandbox.

whether the CFPB was the appropriate agency to administer a regulatory sandbox.[66] The failure of Project Catalyst demonstrated that it would be very difficult to implement a regulatory sandbox in the US based on the UK FCA model.[67] In November 2016, the US Office of the Comptroller of the Currency (the OCC) announced that it was considering a programme to charter certain FinTech companies as 'special-purpose national banks'. According to the white paper published by the OCC, this would help FinTech companies operate in a 'safe and sound' manner to protect customers, business partners, and communities, promote consistency of regulation across the country, and strengthen the national banking system.[68] FinTech companies with such a charter would be exempted from a number of banking and financial services laws and regulations, whether by fitting into already-existing carve-outs for federally chartered banks or by receiving the benefits of applicable federal pre-emption laws. However, other regulators objected to the OCC's proposal on various grounds, including the lack of expertise on the part of the OCC in FinTech, and some parties even brought legal actions against the OCC to prevent it from adopting such rules.[69]

Alternative methods have been used to encourage FinTech innovation in the US. For example, the US Commodity Futures Trading Commission (CFTC) initiative, LabCFTC, provides a forum for FinTech firms to discuss projects with CFTC specialists, and publishes guidance for market participants on FinTech developments.[70] In November 2018, the US Securities and Exchange Commission (SEC) initiated the Strategic Hub for Innovation and Financial Technology (FinHub). According to the SEC, FinHub will facilitate the SEC's engagement with innovators, developers, and entrepreneurs as a resource for information about the SEC's views and actions in the FinTech space.[71] These initiatives focus more on supporting FinTech firms within and through the existing regulatory processes via more traditional processes, rather than introducing new initiatives. Such efforts fail to provide a framework for   **14.45**

---

66   Allen, *supra* note 1, at 37.

67   Patrick McHenry, Bank think CFPB's 'project catalyst' Failed. Fintech Deserves Better, *American Banker* (25 April 2017), available at: https://www.americanbanker.com/opinion/cfpbs-project-catalyst-failed-fintech-deserves-better. See also Lydia Beyoud, CFPB Fintech Group Poised for Renaissance After Restructuring, *Bloomberg BNA* (16 May 2018), available at: https://www.bna.com/cfpb-fintech-group-n73014476056/.

68   Office of the Comptroller of the Currency: *Exploring Special Purpose National Bank Charters for Fintech Companies* (December 2016), available at: https://www.occ.gov/topics/responsible-innovation/comments/special-purpose-national-bank-charters-for-fintech.pdf, at 2.

69   Conference of State Bank Supervisors, *CSBS Sues OCC Over FinTech Charter* (25 October 2018), available at: https://www.csbs.org/ csbs-sues-occ-over-fintech-charter.

70   US Commodity Futures Trading Commission, LabCFTC Primers, available at: https://www.cftc.gov/LabCFTC/Primers/index.htm.

71   See https://www.sec.gov/finhub.

the level of collaboration between regulator and innovator that is characteristic of regulatory sandboxes.

14.46 Finally, in a report on the regulation of FinTech,[72] the US Government Accountability Office (GAO) recommended the consideration and adoption of regulatory models used in other jurisdictions to ease the regulatory burden on innovative companies in the financial services industry, including the introduction of regulatory sandboxes.

2. State-level experiment

14.47 In August 2018, the Arizona Attorney General's Office launched Arizona's FinTech Sandbox (the Arizona Sandbox).[73] Arizona Sandbox participants will be allowed to engage in the testing of products and services on as many as 17,500 residents under certain circumstances and for up to two years (with the possibility of a one-year extension) without additional licensing. After the permitted period, participants will be expected to apply for a license or must stop offering their products and services in Arizona.

14.48 Products or services eligible for Arizona Sandbox testing are expected to include most types of credit extending services, such as peer-to-peer lending, 'innovative products and services for money transmission,' and certain blockchain or cryptocurrency products or services.[74] Ineligible products or services include securities trading, insurance products, and services that provide 'solely deposit-taking functions'.[75] Whilst the eligibility criteria for the Arizona Sandbox appear to be less prescriptive than those for the FCA Sandbox – the Arizona Attorney General 'evaluates applications holistically to determine the applicant's ability to conduct a test that does not place undue risk on consumers' – the list of considerations that the Arizona Attorney General may consider, including capitalisation, compliance or legal support, and cash on hand,[76] are suggestive of a similar vetting process.

---

72 US Government Accountability Office, Financial Technology, Additional Steps by Regulators Could Better Protect Consumers and Aid Regulatory Oversight (March 2018), available at: https://www.gao.gov/assets/700/690803.pdf, at 74.

73 Attorney General of the State of Arizona, Arizona's FinTech Sandbox, available at: https://www.azag.gov/fintech?utm_source=9-25-18+Member+List&utm_campaign=19409af3eb-EMAIL_CAMPAIGN_2018_01_19_COPY_01&utm_medium=email&utm_term= 0_df6f78c247-19409af3eb-345024239.

74 Attorney General of the State of Arizona, Frequently Asked Questions, available at: https://www.azag.gov/fintech/faq.

75 Ibid.

76 Ibid.

The Arizona Sandbox initiative was followed in February 2019 by the State of **14.49**
Wyoming where the Wyoming Governor signed HB0057 which established a
regulatory sandbox programme.[77] Other states, including New York and
Illinois, are also considering adopting state-level regulatory sandboxes mod-
elled after the Arizona Sandbox. In addition, the state bank regulators in New
England (comprising Connecticut, Rhode Island, Massachusetts, Vermont,
New Hampshire and Maine) are reported to have been exploring a regional
regulatory sandbox.[78]

3. Regulatory sandbox implementation issues in the US

For the US, there are profound structural limitations due to the dual federal- **14.50**
state and multi-regulator financial regulatory system. The GAO observed that
'regulatory oversight is fragmented across multiple regulators at the federal
level, and also involves regulatory bodies in the 50 states and other US
jurisdictions'.[79]

In 2018, the Department of the Treasury (the Treasury) recommended **14.51**
updates to the existing regulatory framework, encouraging the embrace of
current technology and consumer practices, and urged for the harmonisation
of regulations to promote innovation.[80] The Treasury also recommended that
federal and state regulators establish a regulatory solution that 'expedites
regulatory relief under applicable laws and regulations to permit meaningful
experimentation for innovative products, services and processes ... in essence,
a "regulatory sandbox"'. Any such regulatory sandbox would be based on a
number of principles, including the promotion, adoption and growth of
innovation and technological transformation in financial services and maintaining financial integrity, consumer protection and investor protection.[81]

The Treasury did not list any agencies to lead the regulatory sandbox implemen- **14.52**
tation effort. Clearly, the creation of any US regulatory sandbox would likely
involve the participation of multiple agencies with regulatory jurisdiction over
FinTech and other non-bank financial services firms. Unlike the UK, which has

---

77 State of Wyoming 65th Legislature, HB0057 – Financial technology sandbox, available at: https://www.
    wyoleg.gov/Legislation/2019/HB0057.
78 Paul Sweeney, Fintech Sandbox? States, OCC Mull Regulatory Options, *deBanked* (2 May 2017), available
    at: https://debanked.com/2017/05/fintech-sandbox-states-occ-mull-regulatory-options/.
79 United States Government Accountability Office, *supra* note 72, at 40.
80 US Department of the Treasury, A Financial System That Creates Economic Opportunities, Nonbank
    Financials, Fintech, and Innovation, available at: https://home.treasury.gov/sites/default/files/2018-08/A-
    Financial-System-that-Creates-Economic-Opportunities—Nonbank-Financials-Fintech-and-Innovation_
    0.pdf, at 10.
81 Ibid., at 169.

only two main financial sector regulators,[82] or Australia, where financial and corporate laws are administered only at the federal level, any implementation of a regulatory sandbox model in the US is likely to be plagued by its aforementioned fragmented regulatory landscape.

14.53 At the state level, certain state regulators may not be technologically or otherwise equipped to oversee regulatory sandbox implementation. Any state-level regulatory sandbox would also not be able to facilitate experimentation beyond that state's borders.[83] In addition, state regulators may even lack the incentive to promote financial stability, which should be a core principle of any sandbox administrator, as doing so may make other states more attractive to FinTech companies.[84] Therefore, it may be necessary for regulatory sandbox administrators in the US to have the power to grant the pre-emption of state-level regulation. To complement this, state-level regulators could be responsible for the direct monitoring of the progress of activity within their borders and initiate necessary enforcement actions against participants.

14.54 Similarly, allocating responsibility for administering the regulatory sandbox to any one US regulatory agency would limit the range of regulatory relief available to participants, as no single agency has the power to grant exemptions from enforcement action by other agencies.[85] It has thus been suggested that the regulatory sandbox will need to be administered by a committee of financial regulators – the admission to the US regulatory sandbox would be decided by the relevant federal regulators collectively, and perhaps include consultation with state regulators, but the day-to-day administration of the regulatory sandbox should be the responsibility of the most suitable federal regulatory agency.[86] Above all, there should be a clear set of objectives and no confusion between the sandbox administrators about the priorities between the objectives of consumer protection, stability of the financial system and promoting innovation. Conflict between sandbox administrators about these objectives could lead to administrative deadlocks.[87]

---

82 The FCA and the Prudential Regulatory Authority. The FCA anticipates that sandbox options for some firms will have to be agreed in consultation with the UK's Prudential Regulatory Authority. See Financial Conduct Authority, Regulatory Sandbox (November 2015), available at: https://www.fca.org.uk/publication/research/regulatory-sandbox.pdf, at 7.

83 Allen, *supra* note 1, at 36.

84 Ibid.

85 Ibid., at 38.

86 Ibid., at 39.

87 Zetsche et al., *supra* note 4, at 63.

On the whole, effective sandbox model adoption in the US remains a distant **14.55** prospect, particularly in light of its fragmented regulatory architecture. Nevertheless, as the Treasury noted, a regulatory sandbox solution has to be implemented 'in a timely manner' – state-level implementation could be a small but necessary step towards wider adoption.

G. A GLOBAL REGULATORY SANDBOX

Since the inception of the FCA Sandbox, the regulatory sandbox model has **14.56** been adopted by many financial services regulators around the world. To name a few, the Hong Kong Monetary Authority (the HKMA), ASIC and MAS each launched their FinTech regulatory sandbox in 2016, the Canadian Securities Administrators regulatory sandbox launched in February 2017 and the Bank of Lithuania launched its regulatory sandbox platform in 2018. There is a clear hype about regulatory sandboxes as the new approach to regulating FinTech developments today and its widespread adoption is expected to fuel competition among financial centres in their bids to become global FinTech leaders.

Nevertheless, being a successful national regulatory sandbox has its limits, **14.57** particularly in the FinTech industry where developers would seek for their innovations to be employed on a cross-border basis. This would particularly be the case for developers in smaller financial markets that lack, by themselves, the market size necessary to support the exploitation of substantial economies of scale. This is why a regional or global regulatory sandbox is a natural progressive step after a stable national regulatory sandbox programme is established.[88] The establishment of a global regulatory sandbox can facilitate the exchange of information, ideas and experiences between national regulators, while also providing a gateway for FinTech firms to test and eventually scale the implementation of their innovative products beyond their national borders.

In a collaborative effort between 11 financial regulators and related organ- **14.58** isations, the Global Financial Innovation Network (GFIN), building upon the FCA's 2018 proposal to create a 'global sandbox', was officially launched in January 2019.[89] The three main functions of the GFIN are: to act as a network of regulators to collaborate and share experiences of innovation in their

---

88 Ibid., at 80.
89 Financial Conduct Authority, Global Financial Innovation Network (GFIN), available at: https://www.fca. org.uk/firms/global-financial-innovation-network.

respective markets; to provide a forum for joint RegTech work and collaborative knowledge sharing; and to provide firms with an environment in which to trial cross-border solutions.[90] As of the date of this writing, GFIN membership includes ASIC, the Central Bank of Bahrain, *Autorité des marchés financiers*, the Guernsey Financial Services Commission, the HKMA, the Hong Kong Securities and Futures Commission, Astana Financial Services Authority, the MAS, the Dubai Financial Services Authority, CFPB and the FCA.

14.59 Implementation is a less optimistic scenario – a global regulatory sandbox will require a consensus amongst all member regulators on the standardisation of such global regulatory sandbox eligibility criteria, which would likely be that of the most stringent member jurisdiction. It is also not clear whether GFIN member nations would be willing to concede any part of their regulatory authority by accepting sandbox testing results from another member state – this might similarly hinge on the extent of the divergence of testing standards between the relevant regulators. In any event, the global regulatory sandbox concept presents national regulators with another strategic decision to make in attracting FinTech investment – a regulator can compete by establishing an extremely accessible regulatory sandbox which is limited to their national market, or a group of regulators may collaborate to achieve a semblance of regulatory convergence, aspiring towards a global regulatory sandbox where successful testing in one jurisdiction paves the way to market penetration in others, and consequentially forge a collective competitive edge in favour of an individual national one.

14.60 In March 2018, the European Banking Authority (EBA) published its FinTech Roadmap,[91] following a discussion paper issued in 2017 regarding the EBA's approach to FinTech (the Discussion Paper).[92] Respondents to the Discussion Paper urged the EBA to promote best practices and convergence in supervisory and regulatory approaches in the European Union, including in relation to regulatory sandboxes.[93] The expressed objectives aspire towards the conception of a regional sandbox and include the need to achieve technological neutrality and innovation across the single market and consistency in the regulatory treatment of FinTech and the operational aspects of regulatory

---

90 Ibid.

91 European Banking Authority, Conclusions from the Consultation on the EBA's Approach to Financial Technology (15 March 2018), available at: https://eba.europa.eu/documents/10180/1919160/EBA+Fin Tech+Roadmap.pdf.

92 European Banking Authority: Discussion Paper on the EBA's Approach to Financial Technology (FinTech) (4 August 2017), available at: https://eba.europa.eu/documents/10180/1919160/EBA+Discussion+Paper +on+Fintech+%28EBA-DP-2017-02%29.pdf.

93 European Banking Authority, *supra* note 91, at 3.

sandboxes[94] so as to prevent 'forum shopping'.[95] The intended result of this process is to make EU member states, collectively, a more attractive destination for FinTech innovation.

H. CONCLUSION

The regulatory sandbox model in the context of FinTech is still a fresh **14.61** innovation itself and has taken on various forms across the globe. Many aspects of this model are in want of fine-tuning to address, amongst other issues, participant selection and scalability. Regulators are constantly challenged by the balancing act of preserving the stability of the financial system, protecting consumers, and promoting (or, more accurately, not hindering) innovation – regulations saddle service providers with compliance costs and expenses that draw resources away from creating innovative products.[96]

The regulatory sandbox model presents a welcome addition to the financial **14.62** regulators' arsenal to manage innovation-associated risks on a case-by-case basis, at an early stage and in real time, before they materialise in the live markets. Nevertheless, it is hoped that the discussions above show that the extent to which the regulatory sandbox model can be exploited depends on a myriad factors, not least the relevant national regulatory structure and a regulator's reputation in terms of experience and regulatory sandbox administration capacity and capability. Regulators that are just joining the regulatory sandbox bandwagon should not bow to pressure to lower their standards just to attract FinTech investment. Rather, a more sustainable approach, and one that will facilitate eventual collaboration on a global level, would be to invest in securing the right expertise, including FinTech experts and economists, to bolster their regulatory sandbox administrative capabilities – this way, the race to the top does not descend into a race to the bottom.

---

94 For example, the objectives, scope, entry and exit conditions, regulatory requirements, typical duration of operation and cooperation arrangements between regulatory sandbox administering authorities.
95 European Banking Authority, *supra* note 91, at 12.
96 Zetsche et al., *supra* note 4, at 34.

15

COMPLIANCE AND WHISTLEBLOWING: HOW TECHNOLOGY WILL REPLACE, EMPOWER AND CHANGE WHISTLEBLOWERS

Kieran Pender, Sofya Cherkasova and Anna Yamaoka-Enkerlin[*]

A. INTRODUCTION

15.01 Whistleblowing is not a new phenomenon. Some scholars have traced the concept to Ancient Greece, drawing parallels with the notion of *parrhēsia*, or fearless speech.[1] Lykourgos, an Athenian orator of the mid-300s BC, is reported to have said that 'neither the laws nor judges can bring any results unless someone denounces the wrong doers'.[2] Laws to incentivise whistle-blowers are not novel either. In the 7th century, a British king declared that 'if a freeman works during [the Sabbath], he shall forfeit his [profits], and the man who informs against him shall have half the fine, and [the profits] of the

---

[*] The authors acknowledge with thanks the helpful comments of Ashley Savage and Jelena Madir on an earlier draft.

1 Michel Focault, *Fearless Speech*, Semiotext(e) (2001); and Alan Chu, In Tradition of Speaking Fearlessly: Locating a Rhetoric of Whistleblowing in the Parrhēsiastic Dialectic, 19 *Advances in the History of Rhetoric* 231 (2016) at 239–48.

2 Transparency International, Providing an Alternative to Silence (2013), available at: http://www.transparency.gr/wp-content/uploads/2013/11/WHISTLEBLOWERS_ENGLISH_LOW.pdf at 13.

labour'.[3] Modern American whistleblower protections, meanwhile, are grounded in the Civil War-era False Claims Act.

The label whistleblowing, on the other hand, is a more recent invention. The **15.02** term was popularised in the 1970s by American political activist Ralph Nader, who described it as 'an act of a man or a woman who, believing that the public interest overrides the interest of the organisation he serves, publicly "blows the whistle" if the organisation is involved in corrupt, illegal, fraudulent or harmful activity'.[4] In the following decades, whistleblowing entered the mainstream lexicon. High-profile whistleblowers drew attention to the considerable public interest in their deeds and the adverse consequences they often suffered. Laws were enacted to encourage whistleblowing and protect those who did so – the Public Interest Disclosure Act 1998, a notable early example in the UK – and charitable organisations were established to advocate the whistleblower cause. There remains, though, no universally-accepted definition of a whistleblower or defined criteria of what constitutes whistleblowing.

Although progress has been slow, by 2019 whistleblowing is beginning to lose **15.03** the societal stigma often attached to it. Whistleblowers have revealed large-scale tax avoidance (Antoine Deltour and LuxLeaks), widespread data misuse (Christopher Wylie and Cambridge Analytica) and multi-billion pound money laundering (Howard Wilkinson and Danske Bank). In recent years Ireland, the Netherlands, France, Italy and Serbia have been among the jurisdictions to pass landmark whistleblower protection regimes – approximately 40 countries globally now have specific legal protections for those who blow the whistle. At the time of this writing, the European Parliament was in the process of enacting European Union-wide whistleblower protection laws.

But just as societies are beginning to appreciate the significant contributions **15.04** whistleblowers make to democratic accountability and corporate compliance, the concept of whistleblowing is being transformed by technology. Such disruption is the focus of this chapter. Technology offers much promise to whistleblowers and whistleblower protections, but also many potential pitfalls. A sober analysis is required to determine where technology might add benefit, and where it could prove problematic.

---

3   International Bar Association, Whistleblower Protections: A Guide (2018), available at: https://www.ibanet.org/Conferences/whistleblowing.aspx, at 5.

4   Ralph Nader, An Anatomy of Whistle Blowing, in Ralph Nader, Peter J Petkas and Kate Blackwell (eds) *Whistle Blowing* (1972), at vii.

15.05   This chapter has three substantive parts. Section B will begin by detailing how data analytics and artificial intelligence (AI) are becoming 'algorithmic whistleblowers', detecting (or even preventing) misconduct before it can be discovered by human whistleblowers. In other words, how is technology replacing whistleblowers? Section C analyses a range of technological solutions that are helping to empower whistleblowers, by protecting them and giving them new avenues for reporting misconduct. The exciting potential for blockchain to offer anonymity, immutability, resilience, compensation and information escrow in the whistleblowing context will be considered. Section D discusses how technology is changing the nature of whistleblowing, given the modern-day ability to distribute terabytes of information with a few clicks. The implications of technological-driven change, including the increasingly blurred lines between whistleblowing, leaking and hacking, are reflected upon. Section E concludes.

B.   TECHNOLOGY REPLACING THE WHISTLEBLOWER

15.06   We live in the age of information. An unprecedented level of openness is demanded from institutions, and the link between data disclosure, transparency and accountability is often assumed.[5] However, disruptive technology is increasingly becoming necessary to harness the power of this data to detect and minimise misconduct in the public and private sector. As this technology becomes more widespread, it is reducing the need to rely on human whistleblowers. This is positive not only from a compliance and supervisory perspective, but also in minimising the personal, financial and professional toll on would-be whistleblowers.[6] However, the benefits of 'algorithmic whistleblowing' must be weighed against risk, requiring trade-offs between transparency, privacy and accuracy.

1.   The 'openness revolution'

15.07   Transparency is a contested concept, but at its heart it 'refers to the notion that information about an individual or organisation's actions can be seen from the outside'.[7] Transparency has become a default policy prescription,[8] often

---

5   Aarti Gupta, Transparency Under Scrutiny: Information Disclosure in Global Environmental Governance, 8 *Global Environmental Politics* 1 (2008), at 1.

6   Adam Waytz, Why Robots Could be Awesome Whistleblowers (2014), available at: https://www.the atlantic.com/business/archive/2014/10/why-robots-could-be-awesome-whistleblowers/381216/.

7   Matthew S. Mayernik, Open Data: Accountability and Transparency, *Big Data and Society* 1 (2017), available at: https://doi.org/10.1177/2053951717718853 at 1.

8   Gupta, *supra* note 5, at 1.

invoked as an essential component of trust and cooperation, as a market efficiency mechanism, as a legitimising procedural tool and, at its broadest, as a value embedded in democracy.

The ascent of transparency as an institutional norm dovetails with the growing **15.08** recognition of the value of whistleblowers as 'the primary source of involuntary transparency',[9] reflected in the development of whistleblower protection legislation worldwide.[10] The need is great. While the global cost of fraud has been estimated to amount to over £3 trillion,[11] nearly half of the respondents to Kroll's *Global Fraud and Risk Report* indicated that instances of detected fraud in their organisation over the past year were uncovered by whistleblowers.[12] According to the World Bank, companies worldwide are cumulatively paying over £300 billion in bribes annually, despite evidence that bribery is ultimately counterproductive (even when no enforcement action is commenced).[13] When compliance claims are brought, penalties can be steep.[14]

Meanwhile, regulators and advocates alike are increasingly pursuing another **15.09** transparency frontier which has, along with whistleblowing, grown from the historical right to information movement: access to data.[15] Open data proponents support the disclosure of data in a way that allows it to be freely used, modified and shared by anyone for any purpose. The OECD identifies open data as a 'key public good' and a powerful tool in the fight against the abuse of power.[16] Efforts are being made to open up government data sets which include public officials' directories, budgets, public procurement, political financing, voting records and land registries.[17]

---

9   Jennifer Shkabatur, Transparency With(out) Accountability: Open Government in the United States 31 *Policy Review* 89 (2012), available at: https://digitalcommons.law.yale.edu/cgi/ at 113.

10   International Bar Association, *supra* note 3.

11   Jim Gee, Financial Cost of Fraud (2018), available at: www.crowe.com/uk/croweuk/insights/financial-cost-of-fraud-2018.

12   Kroll, Kroll Annual Global Fraud and Risk Report 2017/2018 (2018), available at: https://www.kroll.com/en-us/global-fraud-and-risk-report-2018.

13   David Montero, How Managers Should Respond When Bribes Are Business as Usual (2018), available at: hbr.org/2018/11/how-managers-should-respond-when-bribes-are-business-as-usual.

14   Rob Evans, Rolls-Royce to Pay £671m Over Bribery Claims (2017), available at: https://www.theguardian.com/business/2017/jan/16/rolls-royce-to-pay-671m-over-bribery-claims.

15   Katleen Janssen, Open Government Data: Right to Information 2.0 or its Rollback Version? 8 ICRI Research Paper (2012), available at: https://ssrn.com/abstract=2152566 at 4–8.

16   OECD, Compendium of Good Practices on the use of Open Data for Anti-corruption (2017), available at: http://www.oecd.org/gov/digital-government/g20-oecd-compendium.pdf.

17   World Wide Web Foundation and Transparency International, *Connecting the Dots: Building a Case for Open Data to Fight Corruption* (2017) available at: http://webfoundation.org/docs/2017/04/2017_OpenData ConnectingDots_EN-6.pdf.

15.10 The 'openness revolution' is also marching into the private sector.[18] For example, the movement pushing for a global public database featuring country-by-country reporting (CBCR)[19] on the economic activity and tax contributions of multinational corporations achieved a breakthrough in 2017, when the European Commission voted for a second time in favour of public CBCR by multinationals.[20] Another example is the call for beneficial ownership reporting.[21] In 2016, the UK became the first country to publish the identity of those who benefit from, own and control companies;[22] 15 other countries have subsequently committed to introducing beneficial ownership registers. Meanwhile, navigating the regulatory complexity that followed the Global Financial Crisis has 'inevitably required greater granularity, precision and frequency in data reporting, aggregation, and analysis' from corporations, financial institutions and supervisory authorities alike.[23]

15.11 In summary, the demand for open data coupled with an increase in data intensive regulation is adding unprecedented dimensionality to high-volume, high-velocity and high-variety information assets, also known as big data.[24] At the outset, this might appear to be an unreservedly good development from transparency and anti-corruption perspectives, reducing reliance on human whistleblowers. However, there are at least three potential limitations.

2. Challenges

15.12 First, more data does not necessarily mean more transparency. Jonathan Fox distinguishes between two kinds of transparency.[25] Opaque transparency

---

18   The Openness Revolution (2014), *The Economist* available at: www.economist.com/business/2014/12/11/the-openness-revolution.

19   Since 2002, CBCR has become the extractive industry standard in 52 countries, and has since spread to the financial institutions; Alex Cobham et al., What Do They Pay? Towards a Public Database to Account for the Economic Activities and Tax Contributions of Multinational Corporations (2017), available at: datafortaxjustice.net/what-do-they-pay/#extractive-industries-data.

20   Financial Transparency Coalition, Letting the Public In (2015), available at: https://financialtransparency.org/wp-content/uploads/2016/09/OpenData_fullpaper.pdf.

21   According to the World Bank, up to 70% of cases of financial misconduct involve anonymous companies. Open Ownership: *Ending anonymous company ownership*, available at: https://openownership.org/.

22   Jonathan Grey and Timothy Glyn Davies, Fighting Phantom Firms in the UK: From Opening Up Datasets to Reshaping Data Infrastructures? (2015), available at: doi:10.2139/ssrn.2610937.

23   Douglas W. Arner et al., FinTech, RegTech, and the Reconceptualization of Financial Regulation 37(3) *Northwestern Journal of International Law and Business* (2017), available at: https://scholarlycommons.law.northwestern.edu/njilb/vol37/iss3/2, at 388.

24   Doug Laney, 3D Management: Controlling Data Volume, Velocity, and Variety, *Gartner* (2001), available at: https://blogs.gartner.com/doug-laney/files/2012/01/.

25   Jonathan Fox, The Uncertain Relationship between Transparency and Accountability, 663 *Development in Practice* (2007), available at: https://doi.org/10.1080/09614520701469955, at 667.

involves 'the dissemination of information that does not reveal how institutions actually behave in practice, whether in terms of how they make decisions, or the results of their actions', while clear transparency 'sheds light on institutional behaviour permit[ting] interested parties to pursue strategies of constructive change'. Despite a tendency to equate more data with more transparency, clear transparency necessitates not *data* per se, but the ability to extract relevant *information* about the entity in question from that data.[26] Even putting aside data quality issues,[27] the sheer volume of potentially available data[28] and a dearth of data literacy[29] among the general population makes actualisation of the average citizen as auditor doubtful.

Second, the push for transparency has resulted in a fragmented web of **15.13** financial regulations, contributing to ever-increasing compliance costs. The rate of new regulation led one analyst to suggest that 'much like Moore's law in the field of computing there is a "Regulatory Law" that means the operational burden of controlling regulations will double every few years'.[30] Third, regulators are under considerable pressure to effectively supervise with limited resources, even as technology is enabling innovative difficult-to-trace methods for abusing power. For now, reliance on whistleblowers persists. Disruptive technology might provide opportunities for these concerns to be addressed.

3. Opportunity

The use of information and communications technology, including artificial **15.14** intelligence, to spot patterns and make predictions from vast amounts of data is far from new. What has changed is the unprecedented availability of data coupled with the exponential growth of computing power, leading to a dramatic increase in the rate of technological progress.[31] The result has been

---

26 Catharina Lindstedt and Daniel Naurin, Transparency is not Enough: Making Transparency Effective in Reducing Corruption, *International Political Science Review* (2010), available at: https://journals. sagepub.com/doi/abs/10.1177/0192512110377602, at 302.

27 Open Knowledge International Blog: *Open Data Quality – the Next Shift in Open Data?* (2017), available at: https://blog.okfn.org/2017/05/31/open-data-quality-the-next-shift-in-open-data/.

28 Of all data existing today 90 per cent was created in the last two years, amounting to 2.5 quintillion bytes of data being created per day. See Domo, Data Never Sleeps 5.0 (2018), available at: https://www.domo.com/learn/data-never-sleeps-5.

29 Annika Woolf et al., Creating an Understanding of Data Literacy for a Data-driven Society, 12 *Journal of Community Informatics* (2016), available at: http://oro.open.ac.uk/47779/, at 10.

30 Tom Groenfeldt, Taming The High Costs Of Compliance With Tech (2018), available at: www.forbes.com/sites/tomgroenfeldt/2018/03/22/taming-the-high-costs-of-compliance-with-tech/#3f7d5285d3f7.

31 Tom Simonite, How can AI keep Accelerating after Moore's Law (2017), available at: https://www.technologyreview.com/s/607917/how-ai-can-keep-accelerating-after-moores-law/.

the delivery of insights from big data necessary to achieve clear transparency, via algorithmic whistleblowing, coupled with the use of automation to eliminate opportunities for corruption.

15.15 There are many technologies contributing to these advancements, perhaps most significantly AI. AI has been taken to include machines that exhibit aspects of human intelligence like problem solving, making predictions, identifying objects and analysing language.[32] Machine learning is one subset of AI. Supervised machine learning algorithms are 'trained' through the processing of labelled samples of training data by a learning algorithm, before the algorithm is presented with unlabelled test data. Typical applications include the prediction of a label (classification) or a continuous value (regression). Unsupervised learning involves tasks like clustering and dimensionality reduction, in order to 'learn the inherent structure of our data without using explicitly-provided labels'.[33]

15.16 Deep learning is an approach to machine learning which departs from the statistics-based methods that ground the solutions previously described. Deep learning algorithms learn via layers of artificial neural networks imitating the biological structure and functions of the brain.[34] Whereas the performance of trained machine learning algorithms will at some point reach a plateau, the ability of deep neural networks to replicate real world systems has no such theoretical ceiling.[35] Most promising is deep learning's superior potential to discover structures within otherwise unstructured, unlabelled data – the format of most data in the world.

15.17 A combination of these innovations, among others, is responsible for the displacement of whistleblowers: an under-appreciated consequence of the emergent RegTech and Suptech fields. Some of the most advanced RegTech solutions are being applied by financial institutions to automate KYC and AML compliance, analysing customer transactions for anomalies and vastly decreasing the number of false positives which are costly to investigate. This often involves using AI-powered data analytics, in particular deep learning, to

---

32 While beyond the scope of this chapter, the definition and meaning of 'artificial intelligence' is fiercely contested. Shane Legg and Marcus Hutter, A Collection of Definitions of Artificial Intelligence, 157 *Frontiers in Artificial Intelligence Appl.* 17 (2007), available at: https://arxiv.org/pdf/0706.3639.pdf.

33 Devin Soni, Supervised vs. Unsupervised Learning, Towards Data Science (2018), available at: science.com/supervised-vs-unsupervised-learning-14f68e32ea8d.

34 Snezana Agatonovic-Kustrin and Roderic Beresford, Basic Concepts of Artificial Neural Network (ANN) Modeling and its Application in Pharmaceutical Research, 22 *J Pharm Biomed Anal* 171 (2000) available at: https://doi.org/10.1016/S0731-7085(99)00272-1, at 718–22.

35 Ian Goodfellow et al., *Deep Learning*, The MIT Press (2016), at 197.

parse structured and previously inert unstructured data to detect patterns and anomalies that would be otherwise indiscernible to a human analyst.[36]

Within companies, RegTech can prevent and detect asset misappropriations, corrupt schemes and financial statement fraud while reducing the number of false positives, which are often costly to investigate.[37] AI is enabling auditors to analyse data and detect connections between e-mails, pdf documents, expense reporting, social media profiles, criminal record checks, work hour reports, registered attempts to access restricted work areas and more.[38] This could reveal behavioural insights so that 'companies can identify individuals who might pose a higher risk to business'.[39] **15.18**

It follows that in some jurisdictions there may be an incentive to adopt RegTech to minimise the risk of corporate criminal convictions for reasons in addition to an increase in transparency deterring the occurrence of misconduct. For instance, section 7 of the UK's Bribery Act 2010 – one of the strictest examples of international anti-bribery legislation – makes the failure of an organisation to prevent bribery an offence. However, it is a defence under section 7(2) for the organisation to 'show that [it] had in place adequate procedures designed to prevent' such conduct. It is not far-fetched to imagine that a company's demonstration of reliance on a RegTech solution to combat bribery could be sufficient to succeed under section 7(2). **15.19**

RegTech's counterpart, SupTech, is revolutionising the work of supervisory agencies. Instead of periodically collecting aggregated data in reporting templates, 'data pull' approaches source data directly from the operating systems of regulated institutions at intervals ranging from 24 hours to 15 minutes.[40] This allows for the real-time monitoring of transactions, minimising reporting errors, and removing the opportunity for financial misstatements – even allowing automatic incorporation of changes in regulatory requirements into the technological reporting protocols. 'Data-input' approaches, on the other hand, involve reporting institutions submitting data that are encoded into a **15.20**

---

36 Institute of International Finance, RegTech in Financial Services: Technology Solutions for Compliance and Reporting (2016), available at: https://www.iif.com/system/files/regtech_in_financial_services_-_solutions_for_compliance_and_reporting.pdf.

37 Institute of International Finance, Deploying Regtech Against Financial Crime (2017), available at: https://www.iif.com/system/files/32370132_aml_final_id.pdf.

38 Ibid.

39 Ibid.

40 The National Bank of Rwanda (BNR) was one of the first financial institutions to implement this. Bank for International Settlements, Innovative Technology in Financial Supervision (Suptech) – the experience of early users (2018), available at: https://www.bis.org/fsi/publ/insights9.htm, at 6.

human- and machine-readable format that use standardised electronic taxonomies, or 'tags', and sending it to a central database in an unaggregated form.
The US Securities and Exchange Commission (the SEC), for example, has
since 2009 required public reporting in XBRL format.[41] This data is then fed
to its corporate issuer risk assessment dashboard, which analyses the reports to
detect traces of fraud.[42] This functionality should be further developed in the
EU following its adoption of the Single Electronic Format in 2020.[43]

15.21 Data consolidation and analysis is another important focus of SupTech
solutions. For example, the Bank of Italy is combining suspicious activity
reports with natural language processing analysis of press reviews to detect
money laundering. The UK's FCA, meanwhile, has trained algorithms to
model normal trading behaviour and automatically report signs of insider
trading.[44] These are revelations which otherwise might only have been
brought to light by a human whistleblower, if at all.

15.22 Although not typically conceptualised in this context, arguably SupTech can
also be used to refer to the use of technology by governments to supervise their
own agencies, and to assist with the supervisory activities of the public and
independent watchdog organisations.[45] One example is ProZorro, the much-
lauded Ukrainian public e-procurement system, which is being enhanced by
AI to identify procurement violations and tenders with a high risk of
corruption. Unlike orthodox risk management systems, the indicators are not
pre-set beforehand and there is no exhaustive list.[46] Meanwhile, in Spain
researchers have developed a 'corruption early warning system', using a neural
network approach to aggregate and analyse data – including real estate
taxation, unemployment rate and number of years in government – to predict
public sector corruption, helping those combating corruption focus their
limited resources.[47] These researchers suggest that their algorithms, once

---

41 Business Reporting Language, or XBRL, is the international data standard for international business
reporting: Marc. D Joffe, Open Data for Financial Reporting, *Data Foundation* (2017), available at:
https://www.datafoundation.org/xbrl-report-2017/.

42 Institute of International Finance, *supra* note 37.

43 European Securities and Markets Authority, European Single Electronic Format (2018), available at:
https://www.esma.europa.eu/policy-activities/corporate-disclosure/european-single-electronic-format.

44 Bank for International Settlements, *supra* note 40.

45 Global Witness, Three Ways the UK's Register of the Real Owners of Companies Is Already Proving Its
Worth (2018), available at: https://www.globalwitness.org/en/blog/three-ways-uks-register-real-owners-
companies-already-proving-its-worth/.

46 Transparency International Ukraine, Dozorro Artificial Intelligence to Find Violations in ProZorro: How
it Works (2018), available at: https://ti-ukraine.org/en/news/dozorro-artificial-intelligence-to-find-
violations-in-prozorro-how-it-works/.

47 Félix J. López-Iturriaga and Iván Pastor Sanz, Predicting Public Corruption with Neural Networks: An
Analysis of Spanish Provinces, 140 *Social Indicators Research* 975 (2018), available at: https://doi.org/
10.1007/s11205-017-1802-2.

trained on more complex and diverse data sets, could uncover deeply hidden indicators of various legal and economic issues across the EU, including money laundering.

4. Obstacles

Various obstacles to RegTech and SupTech adoption remind that tech- **15.23** nological solutions are no panacea for eliminating the challenges faced by whistleblowers. These include regulatory and legislative barriers to knowledge sharing (such as data protection and localisation laws), legacy IT systems, the lack of integrated data taxonomies and the limited room for financial institutions to innovate while maintaining compliance.[48] There are also at least three potential ethical challenges arising from the proliferation of technology in the present context that merit further examination.

a. Privacy

The first obstacle is the balance between transparency and privacy. As Fox **15.24** quips: 'One person's transparency is another's surveillance.'[49] A survey conducted by Ernst & Young revealed a 'tension between opinions about what channels companies should monitor and the types of surveillance that their employees consider a violation of privacy'.[50] The GDPR, as the global legal standard for data protection and privacy, imposes various duties on data controllers and data processors, including obligations to declare a lawful basis for data collection and processing, and limitations on the export of personal data outside the EU. Special attention to these provisions should be paid by organisations that are effectively outsourcing their RegTech and SupTech compliance solutions to third parties.

b. Bias

The second obstacle concerns the risks of error, bias and the threat of **15.25** algorithmic discrimination.[51] Machine learning algorithms will learn from and perpetuate distortions in training data. Moreover, inherently algorithms are optimised to achieve particular goals, which can lead to biased decision

---

48 Institute of International Finance, *supra* note 37.

49 Fox, *supra* note 25; and Privacy International, Fintech: Privacy and Identity in the New Data-Intensive Financial Sector (2017), available at: https://privacyinternational.org/sites/default/files/2017-12/Fintech %20report.pdf.

50 For example, around 65 per cent of respondents felt that e-mail and phone-call monitoring was a violation of privacy. See *EY Reporting*, What should be Monitored? (2017) available at: https://www.ey.com/ Publication/vwLUAssets/ at 9.

51 Solon Barocas and Andrew Selbst, Big Data's Disparate Impact, 104 *California Law Review* 671 (2016), available at: http://www.californialawreview.org/wp-content/uploads/2016/06/2Barocas-Selbst.pdf.

making. RegTech and SupTech are not immune. For example, fraud detection algorithms have been shown to be biased against certain ethnic minorities, immigrants and even against men.[52] While extensive technical research is being done on identifying and correcting bias in algorithms, others are advocating algorithmic impact assessments and even making a business out of algorithmic auditing.[53] ORCAA, one such consultancy, assesses the quality of training data, testing the algorithms' design, implementation, execution and ethical consequences, and offers training in algorithmic auditing. The resultant seal is 'like an organic sticker for algorithms', on the basis that 'the food we eat has quality certifications. Why shouldn't the algorithms that shape our world?'[54] In the meantime, the question arises: how much less biased than a human does an algorithm have to be before we are willing to let it loose on the work of whistleblowers?

c. Black box

15.26 Finally, the third obstacle is that machine learning algorithms tend to be 'opaque in the sense that … rarely does one have any concrete sense of how or why a particular classification has been arrived at from inputs'.[55] This is known as the explainability or black box problem, and it is particularly acute in deep learning. Some argue that even the technologically-increased accuracy of decisions does not compensate for the inability to explain the weighting of decision-making factors and essentially fails to respect a subject's dignity,[56] offending one's 'right to an explanation',[57] and raising Kafkaeque concerns for fair trial standards.[58] There are a growing number of researchers, business leaders and policy makers who are developing both technical solutions to explainable AI (XAI) and corporate civil regulation for the development of ethical AI.[59] On the other hand, some counter that to the degree that AI

---

52 Adeesh Goel, Algorithmic Bias: Challenges and Solutions (2017), available at: https://mse238blog.stanford.edu/2017/08/adeesh/algorithmic-bias-challenges-and-solutions/.

53 FAT/ML: Principles for Accountable Algorithms and a Social Impact Statement for Algorithms, available at: http://www.fatml.org/resources/principles-for-accountable-algorithms.

54 Katharine Schwabe: This logo is like an organic sticker for algorithms (2018), available at: https://www.fastcompany.com/90172734/this-logo-is-like-an-organic-sticker-for-algorithms-that-arent-evil.

55 Jenna Burrell, How the Machine 'Thinks': Understanding Opacity in Machine Learning Algorithms, *Big Data and Society* (2016), available at: https://journals.sagepub.com/doi/pdf/10.1177/2053951715622512, at 1.

56 Jeremy Waldron, How Law Protects Dignity, 71 *Cambridge Law Journal* 200 (2012), at 210.

57 Reuben Binns, Max Van Kleek, et al., 'It's Reducing a Human Being to a Percentage'; Perceptions of Justice in Algorithmic Decisions (2018), available at: https://doi.org/10.1145/3173574.3173951.

58 Council of Europe, Algorithms and Human Rights (2017), available at: http://rm.coe.int/algorithms-and-human-rights-en-rev/16807956b5.

59 See the 2017 Asilomar principles, which has 1,273 AI/Robotics researchers as signatories. The Future of Life Institute, The Asilomar AI Principles (2017), available at: https://futureoflife.org/ai-principles/?submitted=1&cn-reloaded=1#confirmation.

becomes 'explainable', bad actors may be able to adjust their behaviour to 'game' the system.[60] As it stands, the paradox is that the increase in transparency in the sense of information disclosure is dependent on an opaque mechanism. Minimising harm to whistleblowers requires a trade-off with the potential of harm to the subjects of inexplicable algorithmic outputs.

In the age of information, reliance on disruptive technology is essential to achieving clear transparency and accountability. RegTech and SupTech promise to minimise compliance costs and revolutionise supervision and detect and report misconduct more effectively and efficiently than human whistleblowers. Moreover, algorithms cannot be personally victimised or directly retaliated against. Algorithmic whistleblowing is therefore a positive development insofar as it reduces reliance on whistleblowers who often endure significant personal and professional costs, despite the public interest in their reporting. However, the technology that is enabling these changes also poses new ethical dilemmas, involving the balancing of privacy against transparency and accuracy against dignity. Despite the inherent difficulties, eventual adoption of RegTech and SupTech is likely inevitable, which means that whistleblowing may be just the latest human endeavour to be taken over by machines. **15.27**

C. TECHNOLOGY EMPOWERING THE WHISTLEBLOWER

The barriers to blowing the whistle are widely known and have been extensively analysed, the foremost being the fear of retaliation.[61] The difficulty of ensuring confidentiality and, in some cases, the anonymity of the whistleblower therefore looms large. A related problem is the utilisation of trusted channels of reporting, which must be secure and effective. Technological applications, designed to facilitate the whistleblowing process, offer potential solutions. This section will examine four technologies that empower the whistleblower: hotline services, web portals, mobile apps and blockchain. **15.28**

1. Hotline services

The most widely used technical application are hotline services. These may be internal or external (run by a service provider) and are operated by 'live' call centre staff or an automated voice. Their main advantages are that they offer **15.29**

---

60 Paul B. de Laat, Algorithmic Decision-making Based On Machine Learning from Big Data: Can Transparency Restore Accountability? *P.B. Philos. Technol.* 17 (2017), available at: https://link.springer.com/content/pdf/10.1007%2Fs13347-017-0293-z.pdf.

61 International Bar Association, *supra* note 3.

anonymity, increased accessibility and consequently generate more trust. Downsides include the impossibility of sharing documents and establishing further communication with the investigator unless the whistleblower decides to call again. The capture of all pertinent information may depend on the skills of the operator, and hotlines can become expensive when operated across different languages and time zones.[62]

2. Web portals

15.30 A potentially more effective technology, which increasingly replaces hotlines and direct reporting, are web portals. They give the whistleblower the benefit of remaining anonymous by creating an account with a random username, through which the whistleblower can submit a report from anywhere in the world in a variety of languages, attach any type of document, communicate with an investigative authority and track the progress of the disclosure.[63] Additionally, an automated whistleblowing system allows companies to compile statistical data to analyse problematic areas using technologies described in Section B above.

15.31 Web portals can be established within an organisation or outsourced to a third-party company. A notable example of the latter is Business Keeper AG. It provides a certified secure and private external whistleblowing portal for companies in 197 countries, including administrative bodies such as the Austrian Central Department of public prosecution of economic crimes and corruption and the German Federal Financial Supervisory Authority.[64]

15.32 The perceived effectiveness of web portals has prompted the emergence of companies offering open-source whistleblowing software, providing any organisation with tools to create their own whistleblowing web portal. One example is GlobaLeaks,[65] an Italian-based software that allows any organisation to set up their own website, guaranteeing the security level necessary for a whistleblowing platform. In February 2018, the Italian Anti-Corruption Authority launched its national online whistleblowing platform based on the

---

62 John Wilson, Whistleblowing: What are the Most Effective Speak-up Channels? (2017), available at: http://in-houseblog.practicallaw.com/whistleblowing-what-are-the-most-effective-speak-up-channels/.

63 Mostafa Hussien and Toshiyuki Yamanaka, Whistleblowing at Work. Can ICT Encourage Whistle-blowing?, 27 *Joho Chishiki Gakkaishi* 150 (2017), available at: https://www.jstage.jst.go.jp/article/jsik/27/2/27_2017_017/_article/-char/en at 151.

64 Business Keeper AG, available at: https://www.business-keeper.com/en/whistleblowing-system/references.html.

65 GlobaLeaks, available at: https://www.globaleaks.org/.

GlobaLeaks software.[66] Building on this success, the GlobaLeaks founders established a Digital Whistleblowing Fund, which offers operational, strategic and financial support for journalists and human rights organisations in 'starting a secure digital whistleblowing initiative'.[67]

Another platform that enables the whistleblowing process is SecureDrop, 'an **15.33** open source submission system that organisations can install to securely accept documents from anonymous sources'.[68] Employing the Tor network, it acts as an intermediary between whistleblowers and journalists by allowing the former to download documents to a server and contact journalists using SecureDrop messages.[69] Since its launch in 2013, prominent news organisations such as *The New York Times* and *The Guardian* have used SecureDrop to solicit information.

Wikileaks is another web portal, infamous for its major role in publishing **15.34** millions of leaked documents, including the Iraq War Logs and Hillary Clinton's emails. Wikileaks has garnered significant controversy and the division between public interest whistleblowing and politically-motivated leaking is contested – an increasingly blurred distinction considered further below.

Such web portals have been required to adopt certain technological measures **15.35** to guarantee the security and anonymity necessary for whistleblowing. The majority employ Tor, a 'group of volunteer-operated servers' that constitute a distributed anonymous network. Servers of this network are connected via virtual tunnels, concealing the path of a user's traffic, ensuring privacy and preventing tracking. Whistleblowing portals reliant on Tor adopt its 'onion service' in order to publish a website without revealing its location. This service operates by using random 'rendezvous-points' where a client can go to access the website, using a public key and an onion address, without revealing their identity.[70] Another system often employed to ensure anonymity is The Amnesic Incognito Live System (TAILS), operated through USB or DVD to access the Internet without leaving a footprint on the host computer.[71]

---

66   Lucian Armasu, Italian Anti-Corruption Authority Embraces Tor For Whistleblower Protection (2018), available at: https://www.tomshardware.com/news/italian-anac-tor-whistleblower-platform,36515.html.
67   Digital Whistleblowing Fund, available at: https://www.whistleblowingfund.org/.
68   SecureDrop, available at: https://securedrop.org/.
69   Amy Davidson Sorkin, Introducing StrongBox (2013), available at: https://www.newyorker.com/news/amy-davidson/introducing-strongbox.
70   Tor Project, Tor: Onion Service Protocol, available at: https://www.torproject.org/docs/onion-services.
71   Tails, Privacy for Anyone Anywhere, available at: https://tails.boum.org/.

3. Mobile apps

15.36 A relatively recent promising development is the emergence of whistleblowing mobile apps. These channels combine the advantages of web portals with an accessibility of mobile phones, creating a universal platform that can be employed almost anywhere. The use of mobile apps has been especially prominent in countries with less developed technological infrastructure.

15.37 One example is Wahala Dey, a whistleblowing app launched in 2017 by Nigeria's Independent Corrupt Practices and Other Related Offences Commission (ICPC). This app is intended to track corruption practices across government agencies and in the private sector. It is possible to file an anonymous complaint, attaching pictures and videos, as well as send petitions directly to ICPC. Similar apps, intended to provide a secure and private outlet for blowing the whistle, were launched in May 2018 in Abu Dhabi ('Inform the Prosecution')[72] and in India, exclusively for members of political party Makkal Needhi Maiam in order to flag issues caused by party members ('Maiam Whistle').[73] An app of a more general nature is SpeakingUp,[74] which allows for the submission of an encrypted report from anywhere in the world in English, French or German.

4. Blockchain

15.38 Perhaps the most promising technological development for whistleblowers – albeit the least actualised – is blockchain, which when applied to whistleblowing can offer several important advantages.

a. Anonymity

15.39 Given the ease of tracking the identity of whistleblowers when communicating online,[75] blockchain is a potential solution which can strike the balance between the need for anonymity and the importance of an investigative authority being able to contact the whistleblower for further details. A project called WhistleAI is currently working towards realising this potential by combining the benefits of blockchain, crowdsourcing and AI. To ensure

---

72 Wam, *Abu Dhabi Launches New Whistleblower App* (2018), available at: https://www.khaleejtimes.com/nation/abu-dhabi-launches-new-whistleblower-app.

73 Dharani Thangavelu, *Kamal Haasan Launches Party App to Focus on Key Issues* (2018), available at: https://www.livemint.com/Politics/.

74 Expolink's SpeakingUp mobile app, available at: https://www.expolink.co.uk/whistleblowing-hotline/mobile-app-2/.

75 Owen Bowcott, *Whistleblowers Endangered in Digital Age, Says Lawyers' Report* (2017), available at: https://www.theguardian.com/media/2017/feb/22/.

anonymity their platform relies on zero-knowledge protocols, which entails splitting information into fragmented pieces before sending it to the nodes for verification. This ascertains the protection of whistleblower identity while allowing the members of the network to verify the correspondence of the whistleblower's allegation with the information provided in their report.[76]

b. Immutability

The second advantage of blockchain is its immutability. Data, once uploaded **15.40** on a blockchain-based platform, cannot be deleted or tampered with as it is aggregated into interconnected blocks. This prevents employers or organisations implicated by the disclosure from concealing the whistleblowing report. An additional function of this platform may be public time stamping, which allows whistleblowers to aggregate data for a period of time, before deciding whether to publish the materials or not.[77] Time stamping and immutability of data would mean information could be used in future court proceedings without concern for the veracity of evidence.[78]

c. Resilience

Relying on blockchain for whistleblowing would drastically increase the **15.41** resilience of the whistleblowing platform. Unlike website-based platforms, blockchain would not be susceptible to DDOS attacks or disruption of a domain name and there would be no need to change the hosting servers.[79]

d. Compensation

A unique and arguably controversial feature of blockchain is its ability to offer **15.42** compensation to the whistleblower through smart contracts. This mechanism would not only offer the whistleblower confidence of their identity's security through blockchain, but also provide them with adequate compensation through the use of cryptocurrency, which could be automatically transferred to their account once the 'leaked' data is verified and the appropriate conditions for reward are satisfied. This idea has been implemented in the Crypto Community Watch project (explored further below)[80] and in WhistleAI,

---

76 WhistleAI, available at: https://www.whistleai.io/WhistleAI.pdf.
77 Shafi Goldwasser and Sunoo Park, Public Accountability vs. Secret Laws: Can They Coexist? A Cryptographic Proposal (2017), available at: https://eprint.iacr.org/2018/664.pdf, at 4.
78 Wolfie Zhao, Chinese Supreme Court Admitted Blockchain Evidence as Legally Binding (2018), available at: https://www.coindesk.com/chinas-supreme-court-recognizes-blockchain-evidence-as-legally-binding/.
79 Yochai Benkler, A Free Irresponsible Press: Wikileaks and the Battle Over the Soul of the Networked Fourth Estate, 46 Harv. C.R.-C.L. L. Rev. 311 (2011), available at: http://benkler.org/Benkler_Wikileaks_current.pdf, at 3.
80 Jonathan Kim, Industry Consortium Launches Crypto Community Watch Program (2018), available at: https://cryptoslate.com/industry-consortium-launches-crypto-community-watch-program/.

where a privacy coin named WISL is used both for compensating whistle-blowers and for incentivising crowdsourcing participants that allow the platform to continue operating.[81]

e. Escrow

15.43 Another possible advantage of blockchain is its application as an information escrow. This can be done through a smart contract, programmed to release information only if certain conditions are satisfied. For example, Callisto, initially designed to combat sexual harassment on college campuses, forwards the reported misconduct only when there are at least two complaints about the same perpetrator.[82] Such technology, combined with the other benefits of blockchain, would help eliminate the 'first-mover disadvantage' and lessen the likelihood of retribution.[83]

f. Concerns

15.44 There are, of course, potential disadvantages to blockchain's adoption in the present context. First, employing a distributed network means that all users of a blockchain could have the sensitive data on their nodes (computers), potentially exposing them to liability in some jurisdictions.[84] One way in which this risk may be mitigated is through the use of Enigma secret contracts.[85] These smart contracts use 'secure computation' technologies to compute over the encrypted data, thus concealing sensitive information contained in the report from the other members of the network, but retaining their ability to validate the transactions.[86] Secret contracts, thereby, offer privacy to the whistleblowers, hiding their identity and mitigating the risk of retaliation. A second potential drawback of blockchain is that there has to be an established mechanism of incentives to continue mining and, consequently, verifying the information. Employing cryptocurrencies for this purpose might be one of the solutions, for example, as demonstrated by the WhistleAI project.

---

81 WhistleAI, *supra* note 76.

82 Callisto project, available at: https://www.projectcallisto.org/.

83 Ian Ayres and Cait Unkovic, Information Escrows, 111 *Michigan Law Review* 145 (2012), available at: https://repository.law.umich.edu/mlr/vol111/iss2/1, at 3; and Carsten Tams, Can 'Allegation Escrows' Remedy the Underreporting of Sexual Harassment? (2017), available at: http://www.fcpablog.com/blog/2017/11/20/carsten-tams-can-allegation-escrows-remedy-the-underreportin.html.

84 Roman Matzutt et al., A Quantitative Analysis of the Impact of Arbitrary Blockchain Content on Bitcoin, (2018), available at: https://www.martinhenze.de/wp-content/papercite-data/pdf/mhh+18.pdf, at 7.

85 Enigma Protoco, Overview, available at: https://enigma.co/protocol/.

86 Guy Zyskind, Defining Secret Contracts (2018), available at: https://blog.enigma.co/defining-secret-contracts-f40ddee67ef2.

g. Application

Today there are very few existing blockchain-based whistleblowing platforms. **15.45**
One example is Crypto Community Watch, created in August 2018 by several
major Initial Coin Offering platforms for reporting wrongdoing in the
cryptocurrency industry.[87] The creators of Crypto Community Watch also
created a reward pool of 100 Bitcoins that will be paid out to whistleblowers
whose reports of fraudulent activity lead to an arrest or other punishment of a
wrongdoer.[88] At the time of this writing, over 200 reports have been lodged,
but no information is available on the outcomes of subsequent investigations.[89]

Another broadly analogous platform, Darkleaks, is essentially a black market **15.46**
for information (such as trade secrets and source codes). The leaked document
is presented in the form of several segments, each one hashed with different
Bitcoin addresses.[90] While Darkleaks might not represent a whistleblowing
platform in a traditional sense, it demonstrates the technological possibilities
offered by blockchain in this context.

The growing use of technology to empower whistleblowers coincides with **15.47**
heightened appreciation of the role of whistleblowers in society. These are
welcome developments, albeit they need to be coupled with mechanisms to
ensure that new technologies actually protect whistleblowers. Emergent technology, particularly blockchain, promises not only to facilitate whistleblowing
but also to secure the veracity of information passed on, empowering whistleblowers to a potentially unprecedented degree.

D. TECHNOLOGY CHANGING THE WHISTLEBLOWER

Some 50 years ago, Daniel Ellsberg spent 18 months meticulously copying **15.48**
page after page of incriminating materials to reveal the Pentagon Papers.[91] It
took only one memory card and several clicks for Edward Snowden to expose
gigabytes of data to the masses.[92] Indeed, the most notorious of recent

---

87 Ecoinmerce, Join the Crypto Community Watch! (2018), available at: https://www.ecoinmerce.io/crypto-community-watch.
88 Zane Huffman, Rewarding Whistleblowers with Crypto Community Watch (2018), available at: https://nulltx.com/rewarding-whistleblowers-with-crypto-community-watch/.
89 Crypto Community Watch Responses, available at: https://docs.google.com/spreadsheets/.
90 Mellisa Tolentino, Darkleaks, a Haven for Whistleblowers and Pirates (2015), available at: https://siliconangle.com/2015/02/04/darkleaks-a-haven-for-whistleblowers-and-pirates/.
91 Daniel Ellsberg, *Secrets: A Memoir of Vietnam and the Pentagon Papers* (2003), at 301.
92 Richard J. Aldrich and Christopher R. Moran, 'Delayed Disclosure': National Security, Whistle-Blowers and the Nature of Secrecy, *Political Studies* (2018), available at: https://journals.sagepub.com/doi/abs/10.1177/0032321718764990 at 7.

whistleblowing incidents have taken the form of massive dumps of information to web-sources: Snowden's 2013 disclosure was 60GB in size; Antoine Deltour's 2014 Luxleaks were 4GB; while the 2016 Panama Papers included 2.6TB of information.[93] Moreover, all of them contained massive collections of documents containing a multitude of revelations of which the whistleblowers themselves may have been unaware.

15.49 By radically affecting the sheer amount of information that can be disclosed and the means by which to do so, technology is altering the nature of contemporary whistleblowing by blurring the lines between 'whistleblowers', 'hackers' and 'leakers'. The implications of these developments must be confronted if whistleblower protections worldwide are to be fit for the future.

15.50 Whistleblowing, leaking and hacking do not, in public discourse or as a matter of law, have universally accepted definitions, and often these concepts are conflated. However, 'whistleblowing' has been largely defined as disclosing information about a wrongdoing,[94] while 'leaking' is usually understood as revealing confidential information without official authorisation.[95] As whistleblowing takes the form of increasingly large leaks, these concepts are eliding, Savage suggests that 'unauthorised disclosures made to the public are likely to be considered whistleblowing where there is public interest value in the information disclosed'.[96]

15.51 The third dimension complicating this emergent dynamic is the rise of hackers fulfilling a whistleblower-like function. This is illustrated by the 'rise of cybersecurity whistleblowers',[97] who have been thrust into the limelight following incidents such as the WannaCry ransomware attack, the Equifax breach and the Cambridge Analytica Facebook data breach.[98] Cybersecurity whistleblowers can include a range of actors from non-technical company

---

93 Suelette Dreyfus, Chelsea Manning and the Rise of 'big data' Whistleblowing in the Digital Age (2018), available at: https://theconversation.com/chelsea-manning-and-the-rise-of-big-data-whistleblowing-in-the-digital-age-102479.

94 OECD, Committing to Effective Whistleblower Protection (2016), available at: https://www.oecd.org/daf/anti-bribery/Committing-to-Effective-Whistleblower-Protection-Highlights.pdf, at 18.

95 Ashley Savage, Whistleblowers for Change: The Social and Economic Costs and Benefits of Leaking and Whistleblowing (2018), available at: https://www.opensocietyfoundations.org/sites/default/files/20181120-whistleblowers-for-change-report.pdf, at 7.

96 Ibid.

97 Dallas Hammer and Evan Bundschuh, The Rise of Cybersecurity Whistleblowing (2016), available at: https://wp.nyu.edu/compliance_enforcement/2016/12/29/the-rise-of-cybersecurity-whistleblowing/.

98 Cybersecurity incidents reportedly increased by 47 per cent over the last year. Obtaining information was the objective of attacks in about 40 per cent of cases. Positive Technologies, Compliance Management and Threat Analysis Solutions, available at: https://www.ptsecurity.com/ww-en/analytics/cybersecurity-threatscape-2018-q2/.

employees made aware of security flaws or unreported data breaches, to 'ethical' or 'white-hat' hackers, cybersecurity professionals that use the same techniques as the more notorious 'black-hat' malicious actors to test systems for vulnerabilities.[99] Many companies increasingly rely on white-hat hackers, as evidenced not only by the demand for employees and contractors, but also the burgeoning freelance bounty 'bug-hunter' market.[100] However, there is another category of people which many would also consider to be white-hat hackers: public-spirited security researchers that conduct unsolicited hacks to disclose the vulnerabilities of the system to the public ('full disclosure') or to the company ('coordinated/responsible disclosure'), without exploiting those flaws.[101]

Difficulties arise when, in light of cybersecurity revelations, a company **15.52** responds by suppressing the information to save the remedial expense or conceal a past incident. In these situations, those who make vulnerability disclosures risk reprisals in the form of intimidation, job termination and criminal or civil suits.[102] Outdated laws in this area, such as the US's Computer Fraud and Abuse Act 1984 and the UK's Computer Misuse Act 1990, mean that ethical hackers may be prosecuted relatively easily. Security researchers have reported a chilling effect on their work, admitting that 'facing legal action is just one of those things where it's just not worth it anymore'.[103] This should concern us all. Cybersecurity whistleblowers are an essential aspect of compliance reporting, risk minimisation, and defence of the technological infrastructure that underpins virtually every aspect of modern society.[104] The consequences of the convergence of whistleblowing, leaking and hacking can be broadly divided into three groups: political, ethical and legal implications.

---

99 Jennifer M. Pacella, The Cybersecurity Threat: Compliance and the Role of Whistleblowers, 11 *Brook. J. Corp. Fin. & Com L.* (2016), available at: https://brooklynworks.brooklaw.edu/bjcfcl/vol11/iss1/3/ at 50.

100 Martin Giles, Crowdsourcing the Hunt for Software Bugs is a Booming Business—and a Risky One (2018), available at: https://www.technologyreview.com/s/611892/crowdsourcing-the-hunt-for-software-bugs-is-a-booming-businessand-a-risky-one/.

101 National Cyber Security Centre, Coordinated Vulnerability Disclosure: The Guideline (2018), available at: https://www.ncsc.nl/english/current-topics/responsible-disclosure-guideline.html.

102 Ibid.

103 Zach Whittaker, Lawsuits Threaten Infosec Research—Just When we Need it Most (2018), available at: https://www.zdnet.com/article/chilling-effect-lawsuits-threaten-security-research-need-it-most/.

104 Madrea Matwyshyn, Hacking Speech: Informational Speech and the First Amendment, 107 *North Werstern U. L. Rev.* 795 (2013), available at: https://scholarlycommons.law.northwestern.edu/nulr/vol107/iss2/10/.

1. Political implications

15.53 Whistleblowing, leaking and hacking carry different connotations. In particular, whistleblowing, though controversial, is widely recognised as having positive attributes as a valuable compliance and accountability tool. Leaking and hacking, on the other hand, arguably carry negative, criminal connotations.[105] The conflation of these three phenomena gives rise to the risk of strategically-framed policy decisions to justify undermining whistleblower protections. For instance, while campaigning, Obama expressed support for whistleblowers as one of 'the best source(s) of information about ... abuse in government'. However, his administration proceeded to engage in an unprecedented 'hunt for leakers', and eight individuals were prosecuted under the Espionage Act 1917, more than all previous governments combined.[106] In Australia, meanwhile, the federal government imposed severe potential criminal liability for public servant 'leakers', before implementing whistleblower protection reform. One employment lawyer noted: 'Cracking down on unauthorised disclosure before a robust and effective program for authorised disclosure of official information is illogical at best, and shows a barely disguised contempt for whistleblowers at worst.'[107] These are but two manifestations of a wider issue – the increased politicisation of the distinction between leakers, whistleblowers and hackers in the digital age. This strategy is becoming more prevalent as big data leaks, and the hacks that may enable them, have the potential to do more damage than ever before. As Shkbatur writes, 'the war against leaks can therefore be understood as a response against the new whistleblowing reality created by the Internet'.[108]

2. Ethical implications

15.54 The debate surrounding the justifiability and desirability of whistleblowing, in particular regarding the balance between collateral damage to individuals and the public's right to know, is not new. However, the nexus between leaking,

---

105 Will Ma et al., Whistleblower or Leaker? Examining the Portrayal and Characterization of Edward Snowden in USA, UK, and HK Posts, in Ma et al. (eds) *New Media, Knowledge Practices and Multiliteracies* (2014), available at: https://www.researchgate.net/publication/265121066_Whistleblower_or_Leaker_Examining_the_Portrayal_and_Characterization_of_Edward_Snowden_in_USA_UK_and_HK_Posts.

106 Mary-Rose Papandrea, Leaker Traitor Whistleblower Spy: National Security Leaks and the First Amendment, 94 *B.U. L. Rev* 449 (2014), available at: https://www.bu.edu/bulawreview/files/2014/05/PAPANDREA.pdf, at 451.

107 John Wilson, Whistleblowing isn't Dobbing. It Supports our Democracy (2018), available at: https://www.smh.com.au/public-service/whistleblowing-isnt-dobbing-it-supports-our-democracy-20180203-h0t6cv.html.

108 Shkabatur, *supra* note 9 at 116.

hacking and whistleblowing exacerbates these issues. As new-age whistle-blowers take the form of custodians of huge amounts of data, they arguably have even greater ethical burdens to discharge.

The lack of responsible practices for publishing data leaks has already had **15.55** consequences. For example, in 2016 Wikileaks revealed 300,000 e-mails dubbed the 'Erdogan e-mails'. While subsequent investigation of these e-mails did not yield significant evidence of wrongdoing, sensitive personal information, including current phone numbers, citizenship IDs, addresses and political party affiliations of millions of women, was released.[109] Such data dumps have also revealed the personal information of rape victims and even the identities of several gay men in Saudi Arabia, where homosexuality is illegal.[110]

These dilemmas demand a balancing test, and – perhaps more than ever **15.56** before – there are no easy answers. On the one hand, excessive whistleblower self-censorship is undesirable, in particular from a transparency perspective. On the other hand, there is a need to minimise harm to those who, in the absence of basic responsible data practices, may be unnecessarily compromised as a side-effect of holding the powerful to account.[111]

3. Legal implications

Finally, changes in the nature and methods of whistleblowing are bound to **15.57** affect the drafting of new whistleblower protection laws that are being adopted across the world, as well as the assessment of the extent to which existing whistleblowing laws are fit for purpose. While there are many legal issues that might arise, only a few relating to some of the key elements of whistleblower protection schemes will be highlighted below.

First, as a result of these changes, the whistleblower, the regulator, any **15.58** whistleblowing service provider, and the entity accused of misconduct will commonly be based in different jurisdictions. This puts pressure on jurisdictional inconsistencies between the kinds of disclosure which will attract the

---

109 Zeynep Tufekci, WikiLeaks Put Women in Turkey in Danger, for No Reason, *The Huffington Post* (2017), available at: https://www.huffingtonpost.com/zeynep-tufekci/wikileaks-erdogan-emails_b_11158792.html.

110 Nicky Woolf, WikiLeaks Posted Medical Files of Rape Victims and Children, Investigation Finds (2016), available at: https://www.theguardian.com/media/2016/aug/23/wikileaks-posts-sensitive-medical-information-saudi-arabia.

111 Alix Dunn, Responsible Data Leaks and Whistleblowing (2016), available at: https://www.theengineroom.org/responsible-data-leaks-and-whistleblowing/?fbclid=IwAR0_8kIpLnGmSaCRZHChpbiegf0dWKd1XqXNdm7gSGGKdrIak1Vjc4sNUk.

protection of whistleblower legislation. There is a range of sources of law where whistleblower protections may be found, including bespoke legislation, sectoral laws and laws specifically aimed at the public service. This can result in legal loopholes which may deter potential cybersecurity whistleblowers who are unsure whether they would be protected. Other laws take a more expansive approach, capturing for instance disclosures in the 'public interest' or those which disclose 'abuse of laws'.[112]

15.59　For example, there is no federal statute that directly addresses cybersecurity whistleblowing in the US, rather, protection must be read down from various existing federal or state laws, and depends on the facts of each case.[113] Protection will depend on the facts of each case, but the law is unclear. The SEC has been taking a proactive approach to whistleblowing, and cybersecurity whistleblowing in particular. In 2011, the SEC's Division of Corporate Finance called for the disclosure of cybersecurity incidences materially relevant to a company's operations as a part of regular reporting requirements under the federal securities regulation.[114] In 2018, the SEC reiterated this call and offered further interpretive guidance.[115] However, this is not legally binding, giving rise to a 'grey area' with respect to whether cybersecurity whistleblowers can take advantage of the robust protection under the SEC's whistleblower protection programmes and the Dodd-Frank Act.[116] Meanwhile, potential cybersecurity whistleblowers who work on entities not regulated by these federal statutes are left to fend off potential criminal liability for their actions.[117] By contrast, article 1 of the draft European Union Directive on Whistleblowing 'lays down common minimum standards for the protection of persons reporting (on) unlawful activities or abuse of law' and specifically includes 'protection of privacy and personal data, and security of network and information systems'. While the inclusion of cybersecurity whistleblowers is a positive development, there remains a lack of legal clarity over intersection with criminal laws directed at not dissimilar conduct.[118]

112　OECD, G20: Study of Whistleblower Protection Frameworks, Compendium of Best Practices and Guiding Principles for Legislation (2012), available at: https://star.worldbank.org/document/study-whistleblower-protection-frameworks-compendium-best-practices-and-guiding-principles, at 6.

113　Alexis Ronicker, Cybersecurity Whistleblower Protections (2017) available at: https://www.kmblegal.com/sites/default/files/cybersecurity-whistleblower-protection-guide.pdf.

114　Pacella, *supra* note 99.

115　Securities and Exchange Commission, Statement and Guidance on Public Company Cybersecurity Disclosures (2018) available at: https://www.sec.gov/rules/interp/2018/33-10459.pdf.

116　Pacella, *supra* note 99.

117　Ronickher, *supra* note 113.

118　Centre for European Policy Studies, Software Vulnerability Disclosure in Europe: Technology, Policies and Legal Challenges (2018), available at: https://www.ceps.eu/publications/software-vulnerability-disclosure-europe-technology-policies-and-legal-challenges at 42.

Some question whether even broader whistleblower laws should capture the **15.60** reporting of ethical or immoral conduct, especially where 'these tread the fine line between illegality and morality'.[119] On the one hand, it is argued that extending protections to the disclosure of ethical or moral concerns may introduce too much subjectivity and uncertainty as to the scope of protections.[120] However, as Savage points out, 'if the definition is restricted to the law, and the law is restrictive in scope, this may deter individuals from raising concerns and provide justifications to not protect those that do'.[121] Arguably the restrictiveness of laws may become increasingly problematic for potential whistleblowers as technology rapidly advances, widening the gap between ethically problematic practices and illegality as the law struggles to keep up.

This gap, and the question of whether disclosures of 'immoral' conduct should **15.61** entitle whistleblowers to protection may, for instance, be directly relevant to the joint initiative launched by a whistleblower non-profit 'the Signals Network' in collaboration with international media groups. With a combined audience of 46 million people, this consortium is encouraging whistleblowers who believe that corporations are 'misusing' big data to come forward.[122] Consider the GDPR, which took six years to come into force – although it has been hailed as setting the global standard, some argue that its primary focus on individual privacy rights and the protection of personally identifiable data is already outdated. This on the basis that it fails to 'account for the actual technological landscape unfolding before us', where the scale of big data analysis is such that many of the most powerful applications and risks of harm are directed not at individuals, but at groups.[123] Imagine a data scientist at a start-up who, encouraged by the Signals Network Initiative, came forward disclosing that his/her company was engaged in what he viewed as the use of big data in a way which posed harm to a group.[124] Given the relative underdevelopment of law relating to group privacy harm, it is unlikely to be clear whether the practice disclosed is *unlawful* or 'merely' immoral, and therefore whether whistleblower protections apply. As the law struggles to keep up with technological development and the ethical issues it raises, there will be increased pressure on developing whistleblowing legislation to adopt an

---

119   Savage, *supra* note 95, at 16.
120   International Bar Association, *supra* note 3.
121   Savage, *supra* note 95, at 17.
122   The Signals Network, Global Investigation on the Misuse of Big Data (2018) available at: https://thesignals network.org/press-release/.
123   Linnet Taylor et al., Group Privacy: New Challenges of Data Technologies, available at: https://linnet taylor.files.wordpress.com/2017/01/groupprivacy.pdf at 3.
124   See, e.g., Christopher Wylie, Why I Broke the Facebook Data Story and What Should Happen Now (2018), available at: https://www.theguardian.com/uk-news/2018/apr/07/christopher-wylie-why-i-broke-the-facebook-data-story-and-what-should-happen-now.

expansive approach to the breadth of protection, while intensifying the debate over whether to extend the scope of protection schemes to the reporting of immoral or unethical conduct.

15.62 Another contentious area in the development of whistleblower protection regulation is the relevance, if any, of motive. Many definitions include a 'good faith' requirement.[125] By contrast, the EU's draft whistleblower protection directive only requires that the individual has 'reasonable grounds' to believe that the wrongdoing disclosed falls within the scope of the regime. To many, this is a welcome development, as the good faith requirement can lead to unnecessary scrutiny of whistleblower's motivations rather than focus on the wrongdoing itself.[126] However, whether notions of good faith can or should be abandoned in the context of the changing nature of whistleblowers, is open to question. The question of motive is highly relevant in the context of distinguishing leaking and whistleblowing. In the public discourse, 'whistleblowers' are sometimes regarded as defenders of public interest, while 'leakers' are portrayed as selfish, jealous or overtly competitive.[127] Some also argue that the motive considerations can affect the state authority's decision on the merits of the case, even when the motive *de jure* is not relevant.[128]

15.63 Notions of good faith and the relevance of motive are also inherent in the concept of a whistleblower-as-hacker. Countries where the public prosecutor can exercise discretion in pursuing cases throw this into sharp relief. Article 2 of the EU's Cybercrime Directive and article 3 of the Cybercrime Convention lay down provisions regarding illegal access to information systems. However, the notion of 'ethical hacking' does not exist in the criminal law. In order to decide whether or not prosecution would be in the public interest, prosecutors are relying on assessments of security researchers' 'bona fides' and motives to distinguish 'white-hat' and 'black-hat' hackers.[129] It could be argued that the distinction should instead be drawn by examining the proportionality of the hacker's actions: whether they did more than was necessary to expose the breach. However, this determination is not free from difficulty, and for an ethical hacker this may be impossible to predict in advance. This suggests that an examination of motives and good faith will, in the context of new-age whistleblowers, continue to be relevant.

---

125   International Bar Association, *supra* note 3.
126   Ibid.
127   Leo Wolinski, Leaking, Whistleblowing and the Truth – An Expert's Guide (2017) available at: https://www.sacbee.com/opinion/california-forum/article162331793.html.
128   Papandrea, *supra* note 106, at 38.
129   Centre for European Policy Studies, *supra* note 118.

Finally, the changing whistleblower is challenging policy makers to confront **15.64** the cross-border reality of whistleblowing in 2019.[130] Globalisation is both a consequence and reason for whistleblowing, leaking and hacking. It is a consequence in the sense that the online platforms, discussed above, emerged as a way to allow the disclosure of large amounts of information on a safe platform that would be freely available to all. The distinguishing feature of these platforms is that they lack a territorial connection to one given state as they typically rely on a complicated web of interconnected servers, situated in different parts of the world. It is also a reason: in light of a steady rise of cross-border commerce and financial interactions, leaking and hacking have become ways to bring about transparency and accountability as whistleblowers traditionally have, addressing the demand for information about international transactions, especially in the tax-related area.[131] The technologically enabled opportunity for cross-jurisdictional whistleblowing is heightening the urgency of addressing the challenges that come along with it, including legal uncertainty over which jurisdiction's laws apply (which is crucial where there are significant differences in the level of protection offered and issues to do with conflict of laws).[132] Greater cooperation among regulators and law enforcement is needed, as well as, where possible, the harmonisation of laws. The proposed EU directive is a positive step in this direction.

The lines between whistleblowing, leaking and hacking are being blurred in **15.65** the age of information, changing the nature and methods of whistleblowing. Protection of the whistleblowers of the future will depend not only on addressing the political and ethical implications of these developments, but also a worldwide effort to confront the need for protections responsive to the globalised nature of modern whistleblowing.

E. CONCLUSION

Whistleblowing has changed considerably since the ancient Athenians hailed **15.66** the important function undertaken by those who draw public attention to private wrongdoing. The most dramatic developments have occurred in the

---

130 Ashley Savage, Embracing the Challenges and the Opportunities of Cross-jurisdictional Whistleblowing (2018), available at: http://www.oecd.org/corruption/integrity-forum/academic-papers/Savage.pdf.

131 Shu-Yi Oei and Diane M. Ring, Leak-driven Law, 65 *UCLA Law Review* (2018), available at: https://papers.ssrn.com/sol3/papers.cfm?abstract_id=2918550, at 14.

132 Ashley Savage and Richard Hyde, Whistleblowing Without Borders: The Risks and Rewards of Transnational Whistleblowing Networks, in David Lewis and Wim Vandekerckhove (eds) *Developments in Whistleblowing Research* (2015), available at: http://www.track.unodc.org/Academia/Documents/151110 IWRN ebook 2015.pdf.

past half-century, as whistleblowing went mainstream and regulatory protections became increasingly commonplace. Yet greater societal support for whistleblowers is now coinciding with technological disruption. FinTech, RegTech, SupTech and other innovations have the potential to replace, empower and change whistleblowing, whistleblowers and whistleblower protections. Predicting the future is a notoriously fraught exercise. It is hoped this chapter has provided a helpful summary of recent and forthcoming developments, alongside thought-provoking speculation about 'whistleblowing 2.0'.

16

REGULATION OF ROBO-ADVISORY SERVICES

Lee Reiners

A. INTRODUCTION

The wealth management industry is massive and has historically been very **16.01** profitable. PwC estimates that at the end of 2016, the amount of assets under management by wealth management firms around the world was approximately USD 85 trillion, with this figure expected to reach USD 154.4 trillion by 2025.[1] The industry has traditionally been labor-intensive, with scores of advisers and retail brokers meeting with clients face-to-face on a periodic basis to provide investment recommendations and rebalance client portfolios. Given the industry's size and previous lack of technological sophistication, it is no wonder tech start-ups have begun to put their own spin on the very old business of managing other people's money. These new FinTech firms, commonly called robo-advisors, provide automated, algorithm-driven, financial planning services based on investors' data and risk preferences.

---

[1] PwC, Global Assets under Management Set to Rise to $145.4 Trillion by 2025, *PwC Press Room* (30 October 2017), available at: https://press.pwc.com/News-releases/global-assets-under-management-set-to-rise-to–145.4-trillion-by-2025/s/e236a113-5115-4421-9c75-77191733f15f.

16.02 This chapter is structured as follows: Sections B–E explain what robo-advisors are, provide an overview of the current industry landscape and describe key benefits and risks of robo-advisors. Sections F and G analyse the regulatory framework for robo-advisors in the US and Europe, respectively. Section H concludes.

B. WHAT ARE ROBO-ADVISORS?

16.03 Robo-advisors combine insights from portfolio theory and behavioural economics with modern technology. In the decades since John Bogle – founder of Vanguard – wrote in his 1951 Princeton economics thesis that mutual funds 'may make no claim to superiority over the market averages',[2] many economists and investors have come to agree with Bogle that the average investor is better served by buying and holding a low-cost and broad-based index fund than by attempting to beat the market through actively buying and selling securities. This simple premise has been upheld in numerous studies,[3] including one by Standard & Poor's, who in their year-end 2017 report on the S&P 500, found that 'over the 15-year investment horizon, 92.33% of large-cap managers, 94.81% of mid-cap managers, and 95.73% of small-cap managers failed to outperform' their benchmark index.[4] This insight has led to a mass exodus of investors from actively managed funds to passively managed funds. In 1995, passive funds accounted for 3 per cent of assets under management (AUM) in mutual funds and exchange-traded funds (ETFs) in the US.[5] By year-end 2018, the figure had risen to 48 per cent and is expected to cross 50 per cent in 2019.[6]

16.04 Robo-advisors have capitalised on the rush to low-cost investing by utilising ETFs that track broad market benchmarks, and by reducing, or eliminating,

---

2   John C. Bogle, How the Index Fund Was Born, *Wall Street Journal* (3 September 2011), available at: https://www.wsj.com/articles/SB10001424053111904583204576544681577401622.

3   See, e.g., Stephen Schaefer, Passive Beats Active Management, London Business School (10 April 2018), available at: https://www.london.edu/faculty-and-research/lbsr/passive-beats-active-management-its-not-scepticism-its-arithmetic; and Mark J. Perry, More Evidence that it's very Hard to 'Beat the Market' over Time, 95% of Finance Professionals can't do it, *AEI* (Mar. 20 2018), available at: http://www.aei.org/publication/more-evidence-that-its-very-hard-to-beat-the-market-over-time-95-of-financial-professionals-cant-do-it.

4   Aye M. Soe and Ryan Poirier, SPIVA U.S. Scorecard, S&P Dow Jones Indices (2018), available at: https://us.spindices.com/documents/spiva/spiva-us-year-end-2017.pdf.

5   See Kenechukwu, et al., The Shift from Active to Passive Investing: Potential Risks to Financial Stability?, Federal Reserve Bank of Boston Working Paper (2018).

6   Charles Stein, Shift From Active to Passive Approaches Tipping Point in 2019, *Bloomberg* (31 December 2018), available at: https://www.bloomberg.com/news/articles/2018-12-31/shift-from-active-to-passive-approaches-tipping-point-in-2019.

human involvement in the portfolio selection process. The robo-advising process starts by having consumers fill out an online questionnaire.[7] The questionnaire elicits the consumer's age, income, investing goals, risk tolerance, investing timeframe, and their current financial assets. Once this information is collected, it is fed into the robo-advisor's proprietary algorithm, which then spits out a recommended asset allocation and one or more investment recommendations. Clients with similar investment objectives and risk profiles generally receive the same investment advice and may hold the same or substantially the same investments in their accounts.[8]

Not all robo-advisors are the same, and the level of service offered can vary between firms. In their simplest form, robo-advisors will maintain a list of products and portfolio allocations, and present the most suitable option to each investor based on their answers to a questionnaire. It then falls upon the investor to implement the given allocation and periodically rebalance their portfolio. More sophisticated robo-advisors will develop a comprehensive risk profile for each client based upon their answers to a questionnaire and invest on behalf of the investor in accordance with the recommended investment programme. These robo-advisors may also automatically rebalance client portfolios to stay within target allocations and engage in tax-loss harvesting in order to minimise the client's tax burden. **16.05**

C. INDUSTRY OVERVIEW

The robo-advice industry was launched in the aftermath of the 2008 global financial crisis, with the first robo-advisors, Betterment and Wealthfront, founded in 2008 (they started offering their services to customers in 2010). Both companies manage over USD 10 billion in client assets and are the largest independent robo-advisors globally. With more than 200 robo-advisors, the US is the clear industry leader.[9] Germany is in second place with 31, while the UK and China are tied for third with 20. **16.06**

---

7   See, e.g., David John Marotta, Schwab Intelligent Portfolios: Built on a Faulty Premise, *Forbes* (22 March 2015), http://www.forbes.com/sites/davidmarotta/ 2015/03/22/schwab-intelligent-portfolios-built-on-a-faulty-premise/#776563f01b3b [http://perma.cc/N68Y-T4VQ] (listing the questions on Schwab Intelligent Portfolio's questionnaire); and Wealthfront, Assess Your Risk Tolerance, available at: https://www.wealthfront.com/questionnaire (displaying page one of Wealthfront's initial questionnaire for prospective client).

8   See Melanie L. Fein, Robo-Advisors: A Closer Look (2015) (unpublished manuscript), available at: https://papers.ssrn.com/sol3/papers.cfm?abstract_id=2658701, at 2.

9   See, The US Still Has the Robo-advisor Lead, *Business Insider* (26 April 2017), available at: https://www.businessinsider.com/the-us-still-has-the-robo-advisor-lead-2017-4.

16.07 The robo-advising industry has grown steadily over the past ten years, with total industry assets under management surpassing USD 200 billion in 2017.[10] This number is expected to reach an eye-popping USD 16 trillion by 2025.[11] This growth potential has attracted the attention of traditional money managers who have begun to introduce their own robo-advice platforms that are threatening the long-term viability of standalone robo-advisors. In 2015, Charles Schwab and Vanguard respectively introduced Schwab Intelligent Portfolios[12] (SIP) and Personal Advisor Services.[13] SIP utilises Schwab's own ETFs and cash allocation programmes insured by the Federal Deposit Insurance Corporation (FDIC) to construct client portfolios, and charges no advisory fees and commissions, or account services fees, to Schwab customers. Vanguard's Personal Advisor Services charges 0.30 per cent of assets[14] under management per year and combines 'computerized asset allocation and rebalancing with access to human advisors over the phone and via videoconferencing'.[15] Other asset management, wealth management, and online brokerage firms have followed Schwab and Vanguard's lead and launched their own robo-advice platforms, including: Fidelity, E-Trade, BlackRock, and Credit Suisse.[16]

16.08 Robo-advisors integrated with established financial institutions quickly outgrew standalone robo-advisors like Betterment. Vanguard's Personal Advisor Services has over USD 101 billion in AUM – roughly half of all robo assets – and Schwab is the second largest robo-advisor, with USD 27 billion in AUM across its robo-advice platforms.[17] These integrated platforms were able to grow quickly because they are operated by recognised and trusted brands, with large customer bases, thereby allowing these firms to spend less on client

---

10 See Alex Eule, As Robo-Advisors Cross $200 Billion in Assets, Schwab Leads in Performance, *Barron's* (3 February 2018), available at: https://www.barrons.com/articles/as-robo-advisors-cross-200-billion-in-assets-schwab-leads-in-performance-1517509393.

11 See, The Expansion of Robo-Advisory in Wealth Management, Deloitte (2016), available at: https://www2.deloitte.com/content/dam/Deloitte/de/Documents/financial-services/Deloitte-Robo-safe.pdf, at 1.

12 Charles Schwab, Charles Schwab Launches Schwab Intelligent Portfolios (9 March 2015), available at: https://pressroom.aboutschwab.com/press-release/corporate-and-financial-news/charles-schwab-launches-schwab-intelligent-portfolios.

13 Janet Novack, Vanguard Rolls Out New Robo-Hybrid Advisor Service with $17 Billion in Assets, *Forbes* (5 May 2015), available at: https://www.forbes.com/sites/janetnovack/2015/05/05/vanguard-rolls-out-new-robo-hybrid-advisor-service-with-17-billion-in-assets/#450374b645c0.

14 Personal Adviser Services' 0.30 per cent rate applies to investments below USD 5 million; above that, the rate decreases as the value of assets invested increases. See Vanguard Advisers, Inc., Vanguard Personal Advisor Services Brochure: Form ADV Part 2A (2018) at 4.

15 See Novack, *supra* note 13.

16 See, e.g., Robo-Advisor Upgrade! Installing a Program for Profitability: Digital Advice Raises Profits for Investment Services Industry, Morningstar & Pitchbook (2018), available at: https://www.morningstar.com/content/dam/marketing/shared/pdfs/Research/equityreserach/FinancialServicesObserverRoboAdvisorUpgrade.pdf?cid=EMQ.

17 See, Eule, *supra* note 10.

acquisition. Large money managers are also able to provide robo-advice at a lower cost than standalone robo-advisors due to their ability to sell additional products and services to their robo-advice clients. These competitive dynamics have led many standalone robo-advisors to sell themselves to bigger companies, and those that have not done so, have experienced a significant slowdown in growth.[18] The challenges faced by standalone robo-advisors were crystallised when Wealthfront's 'post-money valuation fell to USD 500 million after its January 2018 fundraising, compared with USD 700 million after its October 2014 fundraising'.[19]

D. BENEFITS OF ROBO-ADVISORS

Robo-advisors are growing in popularity for several reasons. For starters, they **16.09** are cheaper than traditional financial advisers who typically charge each client an annual fee anywhere between 1 and 2 per cent of client assets under management. In contrast, robo-advisors charge between 0 and 0.5 per cent in management fees. Customers are also flocking to robo-advisors because they offer the same, or higher, performance as traditional advisers and reduce the emotional and cognitive biases that human advisers have.[20] Why pay active managers if they perform worse than the market? By utilising passive investment strategies selected by an algorithm, robo-advisors can beat active managers, providing higher returns to their customers at a lower price. Robo-advisors are also an attractive option for those who wish to save for retirement or some other future event but do not meet the minimum net worth requirements that most traditional wealth management firms require. Most robo-advisors require between USD 0 and USD 50,000 to open an account, whereas traditional firms may require a minimum investment of at least USD 250,000.[21]

By utilising algorithms, robo-advisors are also able to rebalance and tax-loss **16.10** harvest more efficiently than human advisers.[22] Periodic rebalancing is required to ensure that each investor's portfolio stays within the original target allocations[23] and is done by human investment advisers at predetermined time

---

18 See, e.g., Robo-Advisor Upgrade!, *supra* note 16, at 12.
19 Ibid., at 7.
20 See, Megan Ji, Are Robots Good Fiduciaries? Regulating Robo-Advisors Under the Investment Advisers Act of 1940, 117(6) *Columbia Law Review* (2017), at 1563.
21 U.S. Gov't Accountability Off., GAO-17-361, Financial Technology: Information on Subsectors and Regulatory Oversight (2017), at 33 (hereinafter 'GAO FinTech Report').
22 Ji, *supra* note 20, at 1563.
23 See, How and When Is My Portfolio Rebalanced?, *Betterment*, available at: https://help.betterment.com/hc/en-us/articles/115004257146.

intervals.[24] Because robo-advisors utilise algorithms that continuously monitor client portfolios, they can automatically rebalance a client's portfolio the moment asset allocations hit certain percentages ('threshold-based rebalancing').[25] Automatic rebalancing ensures that 'investment allocations continuously reflect client-goals.'[26]

16.11 Tax-loss harvesting involves selling a security that has experienced a loss – while simultaneously buying a similar security – so that the investor can incur a capital loss that reduces their tax liability while at the same time keeping their portfolio at the desired allocation.[27] Tax-loss harvesting requires deftly avoiding the 'wash sale rule' which disallows a loss from selling a security if a 'substantially identical' security is purchased 30 days after or before the sale.[28] Robo-advisors are ideally suited for compliance with the wash sale rule because their algorithms can automatically identify and select 'parallel securities' that are not 'substantially identical' but still allow the investors to maintain their target asset allocation at all times.

E. RISKS OF ROBO-ADVISORS

16.12 As with any type of financial advice, whether it is provided by a robo-advisor or traditional financial adviser, consumers face the risk of receiving unsuitable investment advice. While a human adviser may be able to mitigate this risk by probing consumers for more information to assess needs, risk tolerance, or other important factors, a robo-advisor's ability to mitigate this risk may be based on a discrete set of questions to develop a customer profile. Financial advisers of all kinds can also make inaccurate or inappropriate economic assumptions, perhaps due to a failure to factor in changing economic conditions, which could result in flawed investment recommendations. While human advisers may be able to mitigate this risk to some degree based on their ability to adjust to economic conditions, a robo-advisor's ability to mitigate this risk is based on whether its algorithm has been updated to reflect the most recent economic conditions.

---

24 See Ji, *supra* note 20, at 1563.
25 See Michael Kitces, Finding the Optimal Rebalancing Frequency – Time Horizons Vs Tolerance Bands, *Kitces.com: Nerd's Eye View* (4 May 2016), https://www.kitces.com/blog/best-opportunistic-rebalancing-frequency-time-horizons-vs-tolerance-band-thresholds/.
26 See Ji, *supra* note 20, at 1559.
27 See, e.g., White Paper: Tax Loss Harvesting+, *Betterment*, available at: https://www.betterment.com/resources/research/tax-loss-harvesting-white-paper/.
28 Ibid.; see also 26 U.S.C. § 1091 (2012) (codifying the wash sale rule).

Robo-advisors have only been in existence during a record bull-market run,[29]   **16.13**
and there are concerns around how robo-advisors will perform during an
inevitable market downturn. Anecdotal evidence from brief bouts of market
turbulence suggests that robo-advisors may struggle during a financial crisis or
prolonged market downturn. In the aftermath of the UK's vote to leave the
European Union in 2016 (Brexit), popular robo-advisor Betterment halted
trading for two-and-a-half hours without notifying retail customers.[30] Betterment responded to criticism by noting that the firm does not trade into 'highly
unpredictable volatility'[31] and that the firm's 'rights to suspend trading are
spelled out in its client agreement'.[32] Betterment and Wealthfront experienced
additional trouble in February 2018 after the 'Dow Jones Industrial Average
shed more than 1,000 points and the VIX, a gauge of market anxiety, more
than doubled in a matter of hours'.[33] Spooked by the market's decline,
customers tried to access their accounts only to find they could not log in.[34]

These disruptions highlight the fact that no amount of technological innov-   **16.14**
ation can overcome human psychology. When markets experience sharp
declines, investors behave irrationally and may not trust 'the algorithm' to
make decisions that affect their nest-egg. Without the ability to facilitate
face-to-face interaction, some robo-advisors may experience a mass exodus of
customers during the next severe market downturn.[35] As Mary Erdoes, the
head of JP Morgan's asset management unit said: 'Human beings need human

---

29 The record was reached on 22 August 2018. See, Gretchen Frazee, What the Longest Bull Market in
    History Means for the Economy and Yiur Investments, *PBS NewsHour* (22 August 2018), available at:
    https://www.pbs.org/newshour/economy/making-sense/what-the-longest-bull-market-in-history-means-
    for-the-economy-and-your-investments.
30 See Michael Wursthorn and Anne Tergesen, Robo Adviser Betterment Suspended Trading During 'Brexit'
    Market Turmoil, *Wall Street Journal* (24 June 2016), available at: https://www.wsj.com/articles/robo-adviser-
    betterment-suspended-trading-during-brexit-market-turmoil-1466811073?mod=article_inline.
31 Ibid.
32 See Michael Wursthorn and Anne Tergesen, Robo Adviser Betterment Stokes Concern Over Brexit
    Trading Halt, *Wall Street Journal* (2 July 2016), available at: https://www.wsj.com/articles/robo-adviser-
    betterment-stokes-concern-over-brexit-trading-halt-1467403366.
33 Frank Chaparro, Betterment and Wealthfront Crash During Market Bloodbath, *Business Insider* (5 February
    2018) available at: https://nordic.businessinsider.com/betterment-and-wealthfront-crash-during-market-
    bloodbath-2018-2/
34 See Brandon Kochkodin et al., Fidelity Reports Web Issues After Robo-Adviser Sites Crash, *Bloomberg* (5
    February 2018), available at https://www.bloomberg.com/news/articles/2018-02-05/robo-adviser-websites-
    crashed-cutting-clients-off-from-accounts.
35 See, e.g., Samantha Sharf, Can Robo-Advisors Survive a Bear Market?, *Forbes* (28 January 2015), available
    at: https://www.forbes.com/sites/samanthasharf/2015/01/28/can-robo-advisors-survive-a-bear-market/#47
    a410b3e7ec; and Robert Litan andHal Singer, Obama's Big Idea for Small Savers: 'Robo' Financial Advice,
    Wall Street Journal (21 July 2015), available at: https://www.wsj.com/articles/obamas-big-idea-for-small-
    savers-robo-financial-advice-1437521976.

beings to explain the world to them: that is our job.'[36] Such sentiment is why many robo-advisors, particularly those offered by traditional investment firms, are incorporating a hybrid model where the customer has access to a human adviser by phone or online chat.[37] Even robo-advisor pioneer, Betterment, now offers a service – 'Betterment Plus' – that provides customers with an annual consultation with a financial adviser along with advice on portfolio construction from a team of certified financial planners.[38] Some robo-advisors are even expanding their product offerings to further differentiate themselves. This includes offering services like asset aggregation capabilities that enable the provision of 'more holistic advice than fully automated digital wealth managers, based on a comprehensive view of client assets and liabilities, as well as expense-tracking and advice on budgeting and financial-goal planning'.[39]

16.15 As the use of robo-advisors grows more prominent, there are also justifiable concerns around consumers being herded into identical, or similar, financial products. This could result in 'wide swaths of the population' experiencing highly correlated losses during a market downturn.[40] To illustrate this point, Professors Tom Baker and Benedict Dellaert provide the following analogy:

> [c]onsider the impact of Google or Yelp on tourists' search for a restaurant in a new town as compared to the traditional approach of asking the hotel concierge for a restaurant recommendation. Google … provides access to restaurant information to all tourists in all towns, and it is easily accessible to everyone. If it gives systematically bad restaurant advice, the impact will be much greater than bad advice given by any individual concierge … Of course, the consequences of providing poor restaurant advice even on a large scale seem sufficiently small that regulating Google's or Yelp's restaurant reviews seems unlikely to be necessary. However, the consequences of poor financial advice can be severe even in an individual instance, and potentially catastrophic on a large scale.[41]

---

36 Ben McLannahan, JPMorgan Wealth Management Head Casts Doubt on Robo Advisers, *The Financial Times* (28 February 2017), available at: https://www.ft.com/content/2cfc2524-fe0b-11e6-96f8-3700c5 664d30.

37 See, e.g., Clint Boulton, Roboadvisors Stand at the Vanguard of Human-Machine Collaboration, *CIO* (25 March 2016), available at: http://www.cio.com/article/3048318/vertical-industries/roboadvisors-stand-atthe-vanguard-of-human-machine-collaboration.html (describing Vanguard Group's hybrid services); and Bernice Napach, With FutureAdvisor, BlackRock Seeks to Compete with Schwab, Vanguard, *Thinkadvisor* (14 June 2016), available at: https://www.thinkadvisor.com/2016/06/14/with-futureadvisor-blackrock-seeks-to-compete-with/?slreturn=20190023162541.

38 See Ben McLannahan, Pioneer of Robo-advice Industry Opts for Human Touch, *The Financial Times* (31 January 2017), available at: https://www.ft.com/content/c6b3bd9e-e74f-11e6-893c-082c54a7f539.

39 GAO FinTech Report, *supra* note 21, at 32–3.

40 See Benjamin P. Edwards, The Rise of Automated Investment Advice: Can Robo-Advisors Rescue the Retail Market?, 93 *Chi.-Kent L. Rev.* 97 (2018), at 108.

41 Tom Baker and Benedict Dellaert, Regulating Robo Advice Across the Financial Services Industry, 103 *Iowa L. Rev.* 713, 743 (2018), at 743.

Investor herding also creates new cybersecurity risks. If a hacker caused a robo-advice firm 'to suddenly sell substantial assets, it could significantly disrupt markets'.[42]

Robo-advisors rely on passive ETFs to construct client portfolios, which **16.16** means investors do not hold voting rights in the stocks that make up a given ETF. Instead, the voting rights are held by the ETF provider, the largest being BlackRock, Vanguard, and State Street. This means that these firms effectively control an ever-growing share of the stock market, which has led to concerns around declines in corporate governance and corporate accountability.[43]

F. REGULATION OF ROBO-ADVISORS IN THE US

In the US, the provision of investment advice is governed by the Investment **16.17** Advisers Act of 1940 (the Advisers Act).[44] The Securities and Exchange Commission (the SEC) is responsible for regulating investment advisers, 'which generally includes firms that provide digital wealth management platforms'.[45] Therefore, most robo-advisors are subject to the same regulations as traditional investment advisers and robo-advisors that manage over USD 110 million in assets are required to register with the SEC as investment advisers.[46] The Advisers Act defines an investment adviser as any person who, for compensation, engages in the business of advising others, either directly or indirectly through publications or writings, as to the value of securities or as to the advisability of investing in, purchasing, or selling securities.[47] Under Section 203(b)(1), exemption from registration is available to investment

---

42 Edwards, *supra* note 40, at 108.

43 See, e.g., John C. Bogle, Bogle Sounds a Warning on Index Funds, *Wall Street Journal* (29 November 2018), available at: https://www.wsj.com/articles/bogle-sounds-a-warning-on-index-funds-1543504551?mod=trending_now_4; Gita R. Rao, Give Mutual Fund Investors a Voice in Shareholder Proxy Voting, *MarketWatch* (12 December 2017), available at: https://www.marketwatch.com/story/give-mutual-fund-investors-a-voice-in-shareholder-proxy-voting-2017-12-12.

44 The Advisers Act defines an investment adviser as any person (i.e., individual or firm) who is in the business of providing advice, or issuing reports or analyses, regarding securities, for compensation. 15 U.S.C. § 80b-2(a)(11); IA Rel. No. 1092.

45 GAO FinTech Report, *supra* note 21, at 36.

46 Some robo-advisors with less than USD 110 AUM may still chose to register with the SEC, provided they meet certain conditions. SEC Rule 203A-2(e) permits internet investment advisers to register with SEC if the adviser provides investment advice to all of its clients exclusively through the adviser's interactive website, except that the investment adviser may provide investment advice to fewer than 15 clients through other means during the preceding 12 months. See, Exemption for Certain Investment Advisers Operating Through the Internet, Investment Advisers Act Release No. 2091 (12 December 2002), available at: http://www.sec.gov/rules/final/finalarchive/finalarchive2002.shtml.

47 15 U.S.C. § 80b-2(a)(11).

advisers whose clients are all within the same state as the adviser's principal business office and do not provide 'advice or issue analyses or reports' about securities listed on any national securities exchange.[48] However, all investment advisers are still subject to the anti-fraud provisions in the Advisers Act's Section 206.[49] Generally, investment advisers with less than USD 110 million in assets under management will be subject to the registration and oversight requirements of the state securities regulator in the state where the adviser maintains its principle office and place of business.[50]

1. Fiduciary duty for investment advisers

16.18 The Advisers Act imposes a fiduciary duty on investment advisers and there has been considerable debate as to whether robo-advisors are capable of meeting this duty.[51] A fiduciary duty was first read into the Advisers Act in 1963 when the Supreme Court decided *SEC v. Capital Gains Research Bureau, Inc.* ('*Capital Gains*').[52] Although the majority's opinion did not explicitly state that investment advisers have a fiduciary duty, the Court did interpret the Advisers Act's anti-fraud provisions in Section 206 to impose on investment advisers an 'affirmative duty of "utmost good faith and full and fair disclosure of all material facts"',[53] and 'to employ reasonable care to avoid misleading ... clients'.[54]

16.19 Subsequent Supreme Court decisions have interpreted *Capital Gains* as imposing a fiduciary duty on investment advisers. For instance, in *Santa Fe Industries, Inc. v. Green*, the court interpreted the Advisers Act to reflect the intent of the Congress to 'establish federal fiduciary standards for investment advisers'[55] and in *Transamerica Mortgage Advisors, Inc. v. Lewis*, the court

---

48 §203(b)(1) 15 U.S.C. §80b-3(b)(1).

49 *Proposed Commission Interpretation Regarding Standard of Conduct for Investment Advisers*, Request for Comment on Enhancing Investment Adviser Regulation, Investment Advisers Act Release No. IA-4889, note 54 (18 April 2018), available at: https://www.sec.gov/rules/proposed/2018/ia-4889.pdf (hereinafter 'Adviser Conduct Proposal').

50 See Investor Bulletin, Transition of Mid-Sized Investment Advisers from Federal to State Registration, SEC (2011), available at: https://www.sec.gov/files/transition-of-mid-sized-investment-advisers.pdf.

51 Clifford E. Kirsch, Investment Adviser Regulation: A Step-by-Step Guide to Compliance and the Law § 8:8.5 n.180 (2018); and Nicole G. Iannarone, Computer as Confidant: Digital Investment Advice and the Fiduciary Standard, 93 *Chi.-Kent L. Rev.* 141 (2018); David Quest QC, Robo-advice and Artificial Intelligence: Legal Risks and Issues, *Butterworths Journal of International Banking and Financial Law* (January 2019).

52 *SEC v. Capital Gains Research Bureau, Inc.*, 375 U.S. 180, 194 (1963) (hereinafter *Capital Gains*).

53 Ibid., at 194 (quoting William I. Prosser, *Handbook of the Law of Torts* 535 (2d. ed. 1955)).

54 Ibid., (internal quotation marks omitted) (quoting 1 Fowler V. Harper and Fleming James, Jr., *The Law of Torts* 541 (1956)).

55 *Santa Fe Industries, Inc. v. Green*, 430 U.S. 462, 471, n.11 (1977).

stated that the 'Advisers Act establishes federal fiduciary standards to govern the conduct of investment advisers'.[56]

Defining the exact substance of the Advisers Act's fiduciary standard has fallen **16.20** to the SEC, who has issued numerous rules and regulations over the years to provide greater clarity.[57] The outcome of these actions is a clear understanding that an adviser's fiduciary duty encompasses a duty of care and a duty of loyalty.[58]

According to the SEC: **16.21**

> the duty of care includes, among other things: (i) the duty to act and to provide advice that is in the best interest of the client, (ii) the duty to seek best execution of a client's transactions where the adviser has the responsibility to select broker-dealers to execute client trades, and (iii) the duty to provide advice and monitoring over the course of the relationship.[59]

The duty of loyalty requires investment advisers to put their client's interests **16.22** first.[60] To meet the duty of loyalty, an adviser must 'make full and fair disclosure to its clients of all material facts relating to the advisory relationship', 'seek to avoid conflicts of interest with its clients', and 'make full and fair disclosure of all material conflicts of interest that could affect the advisory relationship'.[61]

Traditional investment advisers and some legal scholars have argued that **16.23** robo-advisors are not capable of meeting the Advisers Act's fiduciary duty.[62] Even the Massachusetts Securities Division has stated in a policy statement that it believes that 'fully automated robo-advisers, as currently structured, may be inherently unable to carry out the fiduciary obligations of a state-registered investment adviser'.[63]

---

56 *Transamerica Mortgage Advisors, Inc. v. Lewis*, 444 U.S. 11, 17 (1979).
57 See, e.g., Investment Adviser Codes of Ethics, Investment Advisers Act Release No. 2256 (July 2, 2004); Compliance Programs of Investment Companies and Investment Advisers, Investment Advisers Act Release No. 2204 (Dec. 17, 2003) ('Compliance Programs Release'); Electronic Filing by Investment Advisers; Proposed Amendments to Form ADV, Investment Advisers Act Release No. 1862 (5 April 2000).
58 See Adviser Conduct Proposal, *supra* note 49.
59 Ibid., at 9.
60 Ibid., at 15.
61 Ibid., at 16.
62 See e.g., Fein, *supra* note 8.
63 Mass. Sec. Div., Policy Statement: Robo-Advisers and State Investment Adviser Registration 3, 5-6 (2016), available at: http://www.sec.state.ma.us/sct/sctpdf/Policy-Statement-Robo-Advisers-and-State-Investment-Adviser-Registration.pdf [http://perma.cc/Z9WR-2HVS].

16.24 When it comes to the duty of care, critics contend that an online questionnaire does not gather enough information to allow for suitable investment recommendations.[64] Specifically, questionnaires may miss critical pieces of information and do not capture information on assets outside a client's account with the robo-advisor. In addition, robo-advisors typically have no way of confirming if the information supplied by the client is correct. Combined, these factors make it difficult for a robo-advisor to act in the client's best interest because they lack a comprehensive view of the client's financial circumstances.

16.25 Some believe that only humans can meet the duty because face-to-face conversation is required to pick-up on 'the subtleties of a client's situation'.[65] Robo-advisor critics like to point to the disruption of service after Brexit and the volatility in February 2018 as evidence that only humans can prevent investors from panicking and making investment mistakes.[66]

2. SEC guidance

16.26 Despite the limitations of online questionnaires in providing personalised investment advice, the SEC has made it clear that robo-advisors are still capable of meeting the fiduciary duty's duty of care. Speaking at a conference in 2016, then SEC Chairman, Mary Jo White, stated:

> Just like a conversation with a 'real person' about a client's financial goals, risk tolerances, and sophistication may be more or less robust, so too there is variation in the content and flexibility of information gathered by robo-advisors before advice is given.[67]

Chairman White's statement is an acknowledgment that human advisers face many of the same challenges as robo-advisors in developing a complete picture of a client's financial situation. Just like robo-advisors, human advisers rely on information provided to them by the client, and they may not meet with the client frequently enough to incorporate changes in the client's financial position in a timely manner.

---

64 See Ji, *supra* note 20, at 1565.
65 Ibid., at 1567.
66 Ibid.
67 Mary Jo White, Chair, SEC, Keynote Address at the SEC-Rock Center on Corporate Governance Silicon Valley Initiative (31 March 2016), available at: https://www.sec.gov/news/speech/chair-white-silicon-valley-initiative-3-31-16.html.

Recognising the 'unique challenges and opportunities' presented by robo-advisors, the SEC issued staff guidance in 2017 to help robo-advisors better understand how they can meet their legal obligations under the Advisers Act.[68] The guidance included suggestions for how robo-advisors can use questionnaires in such a way that only suitable investment advice can be provided. The SEC encourages robo-advisors to consider: **16.27**

- Whether the questions elicit sufficient information to allow the robo-advisor to conclude that its initial recommendations and ongoing investment advice are suitable and appropriate for that client based on his or her financial situation and investment objectives;
- Whether the questions in the questionnaire are sufficiently clear and/or whether the questionnaire is designed to provide additional clarification or examples to clients when necessary (e.g., through the use of design features, such as tool-tips or pop-up boxes); and
- Whether steps have been taken to address inconsistent client responses, such as incorporating into the questionnaire design features to alert a client when his or her responses appear internally inconsistent and suggest that the client may wish to reconsider such responses; or implementing systems to automatically flag apparently inconsistent information provided by a client for review or follow-up by the robo-adviser.[69]

3. Conflicts of interest

Robo-advisors and their supporters contend that the use of algorithms to construct client portfolios reduces, or eliminates, the conflicts of interest and biases that are prevalent in human advisors.[70] However, these algorithms are developed by humans, therefore it is possible for biases and conflicts of interests to be embedded in computer code.[71] These conflicts will take the form of firm-client conflict, whereby the algorithm is programmed to do what is in the best interest of the firm as opposed to what's best for the client.[72] **16.28**

Many robo-advisors have an affiliated broker-dealer that is owned by the same parent company and that executes all the robo-advisor's transactions on behalf **16.29**

---

68   Div. of Inv. Mgmt., SEC, IM Guidance Update: Robo-Advisors 2 (2017).
69   Ibid., at 7.
70   See, e.g., Megan Leonhardt, Capital One Launches Robo-Adviser, with Humans on the Phone, *Time* (17 June 2016) available at: http://time.com/money/4371434/capital-one-launches-digital-advice/: 'The robots like to say they have no conflict of interest because a computer dispassionately picks your investments.'
71   See FINRA, Report on Digital Investment Advice 9-10 (2016), available at: https://www.finra.org/sites/default/files/digital-investment-advice-report.pdf, at 13.
72   See Ji, *supra* note 20, at 1573.

of clients.[73] For instance, in their Form ADV submission – the uniform form used by investment advisers to register with both the SEC and state securities authorities – Betterment notes that:

> Clients must establish a brokerage relationship with our affiliated broker-dealer, Betterment Securities, a FINRA member broker-dealer. By entering into an Advisory Agreement with Betterment, Clients authorize and direct Betterment to place all trades in Clients' accounts through Betterment Securities. As such, Betterment Securities will maintain all client accounts and execute all securities transactions in client accounts without separate commission costs or other fees. Betterment Securities exercises no discretion in determining if and when trades are placed; it places trades only at the direction of Betterment. Betterment Securities' procedures are designed to make every attempt to obtain the best execution possible, although there can be no assurance that it can be obtained. Clients should understand that the appointment of Betterment Securities as the sole broker for their accounts under this Wrap Fee Program may result in disadvantages to the client as a possible result of less favorable executions than may be available through the use of a different broker-dealer.[74]

16.30   As Betterment makes clear, all client transactions are routed through their affiliated broker-dealer regardless of whether it is in the client's best interest. As a result of this arrangement, client returns may suffer because Betterment Securities has an incentive to quote less favourable prices – in the form of bid-ask spreads – than a client could achieve elsewhere.[75] While affiliated broker-dealer arrangements are not illegal, and in fact are fairly common across all types of investment advisers, the SEC acknowledges the use of affiliate brokers presents a conflict of interest and therefore must be disclosed in Form ADV Part 2, which is the narrative brochure written in plain English and provided to clients.[76]

16.31   Another conflict of interest prevalent amongst robo-advisors run by traditional investment management firms is the use of propriety products in client portfolios. For instance, Charles Schwab places their SIP clients in a portfolio of 'ETFs combined with the Schwab Intelligent Portfolios Sweep Program, which automatically deposits, or "sweeps", free credit balances to deposit accounts at Charles Schwab Bank (Schwab Bank)'.[77] Schwab acknowledges

---

73   Ibid., noting that this practice is common for all investment advisers, not just robo-advisors.

74   Betterment, Betterment Wrap Fee Brochure: Form ADV Part 2A-Appendix 1, at 15 (2019), available at: https://s3.amazonaws.com/betterment-prod-cdn/agreements/Betterment_LLC_ADV_2019_01_03.pdf.

75   See Ji, *supra* note 20, at 1574.

76   See SEC, Study on Investment Advisers and Broker-Dealers as Required by Section 913 of the Dodd-Frank Wall Street Reform and Consumer Protection Act 27–28 (2011), available at: https://www.sec.gov/news/studies/2011/913studyfinal.pdf, at 29.

77   Charles Schwab & Co., Inc., Schwab Intelligent Portfolios Disclosure, available at: https://www.schwab.com/public/file/CMS-BDL100049, at 4.

that eligible ETFs include Schwab ETFs, which are managed by Charles Schwab Investment Management, Inc.[78] and that clients must pay the operating expense ratios of ETFs used in their portfolios, 'including Schwab ETFs, which affects the performance of SIP Program accounts'.[79] The cash allocation of SIP client portfolios is 'swept' to Schwab Bank, which earns revenue based upon 'the interest rate Schwab Bank pays to clients on such deposits and the amount it can earn from the extension of loans and the purchasing of investment securities with these deposits'.[80] Although SIP clients can request that certain ETFs be excluded from their account, Schwab is not required to accommodate this request. Thus, even if SIP clients wanted to exclude Schwab products and services from their account, they have little say in the matter.

While the above conflicts of interest are not illegal, SEC regulation requires **16.32** they must be adequately disclosed to clients and potential clients. This disclosure is crucial for a client's ability 'to make an informed decision about whether to enter into, or continue, an investment advisory relationship'.[81] While a human adviser can deliver this information in writing as well as in-person to the client, robo-advisors depend on 'electronic disclosures made via email, websites, mobile applications, and/or other electronic media'.[82] In their 2017 guidance to robo-advisors, the SEC encourages robo-advisors to consider:

- whether key disclosures are presented prior to the sign-up process so that information necessary to make an informed investment decision is available to clients before they engage, and make any investment with, the robo-adviser;
- whether key disclosures are specially emphasised (e.g., through design features such as pop-up boxes);
- whether some disclosures should be accompanied by interactive text (e.g., through design features such as tooltips21) or other means to provide additional details to clients who are seeking more information (e.g., through a 'Frequently Asked Questions' section); and
- whether the presentation and formatting of disclosure made available on a mobile platform have been appropriately adapted for that platform.[83]

---

78   Ibid., at 5.
79   Ibid., at 8.
80   Ibid., at 7.
81   SEC, IM Guidance Update, *supra* note 68, at 3.
82   Ibid., at 3.
83   Ibid., at 5 and 6.

4. Examination

16.33 Robo-advisors are examined just like traditional advisers. In its 2018 National Exam Program Examination Priorities document, the SEC noted that it will continue to examine investment advisers – including robo-advisors – that offer investment advice through automated or digital platforms.[84] These Examinations focused on registrants' compliance programs, including oversight of computer program algorithms that generate recommendations, marketing materials, investor data protection, and disclosure of conflicts of interest.[85]

5. Responsibilities of robo-advisors registered as broker-dealers

16.34 Robo-advisory firms can be investment advisers or broker-dealers, both of which employ licensed professionals to assist investors with their financial goals. Brokers are paid through commissions for the trades they make on behalf of their clients and are governed by Financial Industry Regulatory Authority (FINRA) rules. FINRA is a self-regulatory organisation that regulates member brokerage firms and exchange markets. Investment advisers are paid either a straight fee for their time or a percentage of the assets under management and as previously mentioned, are governed by SEC rules and regulations. Many FINRA registered broker-dealers are also registered investment advisers.

16.35 Investment advisers are held to a higher legal standard than brokers. Whereas investment advisers owe a fiduciary duty to their clients, brokers are held to a suitability standard, which means that as long as an investment recommendation meets a client's defined need and objective, it is deemed appropriate.

16.36 In 2016, the US Department of Labor proposed the so-called 'fiduciary rule', which would automatically elevate all financial professionals who work with retirement plans or provide retirement planning advice – in accordance with the Employee Retirement Income Security Act of 1974 (ERISA) – to the level of a fiduciary.[86] The rule would hold persons who provide investment advice or recommendations to an employee benefit plan, plan fiduciary, plan participant or beneficiary, IRA, or IRA owner as fiduciaries under ERISA.

---

84 SEC, 2018 National Exam Program Examination Priorities, available at: www.sec.gov/about/offices/ocie/national-examination-program-priorities-2018.pdf.

85 Ibid., at 5.

86 'Definition of the Term "Fiduciary"; Conflict of Interest Rule-Retirement Investment Advice.' *Federal Register*, The Federal Register (20 April 2015), www.federalregister.gov/documents/2015/04/20/2015-08831/definition-of-the-term-fiduciary-conflict-of-interest-rule-retirement-investment-advice.

Due to the broad scope of advice the fiduciary rule covers, it would effectively elevate all brokers to the level of fiduciary.[87]

The fiduciary rule has been controversial from the beginning,[88] and underwent **16.37** a lengthy legal challenge. The rule was effectively killed in March 2018 when the Fifth Circuit Court of Appeals vacated the rule after finding that the Department of Labor exceeded its statutory authority under ERISA in promulgating the rule.[89]

The death of the fiduciary rule does not mean broker-dealers are entirely 'off **16.38** the hook'.[90] In June 2019, the SEC finalized Regulation Best Interest,[91] which establishes a new 'best interest' standard of conduct for broker-dealers when recommending a securities transaction or investment strategy to a retail customer, including that the broker-dealer act without placing its own interests ahead of the retail customer's interests, and disclose and mitigate certain conflicts of interest. The new 'best interest' standard closes part of the gap between the fiduciary standard that is currently applied to investment advisers and the suitability standard that had previously applied to brokers.[92]

Similar to the SEC, FINRA recognised that many of the broker-dealers it **16.39** supervised were beginning to adopt digital investment advice tools, so in 2016, they issued a report reminding broker-dealers of their obligations under FINRA rules and sharing effective practices related to digital investment

---

87 See Ron Carson, What the Demise of the DOL Fiduciary Rule Means For You: 4 Questions To Ask Your Advisor Now, *Forbes* (5 August 2018), available at: https://www.forbes.com/sites/rcarson/2018/08/05/demise-of-the-dol-rule/#5b26ae7f7318.

88 See, e.g., Iannarone, *supra* note 51, at 146–7.

89 Mark Schoeff Jr., Fifth Circuit Court of Appeals Vacates DOL Fiduciary Rule, *Investment News* (15 March 2018), available at: https://www.investmentnews.com/article/20180315/FREE/180319947/fifth-circuit-court-of-appeals-vacates-dol-fiduciary-rule.

90 The Labor Department plans to issue in September 2019 a revised final fiduciary rule package to replace the one vacated this spring by the US Court of Appeals for the Fifth Circuit, according to Labor's autumn regulatory agenda. See Melanie Waddell, New DOL Fiduciary Rule Coming Next Fall, *ThinkAdvisor* (18 October 2018), available at: https://www.thinkadvisor.com/2018/10/18/new-dol-fiduciary-rule-coming-next-fall/.

91 United States Securities and Exchange Commission, Regulation Best Interest: The Broker-Dealer Standard of Conduct, Release No. 34-86031 (5 June 2019), available at: https://www.sec.gov/rules/final/2019/34-86031.pdf.

92 Note that the best-interest standard doesn't go into effect until June 2020. Also, there is considerable debate as to the level of consumer protection provided under the fiduciary standard compared to the best-interest standard. This debate is partially fueled by the fact that the new rule does not clearly define what 'best interest' is. Nonetheless, it is generally agreed that the fiduciary standard does provide a greater level of consumer protection. See Bob Pisani: A breakdown of whether investors are safer after the SEC passes financial protection rule, CNBC (6 June 2019), available at: https://www.cnbc.com/2019/06/06/a-breakdown-of-whether-investors-are-safer-after-the-sec-passes-financial-protection-rule.html.

advice, including with respect to technology management, portfolio development and conflicts of interest mitigation.[93] The FINRA report on robo-advisors focused on the governance and supervision of investment recommendations in two areas: first, the algorithms that drive digital investment tools; and second, the construction of client portfolios, including potential conflicts of interest that may arise in those portfolios. FINRA recommends that robo-advisors should be able to answer the following questions about their algorithms: 1) Are the methodologies tested by independent third-parties? 2) Can the firm explain to regulators how the tool works and how it complies with regulatory requirements? And 3) Is there exception reporting to identify situations where a tool's output deviates from what might be expected and, if so, what are the parameters that trigger such reporting? FINRA also encourages robo-advisors to have governance and supervision structures in place to review both the customer profiles and pre-packaged portfolios that may be offered to clients.

6. Recommendations to change the regulatory framework

16.40 In July of 2018, the US Department of the Treasury released a report that assessed non-bank financial institutions, financial technology, and financial innovation.[94] Recognising the benefits that digital financial planning tools provide consumers, the report included several recommendations to help simplify the existing regulatory framework for financial planning. Treasury suggests that regulatory oversight for all financial planning services should fall within one – new or existing – federal agency, or a self-regulatory organisation that would be subject to oversight by one or more federal regulators.[95] Treasury believes that a simple and efficient regulatory structure would provide greater legal certainty and avail more consumers – those with 401(k) (defined-contribution pension) accounts in particular – to the benefits of robo-advisors:

> a number of digital financial planning tools do not provide advice on 401(k) accounts, and some participants in outreach discussions indicated that regulatory compliance concerns were a factor in such decisions. Given that 401(k) account balances may account for a significant portion of an individual's investment portfolio, the lack of

---

93 FINRA Report on Digital Advice, *supra* note 71.
94 US Department of the Treasury, A Financial System That Creates Economic Opportunities: Nonbank Financial, FinTech, and Innovation, Report to President Donald J. Trump (2018), available at: https://home.treasury.gov/sites/default/files/2018-07/A-Financial-System-that-Creates-Economic-Opportunities—Nonbank-Financi...pdf.
95 Ibid., at 164.

advice on such accounts will not advance Americans' ability to save for retirement and accumulate wealth.[96]

G. REGULATION OF ROBO-ADVISORS IN EUROPE

Similar to the US, the regulation of robo-advice in Europe is 'technology **16.41** neutral', meaning the same rules apply whether investment advice is provided under a traditional model or an online platform.[97] However, unlike the US, capital markets in the EU are smaller and more fragmented.[98] In addition, European consumers are far less likely than American consumers to invest in the stock market.[99] To counteract these dynamics, the European Commission (the Commission) launched a plan in 2015 for a single Capital Markets Union for all 28 member states.[100] Considering that robo-advisor assets under management in Europe are just 5–6 per cent of what they are in the US,[101] there is potential for robo-advisory firms to expand access to financial services and serve the policy goals of the Capital Markets Union.[102]

1. MiFID

In the EU, robo-advice has primarily been governed by the Markets in **16.42** Financial Instruments Directive (MiFID) which:

> specifies the information that should be provided to clients, including in respect of the financial institution; the services offered; the financial instrument(s); the risks involved; as well as the overarching obligation that all information provided to clients and potential clients should be fair, clear and not misleading.[103]

---

96 Ibid., at 163.
97 See Financial Stability Board, Financial Stability Implications from FinTech (2017), available at: http://www.fsb.org/wp-content/uploads/R270617.pdf, at 27.
98 See, Wolf-Georg Ringe and Christopher Ruof, A Regulatory Sandbox for Robo Advice, European Banking Institute Working Paper Series 2018 – no. 26 (31 May 2018), at 12.
99 According to data from the OECD, US households on average hold 34 per cent of their financial assets in shares and other equity, compared with 22.3 per cent for Italian households, 22 per cent for French households, and 10.5 per cent for German households. See OECD, Household Financial Assets, available at: https://data.oecd.org/hha/household-financial-assets.htm.
100 European Commission, Action Plan on Building a Capital Market Union, COM (2015) 0468 http://eur-lex.europa.eu/legal-content/EN/TXT/?uri=CELEX%3A52015DC0468.
101 See Orçun Kaya, Robo-advice – A True Innovation in Asset Management, *Deutsche Bank Research* (2017), available at: https://www.dbresearch.com/PROD/RPS_EN-PROD/PROD0000000000449125/Robo-advice_%E2%80%93_a_true_innovation_in_asset_managemen.pdf, at 1.
102 See, e.g., Maria Demertzis et al., Capital Markets Union and the Fintech Opportunity, 157 *Journal of Financial Regulation* (2018), at 6.
103 ESMA et al., Report on Automation in Financial Advice, (2016), available at: https://esas-joint-committee.europa.eu/Publications/Reports/EBA%20BS%202016%20422%20(JC%20SC%20CPFI%20Final%20Report%20on%20automated%20advice%20tools).pdf, at 11.

MiFID 2, which came into force in January 2018, strengthened the requirements established in MiFID by requiring all investment firms to ensure that investment advice is suitable for the client or potential client and forcing these firms to disclose additional information to clients about the scope of advice provided.[104]

16.43 To qualify as an investment firm under MiFID 2, the robo-advisory firm must provide *investment advice* or *portfolio management*.[105] MiFID 2 defines 'investment advice' as 'the provision of personal recommendations to a client, either upon its request or at the initiative of the investment firm, in respect of one or more transactions relating to financial instruments'.[106] Portfolio management is defined as 'managing portfolios in accordance with mandates given by clients on a discretionary client-by-client basis where such portfolios include one or more financial instruments'.[107]

16.44 EU member states can exempt some robo-advisors who provide a limited service from the investment firm requirements of MiFID 2. Exempt persons are not allowed to hold client funds or client securities, nor are they allowed to provide any investment service except the reception and transmission of orders to investment firms authorised under MiFID 2.[108] Thus, it is clear that robo-advisors providing portfolio management do not qualify for the exemption. Firms that qualify for an Article 3 exemption under MiFID 2 will still be subject to stringent member state regulations pursuant to the MiFID 2 'analogous' requirement, which stipulates that member states' conditions and procedures for authorisation and supervision, as well as conduct of business requirements, can be no less strict than what applies to investment firms under MiFID 2.[109]

16.45 MiFID 2 requires the relevant authority of each member state to authorise and register investment firms,[110] and to subject investment firms to ongoing supervision. Obtaining authorisation is a rigorous process that involves meeting a number of requirements, including minimum capital requirements.[111] Investment firms that provide investment services are required to act in the best interest of their clients,[112] and firms that provide investment advice or

---

104 Ibid.
105 See Demertzis, et al., *supra* note 102, at 22.
106 Art (4)(1)(4) of MiFID 2.
107 Art (4)(1)(8) of MiFID 2.
108 Art (3)(1)(a–b) of MiFID 2.
109 Art (3)(2)(a–b) of MiFID 2.
110 Art 5 of MiFID 2.
111 See Demertzis, et al., *supra* note 102, at 23.
112 Art 24 of MiFID 2.

portfolio management are required to gather sufficient information from clients so that all recommendations are 'suitable' and in accordance with the investor's 'risk tolerance and ability to bear losses'.[113] In addition, investment firms are required to take all appropriate steps to identify and to prevent, or manage, all conflicts of interest.

Similar to robo-advisors operating in the US, European based robo-advisors **16.46** must take special care to ensure their investment recommendations are suitable for the client and that conflicts of interest are clearly communicated. To help clarify MiFID 2's suitability requirements for robo-advisors, the European Securities and Markets Authority (ESMA) released a consultation paper in 2017.[114] ESMA's guidance makes clear that the 'use of electronic systems in making personal recommendations or decisions to trade' does not change the responsibility of firms.[115] Specifically, ESMA notes that robo-advisory firms 'should be aware that the ability of a client to make an informed decision might be based solely on electronic disclosures made via email, websites, mobile applications and/or other electronic media'.[116] Given this, ESMA encourages firms to present information in 'a clear and simple way' and explain to customers the degree of human interaction available to clients. ESMA also encourages robo-advisors to address any inconsistencies in client answers to the online questionnaire and to provide the client with help when filling out the questionnaire.[117]

2. National competent authorities

Despite the comprehensiveness of MiFID 2, robo-advisory firms still face **16.47** uncertainty as to how they are regulated. Firms 'struggle with the distinction between investment advice and portfolio management and between investment advice and investment intermediation',[118] the latter of which is not covered under MiFID 2 and is therefore subject to domestic law. For instance, in Germany, investment intermediation is not subject to a suitability requirement.[119] This regulatory uncertainty was highlighted in a 2017 mapping exercise conducted by the European Banking Authority (EBA) whereby 282 FinTech firms were sampled to better understand how they are regulated

---

113   Art 25(2) of MiFID 2.
114   ESMA, Guidelines on Certain Aspects of the MiFID 2 Suitability Requirement, Consultation Paper (2017), available at: https://www.esma.europa.eu/sites/default/files/library/2017-esma35-43-748_-_cp_on_draft_guidelines_on_suitability.pdf.
115   Ibid., at 7.
116   Ibid., at 13.
117   Ibid., at 14.
118   See, Demertzis, et al., *supra* note 102, at 24.
119   Ibid.

pursuant to EU or national financial services legislation.[120] For the robo-advisory firms included in the sample, 35 per cent were under no regulatory regime, 41 per cent were regulated under EU law, and 24 per cent were regulated under a national regime.[121]

16.48 To help provide greater regulatory clarity, some National Competent Authorities (NCAs) have released additional guidance pertaining to automated advice tools. For instance, in 2017, the German Federal Financial Supervisory Authority (BaFin) released an article intended to help robo-advisors assess whether they meet the definition of investment advice.[122] The article notes that robo-advice generally meets the definition of investment advice and therefore requires authorisation under German banking or industrial law. In March 2018, the Dutch Authority for the Financial Markets (AFM) released a report clarifying the expectations it has regarding the further development of automated financial services.[123] The report notes that the Dutch Financial Supervision Act makes no distinction between automated and physical service provision. The AFM's report also notes that robo-advisors are encountering grey areas with respect to meeting their duty of care, 'for instance in relation to the client onboarding and the obligation to update client information'.[124] Also in March 2018, the Luxembourg Commission de Surveillance du Secteur Financier (CSSF) issued a communication on robo-advice which notes that digital financial advice services in Luxembourg are subject to the same regulatory requirements as traditional financial advice services.[125] Finally, in May 2016, the UK Financial Conduct Authority (FCA) set-up an Advice Unit to provide regulatory feedback 'to firms developing automated models to deliver lower cost advice and guidance to consumers'.[126]

16.49 The FCA also published guidance in 2017 for firms seeking to offer '"streamlined advice" on a limited range of consumer needs'.[127] In addition, several

---

120 EBA, *Discussion Paper on the EBA's Approach to Financial Technology (FinTech)*, (2017), available at: https://eba.europa.eu/documents/10180/1919160/EBA+Discussion+Paper+on+Fintech+%28EBA-DP-2017-02%29.pdf.

121 *Ibid.*, at 26.

122 BaFin, *Robo-advice – Automated Investment Advice in Supervisory Practice*, (2017), available at: https://www.bafin.de/SharedDocs/Veroeffentlichungen/EN/Fachartikel/2017/fa_bj_1708_RoboAdvice_en.html; jsessionid=D9E8AE0C452E7CBD9986BE859CA343B4.1_cid298.

123 AFM, *Guidance on the Duty of Care in (semi)automated Portfolio Management*, (2018), available at: https://www.afm.nl/en/nieuws/2018/mrt/doorontwikkeling-roboadvies.

124 *Ibid.*, at 3.

125 CSSF, *Robo-advice*, (2018), available at: http://www.cssf.lu/fileadmin/files/PSF/Robo_advice_270318.pdf.

126 https://esas-joint-committee.europa.eu/Publications/Reports/JC%202018%2029%20-%20JC%20Report%20on%20automation%20in%20financial%20advice.pdf at 13.

127 See FCA, *Streamlined Advice and Related Consolidated Guidance, Finalised Guidance* (2017), available at: https://www.fca.org.uk/publication/finalised-guidance/fg-17-08.pdf.

robo-advice firms have been admitted into the UK's regulatory sandbox, which is a safe space in which businesses can test innovative products, services, business models and delivery mechanisms without immediately incurring all the normal regulatory consequences of engaging in these activities.[128] For robo-advisory firms testing their product within the sandbox, the FCA has required additional safeguards to ensure consumers are receiving suitable advice.[129] For some sandbox firms, this has involved: qualified financial advisers checking the automated advice outputs generated by the underlying algorithms, having an experienced adviser being present when a consumer received automated advice, and notifying consumers that they should not act upon the robo-advice until they have received a second notification from a qualified financial adviser confirming that the advice is suitable.[130]

All of the previously mentioned NCAs releases are intended to clarify how **16.50** robo-advisors fit with existing national regulatory frameworks. To date, no NCA has issued new domestic legislation specifically covering automated investment advice or portfolio management and the relevant European Supervisory Authorities have determined that given a lack of material risk, no immediate action is necessary to address robo-advisors at the EU level.[131]

H. CONCLUSION

While regulators in the US and Europe have thus far deemed existing laws **16.51** and regulations sufficiently flexible to cover the provision of automated investment advice and portfolio management, rapid technological developments may soon force a rethink of the existing liability framework. Currently, the legal entity that operates a robo-advisor is held liable for any breaches of laws and regulations in the US or Europe. This liability framework is appropriate given that the technology behind the robo-advisor was developed by the firm – specifically employees working for the firm. But what happens when investment recommendations and decisions cannot be explained by anyone working for the firm? This scenario may sound far-fetched, but advances in machine learning, deep learning, and artificial neural networks

---

128 The UK was the first country to implement a regulatory sandbox, but as of March 2018, 17 countries operate a similar type of sandbox, including the Netherlands, Denmark, and Switzerland. See Demertzis, et al., *supra* note 102, at 31.

129 See FCA: Regulatory Sandbox Lessons Learned Report (2017), available at: https://www.fca.org.uk/publication/research-and-data/regulatory-sandbox-lessons-learned-report.pdf, at 3.

130 Ibid., at 15.

131 ESMA et al., Joint Committee Report on the Results of the Monitoring Exercise on 'Automation in Financial Advice' (2018), available at: https://esas-joint-committee.europa.eu/Publications/Reports/JC%202018%2029%20-%20JC%20Report%20on%20automation%20in%20financial%20advice.pdf, at 4.

may soon allow investment algorithms to scan massive amounts of data and make investment decisions that are unexplainable to the simple human mind.[132] While no jurisdiction is currently considering revising existing liability regimes for robo-advisors, some have begun to grapple with the unique challenges artificial intelligence poses to existing legal frameworks.[133] For instance, the European Parliament has recommended the European Commission create 'a specific legal status for robots' and apply 'electronic personality to cases where robots make autonomous decisions or otherwise interact with third parties independently'.[134] As robo-advisors continue to develop and play a larger role in the financial lives of ordinary consumers, expect more jurisdictions to revisit the existing liability frameworks applicable to robo-advisors.

---

132   See, e.g., John Lightbourne, Algorithms and Fiduciaries: Existing and Proposed Regulatory Approaches to Artificially Intelligent Financial Planners, 67 *Duke L.J.* 651-679 (2017); Quest QC, *supra* note 51.

133   See, e.g., Steve Lohr, How Do You Govern Machines That Can Learn? Policymakers Are Trying to Figure That Out, *The New York Times* (20 January 2019), available at: https://www.nytimes.com/2019/01/20/technology/artificial-intelligence-policy-world.html.

134   Resolution on Civil Law Rules on Robotics, PARL. EUR. DOC. P8 TA(2017)0051, para. 59(f) (2017).

17

PATENTABILITY OF FINTECH INVENTIONS

Mirjana Stankovic

A. INTRODUCTION

Recent years have witnessed the increased use of several disruptive tech- **17.01** nologies in the FinTech landscape, including artificial intelligence (AI), data analytics, the Internet of Things (IoT) and distributed ledger technology (DLT), including blockchain. These innovative developments have transformed significantly the way business processes and transactions are carried out in the financial services sector.

FinTech innovations lie at the intersection of finance and technology, and **17.02** FinTech-related patents can therefore have many different classifications. One possible classification could be based on the type of financial service or product that is addressed by the relevant patent. Thus, patents could possibly be classified on the basis of such financial categories as payments, banking, wealth management, capital markets, insurance and lending. Another possible partitioning of FinTech patents could be based on the technologies used. In this case, possible patent categories would be big data and data analytics, the

IoT, cloud computing, DLT, AI and machine learning.[1] This chapter proposes classifying FinTech patents by the type of financial service that the relevant FinTech innovation addresses, such as electronic payments; investment platforms; insurance and robo-advice; investment advice; banking, securities trading and cryptocurrencies; security, fraud and authentication; and smart contract code.

17.03 Patents are exclusive rights granted to novel inventions. They confer the rights to exclude others from making, using or selling the patented technology. The main argument in favour of patents as monopoly rights is that they can be a valuable part of intangible assets, by potentially increasing the firm's revenue, obtaining or maintaining market share, and acquiring goodwill through attracting investment and licensing. In exchange for granting an inventor a monopoly right, patent applications are published and the technical details of the new technology are revealed to the public. Thus, patents support innovation and knowledge transfer at the same time.

17.04 This chapter examines key issues in the patentability of FinTech inventions. Section B gives an overview of the FinTech patent landscape. Section C describes the main types of FinTech inventions, and provides an overview of the patent eligibility legislation and jurisprudence in the US and under the rules of the European Patent Office (the EPO). It also highlights the successful example of the FinTech fast track initiative of the Intellectual Property Office of Singapore (IPOS). Section D examines key issues in the patentability of blockchain technologies. Section E concludes.

B. OVERVIEW OF THE FINTECH PATENT LANDSCAPE

17.05 As indicated in Chapter 1, in the first half of 2018, global investment in FinTech companies reached USD 57.9 billion across 875 deals.[2] This is a sign that the FinTech market continues to experience significant growth and innovation. In the more mature areas of FinTech, dominant market players were able to attract larger investment rounds. During the first and second quarters of 2018, investments focused on innovative technologies, such as AI and robotic process automation. Interest in InsurTech and RegTech also grew significantly.[3]

---

1 Marcus Malek, Industry Report – Fintech Patents: Where Finance Meets Technology (2015), available at: https://www.iam-media.com/strategy/fintech-patents-where-finance-meets-technology.

2 KPMG, The Pulse of Fintech 2018 Biannual Global Analysis of Investment in Fintech (31 July 2018), available at: https://assets.kpmg/content/dam/kpmg/xx/pdf/2018/07/h1-2018-pulse-of-fintech.pdf, at 3.

3 Ibid.

The FinTech patent landscape consists of various players, such as banks and **17.06** other financial services providers and FinTech companies. According to the 2018 research carried out by Cipher, Bank of America is the front-runner in applying for and obtaining FinTech patents. The Bank of America's patent families cover banking IT infrastructures, transaction data processing technologies, and online and mobile banking.[4] According to the statistics obtained from the IPOS, the US, China and South Korea are the top three country players that account for 83 per cent of the worldwide FinTech patents that are published.[5] In 2018, a total of 12,058 total patent applications have been published. Insurance-related inventions exceeded the 1,000 mark for the first time, with 1,044 patents published in 2018.[6]

Unsurprisingly, the FinTech patent portfolio of Bank of America and other **17.07** banks looks miniscule when compared to the FinTech patent portfolio of technology companies. This is because business strategies of technology companies rely heavily on protecting and managing their FinTech inventions with patents and other intellectual property rights. Just to illustrate, according to Cipher, IBM owns five times more FinTech patents than all the banks together.[7] Most of IBM's patents in FinTech relate to optical character recognition (OCR). Microsoft, Google and Oracle follow suit, by owning FinTech patent portfolios in three major categories: OCR, transaction and data processing and online and mobile banking technologies.[8]

C. PATENT ELIGIBILITY OF FINTECH INVENTIONS

FinTech inventions are software driven: they run on software and business **17.08** methods that rely on using computers and related systems in the provision of financial products and services. The patentability of these computer-implemented inventions has been under great scrutiny in many countries, and many patent applications for computer-implemented inventions have been rejected as containing claims that relate to unpatentable subject matters.

---

4 Cipher, IP Strategy Report Technology Disruption Through a Patent Lens (July 2018), available at: http://cipher.ai/wp-content/uploads/Cipher-IP-Strategy-Report-2018-.pdf?utm_source=IP%20Strategy%20 Report%202018%20ePDF&utm_medium=website&utm_campaign=IP%20Strategy%20Report, at 17–20.

5 Intellectual Property Office of Singapore, FinTech infographic, available at: https://www.ipos.gov.sg/docs/ default-source/resources-library/patents/Guidelines-and-Useful-Information/the-next-wave-fintech—an-infographic.pdf.

6 Ibid.

7 Cipher, *supra* note 4, at 18.

8 Ibid.

17.09   Patents might be an essential ingredient of the FinTech enterprises' commercialisation strategy that looks to disrupt the financial industry by offering innovative products and services. However, in order for patents to lead to a successful commercialisation of FinTech inventions, two hurdles need to be overcome. The first hurdle concerns the fact that not all financial technology-related innovations are patentable *per se*. The patent law statutes and jurisprudence on patentable subject matters related to FinTech are constantly evolving. The second hurdle is related to the fact that FinTech inventions have very short life cycle. Under normal circumstances, it takes up to 16 months for a patent office to take its first action on a patent application, and between one and three years to make a final decision. By that time, the FinTech invention might lose its value and become obsolete. As an illustrative example, the Bank of America's patent application for a cryptocurrency exchange system that converted one digital currency into another was filed in 2014, made public in 2015 and granted in 2017 by the US Patent and Trademark Office (USPTO).[9]

1.   Types of FinTech inventions

17.10   There are various types of FinTech inventions that can be patented. Table 17.1 below provides a schematic overview of FinTech inventions adapted from the overview presented by the IPOS, based on the type of financial service to which the FinTech invention relates.[10]

Table 17.1   Types of FinTech inventions classified by the type of financial service to which the potential FinTech invention relates

Type of financial service	Description of the FinTech invention
Electronic payments	Inventions that use technologies related to the transaction of goods and services over a network, such as mobile payment, streamlined payment, integrated billing and mobile money.
Investment platforms	Inventions that use data analytics to improve the efficiency of online investment or trading platforms, as well as inventions involving cryptocurrency exchanges and market information platforms.

---

9   Malathi Nayak, Blockchain Patent Race Is on, but Hurdles Await, *Bloomberg Law* (30 May 2018), available at: https://news.bloomberglaw.com/ip-law/blockchain-patent-race-is-on-but-hurdles-await.

10   Intellectual Property Office of Singapore, Guidelines on FinTech, Launch of IPOS' FinTech Fast Track Initiative 2018 – New Accelerated FinTech Patent Process in Singapore, Annex A, available at: https://www.ipos.gov.sg/docs/default-source/resources-library/patents/circulars/(2018)-circular-no-3—launch-of-fintech-fast-track-initiative.pdf, at 2.

Type of financial service	Description of the FinTech invention
Insurance and robo-advice	Inventions that use technology to allow consumers to interact directly with insurance providers.
Investment advice	Inventions that use AI or machine learning to provide automated investment advice.
Banking, securities trading and cryptocurrencies	Inventions that improve the security and efficiency of banking operations and securities trading, as well as cryptocurrencies.
Security, fraud and authentication	Inventions that use big data analytics, AI and machine learning to provide digital identification and verification in order to prevent fraudulent payment transactions.
Smart contract code	Computer code, which is recorded as part of a transaction, and automatically executes terms of a contract upon fulfilment of specified conditions.[11]

2. Patent eligibility legislation and jurisprudence in the US

A US patent provides the right to exclude others from making, using, offering **17.11** for sale, or selling 'the invention as claimed in the published patent application' within the US, or importing the invention into the US, for up to 20 years from the date on which the application for the patent was filed.[12] Many companies consider patent rights a core component of their intellectual property (IP) and broader business strategy. In the US, the Patent Act defines the subject matter eligible for patent protection as follows: 'Whoever invents or discovers any new and useful process, machine, manufacture, or composition of matter, or any new and useful improvement thereof, may obtain a patent therefor, subject to the conditions and requirements of this title.'[13]

Abstract ideas, laws of nature, and natural phenomena are considered basic **17.12** tools of scientific and technological work and thus are patent ineligible. If these tools were monopolised by granting patent rights, this might impede innovation rather than promote it. In light of this, the US Supreme Court has established a two-prong test for identifying patentable inventions in the landmark *Mayo Collaborative Services v. Prometheus Laboratories, Inc.* case.[14]

---

11 For example, Alibaba has filed a patent application with the USPTO for a blockchain-based system that allows a third-party administrator to intervene in a smart contract in case of illegal activities. See Ana Alexandre, Alibaba Files Patent for Blockchain System That Allows 'Administrative Intervention', *CoinTelegraph* (5 October 2018), available at: https://cointelegraph.com/news/alibaba-files-patent-for-blockchain-system-that-allows-administrative-intervention.

12 35 U.S.C. §154.

13 35 U.S.C. §101.

14 *Mayo Collaborative Services v. Prometheus Laboratories, Inc* (2012), 566 U.S. 66, available at: https://supreme.justia.com/cases/federal/us/566/66/.

According to this test, courts must first determine whether the claim at issue is directed at a 'patent-ineligible concept' (an abstract idea, a law of nature or a natural phenomenon).[15] If the claim is directed at a 'patent-ineligible concept', the court must then examine the elements of the claim to determine whether the claim contains an 'inventive concept' sufficient to 'transform' the claimed abstract idea into a 'patent-eligible application'.[16] The second prong of the test will be satisfied if a claim includes 'additional features' to ensure 'that the claim is more than a drafting effort designed to monopolize the abstract idea'.[17]

17.13 Two years after *Mayo*, in another landmark decision, *Alice Corp v. CLS Bank International*,[18] the US Supreme Court ruled that a proposed FinTech service delivering online escrow was just an abstract idea not eligible for patent protection. Alice Corp was a FinTech start-up that allowed a third party to reduce settlement risk in financial trading systems. It sued CLS Bank International for using technology that was too similar to the technology covered by the four patents it owned. The Supreme Court considered the validity of patent claims directed at mitigating financial risk using a computer to carry out a method for exchanging obligations between parties to a deal.

17.14 The Court decided that the principle of mitigating financial risk through an intermediary that was not a party to the deal was an economic practice that remained an unpatentable 'abstract idea'. In addition, the Court also ruled that the use of a computer to implement these abstract ideas or the process of transformation of the method into a format necessary for computer implementation did not render the process patent-eligible. Thus, the Supreme Court ruled against Alice Corp, and raised the patent eligibility bar for computer-implemented inventions.[19]

17.15 Based on the *Mayo* two-step test for determining patent eligibility, the *Alice* decision has reiterated the requirement that, in order to be patent-eligible, the software-related claims must contain an element that amounts to 'significantly more' than the abstract computer program. Generic computer implementation

---

15 Laws of nature are not patent eligible, nor are processes that recite a law of nature, 'unless that process has additional features that provide practical assurance that the process is more than [an attempt] to monopolize the law of nature itself'. Ibid., at 8–9.

16 Ibid., at 3 and 9.

17 Ibid., at 8–9.

18 *Alice Corp v. CLS Bank International* (2014), 573 U.S. 208, 134 S. Ct. 2347, available at: https://www.supremecourt.gov/opinions/13pdf/13-298_7lh8.pdf.

19 See Dvorah Graeser, The Top Patent Challenges for Fintech Companies (28 February 2018), available at: https://kisspatent.com/resources/the-top-patent-challenges-for-fintech-companies.

of an otherwise abstract process does not qualify as 'significantly more',[20] as defined by the *Mayo* two-step test described above. Under the second step, when scrutinising the patent eligibility of computer programs, the court has to inquire whether the patent claim includes any element, or a combination of elements, that are sufficient to ensure that the claim amounts to significantly more than an abstract computer programme. However, the Supreme Court did not define what an abstract idea is. Thus, the subsequent jurisprudence had to struggle with defining the concept of an 'abstract idea' under the two-step test devised by the Supreme Court in *Mayo* and *Alice*.

Following *Mayo* and *Alice*, the USPTO has directed examiners to apply a **17.16** two-part test to determine whether a patent claim contains an abstract idea, a law of nature or a natural phenomenon, and if it does, whether any element, or a combination of elements, in the claim is sufficient to ensure that the claim amounts to significantly more than an abstract idea. Thus, examiners would need to look into whether there were other limitations in the claims that showed a patent-eligible application of the abstract idea. In other words, examiners are required to analyse if the claims are more than a mere instruction to apply the abstract idea.[21]

The decisions of the US Court of Appeals for the Federal Circuit that ensued **17.17** after *Alice*, have additionally clarified the requirements related to patent eligibility of computer-implemented inventions. For example, in *Enfish, LLC v. Microsoft Corp*, the Federal Circuit held that the claims in question were not an abstract idea 'because the claims were directed at a particular improvement in the computer's functionality'.[22] In a similar fashion, the Federal Circuit's decision in *Amdocs (Israel) Ltd v. Openet Telecom, Inc*[23] clarified that patent eligibility may be found from generic computer components working together in an unconventional manner to solve a technological problem. In both cases, the Federal Circuit held that claims directed at causing a specific improvement to the way computers operate, or causing computers to operate in unconventional ways to achieve an improvement in functionality, could be considered as elements amounting to 'significantly more' than an abstract idea. These considerations are identical for software used in financial services.

---

20   *Amdocs (Israel) Ltd v. Openet Telecom, Inc* 56 F.Supp.3d 813 (2014), available at: http://www.cafc. uscourts.gov/sites/default/files/opinions-orders/15-1180.Opinion.10-28-2016.1.PDF.

21   Morse, Barnes-Brown & Pendleton, Scrutinizing Biotechnology & Software Patent Eligibility in M&A Deal Valuations (6 January 2015).

22   *Enfish, LLC v. Microsoft Corp.*, 822 F.3d 1327 (Fed. Cir.) (2016), available at: http://www.cafc.uscourts.gov/ sites/default/files/opinions-orders/15-1244.Opinion.5-10-2016.1.PDF.

23   *Amdocs (Israel) Ltd v. Openet Telecom, Inc, supra* note 20.

3. Patent eligibility rules: the European Patent Office perspective

17.18 The main principle that governs patentable subject matter of computer-implemented inventions and business methods at the EPO and under the European Patent Convention (the EPC)[24] was established by the EPO Board of Appeal in its landmark decision *T0641/00 (COMVIK)*,[25] where the EPO Board held:

> An invention consisting of a mixture of technical and non-technical features and having technical character as a whole is to be assessed with respect to the requirement of inventive step by taking account of all those features which contribute to said technical character whereas features making no such contribution cannot support the presence of inventive step.[26]

17.19 Article 52(1) of the EPC stipulates that patents will be granted for any inventions, in all fields of technology, provided that they are new, involve an inventive step and are susceptible of industrial application. An invention is held to involve an inventive step if it is 'not obvious to the skilled person in the light of the state of the art'.[27] The inventive step requirement is intended to prevent exclusive rights, such as patent rights, acting as barriers to normal and routine research and development.[28] In evaluating the inventive step, the EPO uses the 'problem-solution' approach, i.e., whether the solution presented to the problem in the patent application is obvious or not to the person skilled in the art. Depending on the specifics of the case, different factors are taken into account, such as the unexpected technical effect of a new combination of known elements, the choice of specific process parameters within a known range, the difficulty the skilled person has in combining known documents, the fact that the invention solves a long-standing technical problem which there have been many attempts to solve, or the overcoming of a technical prejudice.[29]

17.20 According to Article 52(2) of the EPC, the following are not considered inventions and are excluded from patentability: (a) discoveries, scientific theories and mathematical methods; (b) aesthetic creations; (c) schemes, rules

---

24   The European Patent Convention, available at: https://www.epo.org/law-practice/legal-texts/epc.html.

25   EPO Boards of Appeal, *T 0641/00* (Two identities/COMVIK) (2002), available at: https://www.epo.org/law-practice/case-law-appeals/pdf/t000641ep1.pdf.

26   Ibid., at 1.

27   The European Patent Convention, Art 56.

28   EPO, Guide for Applicants: How to get a European Patent, available at: https://www.epo.org/applying/european/Guide-for-applicants/html/e/ga_b_iii.html.

29   Ibid.

and methods for performing mental acts, playing games or doing business, and programmes for computers; and (d) presentations of information.[30]

As an illustrative example, an element would be considered non-technical, and **17.21** thus unpatentable, if it were related exclusively to a mathematical method. For instance, it can be assumed that any AI application that enables a FinTech solution is based on a mathematical model. Following this line of reasoning, any FinTech invention whose main enabler is an AI application might be excluded from patentability, based on the assertion that the AI application is directed at a mathematical model *per se*. In order to clarify matters and avoid a situation where all FinTech inventions that rely on AI applications are deemed patent-ineligible, the new EPO Guidelines for Examination provide further guidance regarding patentability of AI inventions.[31] Under the EPO Guidelines, computer programs, if claimed as such, are excluded from patentability under EPC Article 52(2)(c) and (3). However, this exclusion does not apply to computer programs having a technical character. In order to have a technical character and be patent eligible, a computer program must produce a 'further technical effect' when run on a computer, i.e., a technical effect going beyond the 'normal' physical interactions between the programme (software) and the computer (hardware) on which it is run. The normal physical effects of the execution of a program (e.g., the circulation of electrical currents in the computer), are not *per se* sufficient to confer technical character on a computer program.[32]

The EPO has devised a 'two-step' approach for analysing patent eligibility of **17.22** computer-implemented inventions. The first step has a rather low threshold, and requires the proposed invention to be of a technical character, i.e., it must show a technically skilled person how to solve a technical problem using technical solutions. The problem solved by the invention must be technical, and not of a purely financial, commercial or mathematical nature. The requirements of this step can be fulfilled by amending the patent claim from a method that is based on the performance of a machine learning algorithm to a computer-implemented method.

---

30   The European Patent Convention, *supra* note 24, Art 52.

31   EPO, *Guidelines for Examination* (November 2018), available at: https://www.epo.org/law-practice/legal-texts/html/guidelines2018/e/g_ii_3_3.htm.

32   EPO Boards of Appeal, *T 1173/97* (Computer program product) of (1 July 1998), available at: https://www.epo.org/law-practice/case-law-appeals/recent/t971173ep1.html#q; see also EPO Boards of Appeal, *G 0003/08* (Programs for computers) (12 May 2010), available at: https://www.epo.org/law-practice/case-law-appeals/recent/g080003ex1.html.

17.23 This reasoning is based on the decision in *T1227/05 (INFINEON)*, in which a mathematical method for generating random numbers according to a specific distribution was found to be technical. Specifically, the Board of Appeal was persuaded that 'simulation of a circuit subject to 1/f noise constituted an adequately defined technical purpose for a computer-implemented method, provided that the method is functionally limited to that technical Purpose'.[33] The technical purpose of the method is determined by the direct technical relevance of the results of the mathematical method, and not by the nature of the data input into the method.[34] Patent claims might also include a mix of technical and non-technical features, and all features contributing to the technical character should be taken into account.

17.24 If the invention has not satisfied the requirements of the first step, the second step (i.e., inventive step) must be satisfied. The presence of an inventive step may only be supported by those features of the claimed invention that contribute to its technical character, i.e., those features that provide a technical solution to a technical problem. There must be a non-obvious technical contribution over the prior art.[35] Thus, the threshold for the second step is higher than for the first step, as it requires a technical contribution to the inventive step. For instance, a mathematical method may contribute to the inventive step if it is applied to a specific technical problem, such as image processing. Another example of satisfying the second step would be claiming a specific technical implementation of a mathematical method that has been adapted to run on a particular hardware configuration.[36]

4. Patent eligibility rules and the FinTech Fast Track initiative of the Intellectual Property Office of Singapore

17.25 In April 2018, the IPOS launched a FinTech Fast Track (FTFT) initiative in order to expedite the file-to-grant process for FinTech patent applications to as fast as six months. Under normal circumstances, it would take an average of 42 months from filing before a patent application could be granted in Singapore.[37] This initiative is unique, as there is no other patent office initiative that focuses exclusively on the fast tracking of FinTech patents.

---

33 EPO Boards of Appeal, *T 1227/05* (Circuit simulation I/Infineon Technologies) (2006), available at: https://www.epo.org/law-practice/case-law-appeals/recent/t051227ep1.html, ¶3.1.

34 See Marks and Clerk, Patenting AI: the EPO's New Guidelines (2 October 2018), available at: https://www.lexology.com/library/detail.aspx?g=4459673e-4c34-41bc-8459-6fc336ff0d53.

35 Prior art is any evidence that your invention is already known. See EPO, What is Prior Art?, available at: https://www.epo.org/learning-events/materials/inventors-handbook/novelty/prior-art.html.

36 See Marks and Clerk, *supra* note 34.

37 Mirandah Asia, Fintech Patent Applications to be Fast-tracked in Singapore (13 May 2018), available at: https://www.lexology.com/library/detail.aspx?g=bea5137d-084b-4007-8f95-c54a653c0fec.

FinTech businesses from all over the world can use this initiative, and there **17.26** are no fees associated with it. The following are the requirements of the FTFT initiative that need to be satisfied:

- the patent application is related to FinTech;
- the patent application is first filed in Singapore;
- the filing of Request for Grant of Patent and Request for Search and Examination are completed on the same day;
- the application contains 20 or fewer claims; and
- a supporting document labelled as 'Fast Track document', stating that the application is related to FinTech, is furnished during the submission of the Request for Search and Examination.[38]

In Singapore, software-related inventions are deemed patent eligible 'if they **17.27** make a contribution beyond the regular workings of the computer hardware executing the software'.[39] Assessments are made in order to determine if the computer or other technical elements contribute to the inventive concept of the software related invention, and if these technical elements can be deemed integral to the inventive concept. Thus, FinTech inventions can be patentable in Singapore if they meet certain conditions. These inventions should also satisfy the requirements pertaining to novelty, the inventive step and industrial application.[40] In order to satisfy the inventive step requirement, the invention must be an improvement over any existing product or process that is already available. The improvement must not be obvious to someone with technical skills or knowledge in the field of the invention.[41]

Computer-implemented business methods can be considered patent eligible if **17.28** sufficient interaction can be demonstrated between the steps of the method and the physical hardware (such as computers and servers) that implement the method in order to address a specific problem. For instance, a patentable FinTech invention in this regard might be a novel 'transaction platform that employs encryption to increase network security for a transaction, a unique software for processing and storing finance-related data that greatly enhances

---

38 Intellectual Property Office of Singapore, Launch of FinTech Fast Track Initiative: An Accelerated File-to-Grant Service for Financial Technology Patent Applications (Circular No. 3/2018) (March 2018), available at: https://www.ipos.gov.sg/docs/default-source/resources-library/patents/circulars/(2018)-circular-no-3—launch-of-fintech-fast-track-initiative.pdf.

39 Chung Ka Yee and Wong Chee Leong, FinTech Innovations: Forging Ahead (6 September 2018), available at: https://journalsonline.academypublishing.org.sg/Journals/SAL-Practitioner/Fintech/ctl/eFirstSALPDF JournalView/mid/595/ArticleId/1291/Citation/JournalsOnlinePDF, at 5.

40 Ibid.

41 IPOS, Application Process, available at: https://www.ipos.gov.sg/protecting-your-ideas/patent/application-process.

computer resource usage, or an innovative interface utilising machine learning for providing automated advice and wealth management'.[42]

17.29 The FTFT applicants are required to respond within two weeks from the date of receipt of an adverse formalities examination report,[43] and within two months from the date of receipt of a Written Opinion.[44] By contrast, under the regular track, applicants are given up to two months to rectify the deficiencies at formalities examination stage and up to five months to respond to a Written Opinion at substantive examination stage.

17.30 Once a notice of eligibility to proceed to the grant of the patent has been issued, applicants have to file a request for the issuance of a patent grant within two months from the date of receipt of the notice.[45] Although the stipulated timeline remains the same for applications under the normal track, applicants are encouraged to file a request for early publication before, or on the same day of, filing the request for the issuance of a certificate of grant, as patent applications will only be published 18 months from the date of filing without such request for early publication.[46]

17.31 This initiative brings Singapore closer to being a smart nation and a business-friendly environment for FinTech companies that would presumably have an increased interest in filing their FinTech inventions in Singapore. Given the fact that FinTech inventions have an extremely brief life cycle, thanks to the FTFT, these inventions can be commercialised in the shortest time possible in Singapore.

D. PATENTING OF A FINTECH TECHNOLOGY: THE CASE OF BLOCKCHAIN

17.32 As described in more detail in Chapters 1 and 6, blockchain is a data structure and a technology that makes it possible to create a digital ledger of

---

42 Yee and Leong, *supra* note 39.
43 This Report is issued if the formalities of the patent application are not satisfied during the preliminary examination by the formalities officer at the IPOS. See Intellectual Property Office of Singapore: *Patents Formalities Manual* (2018), available at: https://www.ipos.gov.sg/docs/default-source/resources-library/patents/infopacks/patents-formalities-manual_1-nov-2018.pdf, at 19.
44 During the examination process, the Patent Examiner may issue a Written Opinion if there are any unresolved objections regarding the patent application. The applicant will be invited to respond and/or amend the specification. Ibid., at 54.
45 Intellectual Property Office of Singapore, *supra* note 38.
46 Ibid.

transactions and share it among a distributed network of computers.[47] It allows parties to verify and record transactions in software code blocks, like links in a chain. Moreover, it involves peer-to-peer or community computer networks where each computer can act as a server for the others with shared data access. Blockchain is different from current operating systems used by banks that use one central server or computer. The most remarkable democratic feature of blockchain is that it is not governed by one single user. The decentralised nature of blockchain, which involves a chain of peer-to-peer or linked actions by multiple parties in transactions, makes it extremely difficult to tie this technology to a patentable subject matter and to determine the scope of the invention.

Notably, the core blockchain technology is already part of the public domain, **17.33** and therefore only novel and non-obvious modifications and improvements to the technology can be patented. Furthermore, blockchain systems, such as Bitcoin and Ethereum, are not yet well-defined from a legal point of view. These fast-developing and complex technologies are still in their infancy, and there is a plethora of unresolved issues regarding what is patentable and how patent law intersects with the mostly open source software[48] used in blockchain systems.

From the very beginning, the blockchain systems have relied mostly on open **17.34** source software – software with a source code that is freely available for anyone to view, use and edit. As such, the open source philosophy is an antipode to the idea of patents, which give the patent owner a right to control the patented invention for a limited period of time. However, the reliance of blockchain on open source software is gradually losing it prominence in the industry. A study conducted by Deloitte and GitHub in 2017 indicated that most open source projects had been abandoned or did not achieve meaningful scale.[49] Open source blockchain projects are not immune to this trend, and it remains to be seen how these developments will affect the patentability of blockchain inventions.

---

47   Cristina Pombo et al., Social Services for Digital Citizens: Opportunities for Latin America and the Caribbean, Inter-American Development Bank (2018), available at: https://publications.iadb.org/en/publication/17374/social-services-digital-citizens-opportunities-latin-america-and-caribbean.

48   Notable blockchain players that have made their software open source are: Ethereum (smart contracts), block.one (commercial applications), Chain (enterprise-grade blockchain infrastructure) and Digital Asset Holdings (financial applications).

49   Deloitte Center for Financial Services, Evolution of Blockchain Technology Insights from the GitHub Platform (October 2017), available at: https://www2.deloitte.com/content/dam/Deloitte/ru/Documents/financial-services/evolution-blockchain-technology.pdf, at 10.

17.35 While the blockchain software might be freely accessible, obtaining patent protection for inventions that use open source software is possible where the technical improvements satisfy the patent eligibility requirements, such as being novel and non-obvious technical contribution over the prior art. However, patents obtained in this context may be subject to licensing commitments, because these inventions might be deemed 'essential' to (or must be used to comply with) a technical standard, obliging the patentees to agree to license them on fair, reasonable, and non-discriminatory (FRAND) terms.[50] The FRAND licenses are used in many jurisdictions around the globe for licensing of 'standard-essential patents.'

17.36 An interesting development in this regard is the 'Blockchain Defensive Patent License', an agreement among mining hardware manufacturers to license their products on FRAND terms.[51] Thus, FinTech companies will need to consider a plethora of issues that pertain to the use of open source software, industry standards, and licensing of IP rights during the course of developing their IP strategy.[52]

17.37 It is a difficult endeavour to present a comprehensive overview of granted blockchain patents by different patent offices around the globe, simply because the statistics are scattered among various patent offices and are not centralised. A few exemplary blockchain patents for the provision of financial services granted by the USPTO are described below:

- *System for tracking and validation of an entity in a process data network:* This patent was granted to Bank of America for providing an innovative system, method, and computer programme for tracking and validating changing user identities via a blockchain database.[53]
- *Method for distributed trust authentication:* Modern businesses make use of a large number of services and applications in day-to-day operations. Requiring employees to maintain multiple authentication credentials for these services and applications would result in significant inconvenience

---

50 A patent that controls any part of the technology used in a standard is called a standard-essential patent (SEP). In order to ensure equitable access to SEPs so that standards can be widely adopted, standard setting organizations (SSOs) have created FRAND – a requirement that SSO members license SEPs under 'Fair, Reasonable, and Non-Discriminatory' terms to other members of the SSO and, very often, to non-members who use the standard. See Jeffrey I. D. Lewis, What is "FRAND" All About? The Licensing of Patents Essential to an Accepted Standard (6 November, 2014), available at: https://cardozo.yu.edu/sites/default/files/Lewis.WhatIsFrandAllAbout.pdf.

51 Blockchain Defensive Patent License, available at: https://blockchaindpl.org.

52 Covington, Intellectual Property Issues in Blockchain and FinTech (December 2018), available at: https://www.cov.com/-/media/files/corporate/publications/2018/12/intellectual_property_issues_in_blockchain_and_fintech.pdf.

53 US9825931B2 US Grant, available at: https://patents.google.com/patent/US9825931B2/en.

and inefficiencies. To address this issue, this patented invention encompasses development of identity providers, which maintain identity information for service users and enable that information to be used for authenticating users with multiple service providers. As a result, identity providers allow users to access many services and applications with a single set of credentials. This invention provides a new and useful method for distributed trust authentication. The patent was granted to Duo Security Inc.[54]

- *System for managing security and access to resource sub-components:* This patent was granted to Bank of America for the blockchain invention that enables the creation of tags that can be applied to blocks so that a designated entity or user can locate the block though the presentation of keywords associated with the tag. In addition, a security token is generated that is assigned or otherwise provided to the designated user. The token is configured to grant the designated entity access to resources in the block.[55]

According to Bloomberg Law, the USPTO has published around 700 blockchain-related applications it received between January 2011 and April 2018. Of those, the USPTO has granted 70 patents on blockchain technology during that time.[56] It appears that Bank of America is the top filer of blockchain patents in the US.[57] Notably, the USPTO has not yet published guidelines for patent eligibility of blockchain inventions.[58] **17.38**

On a global level, the analysis carried out by Wilson, Sonsini, Goodrich and Rosati, points out that IBM and Mastercard hold almost 20 per cent of all patents and patent applications held by the top 45 blockchain and cryptocurrency/token filers. The analysis also suggests that the top five patent filers hold almost 30 per cent of the patents and applications, and the top 12 filers hold over 50 per cent. This concentration suggests that, as blockchain and cryptocurrency industries mature, they might be prone to deploying similar IP strategies as the strategies of more seasoned industries **17.39**

---

54   US9825765B2 US Grant, available at: https://patents.google.com/patent/US9825765B2/en.

55   US9979718 US Grant, available at: http://patft.uspto.gov/netacgi/nph-Parser?Sect1=PTO2&Sect2=HITOFF&u=%2Fnetahtml%2FPTO%2Fsearch-adv.htm&r=1&p=1&f=G&l=50&d=PTXT&S1=9,979,718.PN.&OS=pn/9,979,718&RS=PN/9,979,718.

56   Nayak, *supra* note 9.

57   Ibid.

58   Ibid.

(e.g., licensing programmes, development of large patent portfolios as a defence, deterrent IP strategy, etc.).[59]

17.40 Novel uses of blockchain technologies can avoid the patent ineligibility pitfall only if the patent claims go beyond just a network of standard computers performing standard computer functions. If the claims involve security aspects or novel uses of security aspects, such as encryption, hashing and digital signatures, there is a high probability that the blockchain invention would satisfy the patent eligibility requirements. The claims might also pertain to networking aspects or novel uses of networking aspects, such as consensus protocols and smart contract protocols.[60] By contrast, patent claims that are directed at the pure computerisation of an existing business practice are, in most cases, unpatentable. Similarly, novel inventions aimed at handling human relationships, including financial obligations (such as providing investment advice), are also unpatentable. Automation of prior practices, such as using conventional systems in unforeseeable and novel ways, might be patentable.[61]

17.41 Helpfully, Jon E. Gordon gives an overview of several important guiding principles when patenting blockchain inventions:

- *Improvements embodied in special-purpose hardware, i.e., claims directed at new and special purpose hardware, might be patentable*: it is a common understanding that these types of claims are not directed at applying an abstract idea on generic computer hardware.[62] For instance, the USPTO has granted a patent directed at digital currency mining circuitry with adaptable comparison capabilities for difficulty. Mining is the process of verifying and recording new transactions on a distributed ledger. Upon the completion of the operation, the miner is rewarded with a new cryptocurrency unit. This patent refers to an improved mining system in terms of speed and performance.[63]

---

59   Wilson, Sonsini, Goodrich and Rosati, Overview of the Patent Landscape in the Blockchain, Cryptocurrency, and Cryptographic Token Space (12 October 2018), available at: https://www.wsgr.com/email/Practitioner-Insight/Blockchain/Practitioner-Insight-blockchain-1018-web.html.

60   Paul Haughey et al., 10 Considerations for Blockchain Patent Applications (2018), available at: https://www.kilpatricktownsend.com/-/media/Files/articles/2018/10-Considerations-For-Blockchain-Patent-Applications.ashx.

61   Jon E. Gordon, Can You Patent the Blockchain? That Depends (30 July 2018), available at: https://www.haugpartners.com/app/uploads/2018/07/Can-You-Patent-the-Blockchain.pdf.

62   Ibid.

63   U.S. Patent No. 9,942,046 (Drego et al.), Assignee: 21 Inc., available at: https://patents.justia.com/patent/9942046. See also: The Top Blockchain Patents of 2018 (2019), available at: https://www.munsch.com/Newsroom/Blogs/108602/The-Top-Blockchain-Patents-of-2018.

- *Enhancements related to improved blockchain security or improved and faster processing and indexing might be patentable as well*: an illustrative example in this regard is a patent granted by the USPTO that offers a technical solution to reducing the power consumption of the blockchain while making it more secure.[64]
- *Enhancements related to the enabling features of blockchain, such as improvements to the performance of smart contracts might also be patentable*: for instance, the USPTO-granted patent for the 'system, method and computer program product for privacy-preserving transaction validation mechanisms for smart contracts that are included in a ledger' is directed at controlling the confidentiality of user transaction on the blockchain: information on a particular transaction might be revealed to a restricted number of validating entities and still remain verifiable by public validators and thus be added to the blockchain.[65]
- The method of replacing a database with a blockchain is generally not patentable.[66]

Another predicament related to blockchain-related patent applications is that they need to be drafted in a manner that preempts infringement and allows enforcement. However, the decentralised, peer-to-peer and network nature of blockchain technologies makes it extremely challenging to identify a party deemed to be infringing a particular element of a patent claim. Very similar issues arise in the context of the allocation of liability on blockchain, as described in Chapter 9. Going forward, this is another issue that will need to be addressed by lawmakers and regulators.[67] **17.42**

E. CONCLUSION

This chapter has provided a broad overview of the most prominent issues in the patentability of FinTech inventions by examining the regulation and case law in the US, Europe and Singapore. It has also analysed the key issues and challenges related to the patentability of blockchain inventions. **17.43**

The analysis demonstrates that FinTech inventions, and blockchain inventions in particular, can be patentable, provided that certain patentability **17.44**

---

64 U.S. Patent No. 9,875,510 (Lance Kasper), available at: https://patents.google.com/patent/US9875510B1/en.
65 U.S. Patent No. 9,992,028 (Androulaki, et al.) Assignee: IBM. See also: The Top Blockchain Patents of 2018 (2019), available at: https://www.munsch.com/Newsroom/Blogs/108602/The-Top-Blockchain-Patents-of-2018.
66 Gordon, *supra* note 61.
67 Nayak, *supra* note 9.

requirements have been satisfied. A common feature of the patentability rules pertaining to computer-implemented inventions across all jurisdictions is a two-step test. Very broadly speaking, the first step involves ascertaining that the invention is not directed at an abstract idea. However, even when the invention is directed at an abstract idea, such as a mathematical concept, the patentability hurdle can be overcome if it can be demonstrated that a technical element or a combination of technical elements contributes to the inventive concept of the computer-implemented invention, and if these technical elements can be deemed integral to the inventive concept.

17.45 These regulatory developments offer uniformity and predictability for both FinTech companies and FinTech investors. These developments are also encouraging because they acknowledge one the most important features of FinTech – its cross-border nature.

17.46 From a public policy perspective, patent regulations should be drafted and implemented in a way that does not stifle the growth of the FinTech sector across the globe. There is a clear trend of patenting of FinTech inventions, as shown in Sections B and C above. As the FinTech industry continues to grow and mature, FinTech companies will start deploying different patent management strategies, such as obtaining patent portfolios for cross-licensing or deterrence of competitors.

17.47 When preparing patent applications, FinTech companies should highlight and focus on technical advantages and practical implementation details, emphasising technical improvements that go beyond improvements of general abstract ideas. Also, where inventions are deemed 'essential' to a technical standard, FRAND licenses should be considered as an acceptable practice.

17.48 One of the key ingredients to claiming successful FinTech patents is an understanding of the regulatory requirements for patentability and of the judicial practice in adjudicating patent eligibility cases. The patentability regulations and the jurisprudence are in constant flux, closely following the trends and developments in the FinTech arena.

Part IV

TECHNOLOGICAL INNOVATIONS IN LEGAL SERVICES

18

THE INNOVATION PROCESS IN LAW FIRMS

Sophia Adams-Bhatti and Tara Chittenden

A. INTRODUCTION

18.01 In an ever-changing business climate, lawyers face a future of transformation on a varied scale and at unprecedented speed. Innovation in services and service delivery will become a key determinant of success, as will new skill sets. Law firms face the opportunities and challenges that come from developing new technologies and process solutions, handling more data than ever before, integrating legacy and new systems, a greater need for collaboration (inside and outside the firm) and new start-ups bringing solutions and agility to shake up the sector. The nature of competition in the legal services market has changed and firms' abilities to embrace technological innovation may well manifest as a primary determinant of long-term survival.

18.02 Traditionally, law firms have been viewed by some as conservative, resistant to change and risk averse. This view gives rise to concerns of a negative relationship between the law firm partnership model and innovation, and yet law firms should have incentives to innovate as a means to access new business opportunities. There are, however, inbuilt incentives which might nonetheless enable innovation to take hold – the drive to access new business opportunities, survival and long-term continuity all firmly rely on innovation. Logically, therefore, the case for innovation is inherent, the question remains however as to just when, why and how firms take on this challenge. The typical narrative of a traditional law firm is one where there is a drive to protect partner profits and control, along conservative organisational norms. As would be expected, this would also set the scene and predicate not only the *extent* of the firm's innovation efforts, but also *how* the firm attempts to innovate and the results it achieves. Thus, the question becomes not simply whether law firms innovate more or less than other professional services (such as accountants, financial services, banks, insurance companies), but *how* law firms approach the innovation process.

This chapter contributes to the literature on professional services innovation **18.03** by analysing the drivers and barriers underlying law firm attitudes to innovation and by offering insights into the innovation process in business-to-business (B2B) law firms and, where appropriate, General Counsel (GC) and in-house lawyers as clients of these firms. It questions the processes by which innovation needs are defined and communicated and argues that, at present, the missing cooperation between legal and technology players impedes an effective commercialisation and diffusion of LegalTech innovations. Taking into account the wider themes of this book, Section F considers how technological innovation in law firms compares to FinTech in the financial sector and where the influence of financial sector clients shapes law firms' acceptance of technological innovation. Innovation is about more than technology and many in professional services are beginning to realise that technology is not the 'silver bullet' that will fix broken aspects of underlying processes or business models. Indeed, as this chapter will discuss, even *technological* innovation is as much about a firm's culture and the risk appetites of the firm's decision-makers as it is about the introduction of code and software systems.

Following this introduction, Section B looks at the reality of pressure on law **18.04** firms to change and outlines the drivers and barriers to innovation in Sections C and D, respectively. Section E unpacks the innovation process in action at law firms, from ideas through decision-making and senior management buy-in to costs and expectations around return on investment. This section also considers spaces for innovation and the rise of law firm incubators. In Section F, the chapter considers LegalTech in the context of FinTech, and Section G examines longer-term implications of technological innovation for law firms and the skill sets of future lawyers. Section H concludes.

18.05   Technological innovation has had an impact on industry structure, the formation and development of new firms, and the growth and the survival of existing firms. This wide range of effects has been the focus of increasing discussion and interest.[1] LegalTech has the potential to fundamentally change the legal services sector and the wider business of law. While still early in its evolution, LegalTech can bring new found efficiencies to legal processes and operations, and more broadly reshape the relationship between clients and legal service providers.

18.06   LegalTech is less mature than FinTech where funding and regulatory alignment are more advanced. One of the principal drivers for legal technology adoption has been the need to deliver efficiencies. The starting position of highly manual tasks has provided easy pickings for the application of technology to automate and speed-up processes. Arguably, LegalTech is currently less 'transformative' than other areas of digital disruption, such as InsurTech and FinTech, which often offer distinctly new ways of delivering financial services and more than just efficiency gains. LegalTech solutions have not invariably focused on reimagining the whole service, but on making more efficient a specific portion or task. LegalTech also still has a relatively low penetration rate across all segments of law and even in big law firms where adoption is most advanced, it still only impacts a relatively small proportion of client work.

18.07   Notably, although this chapter talks about B2B law firms, even within this grouping there is a great diversity of practice types – from global corporate law firms to agile boutique law firms and smaller traditional partnership models. Consequently, this chapter should not be taken as applicable to all B2B firms, but instead aims to raise some issues and observations about law firms' innovation processes, with the acknowledgement that there are notable exceptions – daily news feeds highlight new law firm and technology partnerships and evolving business models.[2] What is more universally accepted amongst law firms is that their operating environment is changing. Some will have already felt the effects quite strongly, whilst others suspect impact on their practice is not far off. Change begins to feel inevitable for law firms, but do they only have one choice?

---

1   Robert Cross and Giorgio Castellano, Technology and Innovation in Legal Services, The Legal Services Board (2018); and Robert Brown, Technological Innovation's Impact on Market Structure and Industry Profitability, 5(1) *The Journal of High Technology Management Research* (Spring 1994) at 123–40.

2   See, e.g., feeds from *The Lawyer*; *Artificial Lawyer*; *LegalIT insider*; *Forbes*; *Financial Times*; *Legal Futures*.

B. INNOVATE OR DIE?

'Innovate or die?' This seems to be the hyped challenge levelled at many, **18.08** especially smaller, traditional law firms. However, it may not be so severely binary a decision. 'Innovate' can mean many things ranging from small incremental improvements through to a radical disruption of business models and services. Marquis[3] observed a number of levels of complexity in innovation:

(1) very complex systems which involve many years to implement and resources far beyond those of a single firm;

(2) major breakthroughs in technology which alter the character of a whole industry, usually initiated outside that industry; and

(3) innovation of new products, processes, and product improvements carried out within the firm and vital to its commercial success.

Organisations need to continuously reinvent themselves if they are to survive **18.09** and prosper in dynamic environments. Law firms are no exception. Underlying this strong assertion is the question of whether 'really new' products are crucial to firm survival in the current fast-changing business environment. In other words, for now, technological innovations with a closer fit to firms' current processes and competences tend to be more successful. Interviewees in *Capturing Technological Innovation in Legal Services*[4] spoke of ways for firms and their clients to benefit from technological innovations in terms of processes, communication and client service, but firms were subtly interweaving these tools throughout existing business models to augment rather than rupture services. Yet, cautious attitudes from firms were having a wider impact on the extent to which LegalTech start-ups felt they could radically depart from what firms already knew and did.

Many LegalTech start-ups cannot technically be classified as being 'disruptive' **18.10** where the technology is focused on delivering efficiencies to current processes, rather than offering a 'new route to law'. Contrast this with FinTech and InsurTech, for example, where a significant portion of start-ups are offering new ways of providing financial services or insurance products. The LegalTech solutions gaining most traction in the market are 'horizontals' – tech applications that work in law, but also have experience and application in other sectors (cross-vertical success), such as elsewhere in professional services or in FinTech. Lawyers are increasingly aware of the efficiency gains achieved

---

3 Donald G. Marquis, *The Anatomy of Successful Innovations*, Readings in the Management of Innovation, Ballinger Publishing Company (1988), at 26–33.

4 Tara Chittenden, *Capturing Technological Innovation in Legal Services*, The Law Society (2017), at 110.

across other sectors. Clients who have achieved such gains through the use of technology are pressuring law firms to adopt the same approaches. Agile law firms work with clients and supply chain partners to identify and implement improvements and innovations.[5] Although traditional law firms are likely to perform fewer innovation efforts than new entrants, this does not mean that they do not innovate. Indeed, their competitiveness and long-term survival continue to depend on innovation. The question to answer is what types of innovation best match the differential characteristics of these firms and how sustainable this approach is if it continues to sidestep the automation of processes or machine learning capabilities?

18.11 A firm's choice of which clients to serve has a powerful impact on the capabilities it develops and the strategies it can pursue. 'First-mover advantage' may not hold true in fast-changing industries. It can be hard to find partners within a law firm who are willing to be the first to deploy machine learning or Natural Language Processing (NLP) on a live client project for the first time. They fear the risk of it going wrong, losing the client and damaging the law firm's reputation. Highly profitable firms tend to become conservative and defensive as the market expands beyond their original offer and this is the point at which it becomes difficult for the firm to keep up with rapid market shifts. Eventually firms must accept the inevitability of change by valuing innovation even above past success; one of management's most essential roles is to find a balance between supporting new and established innovations.

18.12 The following two sections highlight forces external to law firms that may encourage or constrain law firm decision-makers' abilities to change their competitive and technological strategies in order to survive.

C. DRIVERS FOR TECHNOLOGICAL INNOVATION IN LAW FIRMS

18.13 The effectiveness of law firms in originating, developing, and implementing technological innovations can be viewed as a function of three sets of factors:

(1) characteristics and drivers within the firm's immediate operating environment;
(2) internal characteristics and culture of the firm itself; and
(3) flows between the firm and its environment – most notably in the form of clients, their needs and expectations.

---

5 Ibid., at 83.

None of these drivers (nor any of the barriers described in the next section) **18.14** operate in isolation, and we can see considerable overlap when looking at how different drivers take effect. Moreover, a driver might also be a barrier in other situations and vice versa.

Current market forces are driving a much greater level of innovation through- **18.15** out the legal sector. In the most active parts of the market, the pace of change and technological innovation is increasing as the legal workforce becomes younger, more mobile and more tech-savvy. The main drivers behind law firm innovation can be summarised as:

- client pressure
- competitive pressure
- hype and publicity
- need to replace legacy systems
- regulatory and compliance drivers
- acceptance of cloud computing
- changing workforce
- government incentives.

Let us look at each of these in more detail:

Client pressure has become the most significant driver for technological **18.16** innovation in the legal services market. Different parts of the market are feeling the impact of this driver in different ways, but fundamentally it is about economics and technology as a means to an end. Law firms are having to deal with the same issues that have faced other sectors in having to do more with less. There is increased pressure on fees particularly from larger client organ- isations with greater buying power looking for increased value for money from their legal budgets. GCs are using the competitive tendering exercises for a place on their legal panels as a trigger for greater innovation and efficiencies. This in turn acts as a prompt for law firms to become much more serious about legal technology and its capabilities.

Lawyers are keen to show how they are innovating in the clients' interests. **18.17** Corporate legal services have traditionally been a high margin activity and for a long period law firms have been able to maximise profits by actively avoiding changes in delivery model. Over time, cost pressure from clients, increased traction by Legal Process Outsourcers (LPOs) and increased regulation and compliance pressures on in-house teams have forced everyone to look again at the cost-to-value ratio of services. The need for cost savings and efficiencies is challenging law firms to consider technology as a key component of service delivery and may ultimately force many law firms to innovate and potentially change their business models.

18.18 The research of the Law Society of England and Wales[6] into the tech adoption landscape found that banking and financial services are more prone to demanding new ways of working than their law firms. The Programme Director at one large law firm observed that big banking clients had been the most assertive at getting law firms to move out of their comfort zone and provide more than just traditional legal services. GCs in banks are demanding new ways of working, requiring more than just 'great lawyers' and wanting to see the use of process experts, technologists, technology solutions, and professional project management – a full service model. Technologies such as blockchain represent a fundamental shift in the way digital data is processed, stored and shared. Consequently, it is likely to create profound legal questions that cross regulatory and industry boundaries. Lawyers are being required to advise on the myriad cybersecurity issues inherent in blockchain, as well as questions around regulatory compliance, consumer protection, privacy, intellectual property and business transactions.[7] Clients in such settings are also increasingly looking for a new way of working with their firms, a move away from a purely transactional, towards a more holistic relationship approach. This is more common among the 'Big Four' accountancy firms[8] and is now increasingly considered by law firms. This cultural and operational shift requires an innovation mindset which allows both cultural and structural norms to be challenged and changed.[9]

18.19 *Competitive pressure* has been intensifying in the legal services market for some time. LPOs with a focus on industrialising processes and driving efficiencies, and have been effective early adopters of legal technology solutions. LPOs have taken market share from law firms in certain activities and have the advantage of being able to line up people, process and technology with a clear focus on lower cost, lower margin activity. In addition, players such as the 'Big Four' accountancy firms and some strategic management consultancies have also been moving into the legal services space. Accountancy providers have been particularly successful at automating large swathes of their business processes, such as audit, and can point to a track record of technology-enabled

---

6 The Law Society, *The LawTech Adoption Landscape* (forthcoming 2019).
7 Keith Fall and Taylor Miller, How Law Firms can Prepare for FinTech Wave (2018), available at: https://walkersearch.com/how-law-firms-can-prepare-for-fintech-wave/.
8 Deloitte; Ernst & Young; KPMG; and PricewaterhouseCoopers (PwC).
9 LexisNexis and Judge Business School, Trust and Transparency Between Law Firms and their Clients (2018).

service delivery that is more advanced than the norm for legal services. For example, all of the 'Big Four' accountancy providers in the UK now have a legal arm.

The *hype and publicity* associated with technologies such as AI, machine **18.20** learning and blockchain, have often been confusing and raised expectations beyond what the technologies can currently deliver, yet have had the positive effect of raising awareness throughout the legal sector. A result of this increased awareness is the shift from an IT industry push to a legal practice area pull, where law firms and legal teams are regularly taking the lead in starting conversations with tech vendors. However, there needs to be greater focus on engagement and getting adoption of existing tools as a priority over more advanced solutions that are a few years away.

Established law firms often have a myriad of *legacy systems* including document **18.21** preparation, document retention and a range of finance-related systems to record time and billing. New entrants and start-ups can begin with a blank sheet. However, for law firms facing the complexity of an array of technologies acquired over years of legacy systems, many of which no longer integrate, this can be a real driver towards technological innovation. Robotic process automation can be adopted to extend the life of existing legacy systems and allow for disparate systems to talk to each other. As these legacy systems come to the end of their life, law firms are naturally forced to come to market for new more advanced systems.

Regulatory and compliance requirements (e.g., AML and KYC requirements) **18.22** have increased significantly and are placing huge burdens on law firms and in-house lawyers. RegTech companies that have already been providing solutions to financial services and banking have started to pivot into the legal space, applying automation technologies to streamline processes like AML and KYC, with a view to reducing the non-billable hours spent on policy checks and client onboarding.

Technological innovation is a potential source of differentiation for smaller **18.23** law firms with ambition to take on larger, more profitable work. *Cloud* and Anything-as-a-Service (XaaS)[10] models bring a lower cost to access technology and mean that smaller firms can compete with larger law firms without needing the scale of staff or IT budget.

---

10 The core idea behind XaaS and other cloud services is that businesses can cut costs and get specific personal resources by purchasing services from providers on a subscription basis.

18.24 The *current generation of lawyers* now entering the workforce is in the main 'digital native'. Their higher level of tech literacy and expectations that technology should be the same in the workplace as it is at home will promote technological innovation and adoption in firms looking to retain talent. Supporting this is an increased focus on LegalTech in law schools and legal education. As described in Chapter 19, new courses will teach the next generation of lawyers both how to use these platforms and algorithmic systems and speak intelligently to the people building them.

18.25 *Government organisations and incentives* around technological innovation are providing avenues for law firms to enter the debate and try out new ideas. For example, in the UK, the 'Next Generation Services' stream of the Industrial Strategy Challenge fund offers up to GBP 20 million of 'pioneer funding' to establish ways in which new technologies could enable the UK accountancy, insurance and legal services industries to transform how they operate and where the greatest impact will be.[11] More initiatives, such as the recently announced research with NESTA to examine ways that technology and innovation can help to meet access to justice needs, can be a catalyst in this sector.[12]

D. BARRIERS TO TECHNOLOGICAL INNOVATION IN LAW FIRMS

18.26 The pace of technological innovation and adoption in law has been slower than in other service industries such as banking. There remain some significant structural barriers to innovation within those traditional law firms wedded to their billable hour and partnership model. The key barriers to be navigated on the path to technological innovation can be summarised as:

- Lack of capital
- Cost centre mentality
- Technical and process barriers
- Billable hour model
- Partnership model
- Market confusion
- Security concerns
- Longer sales cycle
- Regulatory lag.

---

11 See UK Research and Innovation, https://www.ukri.org/innovation/industrial-strategy-challenge-fund/next-generation-services/.

12 See *Artificial Lawyer*, SRA Targets Legal AI A2J Applications with 'Innovate Testbed' (5 October 2018), available at: https://www.artificiallawyer.com/2018/10/05/sra-targets-legal-ai-a2j-applications-with-innovate-testbed/.

Let us look at each of these in more detail.

The need to replace legacy systems can be a driver for change, but a history of **18.27** underwhelming technologies has left some sceptical of the potential benefits. Such systems have often been adapted from accounting systems, resulting in software that fails to reach its potential within a law firm. *Lack of capital* seems to have restricted technology investment within many law firms not structured to free up the same level of capital for investment in things like IT as other businesses. In-house legal departments and IT departments in law firms are often viewed as *cost centres*, and second to 'core operations' when it comes to investment budgets.

Rolling out technology across a law firm requires significant change manage- **18.28** ment that seeks to *align people, processes and technology*. It can be a challenge to find time to train lawyers with already busy schedules to fully implement new technologies or processes; with more senior lawyers there is sometimes the additional challenge of overcoming a cultural reluctance to engage. In large or more traditional law firms, the common pitfalls when considering innovation cluster around delayed participation, a tendency to stay with the familiar and to view any new technologies or innovation through the lens of what worked in the past.[13]

While there has been an increase in fixed fees and alternative models of **18.29** charging for legal services, the *billable hour* remains the *de facto* charging mechanism and can be a powerful barrier to innovation. The billable hour mentality can provide a challenge to efficient legal practices and can also mean that active lawyers have little time to explore innovation and learn new tools. There remains apprehension in some firms that a move away from the billable hour requires a new method of measuring value, which is seen as complex and opens firms to competition with other sectors that offer creative and holistic approaches to problem-solving.

The majority of law firms remain partnerships and money that would be spent **18.30** on technological innovation usually comes direct from the *partner profit pool*, something that can create a high bar to adoption or to high-risk projects. Partnerships also result in dispersion of responsibility, which can make gaining

---

13 Chittenden, *supra* note 4, at 84.

the support of all partners a very difficult task. Partners close to retirement may be less motivated to invest in the future of the law firm.

18.31 The amount of start-up activity and hype associated with legal technology has generated a lot of *confusion within the marketplace*. Larger law firms have the advantage of dedicated innovation teams and IT expertise to help navigate the rapidly changing landscape. Information asymmetries between innovators and lawyers persist, and smaller and resource-deprived firms may struggle to find easy paths toward technological innovation and choose instead to disengage with the issue.

18.32 *Cloud* computing has gained significant traction in the legal services market over the past four years and across a broad range of law firms. However, compared to other sectors, there remains less cloud-based infrastructure in place and some IT departments still default to on-the-premises delivery. In addition, law firms are naturally sensitive around the handling of client data and the associated rigorous security requirements can be a high barrier for LegalTech vendors to overcome during procurement. The need to maintain a secure document environment has been an historical inhibitor as some law firms still perceive internal systems to be safer.

18.33 While some LegalTech providers fear a lengthy *'death by procurement'* when dealing with law firms, others find the Software-as-a-Service (SaaS) model (such as charging for a 'per-deal per-month' basis), a much easier proposition and quicker to secure budget, particularly where the cost is added to the client's bill on a specific deal, effectively passing the cost on.

18.34 One of the possible barriers or deterrents to law firm innovation is the gap between *the Regulator* (e.g., the Solicitors Regulation Authority in England and Wales) and the emerging legal technology ecosystem. Although, compared to other jurisdictions, England and Wales have a fairly liberal professional regulatory approach, as evidenced by the introduction of the alternative business structure (ABS) model,[14] there remains reluctance to take up innovative ways of working for fear of breaching compliance obligations. In contrast, one of the advantages in the FinTech sector is a close alignment with their regulators, in part due to many (including the FCA in the UK) setting up regulatory sandboxes that provide a safe space for firms to test out new ways of working whilst remaining explicitly compliant.

---

14 Introduced by the UK 2007 Legal Services Act, an alternative business structure is an entity that, while providing regulated reserved legal activities, allows non-lawyers to own or invest in law firms.

E. THE INNOVATION PROCESS IN ACTION

In 2017, the Law Society of England and Wales published Capturing **18.35**
Technological Innovation in Legal Services.[15] Part two of this report explored
the innovation processes in law firms, as related by the firms' CEOs,
Innovation Directors and senior partners and by tech vendors. This section
revisits some of the key points on the innovation journey to explore the
practical process and decision-making that underpin many law firms'
approaches to innovation. Putting clients at the heart of decisions around
innovation and starting with what clients need, rather than a technological
solution or IT directive, was an ethos in common across all interviewees. The
ability to break out of the 'this is how we do things' mindset – often by talking
with clients or bringing in non-lawyer executives, with experience outside of
the legal industry – contributes to firms' appetite for innovation, along with
the six key factors set out in the Figure 18.1.

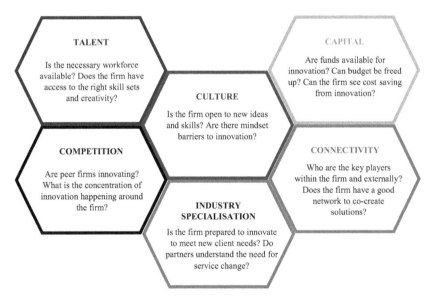

Figure 18.1   Ingredients for innovation in law firms

Productivity gains result from concurrent and often incremental changes in **18.36**
these six factors, some of which are stimulated by changes in the market,
external to the firm and may suggest ways in which service and process
innovation contributes to the renewal of the firm. The relationships between
these key factors begin to identify certain of the firm's characteristics, where

---

15   Chittenden, *supra* note 4, at 79.

the firm can draw on existing competences and where it requires competences and skill sets the firm does not yet have.

18.37 The process of innovation can be considered to occur in three phases: (1) idea generation; (2) decision-making and getting the senior management buy-in; and (3) budget allocation and expectations around ROI. A firm's innovation attempts will depend on differences in the firm's environment and its strategy for competition and growth, and with the state of development of technology used by a firm and its competitors. Each of these phases is described below.

1. Initiating innovation: ideas and insight

18.38 The initiation phase generally includes the following stages:

- identifying the pain points or problems to be addressed and dividing these into separate sub-problems where possible;
- assigning a priority to each sub-problem and determining which ones are critical, as opposed to desirable to address;
- designing alternative possible solutions; and
- evaluating the design alternatives (for feasibility, technical and cultural fit with the firm).

18.39 Success requires that firms learn and adopt new ways of working and problem solving – ideally, it requires flexibility, experimentation and learning on the way: 'we used to think having the right idea was all that matters – that's probably not true. What people like Steve Jobs did was to bypass the feedback loops, they just carried on with good ideas'.[16] By devoting some part of their strategic planning to test new ideas, firms certainly run the risk of increasing the frequency of failure, but they also open up the possibility of generating novel solutions to problems and new ideas for services and innovation. Culturally this requires both firms and clients to be willing to understand and appreciate the value of experimentation, and failure, and the longer-term value of research and development.

18.40 Innovative insight comes from those individuals or firms that are intimately familiar with the client experience and needs, rather than those intimately familiar with new technologies. The two main directions of innovation influence are foresight-driven and client-driven. The former is more likely to result in the automation of existing processes or slightly different ways to do

---

16 Jonathan Sea, Provoke Event Whitepaper: Siri and Cortana have applied for your job: the rise of AI in Marketing, Mando (2016), at 20.

what lawyers already do, while the latter, starting from the point of client need – and informed by the experiences of external industries – presents scope for firms to seriously consider how the world they serve is changing, and question their place within it.[17]

Foresight-driven insight is a top-down approach that seeks to understand the **18.41** complex forces driving change, including emerging and converging trends, new technologies, competitive dynamics, potential dislocations and alternative scenarios. In this case, innovation is driven by senior executives at the firm, based on their reading of these forces to design what they think best fits clients' needs based on the firm's own operating model. A contributing factor to the slow pace of technological change in the legal profession has been a preference for top-down, firm- and lawyer-centric approaches to innovation. Client-driven insight is a bottom-up approach that leverages insights into the behaviours, perceptions and needs of current and potential clients by involving them as true partners in the innovation process. This approach stresses the importance for the firm to build external alignment with, and to gather ideas and insights from, partner organisations by formally making them part of the co-creation process – this could be clients, universities, or technology suppliers. Where client companies are more advanced in their own technology and business models, these clients are often the driver of change at their law firms. Client-driven insight is often a better and more pragmatic approach for identifying genuine areas of need and use cases for technologies which benefit clients and the firm.

An optimum approach for law firms is to articulate an innovation strategy that **18.42** aligns innovation efforts with the overall business strategy. An innovation strategy sets the innovation direction for the firm, giving employees an idea of what new achievements and directions will best benefit the firm in its future and should address how innovation will create value for clients and for the firm. Without such strategy, firms will struggle to gain buy-in (internally and even at some senior roles) and also struggle to weigh the trade-offs of competing business activities.

2. Seeking senior buy-in

Research stresses 'managerial gaps' between law firm needs and the LegalTech **18.43** solutions offered by vendors.[18] A lack of technological knowledge can make it

---

17 Chittenden, *supra* note 4, at 82.
18 Tanel Kerikmäe et al.: 'Legal Technology for Law Firms: Determining Roadmaps for Innovation', *Croatian International Relations Review* – CIRR XXIV (81) (2018), at 91–112.

more difficult for senior decision-makers in law firms to detect risks and flaws. This does not necessarily indicate that such firms are not innovative, but only that they avoid a mode of innovation that is ill-suited to their risk preferences and resources. Here decisions by senior partners and firm executives arguably shape what is available to followers and late adopters – those firms that wait for a product to be more robust and with wider market acceptance before investing – and what the future of the legal services model might ultimately look like. Decisions, certainly at this early stage of the LegalTech market, can have much wider repercussions than within the firm itself.

18.44 The process to secure ideal buy-in calls for a firm-wide effort to make innovation work and stresses the importance of building in time for the rest of the office to stay on the innovation journey. The firm knows how to deal with the risks in its set ways of working, but there are new risks with new ways of working. In the end, it is likely that technology and process innovation will reduce the risk profile, but that is often not perceived at the outset and a firm's risk and insurance team can bring another layer to decision-making. A law firm's time to decision can be hard for start-ups who are used to agile and fast iteration.

3. Budget for innovation and expectations of a return on investment

18.45 Capital constraints can limit the possibility of initiating costly innovation projects. External funding or collaboration may be seen by traditional firms more as a threat to their sources of competitive advantage than as a way of sharing risks and costs and, for fear of losing decision-making control, such firms are little inclined to access capital markets or to allow the entry of other investors. This is a generalisation that draws attention to a number of exceptions where firms have set up as an ABS, brought in the risk strategies of their non-legal industry executives and even invested in LegalTech start-ups themselves (there are also firms that have invested to set up their own incubator space as the chapter discusses in the following section).

18.46 Some law firms are able to target external investment, while others choose to pursue a minimum outlay and quick test route, advocating that large capital expenditure is not essential to innovation. Even large law firms, with perceived reserves of capital to direct towards technological innovation, can encounter some difficulty managing resources around innovations that may not be fully welcomed at senior levels. Law firms 'do not relish taking money from the partners to pay for computer systems that many partners will refuse to use'.[19]

Return on investment is to some extent contingent on the point at which the **18.47** firm enters the LegalTech arena. Depending on its risk appetite, a law firm may attempt to be the first to introduce a specific technologically-enabled process or service (with a view to driving operational efficiency and impressing current and potential clients). Alternatively, it might prefer to watch others innovate, but be prepared to act quickly to adapt and introduce new variations and features to their own offer once market-tested. Others still will maintain reserve and enter the market later, gaining the benefits of a simpler and less expensive fully-tested market solution, yet at risk of always being in a catch-up mode.

The probability that a law firm will adopt a technological product or process is **18.48** thought to be an increasing function of the proportion of firms in the industry already using it and the profitability of doing so, but a decreasing function of the size of the investment required. A 'pioneer' firm with a performance-maximising strategy might be expected to emphasise unique applications of technology (especially machine learning) in the anticipation that a new capability will expand client requirements. A majority of innovations implemented by such firms would be expected to be market-stimulated with a high degree of uncertainty about their ultimate market potential or return on investment.

The measures of success used in most new product research view the **18.49** LegalTech solution in isolation, and its potential benefits for later services (through machine learning or through widening use cases) or for the longer-term value of data collected are not taken into account.[20] Executives should not just look at the achievement of service-specific objectives, but also at how a LegalTech solution builds new competences and serves as a tool for exploring new clients and the additional use of new technologies. For example, a LegalTech solution can generate more data as it operates, permitting it to collect or capture information that was not available before, and thus enabling law firms to predict and understand more about client needs and emerging risks. The number of variables that a firm can analyse has grown dramatically. LegalTech not only affects how individual case activities are performed but, through new information flows, it enhances the firm's ability to utilise

---

19 Kenneth Grady, The Low Cost of Lean (Part 4) (June 2016), available at: https://www.seytlines.com/2016/06/the-low-cost-of-lean-part-4/.
20 See: Michael J. Mauboussin, The True Measures of Success (October 12), available at: https://hbr.org/2012/10/the-true-measures-of-success.

connections between activities, both within and outside the firm. Therefore, measures of organisational learning may be more appropriate for technological innovation projects than financial measures of performance.

18.50 Many LegalTech solutions are geared to 'Big Law' (the industry's largest law firms) and solutions which are suited to smaller firms often require a significant degree of customisation. Consequently, seduced by the technology, a lot of small- to medium-sized firms end up paying for a lot of features they do not use and getting a poor return on their investment. Before going near technology and especially any form of automation, a full process mapping review ensures a better return or acquired value from technology investment. In addition, a rigorous decommissioning to remove legacy systems avoids individuals across the firm reverting back to using their preferred systems and perpetuating a mix of technologies and stifling potential returns.

4. Law firm incubators and dedicated space for innovation

18.51 Large corporate law firms have noted a tension between the need to identify and cultivate innovation projects and the need to integrate them with the rest of the firm's activities across teams, offices and countries. In a form of knowledge and technology brokerage, law firm incubators (e.g., MDR Labs;[21] Fuse;[22] Nextlaw Labs[23]) or LegalTech labs (e.g., Barclays' EagleLabs;[24] the University of Helsinki's LegalTech Lab[25]), play a crucial role in establishing and governing a closer collaboration and in fostering knowledge flows between start-ups and law firms (or in-house legal departments). The articulation of needs and options, the alignment of relevant players and the support of learning processes have been found to be important traits of these incubators in transforming law firm processes. They now directly engage in innovation agency, organising cooperation amongst the major players (law firms, clients, tech vendors and start-ups) to help establish a wider market for legal process innovation. For some law firms, having start-ups on site as part of an incubator has also informed investment decisions. For example, Allen & Overy made an equity investment in Nivaura, a FinTech company and the first start-up invited to work in their Fuse incubator.[26] Here the incubator

---

21   See: https://lab.mdr.london/.
22   See: http://www.allenovery.com/advanceddelivery/fuse/Pages/default.aspx.
23   See: http://www.nextlawlabs.com/.
24   See: https://labs.uk.barclays/community/law-society.
25   The Legal Tech Lab is a non-profit interdisciplinary project at the Faculty of Law, University of Helsinki, which examines and experiments on legal tech and digitalisation of legal practices. See: https://www.helsinki.fi/en/networks/legal-tech-lab/about.
26   See: http://www.allenovery.com/news/en-gb/articles/Pages/Allen-Overy-makes-equity-investment-in-fintech-company-Nivaura.aspx.

serves not only to give the host institution access to shape relevant process solutions, but also to off-set potential losses from automation via equity investment in these products. Despite conceptual evidence that institutional intermediaries at the intersection of private research and development and commercialisation have beneficial effects,[27] data on the ability of law firm incubators to address barriers in the LegalTech innovation space remains nascent.

If law as profession 'has to be perfect' and is driven towards arguments and **18.52** contracts with no loopholes, this might explain why firms struggle to trial new LegalTech solutions that are not 'perfect' from the outset. One law firm CEO created a 'sandpit' at his firm where new ideas could be tested and improved through iteration, helping to build confidence around innovation, while also meaning the firm 'does not wait forever to deliver'.[28] In April 2018, the England and Wales Solicitors Regulation Authority announced plans to formalise its innovation 'safe space', which allows firms to 'develop new ideas for business lines and products that could test regulatory boundaries'.[29]

F. COMPARISONS BETWEEN LEGALTECH AND FINTECH

FinTech has a number of barriers to adoption that are highly comparable to **18.53** what we see in LegalTech.[30] Financial services institutions have a shortage of funds to invest, a shortage of the right people and a shortage of time to make the necessary changes. As with law firms grappling with LegalTech, the financial services sector has struggled to analyse which is the best technology to use and who is best to implement it, what it should cost and what should be done first. All these barriers are consistent across the different sectors, as is the need to drive adoption throughout a financial services institution with effective project management, project initiation and project assessment – all major issues within any organisation that is looking to make transformative changes.

While many of the drivers and barriers to the adoption of disruptive tech- **18.54** nologies in the legal and financial services sectors overlap, the role of the

---

27 Shahid Yusuf, Intermediating Knowledge Exchange Between Universities and Businesses, 37(8) *Research Policy* (2008), at 1167–74.

28 Chittenden, *supra* note 4, at 79.

29 Thomas Alan, 'A Safe Space': SRA Pushes Ahead with Innovation Agenda, *Legal Business* (April 2018), available at: https://www.legalbusiness.co.uk/blogs/a-safe-space-sra-pushes-ahead-with-innovation-agenda/.

30 Insights in this section come from Law Society research into the LegalTech adoption landscape (forthcoming 2019); part of the project examined how the growth and adoption of LegalTech compared with that of FinTech, RegTech and InsurTech.

regulator has been very different. For example, in the UK, the FCA has taken a very hands-on approach to the development of FinTech, by regulating many of the start-ups directly, on the one hand, and pushing for the use of technology as a positive means to drive compliance through the promotion of RegTech, on the other hand. For decades, banks have been embracing technology to deliver efficiencies into their business processes. Over the last five years regulation has become a great spur to adopt new technology within financial services, a feat yet to take effect in the LegalTech space.

18.55 FinTech has become a central focus for financial services institutions, as a new set of competitors such as Monetize, Amazon and Monzo have entered the market and acquired market share. Whereas the adoption of LegalTech is being primarily driven by large law firms and their clients searching for efficiencies, FinTech increasingly features novel operating models designed to deliver new services underpinned by technology and consequently displace incumbent financial institutions. This shift in market players has created the need for big financial services providers to have an interface with FinTech to bring these organisations together via an innovation framework that encourages collaboration. Companies such as Temenos and Finastra have developed platforms on which FinTech applications can sit, designed to allow financial services institutions to access the technology in a way that protects FinTech start-ups. The rise of platforms for FinTech, together with open APIs, has the power to seamlessly and intelligently connect banking apps and financial products and services, to create new finance experiences and lead to the rise of the 'super aggregator' within financial services. One such example is 'bud' an independent banking and aggregator platform.[31] Bud describes itself as a 'plug and play financial services platform' to make all of an individual's financial streams accessible with the tap of a screen.

18.56 There are FinTech start-ups which want to connect with banks and are partnership-focused with bank-adjusted offerings, but the other side of FinTech wants nothing to do with banks. The latter category can and is exploring more radical departures from traditional banking. This has resulted in a divide in the FinTech sector that is not (yet) observable in the LegalTech sector, probably because of the high barriers of entry into the provision of legal services. However, while some areas of legal practice remain restricted to be undertaken by qualified solicitors only,[32] there are many other parts of legal

---

31 See: https://thisisbud.com/.
32 In England and Wales these are known as 'reserved activities' and include: the exercise of a right of audience; the conduct of litigation; reserved instrument activities (e.g. transfer of land title); probate activities; notarial activities and the administration of oaths. See also: https://www.legalservicesboard.org.uk/can_we_help/faqs/Reserved_Legal_Activities.htm.

and professional services ripe for LegalTech start-ups looking to reinvent services and service provision (e.g., will-writing, divorce, some areas each of dispute resolution, commercial contracts and tax work, to mention a few). Moreover, the growth of distributed trust networks may revolutionise the way information is stored and how transactions are processed, but in so doing removes the need for trusted intermediaries such as lawyers.

G. TO INNOVATION AND BEYOND

18.57 Innovations that involve the ability to process data will have the greatest opportunity for success in the near term. Above all, technological innovation calls for a change in firm thinking and culture and the inertia that comes from practising in the same way for sustained periods. Exploiting mass data and intelligent FinTech systems to automate financial tasks around tax and audit seems relatively unproblematic (in terms of the accuracy of the output, rather than what this means for employment). There also appears a greater ability to anonymise and aggregate data in financial services in order to train the systems on the volumes necessary for optimum accuracy. In the legal sector, law firms face client sensitivity and unwillingness to consent to their data being used with others to train machine learning systems, even though the clients want the benefits of the better trained system. Although all law firms have pools of data, the extent to which a firm's data may be useable and sufficient to see the gains of expert machine learning systems is limited.

18.58 Machine learning systems can analyse vast volumes of data to derive patterns used to predict behaviour and arguably mimic human decisions. However, alongside questioning what this might mean for human jobs, deeper questions arise around the impact of the use of data such as bias encoded in these systems, explainability, transparency, data privacy and 'ownership', and the nuances and subjectivity missing from interpretations of circumstances if rendered solely by an AI system. To innovate will increasingly mean to initiate new ways of working with machines, new processes of interaction and exchange where machines complete routine tasks and help lawyers find relevant information from a mass of noise, leaving the lawyer to focus on interpreting and applying reasoning. Across the economy, there are concerns of the dampening effects of a lack of consensus and agreed framework to some of these fundamental building blocks of data governance and management. Many organisations such as the Royal Society, British Academy, Turing Institute, Ada Lovelace Institute, Centre of Data Ethics and Innovation, and Office of AI, to name a few, have emerged to seek to provide clarity, although this will necessarily take some time.

18.59 The point where general AI replaces lawyers is still a long way off, if it ever truly takes root in the legal profession at all; we might expect more radical change in legal processes to take over before that point. The emergence of a dominant LegalTech industry will mark a clear milestone in the competitive landscape of the legal sector. The predominant adoption of LegalTech will plausibly lead to a decrease in the number of firms in the industry, will undoubtedly change the nature of work and the value offered by law firms, and will impact heavily on administrative and process-led roles.

18.60 Skills and experience will play a vital role in the ability to maximise on the opportunities. This is relevant both for the existing workforce in law (in firms or in-house) and the new generation of lawyers. Increasingly, as described in Chapter 19, the university sector is interested in delivering broader competency-based learning, experiential or otherwise, in conjunction with STEM based disciplines. However, the norm is still a way from a reimagined legal education route which enables the sector to master the opportunities of the technology and to innovate more widely. There appears to be a perceived trade-off between the expectations of 'traditional' academic rigour and the practical insights of legal skills which deliver competency in areas such as AI and legal innovation. There exist opportunities to create the capabilities of an innovation mindset, beyond the simple use of technology, amongst the incoming generation of legal professionals, which would benefit the sector as a whole.

18.61 Retraining the existing workforce also has challenges, as in any other sector. It is likely that the response will be driven by needs – those of the clients in specific sectors. Financial services clients will expect a greater 'literacy' in the technology applications in their sector, as might large corporates who will see peers and law enforcement using technology assisted review (TAR)[33] to support their work. Innovation mindset in the existing workforce is harder to achieve, or at least faces a greater number of barriers. The institutional norms, organisational culture, incentive and reward packages, incumbency and organisational structure and design, are all invariably optimised for aspects of excellence described in terms of expertise, accuracy, reliability, and not innovating, changing and experimenting.

---

33   Technlogy assisted review uses artificial intelligence to identify and tag potentially discoverable documents, focusing and expediting the human review process.

H. CONCLUSION

This chapter has touched on the value, and at times necessity, of technological **18.62** innovation in a changing legal sector. It has outlined the drivers of innovation and the influence of clients and sectors such as FinTech, on shaping the evolution of service provision. Yet, innovation is not without challenges and, in featuring the barriers to innovation, this chapter indicated the tensions firms face in attempts to align their practices for the future. The growth of law firm incubators and the use of machine learning and automation across other industries points to possibilities for how law firms might transform. However, as this chapter has discussed, the process of innovation – from ideas to senior management buy-in and budget allocation – remains a strategic strain for many law firms.

Law firms cannot evolve in a vacuum. Innovation is inextricably linked with **18.63** changes in the market and client behaviours. With collaboration comes the idea of breaking down the borders that contain and define the firm and this is still new for many law firms. Increasingly, firms are also being asked to collaborate with other lawyers so that the client has the benefit of a wider range of expertise. Collaboration enables a firm to capitalise on its own strength while harnessing the capabilities and assets of others, yet raises more questions around professional boundaries and what it will mean to think like a lawyer in the future.

19

FUTURE LAWYERS: HOW TO STAY UP TO DATE WITH THE LEGAL TECH REVOLUTION

Mark Fenwick, Wulf A. Kaal and Erik P.M. Vermeulen

A. INTRODUCTION

19.01   We live in an age of 'ubiquitous computing'.[1] Consider how much of our time is spent interacting with devices that are, at some level, structured by, and operate, a computer code. Think work, recreation, communication, consumption, travel, and education/research. Such interactions with code-based technologies can be direct and intimate – interacting with a smartphone or PC, for instance – or more 'distant' – travelling to work on an underground system that is automated in various ways. In both cases, it is code that makes the experience possible and code that, ultimately, provides the structure for that experience.[2]

19.02   The world today is, therefore, organised by and around computer code. Or, as the venture capitalist and serial entrepreneur, Marc Andreessen, dramatically

---

1   A concept first coined by Mark Weiser, chief scientist at XEROX, in the late 1980s.
2   See Larry Lessig, *Code, and Other Laws of Cyberspace, Version 2.0*, Basic Books (2006); and William Mitchell, *City of Bits: Space, Place and the Infobahn*, MIT Press (1996).

puts it, 'software is eating the world'.[3] Code provides the fundamental architecture that sets the terms on which life in a digital age is lived. The code determines how easy it is to protect personal information or express ourselves. It determines whether access to information is open or whether specific information or space is zoned, and access limited. The code affects who sees what, or who or what is monitored. It determines how machines communicate in the Internet of Things. The deep architecture of a digital world can regulate in a host of ways, ways that one cannot begin to see (or understand) unless you consider the nature of such code and how it operates.

As a consequence, the 'authors' of code – software developers – play an increasingly important role in society. As the Microsoft CEO, Satya Nadella put it: **19.03**

> In short, developers will be at the centre of solving the world's most pressing challenges. However, the real power comes when every developer can create together, collaborate, share code and build on each other's work. In all walks of life, we see the power of communities, and this is true for software development and developers.[4]

The prevalence of code across multiple domains of social and economic life raises all types of legal issues. Moreover, computer code and digital technologies are transforming what it means to be a lawyer. In that respect, all lawyers are being and will continue to be affected by the on-going digital transformation.[5] And, if Satya Nadella is right that developers will be at the 'centre' of solving the problems of this new world, then lawyers must be able to 'speak' the language of code to participate in the crucial task of designing and developing solutions to the 'world's most pressing challenges'.[6] **19.04**

Historically, lawyers have been at their most effective – and socially useful – when they facilitate new forms of business or other social relationships. It seems clear that, in the near future, this function will, to a large extent, be **19.05**

---

3   Marc Andreessen, Why Software is Eating the World, *Wall Street Journal* (20 August 2011), available at: https://www.wsj.com/articles/SB10001424053111903480904576512250915629460; and Jeetu Patel, Software is Still Eating the World, *TechCrunch* (7 June 2016), available at: https://techcrunch.com/2016/06/07/software-is-eating-the-world-5-years-later/.

4   Satya Nadella, Microsoft + Github = Empowering Developers, *Microsoft Official Blog* (3 June 2018), available at: https://blogs.microsoft.com/blog/2018/06/04/microsoft-github-empowering-developers/.

5   Daniel Newman, Top 5 Digital Transformation Trends in Legal, *Forbes* (29 August 2017), available at: https://www.forbes.com/sites/danielnewman/2017/08/29/top-5-digital-transformation-trends-in-legal/#2610caac76f8.

6   Erik P.M. Vermeulen, Why I Want My Students to Code: The Importance of Coding in Education, *Medium: Hackernoon* (1 April 2018), available at: https://hackernoon.com/why-i-want-my-students-to-code-b358a2b97770.

'code-based' in some way.[7] This does not mean that lawyers will be rendered irrelevant or that they will disappear. Rather, the digital transformation will disrupt the legal profession and demand a different set of skills and capacities than have traditionally been taught in law schools or employed in legal practice.

19.06 It is for this reason that we decided to introduce a 'Coding for Lawyers' course in our legal education programmes. We are convinced that 'coding' can help us in solving many contemporary economic, environmental and social issues and that to participate in the 'multi-disciplinary' teams of the future, all lawyers will need to develop an understanding of coding. This chapter is structured as follows: Section B outlines the broader context of the transformation of education in a digital age; Sections C–E describe the importance of computer code in a legal context, particularly in terms of technology-driven changes to the legal profession; Section F introduces the main features of the 'Coding for Lawyers' course and lessons learned from its initial reception; Section G describes in more general terms the skills that the lawyer of the future will need to acquire to remain relevant and competitive; and Section H concludes.

19.07 It is perhaps not entirely surprising to note that this initiative and the broader argument on which it is based have been met with a certain degree of scepticism. 'Is it really necessary for law students or practicing lawyers to learn how to code?;' 'What is the value-added for us (non-technologists) of understanding code?;' or, 'Isn't this all just a waste of time?' These are some of the typical reactions of more cautious and conservative colleagues. No doubt, there is some merit to these concerns. After all, we do not need to have a deep understanding of code to successfully navigate the digital world. 'Users' of digital devices do not need to be able to code for themselves. We use technology all the time, without ever really understanding it. We can drive a car perfectly well, without understanding much about how a combustion engine works and the overwhelming majority of internet users do not necessarily understand the nuances of TCP/IP protocols. Moreover, coding is not easy. Acquiring competency takes a significant investment of time, and even if law students or practicing lawyers feel the need to learn how to code, readily available resources (on and offline) can teach them. In short, perhaps it is not effective or necessary to add 'another course' to the law school curriculum, or to the already busy schedule of practicing lawyers, focused as they are on billable hours.

---

7   Dan Mangan, Lawyers Could be the Next Profession to be Replaced by Computers (17 February 2017), available at: https://www.cnbc.com/2017/02/17/lawyers-could-be-replaced-by-artificial-intelligence.html?& qsearchterm=lawyers%20could%20be%20replaced%20by%20artificial%20intelligence.

But, to be clear from the start, we are not suggesting that law students or **19.08** lawyers should become professional coders, just like professional coders should not become lawyers. After all, coding is complicated and to become a serious coder takes a significant investment of time. However, we do believe that the ability to understand and communicate with coders is a necessary skill for the lawyer of the future. As such, we think that law students and practicing lawyers alike will benefit from understanding the basic concepts and power of coding. Not only by reading or hearing about it but by participating in and experimenting with coding projects in a classroom or training environment. This basic literacy is just one of several new technology-related skills that the lawyer of the future will need to develop to survive and flourish in a 'digital age.'

B. EDUCATION IN A DIGITAL AGE

As a result of the global proliferation of new technologies, we live in a 'digital **19.09** world' that is characterised by fast-paced, technology-driven social, economic and cultural change.[8] And, with ever-shorter innovation cycles, it seems obvious that new technologies will continue to transform every aspect of social life. Constant technological disruption is the 'new normal' and, as a consequence, 'old world' concepts, paradigms, and ideas are becoming increasingly less relevant.[9] At least, they are being challenged and disrupted in a new networked, global world of interconnected digital technologies. The resulting uncertainties create a massive challenge for all educators and other professionals (and not just lawyers): what should we be teaching law students today to prepare them for the complex and uncertain world of tomorrow? How should all professionals, including mid-career lawyers, acquire the skills necessary to operate successfully in this new digital environment? Beginning with some general thoughts on education in a digital age seems appropriate to provide some context for the law-specific discussion that follows.

Teaching has always tended to be 'backward-looking' and knowledge-based.[10] **19.10** Transmitting the settled knowledge of the past has been the starting point for our whole approach to education. For instance, in a legal context, students

---

8 Erik P.M. Vermeulen, Technology is Changing Us: We Must Be Much Smarter About the Digital Transformation, *Medium: Hackernoon* (27 May 2018), available at: https://hackernoon.com/technology-is-changing-us-e3c6bf7f9888.

9 Erik P.M. Vermeulen, Education in a Digital Age: How to Prepare the Next Generation for the Uncertain Things to Come, *Medium* (22 February 2018), available at: https://mystudentvoices.com/education-in-a-digital-age-by-professor-vermeulen-7d3b69f43de3.

10 Ibid.

have traditionally analysed existing laws, regulations and cases. The idea has been that if you understand and examine historical developments, you will be able to solve future problems by applying old doctrines and precedents to the new situation.

19.11 The responsibility of the educator was to transmit a settled body of information/knowledge. In a world of information asymmetries, the educator-student relationship was, by necessity, a hierarchical one. After all, the teacher had all of the knowledge and experience. This was the source of their authority and credibility as an educator. But this model seems ill-suited to a world of fast-paced change and easy access to information. Prior experience may not be relevant to a fast-changing reality where information is only ever one Google search away.

19.12 If the future is radically different from the present, it does not make sense to focus too much attention on transmitting information that seems likely to become less and less relevant. Especially when that information is readily available online. Instead, education needs to become much more 'forward-looking' and skills- rather than content-based. How do we prepare the next generation for dealing with unknown future problems? This is the question that everyone involved with education, including practicing professionals, now needs to be asking.

19.13 Here are a few general suggestions. For a start, everyone is going to need a much better technical grasp of the core technologies surrounding computers, communication networks, and AI. For many of us, the underlying technologies that are driving social change remain a mystery, and that is a problem. Practical technical knowledge needs to be integrated into many fields of education (and not just law), particularly in the social sciences. Coding and data analysis seem a good starting point. But we also need to think about other skills and capacities that are important in a world of constant change. The focus should be on building skills that will assist the next generation in making 'better' decisions under conditions of cognitive and normative uncertainty.

19.14 In the legal context, lawyers, both the current generation of practicing lawyers and the next generation, have to be able to think fast and 'out of the box'. Dynamic analysis of complex situations and the ability to communicate solutions, in presentations or video form, will become increasingly important.

In the future, we will see looser organisations and social platforms.[11] It is therefore important that the next generation finds ways to become more productive and self-motivating. They must find a way to operate without a 'boss' or supervisor telling them what to do. A premium is therefore put on the capacity to think creatively rather than comply with established ways of operating. This is particularly important for practicing lawyers confronted with multiple emerging practice fields that simply did not exist even five years ago. Consider FinTech, algorithm bias, augmented reality, dark web issues, implantable microchips, biometric privacy, or e-sports, to take some diverse examples of emerging new fields of legal practice.

As traditional concepts of a 'career' become much less relevant in the so-called   **19.15** gig economy,[12] it will become increasingly important to build and communicate a personal 'brand' by telling the right kind of story.[13] More and more businesses are adopting a more open form of 'ecosystem' style organisation in which internal divisions are blurred and partnering with 'outsiders' becomes deeper and more significant.[14] This will mean having to work in teams of strangers, often from diverse national or disciplinary backgrounds. The ability to work in such teams, continually adapting to new situations and working patterns, becomes crucial. Finally, many of the problems of the future will be ethically complex. This seems particularly true in the context of robotics and AI, but all new technologies raise difficult moral issues.[15] Building the capacity of students to think about ethical issues, therefore, seems another way that educators can add value. This would seem to put a premium on more inter- and multidisciplinary forms of study. Again, these are the skills that practicing lawyers will similarly need to develop to remain competitive in the market for legal services.

C. THE LAWYER OF THE FUTURE AS 'TRANSACTION ENGINEER'

When thinking about legal education and legal practice, it is essential to   **19.16** consider the general function and needs of the legal profession in a digital age.

---

11   Mark Fenwick et al., The End of 'Corporate' Governance (Hello Platform Governance), European Corporate Governance Institute Working Paper No 430/2018 (2018), available at: https://papers.ssrn.com/sol3/papers.cfm?abstract_id=3232663.

12   The 'gig economy' is a labour market characterised by the prevalence of short-term contracts or freelance work, as opposed to permanent jobs.

13   Erik P.M. Vermeulen, Hello Gig Economy, *Medium: Hackernoon* (2 September 2018), available at: https://hackernoon.com/hello-gig-economy-get-ready-for-our-digital-relationships-b885b3a43fb4.

14   Mark Fenwick and Erik P.M. Vermeulen, The New Firm, 16 *European Business Organization Review* 593 (2015) at 601.

15   Marcelo Corrales et al., *Robotics, AI & the Future of Law*, Springer (2018), at 6.

In this regard, it is helpful to examine the role of lawyers in earlier periods of technological change. Crucially, lawyers can play an important role in co-creating solutions around the deployment of new technologies. In this context, the history of the legal profession can provide some guidance as to the type of role that lawyers can play.

19.17 From a historical perspective, lawyers have been most important when they have operated as 'transaction engineers' that create opportunities for new forms of business and other social relationships. Consider the development and growth of Silicon Valley as a centre for digital technologies in the early 1970s. While the idea of the 'clustering' of similar businesses was a significant source of innovation, there is a broad consensus that the legal industry was also important in the development of technology firms and facilitating innovation.[16] For example, lawyers were responsible for drafting the innovative contractual provisions that protected high-risk investors – for instance, angel investors and venture capitalists – from the relational and performance risks associated with investing in young companies and inexperienced founder-entrepreneurs.[17] Moreover, the involvement of lawyers in both non-legal and legal activities, such as deal making and conciliating, also served as an important 'sorting device' for entrepreneurs that needed more than just investors to start and scale their young businesses.

19.18 We can see from the Silicon Valley example how lawyers functioned as 'transaction engineers'. Law firms operated as crucial intermediaries that brought together, in a 'safe' space, various parties with different but mutually compatible interests and novel forms of expertise. On this type of account, the often-neglected contribution of local law firms to the institutionalisation of venture capital and venture capital contracting goes some way in explaining the success of Silicon Valley.[18]

19.19 The problem, however, is that lawyers have often failed to perform this function of being proactive transaction engineers that add value. Instead, they have often become a hindrance or obstacle to any form of transacting.[19] This can happen for multiple different reasons, but the tendency to 'proceduralise' solutions and to employ standard form 'templates' is one major factor. Fixed

---

16   Anapum Chander, How Law Made Silicon Valley, 63 *Emory Law Review* 639 (2014), at 639.

17   Lisa Bernstein, The Silicon Valley Lawyer as Transaction Cost Engineer?, 74 *Oregon Law Review* 239 (1995), at 245–51.

18   Joseph A. McCahery et al., Corporate Venture Capital: From Venturing to Partnering, in D. Cummings (ed.) *Oxford Handbook of Venture Capital*, Oxford Handbooks (2012), at 211.

19   Frederic A. Rubinstein and Audrey M. Roth, The Life Cycle of a Venture-Backed Company, in *Deal Strategies for Venture Capital and Private Equity Lawyers*, Aspatore Books (2007), at 3.

and standardised solutions are often imposed on complex, dynamic transactions resulting in frustration and difficulties, especially for clients.[20] The list of complaints is familiar: lawyers are verbose; they do not listen; they are unresponsive; they are constantly saying 'no'; they charge too much; they are not commercially minded; they spend too much time on trivial issues; they do not keep clients informed; they constantly 'over-lawyer'; and they do not communicate clearly and concisely. As a result, lawyers have developed a reputation as one of the least trusted professions.[21]

In a highly competitive and fast-changing environment, law firms need to **19.20** focus on re-discovering their function as effective transaction engineers that can help parties to facilitate interactions and reduce costs. After all, the FinTech (r)evolution is premised on the multiple costs that could and should be cut: agency costs; transaction costs; monitoring costs; regulatory costs; and (the increasingly important category of) compliance costs. In that respect, the potential for lawyers to add value is enormous. As such, lawyers can play a crucial role in the 'co-creation' of the infrastructure for the deployment of new technologies. Such co-creation involving partnerships between multiple actors can be crucial to building a 'better' digital future.[22]

In contrast, one hears many commentators suggesting that the digital trans **19.21** formation may mark the beginning of the end for lawyers and legal advisers.[23] We certainly do not agree with this argument. Nevertheless, we do think that if lawyers of the future are to function as effective transaction engineers playing a socially productive role in the deployment of digital technologies, it is clear that the legal profession is going to need to adapt in various ways. Here are three adaptations that seem particularly relevant and urgent:

---

20   Open Law, *Decentralizing the Deal, Medium* (25 September 2017), available at: https://media.consensys.net/decentralizing-the-deal-e6af1c0cfdab; and Michael G. Parsomanikas, Frustration of Contract in International Trade Law and Comparative Law, 18 *Duquesne Law Review* 551 (1980), at 605.

21   Felicity Nelson, Why Do People Hate Lawyers So Much?, *Lawyers Weekly* (18 February 2015), available at: https://www.lawyersweekly.com.au/folklaw/16179-why-do-people-hate-lawyers; and Derek Thompson, The Least-Trusted Jobs in America: Congress Members and Car Salespeople, *The Atlantic* (3 December 2012), available at: https://www.theatlantic.com/business/archive/2012/12/the-least-trusted-jobs-in-america-congress-members-and-car-salespeople/265843/.

22   William Callison et al., Corporate Disruption: The Law and Design of Organizations in the Twenty-First Century, 19 *European Business Organization Law Review* 737 (2018), at 766; and Fenwick and Vermeulen, *supra* note 14 at 611.

23   For examples of this argument, see Jason Koebler, Is AI Making Lawyers a Disappearing Profession, *Financial Review* (24 April 2017), available at: https://www.afr.com/business/legal/is-artificial-intelligence-making-lawyers-a-disappearing-profession-20170418-gvmzbs; and Richard Susskind, *The End of Lawyers: Rethinking the Nature of Legal Services*, Oxford University Press (2010).

19.22 First, lawyers of the future will need to be able to assume the role of 'project managers' or, at least, active participants in multi-disciplinary teams that will design new solutions for the problems of the future. As such, a capacity to operate effectively in diverse teams will take on a much greater significance than has previously been the case for lawyers. The ability to work with and communicate with a range of 'partners' will be increasingly required. In the digital world, this means that lawyers will have to work closely not only with their traditional professional 'partners' such as accountants or financial advisers but also with engineers, designers, architects and other technical experts and specialists (depending on the particular project/transaction at hand). In this new model of legal services, law firms will become more like 'platforms' with an emphasis on connecting legal and other experts and managing the resulting collaboration and transactions.[24] In a new world of platforms, this type of 'matchmaking' and project-based partnership will mean that lawyers and other legal advisers need to be aware of the way network technology and other code-based technologies operate.

19.23 Second, in pursuing these new solutions, lawyers will be confronted with a very different type of client with a different set of 'needs'. Fast-growth technology companies with few assets and fewer employees are increasingly central in a digital environment. The most successful companies today have leveraged the opportunities of networked digital technologies to develop new business models. Trust, value and wealth are created through such platforms, connections, and networks, instead of the (more traditional) management of workers or physical assets.[25] Crucially, many firms in this new innovation-driven economy adopt new organisational forms and governance structures to deliver their new products and services.[26]

19.24 What then are the main features of these new organisations? To appeal to millennial 'talent' and consumers, younger firms have often embraced more mission-driven and inclusive organisational cultures and practices in which a 'best-idea-wins' culture replaces formal hierarchies. Significantly, however, many such 'new' firms have often struggled to maintain this new governance model and fulfil their initial promise. As firms scale, they often find themselves transforming into the very thing that they were initially designed to avoid, namely a corporate dinosaur. Lawyers of the future will need to understand the opportunities and challenges of the digital world and help

---

24 Fenwick et al., *supra* note 11.
25 Erik P.M. Vermeulen, We All Struggle!, *Medium: Hackernoon* (19 August 2018), available at: https://hackernoon.com/we-all-struggle-adb0cfc65773.
26 Callison et al., *supra* note 23.

firms to maintain their more open and inclusive governance structures even after they have become bigger and more successful.

Third, many of the 'solutions' that the lawyer of the future will be expected to **19.25** help design will be technology-based. The transactions that lawyers will be facilitating will be dependent on computer code. It is in this context that blockchain and smart contracts become particularly important. To enable lawyers to perform this function, legal education will need to undergo some important changes to prepare prospective legal professionals to perform this function. For example, in the context of the digital transformation, an understanding of code is going to be crucial for the lawyer of the future to perform their transaction engineer function effectively.[27]

So, what can be done to facilitate law firms in meeting these new challenges **19.26** and re-focusing on being active and effective transaction engineers? What seems clear is that, in the context of the digital transformation, an understanding of code is going to be crucial for the lawyer of the future to perform this function effectively. Two issues seem particularly relevant:

(1) LegalTech will disrupt the legal profession and, as described in 19.29 **19.27** below, since LegalTech is code-based, lawyers need to be able to understand and talk about code to participate in the design of such legal technologies and to maximise their usefulness in supporting all legal work.

(2) More and more businesses and industries revolve around code-based products or services. Since all companies are now increasingly managed by, and run on, software code, transaction facilitation would benefit from lawyers having some knowledge or, at least, a better understanding of coding. The development of blockchain technologies and smart contracts are particularly relevant in this regard.

The next two sections consider these issues in turn.

D. LEGALTECH

LegalTech has evolved from support systems to fully integrated and auto- **19.28** mated services for lawyers that increasingly disrupt the practice of law. As

---

27 Mark Fenwick et al., Regulation Tomorrow: Strategies for Regulating New Technologies, in T. Kono, et al. (eds) *Transnational Commercial and Consumer Law: Current Trends in International Business Law*, Springer (2018), at 153.

such, LegalTech can be defined as the integration of information technology services and software in the legal context, as well as the development of legal platforms and their applications.[28] Since the 1970s, with the invention of the first legal databases, LegalTech has supported lawyers in their work, reducing costs and improving performance. The success of these earlier efforts and developments in information technology have attracted investment in this field, further bolstering potential efficiency gains.[29]

19.29   As such, LegalTech has made law firms and lawyers more efficient in performing their activities. Examples include automated billing, document storage, practice management, and accounting software.[30] But, from the early 2010s, LegalTech became more advanced and started to incorporate technology that assisted legal professionals in due diligence and e-discovery processes.[31] Since around 2015, LegalTech has continued to evolve in unprecedented ways. Many start-ups and their investors have started to capitalise on technologies, and their applications are already replacing some junior lawyers and disrupting the existing parameters for the practice of law.[32] In order to play a meaningful role in designing and implementing these solutions, practicing lawyers will likely need to have some understanding of the underlying technologies, specifically the code. Not every lawyer will be involved in the design of such technologies, but almost all lawyers will be users and the more feedback that lawyers can provide, the more such technologies will be able to develop and improve with each iteration. As LegalTech becomes more sophisticated and pervasive, this need for user-feedback will only increase.

19.30   Four types of LegalTech start-up can be distinguished – the first category includes start-ups that offer a range of online legal services, removing the

---

28   Joshua Lenon and Bryce Tarling, The Next Phase of Legal Technology has Already Been Built, *Above the Law: Evolve the Law* (7 December 2017), available at: https://abovethelaw.com/legal-innovation-center/2017/12/07/the-next-phase-of-legal-technology-has-already-been-built/.

29   Catalyst Investors, Legal Tech is Primed for Growth Investments, (2018), available at: https://rossintelligence.com/legaltech-growth-investments/; and Edgar Alan Rayo, AI in Law and Legal Practice: A Comprehensive View of 35 Current Applications, *Tech Emergence* (29 November 2017), available at: https://www.techemergence.com/ai-in-law-legal-practice-current-applications/.

30   Wells H. Anderson and JoAnn Hathaway, All-in-One Practice Management Applications, 31 *GP Solo* 4 (2014), available at: https://www.americanbar.org/publications/gp_solo/2014/july-august-2014/allinone_practice_management_applications.html; and Eileen O'Loughlin, Legal Document Management Software Buyer's Guide: Software Advice (3 August 2018), available at: https://www.softwareadvice.com/legal/document-management-comparison/.

31   Robert Ambrogi, The 10 Most Important Legal Technology Developments of 2015, *Law Sites* (28 December 2015), available at: https://www.lawsitesblog.com/2015/12/the-10-most-important-legal-technology-developments-of-2015.html.

32   Ibid.; see also 3 Reasons Why Tech Companies Need a New Kind of Lawyer, *Cornell Tech: Law Tech Blog* (17 February 2016), available at: https://tech.cornell.edu/news/3-reasons-why-tech-companies-need-a-new-kind-of-lawyer/.

'in-person' legal consultation process and guidance for clients.[33] The second category involves online 'matching' platforms that connect lawyers with clients.[34] Such platform start-ups help consumers find an appropriate lawyer without the involvement of a law firm. The third category entails start-ups that use AI tools to take over their lawyer's time-consuming and expensive legal research activities such as reviewing, understanding, evaluating, and reapplying contracts.[35] Finally, start-ups with expertise in blockchain technology are attempting to replace lawyers as intermediaries in certain types of transactions, notably real estate and intellectual property.[36]

The central purpose of these start-ups seems to be the disruption of existing **19.31** legal practices, and this has broad repercussions for the legal profession. In particular, junior legal professionals and legal support staff are likely the first victims of the development of LegalTech,[37] which will soon be able to perform much of the work of junior lawyers – such as document review – without the human elements that introduce imprecision, flaws, inaccuracies, possible lawsuits, and delay.[38] Second, and more importantly, the legal profession will be forced by such start-ups to innovate, a task that is not easily accomplished by overextended legal organisations that have deeply entrenched operating procedures and limited capacity for rapid re-invention.[39] Innovation trends in law firms are described in more detail in Chapter 18.

More speculatively, LegalTech has the potential to rapidly transform law firms **19.32** and legal departments into virtual law firms. Virtual law firms may dominate in the future. A virtual law firm is a platform with an emphasis on connecting legal and other professionals in a collaborative online environment involving human and machine actors. When implemented successfully, the effect of the platform model will be the creation of a flexible and accessible community of professionals with different skills and experience. The bigger the community, the easier it is to offer solutions tailored to the needs of the clients. The virtual law firm model attracts a broad spectrum of law firms. One extreme is represented by the traditional law firm characterised by a hierarchy with

---

33 Zoe Andreae, Legal Tech Start-ups, *Medium: Legal Tech Insights* (29 May 2017), available at: https://medium.com/legal-tech/legal-tech-startups-9755b18f93ac.

34 Ibid.

35 Ibid.

36 Erik P.M Vermeulen, There is No Escape from Blockchains and Artificial Intelligence … Lawyers Better Be Prepared!, *Medium* (23 January 2017), available at: https://medium.com/@erikpmvermeulen/there-is-no-escape-from-blockchains-and-artificial-intelligence-lawyers-better-be-prepared-2d7a8221c627.

37 Ibid.

38 Ibid.

39 Ibid.; see also Erin Winick, Lawyer-Bots are Shaking Up Jobs, *MIT Technology Review* (12 December 2017), available at: https://www.technologyreview.com/s/609556/lawyer-bots-are-shaking-up-jobs/.

partners at the top and varying levels of associates, paralegals, and non-lawyers below them. On the other end of the spectrum are those firms that adopt an 'Airbnb-type' platform organisation, mainly providing a matchmaking/ coordination service. Enormous variations exist between the two extremes, depending on the level of implementation of LegalTech.

19.33 Some start-ups are already looking to develop as legal platforms that add value by connecting lawyers and clients. At the moment, the focus is primarily on matchmaking but integrating AI or machine learning is explicitly mentioned as a key near-future goal. For instance, UpCounsel offers entrepreneurs on-demand access to experienced lawyers.[40] LawyerlinQ[41] in the Netherlands and Digitorney[42] in Germany offer law firms the possibility to insource[43] special knowledge and skills for more complex projects. Digitorney aims to disrupt the traditional relationship between companies and corporate law firms by providing a platform or matchmaking function that connects companies with the law firm that is best placed to meet a company's specific needs. As such, it helps companies overcome the lack of transparency or comparability in the legal market services, as well as the greater degree of specialisation in the business law context.[44]

19.34 In many ways, LegalTech is replacing – or at least, supplementing – the traditional role of law professionals. Law professionals play a crucial role in establishing trust and truth in legal transactions. They negotiate, draft, and interpret contracts and help enforce them; they create laws and regulations that protect the weaker parties, and they design structures that enable the registration and transfer of tangible property and intellectual property. Well-drafted legal contracts help establish confidence in the validity of the transaction and the economic benefits of the transaction for the contracting parties. Important matters, such as the truth about ownership and control, the transfer of ownership, and the allocation of risk and control, are typically covered in a contract. However, such deal-making, matchmaking, gatekeeping, and enforcing roles are increasingly performed by – or, at least, with the assistance of – technology. This trend is likely to accelerate soon, enabled by new technologies (such as blockchain technology) and smart contracts.

---

40 Upcounsel: https://www.upcounsel.com.
41 LawyerlinQ: https://about.lawyerlinq.com.
42 Digitorney: https://www.digitorney.com/.
43 'Insourcing' refers to the practice of using an organisation's own staff or other resources to accomplish a task that was previously outsourced.
44 See Digitorney, White Paper (14 December 2018) available at: https://group.digitorney.com/wp-content/uploads/2018/12/Digitorney-STO-Whitepaper_20181214.pdf.

But it will not stop here. Near future technological advances – most obviously, **19.35** machine learning and deep learning – have already started to replace lawyers and other legal professionals. Artificial intelligence tools help clients to review, understand and even draft legal documents.[45] Data analytics, machine learning, and deep learning are not only used to do legal research but also assist in legal decision-making and the prediction of legal cases.[46] As such, there is no doubt that LegalTech will automate 'legal work,' such as contract drafting, legal risk management, and dispute resolution. If legal work is dependent on and performed by algorithms in the future, it will soon be crucial for all lawyers to have a better understanding of 'data analytics' and 'artificial intelligence.'

E. BLOCKCHAIN SMART CONTRACTS

Bearing in mind that blockchain is described in more detail in Chapters 1 and **19.36** 6, this section explains why blockchain is relevant in the business context and its relevance to the legal profession. What makes the blockchain such a revolutionary technology is that the ledger or database is distributed to a countless number of participants ('nodes') around the world in public peer-to-peer networks (similar to the internet) or private (or permissioned) peer-to-peer networks (similar to an intranet).[47] These participants can be individuals or organisations (and even things). The only condition is that they have a mobile phone and internet connection. Such 'peer-to-peer' transactions are possible because the technology uses a 'distributed consensus model' where the network 'nodes' verify, validate and audit transactions before and after they are executed. This is safer than a traditional model in which transactions can only be accomplished through third-party intermediaries, such as a bank, judiciary or notary.

Network connectivity is also important because it allows for multiple copies of **19.37** the blockchain to be available across a distributed network. This makes it practically impossible to alter or erase information in the blockchain. The use of cryptographic hashes makes tampering with blockchain records even more difficult, if not impossible.

---

45 For example, Beagle: https://www.beagle.ai, Legalzoom: https://www.legalzoom.com, and Legal Robot: https://www.legalrobot.com/.

46 Beverly Rich, How AI Is Changing Contracts, *Harvard Business Review* (12 February 2018), available at: https://hbr.org/2018/02/how-ai-is-changing-contracts.

47 Saurabh Gupta, Blockchain: The Next Big Revolution, *Medium: Blockchain Musings* (3 July 2017), available at: https://medium.com/blockchain-musings/blockchain-the-next-big-revolution-dabb748d33fa.

19.38 In short, blockchain technology creates an independent and transparent platform for establishing truth and building trust.[48] Intermediaries, bureaucracy and old-fashioned procedures are replaced by the four Cs: code, connectivity, crowd, and collaboration.[49] The technology increases openness and speed, while at the same time significantly reducing costs.

19.39 But perhaps the most significant feature of blockchain is that it is very adaptable. There are multiple possible applications relevant in a business context. Most obviously, blockchain can be used to provide new methods of processing digital transactions.[50] But blockchain can also be used for cryptocurrencies, records management (e.g., real estate, corporate or medical records), e-voting and identity management. It is for this reason that blockchain technology has been mentioned as one of the most significant disruptive technological innovations since the emergence of the internet.[51]

19.40 Blockchain becomes particularly attractive in the legal context when combined with smart contracts, described in Chapter 7. In the business context, a smart contract could be an essential part of, for instance, a car loan. For example, if the borrower misses a payment (tracked via a blockchain-like technology), the contract will not allow the use and operation of the car ('enforced' via networked technologies that 'disable' the car automatically, rather than a 'repo man' physically depriving a driver of access to their car).[52] Such smart contracts will become more prevalent in the growing world of the Internet of Things. The more devices are connected, the more smart contracts will be used to execute and enforce legal transactions.

19.41 A more complex example is the set-up of the so-called 'decentralized autonomous organizations' (DAOs) built on software, code, and smart contracts, challenging traditional corporation laws. DAOs do not have any directors, managers or employees. The governance structure is built with and on software, code and smart contracts that run on a public decentralised blockchain platform. This automated structure is intended to give 'participants/ investors' in the DAO direct real-time control over contributed funds and where such funds would be distributed. DAOs fit in the flatter, decentralised and automated world. Unfortunately, law school programmes have been slow

---

48 Ibid.

49 Vermeulen, *supra* note 36.

50 Gupta, *supra* note 47.

51 Martin Hiesboeck, Blockchain is the Most Disruptive Invention Since the Internet Itself: Not Just in Finance, *Digital Doughnut* (6 April 2016), available at: https://www.digitaldoughnut.com/articles/2016/april/ blockchain-is-the-most-disruptive-invention-since.

52 Felix Küster, What Are Smart Contracts in Blockchain Technology, *Captain Altcoin* (14 July 2017), available at: https://captainaltcoin.com/blockchain-smart-contracts.

to adapt to these technological developments. Most students are still being prepared for a hierarchical, centralised and 'proceduralised' world. In the labour market of the future, however, a premium will be placed on a person's capacity to design and communicate innovative solutions, rather than comply with pre-established procedures. And since these new solutions will be code-based, an understanding of code and coding will be essential to participate effectively in our digital world.

Teaching students and experienced lawyers the basics of 'how to code' and **19.42** inspiring them to get out of their comfort zone, will be a necessary first step to help them embrace the many future opportunities of a 'software-based' environment. Blockchain and smart contracts can solve multiple societal challenges and – in doing so – to facilitate new opportunities for disruptive business models. Consider the following real-world implementations of these technologies that will impact on legal practice:

- *Health and wellbeing*: blockchain technology has the potential to trans- **19.43** form healthcare, giving the patient more control in the healthcare ecosystem by increasing the security, privacy, and interoperability of health data.
- *Agriculture and food security*: consumers increasingly favour 'clean' food, but it can be difficult to verify the integrity of products. A distributed ledger replacing the current supply chain would provide greater transparency and trust.
- *Safe, clean and efficient energy supplies*: we are facing a rapid growth in distributed energy resources. Think rooftop solar and electric vehicles, for example. Governments, utilities, and other stakeholders need to find new ways to regulate better and manage the electricity grid. Blockchain has the potential to offer a reliable, low-cost solution for financial or operational transactions to be recorded and validated across a distributed network.

In each of the above examples, a major societal problem could potentially be **19.44** solved more effectively by the use of blockchain technology and smart contracts. From a legal perspective, an interesting feature of such technologies is how they deliver new mechanisms for trusting. In a 20th-century business context, trust was typically created and maintained by rules, regulations, or contracts.[53] One way of thinking about the law is as a mechanism for stabilising expectations and building trust and reputation when interacting

---

53   Vermeulen, *supra* note 6.

with strangers.[54] 'I may not know you or even like you, but the fact that we have a contract means that I can (to a certain extent) trust you.' In a digital environment, trust can be achieved through software code agreed upon between the parties that reduces the need for (or at least, the scope of) traditional contracts. Recent interest in smart contracts suggests that this is going to be a significant growth area in the near future. Moreover, building trust via code is also crucial in machine-to-machine (M2M) based transactions. As M2M interaction becomes normalised in an Internet of Things environment, the issue of trust is re-imagined as a technical and design problem.

19.45 Such code-based solutions are increasingly delivered through online/cloud-based services. Again, this trend will only increase with the proliferation of M2M interactions. In this context, cybersecurity becomes an important issue, as described in Chapter 10. But instead of combatting cybersecurity with the introduction of 'more law in books', the lawyer of the future will need to engage with more technology-based solutions. At the very least, lawyers will need to acquire the necessary knowledge to evaluate technology-based solutions and compare them with more traditional alternatives.

19.46 Finally, there are the myriad ethical issues that are created in a code-based world and being aware of these issues is again essential for the lawyer of the future. Consider the example of the driverless car. How do we want our driverless vehicle to react when confronted with an unavoidable accident? Should it minimise the loss of life, even if that means sacrificing the occupants of the car or should it prioritise the lives of the occupants at any cost? Alternatively, should the choice be a random one? This is just one (well-known) example of an ethical challenge associated with new technologies. There are already multiple ethical questions involved with the dominant position of software code in our society.[55] Building the capacity of the lawyers of the future to think about the social and ethical implications of code is both essential and inevitable. But, to say something sensible about the ethical aspects of technology, it is necessary to understand more about the capacities and limits of coding.

---

54 Ibid.
55 See, e.g., Julia Bossmann, Top 9 Ethical Issues in Artificial Intelligence, World Economic Forum: Agenda (21 October 2016), available at: https://www.weforum.org/agenda/2016/10/top-10-ethical-issues-in-artificial-intelligence.

F. 'CODING FOR LAWYERS'

The above discussion provides the background for why coding will become **19.47** increasingly important for lawyers. So, what does the 'Coding for Lawyers' course entail and what lessons has the experience of offering such course taught us?

Two defining features of this course are its interdisciplinary and dynamic **19.48** character. Most obviously, the course is taught by a team of lawyers, coders, and mathematicians, and the curriculum has been constantly adapted in pursuit of an appropriate balance between the various disciplinary elements. The need for constant 'experimentation' by multidisciplinary teams – both regarding course content and teaching method – is one of the most important takeaways we have gained from the experience of offering this course. And, this is something all educators (as well as law firms and policymakers) should consider integrating into their practice.[56]

In the course, we first introduce the main features and advantages of block- **19.49** chain and smart contract-based applications. We explain how these applications inhibit 'rent-seeking' and offer greater transparency and security. In particular, the organisation of DAOs is introduced in more detail to show how traditional forms of business organisation are being disrupted by blockchain based technology. The open-source governance protocols used in DAOs are outlined to highlight how an openly readable ledger means anyone can monitor the integrity of transactions. The distributed cooperation component highlights a key advantage of such technologies, namely that 'attackers' must be able to 'out-compute' the entire network (which is difficult). Moreover, since DAOs are cheap and straightforward to 'clone', this will potentially lead to more competition and improvement in the model. The distributed and anonymous nature of the organisations prevents natural and political monopolies.

Of course, DAOs and other blockchain-based technologies still have signifi- **19.50** cant technical and operational shortcomings, and, in our discussion, the following weaknesses are highlighted. There is still a lack of decentralisation (there are currently no 'true' DAOs). For instance, Bitcoin's proof of work protocol has led to 'mining pools' because of economies of scale and unbalanced reward structures. Also, the anonymity in blockchain organisations

---

56 Fenwick et al., *supra* note 27.

means that they are prone to 'Sybil attacks' and '51% attacks'.[57] We also discuss the many examples in which the anonymity (and autonomy) have led to hacks.

19.51 Next, we introduce the mathematics behind cryptography, namely the role of hash functions, and Merkle trees. Several recent real-world blockchain initiatives are introduced. For instance, we present a blockchain-based 'reputation verification platform' (Semada.io) that rewards trustworthy parties and punishes bad actors.[58] The Semada Proof of Stake protocol (SPoS) is presented as a recent example that uses its reputation-verification platform to solve the centralisation, efficiency and security problems that afflict existing blockchain consensus protocols.

19.52 Finally, students are introduced to the Ethereum platform and given a basic introduction to coding on that platform. Assessment for the course involves students coding for themselves. Here are some examples of the kind of project that students have submitted:

- a blockchain-based dispute resolution procedure;
- a blockchain-based land and real estate registration system;
- blockchain-based digital identities for refugees or other stateless persons;
- blockchain-based 'ride-sharing';
- smart contracts for political campaign funding; and
- blockchain solutions for art traders.

19.53 In an increasingly software-driven world, we need to remain smart about technology. And this is what the 'Coding for Lawyers' course is aiming to achieve. It is not about teaching students how to become professional coders, but about making them realise how important it is to think about our relationship with new technology and technology experts. It is about encouraging a new level of technological literacy. In this way, students can see the new opportunities that technology creates, but also think about the new issues (practical and ethical) that such technologies create. Such an informed, but critical approach toward technology seems important for all lawyers and practicing lawyers would also benefit from learning more about current trends in technology, particularly in legal settings. In this respect, law

---

57 A '51% attack' refers to an attack on a blockchain in which hackers gain control of more than 51 per cent of the network's mining rate allowing them to prevent new transactions from receiving confirmation or to reverse transactions that had already been completed.

58 Craig Calcaterra et al., Semada Technical Whitepaper: Blockchain Infrastructure for Measuring Domain Specific Reputation in Autonomous Decentralized and Anonymous Systems (2018), available at: https://papers.ssrn.com/sol3/papers.cfm?abstract_id=3125822.

firms have some obligation to institutionalise life-long learning mechanisms and processes that ensure all of their employees are given the necessary core knowledge to understand, deploy and provide meaningful feedback on technology-based solutions.

G. THE CYCLE OF SELF-LEARNING

The risk of any form of education, including legal education, in a fast-changing and complex world is that it becomes overly 'standardised', and the result is that students expect, or even demand, to be 'spoon-fed'. Of course, there is an upside to having standards in place. Most obviously, it helps guarantee a certain uniform quality. However, the unintended downside of such an approach is that we 'programme' students to operate in a predetermined way, according to settled practice. In general, everything focuses on the reproduction of pre-given knowledge in a test. The result? Students want to know which pages of the 'textbook' they must read to succeed. And these pages should directly match the content of the lecture and examinations. Stated bluntly, students demand to be told what and how to think. Students do not see education as the cultivation of life-enhancing abilities, but as a means of gaining the necessary credentials (e.g., a degree or diploma from a good university/programme) to enter the marketplace as quickly as possible. **19.54**

There are parallel dangers of an unhealthy 'proceduralisation' developing within the culture of a law firm. For example, if previous practice or prior experience becomes the dominant consideration in decision-making, there is a risk that decisions can become overly cautious and conservative. This seems especially problematic in circumstances where a decision concerns an unprecedented set of circumstances and prior experience is either a potential distraction from a 'better' solution or prior experience is not relevant. As described in Chapter 18, another potentially damaging aspect of an overly proceduralised law firm culture is the dominance of hierarchical, rule-bound organisational structures and practices. Rather, encouraging a 'best idea wins culture' is vital. None of this is meant to suggest that procedural forms of organisation are inherently problematic. However, developing a critical awareness of how proceduralisation might be potentially damaging, especially in a fast-changing environment where more dynamic action is often necessary, is an important capacity for individual lawyers and law firms to cultivate and maintain. **19.55**

So, how can we resist the dangers of proceduralisation in this context? How can we instil in law students a capacity for 'self-learning' that will enable them **19.56**

437

to operate as effective 'transaction engineers?' How do we ensure that practicing lawyers also develop and retain a similar capacity throughout their careers? Here we offer a brief overview of a 'matrix' of skills necessary for surviving in a digital age, which we describe as a 'cycle of self-learning'.[59] These are the capacities that we believe students and practicing lawyers need to develop to be prepared for the new challenges facing legal professionals in the future. They are the skills that any 'future lawyer' and law firm needs to cultivate to remain relevant in a technology-driven environment where a premium is placed on the capacity to adapt to new situations and fast-changing circumstances:

- *Collection*: future lawyers will need to know *how* to collect the information necessary to deal with the 'digital' problems/issues/challenges, at hand. As such, 'navigating' the digital information highway becomes an indispensable skill. We tend to assume that 'digital natives' already have this skill or are quick to acquire it, but this often is not the case and certainly should not be assumed. Passive use is not the same as active, goal-oriented 'collection' of data-facts, and a new form of 'literacy' needs to be acquired and constantly honed. In part, this can be done through lifelong training programmes – particularly when we are concerned with the effective use of legal databases and other resources – but we should not underestimate the importance of other more diverse sources of information, such as social media and the internet generally.
- *Consumption*: future lawyers need to spend time, 'consuming' the diverse content that they have collected. This is an integral part of being successful in a digital age. Exposure to diverse information not only feeds curiosity, but also provides the intellectual resources necessary to develop better ideas and solutions.
- *Curation*: future lawyers need to be able to filter out ('curate') the relevant information from the multiple sources that they 'consume'. Identifying and selecting the 'right' information is particularly challenging in a world of seemingly infinite information where it can be difficult to make accurate judgments as what is valuable and what is merely noise.
- *Co-creation*: future lawyers must be able to take the 'curated' information that they gathered and create and (in particular) 'co-create' new content or solutions based on that information. The creation of new content helps build a unique and focused skill set around which an individual lawyer can build and then project a personalised brand. This is particularly important in the modern workplace where traditional jobs are being transformed and some are slowly disappearing, while the idea

---

59   Erik P.M. Vermeulen, Education is the Key to a Better Future, But … , *Medium: HackerNoon* (16 September 2018), available at: https://hackernoon.com/education-is-the-key-to-a-better-future-but-6516903c547f.

of 'lifetime employment' has become rather obsolete. Branding becomes important for individual lawyers looking to maintain some coherence in their (more individualised) career development and growth.

- *Communication*: the capacity for 'communication' of new content and solutions is essential in a digital age. The ability to communicate 'solutions' in a clear and persuasive way is at a premium in a world where following the traditional method of operating will no longer cut it. In a world where solutions are non-obvious, the ability to persuade others that your answer is 'best' becomes crucial. Again, this connects to the culture of the firm and the importance of the environment in which open communication is fostered and the 'best idea wins'.
- *Correction*: finally, there is the capacity to reflect on and incorporate feedback and iterate solutions. This final step refers to the ability to adjust and develop (i.e., 'self-correct') constantly. Again, in a fast-changing digital environment, the ability to adapt to new information or circumstances becomes essential in iterating improved solutions to par-ticular problems and situations.

What makes this 'Collection-Consumption-Curation-Co-creation-   **19.57** Communication-Correction' model so different from the current curriculum of law schools is that it is not about instant gratification (passing a course/ exam or gaining credits), the reproduction of knowledge, or measuring 'success' by grades on a test. Instead, it is about appreciating the value of more open-ended ('free') self-learning, as well as the life-changing capacities that it offers. Of course, it is more difficult both for students and educators, lawyers and law firm, to institutionalise and evaluate such an approach, but these are the capacities necessary to identify and develop legal solutions appropriate for the uncertainties and complexities of a digital age.

H. CONCLUSION

Neither currently practicing nor future lawyers should feel threatened by the   **19.58** exponential growth of new technologies and the subsequent social and economic change that they bring. But they should not deny such change and cling to traditional ways of operating. Instead, they should view new tech-nology as a source of opportunity. The opportunities for lawyers and other legal professionals seem obvious. If machines can perform much of the standardised legal work, there will be more time for assisting the client with the new and specific challenges of navigating the complexities of a digital environment. However, to enjoy the benefits of these opportunities, it will be necessary to possess (and then leverage) a level of literacy in the basic building blocks of this new world. In an age of 'ubiquitous computing', a crucially important element is code and coding. As such, emerging technologies oblige us to rethink legal education and lifelong learning for practicing lawyers. The task seems clear: creating new courses – both inside and outside universities – that ensure that students and practicing lawyers possess the skills to remain relevant in a society that is characterised by the exponential growth of technology.

INDEX

'*An excellent review of the key topics in the developing world of FinTech. Easily digestible chapters that identify and demystify legal issues surrounding this rapidly expanding subject matter.*'

James M. Klotz, Miller Thomson LLP, Canada; Vice-President, International Bar Association; Immediate Past-Chair, IBA Task Force on the Future of Legal Services

FinTech: Law and Regulation *makes an important and welcome contribution to the literature in the growing financial technology industry. It covers every area from open banking to smart contracts whilst neatly combining analysis of the technical considerations as well as the pertinent legal and regulatory issues. This book will be hugely beneficial to practicing lawyers, law students, technologists and academics. Highly recommended.*'

Peter Hunn, Founder and CEO, Clause Inc., USA